CRITICAL SURVEY
OF
LONG FICTION

CRITICAL SURVEY
OF
LONG FICTION

English Language Series

Authors

Stur-Z

7

Edited by
FRANK N. MAGILL

Academic Director
WALTON BEACHAM

LIBRARY OF CONGRESS CATALOG CARD NUMBER: 83-61341

Complete Set: ISBN 0-89356-359-5
Volume 7: ISBN 0-89356-366-8

LIST OF AUTHORS IN VOLUME 7

	page
Sturgeon, Theodore	2579
Styron, William	2589
Swift, Jonathan	2604
Thackery, William Makepeace	2613
Theroux, Paul	2628
Tolkein, J. R. R.	2635
Trollope, Anthony	2648
Twain, Mark	2660
Tyler, Anne	2671
Updike, John	2686
Van Vechten, Carl	2705
Vidal, Gore	2712
Vonnegut, Kurt, Jr.	2722
Wain, John	2733
Walker, Alice	2746
Wallant, Edward Lewis	2758
Warren, Robert Penn	2767
Waters, Frank	2781
Waugh, Evelyn	2793
Wells, H. G.	2805
Welty, Eudora	2817
Wescott, Glenway	2830
West, Nathanael	2840
Wharton, Edith	2848
White, Patrick	2859
Wilder, Thornton	2880
Wilkinson, Sylvia	2889
Wilson, Angus	2897
Wilson, Ethel	2907
Wodehouse, P. G.	2917

		page
Wolfe, Thomas	.....	2927
Woolf, Virginia	.....	2940
Wouk, Herman	.....	2961
Wright, Richard	.....	2974
Yerby, Frank	.....	2985
Yglesias, José	.....	2993
Young, Al	.....	3004

CRITICAL SURVEY
OF
LONG FICTION

THEODORE STURGEON

Born: Staten Island, New York; February 26, 1918

Principal long fiction

The Dreaming Jewels, 1950 (also known as *The Synthetic Man*, 1957); *More Than Human*, 1953; *I, Libertine*, 1956 (as Frederick R. Ewing); *The Cosmic Rape*, 1958; *Venus Plus X*, 1960; *Some of Your Blood*, 1961; *Voyage to the Bottom of the Sea*, 1961.

Other literary forms

While Theodore Sturgeon is not as prolific as some of the science-fiction fraternity, by 1977 he had written more than 190 short stories, 130 articles, and a number of radio and television scripts.

Achievements

Theodore Sturgeon's work has been called "the single most important body of science fiction by an American to date." A founder of modern American science fiction, he has contributed to and survived the genre's transition from underground to mainstream literature. He is the recipient of Argosy (1947), International Fantasy (1954), Nebula (1970), and Hugo (1971) awards.

Biography

Theodore Sturgeon was born Edward Hamilton Waldo, on February 16, 1918, on Staten Island, New York. His parents were divorced, and, after his mother remarried in 1929, his name was legally changed when he was adopted by his stepfather. After he was graduated from high school, where his career as a gymnast was ended by rheumatic fever, he finished a term at Penn State Nautical School and then spent three years at sea. During that time he began to write, producing some forty conventional short stories for McClure's Syndicate before turning to science fiction, which he began to publish in John W. Campbell, Jr.'s *Astounding Science Fiction* in 1939.

Sturgeon has recalled that science fiction was "the pornography of its day," and recounts how his stepfather discovered and destroyed his 1935 issues of *Amazing*. When he took up science fiction, Sturgeon was both breaking with the strictures of his early home life and making a commitment to a literary form which promised little prestige and very modest financial returns. He married in the same year he launched his science-fiction career and contributed regularly to *Unknown* and *Astounding Science Fiction* in order to support his family. Although he produced highly regarded stories, such as "It" (1940) and "Microcosmic God" (1941), he had to seek employment outside of writing to earn a living.

After operating a hotel in the British West Indies in 1940, Sturgeon worked as a door-to-door salesman, as Assistant Chief Steward at Fort Simonds, and as a bulldozer operator. In 1942, he pursued the latter occupation in Puerto Rico. Except for *Killdozer*, a novelette about a machine possessed by a malignant force, his literary output declined sharply between 1942 and 1944, when he returned to the United States and became a copy editor. These were difficult years for Sturgeon, financially and emotionally. Not until 1946, after his marriage ended in divorce, did he fully resume his career under the encouragement of John Campbell.

While continuing to write, Sturgeon tried his hand at running a literary agency and producing advertising copy. The first substantial public recognition for his work came in 1947 when he won a thousand-dollar prize for "Bianca's Hands." (The runner-up in the contest, sponsored by the British magazine *Argosy*, was Graham Greene.) "Bianca's Hands" had been written on Sturgeon's honeymoon years earlier but had found no market because of its bizarre treatment of a "passionate human attachment." Its acceptance marked a turning point for Sturgeon, which was closely followed by the publication of the first of his many anthologies, *Without Sorcery* (1948), with an introduction by Ray Bradbury.

As he entered the period of his greatest creativity, Sturgeon's personal life again underwent change, with a second marriage in 1949 and a third in 1951. His output of fiction was unabated, however, with *The Dreaming Jewels*, his first novel, appearing in 1950, and *More Than Human*, published in 1953, winning the 1954 International Fantasy Award, a confirmation of his rank as one of America's foremost writers of science fiction. His stories continued to be anthologized in his own collections and those of others, and he engaged in a broad range of literary activity, from a hoax with Jean Shepard, *I, Libertine* (1956), published under the name Frederick R. Ewing, to a fictional case history of vampirism, *Some of Your Blood* (1961), and a novel depicting an androgynous utopia, *Venus Plus X* (1960).

As a major author of speculative fiction, he helped to create a climate of acceptance for the genre among the general public. In his book reviews for the *National Review* (1961-1973), for example, he explained and defended his art while introducing some of contemporary science fiction's finest authors to an audience who might otherwise not have learned of them. He was involved in science fiction's growth in other media also, in 1966 moving to Los Angeles to write for *Star Trek*. While he no longer publishes much new fiction, Sturgeon continues to compile anthologies of his previous work for new audiences. He resides in California with his fourth wife, Wina, whom he married in 1969.

Though Sturgeon has deplored the "inexcusable invasions into . . . authors' most intimate motivations" by academic critics, there are nevertheless certain definite biographical influences on his work. Beverly Friend has called him "a highly personal writer drawing from his own suffering for his craft." She cites his parents' divorce, his estrangement from his stepfather, his illness in adolescence, and his marital and professional problems as sources for his art. Since a full biography is not yet available, however, the reader does best to focus on these influences mainly as they manifest themselves as themes in Sturgeon's major fiction.

Analysis

Theodore Sturgeon has said, "All great literature is great because it is fable—because it creates typical and archetypical characters and situations which can be applied outside the work to illuminate the human condition." He has repeatedly insisted that he does not undervalue the science of science fiction, but he clearly inclines toward minimizing technology as a focus for his work; rather, he concentrates upon fable, often premising his work on occult matters upon which science has had little to say. He has said that "in teaching, reviewing, and enjoying science fiction, my emphasis is always on the fiction." This is, he says, "because I like writers to be read and remembered and (when they can) to move people and shake them; to ignite, to increase their ability to share their visions and their joy and their terror, as well as their knowledge." Sturgeon's criteria for art are more affective than cognitive, and he generally concentrates upon rites of passage rather than technological extrapolation.

Whatever Sturgeon's premise for a story, scientific, psychological, or occult, he wishes the work to reflect essential human experiences: "love, and pain, and greed, and laughter, and hope, and above all loneliness." Loneliness is most significant since he feels "what I have been trying to do all these years is to investigate this matter of love, sexual and asexual," and his major fictions are fables of growth toward community and maturity.

The four science-fiction novels which are the heart of Sturgeon's work (*The Dreaming Jewels*, *More Than Human*, *The Cosmic Rape*, and *Venus Plus X*) develop the idea that "our strange species has two prime motivating forces: sex, of course, and worship." Throughout his writing, the latter is the more important, and Sturgeon has been unwilling to see the highest self-sacrificial and altruistic acts as having any foundation in sexuality. Sturgeon's center of worship, however, is not to be found outside man but in humanity.

Sturgeon's first novel, *The Dreaming Jewels*, is an exploration of what it means to be human. Its premise is the creation of a "synthetic man" by the action of alien crystals which have a deep collective life of their own, apparently unrelated to the affairs of men. These crystals, seemingly without purpose, "dream" ojbects into existence, sometimes imperfectly, creating freaks and monsters, and sometimes—when they are mating—perfectly, creating creatures with the power of self-transformation. Such materials are better suited to psychological symbolism than scientific discussion. This is precisely the direction of Sturgeon's art; since he finds "more room in inner space than in outer space," his fables are essentially paradigms of psychological growth which begin with the frustrations and alienation of youth and end in maturation and integration. On a number of occasions, he has defined science fiction in terms of the derivation of the word "science" from the Latin "to know." "Science fiction is knowledge fiction," he has written, adding that "by far most of the knowledge is psychological."

In *More Than Human*, Sturgeon makes significant use of syzygy, a concept of nonreproductive union signified by a strange word. A collective identity is formed by a group of persons who retain their individuality while contributing to a gestalt which has the ultimate promise of a god. The collective person remains distinctly human, however, and the worship due it is finally worship of humanity. Here the components of the human being, conscience being the highest, are integrated and raised to the highest power. So, too, in a novel which deals directly with sexuality, *Venus Plus X*, the integration of the human personality and worship become paramount, with Sturgeon using androgyny as a symbol of wholeness and providing his utopia's inhabitants with a religion which worships the promise of man.

The form of Sturgeon's novels can present the critical reader with problems. Sturgeon is perhaps most at home as a writer of short stories, and his techniques of composition reflect at times an incomplete transition to the novel's demands. He seemingly pieces together sections which finally form the whole. This is not to say that the structuring of his books is unskillful, for he does finally bring to focus elements which run through them in parallel directions. Also, such a method can be seen as organic to Sturgeon's themes of integration, with loosely related parts finally encompassed in a total vision. Whatever a reader's verdict on form, however, his principal response will probably be to Sturgeon's handling of theme.

Sturgeon's work takes seriously his claim that "the best of science fiction is as good as the best of any modern literature—articulate, poetic, philosophical, provocative, searching, courageous, insightful." He once complained that though the finest science-fiction writers "open their veins into their typewriters, taking their craft and their readers seriously, they seem to be categorically disqualified from the serious attention of mainstream critics and readers." Fortunately, this is no longer the case, in part because of Sturgeon's fables of human nature.

The reprinted title of *The Dreaming Jewels* is *The Synthetic Man*, a title which more clearly reflects the subject matter of Sturgeon's first novel but which loses some of the symbolic suggestiveness of the original. Paul Williams has commented that the work is in part based on Sturgeon's resentment of his stepfather and has pointed out the significance of the dream to the creative act of writing science fiction. To this might be added the importance of jewel symbolism in the light of Sturgeon's view of science fiction as "knowledge fiction."

Jewels often symbolize arcane knowledge and spiritual transformation; here they are connected with an unconscious dream-power that can be brought to light for good or ill, and in which reside keys to transformation and regeneration. Contesting for this power are Horty, the "synthetic man," and Pierre Monetre, a most thoroughgoing misanthrope who would delight in the destruction of mankind. Horty's victory over Monetre (called "maneater" by his subordinates) comes about through his capacity to tap the power of the unconscious, and through the willing sacrifice of Zena, whose education of Horty to human values keeps him from becoming like the alienated Monetre.

Horty's potential alienation comes from abuse by a cruel stepfather, Armand Bluett, a figure Sturgeon has himself identified with "a lot of bitterness and hostility that I wanted to get out." Bluett's viciousness results in the accidental loss of three of Horty's fingers, and the young boy flees after bidding farewell to Kay Hallowell, a girl whose love balances Bluett's hatred. In his flight, Horty is befriended by carnival people, especially Zena, a midget, who notices the boy's sympathetic connection with his only possession, a jack-in-the-box with strange jewels for eyes. These gems prove to have had their effect on the child, gradually transforming him into a creature capable both of communicating with the inner life of the jewels and of transforming himself at will.

Horty's identity is hidden from Monetre, who owns the carnival. Zena disguises him as a girl and warns him never to reveal that he has regenerated his three lost fingers, which Monetre had treated upon his arrival. During his years with the carnival, Horty fails to grow and is only forced to leave when the owner discloses some curiosity about his hand. After leaving, he discovers his gift of transformation, which is useful when he encounters Armand Bluett, now a judge, victimizing Kay Hallowell. Horty cools off the sexually aggressive Bluett by taking Kay's place and slicing off his regenerated fingers, at which sight Bluett passes out. Horty thus becomes the woman who represents love for him so that he might perform a sacrificial mutilation which is both saving and vengeful.

In a series of improbable events, Kay comes under the power of Bluett and Monetre, who is clearly contrasted with Horty. While both are brilliantly gifted, Horty's mind, under Zena's guidance, has been shaped by "humanity and the extensions of humanity," as against Monetre's, which has been twisted by hatred and desire for power. In the confrontation between Horty and Monetre in a psychic duel, Zena sacrifices herself, instructing Horty to use his power to destroy jewel-created creatures. Since Monetre's character is so inhuman, he is assumed to be one. Ironically, Monetre is biologically human, without possessing any spirit of humanity, while Zena, a synthetic creature, sacrifices herself. In the end, however, Horty kills his adversary, resurrects Zena, who becomes his wife, and assumes Monetre's identity while traveling about trying to undo some of the harm he has done.

Sturgeon has assessed *The Dreaming Jewels* as "a rotten novel." Its chief faults are a terribly contrived plot and a style which lacks the energy of the best of his stories of the 1940's. The use of psychological materials is compelling, however, making it one of Sturgeon's most popular works. Horty's series of transformations are representative of his possession of the secret of the unconscious, the capacity to convert revenge into sacrificial love, whose highest exemplar is Zena. The novel moves from mutilation to regeneration, from revenge to love, with Horty progressing toward wholeness by overcoming alienation and linking the transforming power of the unconscious to positive human values.

More Than Human, Sturgeon's second and best novel, has at the center of its three-part structure a section entitled "Baby Is Three," which was published separately a year before the novel appeared. According to Sam Moskowitz, Sturgeon wrote a prologue and epilogue to this section to compose the novel. Like *The Dreaming Jewels*, "Baby Is Three" is about an alienated superman, fifteen-year-old Gerry Thompson, who in a strong first-person narration relates his visit to a psychiatrist, to whom he reveals his murder of his guardian, Miss Alicia Kew. Gerry also explains that he is part of a composite being, *homo gestalt*, a uniting of persons with extraordinary telepathic and telekinetic powers. Gerry has the capacity to probe the minds of others—he does this with the psychiatrist to make sure that he will not remember his visit—but he lacks human sympathy and moral awareness.

Sturgeon has said that "you cannot write stories about ideas—which is why so much hard-core, nuts-and-bolts science fiction fails as literature." In *More Than Human*, however, he is fortunate in combining a powerful idea with a sure grasp of style and an effective structure. The first section of the novel, "The Fabulous Idiot," focuses on Lone (a shortened form of *alone*), who is an idiot in the root sense of the word. He is aware of himself alone. He gradually becomes aware of others, first through Miss Kew's sister, Evelyn, who along with Alicia had been the victim of a demonically sexually repressive father, and then through the Prodds, a pathetic couple who take him in, and whose retarded child,"Baby," becomes the center of the gestalt being.

Lone becomes aware of a human community to which he has at least rudimentary obligations and of a more specialized group, composed of abandoned or runaway children, to which Gerry belongs, and which is destined to become a new being. By the end of the novel, this group has become a potential god, "not an exterior force, not an awesome Watcher in the sky, but a laughing thing with a human heart and reverence for its origins." In the book's last section, "Morality," Hip Barrows, the being's final component, its conscience, confronts and converts the ruthless Gerry; Hip sees himself as "an atom and his gestalt as a molecule. He saw these others as cells among cells, and he saw the whole design of what, with joy, humanity would become."

His response is a "sense of worship." He participates in a vision not unlike that shared by many Romantic writers of the nineteenth century, what Walt Whitman's follower R. M. Bucke called "Cosmic Consciousness." Sturgeon has said that the willingness of science-fiction writers to treat religious themes, "to invent and extrapolate and regroup ideas and concepts in this as in all other areas of human growth and change delights me and is a source of my true love for the mad breed." *More Than Human* is Sturgeon's best illustration that such themes can be explored profitably.

More Than Human, like *The Dreaming Jewels*, traces the progress of the growth and integration of the person. In each novel, characters move from alienation to wholeness, but in *More Than Human*, the key conflict between misanthropy and humanity is handled with greater dramatic skill. In general a more sophisticated work in conception and structure, *More Than Human* manages to present the idea of a collective entity without losing sight of individual characters or the dynamics of personality. As a speculative fiction, it deserves the praise and popularity it has enjoyed.

The Cosmic Rape also employs the gestalt theme of *More Than Human*, extending the union to all of mankind, which in turn is joined to Medusa, an intergalactic composite creature. While the underlying theme of the book is essentially the same as that of *More Than Human*, it is by no means as successful. Its premises are extrapolated in far less believable fashion and its structure is not dramatically engaging. Intercut scenes which range from the United States to Rome to Africa, are skillfully coordinated, but character development suffers in the effort to show individuals becoming a part of the whole.

In *The Cosmic Rape*, Sturgeon attempts to put love into the largest terms, but, ironically, he employs a character most unlikely to initiate cosmic harmony. One Dan Gurlick, a loathsome bum, has become an atom in Medusa by ingesting a sort of seed concealed in a fragment of hamburger. Through him, Medusa seeks to take over the Earth telepathically. Medusa is at first thwarted, having dealt only with collective minds elsewhere in the universe. This lack in humanity is repaired, however, as psychic unity among men appears as they cooperate in the destruction of invading machines created by Medusa. In the course of attaining collective consciousness, a variety of characters emerge from sexual repression and exploitation or social alienation to sacrifice themselves. Notable is the metamorphosis of Guido, a misfit who has turned to anarchism because his musical genius has been suppressed by a wicked stepfather.

Ultimately, Medusa is joined to the human collective mind. This connection occurs when Gurlick, himself excluded from the universal intelligence, is permitted to act out the sexual fantasies which Medusa has used to control him. What Gurlick intends as rape is welcomed by a woman now sexually liberated as a part of a larger design; likewise, the joining of humanity to

Medusa is transformed from rape to consent. Medusa is in fact possessed by humanity rather than possessing it.

The Cosmic Rape extends the ideas of *More Than Human* as far as they can go. Unfortunately, the extrapolation is ultimately too fanciful and the dramatic power of Sturgeon's myth of human integration is diffused. There is a sense of his recognition of this in his next book, which he calls "a tract"; the social criticism of *Venus Plus X* gives ballast to an imagination which had overextended iteself.

Sturgeon has responded to the charge that "science fiction is characteristically asexual and unaware of love in its larger and largest senses." He believes that this impression has sometimes arisen because writers of science fiction often "work in geological or astronomical time rather than in biographical or historical perspective." Sturgeon had dealt with themes of love in both cosmic and personal perspectives in his earlier novels, but in *Venus Plus X* he turned to utopian fiction to keep the action on a more human scale.

Though Sturgeon had written stories on sex before—"The World Well Lost" (1953) deals with homosexuality, for example—*Venus Plus X* is his most extended statement on sexism and sexual taboos. While the book has been praised for its pioneering study of sex roles, preceding Ursula K. Le Guin's much discussed *The Left Hand of Darkness* (1969) by nine years, *Venus Plus X* is also notable for its skillfuly ironic employment of science-fiction conventions and for its handling of the symbolism of androgyny.

The novel is structured in alternating chapters of action which are connected only by theme. The first set of chapters deals with suburban life and the questions of sexual identity posed to America in the 1950's. Along with standard problems of sex-role definition for children and general sexism, there are hints of change; Herb Raile comes to realize how Western culture has degraded women and catches glimpses of the significance of androgyny in the style of a rock singer. Contrasted with suburban America is Ledom (*model* inverted), a utopia founded upon the fact that its inhabitants are biologically hermaphrodites. Here, sex-role definition is no problem, and the wholeness of the human being in assuming all social duties is stressed. Against the predatory capitalism and commercialized worship of the suburbs is posed charitable religion and universal sharing.

Androgyny is used by Sturgeon as a symbol of wholeness. Like the universal man of *More Than Human*, androgyny can be found in mystical thought as signifying the primordial unity of mankind. In order to stress this aspect of his work, Sturgeon provides the Ledomites with a religion that is an ecstatic celebration of the child. "We keep before us," says the guide to this utopia, "the image of that which is malleable and growing—of that which we have the power to improve. We worship that very power in ourselves, and the sense of responsiblity which lives with it." Here again is Sturgeon's drive toward totality, a worship of human potential, yet in order to present this theme, he undercuts a number of science-fiction conventions to make his readers more aware of the symbolic nature of his statement.

The reader discovers that the book's nominal hero, Charlie Johns, is not a time-traveler as he first believes. Ledom does not exist in the distant future as it first appears; rather, it is a society hidden from the eyes of men. The Ledomites wish to test the reaction of the outside world to their culture, and use Charlie Johns's responses as a gauge. After overcoming his initial bewilderment, Charlie embarks on a course of education, learning that Ledom's technical superiority consists in a machine that can inscribe thought patterns and has revolutionized learning, and a power supply that makes the community self-sufficient. Charlie's approval of technology comes to a screeching halt, however, when he discovers that the hermaphroditism of Ledomites is biologically engineered. His reaction convinces utopian planners that the world is not ready for the revelation of Ledom.

Charlie now regards Ledom as a den of perversion and indicates that it ought to be destroyed. His education, however, has been limited: he has not detected the hints throughout that the whole culture is symbolic, that its essence is "transition." It has been designed to preserve human values while the outside world destroys itself. The novel's disquisition on religion, in fact, suggests that if one human generation could adopt the religion of Ledom, it would be saved. No hermaphroditism would be necessary for a sense of human wholeness.

The final emphasis given Ledom's symbolic nature is the revelation that Charlie Johns is not actually Charlie Johns at all, but merely a collection of his memories, obtained when he was dying after a plane crash and inscribed on the previously blank mind of a biological control. The plot, however, first permits Johns to attempt the standard escape from a dystopia. He finds the one girl who has not been biologically altered, and he tries to leave in what he thinks is a time machine. When he does so, the Ledomites are forced to tell him the truth. He and his girl therefore take up life somewhere between the two worlds, trying to sort out their identities, presumably overcoming the sexism of the man Charlie was, and learning from the wisdom of Ledom. At the same time, on the other side, Herb Raile is working his way slowly and painfully to gain some of Ledom's values.

In spite of some dated writing in the sections on suburbia in the 1950's, this is a book which powerfully anticipates many of the themes taken up by feminists in the 1960's and 1970's. Sturgeon also makes fine use of the conventions of utopian fiction only to undercut them, which is most appropriate to his major points about the nature of dynamic evolutionary change throughout his fiction. Utopia, he has written, "must be life-oriented and recognize that life is change, which is why utopias, be they by Plato or Sir Thomas More, or Joanna Russ, have hidden in them the characteristics of the necropolis." He avoids this by permitting his own utopia to self-destruct, leaving behind the impact of its symbols, and providing what Sturgeon saw in William Golding's *Lord of the Flies* (1954), "a fable of cultural structures, with a meaning—a 'moral' if you like—far greater than the narrative itself."

Major publications other than long fiction

SHORT FICTION: *Without Sorcery*, 1948; *E Pluribus Unicorn*, 1953; *A Way Home*, 1955; *Caviar*, 1955; *A Touch of Strange*, 1958; *Aliens 4*, 1959; *Beyond*, 1960; *Sturgeon in Orbit*, 1964; . . . *And My Fear Is Great/Baby Is Three*, 1965; *The Joyous Invasions*, 1965; *Starshine*, 1966; *Sturgeon Is Alive and Well*, 1971; *The Worlds of Theodore Sturgeon*, 1972; *To Here and the Easel*, 1973; *Sturgeon's West*, 1973; *Case and the Dreamer*, 1974; *Visions and Venturers*, 1978; *The Stars Are the Styx*, 1979; *The Golden Helix*, 1980.

Bibliography

Delaney, Samuel R. "Introduction" to *The Cosmic Rape*, 1977.
Diskin, Lahna F. *Theodore Sturgeon: A Primary and Secondary Bibliography*, 1980.
Friend, Beverly. "The Sturgeon Connection," in *Voices for the Future: Essays on Major Science Fiction Writers*, 1976.
Moskowitz, Sam. *Seekers of Tomorrow: Masters of Modern Science Fiction*, 1966.
Williams, Paul. "Introduction" to *The Dreaming Jewels*, 1978.
——————— . "Introduction" to *Venus Plus X*, 1976.

Henry J. Lindborg

WILLIAM STYRON

Born: Newport News, Virginia; June 11, 1925

Principal long fiction
Lie Down in Darkness, 1951; *The Long March*, 1952, 1956; *Set This House on Fire*, 1960; *The Confessions of Nat Turner*, 1967; *Sophie's Choice*, 1979.

Other literary forms
William Styron's career has been curiously one-sided, and he is one of the few major modern literary figures who bears discussion only in a single genre—the novel. Except for a slight and rather curious play, *In the Clap Shack* (1973), and a recent collection of essays, *This Quiet Dust* (1982), Styron's four major novels and his short one, *The Long March*, constitute his entire significant production. Styron lectures and reads frequently on college campuses, and he has been the subject of a substantial number of interviews and articles in which he has spoken of writing, literature, and politics. He has published a section of a novel in progress about a career officer in the Marines, tentatively entitled *The Way of the Warrior*, in *Esquire* (1971).

Achievements
Until the publication of *The Confessions of Nat Turner* in 1967, Styron was well-known in literary circles as a young novelist of great talent but largely unrealized potential. *The Confessions of Nat Turner*, riding the crest of a wave of social activism in the late 1960's and capitalizing on a national interest in black literature and history, gave Styron a major popular reputation as well as making him the center of a vitriolic controversy between academic and literary critics on one side, who tended to see the novel as an honest attempt to come to terms with history, and a small group of strident black critics on the other hand who questioned, often abusively, the ability of any white writer to deal with the black experience, and who called Styron's portrait of Nat Turner unflattering and inaccurate. The book and the debate it engendered made Styron a major voice in twentieth century fiction, as well as a rich man.

Despite the twelve-year hiatus between the publication of *The Confessions of Nat Turner* and that of *Sophie's Choice*, Styron's reputation grew, particularly in terms of his role as an interpreter of the South. *Lie Down in Darkness* was recognized as one of the finest presentations in fiction of the modern Southern family, haunted by memory, guilt, and time, and *The Confessions of Nat Turner* came to be seen as representative of the concern of Southern writers with the burden of history. *The Confessions of Nat Turner* was accepted as a rhetorically beautiful evocation of the past, whatever its historical inaccuracies.

The publication of *Sophie's Choice* in 1979 cemented Styron's position as one of the major figures of contemporary literature. Although several major critics had reservations about the novel, its ambitious confrontation of a moral theme of enormous implication—the Holocaust—and Styron's compelling, lyrical prose made the novel the literary event of the year. With *Sophie's Choice*, some of Styron's lifelong concerns as a novelist become clearer: the unanswerable problem of pain and suffering, the elusive nature of memory, the ambiguous legacy of history.

Biography

William Styron was born June 11, 1925, in Newport News, Virginia, which he later called "a very Southern part of the world." His mother, Pauline Margaret Abraham Styron, was from the North, but his father, William Clark Styron, a shipyard engineer, came from an old, if not aristocratic, land-poor Virginia family, and Styron remembers his grandmother telling him as a little boy of the days when the family owned slaves, a memory he was to incorporate years later into *Sophie's Choice*. Styron's father was a "Jeffersonian gentleman," liberal in his views for a Southerner, who implanted in his son much of the philosophical curiosity which characterized the young Styron's novels. His mother, a gentling influence, died when Styron was twelve after a long, painful siege with cancer, an experience which was also to leave a mark on his fiction in the form of an almost obsessive concern with physical pain and suffering and the vulnerability of the flesh. After his mother's death, Styron began "going wild," and his father sent him to an Episcopal boys' school in Middlesex County, where he was an indifferent student but a voracious reader. Graduating, he enrolled in Davidson College during World War II but soon dropped out to enlist in the marines.

Styron's stint in Officers Candidate School marked the beginning of his writing career, for while there, he enrolled in a creative writing course at Duke University under William Blackburn, whom Styron acknowledges as the most powerful formative influence on his work. One of his stories, about a Southern lynching, similar in tone and execution to William Faulkner's "Dry September," appeared in a student anthology, Styron's first published fiction. At the tail end of the war, Styron was commissioned and sent to the Pacific, arriving on the island of Okinawa after the fighting was over. Styron was to speak later of his sense of guilt at not having seen action, as well as his feeling of horror at the waste and destruction of the war and the terrible, almost casual way in which life could be lost. Back in America, Styron resumed his program at Duke and was graduated in 1947. He took a job in New York as an associate editor in the book division at McGraw-Hill. His senior editor and immediate superior was Edward C. Aswell, the august second editor of

Thomas Wolfe and an éminence grise to rival Maxwell Perkins; Aswell was to appear grotesquely as "The Weasel" in an autobiographical passage in *Sophie's Choice* nearly thirty years later. The callow young Styron found McGraw-Hill humorless and confining, and after six months he was fired.

Living in a Brooklyn boarding house on a tiny legacy from his grandmother, Styron took another creative writing course, this time from Hiram Haydn at the New School for Social Research. He began work on his first novel, *Lie Down in Darkness*, the story of a star-crossed upper-middle-class Southern family whose failure to find love and meaning in life drives the sensitive daughter, Peyton Loftis, to insanity and suicide. The complex treatment of time in the novel and its high Southern rhetoric showed the influence of William Faulkner, whom Styron had been reading intensely, but *Lie Down in Darkness* was manifestly the work of a powerful and original talent. Styron found that the writing of the book, although exhausting, went surprisingly fast, and he finished it and saw it accepted for publication by Bobbs-Merrill before he was recalled by the marines for service in the Korean War. The novel was published in 1951. Styron was then on active reserve duty, from which he was eventually discharged for an eye problem, but which became the basis for his second novel, *The Long March*.

Lie Down in Darkness was an immediate critical success and a moderate popular one, winning the prestigious Prix de Rome in 1952. At that time, Styron had decamped to Paris and fallen in with a young crowd of American expatriate intellectuals, many of whom would later make names for themselves in literature. George Plimpton and Peter Matthiessen were at the center of a moiling, motley, talented crowd that included Harold Humes, John P. C. Train, Donald Hall, and, on the fringe, writers such as James Baldwin, James Jones, and Irwin Shaw. In 1952 and 1953, the group began compiling a literary magazine, *The Paris Review*, which was to become one of the most influential literary periodicals of the postwar period. Plimpton became the first editor and Matthiessen the fiction editor, and Styron wrote the statement of purpose for the first issue. He also gave the periodical one of the first of its famous "Writers at Work" interviews. It was recorded by Matthiessen and Plimpton at Patrick's, the *Paris Review* crowd's favorite bar, and in it Styron claimed that "this generation . . . will produce literature equal to that of any other generation . . ." and that "a great writer . . . will give substance to and perhaps even explain all the problems of the world. . . ." From the start, his ambitions were large.

Although he later said he drank enough brandy in bistros to develop a *crise de foie*, and spent months in the summer of 1952 on a sybaritic "Ovidian idyll" on the Riviera with Humes, Styron was also writing at top speed during this period. In just six weeks, he wrote a novella based on his marine corps training-camp experience, *The Long March*, and it was accepted for publication in the fall by *discovery*, a literary magazine (Knopf would publish it as a book *The Long March* four years later). In 1953, he used the money from his Prix de Rome to travel in Italy, an experience that laid the groundwork for his 1960 novel of expatriates, *Set This House on Fire*, and during this time he met Rose Burgunder, a Jewish poet with some family money from Baltimore, whom he soon married. They returned to America, to Roxbury, Connecticut, which has been Styron's home ever since, and where he began work on the "big novel" that he planned to follow up the success of *Lie Down in Darkness*.

This was *Set This House on Fire*, a sprawling account of American intellectuals living a life of self-indulgence and self-destruction in postwar Italy. The book contained fine lyrical passages of description, particularly of the physical beauty of Italy and the horrifying squalor and suffering of its people, but as Styron later admitted, the novel was seriously flawed—undisciplined and melodramatic. The reviews were very mixed, and some of them savage. Styron's former friend, Norman Mailer, called *Set This House on Fire*, "a bad, maggoty novel," suggesting that Styron could "write like an angel about landscape, but like an adolescent about people." The novel was better received by Styron's European critics—it is still highly regarded in France— but Styron was wounded by his first really bad press, and he retreated to Roxbury to work on his next book, a novel he resolved to make so thoroughly a work of craftsmanship as to defy criticism.

The Confessions of Nat Turner took years to research and write, and true to Styron's expectations, it was immediately acclaimed as a masterpiece. For years, Styron had had his mind on Nat Turner's 1831 slave rebellion as a subject for fiction. It had taken place close to his own Tidewater Virginia home, and Styron saw the suffering, the violence, and the misunderstanding of the revolt as emblematic both of the South's guilt and pain and of his personal concerns as a writer. Styron claimed that reading Albert Camus' *The Stranger* (1942) furnished him with the technique he was to use in presenting Nat Turner's story—the narrative persona reflecting from jail—and there is no doubt that much of the novel's perspective on black people and black problems was derived from Styron's friend, the black writer James Baldwin, who was a guest of Styron for months while he was writing *Another Country* (1962), Baldwin's first major novel about black/white relations. Styron called *The Confessions of Nat Turner* "less an 'historical novel' than a meditation on history," but despite almost unanimous critical accolades, including the praise of Baldwin, who suggested that the novel might be considered the beginning of a black/white "mutual history," Styron became the target of a group of black critics who protested vehemently the right of a white man to consider himself qualified to interpret the black experience. These critics assaulted Styron in print, accused him of racism and of attempting to demean the reputation of a great hero of black history, and hounded him at meetings, readings, and lectures, rising up and screaming "filthy honky liar," among less kindly epithets. Ironically, Nat Turner, as Styron presented him, was a strong and sensitive character, unquestionably the hero of the novel, but so volatile was the political climate of America in the late 1960's that for some critics, any black character who was not a warrior saint was unacceptable as a fictional creation, particularly the creation of a white writer.

The critical assaults provoked by the *The Confessions of Nat Turner* left Styron bruised, but he was encouraged by the praise for the novel's powerful rhetoric and masterly structure, not to mention its enormous financial success. Of the controversy, he said, "It really had very little effect on me . . . largely because of the fact that I knew that it was politically motivated and hysterical, and that I had not violated any truth that a novelist is capable of doing." He turned to new work, first to a lengthy projected novel exploring the psyche of a career army officer, which he finally shelved, then to *Sophie's Choice*, his latest novel. The book began as an autobiographical reminiscence of his aimless days as a junior editor at McGraw-Hill, when he found himself frustrated artistically, philosophically, and sexually. As he worked through his memories in the character of his narrator, Stingo, whose fictional background is almost identical to Styron's own, he found his real theme: the life and eventual death by suicide of a woman who survived the Nazi concentration camps, but emerged terribly scarred emotionally. This woman, the Sophie of the title, becomes the vehicle through which Stingo confronts the potential horror of life, and through whom he matures.

Sophie's Choice was five years in the writing, but Styron was richly rewarded when it was finally published in 1979. A few critics, notably John Gardner, raised questions about its structure, and about the sometimes jejune intrusions of the shallow Stingo, but for the most part the novel was accepted as a fine and satisfying offering by a major writer. "It has the feel of permanence," Peter Prescott wrote. The gratifyingly large sales were capped by a spectacular sale of the film rights. In 1983, Meryl Streep won an Academy Award for Best Actress for her portrayal of Sophie in that film.

Analysis

The informing patterns of William Styron's fiction are by no means self-evident, and they may not yield themselves readily to the casual critic. Unlike William Faulkner, whom he often resembles in style and technique, his subjects are radically diverse—a doomed Southern family, the intellectual jet set of American expatriates, a historical slave revolt, the horror of the Holocaust. He can shift stylistically from the direct "plain style" of *The Long March* to the purple rhetoric of sections in *Set This House on Fire*, and he moves easily from romantic abstraction to concrete objectivity.

Styron is preeminently, almost self-consciously, a writer of "big" novels of weighty moral significance—a fictional *homme sérieux*, as the French say (which may account for some of Styron's great popularity with French critics).

The eternal verities embody themselves relentlessly in Styron's writing. Death, suffering, the silence of God—grave truths lumber ponderously and insistently at the reader in each novel, mercifully relieved by flashes of humor and lyrical passages of poetic beauty, which spare Styron the gray fate of being a sort of American Thomas Mann. Still, the metaphysical predominates in Styron's books.

Strongly underlying all of his novels is a concern with the past, not so much in the form of the passage of time, but rather an awareness that it is either lost or potentially reclaimable. Each of the four major novels moves from the present to the past in an attempt to explain or understand how things came to be as they are. *Lie Down in Darkness*, with its relentless burrowing in the Loftis family past, looks backward to explain Peyton's death. In *Set This House on Fire*, Peter Leverett moves very deliberately into the past in pursuit of a piece of himself that is missing, and his whole purpose in dredging up the Italian incidents that form the body of the novel is to reveal the past so that he may deal with the present. Both *The Confessions of Nat Turner* and *Sophie's Choice* are historical novels concerned with the actual past and with what Robert Penn Warren has called "the awful burden of history."

Styron's fiction is historical, but in an intensely personal and psychological way. Each exploration of the past is filtered through the consciousness of a protagonist—Milton Loftis, Cass Kinsolving, Nat Turner, Sophie—and strongly colored by the neuroses of those characters. The alcoholism of Milton and Cass, Nat's brooding rage, and Sophie's aching guilt over her murdered child—at the core of each novel is psychological exploration rather than historical exposition. Historical process is only the context within which individual psychologies grope for resolution. Each of Styron's characters lives on the verge of apocalyptic catastrophe, always on the edge of mental breakdown. Each of his protagonists is close to outright insanity. Two actually commit suicide (Peyton and Sophie); Nat Turner essentially does; and Cass Kinsolving of *Set This House on Fire* is only saved from it by the thinnest of margins. His people may be constantly close to madness, yet Styron makes the reader feel that the madness is legitimate, for his characters search for meaning in a mad world, and only when they fail to find it do they become deranged. Peyton Loftis' loveless family, Nat Turner's unjust world, and the horrors of the concentration camp for Sophie are atmospheres in which genuine sanity is difficult, if not impossible. Perhaps the most representative Styron "hero' though, is Cass Kinsolving of *Set This House on Fire*, the only protagonist who is a philosopher as well as a sufferer. Cass's madness derives from his contemplation of the horror of human life and misery, and he staggers drunkenly around postwar Italy demanding a teleological answer for the chaos of existence in which God is silent; "you can shake the whole universe and just get a snicker up there."

Perhaps it is this tendency to project the struggles of his characters beyond the ordinary world and to magnify them to the borders of melodrama that gives all of Styron's novels powerful religious overtones. Some of this tendency derives from Styron's own Episcopalian background, which is strongly echoed in the style of *Lie Down in Darkness* and *Set This House on Fire* and is particularly evident in the rhetoric of Nat Turner, who is stylistically more Anglican than Baptist. The central problem in these novels is the conspicuous absence of God from human life. Styron's world is one in which, as Cass says in *Set This House on Fire*, "God has locked the door and gone away to leave us to write letters to Him." They are unanswered. By the time Styron comes to reflecting on the horror of the Holocaust in his last book, it seems no answer is possible.

This is Styron's theme—the absence of God and the meaninglessness of life. Consistently, he approaches it through a single technique, the presentation and contemplation of pain and suffering. Styron's novels are a catalog of the slings and arrows of outrageous fortune, some physical, some mental, and some simply the result of an empathetic identification with the suffering state of mankind.

On its most elemental level, Styron's depiction of suffering is as pure physical pain, Peyton Loftis is tortured by the ache in her womb, the soldiers of *The Long March* by the agony of their exhausted bodies, Nat Turner by the cold of his cell and the torments of his imprisonment, and Sophie by the tortures of the concentration camp. In *Set This House on Fire*, physical suffering is Styron's primary metaphor for the pain of man's empty relationship with the universe, and the novel is shot through with characters in various stages of suffering from "abuse of the carnal envelope."

Vivid as the physical suffering of Styron's characters is, it is nothing compared to their mental and emotional anguish. Often, this mental anguish derives from their acute sense of alienation—from one another and from God. Milton Loftis, Peyton, Cass Kinsolving, Nat Turner, and Sophie writhe painfully and actively, aware of a pervasive emptiness in their lives.

The structural complexities of *Lie Down in Darkness*, combined with the florid rhetoric of the novel, obscure for many readers the essentially simple causality which underlies the book. It is the story of how and why Peyton Loftis becomes insane and kills herself, tracing the roots of her tortured madness to her father's weakness and her mother's inability to love. Peyton's father, Milton, showers her with an excessive adoration that is one facet of his alcoholic self-indulgence; he smothers his daughter with a sloppy, undemanding adulation that counterpoints his wife Helen's psychotic frigidity. Helen is only able to show love in terms of compulsive formal discharge of parental obligations, bitterly resentful of the martyr role she has chosen to play. Eventually, Peyton instinctively rejects both her father's almost unnatural affection and her mother's unnatural lack of it. By the time Peyton cuts herself loose, however, she has been emotionally crippled, unable to accept any genuine love from a series of lovers, including the Jewish artist she marries and who might have brought her peace. She retreats deeper and deeper inside herself, watching first other people and finally the real world recede before her disintegrating mind. The last major section of the novel is her tormented, insane monologue, a brilliant tour de force reminiscent of the Benjy sections of Faulkner's *The Sound and the Fury* (1929).

When *Lie Down in Darkness* was published in 1952, it was widely hailed as a significant addition to the "Southern" school of writing led by Faulkner, Ellen Glasgow, Flannery O'Connor, and Thomas Wolfe. Thematically, *Lie Down in Darkness* is not a markedly "Southern" novel. Although the Loftis family is from Tidewater, Virginia, and there are mannerisms described in the book that are definitively Southern, Milton Loftis' weakness, his wife's cold rage, and their daughter's breakdown are in no way regional. The story could as easily be that of a New England family, such as Eugene O'Neill's Manions. What is actually distinctive about the tragedy of the Loftises is how much it is exclusively their own, rather than a product of the dictates of fate or society. In this respect, the novel differs from Styron's later works, in which he increasingly attributes man's sufferings to forces beyond the individual.

If Styron traces a source of the Loftis family's deterioration, it is perhaps in their life-style. On one level, *Lie Down in Darkness* is almost a novel of manners, for in keeping with the Loftises' "country club" lives, much of the novel delineates social activity—parties, dances, dinners. Emblematic of this are three scenes in which Milton, Helen, and Peyton go through the motions of conventional social rituals while they are torn by violent emotions lying beneath the facade of meaningless behavior. The first of these is a dance at the country club at which Peyton tries to play the role of belle-of-the-ball while her father makes drunken love to his mistress in a cloakroom and Helen seethes at both father and daughter in a jealous rage. Later, a Christmas dinner turns into a grotesque, painful fiasco, as Helen screams insults at her daughter while Milton slobbers drunkenly. Finally, Peyton's wedding becomes a nightmare when Milton again gets drunk and sloppy, and Helen, as always thinly concealing a bitter resentment of Peyton, finally cracks, screaming "Whore!" at her daughter. In a rage, Peyton claws her mother's face with her nails and flees the family forever.

The loss of love, or rather the failure to find it, informs the entire book. The three Loftises grope at one another in despair, reaching out to one another in their separate, psychologically crippled ways for an understanding and affection that will bring them some sort of emotional peace. That peace, though, is impossible because their psychic natures are flawed beyond redemption. Sigmund Freud spins the plot: Milton loves Peyton not wisely, but too well, as she uncomfortably senses, so his love of her must always seem unrequited, and he is destined to be deserted by her at the last; Helen suffers a patent jealous hatred for Peyton, who has a capacity for love that Helen lacks, and who is stranded between the two poles of her parents' emotional inadequacy. The result is endless pain and ultimately annihilation. As Milton wails, "It was awful not to be able to love. It was hell."

It is not hell, though, but obliteration—nothingness—that truly underlies this novel. In the opening scene, Milton meets the train that brings Peyton's body home for burial. The final scene is her throwing herself to her death from a New York City rooftop. Everything between, the whole body of the novel, is an explanation of that death, and the knowledge of Peyton's unavoidable extinction hangs heavily during the entire book. The title is taken from Sir Thomas Browne's gloomy *Hydriotaphia: Or Urn Burial* (1658), a seventeenth century meditation on the inevitability of death, and the "darkness" of the title is that of the grave. Images of death haunt the dreams of the tortured characters, and the reader is never allowed to forget the ultimate negation implicit in the agony of life.

The agony of life, more than the nullity of death, became the focus of Styron's fiction following *Lie Down in Darkness*. His short novel *The Long March* serves almost as a précis for the motif of pain that came to dominate Styron's writing. Not much longer than a substantial short story, *The Long March* stands between the turgid psychological weight of *Lie Down in Darkness* and the ponderous solemnity of *Set This House on Fire* like a breath of fresh air. Short, clean, concise, and plotted without a wasted word, this unpretentious novella contains some of Styron's most disciplined and readable prose. He trimmed away all the heavy rhetorical and philosophical baggage of his "big" novels, leaving before the reader only his lean and awful central subject—pain and suffering. Appropriately, the pain here is of the most basic and primitive sort—pure physical agony. Stylistically, Styron's writing of the book in 1952 was anomalous in the development of his career, for it was at this period that he was gearing up to write *Set This House on Fire*, and the stylistic and structural complexities of *Lie Down in Darkness* were being inflated to match the ambitious range of the novel to come.

Like the best of Ernest Hemingway, *The Long March* is deceptively simple—a step-by-step account of a thirty-six-mile forced march inflicted on some marine reserves by their mindless officers and endured by the men with varying degrees of courage or cowardice, acceptance or rejection, but mainly endured with pain. The march itself is relentlessly real for the reader on page after page, the physical pain of the characters becoming a kind of rhythmic pattern in the book. If the novel has a "message," it is embodied in the final lines, in which Captain Mannix, who has undergone the march protesting its sadistic insanity, swollen and aching, confronts a sympathetic barracks maid who asks if it hurts: "His words [were] uttered . . . not with self-pity, but only with the tone of a man who, having endured and lasted, was too weary to tell her anything but what was true. 'Deed it does,' he said."

After the critical success of *Lie Down in Darkness* and the artistic success of *The Long March*, there followed the better part of a decade before the 1960 publication of *Set This House on Fire*. Comfortably ensconced in Roxbury, Connecticut, prosperous, rearing a family, and moving into the center of the New York literary world, Styron's reputation grew steadily, although his literary output did not. His house, along with George Plimpton's New York City apartment, became one of the new camping grounds for the old *Paris Review* crowd, and Peter Matthiessen, James Jones, and James Baldwin were frequent visitors. Throughout the late 1950's, word of his forthcoming "big" novel spread as Styron gave private readings from it, and the publication of *Set This House on Fire* was eagerly awaited.

The novel was indeed big; actually, it sprawled embarrassingly. In place of the personal, family tragedy of *Lie Down in Darkness*, Styron broadened his scope by giving the suffering in this novel a universal dimension and by exploring the metaphysical bases of it. It is not a family that suffers, but the world. The reader sees this world through the eyes of Peter Leverett, a Styron surrogate, but the real protagonist is Cass Kinsolving, a sensitive, drunken American artist in Italy in the 1950's who is aghast by the suffering of humanity. Much of the story is told to Leverett (and the reader) by Cass, who looks for the ultimate implications of every grain of sand. Looking back, he tells Leverett that he remembers Italy as "an infinity of remembered pain," and he finds divine aspects even in his drunkenness: "God surely had clever ways of tormenting a man, putting in his way a substance whereby He might briefly be reached, but which in the end . . . sent Him packing over the horizon trailing clouds of terror." To achieve this broadened projection, Styron enlarges his cast of characters, heightens his rhetoric, and throws the whole show on an enormous stage. A vast parade of people moves through *Set This House on Fire*, many of them poor, sick, or abused, the rest venal and contemptible. The action is lifted from the commonplace to the melodramatic; rape, murder, and mystery dominate. The characters, except for Leverett and Cass's bovine, Faulknerian wife, Poppy, are exotic. Mason Flagg is a monstrous idiot typifying Victor Hugo's Quasimodo of *The Hunchback of Notre Dame* (1831). He is the "super bastard" aesthete rich boy, whose cultivated corruption is nauseating but still rich and strange. Cass deteriorates theatrically, staggering about and raving lines from Greek tragedy, a far cry from the humdrum drunkard Milton Loftis.

Heightened rhetoric is Styron's principal method of extending the scope of *Set This House on Fire*. Much of the novel reads like Gothic Thomas Wolfe, from Mason's mother's description of "the horror" of her son's expulsion from prep school to Leverett's account of one of the book's several nightmares: "an abomination made of the interlocking black wings of ravens crawling and loathsome with parasites . . . a country in cataclysm and upheaval." Cass spends much of the book in deliberate blasphemy, "raving at that black, baleful, and depraved Deity who seemed coolly-minded to annihilate His creatures," when he is not suffering from delirium tremens and seeing visions of a boiling sea, or giant spiders on Mt. Vesuvius.

This rhetoric not only complements, but makes possible, the projection of much of the novel on a dream level. Styron had done this before, in a Freudian fantasy of Helen Loftis', in one of Peyton's lover's dreams of babies burning in hell, and in Peyton's entire closing soliloquy. In *Set This House on Fire*, though, the use of dream, vision, and hallucination is so pervasive that much of the novel approaches phantasmagoria. Leverett dreams of a malevolent fiend for several pages, and has recurrent, elaborately described nightmares; Cass is repeatedly haunted, and his drunken ordeal ends with an extended vision of disaster, a passage drawing heavily on Dante and the Book of Revelation. So extensive is Styron's use of dramatic and fantastic imagery that it is often difficult to tell whether he is presenting the reader with a metaphor or a dream, and at one point, when Cass describes himself first making love to a beautiful girl, then suddenly "groping for an answer on some foul black shore," it is impossible to tell whether he is just thinking or hallucinating again. Cass himself probably does not know.

Although they differ in scope and ambition, *Lie Down in Darkness* and *Set This House on Fire* are essentially the same kind of novel. Both are studies in personal alienation and deterioration. Both work through an elevated rhetoric and through psychological revelation. Although *Set This House on Fire* reaches self-consciously for transcendence and philosophical universality, the novel centers upon the psychological aberrations of two characters, Cass Kinsolving and Mason Flagg: similar to the tragedy of the Loftis family in *Lie Down in Darkness*, it is still their individual tragedies rather than a universal one. It may have been the critical failure of *Set This House on Fire* that led Styron to shift from his probing of purely personal disaster, or perhaps it was an increasingly sensitive social conscience that was responsible.

Styron called *The Confessions of Nat Turner* "a meditation on history." Its subject is not only the character of Nat, but also the meaning of slavery itself—what it does to people, and to society. Like Styron's previous novels, the book is a contemplation of horror, with a protagonist who becomes a victim of that horror, but in this case, the horror is not a purely personal one. Significantly, unlike the Loftises and Cass Kinsolving, Nat does not deteriorate, but grows through the course of the book as his comprehension of society and life grows. Nat Turner is the richest and most psychologically complex of Styron's characters, and the historical subject matter of the work is filtered through his sensitive consciousness to produce a visionary "meditation" on the world of slavery, dreamlike in quality and poetic in execution. Southern Virginia of the 1830's, the novel's world, is very much a projection of Nat's mind—a mind produced by that world, and savaged by it.

To develop the subtlety of Nat's mind, Styron drew on all his technical and rhetorical resources. His mastery of time-shifts and dream sequences, already amply demonstrated, was enhanced in this novel, and he explored a variety of rhetorical styles, varying from rural black dialect to a high Anglican style echoing Joan Didion's *A Book of Common Prayer* (1977) for Nat's more poetic utterances. Nat's mind ranges with astonishing virtuosity over his universe—the natural world, the complexities of human relations, the elusive mysteries of God, and the bitterness of mortality. An enormously sophisticated narrative persona, Nat moves fluidly across time, contemplating the painful mystery of the past, represented by his long-dead African grandmother, and of the future, represented by his own forthcoming death. Nat tells the entire novel in flashback, remembering his abortive slave rebellion and the personal and historical events leading up to it, constantly trying to cipher out the meaning of those events. The novel is a study of the growth of knowledge and of the growth of Nat's mind. In the introspective isolation of his anguished imprisonment, he reconstructs his lifelong struggle to understand the meaning of existence. He recalls his progression from childhood, when he had no comprehension of what slavery meant, to an early adult period when he accepted his condition either bitterly or philosophically, to a final understanding of slavery in personal, societal, and moral terms. Ironically, as Nat becomes more morally and aesthetically sensitive, he becomes more insensitive in human terms, gravitating toward an acceptance of the violence that finally characterizes his revolt. Only a sudden, visionary conversion to a God of love at the end of the novel saves him from closing the book as an unrepentant apostle of retributory cruelty.

In the process of expanding his knowledge and developing his terrible vision of deliverance from slavery by violence, Nat becomes the spokesman for two familiar Styron themes—the complexity of human psychology and the mystery of human suffering. The most self-searching of Styron's characters, Nat exhaustively explores the ambivalence and ambiguity of his feelings about race, sex, religion, and violence. Although he casts himself convincingly as a Christian prophet, Nat is no simplistic fundamentalist, for he recognizes in his own emotional turmoil personal depths that he can plumb with only partial understanding. His psychology is the battleground of conflicting feelings, symbolized by his powerful attraction to his master's gentle daughter and his vitriolic hatred for all she represents. When he eventually kills her, neither he nor the reader can discriminate his motives. She dies imploring, "Oh, Nat, it hurts so!", and his realization of her pain is the climax of his apprehension of the myriad pains of all mankind, particularly those of his own people. In this concern, he is representative of all Styron's protagonists.

It is almost impossible to deal with *The Confessions of Nat Turner* without mentioning the storm of controversy that followed its publication and success. A number of critics, primarily black, maintained that the novel was historically inaccurate (for example, it portrayed Nat as having homosexual tendencies, but never mentioned that there are records indicating that the real Nat Turner had a wife). Styron was also accused of demeaning a black hero, in that his Nat has reservations about his mission and is squeamish about wholesale slaughter. The real complaint against Styron, though, most thoroughly summarized in a casebook edited by John Henrik Clarke, *William Styron's Nat Turner: Ten Black Writers Respond* (1968), was that he was a white man attempting a theme that should be the sole province of black writers. In answer to the historical criticism, Styron and his defenders point out that *The Confessions of Nat Turner* is a work of fiction which does not pretend to be straight history, and that it violates no factual information known to Styron at the time of writing. The second complaint, that it degrades a black hero, is more difficult to understand. Unquestionably, Styron, like any true artist, presents his hero with his neuroses, self-doubts, and weaknesses. In the main, however, Nat is without doubt a positive and even heroic character, arguably the most admirable in all Styron's fiction. Only a critic in search of a black plaster saint *sans peur et sans reproche* could consider the creation of as rich and sensitive a character as Nat a slur. Regrettably, though, some readers are still looking for a black Natty Bumpo, however anachronistic he may seem in modern literature. As to the argument that Styron is not black, Homer did not serve at Troy nor was Molly Bloom's soliloquy written by a woman.

Styron's novel *Sophie's Choice* was some twelve years in the works, if somewhat less in the writing, and is in every way as ambitious a novel as *The Confessions of Nat Turner*, although its rank in the Styron canon is still in question. Having dealt in earlier novels with suicide, physical agony, existential despair, and slavery, Styron chose the Holocaust as the logical next state of human misery suitable for artistic contemplation. For a long time, Styron had been moving his narrative personae closer toward the subjects of his novels, introducing clearly autobiographical narrators in *The Long March* and *Set This House on Fire*, and making *The Confessions of Nat Turner* an intensely personal first-person narrative. For *Sophie's Choice*, Styron turned to the confessional form plied by novelists as various as Saul Bellow and Norman Mailer and poets such as Robert Lowell. The narrator of *Sophie's Choice*, a young Southerner named Stingo, is, for all intents and purposes, indistinguishable from the young Styron. A young artist *manqué* in New York, Stingo meets and is fascinated by a beautiful survivor of a Nazi concentration camp, Sophie, who is permanently psychologically scarred by the horror she has undergone, the most ghastly aspect of which was being forced to decide which of her two children would live and which would die. Stingo is the ultimate naïf: sexually, emotionally, morally, and artistically immature. As he comes to know Sophie, he comes to know himself. Stingo is an artist in search of a subject, as Styron evidently felt that he himself had been. Styron's problems with finding subject matter commensurate with his talents as a technician have been pointed out by William Van O'Conner in "John Updike and William Styron: The Burden of Talent" (1964) and by other critics. Styron himself acknowledged his concern with finding a fit subject for his early fiction, but he also felt that a concern with pain had been central to his earlier work. In 1970, he said, "Consciousness of pain and suffering has informed my work . . . I hope my present work will not be so preoccupied." At that time, he was working on his military novel, *The Way of the Warrior*, which he eventually abandoned to write a book that returned to the pain motif with a vengeance, along with the other *leitmotiv* of *Sophie's Choice*, that of the artist's artist's finding of himself.

The emotional pain of Peyton Loftis is alienation from family and love. Cass Kinsolving suffers from guilt brought on by self-hatred and contemplation of human suffering. Nat Turner's ultimate pain derives from his isolation from all mankind and God. Sophie and Stingo suffer the pain of guilt. Stingo, the apotheosis of Styron's autobiographical WASP characters, feels he has not "paid his dues," suffered as others have suffered, and he learns of Sophie's anguished life with a guilty voyeurism. Sophie's guilt has a specific origin in her hideous choice to doom one of her children. She also feels ashamed that in Auschwitz she somehow "suffered less" since she was the commandant's mistress and finally survived when others died. Constantly and compulsively her mind plays over the fates of those dead—her little girl, her tortured friends, and the gassed millions whom she never knew. Even memories of her murdered husband and of her father, both of whom she despised, bring her reproach and grief. The knowledge that she did what she had to gives no relief. She says, "I see that it was—beyond my control, but it is still so terrible to wake up these many mornings with the memory of that, having to live with it . . . it makes everything unbearable. Just unbearable." Soon, she will kill herself to stop the pain.

After Sophie's death, the shattered Stingo, who had just become her lover, walks on the beach trying to find some sort of personal resolution and acceptance of a world in which horror and anguish such as Sophie's exist. Her message, though, has been clear: there is no resolution. Madness and suffering of the magnitude represented by the Holocaust can neither be accepted nor understood. Sophie, like Herman Melville's Ishmael, realizes that "there is a wisdom that is woe, and there is a woe that is madness." Stingo has come to know it, too.

With the death of Sophie, Styron seems to have come full circle in his exploration of human suffering and his search for meaning in a flawed and painful world. Both Sophie and Peyton Loftis find death to be the only release from lives so agonizing and painful as to be unbearable. In both his first novel and this one, Styron leads the reader to the edge of the grave and points to it as the goal of life—"therefore it cannot be long before we lie down in darkness, and have our light in ashes." The crucial difference between *Sophie's Choice* and *Lie Down in Darkness*, however, is the character of Stingo, who like Ishmael escapes to tell the tale. The earlier novel leaves the reader in desolation, but the latter, through Stingo, holds forth the possibility of an alternative existence, one not horribly haunted by the knowledge of pain. Stingo's life is hardly one of euphoria, but it is a tenable existence compared to Sophie's untenable one. To some degree, Stingo has paid his dues through her; he has come to know pain and evil through her sacrifice, and therefore he is sadder and wiser, but not destroyed as she is. His survival counterpoints her destruction; the novel that Stingo will write grows out of her ashes and becomes her immortality.

Sophie's Choice is not a cheerful novel, or even an affirmative one, but it is not nihilistic. Perhaps Stingo's optimism at the close is unjustified. A number of critics feel that when Stingo walks on the beach after Sophie's death and finds the morning "excellent and fair," anticipating his own promising career, Styron is simply tacking on an upbeat ending hardly defensible in view of the horror explored by the novel. Similarly, Cass Kinsolving in *Set This House on Fire* never satisfies his thirst for metaphysical answers to terrible questions, but simply decides to stop thirsting and take up fishing. Whether convincing or not, though, Stingo's survival leaves William Styron's literary career for the moment pointed in a new direction, away from the contemplation of pain and the abyss.

Major publications other than long fiction
PLAY: *In the Clap Shack*, 1973.
NONFICTION: *This Quiet Dust*, 1982.

Bibliography
Clarke, John Henrik. *William Styron's Nat Turner: Ten Black Writers Respond*, 1968.
Fossom, Robert. *William Styron: A Critical Essay*, 1968.
Friedman, Melvin J. *William Styron*, 1974.
_____ , and Irving Malin, eds. *William Styron's "The Confessions of Nat Turner:" A Critical Handbook*, 1970.
Morris, Robert K., and Irving Malin, eds. *The Achievement of William Styron*, 1974.
Pearce, Richard. *William Styron*, 1971.
Ratner, Marc L. *William Styron*, 1972.

John L. Cobbs

JONATHAN SWIFT

Born: Dublin, Ireland; November 30, 1667
Died: Dublin, Ireland; October 19, 1745

Principal long fiction

A Tale of a Tub, 1704; *Gulliver's Travels*, 1726 (originally entitled *Travels into Several Remote Nations of the World . . . by Lemuel Gulliver*).

Other literary forms

Jonathan Swift's oeuvre includes a large and important body of verse, best assembled in *The Poems of Jonathan Swift* (1958), edited by Harold Williams. His letters may be found in *The Correspondence of Jonathan Swift*, also edited by Williams. Outstanding among a variety of political writings are Swift's contributions to *The Examiner* (1710-1711), the treatise called *The Conduct of the Allies* (1711), and the important *The Drapier's Letters to the People of Ireland* (1724-1735). His prose, collected in *The Prose Works of Jonathan Swift* (1939-1968), is a fourteen-volume collection edited by Herbert Davis.

Achievements

It is generally conceded that Swift is the greatest English satirist, possibly the most brilliant ironist and acerb wit in any language. Yet the force of his satiric barbs has rendered him controversial, and many critics have retaliated against his potent quill by claiming that Swift is wreckless, uncontrolled, spiteful, insensate, heathenish, and insane. Such rash responses merely demonstrate the powerful effect his writing instigates.

Swift is not an overt lampooner, diatribe-monger, or name-caller. Curiously, he never utilizes the direct approach: he almost always speaks through a defective mouthpiece, a flawed, self-incriminating persona who forges a case against himself. Indeed, Swift is to be remembered as a grand satiric mimic, finely shaping and generating the voices of knaves and fools alike (the "modern" hack writer in *A Tale of a Tub*, the ignorant serving-woman Frances Harris, the idiot astrologer Isaac Bickerstaff, the callous and mathematical Modest Proposer, the proud but demented simpleton Lemuel Gulliver).

Swift's ear for clichés and inflections of dullness is almost perfect, and an author such as Herbert Read (in *English Prose Style*, 1928) hails Swift as the inevitable and clear master of "pure prose" style. Swift is, without doubt, the major satirist in prose, yet he is also a first-rate light poet (in the manner of Horace and the coarser Samuel "Hudibras" Butler), and, if anything, his reputation as a poet is rising. Furthermore, Swift wrote political pamphlets with ruthless force, and his prose in sermons, letters, and treatises is virile and direct. Finally, Swift should not be forgotten as wit and jester. He invented a child-language when corresponding with Stella, wrote mock-Latin sayings, devised wicked epigrams, created paraphrases of Vergil and Ovid, and could even toy with versifying when devising invitations to dinner. In a word, Swift is the all-around English expert in straightforward exposition—especially when it is bent to provoke savage mockery and the *jeu d'esprit*.

Biography

Jonathan Swift was born in Dublin on November 30, 1667, after the death of his father, a lower-middle class Anglo-Irishman. His grandfather, the Reverend Thomas Swift, had been a vicar in Herefordshire. His father, Jonathan, had settled in Ireland to work as a steward of the King's Inns in Dublin. His mother was Abigail Erick, the daughter of a Leicestershire clergyman. Swift's mother had entrusted her young son to a nurse; the nurse had spirited the infant Swift away from Ireland for several years, and though he was eventually returned, Jonathan was peculiarly linked with Ireland throughout his life. In any case, it was his fancy to picture himself a lonely outcast amid barbarians. He attended Kilkenny School in his youth and Trinity College, Dublin, obtaining a Bachelor's degree in 1686. He spent most of the following decade at Moor Park, Surrey, in the household of Sir William Temple, the distinguished Whig statesman. It was at Moor Park that Swift met, in 1689, the child of Esther Johnson (whom Swift later immortalized as "Stella"), the daughter of Temple's widowed housekeeper. Swift helped in supervising her education and inaugurated a lifelong (and little understood) relationship, for Stella later immigrated to Dublin and spent her life near the Anglican Dean Swift. Naturally, under Temple's aegis, Swift hoped for introductions and advancement, but little came of promises and possibilities; and in 1694, he returned to Dublin long enough to be ordained an Anglican priest (in 1695). He subsequently was reunited with Temple until the latter's death in 1699. Thereafter, he returned to Ireland as chaplain to the Earl of Berkeley. His reputation for talent and wit was rapidly growing.

Swift's great political period took place in London from 1708 to 1714. He became the chief spokesman, apologist, and pamphleteer for the powerful Tory leaders then in power, Robert Harley and Henry St. John Bolingbroke. Their fall and disgrace ushered in a lengthy era of Whig dominance that permanently drove Swift back to what he must have considered exile in Ireland. Swift had been finally rewarded (although he would have perceived it as a paltry recognition) with the Deanery of St. Patrick's Cathedral in Dublin, where he served for the remainder of his life. His powerful satires had earned him powerful enemies, and significant advancement in the Church or in England was never permitted to him.

In any event, Swift served with precision, justness, and rectitude as a clergyman, and continued throughout his career to be an admirable satirist and wit. He even elected to champion the rights of the maltreated Irish, and he came to be admired as their avatar and protector, a "Hibernian Patriot."

In his last years, Swift suffered increasingly from deafness and vertigo (the results of a lifelong affliction by Ménière's Syndrome, a disease of the inner ear), which resulted in senility, and most likely a stroke. Guardians were appointed in his last years, and he died in 1745, shortly before his seventy-eighth birthday.

Swift's last ironic jest was played upon mankind in his will, which committed the bulk of his estate to the founding of a "hospital" for fools and madmen, just as he had pronounced the plan in his *Verses on the Death of Dr. Swift*, 1731:

> He gave the little Wealth he had,
> To build a House for Fools and Mad:
> And shew'd by one satyric Touch,
> No Nation wanted it so much

Analysis

Initially, it must be noted that Jonathan Swift's "fictions" are nothing like conventional novels. They seldom detail the "adventures" of a hero or even a protagonist and never conclude with his romantic achievement of goals or fulfillment of desires. Indeed, Swift is the great master of fictionalizing nonfiction. His satires always purport to be something factual, humdrum, diurnal, unimaginative: a treatise, a travel diary, an annotated edition, a laborious oration, a tendentious allegory, a puffed-out "letter-to-a-friend." Extremist Protestant sects condemned fiction, and "projectors" and would-be investigators in the dawning Age of Science extolled the prosaic, the plodding, the scholarly, the methodical, and the factual. At the same time, urban population growth and the rise of the middle class created a growing new audience, and printing presses multiplied in accordance with demand. Many "popular" and best-seller art forms flourished: sermons, true confessions, retellings (and Second Parts) of hot-selling tales and political harangues, news items, hearsay gossip, and science all became jumbled together for public consumption, much of which led to spates of yellow journalism. Throughout his life Swift rebelled against such indelicacies and depravities, and his satiric procedure included the extremist parody of tasteless forms—*reductio ad absurdum*. It was by such means that Swift secured his fame as an author.

Doubtless his most dazzling prose performance of this kind was his earliest, *A Tale of a Tub*, which appeared anonymously in 1704. (Swift, in fact, published most of his satires anonymously, although his work was usually instantly recognized and acclaimed.) *A Tale of a Tub* is actually a "medley" of pieces imitating the penchant for an author's combining fiction, essays, letters, verse, fragments, or anything to enable him to amass a booklength manuscript. It contained "The Battle of the Books," a wooden allegorical piece in the manner of Aesop's Fables, detailing the "quarrel of ancients versus moderns" and a fragmentary treatise upon "The Mechanical Operation of the Spirit," trussed up in the inept form of a casual letter to a friend.

The treatise mocked the new "scientific" trend of reducing all things to some species of Cartesian (or Newtonian) materialism. Rather comically, it deploys in a blasé manner the language of ancient Greek and Roman atomists—Democritus and Epicurus—as if they were contemporary modernists. Indeed, one pervasive theme throughout this volume is the ridiculousness of the modernist position of "independence"—although they might be ignorant of the past, the ideas and genres of classical antiquity keep recurring in their works, a fact which belies the Moderns' supposed originality (even while demonstrating that, as a result of solipsism, their form and control disintegrate into chaos).

Clearly, the titular piece, "A Tale of a Tub," is Swift's early masterpiece, and one of the great (and most difficult) satires in any language. In its pages, an avowed fanatic "modern" aspires to "get off" an edition, to tout and sell himself, to make money, to demonstrate his uniqueness and, however evanescently, tyrannically to be "the latest modern." He seeks to reedit an old tale of three brothers and their adventures. Naturally, he decorates and updates such a version to give it the latest cut and fashion, the style and wit and jargon of the moment. (It is perhaps an accident that this tale of the dissensions of Peter, Martin, and Jack parallels the vicissitudes of the history of Christianity, as it splinters into differing and quarreling religious sects. The Modern appears ignorant of historical sense.)

The new version of the old story, however, is fragmented: every time the Modern's imagination or his fancy supplies him with a spark, he promptly follows his rather meandering Muse and travels into an elaboration, an annotation, or a digression. In fact, the opening fifty pages of the work is cluttered with the paraphernalia of "modern" publishing: Dedications, Publisher's Comments, Introductions, Apologies, and Gratulations, Notes to the Second Edition, Acknowledgements, Prefaces, and Forewords. Thereafter, when such a cloud of ephemeral formalities would seem to have been dispensed with, the author still manages to interject a plethora of digressions—afterthoughts, asides, cute remarks *à propos* of nothing, commentary, snipings at critics, obsequious snivelings for the reader, canting pseudophilosophy for the learned, and pity and adoration for himself. In no time at all, the entire tale is awash in detours, perambulations, and divagations.

This modern storyteller is nothing if not effervescent, boorish, and chronically self-indulgent. He claims that his pipe dreams and diversions are in essence planned excursions and in fact deliberately philosophic meditations, rich with allegorical meanings. The opposite is also true, and the Modern's Tub is like an empty cart—rattling around most furiously in its vacuity, making the most noise. Furthermore, the digressions become unwieldy. The tale is disrupted more and more frequently and the digressions become longer and longer. The Modern is his most penetrating in the trenchant Section IX—a digression in praise of madness—as he coyly confesses that his reason has been overturned, his intellectuals rattled, and that he has been but recently confined. The continued multiplication of digressions (until they subvert sections of the tale) and the finale when the Modern loses his notes and his ramblings give out entirely are easily understood as the wanderings of a madman—a Modern who suppresses the past, memory, reason, and self-control.

If Swift's warning about the growing taste for nowness, modernity, and things-of-the-moment appears madcap and farcical, it is nevertheless a painfully close nightmare preview of future fashions, fantasms, and fallacies that subsequently came to be real.

A Tale of a Tub clearly demonstrates several of Swift's most common fictional ploys and motifs. Some representative of the depraved "moderns' is usually present, always crass, irreligious, ignorant, arrogant, proud, self-adulatory, concerned with the events of the moment. Indeed, Swift was fond of scrupulously celebrating every April 1 as All Fool's Day, but he also recognized April 2: All Knave's Day. He doubtless felt that both halves of mankind deserved some token of official recognition. Yet Swift also favored mixing the two: he frequently shows readers that a man who is manipulator, con-man, and knave in one set of circumstances is himself conned, befooled, and gulled in another. As such, the Modern reveals an unexpected complexity in his makeup; he also illustrates the era (as Swift imagines it) that he inhabits: a period overfull of bad taste and poor writing which are the broad marks of cultural decadence.

In the work of a satirist, the world is regularly depicted as cyclic in historic periods, and usually in decline. Swift and Sir William Temple both stressed some trend toward decay in the modern era, and spoke often of barbarians and invasions; it was a type of satiric myth suitable to the disruptive fictions that the satirist envisions. In Section IX of *A Tale of a Tub*, the Modern vacillates between viewing all mankind as being "curious" or "credulous," as busy probers, analysts, and excavators, and the superficial and the inert: knaves versus fools. As is typical of Swift, the fool and knave personas are infused with enough familiar traits to suggest that all men partake of either. Further, Swift entraps his reader by implying that there are no other categories: one is either fool or knave or both. His irony is corrosive and inclusive, capturing the reader in its toils. In that sense, Swift is deliberately disruptive; he seeks to startle and to embroil the reader in his fictions about stupidity and depravity. To such an end, he tampers with logic to make his case appear substantial and manipulates paradox to keep his readers off balance. Such techniques lend Swift his volatile force.

These strategies are to be found in Swift's best verse; the same may be said for his two great, ironic short-prose pieces: *An Argument Against Abolishing Christianity* (1708) and *A Modest Proposal for Preventing the Children of Poor*

People in Ireland from Being a Burden to Their Parents (1729). Both of these works seek to shock the reader and to propose the discomforting, the alarming, the untenable.

Swift's undisputed masterpiece is the *Travels into Several Remote Nations of the World . . . by Lemuel Gulliver*, better known as *Gulliver's Travels*. This fictional work accommodates all of Swift's perennial themes and does so effectually. First, the work is perhaps the definitive study of new middle-class values, specifically the preoccupation with slang, cash, smug self-righteousness, self-assertion, and self-gratulation. Second, it might not be considered a "novel" in the conventional sense of the term, but it is a delightfully fact-filled simulation of adventure fiction, and it stems assuredly from the satiric picaresque tradition (in Spain and France) that greatly contributed to the formulation of modern novelistic techniques and themes.

Swift's Lemuel Gulliver (a mulish gull) is a model representative of the fool and the knave: he aspires to befool others but nevertheless befuddles himself. His medium is the very popular literary genre of the travelogue or record of a "voyage of discovery." The genre grew popular through its Cartesian emphasis upon an inductive observer-self and the romantic subject of adventures in far-off lands. Such a travelogue format allows the narrator to take his readers on a vicarious journey of adventure and concludes by suggesting that the traveler has fulfilled the pattern of the *Bildungsroman* and has attained education, growth, experience, and Aristotelian *cognitio* (insight, maturation, the acquisition of new knowledge). As might be expected in an exemplary case manipulated by Swift, Gulliver is anything but the apt learner. He is a crass materialist for whom experiences consist of precise measurements of objects observed, a tedious cataloging of dress, diet, and customs, and an infinite variety of pains in note-taking, recording, transcribing, and translating. He is superficiality and rank objectivity incarnate. Naturally, therefore, his everyday mean density prevents his acquisition of any true understanding.

Gulliver is a minor physician, the mediocre little man, anxious, like Daniel Defoe's Robinson Crusoe, to make sight-seeing tours and to acquire cash. His first of four voyages carries him to the land of six-inch mites, the Lilliputians, and his Second Voyage to the land of gargantuan giants, the Brobdingnagians. Gulliver remains myopic in either location, for he can hardly consider that little midgets can (and do) perpetuate monstrous deeds; and, once he perceives that the giants are rather tame, he leaps to the conclusion that they are infinitely superior to other human types (even though their political and social institutions are no better than they should be, given the quirks and flaws of human nature).

In sum, the tour from very small to very large merely stimulates in Gulliver a sense of wondrous contrast: he expects in these different worlds wondrous differences. Amusingly, what the reader finds is much the same, that is the uneven and imperfect human nature. Equally amusing, Gulliver behaves much the same himself in his attempts to ingratiate himself with his "superiors": he aspires to become a successful competitor in all worlds as a "titled" nobleman, a Nardac, a "courtier" with "connections" at court. Like many middle-class people, he is a man in the middle, aspiring above all for upward mobility, mouthing the commonplaces of the day, utterly incapable of judging men and events. He is also the worst sort of traveler; he is a man who sees no farther than his own predilections and preconceptions and who imitates all the manners that he sees around him. Actually, the realms of big and little are merely distortions of the real world. Here, one of the work's central ironies is found in the fact that Gulliver could have learned as much, or as little, if he had stayed at home.

The world of sizes is replaced in the Third Voyage by the world of concepts: the muddled peoples he visits are victims of mathomania and abstraction-worship. At the same time, it is revealed that the world of the past, like the world of the present, has been tainted and corrupt. Even the potentially ideal Struldbruggs—immortals who live forever—are exposed as being far from lucky. They are, rather, especially accursed by the afflictions of impotence, depression, and senility. Swift has, with cartoon facility, carted Gulliver all around the world, showing him the corrosive face of fallen humanity, even among the various robbers, cowards, pirates, and mutineers that had beset him as he traveled in European ships; but Gulliver does not see.

The stage is properly set for the Fourth Voyage. Utilizing his favorite ploys of reversal and entrapment, Swift puts Gulliver into a land of learned and rational horses (the Houyhnhnms) and debauched hairy monkey-like beasts (the Yahoos). Once again, there is no middle ground: all in this world is rational horse or wolfish (and oafish) bestiality. Obviously, Gulliver chooses the equestrian gentlemen as his leaders and masters. (Indeed, throughout all the voyages, Gulliver the conformist has been in quest of a staid position and "masters" who will tell him what to do and grant him praise and sustenance for his slavish adulation.)

Slowly it is revealed, however, that the Yahoos are men: Gulliver *is* a debased, gross, and deformed member of the Yahoo tribe; as Swift sweetly and confoundingly phrases it, Gulliver is a "perfect yahoo." The horses themselves rebuff this upstart, and Gulliver, who has undergone every other sort of ignominy in the course of his travels, is finally evicted as an undesirable alien from the horsey paradise. At last, Gulliver thinks he has learned a lesson; he aspires to be a horse, and, back in Europe, he shuns the human species and favors the environs of straw and stables. He has hardly acquired the rationality of his leaders and appears quite mad. Swift's ultimate paradox seems to imply that men can "know" about reason and ideals but can never master or practice them. Yet, even here, Swift cruelly twists the knife at the last moment, for the fond Gulliver, several years later, is revealed as slowly forgetting his intense (and irrational) devotion to the Houyhnhnms and is slowly beginning to be able to tolerate and accept the loathly human race that he had earlier so intransigently spurned. Gulliver cannot even stick to a lesson painfully and rudely learned during many years; he has neither the brains, drive, ambition, nor consistency to keep him on any course. Gulliver's travels eventually get him nowhere.

In sum, *Gulliver's Travels* makes a huge tragicomical case for the absurdity of pretentious man. Gulliver is fool enough to believe that he is progressing and knave enough to boast about it, and to hope to gain some position and affluence from the event. Yet, at his proudest moments, he is little more than a driveller, a gibbering idiot who is raveningly insane. Gulliver's painful experiences and the brute instruction his readers acquire are a caustic finale to much of the heady and bold idealism of the Renaissance, and a cautionary plea for restraint in an era launched on celebrating reason, science, optimism, and enlightenment. Time has shown that Swift was largely in the right: blythe superconfidence in man, his sciences, and his so-called "progress" is very likely to come enormously to grief. *Gulliver's Travels* speaks to everyman because it addresses crucial issues about the human condition itself.

Major publications other than long fiction

POETRY: *Cadenus and Vanessa*, 1713; *Verses on the Death of Dr. Swift*, 1731; *On Poetry: A Rapsody*, 1733; *The Poems of Jonathan Swift*, 1958 (Harold Williams, editor, 3 volumes).

NONFICTION: *A Discourse of the Contests and Dissensions Between the Nobles and the Commons in Athens and Rome*, 1701; *The Battle of the Books*, 1704; *An Argument Against Abolishing Christianity*, 1708; *A Project for the Advancement of Religion, and the Reformation of Manners*, 1709; *The Conduct of the Allies*, 1711; *A Proposal for Correcting, Improving and Ascertaining the English Tongue*, 1712; *The Public Spirit of the Whigs*, 1714; *An Enquiry into the Behaviour of the Queen's Last Ministry*, 1721, 1765; *Letter to a Young Clergyman*, 1721; *The Drapier's Letters to the People of Ireland*, 1724-1735; *Letter to a Very Young Lady on Her Marriage*, 1727; *A Modest Proposal for Preventing the Children of Poor People of Ireland from Being a Burden to Their Parents*, 1729; *The History of the Four Last Years of the Queen*, 1758; *Journal to Stella*, 1766, 1768; *The Correspondence of Jonathan Swift*, 1963-1965 (Harold Williams, editor, 5 volumes).

MISCELLANEOUS: *Miscellanies in Prose and Verse*, 1711; *Miscellanies*, 1727-1732 (by Swift, Alexander Pope, and other members of the Scriblerus Club, 4 volumes); *Complete Collection of Genteel and Ingenious Conversation*, 1738; *Directions to Servants in General. . .* , 1745; *The Prose Works of Jonathan Swift*, 1939-1968 (Herbert Davis, editor, 14 volumes).

Bibliography

Davis, Herbert J. *Jonathan Swift: Essays on His Satire and Other Studies*,

1964.
Ehrenpreis, Irvin. *Swift: The Man, His Works, and the Age*, 1962—.
Pons, Emile. *Swift: les années de jeunesse et le "Conte du tonneau,"* 1925.
Price, Martin. *Swift's Rhetorical Art*, 1953.
Quintana, Ricardo. *The Mind and Art of Jonathan Swift*, 1936, 1954.
Tuveson, Ernest Lee, ed. *Swift: A Collection of Critical Essays*, 1964.

John R. Clark

WILLIAM MAKEPEACE THACKERAY

Born: Calcutta, India; July 18, 1811
Died: London, England; December 24, 1863

Principal long fiction
Catherine: A Story, 1839-1840 (as Ikey Solomons, Jr.); *Vanity Fair: A Novel Without a Hero*, 1847-1848; *The Great Hoggarty Diamond*, 1848; *The History of Pendennis: His Fortunes and Misfortunes, His Friends and His Greatest Enemy*, 1849-1850 (2 volumes); *Rebecca and Rowena: A Romance upon Romance*, 1850 (as M. A. Titmarsh); *The History of Henry Esmond, Esquire, a Colonel in the Service of Her Majesty Q. Anne*, 1852 (3 volumes); *The Luck of Barry Lyndon: A Romance of the Last Century*, 1852 (2 volumes); *The Newcomes: The Memoirs of a Most Respectable Family*, 1854-1855, 1863 (2 volumes); *The Virginians: A Tale of the Last Century*, 1858-1859 (2 volumes); *Lovel the Widower*, 1861; *The Adventures of Philip on His Way Through the World, Shewing Who Robbed Him, Who Helped Him, and Who Passed Him By*, 1862 (3 volumes); *Denis Duval*, 1864.

Other literary forms
William Makepeace Thackeray's career as a satirist and journalist contributed to his novelistic style. His works appeared in a number of periodicals, including *The National Standard*, which he owned, *The Constitutional*, for which he was Paris correspondent, and *The New Monthly Magazine*. More important, however, the bulk of his writing appeared in *Fraser's Magazine* and in *Punch*, until, in 1860, he became editor of the *Cornhill Magazine*. In many of his reviews, short stories, burlesques, and travel writings, he adopts facetious pen names that reveal the snobbish preconceptions of his personae. "The Yellowplush Correspondence" appeared in *Fraser's Magazine* in 1837-1838 as the supposed diary of Charles James Yellowplush, an illiterate footman who betrays all of the social prejudices of his employers. The story was later published as *Memoirs of Mr. C. J. Yellowplush* in 1856. Thackeray assumed two pseudonyms for some of his comic pieces. As Michael Angelo Titmarsh, Thackeray published *A Legend of the Rhine* (1845), *Mrs. Perkin's Ball* (1847), and *The Rose and the Ring: Or, The History of Prince Giglio and Prince Bulbo* (1855) among others, in addition to some nonfiction works such as *The Paris Sketch-Book* (1840), *The Irish Sketch-Book* (1843), and *Notes of a Journey from Cornhill to Grand Cairo . . .* (1846); as George Savage Fitz-Boodle, an aging and susceptible bachelor, Thackeray wrote *The Fitz-Boodle Papers* (1852), *The Confessions of George Fitzboodle* (1843), and *Men's Wives* (1852). "Punch's Prize Novelists," which appeared in *Punch* magazine, was a series of parodies of popular novelists of the day, such as Benjamin Disraeli and James Fenimore Cooper, and was perhaps even more

effective than the burlesque *Catherine* (which he wrote as Ikey Solomons, Jr.). Thackeray's other achievements include *The English Humorists of the Eighteenth Century* (1853) and *The Four Georges: Sketches of Manners, Morals, Court and Town Life* (1860); a number of tales and short stories, including *A Shabby Genteel Story* (1857), and a series of ballads and verses, such as the nostalgic "The Ballad of Bouillabaisse" (1849).

Achievements

Long remembered as a social satirist *par excellence*, Thackeray wrote more in the manner of Henry Fielding than of Samuel Richardson and more in the realistic vein than in the style of the "novel of sensibility," that production of the early nineteenth century that sought to achieve heightened emotional effects at the expense of believable plot and characterization. Both in his miscellaneous writings and in his first great novel, *Vanity Fair*, Thackeray sought to counter the kind of melodramatic and pretentious entertainment provided by such authors as Edward Bulwer-Lytton, William Harrison Ainsworth, and even the early Charles Dickens. He attempted, instead, to make his readers see through the social and literary hypocrisy that, as he believed, characterized the age. To this end, he adopted a number of pseudonyms in his early essay writing, pseudonyms that can be said to foreshadow the personae he used in his fiction.

In reviewing both art and literature for such magazines as *Fraser's Magazine* and *The New Monthly Magazine*, Thackeray adopted the Yellowplush and Titmarsh signatures; he was thus able to ridicule in a lively way what he found false. His reviews were no less devastating to the current trend of idolizing criminals and rogues, as seen in the series of popular "Newgate Novels." As Ikey Solomons, Jr., he produced *Catherine*, the tale of a murderess, but even here, his attempt to deglamorize the account was mitigated by his growing sympathy for his created characters. Again, *A Shabby Genteel Story* attempted to deal with the middle class in unvarnished terms. His first sustained narrative, *The Luck of Barry Lyndon*, features an Irish adventurer recounting his own life; the novel follows the rise and fall of its picaresque hero to illustrate the specious nature of worldly success. Perhaps most telling in his ten-year preparation for fiction writing were two series that appeared in *Punch*. "The Snobs of England" was a series of verbal portraits of social types, most drawn for their pretension; "Punch's Prize Novelists" was a collection of parodic rewritings of popular novelists' works.

In his sustained works, however, Thackeray leaves his readers not with a collection of isolated vignettes but with a panoramic study of mankind under the guidance of a witty persona whose satirical bent is tempered by the realization that he himself partakes of the foibles of his own characters. Thackeray's characteristic persona derives not only from Fielding and his prefaces to the various books of *The History of Tom Jones, a Foundling*

(1749), but also from Samuel Johnson, who ends *The History of Rasselas, Prince of Abyssinia* (1759) by suggesting that since an ideal world is impossible, a wise individual will stoically accept the one that exists. Certainly, Thackeray's experimentations with the persona in *The History of Henry Esmond, Esquire*, for example, a novel written in the memoir form, laid the groundwork for such masters of psychological realism and irony as Henry James and James Joyce. In addition, Thackeray's experimentations with the generational form, in which several novels are melded together through the familial relationships of their characters, look forward to such productions as John Galsworthy's *The Forsyte Saga* (1922). In presenting the affairs of Henry Esmond's grandsons and the development of the beautiful Beatrix Esmond into a worldly old woman in *The Virginians*, he was also implicitly exploring the kind of genetic and environmental influence that the naturalists defined as determinism.

While many modern readers are perhaps not as comfortable as their nineteenth century forebears with the conception of the authorial voice as a constant, even necessary factor in the plot, Thackeray nevertheless remains noteworthy, especially in his early novels, both for the realistic renderings of individuals in all social walks and for his moral standpoint, best expressed in the Preface to *Vanity Fair* as a charitable outlook on human foibles.

Biography

William Makepeace Thackeray was born on July 18, 1811, in Calcutta, India. His father, Richmond Thackeray, pursued a family career in the East India Company; his mother, Anne Becher, traced her ancestry back to a sixteenth century sheriff of London. The senior William Makepeace Thackeray and John Harman Becher had extensive interests in India. After his father's death in 1815, Thackeray's mother married Major Henry Carmichael-Smith, a former suitor. As was the custom, Thackeray was sent to England at the age of five for reasons of health and education. His unhappy, early experiences at the Arthurs' school and at Chiswick were later rendered in "Dr. Birch and his Young Friends" (1849). At Cambridge, as a member of a privileged class, he was trained in the standards and preconceptions that he later pilloried in his *The Book of Snobs* (1848, 1852) and in many other works. He was left with a distaste for bullying and with a distrust of his own intellectual abilities. After two years at Cambridge, Thackeray abandoned the pursuit of academic honors. Although he believed that his education had, on the whole, served him ill, it nevertheless had given him a background in history and culture, a double appreciation that is well evidenced in *The History of Henry Esmond, Esquire*; it also convinced him of his social status, although his expensive aristocratic habits were to prove difficult to control.

The gentle satire evident in *Vanity Fair*'s Pumpernickel chapters reflect Thackeray's happy six-month tour of Germany before he undertook to study law in London. While the discipline soon proved not to his taste, his life as a gentleman of fashion (a life that included large gambling debts) was congenial, at least until the collapse of many of the Indian commercial houses reversed his inheritance prospects. Almost relieved to be forced to make his own way, Thackeray decided to develop his talent for drawing, making friends with Daniel Maclise and being tutored by George Cruikshank. While in Paris studying art, he met and married Isabella Shawe, the daughter of a Colonel in the Indian army. He endeavored to support his family through journalistic activities, even offering to illustrate Charles Dickens' *Pickwick Papers* (1836-1837). His friendship with Daniel Maginn made his "Yellowplush Papers" welcome in the columns of *Fraser's Magazine*, whose readers were regaled with the malapropisms of a rascally footman. In addition, he wrote for the London *Times* and for a number of obscure journals. His first long attempt at fiction was *Catherine*, a parody of the "Newgate Novel"; in quick succession he produced *A Shabby Genteel Story* and *The Paris Sketch-Book*.

In 1840, Thackeray was visited by domestic calamity; upon the birth of their third daughter, his wife, Isabella, went insane and required institutionalization. The child-rearing was assumed by Thackeray's parents, leaving him to recoup his writing career, initially with *The Great Hoggarty Diamond* and shortly with contributions to *Punch* and the *Morning Chronicle*. During these middle years, Thackeray solaced himself for the want of domestic connections with a series of friendships with old Cambridge acquaintances such as Alfred Tennyson and W. H. Brookfield, as well as with journalistic brethren such as Francis Sylvester Mahoney (the "Father Prout" of *Fraser's Magazine* fame) and with Dickens himself, whom Thackeray could, however, never accept as a "gentleman." His travel literature was published at this time. His connection with *Punch*, begun in 1842, was an important one. From contributing fillers, he went on to write a number of series; moreover, Thackeray's rivalry with the other principal writer, Douglass Jerrold, was to affect the course of *Punch*'s publishing history, turning the tide from radicalism and democracy to a Whiggish conservatism of which Dickens himself much disapproved.

The year 1847 was crucial for Thackeray. He began to parody novels for *Punch* in the "Punch's Prize Novelists" series, he began a long platonic affair with Jane Brookfield, and he published *Vanity Fair*, the novel that has achieved abiding interest for its panoramic social view and its narrator's satirical viewpoint. His four-year relationship with Jane Brookfield certainly affected his writing; much of the nostalgia and agonizing provoked by the affair are reproduced in *The History of Henry Esmond, Esquire*. Just as important was his entreé into aristocratic circles, for he, along with his daughters Anny and Minnie, with whom he had set up an establishment in Kensington, were welcome not only at Holland House but also in the demirep world of Lady Blessington. Leaving his daughters was the only blight on his first American tour in 1852, when he lectured about "English Humorists of the Eighteenth Century" and marveled at the way in which the *nouveau riche* mingled with the best society.

Upon his return, Thackeray entered the height of the London social season and visited his daughters in Paris. He began *The Newcomes*, a novel much interrupted by illness but, even as its title suggests, much influenced by his social experiences. His work on the "Four Georges," an indictment of the House of Hanover as well as of the monarchy and the upper classes, indicated his changed attitudes. After his second American tour (undertaken, like the first, to provide stipends for his daughters), Thackeray not only published *The Virginians*, but also became editor of *Cornhill Magazine*, a project that allowed him to move "out of novel-spinning back into the world" of the essay. The periodical was an immediate success, publishing such authors as Anthony Trollope and George Henry Lewes. Although Thackeray retired as editor in 1862, he continued to publish his "Roundabout Papers" there until the year after. Indeed, his last unfinished novel, *Denis Duval*, appeared in *Cornhill Magazine* posthumously in 1864, after Thackeray had died on December 24, 1863, in London.

Analysis

While William Makepeace Thackeray may indeed be best known as the author of *Vanity Fair*, to examine all of his novels is to understand why his contribution to the history of the novel is singular. His use of the intrusive narrator, although presaged by Henry Fielding, was developed so carefully that it became a new form of fiction, a "genuine creation of narrative experiment," as critic Alexander Welsh calls it. In addition, his panoramic realism— although creating that anathema of Henry James, the novel that is "a loose and baggy monster"—explored, both seriously and satirically, a number of topics from which other Victorian writers shied away, such as married life and the development of the middle-class gentleman.

Quite aside from the interest generated by the story line, many of Thackeray's novels offer explanations of the art of creating fiction as well as criticism of some of his contemporaries' inadequacies. When Amelia in *Vanity Fair*, for example, tries to visualize George's barracks, the doors are closed to her, for the romantic imagination is in all respects inadequate to the exigencies of real life. In *The Newcomes*, Thackeray compares his method of character-building to the work of the paleontologist who discovers a series of bones and who must construct the habits, behavior, and appearance of his subject from a mere skeleton. He thereby suggests that any such "reality" is merely an illusion, for like the paleontologist, the author must work with probabilities. Insofar as his characters follow a probable course of events, they are true to life and, in a sense, interact without the help of the author. That Thackeray meant his novels to be something more than believable illusionary worlds is clear when his conclusions are examined. In *The Newcomes*, for example, Thackeray retreats at the end from Pendennis' narrative to suggest that the sentimental world he has created has no basis in fact, although the reader may believe so if he wishes to delude himself, and in the well-known ending to *Vanity Fair*, Thackeray puts his "puppets"—his characters—back into their box.

Rather than following Samuel Taylor Coleridge's idea of "willing suspension of disbelief," Thackeray is philosophical, inviting the reader into a reconsideration of his own or of conventional beliefs and preconceptions. Certainly, Thackeray's satire is operative here, particularly in his *Punch* series, in *Catherine*, and in *The Luck of Barry Lyndon*, in which he deliberately spoofed popular historical, crime, and romantic novels, respectively. The reader is asked to look at more than literary conventions, however; he is asked to examine his own degree of hypocrisy and snobbery. In so doing, the reader is reminded again and again that if he laughs at his neighbors, he condemns himself. Thackeray's work is thus truly homiletic, both in a literary and in an extraliterary sense. Unlike many of his predecessors, he examined in detail the difficulties occasioned not only by marriage but also by other personal relationships; rather than assuming that a novel should end with marriage, he makes it his subject. Certainly, his personally tragic domestic situation and his affair with Jane Brookfield are reflected in Rachel Esmond's trials with her reckless husband in Henry Esmond's growing love for her. In the family chronicle *The Newcomes*, Thackeray looks at the misery occasioned by parental marriage choices; Mrs. Mackenzie (known as the "Campaigner"), a strong-minded virago who runs her daughter's life, is modeled on Mrs. Shawe, Isabella's termagant mother. Finally, in *The Virginians*, he traces the development of family characteristics and family ties.

Another one of the many senses in which Thackeray's novels are educative is the way in which he redefines the word "gentleman" to apply not to a member of a particular social class, but rather to one who possesses a set of personal characteristics, such as clear-sightedness, delicacy, generosity, and humanitarianism. His upper-class upbringing in India as well as his Cambridge education coupled with his love of the high life would seem to mitigate against such a redefinition, but, in fact, it is the greengrocer's son, Dobbin, in *Vanity Fair* who is the gentleman, rather than the pompous, vain George Osborne, and it is Colonel Newcome who, despite his misguided attempts to settle his son Clive's happiness, emerges as the paradigmatical enemy to snobbery and to greed.

Vanity Fair, whose title is taken from John Bunyan's *The Pilgrim's Progress*, (1678, 1684), proved to be Thackeray's most successful novel. Indeed, its attention to realistic detail and its panoramic sweep, to say nothing of the constant presence of the author-cum-narrator, caused many reviewers to label Thackeray "the Fielding of the nineteenth century." While neither the initial reviews nor the sales were immediately promising, interest in the serial grew steadily until the publication of the hard-backed volume guaranteed the author a financial as well as a critical success. Rivaling Thackeray at the time was Charles Dickens, whose *Dombey and Son* (1848) appealed to a wide audience; even Thackeray himself, upon reading the number containing little Paul's death, despaired about writing "against such power." Thackeray, however, had his own power, that of the saritist who created "A Novel Without a Hero" and thus ran counter to his readership's expectations, and that of the moralist who included his reader and himself in his reflective view of society.

The hero that *Vanity Fair* must do without is the typically romantic hero. George Osborne (whose first name conjures up the dandified Regency court) is handsome, dashing, and well-loved, but he is also vain, shallow, and pompous. After Joseph Sedley has gone bankrupt, George marries the pining Amelia Sedley only at the urging of his friend William Dobbin; during their honeymoon, he engages in a flirtation with Becky Sharp, herself newly married to Rawdon Crawley. Killed at the battle of Waterloo, George is cherished as a hero only by Amelia. Dobbin is at the other extreme: gangly, awkward, and low in social standing, he is nevertheless possessed of compassion and understanding, yet he is so blinded by his selfless love for Amelia that he does not see until the end of the novel on how slight a character he has set his affection. Even Rawdon, who develops from a typical "heavy dragoon" who lives by his gambling into an affectionate father for his neglected son, lacks intellectual acumen, and, after his separation from Becky, accepts the post that her prostitution to Lord Steyne earned him.

As A. E. Dyson suggests, Thackeray is indeed writing "an irony against heroes"—and against heroines as well. Amelia and Becky are as different as George and Dobbin. Initally, Amelia seems to be a conventional heroine, but the reader who views her in that light will be shocked to discover that he is idealizing the passivity, self-sacrifice, and hero-worship that are the earmarks of neuroticism, the three characteristics well seen in her treatment of her son Georgy, who is absurdly spoiled despite Amelia's and her parents' penury. No wonder, then, that readers preferred "the famous little Becky puppet" for her wit and ambition. From the moment she rides away from Miss Pinkerton's finishing school, leaving Dr. Johnson's dictionary lying in the mud, her energy in making a place for herself in society is impressive. Failing to entangle Amelia's brother Jos, she eventually marries Rawdon, the favorite of his wealthy aunt, and only repines when Lord Crawley himself proposes—too late. She turns her very bohemianism into an asset as she gains entry into the best society, and while she claims that she too could be a "good woman on £5000 a year," her energy in luring dupes to Rawdon's card table, wheedling jewels from Lord Steyne, being presented to the king, and playing charades at a social affair, belies her claim. As John Loofbourow shows, as Becky comes into social ascendency, Amelia declines into obscurity. Amelia lacks Becky's energy, while Becky lacks Amelia's morality. In the end, when

Dobbin has won his prize, Becky has devolved into a female picaresque rogue, traveling across the Continent from disreputable gaming table to questionable boarding house. Neither she nor Amelia qualifies as a heroine.

It is Thackeray's Preface that reveals the moral purpose behind his satire. Posing as the "Manager of the Performance," Thackeray reminds his readers that they are embarked on a fictional journey through an emblematic Vanity Fair, an evocation related only partly to the original in Bunyan's work. Vanity Fair, for Thackeray, is a representation of the human condition; it is not for the reader, like Bunyan's Christian, to pass through and eschew its lures, but rather to experience it "in a sober, contemplative, not uncharitable frame of mind," for the reader and author alike are part of the fair. Thackeray's comments throughout serve the purpose of distancing the reader from the characters and forcing him to judge not only the created "puppets" but also his own preconceptions. If everyone is indeed part of the fair, to condemn the booth-owners' hypocrisy, or social climbing, or snobbery, or mendacity, is to condemn one's own failings. To be possessed of "charity"—to be able to pity others with the same care one has for oneself—this, Thackeray suggests, is the best that can be expected when the puppets are put back in the box.

The subtitle of *The History of Pendennis*—"His Fortunes and Misfortunes, His Friends and His Greatest Enemy"—gives ample indication that the novel is a *Bildungsroman*. As Juliet McMaster points out, however, it is also a *Künstlerroman*; that is, a tale about the development of an artist. It is perforce autobiographical, detailing as it does the way in which a young man learns enough about the world and himself to become a writer of "good books." The novel is important in a study of Thackeray's technique, presenting, as it does, the background for the persona who was to narrate *The Newcomes* and showing Thackeray's struggles with Victorian prudery. Indeed, in his Preface he complains that his readers, unlike those of Fielding, are unwilling to accept a truthful portrayal of human beings unless they are given "a conventional simper." Thackeray's reviewers, however, welcomed the novel, their only complaint being the cynicism with which he endowed Pen. Such cynicism refutes Henry James, Sr.'s remark that Thackeray "had no ideas," for Thackeray's wryness results from a consideration of political and religious turmoil, from the "skepticism" brought about by the 1848 French Revolution, and from the controversy occasioned by the Oxford movement and Cardinal John Henry Newman's conversion from Anglicanism to Catholicism. Clearly, one reason for Thackeray's contemporary appeal was that he reflected the very doubts of his own readers, for whom belief was an exercise in paradox.

The tension between the heart and the world that animates *The History of Pendennis* is well represented by the frontispiece to the first volume, in which a youthful figure is clasped on one side by a woman representing marital duty and on the other by a mermaid representing the siren lure of worldly temptations. Within the dictates of the plot, the same tension is demonstrated by the demands of Pen's sentimental mother, Helen Pendennis, who urges her son to marry the domestic Laura, her ward, and those of his uncle, Major Pendennis, who is willing to blackmail his acquaintance, Sir Francis Clavering, so that Pen can have a seat in Parliament and the hand of Clavering's wealthy but artificial daughter Blanche. Between the two, Pen must, as McMaster points out, find his own reality; he must acquire "his uncle's keen perception without the withering selfishness" and participate in his mother's world of emotions without engaging in "romantic illusion." Pen's education progresses primarily through his amours, but also through his choice of career, for to be a writer, he must determine the relationship between fact and fiction.

Pen's abiding interest in the nature of experience makes his involvement with an actress allegorical in nature. His first affair is with Emily Costigan (known as "the Fotheringay"), an Irish actress older than he and one who plays her parts serenely unconscious of their philosophical implications; her ignorance Pen passes off as "adorable simplicity." Extricated by his uncle, who "lends" Emily's father a small sum in return for Pen's love letters, Pen next enters Oxbridge, and then, influenced by his roommate, George Warrington, determines to study law and to become a writer. His affair with Fanny Bolton, the daughter of his landlady, is again one of an attraction to "adorable simplicity," and his consequent illness a kind of purgation. His attachment to Blanche Clavering is more serious and more dangerous, for Blanche is a social "actress" with whom Pen plays the role of world-weary lover. With her he believes he has matured because he is willing to compromise with disillusionment. His real moment of maturity comes, however, when he finds that he cannot put up with his uncle's worldliness, for in discovering that Clavering's second marriage is bigamous and that the Baronet is paying blackmail money to his wife's first husband, the Major in turn blackmails Clavering to give up his seat in Parliament to Pen and to cede his estate to Blanche.

Pen's responsible decision to honor his proposal to Blanche despite the resultant scandal is, in fact, unnecessary, for she jilts him for a more suitable match, freeing him to marry Laura, whose steadfast, honest devotion represents the alternative to Blanche's sham affection. Laura, in fact, is Pen's muse, his living "laurel wreath"; she has insight and a critical faculty that force Pen to come face to face with himself. With her, Pen finally frees himself from both romantic illusion and worldly disillusionment.

Like Dickens, who turned from the largely unplotted "loose and baggy monsters" of his novelistic apprenticeship to produce the tightly controlled *Dombey and Son*, Thackeray moved from the looseness occasioned by serial publication to the careful construction of *The History of Henry Esmond, Esquire*, more commonly known as *Henry Esmond*. While the novelist Anthony Trollope agreed with Thackeray that the book was his "*very* best," initial critical reaction was mixed, ranging from high praise for Thackeray's realism to a scandalized outcry against what Gordon Ray calls the "emotional pattern" of the work—Esmond's marriage to Lady Castlewood, his cousin and senior by eight years. All agreed, however, that the novel was profoundly moving. Much of its power is owing to its genesis: written when Thackeray was recovering from his alienation from Jane Brookfield, the novel reflects his own emotional current, his nostalgia, his suffering, and his wish-fulfillment. In addition, *Henry Esmond* may be read on many levels—as historical fiction, as novel of manners, and as romance.

Superficially, Thackeray might seem an unlikely figure to write a historical novel, inasmuch as he composed a series of parodies of "costume dramas" (as he called them) for *Punch* and inasmuch as the historical novel was going out of fashion by 1852. Nevertheless, because Thackeray was steeped in seventeenth century history, the work has a verisimilitude that, in the view of some critics, allowed him to outstrip even Sir Walter Scott. The point of view he adopts, that of the first-person narrator, adds to the illusion. This tour de force is accomplished with a success that even Henry James, the master of psychological realism, might envy. The entire story is presented from the limited point of view of Esmond, the cheated heir of the Castlewood estate, who is adopted by his cousins, falls in love with the beautiful but irresponsible Beatrix Esmond, and for her sake joins the Jacobite cause; then, when Beatrix becomes the Pretender's mistress, he realigns himself on the side of the Stuarts, marries Beatrix's mother, and emigrates to America.

That Thackeray could, through a limited narrator, represent the complexity of Lady Castlewood's growing love for the innocent and unconscious Henry is remarkable in its own right. Thackeray's own memories of his boyhood helped him to re-create Henry's loneliness; his relationship with Jane Brookfield shaped his characterization of Lady Castlewood. As John Tilford points out, Thackeray prepares carefully for the marriage, doubtless aware that it challenged many readers' expectations and moral assumptions. Through nuances of dialogue, Rachel Castlewood's awareness of her feelings and of Henry's is revealed. A number of crucial scenes prepare for the denouement: Rachel's hysterical reaction to Henry's early affair with the blacksmith's daughter, an affair that brings smallpox to the family; her vituperation of Henry as he lies in prison for his involvement in a duel that killed Lord Castlewood, whose drinking, gambling, and hunting had contributed to a loveless marriage; and, finally, her overwhelming joy when she sees Henry after his long period of military service.

One early criticism of the novel was recorded by William Harrison Ainsworth, with whom Thomas Carlyle joined in objecting to the exultation of "sentiment above duty" in the novel; other critics found the comparison between the excitement of romantic love and marital unhappiness to be dangerous. The more sophisticated analysis of McMaster registers an "ironic tension" between "Rachel's moral rectitude and . . . the psychological damage" it can cause.

Like Henry James's Mme. de Mauves, Rachel is possessed of a cool virtue based on a conviction of moral and intellectual superiority; as McMaster suggests, she may indeed welcome evidence of her husband's coarseness as a way of rationalizing her affection for Henry and may therefore be responsible for exacerbating her husband's untoward behavior. Thackeray does give both sides: while Castlewood, like Fielding's Squire Western, is rough and careless, pursuing a prodigal, adulterous life once his wife has lost her beauty to smallpox, he accuses her of pride and of a blighting coldness, and pleads for "the virtue that can forgive." Even Beatrix complains that her mother's saintliness provided so impossible a model that she was driven to ambitious selfishness. Such complaints themselves sound like rationalizations, however, for at the end of the novel, Rachel has undergone a long period of repentance. Having sent her temptation—Henry—away, she lives with the renunciation of happiness while he matures. Upon his return, then, she is no longer an angel, but, as he says, "more fondly cherished as woman perhaps than ever she had been adored as divinity."

Subtitled *The Memoirs of a Most Respectable Family*, *The Newcomes* is a novel of manners that explores the way in which four generations of a nouveau riche family acquire social respectability. The novel, the first third of which is densely packed with background material and consequently slow-moving, is a deliberate return to the serial format that Thackeray had abandoned in *Henry Esmond*. While some modern critics object to the pace of this "monster," nineteenth century reviewers believed that with this novel, Thackeray had outstripped even Dickens, whose antiutilitarian manifesto, *Hard Times* (1854), was running concurrently. To be sure, a number of reviewers noted some repetition in theme and characters, a charge against which Thackeray defended himself in the "Overture" but admitted to in private, acknowledging a failure of invention because of sheer exhaustion. One such "repetition," which is, in fact, a way of extending the scope of the novel, is that Pendennis is the "editor" of the Newcome memoirs. This device allows Thackeray not only to assume an objective stance from which his satire is more telling, but also to criticize the very social punctiliousness that Pendennis reveals, thereby achieving an advanced form of psychological analysis.

What provides the novel's "unifying structural principle," as McMaster notes, is "the repetition of the mercenary marriage and its outcome between various couples." This theme, however, is a manifestation of the larger examination of the nature of "respectability," as the subtitle implies. For Barnes Newcome, the banker, for the aristocratic Lady Kew, and even for her granddaughter, Ethel Newcome, affection and generosity are weighed against wealth and social position and found wanting. The touchstone figure is Colonel Thomas Newcome, Barnes's half brother; unworldly, honest, and loving, he is seen by Gordon Ray as a model of Christian humility. The underlying cynicism of the novel is underscored by the inability of the characters to gain happiness, whether they satisfy their acquisitiveness or rebel against such a value, for Thackeray reminds his readers that real fulfillment only exists in "Fable-land."

To pursue the marriage theme is to understand that in Thackeray's world even the best intentions go awry. Certainly, the unhappiness that accrues in some relationships seems self-created: while the joining of money and class in Barnes's marriage to Lady Clara Pulleyn satisfies the dictates of the marriage market, Barnes's brutality drives his wife to elope with a former suitor. In contrast, Clive Newcome, the Colonel's son, is forbidden by Lady Kew to marry Ethel because his profession as an artist is unacceptable. Even Clive himself is infected by the view, for he neglects his modest muse to devote himself to society. For his part, the Colonel, seeing Clive's unhappiness, schemes to marry him to the sweet but shallow Rosey Mackenzie, the niece of his old friend James Binnie. The loveless though well-intentioned match is unhappy, for Clive longs for Ethel's companionship and the couple is tormented by the dictatorial Mrs. Mackenzie after the Colonel's bankruptcy.

Ethel, like Becky Sharp and Beatrix Esmond, is a complex heroine, one who, through much trial and error, weans herself from the respectable avarice she was reared to accept. In love with Clive despite her relations' objections, she nevertheless admits that she delights in admiration, fine clothes, and jewelry, and, although she despises herself for it, that she enjoys being a coquette. Her fine sense of irony about the marriage market, however, prompts her to wear a "sold" ticket pinned to her dress, much to the annoyance of her respectable relatives. At first affianced to Lord Frank Kew, she breaks the engagement; then, capitulating to social pressure, pursues the feeble-minded Lord Farintosh, only to repent at the last moment when the devastation of Barnes's marriage, on which her own is to be patterned, is borne in upon her. In revulsion from her family's values, she devotes herself to Barnes's children and manages to divert some of the Newcome fortune to the impoverished Colonel and his son.

Ethel's "conversion" and Rosey's death do not, however, lead necessarily to a happy ending, for in the years of following Ethel hopelessly, of neglecting his painting, and, finally, of engaging in a loveless marriage, Clive has become less resilient, more demoralized. Indeed, a conventional ending to *The Newcomes* would be as unwieldy as the happy denouement that Dickens was persuaded to tack on to *Great Expectations* (1860-1861). All Thackeray does promise is that in "Fable-land . . . Ethel and Clive are living most comfortably together." As McMaster points out, "poetic justice does not operate in life, however it operates in romance and fairytale." In the end, Thackeray refuses to cater to weak sentimentality.

Written while Thackeray was fighting a lingering illness, *The Virginians* is a long, formless novel, many of whose characters appear in earlier works. The weight of critical opinion, both contemporary and twentieth century, implies that Thackeray, as he well suspected, was at the end of his fictional powers. To Walter Bagehot, the novelist merely presented an "annotated picture," and, indeed, many complained about the plethora of details that substituted for imaginative creation. Thackeray's habit of digressing grew more pronounced, aided by his failure to preserve a distance between himself and his persona for the second half of the novel, the sardonic George Warrington. Connected with such digressions was Thackeray's increasing propensity to justify himself in the eyes of his critics; such justification introduced in a work of fiction was as gratuitous, many felt, as the air of mordant rumination that colored the novel.

On the other hand, Thackeray's supporters cited his adept portraiture of character and his classical style. Geoffrey Tillotson's suggestion that all of Thackeray's works are like one long novel well represents this point of view. In reviving earlier characters and in introducing their descendants, Thackeray studies the development of character traits as well as repetitive familial situations. Beatrix Esmond, for example, having been mistress to the Pretender and the King and having buried two husbands, one a bishop, reappears as a fleshy old woman with a caustic tongue and piercing black eyes. The enigmantic George Washington in *The History of Pendennis* reappears in the person of his namesake; George and Henry Warrington are twin sons of Rachel, Henry Esmond's daughter.

Unfortunately, Thackeray was unable to pursue his original plan, which was to place the brothers on opposite sides in the Revolutionary War and to insert real-life sketches of such figures as Oliver Goldsmith and Dr. Samuel Johnson. The American section was foreshortened, although Thackeray's prodigious reading in American history lends it a remarkably realistic air— so realistic that some American readers were initially incensed that George Washington should be portrayed in so commonplace a light. The book falls into halves, the first reserved for the English adventures of the innocent, gullible Henry. As Gordon Ray points out, the theme, although difficult to discern, is "the contrast between American innocence and Old World corruption."

Henry becomes involved with his cousins at Castlewood, who welcome him as the heir of the Virginia estates, on the supposition that George has died in the battle of Fort Duquesne. Enticed into a proposal by the elderly Maria and encouraged to dissipate his fortune by his infamous cousins, Henry is rescued from debt by his twin, who had not died but was taken prisoner by the French. Deceived by his fortune-seeking relatives, Henry returns to Virginia to marry the housekeeper's daughter. The second half, narrated by George, details his adventures in London. Kept on short funds by his mother, he marries Theo Lambert, the daughter of the gentlemanly General Lambert, a figure much like Colonel Newcome.

Even a brief plot outline of *The Virginians* reveals a number of Thackeray's recurring themes. The attraction of young men to older women is one: just as Henry Esmond married Rachel, many years his senior, so his grandson becomes attached to Maria, and, conversely, so his mother, Mrs. Esmond Warrington, becomes attached to a much younger suitor. The dogmatic and clinging nature of the parent-child relationship is another, much-explored theme: Hetty Lambert gives up her love for Harry to nurture the General, who is loathe to let either of his daughters leave; Mrs. Esmond Warrington throws impediments in the way of George's marriage to Theo; even George himself meditates on his fear that his own daughters will eventually marry. In the final analysis, while *The Virginians* is justly faulted for its digressiveness, Thackeray's treatment of character and his mellow, pure style grant to this work what Gordon Ray calls "a modest vitality."

Overshadowed in modern assessments by his great contemporaries, Dickens and George Eliot, Thackeray is an essential figure in the history of the English novel, and his masterpiece, *Vanity Fair*, is among the great novels in the language. It is with this work that Thackeray is assured a place among the great authors in British literature.

Major publications other than long fiction

SHORT FICTION: *Some Passages in the Life of Major Gahagan*, 1838-1839; *Stubb's Calendar: Or, The Fatal Boots*, 1839; *Barber Cox and the Cutting of His Comb*, 1840; *The Bedford Row Conspiracy*, 1840; *Comic Tales and Sketches*, 1841 (2 volumes); *The Confessions of George Fitzboodle*, 1843; *A Legend of the Rhine*, 1845 (as M. A. Titmarsh); *Jeame's Diary: Or, Sudden Wealth*, 1846; *Mrs. Perkin's Ball*, 1847 (as M. A. Titmarsh); *'Our Street,'* 1848 (as M. A. Titmarsh); *The Book of Snobs*, 1848, 1852; *A Little Dinner at Timmins's*, 1848; *Doctor Birch and His Young Friends*, 1849 (as M. A. Titmarsh); *The Kickleburys on the Rhine*, 1850 (as M. A. Titmarsh); *The Fitz-Boodle Papers*, 1852; *Men's Wives*, 1852 (as George Savage Fitz-Boodle); *Miss Tickletoby's Lectures on English History*, 1852; *The Rose and the Ring: Or, The History of Prince Giglio and Prince Bulbo*, 1855 (as M. A. Titmarsh); *Memoirs of Mr. C. J. Yellowplush* [with] *The Diary of C. Jeames De La Pluche, Esqr.*, 1856; *A Shabby Genteel Story*, 1857.

PLAY: *The Wolves and the Lamb*, 1854.

POETRY: *The Chronicle of the Drum*, 1841.

NONFICTION: *The Paris Sketch-Book*, 1840 (as M. A. Titmarsh, 2 volumes); *The Irish Sketch-Book*, 1843 (as M. A. Titmarsh, 2 volumes); *Notes of a Journey from Cornhill to Grand Cairo. . .* , 1846 (as M. A. Titmarsh); *The English Humorists of the Eighteenth Century*, 1853; *Sketches and Travels in London*, 1856; *The Four Georges: Sketches of Manners, Morals, Court and Town Life*, 1860.

Bibliography

Loofbourow, John. *Thackeray and the Form of Fiction*, 1964.
McMaster, Juliet. *Thackeray: The Major Novels*, 1971.
Rawlins, Jack P. *Thackeray's Novels: A Fiction That Is True*, 1971.
Ray, Gordon N. *Thackeray: The Age of Wisdom, 1847-1863*, 1958.
_____ . *Thackeray: The Uses of Adversity, 1811-1846*, 1955.
Welsh, Alexander, ed. *Thackeray: A Collection of Critical Essays*, 1968.

Patricia Marks

PAUL THEROUX

Born: Medford, Massachusetts; April 10, 1941

Principal long fiction

Waldo, 1967; *Fong and the Indians*, 1968; *Murder at Mount Holly*, 1969; *Girls at Play*, 1969; *Jungle Lovers*, 1971; *Saint Jack*, 1973; *The Black House*, 1974; *The Family Arsenal*, 1976; *Picture Palace: A Novel*, 1978; *The Mosquito Coast*, 1982.

Other literary forms

In addition to a steady stream of novels, Paul Theroux has also published three collections of short stories, *Sinning with Annie* (1972), *The Consul's File* (1977), and *World's End* (1980); a volume of criticism, *V. S. Naipaul: An Introduction to His Work* (1972); two travel books, *The Great Railway Bazaar: By Train Through Asia* (1975) and *The Old Patagonian Express: By Train Through the Americas* (1979); and two collections of children's stories, *A Christmas Card* (1978) and *London Snow: A Christmas Story* (1980). In addition to his books, Theroux has also written numerous reviews and articles, many of them based on his perceptions of events in the non-Western world; these are to be found in newspapers and periodicals such as *The New York Times Magazine*, the *Sunday Times* (of London), *Harper's*, and *Encounter*.

Achievements

It is in the quirky nature of fame that Theroux, a prolific writer of novels, should be better known for his travel writing than for his fiction. *The Great Railway Bazaar* became a best-seller in 1975, gaining for Theroux both popular and commercial success. A second travel book, *The Old Patagonian Express*, published four years later, firmly established his popular reputation. Both offer the reader elegant and humane examples of a genre widely practiced between the world wars but not much seen today.

In the long run, however, Theroux's achievement will rest upon his fiction. At forty, Theroux has earned a reputation as a serious novelist and short-story writer, and he has won a small share of awards for his work: during the past decade, he has collected four Playboy Editorial Awards for fiction (1972, 1976, 1977, and 1979), the Literature Award from the American Academy of Arts and Letters (1977), and the Whitbread Prize for Fiction (for *Picture Palace*, 1978).

Theroux writes in the best tradition of English literature, demonstrating a mastery of fictional conventions as well as a willingness to grapple with some of the thornier issues of modern life. Critics have compared him to, among others, Charles Dickens, Joseph Conrad, Somerset Maugham, Graham

Greene, and Evelyn Waugh. Interested in neither the splashy innovations of a Donald Barthelme nor the lurid headline material of a Norman Mailer, Theroux will nevertheless be a novelist to follow as he continues to engage the essential dilemmas of the late twentieth century.

Biography

Paul Edward Theroux was born of French-Canadian and Italian parentage in Medford, Massachusetts, in 1941, the third of the seven children of Albert and Anne Theroux. Literature and writing were important aspects of his early life. Albert Theroux, a leather salesman, read daily to the family from the classics and encouraged the publication of family newspapers. For his efforts, he was rewarded with two novelists: Paul, and his brother Alexander.

After conventional public schooling and a B.A. in English from the University of Massachusetts, Theroux volunteered for the Peace Corps in 1963 to escape the draft. He taught English in Malawi for two years until he was expelled for his unwitting involvement in the convolutions of African politics. From Malawi, Theroux went to Makerere University in Kampala, Uganda, where he lectured on seventeenth century English literature and maintained a careful political stance during the beginnings of Idi Amin's rise to power. At Makerere, Theroux met V. S. Naipaul, who became for a time his literary mentor. Theroux left Uganda in 1968 after being trapped in a street riot and went to Singapore, where he spent the next three years lecturing at the university.

Throughout this period, Theroux was writing prodigiously, both fiction and reportage, which he published in a variety of journals, both African and European. In 1967, he married Anne Castle, then also a teacher, and fathered two sons, Louis and Marcel. In 1972, judging himself able to earn his living by his pen alone, Theroux gave up teaching and moved his family to London, where he still lives most of the time, summering on Cape Cod.

The Catholic background, the leftish political interests, the ten years in Africa and Asia, the friendship with V. S. Naipaul—these heterogeneous influences have all left their mark on Theroux's fiction. At the same time, one notes how Theroux secularizes, liberalizes, and makes contemporary the Catholic ethic; turns the African experience into a metaphor for all social experience; and absorbs and makes his own the lessons of Naipaul.

Analysis

Paul Theroux approaches his major theme—the ethical behavior of man in society—by way of postcolonial Africa and Southeast Asia, in stories that explore cultural interaction and the meaning of civilization. The three early African novels, *Fong and the Indians*, *Girls at Play*, and *Jungle Lovers*, set the scene, as it were, and suggest the terms for nearly all of his later fiction. These African novels offer not only a fictional portrait of the Third World struggling toward independence, but also a metaphor for all modern society and social ethics. In the apparently simpler world of East Africa, where white ex-patriot confronts black African, where Chinese meets Indian meets German meets American meets Australian, Theroux explores the ways individuals interact to form a social unit and the results, often absurd, of attempts to impose foreign values and ideas of civilization upon the primitive life of the jungle.

Although the later novels leave behind the specifically African setting, they continue to explore the theme of civilization versus jungle, expanding in particular upon the moral and ethical implications of certain kinds of social behavior. *The Family Arsenal* and *Saint Jack* provide instructive examples. In the former, Valentine Hood, an American ex-diplomat from Vietnam living in London, is struck by the domesticity displayed by the members of the terrorist band with which he lives: it is like a family. From this insight develop both the central theme of that novel and its plot structure. In *Saint Jack*, Jack Flowers creates a secular religion out of "giving people what they want." In *The Black House* and *The Mosquito Coast*, Theroux spearates his protagonists from society to explore the meaning of exile, foreignness, and individualism. Yet, underlying all of these fictions will be found the basic assumption that every human experience, from death to redemption, from fear to loneliness, from love to murder, must be understood in a social context.

Fong and the Indians, the first of Theroux's African novels, is the witty tale of the business partnership between Sam Fong, a Chinese grocer, and Hassanali Fakhru, the Indian entrepreneur who rents him the store, supplies his goods, and, when business is poor, even becomes his customer. Fakhru dominates Fong's economic life, manipulating it for his own benefit by taking advantage of Fong's innocent incompetence as a businessman. Yet as the plot unfolds, it becomes clear the the relationship between Fong and Fakhru is far from one-sided. Moreover, it also becomes clear that this relationship is representative of all social and economic relationships. Each individual in a society suffers limitations of understanding that arise both from his own prejudices and from his cultural heritage. When two people meet to do business, they may well be speaking different languages, either literally or metaphorically. Misunderstandings are unavoidable, and the outcome of any action is unpredictable: good intentions may or may not result in good consequences; the same is true of bad intentions. Chaos and absurdity reign when no one quite understands what anyone else is doing.

The plot of *Fong and the Indians* is an intricate comedy of errors involving Fong, the unwilling grocer; Fakhru, the capitalist swindler; and two CIA agents on a mission to convert suspected Communists. The fiction works as both a satirical portrait of African society today and an allegory in which the grocery business, the swindles, and the "good will" mission—artifices of civilization—are, in the context of African reality, revealed to be absurd. In

Fong and the Indians, Theroux explores "civilization"; in later books, *Jungle Lovers*, *Girls at Play*, *The Black House*, and *The Mosquito Coast*, he explores the meaning of "Africa"—the reality of the jungle. At no time does Theroux become an apologist for the Third World, elevating primitive civilization over modern. Rather, he turns "jungle" into a metaphor for man's natural environment: the jungle is both dangerous and nurturing; it demands that its inhabitants concentrate upon basic human needs. Although the metaphor is most easily understood when Theroux sets his story in the literal jungle of Africa or Central America, there is "jungle" too in South London, in an English village, even in Florida.

In *Fong and the Indians*, Fakhru swindles Sam Fong by convincing him that canned milk represents a victory of civilization. In Africa, however, canned milk makes no sense. Africans do not need it; Europeans prefer the fresh milk from Nairobi. Fong's only hope of becoming rich rests upon the wild improbability that the milk train will one day be wrecked. Aware of the absurdity, Fong accepts both the hope and the improbability of its fulfillment. Fong triumphs because he learns to love what he does not understand. He has the patience to submit, to accommodate his life to the requirements of survival. His change of diet, from the traditional Chinese cuisine he has maintained for all his thirty-seven years in Africa to a free, native one based on bananas and fried locusts, is at once a measure of his economic decline and an assurance of his ultimate triumph.

Theroux's ethic, then, appears to be based upon the virtue of inaction. Because human understanding is limited, all events appear ambiguous. Even innocently motivated attempts to improve the lot of humanity may prove unexpectedly destructive, such as Marais' attempt to bring revolutionary ideals to Malawi in *Jungle Lovers*, Valentine Hood's murder to rid the world of Ron Weech in *The Family Arsenal*, or even Maud Coffin Pratt's photographs of the pig feast and of her brother and sister in the mill in *Picture Palace*. Because all events are ambiguous, it is impossible to predict which actions will prove evil and which actions will prove good. Therefore, the only possible moral strategy is to take no action at all, to be patient and accommodate oneself to the unknowable mystery of the jungle.

Inaction, however, should not be confused with selfish laziness; rather it is an active, morally motivated inaction akin to the traditional Christian virtue of patience. Patience redeems the absurdity of the modern world, protecting man from despair and leading ultimately to a triumph of innocence and virtue that will in turn redeem society. This is the lesson of *Saint Jack*.

A middle-aged, balding, American ex-patriot, full of muddle, fear, and loneliness, Jack Flowers jumps ship in Singapore. A stranger and a misfit, Jack sees no hope of rescue; he does not believe in miracles. He is modern man making a realistic appraisal of his chances in an unfriendly and dangerous world. Yet Jack wrests from this vision of despair an ad-lib ethic based upon fulfilling the desires of others. He becomes what others would have him be. Condemning no one, pardoning all, Jack participates in each man's unique fantasy. In the public world, he is called a pimp—he may even be a spy— but in his own private world, Jack is a saint: thoroughly reliable and incapable of cultural misunderstanding. He gives to each what every man needs— pleasure, security, and forgiveness—and stands ready with whatever is needed to meet even an unexpected desire—be it pornographic pictures, the kind attentions of a good girl, or a game of squash. Jack shapes his own needs to match his companion's: he is the perfect friend and protector.

Jack's tattooed arms, emblazoned with Chinese obscenities and curses disguised as flowers, symbolize the way he eases the pain of human loneliness and fear by providing an illusion of hope and friendship and the reality of a temporary pleasure taken in safety. Pity, compassion, and a stubbornly innocent vision of human needs save Jack himself from doing evil and redeem the actions of all those he takes care of, even General Maddox himself.

The terms of this novel are coyly religious—Saint Jack, the manager of Paradise Gardens—but God is not really present in Singapore. What might in a Christian fiction be termed grace, is here good luck, and even Jack's redeeming power itself results, in the end, from his own fantasy. The effect is, on the one hand, tongue in cheek, and on the other, quite serious. Theroux appears to be walking the delicate line between a modern recognition that, in this absurd world, good and evil are meaningless categories and a commonsense realization that people need moral categories and at least an illusion of meaning in order to survive relatively sane.

The search for meaning and moral categories provides both the theme and the structure of *The Family Arsenal*. When the story opens, Valentine Hood has come to live with a group of unrelated people in South London. Their domesticity makes them a parody of the typical middle-class family: Mayo, the mother, a thief; Valentine, the father, a murderer; and Murf and Brodie, the teenage children, terrorist bombers. Early in the novel, many odd characters are introduced: Ralph Gawber, an accountant with a fondness for puzzles and a doomsday foreboding; Araba Nightwing, a radical actress who plays Peter Pan; Ron Weech, the hoodlum whom Hood chases and murders; Lorna Weech, his wife; Rutter, a gunrunner; and Lady Arrow. Initially, the relationships among these characters appear obscure if not irrelevant; yet as the plot develops, groupings take shape until the reader discovers, with Valentine Hood, that all are inextricably bound together by all sorts of dirty secrets, making them, in the words of one character, like one big family no one can quit.

The puzzlelike structure of this novel parodies the conventional thriller plot. Its purpose is, however, not action-packed adventure, but rather the slow revelation that, as Hood has suspected all along, inaction is best because all events (be they murder, theft, or bombing) are morally ambiguous. Thus,

Hood changes from social avenger to listener. He develops an innocent vision of pity and love akin to Jack Flowers' that not only reveals the human bonds among all members and classes of society but also redeems his own guilt and saves at least some from the dangers and death that threaten them. By the end of the story, all is discovered and characters are regrouped into more pleasing families based on love rather than convenience.

Paralleling the revelation of relationships in the plot of *The Family Arsenal* is Hood's changing perception of the artistic organization of the stolen Van der Weyden that hangs in Mayo's closet. Mayo stole the painting believing that its theft would signal the beginning of social revolution. It does not: the world cares little about stolen artworks except as an interesting excuse for a headline. Yet, in an unexpected and very personal way, the painting does, in the end, play a revolutionary role in the story: it becomes the symbolic focus for the way art can organize seemingly disparate shapes and colors into a single beautiful whole. The Van der Weyden, like the tattoos on Jack's arms, suggests the resemblance between the personal vision of innocence that can redeem through pity and love and the vision of the artist that can change brutal reality into beauty.

The most extensive development of this theme occurs in *Picture Palace*, which becomes less a song of triumph for the artist's vision than a warning of the danger that arises when that vision becomes separated (as it necessarily must) from its real social context. Civilization versus the jungle, art versus reality—in Theroux's fiction these themes become almost versions of each other. The ethical effects of efforts by either art or civilization to improve human society are always unclear, dependent as much upon luck as fantasy. Instinctively, Maud Coffin Pratt seems to realize this tenet and locks away her photograph of Phoebe and Orlando in an incestuous embrace: to her, the picture represented love and innocent fulfillment, but when her brother and sister find it, they see only their own guilt and death. Unlike Jack Flowers (who can grab back his photographs of General Maddox) or Valentine Hood (whose revelations of family secrets save them in the end), Maud's personal vision of innocence redeems no one; indeed, it backfires completely, and she is left alone at the end of her life, famous but anonymous.

In *The Mosquito Coast,* Theroux returns to the jungle milieu to explore further the consequences of extreme individualism, the separation of self from society and environment. With his perpetual motion ice machine, Allie Fox expends a mad energy trying to produce icebergs in order to impress the Indians with the superiority of his civilized genius. Needless to say, whether he floats the ice downstream to a native village or carries it by sledge across the mountains, the ice melts: the impressiveness of civilization disappears in the heat of the sun. Relying completely upon his own creativity, Fox, the Yankee inventor, may be seen as a type of the artist. His attempt to impose his personal vision of utopia upon the brutal reality of the jungle fails utterly;

his story reads as a warning of the danger of art without social context.

Like Sam Fong's canned milk in *Fong and the Indians*, Fox's ice machine in *The Mosquito Coast* represents an absurd attempt to civilize the jungle; yet Fong is rewarded with riches (the milk train does wreck), while Fox dies mad and beaten on the beach of Central America. Both may be seen as emblems of modern man, alone in a strange land, possessing nothing, trying to shape a life out of events that are mysterious, ambiguous, possibly dangerous, and probably absurd. Their differing responses to the jungle environment determine their different ends and provide the reader with the key to Theroux's view of social ethics.

Allie Fox rejects patience and accommodation; he rejects the mystery and the ambiguity of the jungle. He will build a bugless outpost of civilization; he would rather starve than eat a banana. In Theroux's world, it is poetic justice that Fox should misinterpret events and bring about the ruin of all that he has built. With true tragic irony, Fox learns from his failure not the value of accommodation, but only the need for an increased purity, an increased separation from the jungle, a separation doomed to failure. If Fong is the comic face of humanity, then Fox must be the tragic face.

The progression of Theroux's novels since 1967 demonstrates a marked coherence of interest and an increasing complexity of thematic and structural development. Although Theroux draws freely from the modern storehouse of pornography, violence, and antiheroism, he displays at the same time a real if not profound interest in some of the classic themes of Western literature—the source of good and evil, the use of pity and love in society, art, and reality. Technically, his work shows a similar melding of popular fiction (the Gothic horror story, the thriller) with the structure and conventions of the classic novelists.

Major publications other than long fiction

SHORT FICTION: *Sinning with Annie and Other Stories*, 1972; *The Consul's File*, 1977; *World's End*, 1980.

NONFICTION: *V. S. Naipaul: An Introduction to His Work*, 1972; *The Great Railway Bazaar: By Train Through Asia*, 1975; *The Old Patagonian Express: By Train Through the Americas*, 1979.

CHILDREN'S LITERATURE: *A Christmas Card*, 1978; *London Snow: A Christmas Story*, 1980.

Bibliography

Bell, Robert F. "Metamorphoses and Missing Halves: Allusions in Paul Theroux's *Picture Palace*," in *Critique*. XXII (1981), pp. 17-29.

Coale, Samuel. "'A Quality of Light': The Fiction of Paul Theroux," in *Critique*. XXII (1981), pp. 5-16.

Linda Howe

J. R. R. TOLKIEN

Born: Bloemfontein, South Africa; January 3, 1892
Died: Bournemouth, England; September 2, 1973

Principal long fiction

The Hobbit, 1937; *The Lord of the Rings*, 1955 (includes *The Fellowship of the Ring*, 1954; *The Two Towers*, 1954; *The Return of the King*, 1955); *The Silmarillion*, 1977.

Other literary forms

J. R. R. Tolkien's novels represent only a small part of the complicated matrix from which they evolved. During his lifetime, he published three volumes of novellas and short stories, *Farmer Giles of Ham* (1949), *Tree and Leaf* (1964), and *Smith of Wootton Major* (1967). Some of these tales had originally been bedtime stories for his own children, such as the posthumous *The Father Christmas Letters* (1976). *The Silmarillion* (1977) and *Unfinished Tales* (1980) both contain stories Tolkien composed early in his life, material that sets the stage for the events in his novels. His poetry collections, *Songs for the Philologists* (1936), *The Adventures of Tom Bombadil* (1962), and *The Road Goes Ever On: A Song Cycle* (1967) link Tolkien's poetic formulations of Middle-earth's themes with the historical and linguistic themes of which both his professional work and much of his dreams were made, "the nameless North of Sigurd of the Völsungs, and the prince of all dragons." Tolkien's academic publications dealt with the history of the English language and Middle English literature: *A Middle English Vocabulary* (1922) and editions of *Sir Gawain and the Green Knight* (1925) with E. V. Gordon and the *Ancrene Wisse* (1962). His seminal essay "Beowulf: The Monsters and the Critics" (1936) and his only play, *The Homecoming of Beorhtnoth Beorhthelm's Son* (1953), offer fresh interpretations of ancient English epic poems. Tolkien's novels have been adapted for cinema and television, and many, though not all, of his fragmentary stories, articles, and letters have been published since his death.

Achievements

Tolkien's fiction dismayed most of his fellow scholars at Oxford as much as it delighted most of his general readers. Such reactions sprang from their recognition of his vast linguistic talent, which underlay both his professional achievements and his mythical universe. Tolkien led two lives at once, quietly working as an Oxford tutor, examiner, editor, and lecturer, while concurrently Middle-earth and its mythology were taking shape within his imagination.

For twenty years after he took First Class Honours in English Language and Literature at Oxford, Tolkien's teaching and linguistic studies buttressed his scholarly reputation. Editing the fourteenth century text of *Sir Gawain and the Green Knight* with E. V. Gordon helped bring Tolkien the Rawlinson and Bosworth Professorship of Anglo-Saxon at Oxford in 1925. His lecture "Beowulf: The Monsters and the Critics" approached the Anglo-Saxon epic poem from an entirely new perspective and is considered a landmark in criticism of Western Germanic literature. As he was shaping his linguistic career, however, Tolkien was also formulating an imaginary language, which as early as 1917 had led him to explore its antecedents, its mythology, and its history, all of which he molded into the tales of *The Silmarillion*. Over the years, he shared them with friends, but he never finished putting them into a unified structure.

His preoccupation with Middle-earth and the practical demands of his teaching distracted Tolkien from scholarship, and between his celebrated essay *On Fairy Stories* in 1939 and his edition of the Middle English *Ancrene Wisse* in 1962, Tolkien published only fiction, a circumstance acknowledged with polite forebearance by most of Oxford's scholarly community, although his novels eventually met with astonishing popular success. *The Hobbit*, originally a children's story, was published in 1937 after a six-year gestation, and by 1949, *The Lord of the Rings* was complete. Its sales, though steadily increasing after its publication in 1954-1955, did not soar until 1965, when an unauthorized American printing proved a disguised blessing, resulting in a campus cult responsible for the sale of three million copies by 1968.

Most critics of *The Lord of the Rings* have not achieved moderation. As W. H. Auden observed, "People find it a masterpiece of its genre, or they cannot abide it." Auden himself and C. S. Lewis, Tolkien's Oxford friend, headed the "masterpiece" faction, while Edwin Muir in England and Edmond Wilson in America deplored Tolkien's style and aims.

Honorary fellowships, an honorary Doctorate of Letters from Oxford University, and a C.B.E. from Queen Elizabeth all descended upon Tolkien with the unexpected wealth of his last years, which were nevertheless darkened by his reluctance to complete *The Silmarillion*. His reputation rests not on his academic talent or scholarly production, nor even on his brilliant linguistically oriented "mythology for England," but upon the novels that began as tales for his children and blossomed into a splendid imaginative tree of fiction whose roots feed upon the archetypes of northern European civilization and whose leaves shelter its finest aspirations.

Biography

John Ronald Reuel Tolkein was born in Bloemfontein, South Africa, on January 3, 1892. The piano manufacturing firm of his father's family, originally from Germany, had gone bankrupt, and the elder Tolkien had taken a South African bank position in hopes of improving his shaky finances. Tolkien's mother, Mabel Suffield, joined her husband at Bloemfontein, but when the climate strained Ronald's health, she took their two sons home to England in 1895. Less than a year later, Arthur Tolkien died in South Africa, leaving his widow and children nearly penniless.

In the summer of 1896, Mabel Tolkien rented a rural cottage at Sarehole Mill, close to Birmingham, and for the next four years she taught her boys French, Latin, drawing, and botany, to save school expenses. Much later, Tolkien called these "the longest-seeming and most formative part" of his life. Mabel Tolkien's attraction to Roman Catholicism led to her conversion in 1900, and she moved to a Birmingham suburb from which Ronald began to attend one of England's then leading grammar schools, King Edward's, on a scholarship . His mother's unpopular religion meant that she and her sons received even less help from her own family and the Tolkiens than previously, and her health began to decline rapidly. In 1904, she died at thirty-four, leaving her children in the care of Father Francis Morgan, her friend and pastor. Tolkien's devotion to his mother was inextricably intertwined with his own Catholic faith, and both played vital roles in the development of his fiction.

At sixteen, Ronald Tolkien looked back upon a series of grievous losses: his father, whom he considered as "belonging to an almost legendary past"; the Sarehole countryside he loved; his mother, whom he considered a martyr to her faith. Not surprisingly for a lonely boy, Tolkien fell in love early when he met Edith Bratt, another orphan, in his Birmingham boarding house. She was three years older than he, and she had just enough inheritance to support herself modestly while she dreamed of becoming a musician. Recognizing the boy's scholarly talent and fearing for his future, Father Morgan finally stopped all communication between Ronald and Edith until Ronald was twenty-one. Tolkien himself commented thirty years later, "Probably nothing else would have hardened the will enough to give such an affair (however genuine a case of true love) permanence."

The early fascination with language Tolkien's mother had fostered led him to the ancient languages of the North, Finnish, Welsh, and Old Icelandic, as well as the Anglo-Saxon and Middle English in which he specialized. At Oxford, he was steeped in an all-male academic atmosphere, and when he and Edith were reunited in 1913, they seemed to have little in common. On the eve of his military departure to France in 1916, however, they were married. After some months on the Western Front, Tolkien convalesced from trench fever in England until the Armistice.

In a military hospital in 1917, Tolkien began "The Book of Lost Tales" which would become *The Silmarillion*, as he envisioned it, "a body of more or less connected legend." By 1923, it was essentially complete, but he could not seem to bear finishing it—and losing it. From then on, he looked outward to the male academic company of his fellows at Oxford and inward to Middle-earth, which rapidly became his refuge and his strength. All at once, in the late 1920's, from "the Suffield side of his personality" came a startling thought: "In a hole in the ground there lived a hobbit," and for the rest of Tolkien's creative life, the "hobbit" and his adventures against the backdrop of Middle-earth and its myths dominated his attention.

Toward the end, he said, "The Silmarils are in my heart," and of *The Lord of the Rings*, "It is written in my life-blood." Perhaps little room seemed to remain in Tolkien's life for Edith, his companion for more than fifty years, but at his death in 1973, the names of Beren and Lúthien, taken from the chief story of *The Silmarillion* and carved upon the Tolkiens' headstones, testified to great sacrifices and greater love for all time to come.

Analysis

Looking back around 1951 upon his Middle-earth, J. R. R. Tolkien commented, "I do not remember a time when I was not building it . . . always I had the sense of recording what was already 'there,' somewhere: not of inventing." He conceived of fantasy as a profound and powerful form of literature with intense philosophical and spiritual meaning, serious purposes, and eternal appeal. He believed the imagination, the mental power of making images, could be linked by art to "sub-creation," the successful result of image-making, and so he regarded the genuine artist as partaking in the Creator's divine nature.

Three major factors of Tolkien's personality and environment combined to shape the theory of fantasy underlying his novels, as first enunciated in the essay "On Fairy-Stories" (1938). His love of language for its singular rewards, his brief delight in the English countryside at Sarehole, and his shattering experience of trench warfare during World War I all provided the seeds for his three longest pieces of fiction. They also contributed to the points of view, astonishingly nonhuman and yet startlingly convincing, of *The Silmarillion*, *The Hobbit*, and *The Lord of the Rings*, where Elves and Hobbits illuminate the world of Men.

Even as a boy, Tolkien had been enchanted by Welsh names on railway coal cars, a sign of his unusual linguistic sensitivity, and as a mature scholar, he devoted himself to the mystery of the word in its northern manifestations. In "On Fairy-Stories," he wrote that "*spell* means both a story told, and a formula of power over living men." Tolkien cast his spells in the building blocks of words drawn from the imaginary languages he had been constructing as long as he could remember. The two languages he formulated for his Elves, the Elder Race, both derived from a common linguistic ancestor as human languages do, and this "nexus of languages" supplied the proper names for his novels, so that despite their considerable length and complication they possess "cohesion, consistency of linguistic style, and the illusion of historicity." The last was possibly the greatest achievement of Tolkien's mastery of language in his novels, fostering vital credence in his imaginary world. He felt that the finest fairy stories "open a door on Other Time, and if we pass through . . . we stand outside our own time, outside Time itself, maybe." In his own childhood, a "troublous" one Tolkien said, he had "had no special 'wish to believe'"; he instead "wanted to know," as, perhaps, do his readers, aided by the resonance of his masterful use of words.

The memory of his years at Sarehole, the happiest of his boyhood, gave Tolkien an abiding love of nature, "above all trees," which formed the basis for one of his principal concepts, "the inter-relations between the 'noble' and the 'simple.'" He found "specially moving" the "ennoblement of the ignoble," a theme which recurs throughout his fiction. Tolkien's Elves practice love and respect toward nature, as do his Hobbits, "small people" connected closely to "the soil and other living things" who display both human pettiness and unexpected heroism "in a pinch." The Elves, Hobbits, and good Men are countered in Tolkien's Middle-earth by the threat of the machine, by which he meant "all use of external plans or devices," as opposed to "the development of inner powers or talents." The evil of the machine in Tolkien's eyes (he did not own a car after World War II) derived from the misguided human desire for power, itself a rebellion against the Creator's laws, a Fall from Paradise, another recurring theme in his fiction.

The horrors of World War I must have struck Tolkien as evil incarnate, with new military technology that devastated the countryside, struck down the innocent, and left no place for chivalry, heroism, or even common decency. Unlike Andrew Lang, an early Scottish collector of fairy tales, who felt children most often ask, "Is it true?", Tolkien declared that children far more often asked him of a character, "Was he good? Was he wicked?" Tolkien shared G. K. Chesterton's conviction that children "are innocent and love justice; while most of us are wicked and naturally prefer mercy." The child's stern perception of right and wrong, as opposed to the "mercy untempered by justice" which leads to "falsification of values," confirmed Tolkien's long-held inclination toward the steely world of the northern sagas, where human heroism faces inevitable defeat by the forces of evil, and the hero, according to Edith Hamilton, "can prove what he is only by dying." From his basic distrust of the machine and his firsthand memories of Verdun, Tolkien drew one of the major lessons of his fiction: "that on callow, lumpish and selfish youth peril, sorrow, and the shadow of death can bestow dignity, and even sometimes wisdom."

Reconciling this harsh northern *Weltbild* with his Roman Catholic faith did not seem to be difficult for Tolkien. An indispensable element of his theory of fantasy is the "sudden joyous 'turn'" of a "eucatastrophic" story, a moment in fiction accompanied by "a catch of the breath, a beat and lifting of the heart, near to (or indeed accompanied by) tears." By inserting the "turn" convincingly into his tale, the sub-creator "denies universal final defeat" and give "a fleeting glimpse of Joy, Joy beyond the walls of the world, poignant as grief." Hence, Tolkien believed that such a joy was the "mark of the true fairy story," the revelation of truth in the fictional world the sub-creator built. It might even be greater,"a far-off gleam or echo of *evangelium* in the real world." Tolkien was able to see the Christian Gospels as "the greatest and most complete conceivable eucatastrophe," believing that in fantasy the human sub-creator might "actually assist in the effoliation and multiple enrichment of creation."

Tolkien's *The Silmarillion*, *The Hobbit*, and *The Lord of the Rings*, form, as he always hoped, one coherent and archetypal whole. His "creative fantasy" effectively shows the three dissimilar faces his theory demanded: "the Mystical towards the Supernatural; the Magical towards Nature; and the Mirror of scorn and pity toward Man." Man's "oldest and deepest desire," the "Great Escape" from death, is satisfied in Tolkien's major fiction, not by denying Mortality but by accepting it gracefully as a gift from man's Creator, a benefit to man that Tolkien's immortal Elves envied. The Elves' own magic is actually art, whose true object is "sub-creation" under God, not domination of lesser beings whose world they respectfully share. Scorn for fallen men (and fallen Elves and Hobbits as well) abounds in Middle-earth, but pity, too, for guiltless creatures trapped in the most frightful evil Tolkien could envision, evil that he believed arises "from an apparently good root, the desire to benefit the world and others—speedily—and according to the benefactor's own plans." Middle-earth lives forever in Tolkien's novels, and with it an affirmation of what is best, most true, and most beautiful in human nature.

Both in Tolkien's life and in the chronology of Middle-earth, the tales of *The Silmarillion* came first, but the book was not published until four years after his death. The volume called *The Silmarillion* contains four shorter narratives as well as the "Quenta Silmarillion," arranged as ordered chronicles of the Three Ages of Tolkien's middle-earth by his son Christopher, following his father's explicit intention.

Tolkien began parts of *The Silmarillion* in 1917 after he had been invalided home from France. The work steadily evolved after more than forty years, and, according to Christopher Tolkien, "incompatibilities of tone" inevitably arose from his father's increasing preoccupation with theology and philosophy over the mythology and poetry he had originally favored. Tolkien himself never abandoned his work on *The Silmarillion*, even though he found himself unable to complete it. As Christopher Wiseman had suggested to Tokien, "'why these creatures live to you is because you are still creating them,'" and so Tolkien painstakingly revised, recast, and polished these stories, unwilling to banish their characters from his imagination.

The Silmarillion opens with "Ainulindalë," a cosmogonical myth revealing the creation of Middle-earth by God ("Iluvatar") in the presence of the Valar, whom Tolkien described as angelic powers. He wanted "to provide beings of the same order . . . as the 'gods' of higher mythology" acceptable to "a mind that believes in the Blessed Trinity." The universe to which Middle-earth belonged was set in living motion by music, "beheld as a light in the darkness."

The short "Valaquenta" enumerates the individual Valar, whose personal responsibilities covered all created things of Middle-earth, stopping short of the act of creation itself. One of the Valar, Melkor, rebelled in the First Age; Tolkien believed that "there cannot be any 'story' without a fall." Melkor "began with the desire of Light, but when he could not possess it for himself alone, he descended . . . into a great burning." One of Melkor's servants was Sauron, who later embodied evil in the Third Age of Middle-earth.

The twenty-four chapters of the "Quenta Silmarillion" recount the legendary history of the immortal Elves, the First-Born of Iluvatar, whom Tolkien elsewhere called "rational incarnate creatures of more or less comparable stature with our own." After writing *The Lord of the Rings*, Tolkien clearly indicated that the Elves were "only a representation of an apprehension of a part of human nature" from which art and poetry spring, but, he said, "that is not the legendary mode of talking." The Elves originally share the Paradise of the Valar, Valinor, but the Elves suffer a fall from that grace in the "Quenta Silmarillion," the rebellion and exile to Middle-earth of one of the great families of Elves, led by their chief, the artificer Fëanor, who has captured the primal light of Iluvatar in the three Silmarils. Tolkien described these great jewels as aglow with the "light of art undivorced from reason, that sees things both scientifically (or philosophically) and imaginatively (or subcreatively) and 'says that they are good'—as beautiful." Fëanor's lust to possess the Silmarils for himself leads to their capture by Melkor, and in the struggle to redeem them, splendid deeds are performed by Beren, a Man of Middle-earth beloved of the Elvish princess Lúthien. Tolkien called this "the first example of the motive (to become dominant in Hobbits) that the great policies of world history . . . are often turned . . . by the seemingly unknown and weak." The union of Beren and Lúthien is the first between mortal Man and immortal Elf; they win Paradise together, and eventually Earendil the Elven Mariner closes the "Quenta Silmarillion" by bringing the gem Beren painfully rescued from Melkor to the land of the Valar. His Silmaril was set into the sky as its brightest star, while the others were lost in the depths of the earth and sea, and the First Age of Middle-earth came to its end.

Tolkien saw the Second Age of Middle-earth as dark, and he believed "not very much of its history is (or need be) told." The Valar continued to dwell at Valinor with the faithful Elves, but the exiled Elves with Fëanor were commanded to leave Middle-earth and live in the lonely Isle of Eressëa in the West. Some of them, however, ignored the order and remained in Middle-earth. Those Men of Middle-earth who had aided the Elves to redeem the Silmarils were given the Atlantis-like realm of Númenor as their reward, as well as lifespans three times the normal age of Men. Though Melkor was chained, his servant Sauron remained free to roam Middle-earth, and through his evil influence, both Men of Númenor and the Delaying Elves came to grief.

The decay of Númenor is told in the "Akallabeth," an illustration of Tolkien's belief that the inevitable theme of human stories, is "a Ban, or Prohibition." The long-lived Númenoreans were prohibited by the Valar from setting foot on "immortal" lands in the West. Their wrongful desire to escape death, their gift from Iluvatar, causes them to rebel and bring about their own watery destruction through the worship of Sauron, Melkor's servant. At the same time, the Elves who delayed in Middle-earth suffered the painful consequences of their flawed choice. Tolkien said they "wanted to have their cake without eating it," enjoying the perfection of the West while remaining on ordinary earth, revered as superior beings by the other, lesser races. Some of them cast their lot with Sauron, who enticed them to create three Rings of Power, in the misguided hopes of making Middle-earth another Valinor. Sauron secretly made another ring himself, one with the power to enslave all the others. The ensuing war between Sauron and the Elves devastated Middle-earth, but in the Last Alliance of Elves and Men against Sauron, the One Ring was lost. Tolkien calls this the "catastrophic end, not only of the Second Age, but of the Old World, the primeval age of Legend."

The Posthumous collection called *The Silmarillion* ends with Tolkien's résumé "Of the Rings of Power and the Third Age," which introduces the motives, themes, and chief actors in the next inevitable war between Sauron and the Free Peoples of Middle-earth. Although *The Hobbit* and *The Lord of the Rings* have proved vastly more popular, and both can be enjoyed without the complicated and generally loftily pitched history of *The Silmarillion*, its information is essential to a thorough understanding of the forces Tolkien set at work in the later novels. Even more important, *The Silmarillion* was for Tolkien, as his son Christopher has said, "the vehicle and depository of his profoundest reflections," and as such, it holds the bejewelled key to the autobiography Tolkien felt was embedded in his fiction.

Around 1930, Tolkien jotted a few enigmatic words about "a hobbit" on the back of an examination paper he was grading. "Names always generate a story in my mind," he observed, and eventually he found out "what hobbits were like." The Hobbits, whom he subsequently described as "a branch of the specifically *human* race (not Elves or Dwarves)," became the vital link between Tolkien's mythology as constructed in *The Silmarillion* and the heroic legend that dominates *The Lord of the Rings*. Humphrey Carpenter, Tolkien's official biographer, believes that Bilbo Baggins, hero of *The Hobbit*, "embodied everything he [Tolkien] loved about the West Midlands." Tolkien himself once wrote, "I am in fact a hobbit, in all but size," and beyond personal affinities, he saw the Hobbits as "rustic English people," small in size to reflect "the generally small reach of their imagination—not the small reach of their courage or latent power."

Tolkien's Hobbits appear in the Third Age of Middle-earth, in an ominously quiet lull before a fearful storm. Sauron had been overthrown by the Elf-lord Gil-galad and the Númenorean King Elendil, but since evil is never completely vanquished, Sauron's creatures lurk quietly in the north of Middle-earth, Mordor, while a few Elves keep watch on its borders. Descendants of a few Númenoreans were saved from their land's disaster (Atlantean destruction was a recurrent nightmare for both Tolkien and his son Christopher), and they rule in the Kingdoms of Arnor in the North of Middle-earth and Gondor of the South. The former Númenoreans are allies of the Homeric Riders of Rohan, whose human forefathers had remained in Middle-earth when Númenor came to be. The three Elven Rings of Power secretly guard Rivendell and Lothlórien, which Tolkien called "enchanted enclaves of peace where Time seems to stand still and decay is restrained, a semblance of the bliss of the True West."

The Hobbits live in The Shire, in "an ordered, civilised, if simple rural life." One day, the Hobbit Bilbo Baggins receives an odd visitor, Gandalf the Wizard, who sends Bilbo off with traveling dwarves in search of Dragon's Gold, the major theme of the novel. In the process, Tolkien uses the humble Hobbit to illustrate one of his chief preoccupations, the process by which "small imagination" combines with "great courage." As he recalled from his months in the trenches,"I've always been impressed that we are here, sur-viving, because of the indomitable courage of quite small people against impossible odds."

Starting from the idyllic rural world of The Shire, *The Hobbit*, ostensibly a children's book, traces the typical quest of the northern hero about whom Tolkien himself had loved to read in his youth. Gandalf shares certain char-acteristics with the Scandinavian god Odin, said to wander among men as an "old man of great height," with a long grey cloak, a white beard, and super-natural powers. Gandalf, like Odin, understands the speech of birds, being especially fond of eagles and ravens, and his strange savage friend Beorn, who rescues the Hobbits at one critical point, recalls the berserkers, bearskin-clad warriors consecrated to Odin who fought with superhuman strength in the intoxication of battle. The Dwarves of Middle-earth distinctly resemble their Old Norse forebears, skilled craftsmen who made treasures for the gods. Smaug the Dragon, eventually slain by the human hero Bard, is surely related to "the prince of all dragons" who had captured Tolkien's boyish imagination. The Germanic code of the *comitatus*, the warrior's fidelity unto death, cel-ebrated in the tenth century Anglo-Saxon poem "The Battle of Maldon," inspired Tolkien's only play and applies to *The Hobbit*, too, since Bilbo's outward perils are overshadowed by the worst threat of all to the northern hero, the inward danger of proving a coward. After Bilbo overcomes his fear and slays a giant spider, "He felt a different person, and much fiercer and bolder in spite of an empty stomach."

Bilbo's hard-won self-knowledge allows him to demonstrate the "idomitable courage of small people against great odds" when he saves Dwarves, Men, and Elves from suicidal war against one another. *The Hobbit* far exceeded its beginnings as a bedtime story for Tolkien's small sons, since it is also a fable about the child at the heart of every man, perceiving right and wrong as sternly as did the heroes of the North.

In late 1937, at the suggestion of his British publisher, Tolkien began a sequel to *The Hobbit*. To the East, a malignant force was gathering strength in the Europe that even the mammoth sacrifices of World War I had not redeemed from oppression, and while Tolkien often cautions against interpreting his works allegorically, the apprehensive atmosphere of prewar England must have affected his own peace of mind. He described his intention in *The Lord of the Rings* as "an attempt to . . . wind up all the elements and motives of what has preceded." He wanted "to include the colloquialism and vulgarity of Hobbits, poetry and the highest style of prose." The moral of this novel, not a "trilogy" but, he stressed, "conceived and written as a whole," was "obvious": "that without the high and noble the simple and vulgar is utterly mean; and without the simple and ordinary the noble and heroic is meaningless.

The Lord of the Rings is a vast panoramic contest between good and evil, played out against the backdrop of Tolkien's mythology as presented in *The Silmarillion*. The One Ring of Sauron, long lost, was found by little Bilbo Baggins, and from him it passed to his kinsman Frodo, who becomes the central figure of the quest-in-reverse: having found the Ring, the allied Men, Elves, Dwarves, and Hobbits must destroy it where it was forged, so that its power can never again dominate Middle-earth. Another quest takes place simultaneously in the novel, as the mysterious Strider who greets the Hobbits at Bree on the first stage of their perilous journey is gradually revealed as Aragorn, son of Arathorn and heir to Arnor in the North, descendent of Elendil who kept faith with the Valvar; he is the human King of Middle-earth who must reclaim his realm. Sauron's minions rise to threaten the Ringbearer and his companions, and after many adventures, a great hopeless battle is fought before the Gates of Mordor. As Tolkien stated in "Of the Rings of Power and the Third Age," "There at the last they looked upon death and defeat, and all their valour was in vain; for Sauron was too strong." This is the paradoxical defeat-and-victory of the northern hero, whose glory is won in the manner of his death. As a practicing Christian, though, Tolkien had to see hope clearly in the ultimate struggle between right and wrong, "and help came from the hands of the weak when the Wise faltered." Frodo the Hobbit at last managed to carry the Ring to Mount Doom in spite of Sauron, and there it was destroyed, and "a new Spring opened up on Earth."

In retrospect, Tolkien acknowledged that another central issue of *The Lord of the Rings* was "love in different modes," which had been "wholly absent from *The Hobbit*." Tolkien considered the "simple 'rustic' love" between

Sam, Frodo's faithful batman, and his Rosie was *"absolutely essential"* both to the study of the main hero of the novel and "to the theme of the relation of ordinary life . . . to quests, to sacrifice, causes, and the 'longing for Elves,' and sheer beauty." The evidence of Tolkien's own life indicates the depth of his ability to love, like Beren, always faithful to his Lúthien. Such love that made all sacrifice possible forms the indestructible core of *The Lord of the Rings*, which moved C. S. Lewis to speak of "beauties which pierce like swords or burn like cold iron . . . a book that will break your heart."

Love exemplified in two important romances softens the necromancy and the battles of *The Lord of the Rings*: the poignant "mistaken love" of Eowyn for Aragorn, as Tolkien described it, and the novel's "highest love-story," The tale of Aragorn and Arwen, daughter of Elrond, leader of the Elves of Middle-earth. Eowyn is niece to Theoden, King of Rohan, the land of the horsemen Tolkien patterned after ancient Anglo-Saxon tribes he had first encountered through William Morris' *House of the Wolfings* (1889). In Theoden's decline, the shield-maiden Eowyn gives her first love to the royalty-in-exile she senses in Aragorn, and though he in no sense encourages her, Eowyn's tragedy is one only he can heal once he is restored as King. In contrast, Tolkien merely alludes to the love of Aragorn and Arwen in *The Lord of the Rings*, since it seems almost too deep for tears. Arwen must forsake her Elven immortality and join Aragorn in human death. Like Tolkien's own love for Edith, Aragorn's for Arwen is temporarily prevented from fruition until he can return to her in full possession of his birth-right. The shadow of her possible loss lends stature to the characterization of Aragorn, the hero of *The Lord of the Rings*.

In 1955, Tolkien observed that "certain features . . . and especially certain places" of *The Lord of the Rings* "still move me very powerfully." The passages he cited sum up the major means by which the novel so strongly conveys love, redemption, and heroism achieved in the face of overwhelming odds. "The heart remains in the description of Cerin Amroth," he wrote, the spot where Aragorn and Arwen first pledged their love and where, many years later at the beginning of his fearful quest, "the grim years were removed from the face of Aragorn, and he seemed clothed in white, a young lord tall and fair." Tolkien magnifies this small epiphany of love through the eyes of the Hobbit Frodo. Another key episode, the wretched Gollum's failure to repent because Sam interrupts him, grieved Tolkien deeply, he said, for it resembled "the *real* world in which the instruments of just retribution are seldom themselves just or holy." In his favorite passage, however, Tolkien was "most stirred by the sound of the horses of the Rohirrim at cockcrow," the great "turn" of *The Lord of the Rings*, a flash of salvation in the face of all odds that comes beyond hope, beyond prayer, like a stroke of unexpected bliss from the hand of the Creator.

The "turn" that makes *The Lord of the Rings* a "true fairy-story" in Tolkien's definition links fidelity to a vow, a Germanic value, to the Christian loyalty that animated many of the great Anglo-Saxon works Tolkien had spent his scholarly life studying. By weaving the immensely complex threads of Elves, Hobbits, Men, and Dwarves into his heroic legend of the last great age of Middle-earth, he achieved a valid sub-creation, sharing in the nature of what for him was most divine.

For almost fifty years, mostly in the quiet academic atmosphere of Oxford, Tolkien built his resounding tales of "a body of more or less connected legend, ranging from the large and cosmogonic, to the level of romantic fairy-story." He consciously dedicated it simply "to England; to my country." The intellectual absorption with language he had always enjoyed gave him the starting-place for his mythology, which he implemented in *The Silmarillion*, whose unifying theme is the Fall of Elves and Men. His brief happiness in the English countryside at Sarehole and his West Midlands family background seem to have provided him the landscape from which *The Hobbit* grew, perhaps his most approachable "fairy-story" for both children and adults, illustrating the happiness to be gained from simplicity and the acceptance of the gift of mortality. The chivalric dreams of noble sacrifice shattered for Tolkien's generation by World War I were redeemed for him by his realization that the humble may effectively struggle against domination by the misguided technological values of modern civilization. The heroic legend of *The Lord of the Rings* best illustrates Tolkien's resolution of the conflict between the northern values he had admired from youth and the Roman Catholic religion of hope and consolation to which he was devoted. Tolkien wanted to illuminate the simplest and the highest values of human existence, found in a human love that accepts and transcends mortality. Tolkien's "mythology for England," a unique gift of literature and language, has earned its immense popular success by appealing to man's eternal desire to understand his mortal lot. As Hilda Ellis Davidson commented of the great northern myths, so like Tolkien's own, "In reaching out to explore the distant hills where the gods dwell and the deeps where the monsters are lurking, we are perhaps discovering the way home."

Major publications other than long fiction

SHORT FICTION: *Farmer Giles of Ham*, 1949; *Tree and Leaf*, 1964; *The Tolkien Reader*, 1966; *Smith of Wootton Major*, 1967; *The Father Christmas Letters*, 1976; *Unfinished Tales*, 1980 (Christopher Tolkien, editor).

PLAY: *The Homecoming of Beorhtnoth Beorhthelm's Son*, 1953.

POETRY: *Songs for the Philologists*, 1936 (with E. V. Gordon et al.); *The Adventures of Tom Bombadil*, 1962; *The Road Goes Ever On: A Song Cycle*, 1967.

NONFICTION: *A Middle English Vocabulary*, 1922; *Sir Gawain and the Green Knight*, 1925 (edited with E. V. Gordon); *Ancrene Wisse: The English Text of the Ancrene Riwle*, 1962 (edited); *Letters of J. R. R. Tolkien*, 1981.

Bibliography
Carpenter, Humphrey. *Tolkien: The Authorized Biography*, 1977.
———————— . *The Inklings*, 1978.
Foster, Robert. *A Guide to Middle-Earth*, 1978.
Grotta-Kurska, Daniel. *J. R. R. Tolkien: Architect of Middle-Earth*, 1976.
Kocher, Paul H. *Master of Middle-Earth: The Fiction of J. R. R. Tolkien*, 1972.
Nitzsche, Jane C. *Tolkien's Art: A "Mythology for England,"* 1979.
Noel, Ruth S. *The Mythology of Middle-Earth*, 1977.
Shippey, T. A. *The Road to Middle-Earth*, 1982.

Mitzi M. Brunsdale

ANTHONY TROLLOPE

Born: London, England; April 24, 1815
Died: London, England; December 6, 1882

Principal long fiction

The Macdermots of Ballycloran, 1847; *The Kellys and the O'Kellys*, 1848; *The Warden*, 1855; *Barchester Towers*, 1857; *The Three Clerks*, 1858; *Doctor Thorne*, 1858; *The Bertrams*, 1859; *Castle Richmond*, 1860; *Framley Parsonage*, 1861; *Orley Farm*, 1862; *Rachel Ray*, 1863; *The Small House at Allington*, 1864; *Can You Forgive Her?*, 1864; *Miss Mackenzie*, 1865; *The Belton Estate*, 1866; *The Last Chronicle of Barset*, 1867; *The Claverings*, 1867; *Phineas Finn, the Irish Member*, 1869; *He Knew He Was Right*, 1869; *The Vicar of Bullhampton*, 1870; *The Eustace Diamonds*, 1873; *Phineas Redux*, 1874; *The Way We Live Now*, 1875; *The Prime Minister*, 1876; *The American Senator*, 1877; *Is He Popenjoy?*, 1878; *John Caldigate*, 1879; *The Duke's Children*, 1880; *Ayala's Angel*, 1881; *Dr. Wortle's School*, 1881; *The Landleaguers*, 1883; *Mr. Scarborough's Family*, 1883.

Other literary forms

Anthony Trollope's novels were frequently serialized in various periodicals such as *Cornhill Magazine* and *The Fortnightly Review*. They appeared subsequently in a two- or three-volume format. Trollope wrote several books of cultural reportage which were more than mere travelogues: *The West Indies* (1859), *North America* (1862), *Australia and New Zealand* (1873), and *South Africa* (1878), along with the more impressionistic *Travelling Sketches* (1866). Three volumes of short stories appeared: *Lotta Schmidt and Other Stories* (1867), *An Editor's Tales* (1870), and *Why Frau Frohmann Raised Her Prices and Other Stories* (1882). He wrote sketches of clerical men in *Clergymen of the Church of England* (1866) and detailed biographies of William Makepeace Thackeray, a long-time friend (1879), and Lord Palmerston, the prominent politician (1882). His own *Autobiography* appeared posthumously in 1883. He tried his hand at classical translation in an edition of *The Commentaries of Caesar* (1870). Trollope's letters were edited by Bradford A. Booth (1951) but 205 complete and three fragmentary letters remain unpublished at Princeton University. *The Oxford Trollope* (1948), in multiple volumes, edited by Michael Sadleir and Frederick Page, is the most complete edition of his novels.

Achievements

Trollope was acknowledged during his lifetime as a prominent though not necessarily a weighty or enduring writer. He wished to entertain and he did so, at least until the late 1860's when *He Knew He Was Right* turned out to be a failure. His posthumous reputation was harmed by his *Autobiography*, which claimed that he wrote automatically, that his characters were imitations of commonly observed types, that he transcribed reality without much aesthetic control, and that he forced his production by his methodical habits of composition whatever the circumstances. These admissions brought upon him the wrath of the next generation of writers in the 1880's and 1890's who were imbued with more aesthetic doctrines of carefully contrived and consistent viewpoints, detailed representation of interior states, a conscious interplay of ideas, and a complex style to suit a more complex method of storytelling.

Later, Trollope suffered from those who deemed him a pedestrian realist padding his work with creaking plots, flat characters, prosaic situations, and dull prose. He was, and still is for much of the public, the novelist of a single work, *Barchester Towers*, but other writers and critics have not forgiven him for writing more than thirty novels and setting himself a goal to exceed in quantity if not in quality. Despite what seems to be a simple theory of fiction— the writer tries as closely as possible to make the reader's experience approximate his own, to make his characters and events appear to parallel actual life—Trollope was more sophisticated than he allows.

Walter Kendrick finds that before Trollope's *He Knew He Was Right*, his inner thought is not distinguished from outer events, consciousness is presented chronologically; and characters, at least by implication, appear without authorial intervention. Afterward, character becomes "a zone of space on a canvas" with changes of age, feeling, and appearance even while outside the narrative. Various linear plots create a spatial unity for the reader, and they become a mosaic on which the character exists. Fiction writing becomes a subject in the novel, and the characters are a warning against efforts to define their existence with the narrative. This view sees the characters as a complex interplay between narrative and reader. Nathaniel Hawthorne had a very different view of Trollope, equating him to a giant hewing a great lump out of the earth as the earth's inhabitants go about the business of putting it under a glass case. This comment leads, unfortunately, in the direction of Henry James's evaluation after Trollope's death that he had "a great deliberate apprehension of the real" but that his "great fecundity is gross and importunate."

Trollope is a mixture of several kinds of writer, sometimes realistic in the sociological way of Honoré de Balzac, analyzing class and caste, sometimes a comedian of manners and mores like Henry Fielding, at times a sentimental melodramatist like Charles Dickens, fairly often an ironist deliberately breaking fictional illusions like Thackeray, often introspective if not as equally learned as George Eliot, and periodically a brilliant chronicler of dementia like Joseph Conrad. This mixture is what creates havoc with critical response. Trollope is a master of convincing and accurate dialogue, good at retrospective interior analysis, and gifted with varieties of ironic voices. The building of his reputation, aided by Michael Sadleir's biography in the 1920's, was materially assisted by *The Trollopian* (now *Nineteenth Century Studies*), a journal devoted to studies of his novels, further work by scholars, such as Ruth apRoberts, Robert M. Polhemus, and James R. Kincaid, and new critical techniques, which have given Trollope his present reputation as a leading English novelist.

Biography

Anthony Trollope, born on April 24, 1815, in London, seems to have owed his boisterous energy, booming voice, quarrelsome touchiness, and reticent sensitivity, to a childhood of off-handed upbringing. C. P. Snow refers to him as "weighed down by 20 years of neglect and humiliation." His father was a tactless and impractical barrister who had pretensions about being a land-owner in Harrow. There, he established his family in an elegant though quickly declining farm, Julians, later the model for the experimental Orley Farm in the novel of that name. Trollope's mother, Frances, was the driving force of the family; she was closer to Trollope's oldest brother, Tom, than to Anthony: Anthony received neither much encouragement nor much regular affection from her. After starting his education at Sunbury School, with a brief stint at Harrow, Anthony was sent to Winchester, his father's old school, for three years. In 1827, the family was forced to move into a smaller house in Harrow for financial reasons.

Meanwhile, his mother made the acquaintance of a zealous Utopian reformer, Fanny Wright, and went with her and three of her children—Henry, Cecilia, and Emily—to America. Their experiences there border on black comedy. Among other misfortunes, Frances, without past experience or common sense, started a fancy emporium or bazaar in Cincinnati, the building evolved into a grand structure modeled upon an Egyptian temple. The enterprise only succeeded in making the family penniless. Through the efforts of a painter friend, her husband, and son Tom, they managed to piecemeal their way home to England.

Anthony was removed from Winchester in 1830, which deprived him of the chance to enter Oxford University from which he might have entered into the clergy, the usual course at that time. He returned as a day student to Harrow School where the intense and entrenched snobbery made the shabby boy the butt of ridicule and persecution, and perhaps began his lifelong pattern of irritability. Also at that time, Trollope's father sank into petty miserliness and self-pitying moroseness, becoming more obsessively preoccupied with his scholarly work, an ecclesiastical encyclopedia.

The success of Frances' *The Domestic Manners of the Americans* (1832), a book adversely critical of American society, temporarily kept the family from bankruptcy, but her husband's financial mismanagement created more debts. To prevent his arrest for bankruptcy in 1834, the family, without Anthony, went to Bruges, Belgium. Any possible happiness they might have found was destroyed by tuberculosis, which killed Anthony's father, brother Henry, and sister Emily between 1834 and 1836. Frances Trollope was obviously too occupied with nursing to pay much attention to Anthony, but she did get him a tutoring position in Belgium for a short time. He returned to England where he survived in squalid lodgings in Marylebone, London, at a clerk's job in the main post office for seven years. At age twenty-six, he got the chance which changed his life, obtaining the post of deputy surveyor, the overseer of mail service, in western Ireland.

At Banaghar, he found a comfortable social milieu for the first time, though his manner with carriers and postmasters was brusque and his temper was at times violent. Trollope became a man jovial with companions, truculent with superiors, bullying with inferiors, and tender with close friends and family. In 1842, he married Rose Heseltine, an Anglo-Irish woman. Her bank-manager father, like one of Trollope's own shady characters, was an embezzler. A trusted partner, Rose handled Trollope's financial affairs, edited his manuscripts, and accompanied him on his journeys around the world. The portraits of solid, sensible, and compassionate wives and mothers found throughout his work, such as Lady Staveley in *Orley Farm*, suggest the type of woman Trollope had found in Rose.

Irish scenery and politics, and the models of his mother and his brother, Tom, led Trollope to his own fiction writing. Thus, not coincidentally, his first two novels have an Irish theme. In these years, Trollope also began rearing a family, two sons. Henceforth, Trollope's career ran on a dual path, pursuing his duties for the postal service and his writing.

Posted to southwest England in 1851 to correct faults in rural delivery, Trollope and his family led a roving existence for three years until he became his own boss as full surveyor in Belfast, at age thirty-nine. The experience of sleepy country towns and a current topic—the Anglican Church's misuse of endowed charity funds to create sizable incomes for administrators—resulted in the writing of *The Warden*, finished in Belfast and published in 1855; it was his first major success. When Trollope moved his family to Dublin, he established a daily routine of writing. The successor to *The Warden*, *Barchester Towers*, his best-known novel, is a social comedy in the eighteenth century mock-heroic vein of Henry Fielding or Oliver Goldsmith.

During a visit to see his mother and brother in Italy, Trollope met a young American woman, Kate Field, and began a long and close friendship, mostly carried out by correspondence. C. P. Snow thinks that Trollope was impressed by the independent and self-assertive woman, who was rather unlike English women. Intrigued by Kate's advocacy of feminine freedom, in *Orley Farm* (1862), Trollope presents a woman who affronts social and moral conventions by an act of forgery to save the inheritance of her infant son. The motivation is a bit slick, but the fact that the resolute heroine succeeds against a determined male antagonist suggests that Kate's independence was sympathetically perceived.

Trollope went to North America during the early Civil War (1861-1862); a trip which resulted in a travel book. Like his mother's work, the book took a negative stance toward American institutions. He then published, among others, *Rachel Ray*, *The Last Chronicle of Barset*, and *The Claverings*, which gained Trollope his biggest sales price ever. His works were also being serialized in various periodicals, such as *The Fortnightly Review*. It became obvious, however, that Trollope's continued output led him to repeat themes and recycle characters.

Immersed as he was in writing and somewhat resentful of his position at the post office, Trollope resigned in October, 1867, after the offer of the editorship of a new journal, *St. Paul's Magazine*. He continued to do some work on behalf of the post office, however, since he went to Washington to negotiate a postal treaty in 1868. Trollope ran *St. Paul's Magazine* for three years before it went under financially. He was not temperamentally suited to deal with authors.

In his own writing, Trollope tended, as Walter Kendrick sees it, to turn toward more sensational materials, which other authors had discarded, but he was also experimenting in the psychological novel. In *He Knew He Was Right*, Trollope treats the subject of insanity and he presents a fascinating study of psychosis. Ruth apRoberts praises the novel for its economy and the supporting relationships of closely knit characters. Yet, Trollope's work began to command less popular attention, and he increasingly turned to the political world. He created Phineas Finn, an Anglo-Irish politician, who appears in the novel of that name in 1869 and reappears in *Phineas Redux*, part of the loose series sometimes referred to as the Palliser novels. Trollope, however, did not give up what is really his chief subject: conflict between the sexes.

In 1871, having sold Waltham House and given up his editorship, Trollope and his wife embarked on an eighteen-month visit to New Zealand and a stay with their son, Fred, a relatively unprosperous sheep-farmer in Australia. Trollope continued to write during their stay in the primitive sheep-station. A travel commentary and materials for *John Caldigate* were the result of the voyage, as well as further work on the novel *The Eustace Diamonds*. The Trollopes then settled in London where he wrote on the current topic of "the condition of England" in *The Way We Live Now* and *The Prime Minister*. Trollope presented his skeptical views about the ability of a democratic society to govern itself effectively.

The final stage of Trollope's life was a restless one in his sixties. He took another trip to Australia for eight months in 1875, returning through the United States and meeting with Kate Field. Then, he immediately went to South Africa to inspect the Boer territory with the encroaching British settlement based on gold and diamond exploitation. The Trollopes again returned to the land by moving into a refined farmhouse at Hartung, near

Hastings, where Trollope worked on his autobiography. Along with other fiction, he wrote a mystery novel, *Mr. Scarborough's Family*, which was serialized before his death but published posthumously in 1883. Farm living sparked Trollope's asthma which drained his energy, thus causing him to return to London. He was enjoying club life, dinners, and letters to his son, Henry, who was also a writer, when Trollope suffered a sudden stroke in the fall of 1882 that left him paralyzed, and a month later, on December 6, 1882, he died, at the age of sixty-seven.

Analysis

Recent criticism of Anthony Trollope has acknowledged his affinity with comic satirists of the eighteenth century, and this affinity is reflected in his best-known work, *Barchester Towers*. There are two distinct worlds in the novel: that of London vanity, represented by Mr. Slope, the London preacher who comes to Barchester as the protégé of Mrs. Proudie; and that of the smaller, conservative rural world, represented by Archdeacon Grantly of Barchester Cathedral who opposes Mr. Slope with "high and dry" Anglicanism. At the end, Slope is rejected but so is the siren of the comic interlude, Signora Madeleine Vesey Neroni, daughter of the gentlemanly but parasitic, self-indulgent Dr. Vesey Stanhope, canon of the Cathedral.

The novel is concerned with the pursuit of Eleanor Bold, a young prosperous widow and daughter of Mr. Harding, by Obadiah Slope, a brash and unctuous social climber. The newly vacant position of warden provokes a struggle between the Grantly forces and the Proudie forces (including Mr. Slope), with Mrs. Proudie, at the head. In this strand of the plot, the mock-heroic or mock-epic combat parodies the Miltonic epic tradition, with Grantly and his supporters as the rebel angels struggling against the tyrant Mrs. Proudie, with Slope as a kind of fallen angel. Slope is first supported by Mrs. Proudie in his efforts to prevent the return of the vacant post to Harding, but Slope, in his effort to attain favor with Eleanor Bold, eventually gets the position for Harding.

Slope is emasculated by Signora Neroni, who transfixes him with her bright eyes and silvery laughter during rural games and festivities at Ullathorne, the ancient seat of the Thornes and center of a static pastoral world. Seduced by her witchery, he is humiliated by this demoniac Eve and defeated by Eleanor's godlike rebuff, who slaps his face as he presses his suit upon her. Further, he incurs the wrath of his patroness, Mrs. Proudie, with his attentiveness to Signora Neroni, who, although crippled, rules from a couch where she resides in state like Cleopatra. In this world of sham battles, Grantly celebrates his triumph, including a dean's position for Mr. Harding in a solemn conclave of the clergy.

The disputants in these mock-exercises practice their feints around innocent third parties: Bishop Proudie between Slope and Mrs. Proudie; Quiverful, the other candidate for the wardenship, a pathetically comic father of numerous children, between his determined wife and Slope; and Harding between Slope and Grantly. In this formally ordered structure, it is appropriate that Eleanor and Frances Arabin, the naïve Oxford academician, be matched by Miss Thorne, reaffirming the power of the old order, yet still contending with Proudies. The marriage of Eleanor and Arabin asserts the two worlds, old and new, country and city, innocent and corrupt.

The novel has a rich galaxy of minor characters. For example, there is Bertie Stanhope, the dilettante sculptor, who is pressed into proposing to Eleanor, but he undermines his own courtship by the candid admission of his motives; Mr. Harding, the unwilling tool of both Slope and Grantly, who takes such delight in the cathedral music that he mechanically saws an imaginary cello during moments of partisan plots and counterplots; and Mrs. Quiverful, who functions like a wailing chorus in a Greek tragedy, piteously reminding the world and Mrs. Proudie of the cruel difficulties of pinched means and a large family. Although Trollope did write important novels on more serious themes, *Barchester Towers* remains his best known, with its effective comic scenes, the balletlike entrances and exits, the lively irony, and the mock-heroic bathos. The orchestration of speaking styles ranging from the pomposity of the Archdeacon to the vacuity of Bertie Stanhope is another example of the buoyancy and playful wit that Trollope achieved only intermittently thereafter.

Orley Farm was written during Trollope's middle period. Its central situation revolves around the plight of Lady Mason, the second wife of a rich man, who, twenty years earlier, forged a codicil to her dying husband's will so that it leaves Orley Farm, her sole economic support, to her and her young child, Lucius. The possession of the farm has become a matter of regret, as the suspicions of the legitimate heir, Joseph Mason, otherwise the inheritor of considerable wealth, eventuate in a trial to break the will. The effort fails only because Lady Mason commits perjury. Using the omniscient viewpoint, Trollope shows both her guilt and her anguish in trying to provide security for her infant son. Lucius, as the novel opens, is a proud, priggish young man given to notions of scientifically reforming agricultural practice; he is well-educated, theoretical, and self-righteous.

The novel's unusual perspective poses two main themes: first, how justice can be accomplished, and second, whether justice can actually be achieved. In setting human rights against legal rights, Trollope portrays Lady Mason's crime in the light of vested interests and the selfish motives of various people. Like C. P. Snow in a novel such as *The Masters* (1951), Trollope displays in *Orley Farm* an abstract ideal distorted and transformed by human emotions, calculations, and egotism. Joseph Mason is more concerned with defeating Lady Mason than enjoying the actual property; Sir Peregrine Orme, a highly respected landowner, proposes marriage to Lady Mason in order to extend the protection of his name, but even he is forced to realize the stain upon his honor if the truth should come out, and after Lady Mason refuses his offer, he, having been told the damning truth, keeps his promise to support her in her new trial. Another perspective is provided through Mr. Dockwrath, the country lawyer who discovers the evidence which necessitates the new trial, hopes it will prove lucrative and will enhance his legal reputation. Lady Mason's solicitor, Mr. Furnival, carefully avoids definite knowledge of her guilt, though he suspects it, while also wishing she were proven guilty so that he might forgive her with pleasure. A less selfish attitude is seen in Edith Orme, Sir Peregrine's widowed daughter-in-law, who recognizes with compassion the necessity for Lady Mason's crime and the suffering it has entailed for her.

Trollope reveals some of his other typical thematic concerns in the subplots of *Orley Farm*. He explores various attitudes toward marriage and money in the romances of Peregrine Jr., Lucius Mason, and Felix Graham, a poor barrister, with a variety of modern young women. The women's responses to the gentlemen's advances run from prudent calculation of worldly advantages to prudent reticence in acknowledging love until family wisdom approves it. Also, Trollope's impulses toward indulgence of children are exemplified in Lord and Lady Staveley, who, having made their way without worldly advantages, are willing to offer the same chance to their children by permitting the engagement of a daughter to Felix Graham, whose success has been impeded by his honesty. Trollope's conservatism is revealed through the reluctance of these young people to avow their love until they have consent from the Staveleys.

With regard to the central theme of moral and legal justice, purely through the oratorical skills of the trial lawyer, Lady Mason is found innocent of perjury, a finding wholly incorrect. The trial frees the guilty, turns the truthful into villains, makes the innocent bear the burden of deceit, challenges the loyalty of lawyers, and implicates the idealists posturings. The system has turned Lady Mason's desperate chicanery into heroism. It is somewhat anticlimactic that Trollope has the pure Edith Orme take Lady Mason to her heart and, from a sense of Christian charity, refuse to render judgment against her.

Meanwhile, Lady Mason's greatest trial has been alienation from Lucius who, unaware of her guilt, has attempted vigorous countermeasures to defend her honor rather than respecting her dignified silence. His discovery of the truth cuts deeply into his priggish pride, destroys his dreams of becoming a gentleman-farmer, and makes him restore the farm to Joseph Mason before departing abroad with his mother. Again, Trollope makes an ambivalent statement through this conclusion. Although forgiveness implies repentance and restitution, Lady Mason has not been, at least in public, repentant, and the restitution is as much a matter of pride as of justice. The effect is a tacit denial of Lady Mason's innocence and thus the aborting of the whole effort to save her reputation.

If the power of money, or the distortions of human choice and desire which money brings, is Trollope's major concern, the warfare of the sexes and the frustrations which that warfare brings are secondary themes in his novels. *Can You Forgive Her?*, the first of the Palliser series—which includes *Phineas Finn*, *Phineas Redux*, and *The Prime Minister*, each grounded in politics—raises the issue of what sort of love a woman wishes in marriage or indeed whether marriage is a suitable institution. The novel presents the case of Alice Vavasour, a "new woman" who does not know what she wants in life but resents the demands of social propriety. She especially resents the expectation that she accept the marriage proposal of John Grey, whom she really does love, merely because everyone knows him to be a suitable partner. Her cousin, the heiress Lady Glencora McCluskie, has married Plantagenet Palliser, the dull younger son of a ducal family, to support his Liberal political career with her money; but she has fallen in love with the handsome Burgo Fitzgerald, an unconventional, ruinous, yet passionate charmer. Alice reinstitutes her former affection for her cousin George Vavasour, another charmingly irresponsible man who needs her money to campaign to keep his seat in Parliament. For Alice, the masculine excitement of politics makes George attractive, although she honestly admits his desire for her money.

The novel has low-comedy relief in Alice's aunt, Arabella Greenow, and her two suitors, a grocer with money and a retired military officer without it. Arabella means to have her own way, giving her lovers only as much liberty as she desires, choosing the officer because of "a sniff of the rocks and the valleys" about him. The comedy underscores the desire of Alice and Glencora, who, if they had a choice, would put themselves at the mercy of weak men.

In a melodramatic turn of the main plot, George knocks down his sister, Kate, for refusing to assist him in overturning their grandfather's will, which had left all the family property to her. This turn of the plot demonstrates, through George's furious masculine rage, the falsity of the normal economic subjugation of women, which has been reversed in Kate's case. Arabella Greenow, for her part, is also financially independent and can bargain her way into a satisfactorily romantic liaison balancing "rocks and valleys" against "bread and cheese."

Glencora, aware of being sold into matrimony, almost runs off with Burgo but is dissuaded at the last minute by the vigilance of Alice, who makes clear to Plantagenet the temptation he has given to his wife by his conduct. In an improbable reversal that displays Trollope's own romanticism, Plantagenet sacrifices his political hopes for a cabinet appointment in order to take her away from the scenes of her misery after she has confessed her infatuation. Indeed, he is even willing to provide Burgo, who becomes a frequenter of gambling tables, with an allowance at her behest when they encounter him abroad.

Plantagenet can make a sacrifice for Glencora because he has money and social position; George Vavasour, by contrast, is defeated in politics and exiled for lack of money. John Grey, meanwhile, has interposed himself in Alice's arrangement with George so that her fortune is not at stake. This conduct, chivalrous in one sense, paternalistic in another, results in George's challenging him to a duel. The Victorian world is not that of Regency rakes, however, and George's blustering challenge is physically rebuffed, and he is sent away degraded. Alice finally accepts John Grey in a contrite mood. although Grey has kindly intentions, Alice's undefined longings for autonomy anticipate those Henrik Ibsen made memorable through Nora Helmer in *A Doll's House* (1879), where Nora sacrifices love in the effort to mould her own destiny.

If the future of his heroines seems to lie within conventional marital arrangements or respectable spinsterhood secured by inherited money, Trollope's questioning title for the novel seems to turn the issue of feminine aspiration somewhat ambivalently to the reader. He has shown women challenging the decorum of prudent emotions and affections based on money, but only the ungenteel Mrs. Greenow succeeds in mastering her destiny through financial manipulation.

In *The Eustace Diamonds*, Trollope shows the psychologically damaging effects of survival in an upper-class and aristocratic hierarchy. A society that channels affections and loyalties in terms of property and money, where people struggle for ascendancy, domination, and power, while subscribing to romantic illusions of unfettered expression and creative self-development. The narrator ironically undercuts the Romantic pretensions as the novel delineates the unrealistic strategies of men and women coping with the moral corruption of social ambition. They seek security, status, prestige, and elegance while evincing pretentiousness, snobbery, envy, and parasitism. Trollope takes an anarchic pleasure in those egotistical characters who subvert institutions by undermining the rules of conduct, stretching them to the point of fatuity.

In the novel, Lizzie Eustace appropriates the diamonds without specific authority from her late husband, Sir Florian, and uses them as weapons against the respectable family lawyer, Mr. Camperdown, and the man she intends as her second husband, the morally honorable Lord Fawn. The diamonds become a symbol of Lizzie's inner rage against the world, a rage arising from self-doubt prompted by the excessive demands of her own idealized views of herself. While denying that ownership of the necklace gives her any pleasure, Lizzie simultaneously insists that she will throw the diamonds away while guarding them zealously. When the box in which she ostentatiously houses them is stolen, Lizzie claims that the necklace has been stolen as well. The lie is psychologically predictable. The diamonds exemplify her attitudes toward herself, toward Lord Fawn whom she despises for his complete disdain of the diamonds, and toward Frank Greystock, her champion before the world, whom she has lured away from his serious attentions to Lucy Morris. The supposed theft is Lizzie's symbolic punishment for a guilt which will be lessened if the diamonds are believed stolen, but it is also an aggrandisement of her own self-esteem since secretly she knows they are still in her possession. The diamonds, however, are stolen in a second robbery, which ends Lizzie's control of the situation.

Lizzie's desire for social domination gains dimension through the narrator's ironic moral judgment and through the close-ups of the omniscient viewpoint that reveal her own rationalizations and fears. Seeking support, Lizzie confesses to Lord George, hoping that he will be cynically brutal, but instead she receives his weak acknowledgment of her supposed cunning. When the police discover the truth, Lizzie prefers the illusion of submitting to the police administrator to the reality of confronting her own self-destructive behavior. Lizzie then tries desperately to reestablish control by triumphing over someone: she reproaches Mrs. Carbuncle, her friend; breaks her engagement with Lord Fawn, ignoring his earlier efforts to end the relationship and pretending to be heartlessly jilted, offers herself to Lord George, who also refuses her; and finally bids for the attentions of Frank Greystock through his need for money, yet Frank is simply provoked into promising he will abandon her utterly if she persists.

Yielding to a fantasy logic, Lizzie entertains a marriage proposal from Mr. Emilius, an impudent and sanctimonious popular preacher whom she had once refused. She deliberately accepts him knowing that he is a fraud and admitting that his bogus qualities attract her. Lizzie's limited knowledge of how the world operates is supported by Emilius's brazen effrontery, which will offer her a new chance for social domination.

The secondary characters are drawn with an equal sense of psychological aberration. For example, there is the cynical honesty of Lord George, which conceals a fearful vacillation that abhors responsibility yet is resolute in pushing his companion, Sir Griffin Tewett, into marriage with Lucinda Roanoke. Alternately submissive and aggressive, he turns vindictive in denouncing Lizzie for the damage she has caused his reputation by creating suspicions of his complicity in her concealment of the necklace. He is also forgiving, on the other hand, of Mrs. Barnacle, his former mistress, for her good intentions in encouraging her niece, Lucinda, to marry for money. Lord George appears cognizant of obligations assumed by others though irresolute in taking them upon himself. Further, he shows the unreality of Lizzie's dreams; but his own conduct is the model of a romantic neurosis. Other examples of psychologically crippled characters are Lucinda, who suffers from strong sexual repression and emotional sterility, and Sir Griffin, cool, vindictive, and arrogant, who is repelled by anyone who would love him.

These characters are set up in contrast to the more conventional ones, such as Mrs. Hittaway, who reflect the pathological tendencies that a materialistic society encourages. The baffled efforts of Lizzie, Lord George, Sir Griffin, and Lucinda to deal with destructive self-deception reflect the results of social forces inhibiting real creative growth in understanding. V. S. Pritchett has criticized Trollope for being "a detailed, rather cynical observor of a satisfied world," and that "we recognize that he [Trollope] has drawn life as people say it is when they are not speaking about themselves." C. P. Snow commented that an exploratory psychological writer such as Trollope "has to live on close terms with the blacker—including the worse—side of his own nature." *The Eustace Diamonds* is the record of Trollope's endurance of a mental nature that was divided. Pritchett has accused Trollope of not capturing or presenting the depth of moral experience. This may reflect a demand for a more complex style, a more intensive depiction of the intricacies of moral struggle, and a more insistent emphasis on values. Snow, however, perceived the simple, direct style as cutting out everything except the truth. Trollope was not temperamental or self-advertising, but as a novelist, he covers a wide range of social, institutional, and religious issues and controversies constituting the fabric of Victorian society. He dramatizes the moral and intellectual dilemmas often arising from them and has considerable insight as well as the ability to present the sheer flux of mental life, which anticipates later developments in the work of James Joyce, Virginia Woolf, and Dorothy Richardson.

Major publications other than long fiction

SHORT FICTION: *Tales of All Countries*, 1861, 1863; *Lotta Schmidt and Other Stories*, 1867; *An Editor's Tales*, 1870; *Why Frau Frohmann Raised Her Prices and Other Stories*, 1882.

NONFICTION: *The West Indies*, 1859; *North America*, 1862; *Travelling Sketches*, 1866; *Clergymen of the Church of England*, 1866; *The Commentaries of Caesar*, 1870 (translation); *Australia and New Zealand*, 1873; *South Africa*, 1878; *Thackeray*, 1879; *Lord Palmerston*, 1882; *Autobiography*, 1883; *The Letters of Anthony Trollope*, 1951 (Bradford A. Booth, editor).

Bibliography

apRoberts, Ruth. *The Moral Trollope*, 1971.
Booth, Bradford A. *Anthony Trollope*, 1958.
Kendrick, Walter M. *The Novel Machine*, 1980.
Kincaid, James R. *The Novels of Anthony Trollope*, 1977.
Polhemus, Robert M. *The Changing World of Anthony Trollope*, 1968.
Pope-Hennessy, James. *Anthony Trollope*, 1971.
Smalley, Donald, ed. *Trollope: The Critical Heritage*, 1969.
Snow, C. P. *Trollope: His Life and Art*, 1975.

Roger E . Wiehe

MARK TWAIN
Samuel Langhorne Clemens

Born: Florida, Missouri; November 30, 1835
Died: Redding, Connecticut; April 21, 1910

Principal long fiction

The Gilded Age, 1873 (with Charles Dudley Warner); *The Adventures of Tom Sawyer*, 1876; *The Prince and the Pauper*, 1882; *The Adventures of Huckleberry Finn*, 1884; *A Connecticut Yankee in King Arthur's Court*, 1889; *The American Claimant*, 1892; *Tom Sawyer Abroad*, 1894; *The Tragedy of Pudd'nhead Wilson*, 1894; *Personal Recollections of Joan of Arc*, 1896.

Other literary forms

In addition to his novels, Mark Twain wrote a great deal of short fiction, which can be divided, although often only very arbitrarily, into short stories, tales, and humorous sketches. One of the best examples of his short stories is "The Man That Corrupted Hadleyburg," and one of the best examples of his humorous sketches is "The Jumping Frog of Calaveras County." Somewhere between the story and the sketch are tales such as "Captain Stormfield's Visit to Heaven." Twain also wrote speeches and essays, both humorous and critical. Representative of his best satiric essays, which range from the very funny to the very sober, are "Fenimore Cooper's Literary Offenses" and "To the Person Sitting in Darkness." The first of these is a hilarious broadside against Cooper's style and invention in which Twain is obviously enjoying himself while at the same time continuing his ongoing war against the romanticizing of the past. "To the Person Sitting in Darkness," considered by some to be his finest piece of invective, is his attack upon what he saw as the exploitation of the Philippines following the Spanish-American War by, in his words, "The Blessings-of-Civilization Trust." Early in his career, he wrote the travel sketches and impressions, *The Innocents Abroad* (1869) and *A Tramp Abroad* (1880), and later, *Following the Equator* (1897). Two of his most important books are autobiographical, *Life on the Mississippi* (1883) and *Mark Twain's Autobiography*, published after his death in various editions in 1924.

Achievements

The coincidental appearance of Halley's comet in the years of Twain's birth and death, 1835 and 1910, has been much remarked. A historical event, however, in contrast to the cosmic one, occurring very near the midpoint of his life, provides a better symbol for his career and his achievement than does the mysterious, fiery comet. In 1869, at Promontory Point, Utah, a golden spike was driven to complete the first North American transcontinental railroad. The subsequent settling of the great midwestern center of the continent and the resulting transformation of a frontier society into a civilized one, a process people thought would take hundreds of years, was to be effected in several decades. Twain's life spanned the two Americas, the frontier America that produced so much of the national mythology and the emerging urban, industrial giant of the twentieth century. At the heart of Twain's achievement is his creation of Tom Sawyer and Huck Finn, who embody that mythic America, midway between the wilderness and the modern super-state.

Tom and Huck, two of the nation's most enduring characters, give particular focus to Twain's turbulent, sprawling, complex career as journalist, humorist, entrepreneur, and novelist. The focus is dramatic because the two characters have made their way into the popular imagination with the abiding vitality of legend or folklore. They have been kept before generations of Americans in motion pictures, television, cartoons, and other popular art forms as well as in their original form in the novels. The focus is also symbolic because of the fundamental dualism which the two characters can be seen to represent on the personal, the literary, and the cultural planes.

On the personal plane, Tom and Huck represent aspirations so fundamental to Twain's life as to make them seem rather the two halves of his psyche. Like good and bad angels, they have been taken to represent the contending desires in his life: a strong desire for the security and status of material success on the one hand, set against the deeply ingrained desire for freedom from conventional social and moral restraints on the other. It has been conjectured that riverboat piloting was perhaps the most satisfying of Twain's occupations because it offered him high degrees of both respectability and freedom. Although the character of Tom, the symbol of perennial boyhood, can be easily overburdened by this perspective, there is in him the clear outline of the successful, settled, influential man-of-affairs-to-be. If Tom had grown up, he might well have made and lost a fortune in the publishing business and through investments in the Paige typesetter. He almost certainly would have been a successful professional or businessman. He would likely have traveled abroad and would have been eager to associate with nobility at every opportunity. It is relatively easy to imagine Tom growing up. It is instructive to realize that it is almost impossible to imagine Huck's doing so.

On the literary plane, the two may also be seen as representing contending forces, those of the two principal literary schools of the period, the Romantic and the realistic. Surely, Twain's pervasive attacks upon romantic literature are somewhat compulsive, reminiscent of Nathaniel Hawthorne's preoccupation with the Puritans. Both protest too much. Twain is one of America's foremost Romantics, even if he did see himself as a realist, and even if he did engage much of his time in puncturing the sentimental balloons of the disciples of Sir Walter Scott, Cooper, and the graveyard poets. He was both Romantic and realist, and Tom and Huck emerge almost allegorically as symbols of the two major literary schools of the late nineteenth century.

Tom as the embodiment of socially conforming respectability and as a disciple of Romantic literature contrasts illustratively with Huck as the embodiment of the naturally free spirit, who is "realistic" in part because of his adolescent honesty about such things as art, royalty, and the efficacy of prayer. It is the symbolic dualism on the historical plane, however, that brings into sharpest focus the nature of Twain's central and most enduring achievement. On the historical plane, his two central characters reflect most clearly Twain's principal legacy to posterity: the embodiment in fiction of that moment in time, a moment both real and imaginary, given some historical particularity by the driving of the golden spike at Promontory Point in 1869, when America was poised between the wilderness and the modern, technological state. In this context, Tom represents the settlements that were to become the towns and cities of the new century, and Huck represents the human spirit, freer, at least in the imagination, in the wilderness out of which the settlements were springing. At the end of *The Adventures of Huckleberry Finn*, Twain sends Huck on that impossible mission that has been central to the American experience for centuries, when he has him decide to "light out for the territory" before Aunt Sally can "adopt" and "civilize" him.

Twain the humorist and satirist, Twain the silvermining, Paige-typesetting entrepreneur, Twain the journalist, the family man, the anguished, skeptical seeker after religious faith—all must be taken into consideration in accounts of the nature of his achievements. Without Tom Sawyer and Huck Finn, he would have made his mark as a man of his time, a man of various and rich talents. Most likely, his reputation would rest today largely upon his talents as a humorist and satirist, and that reputation still figures largely in assessment of his overall achievement. With Tom and Huck, however, his achievement is given the depth and dramatic focus of a central contribution to the national mythology. Huck's "voice" is frequently compared to the voice of Walt Whitman's "Song of Myself." Such comparisons rest in part upon rhetorical similarities between the two voices, similarities in what has been called the "vernacular mode." More significantly, they derive from the similarities of the achievements of the poet and the novelist in the establishing of historically and culturally distinctive American "voices" in poetry and fiction. Tom Sawyer and Huck Finn loom large on the nineteenth century literary horizon. They stand, along with Cooper's Natty Bumppo and Chingachgook, Hawthorne's Hester Prynne and Arthur Dimmesdale, and Whitman's persona in "Song of Myself," as the principal characters of the emerging national literature. Twain's contribution to that body of literature is at the deepest center of his achievement as a major American writer.

Biography

Mark Twain was born Samuel Langhorne Clemens in Florida, Missouri, in

1835. He first used the pen name "Mark Twain," taken from the river boatmen's cry for two fathoms of safe water, in 1862.

Twain's father was a Virginia lawyer, and the family was of poor but respectable Southern stock. In 1839, the family moved to Hannibal, Missouri, the Mississippi River town that provided the source material and background of some of Twain's best-known fiction. After his father died in 1847, Twain left school to become an apprentice in the printing shop of his brother, Orion. From 1855 to 1856, Twain worked as a journeyman printer in St. Louis, New York, Philadelphia, Keokuk, and Cincinnati. Between 1857 and 1860, he acquired much of his knowledge of the Mississippi River as a pilot, beginning that short though richly productive career under the tutelage of a senior pilot, Horace Bixby. He was a Confederate volunteer for several months after the Civil War began. In 1861, he left for the Nevada territory with his brother Orion, where he drifted into prospecting and journalism, beginning his career as a reporter with the *Virginia City Territorial Enterprise*, and continuing it with the San Francisco *Morning Call*.

Twain's literary career and the beginning of his fame might be said to have begun in 1865 with the publication in the New York Saturday Press of "The Jumping Frog of Calaveras County." As a journalist, he went to the Sandwich Islands in 1866 and to Europe and the Holy Land in 1867. The latter of the two provided him with the experiences which he shaped into his first book, *The Innocents Abroad*. *Roughing It*, his narrative of pioneers striving to establish civilization on the frontier, appeared in 1872, and his first novel-length fiction, written with Charles Dudley Warner, *The Gilded Age*, came in 1873.

In 1870, Twain married Olivia Langdon. They finished their Hartford mansion and moved into it in 1871. Their infant son Langdon died in 1872, the year Susy, their first daughter, was born. Her sisters, Clara and Jean, followed in 1874 and 1880. Twain's most productive years as a novelist came in this middle period when his daughters were young and he was prospering. *The Adventures of Tom Sawyer*, *The Prince and the Pauper*, *The Adventures of Huckleberry Finn*, and *A Connecticut Yankee in King Arthur's Court*, were all written during this highly productive period.

By 1890, Twain's financial fortunes were crumbling, mostly owing to bad investment in a publishing firm and in the Paige typesetter. In 1891, Twain closed the Hartford mansion, sold the furniture, and went to Europe to economize. While he was lecturing in Europe, his daughter Suzy died, and his wife, Livy, shortly afterward suffered a nervous collapse from which she never recovered. Twain blamed himself for bringing on his beloved family the circumstances that led to both tragedies. His abiding skepticism about human nature deepened to cynicism and found expression in those dark stories of his last years, "The Man That Corrupted Hadleyburg," "The Mysterious Stranger," and in the essay "What Is Man?" He died in 1910 at the age of seventy-four in Redding, Connecticut.

Analysis

It is instructive to note that the most pervasive structural characteristic of Mark Twain's work, of his nonfiction as well as his fiction, is dualistic. That observation is not worth much without detailed application to specific aspects of particular works, but even before turning to particulars, it is useful to consider how many "pairs" of contending, conflicting, complementary, or contrasting characters, situations, states of being, ideas, and values run through Twain's work. One thinks immediately of Tom and Huck, of Huck and Jim, of Huck and Pap, of Aunt Sally and Miss Watson, of the prince and the pauper, of the two sets of twins of *The Tragedy of Pudd'nhead Wilson.* One thinks of boys testing themselves against adults, of youth and adulthood, of the free life on the river contrasted with the settled life of the river towns, of the wilderness and civilization, of the promises of industrial progress against the backdrop of the humbler, traditional rural setting, of Eden and everything east of Eden, and, finally, of good and evil.

The tonal quality of Twain's works is also dualistic. "The Jumping Frog of Calaveras County" is almost pure fun. "The Mysterious Stranger," published after Twain's death, is almost pure gloom. Most of Twain's fiction comes between the two, both chronologically and thematically. Except for *The Gilded Age,* which he wrote with Charles Dudley Warner, the novels, from *The Adventures of Tom Sawyer* to the final two, *The Tragedy of Pudd'nhead Wilson* and *Personal Recollections of Joan of Arc,* fall within the thematic and tonal extremes established by the short fiction. That is, Tom's adventures take place in the hallowed light of innocence and virtue beyond the reach of any truly effective evil forces, while Roxy's adventures in *The Tragedy of Pudd'nhead Wilson,* are of almost unrelieved gloom. *The Adventures of Huckleberry Finn* is midway between the extremes, with its blending of the light and affirmation that shine so brightly in Twain's childhood idyll with the darkened vision of the later years.

Nearly everyone agrees that *The Adventures of Tom Sawyer,* Twain's second novel, is an American classic, and nearly everyone agrees that there is no accounting for its success. It is at the same time a novel of the utmost simplicity and of deep complexity. The novel is a marvelous boy's adventure story, a fact given perspective by Twain's observation that "it will be read only by adults." That is, the essence of childhood can be savored only after the fact, only after one has passed through it and can look back upon it. Popularizations of Tom's adventures are produced for children, but the continuing vitality of the novel depends upon the adult sensibility and its capacity and need for nostalgic recollection. Twain plays on all the strings of that sensibility as he guides the reader through Tom's encounters with the adult world, represented by Aunt Polly and Judge Thatcher, through Tom's romance with Becky, and finally to the adventurous triumph over evil in the person of Injun Joe.

Aunt Polly is the perfect adult foil for a perfect boyhood. Not only does she provide the emotional security that comes from being loved in one's place, but she also serves as an adult Tom can challenge through his wits, thereby deepening his self-confidence about his place in the adult world. The fence whitewashing episode is surely one of the best-known in American literature. In it, Tom not only outwits his friends, whom he dupes into whitewashing the fence for him, but also successfully challenges the adult world which, through Aunt Polly, assigned the "boy's chore" to him in the first place. The episode also provides Twain an opportunity to exercise his irony, which, in contrast to much that was to come in the later fiction, is serenely gentle here. Judge Thatcher represents the secure, if somewhat pompous, authority of the adult world beyond the domestic circle. The much desired recognition of that authority is achieved with decisive pomp when the Judge makes the treasure found in the cave legally Tom's and Huck's.

The romance with Becky is almost pure idyll, although the young lovers' descent into the cave inevitably raises speculations about deeper implications. While Injun Joe as evil incarnate is believable enough to raise the hair along the back of the necks of adults as well as children, especially when the torch goes out in the cave, there is never any doubt that Tom and Becky will be saved, that good will triumph—never any doubt, that is, for the adult sensibility, secure beyond the trials and tribulations of adolescent infatuation and terror.

The book as childhood idyll is really a simple matter, but that does not diminish the significance of that dimension of the work. Rather, it affirms an understanding of the book's success on that level. There is more to be considered, however, especially in terms of the companion piece to come, *The Adventures of Huckleberry Finn*. The poignance of *The Adventures of Tom Sawyer* is attributable in part to the fact that it is an imaginative reconstruction of youthful experience from the perspective of early middle age. The actual historical frame of the re-creation adds its own deeply poignant dimension to the book. The American national experience was clearly in the transitional state between frontier and modern society when the novel was published in 1876. Twain's idyll of boyhood is set in a time and place in history calculated to deepen the significance of the adult's backward recollection of a time of innocence and joy. The American wilderness was never Eden, but that image has haunted the American imagination from at least the time of James Fenimore Cooper's creation of his frontiersman, Natty Bumppo, down to at least the time of Robert Frost's creation of his travelers through the dark, lonely woods.

Finally, in part because it is one of those many pairings of characters so pervasive in Twain's work, Tom's relationship with his half-brother Sid should be noted. The relationship is instructive in that it foreshadows that of the later Tom-Huck relationship. Sid is the "good" boy who serves as Twain's foil for Tom's adventuresome independence. While Tom is never good in the subservient, lap-dog sense that Sid is, there is a kind of lateral movement of his character from the early to the later novel; in *The Adventures of Tom Sawyer*, Tom plays off the foil of Sid's pious "respectability," while in *The Adventures of Huckleberry Finn*, Tom, himself, has moved over to provide a similar foil for Huck's freedom.

Unlike its predecessor, *The Prince and the Pauper* is a "children's book" which has remained simply that, a book for children. Twain professed to have taken great joy in the writing of it, probably in part because of the relief he felt upon completing the troublesome *A Tramp Abroad*. His wife and children admired the book, as did William Dean Howells and the reviewers for the New York *Herald*, the Boston *Transcript*, *The Atlantic*, and the *Century*. Nevertheless, the novel holds little interest for the mature reader except in terms of its relationship to the two superior novels which preceded and followed it.

Its plot hinges upon one of Twain's most explicit pairings, that of Prince Edward with the pauper Tom Cantry. The switching of these look-alike adolescents in the England of Henry VIII allows the Prince to learn what poverty and hardship are like in the alleyways of his kingdom and the pauper to satirize, through his innocence, the foibles of royalty and court life. Neither the satire nor the compassion, however, ring true. It is almost as if Twain were finding his way from his first classic to his second through this experiment, set in a time and place far removed from his native Mississippi River valley.

With that contrast in mind, it is perhaps reasonable to see the prince and the pauper as another Sid and Tom, another Tom and Huck, all of the sets representing at various removes those two basic drives of Twain's nature for respectability and freedom. Huck and Tom Cantry, the pauper, are "freer" than are Tom and Prince Edward, although the relationships are not that simple, since the members of each pair are attracted like magnetic opposites to their mates. This attraction is made most explicit in *The Prince and the Pauper*, where the two actually exchange places. Later in his career, in *The Tragedy of Pudd'nhead Wilson*, Twain made a comparably explicit exchange with wholly tragic consequences. In *The Prince and the Pauper*, it is all play with little consequence at all except for the exigencies of a contrived, melodramatic plot. Twain's truest pairing, that of Huck and Jim, was yet ahead of him.

The Adventures of Huckleberry Finn is almost universally hailed as Twain's best book, as well as one of the half dozen or so American classics of the nineteenth century. This is not to say that the novel is without defects. The ending, in particular, presents some very real problems, structurally, thematically, and rhetorically. The very high place of the novel, however, is generally conceded. This success depends upon several considerations. In the first place, the novel continues the mythic idyll of American boyhood begun with *The Adventures of Tom Sawyer*. That connection and that continuation by itself would have insured the book a place in the national archives if not the national heart. Most agree, however, that its success derives from even deeper currents. *The Adventures of Huckleberry Finn* is Twain's best book because, for whatever reasons, he brought together in it, with the highest degree of artistic balance, those most fundamental dualities running through his work and life from start to finish. The potentially destructive dualities of youth and age, of the need for both security and freedom, of the wilderness and civilization, of innocence and corruption, all are reconciled by means of an aesthetic transformation. Historical, realistic dualities as well as psychological and moral dualities are brought into an artistic synthesis, into a novel, the most distinctive feature of which, finally, is its own modal duality, played out in the terms of a delicate balance between lyricism and satire.

Huck's relationship with Jim, the runaway slave, is central to the novel's narrative, to its structure, and to its theme. Escaping "down" the river, a cruel irony in itself, provides the episodic structure, which is the narrative thread that holds together the developing relationship between the two runaways on the raft. The escape, the quest for freedom, is literal for both Huck and Jim as they flee from Pap and Miss Watson. It may also be seen as symbolic on several planes: historical, philosophical, and moral. The historical setting of the novel is that pivotal era in American history when the new nation was being carved out of the wilderness. The flight down the river is a flight from the complexities of the ever-expanding, westward-moving settlements of the new civilization. The continuing vitality of the novel depends in part upon the survival in the twentieth century of the need for that imaginative escape. Like Henry David Thoreau's Waldon Pond, Huck's Mississippi River, originally an escape from what may now seem some of the simpler strictures of society, continues to serve the American psyche as an imaginative alternative to modern civilization.

The philosophical dimensions of the rapidly disappearing frontier are those of nineteenth century Romanticism. Celebrating their freedom on the raft from the legal and social strictures of the town along the river, Huck and Jim are at the same time affirming the central Romantic thesis concerning man's need to return to nature and to the natural self. There are two kinds of Romanticism in the novel: that which Tom espouses in his adolescent preoccupation with adventure, and that which Huck practices on the river under the stars and, most significantly, in the final resolution of the problem of Jim as a runaway slave. Twain holds up Tom's bookish Romanticism as childish at best and, for the most part, as silly. This attack on Romanticism—a secondary theme in *The Adventures of Huckleberry Finn*, where Twain sends the derelict steamer, the *Walter Scott*, to its destruction on a sandbar—was one of Twain's lifelong preoccupations. It was continued with a vehemence later in *A Connecticut Yankee in King Arthur's Court*, but its deep-running, destructive potential for Twain is harnessed in *The Adventures of Huckleberry Finn*. The satire is there, but it is in the largely playful terms of the antics of the King and the Duke, their mangling of Shakespeare, and the graveyard art of Emmaline Grangerford. This playful treatment of one of his serious themes results in part from the fact that Twain is here working a deeper vein of Romanticism in the person of his supreme fictional creation, Huck.

The moral climax of the novel comes in chapter 31, when Huck decides that he will "go to hell" rather than turn in Jim. The difficulties with the ending of the book derive largely from that relatively early resolution of its central theme. Shortly thereafter, Huck is reunited with Tom, who is responsible for all the preposterous plans to save Jim, who, ironically, no longer needs to be saved. There are real problems here with the plot, with motivation, and with the prose itself, which is no longer sustained by the lyricism of Huck's accounts of life on the raft. The artistic achievement of the climax, however, makes such problems pale into relative insignificance. Twain embodies in Huck and dramatizes in his decision a principle line of American political and moral thought which has its roots in Thomas Jefferson and Thomas Paine, its "philosophical" development in Ralph Waldo Emerson and Thoreau, and its aesthetic transformation at the hands of Twain and Whitman. Huck is the embodiment of both the political and the Romantic ideals of the common man, with no past or roots, whose principal guide is experience rather than tradition. He is one of the principal literary symbols of that fundamental American mythical dream of moral rejuvenation in the Edenic wilderness of the "new" continent. He stands at the center of nineteenth century American literature and at the center of Twain's achievements.

In *The Adventures of Huckleberry Finn*, Twain's attack upon the romantic glorification of the past is a peripheral theme. In *A Connecticut Yankee in King Arthur's Court*, it is central and devastating, both in the novel itself and in its signaling of the direction in which Twain's thought and creative energies were heading. Although this too is a boy's book of a kind, there is about it none of the idyllic radiance of *The Adventures of Tom Sawyer* nor the harmonious balancing of opposites of *The Adventures of Huckleberry Finn*. Rather, there is finally outright war between the forces of the feudal past and those of the progressive present, with considerable ambiguity about which is to be considered the good and which the evil.

There is no doubt that the reader's sympathies at the outset are with the Yankee mechanic, Hank Morgan, who, after a blow on the head, wakes up in King Arthur's England of A. D. 528. After saving himself from execution as a witch by "prophesying" a total eclipse of the sun, he vies successfully with Merlin for power and prestige at court. He is like Huck in his commonsense responses to life in general, and in particular to the romantic claims of the feudal society in which he finds himself. He is unlike Huck in his vigorous progressivism, in his determination to bring the fruits of nineteenth century democracy and technology to feudal England. He introduces explosives, sets up schools to train workmen in the mechanical arts, gives instruction in journalism to his page with an eye to a national press, and stretches telephone lines haphazardly across the countryside. His talents, taken for magic for the most part, earn for him the title "Boss," and the abiding enmity of Merlin, whom he replaces at court. He plans to declare a republic after Arthur's death, and the sixth century kingdom enjoys all the fruits of progress: schools, trains, factories, newspapers, the telephone and telegraph. The end of the story, however, just before Hank returns to his own century, pictures anything but the envisioned utopia. Arthur dies in a battle with Lancelot, Camelot is reduced to shambles, and Hank fortifies himself in a castle against the surviving chivalry of England. One of his final concerns is with the pollution caused by the dead bodies piled in the trenches around his fortress. The repressive, superstitious nightmare of feudal society has been compounded by the fearful efficiency of nineteenth century technology.

The ambiguity of the ending of the novel is symptomatic. The artistic balance of *The Adventures of Huckleberry Finn* is no longer in evidence. Twain, always something of an allegorist, was by 1889 becoming more and more a polemicist, increasingly more interested in conflicts between abstract ideas and values than in the development and portrayal of human characters in all their complexities. Hank can be identified with Huck in terms of their common sense and their human values, but the big difference between them is that Huck's chief concern is with another human being while Hank's is with an abstraction called feudalism.

Twain was to do some of his most important writing in the last two decades of his life, including short fiction and social and moral criticism. His best novels, however, were completed in 1876 and in the 1880's. Of those coming after 1889, *The Tragedy of Pudd'nhead Wilson* is the most readable and the most consistent with the principal direction of his deepening cynicism about the "damned human race." The novel's only really interesting character is Roxy, a slave woman who switches her son with that of her owner Percy Driscoll to save her child from eventually being sold "down river." The whole of the dark tale that follows indicates, in Maxwell Geismar's words, how much "irony and tragedy have taken over the center stage in [Twain's] comic proscenium of life."

Major publications other than long fiction

SHORT FICTION: *The Celebrated Jumping Frog of Calaveras County, and Other Sketches*, 1867; *Mark Twain's Sketches: New and Old*, 1875; *The Stolen White Elephant*, 1882; *The £1,000,000 Bank-Note and Other New Stories*, 1893; *The Man That Corrupted Hadleyburg and Other Stories and Essays*, 1900; *A Double Barrelled Detective Story*, 1902; *The $30,000 Bequest and Other Sto-*

ries, 1906; *A Horse's Tale*, 1907; *The Mysterious Stranger and Other Stories*, 1916; *The Complete Short Stories of Mark Twain*, 1957 (Charles Neider, editor); *Selected Shorter Writings of Mark Twain*, 1962 (Walter Blair, editor).

NONFICTION: *The Innocents Abroad*, 1869; *Roughing It*, 1872; *A Tramp Abroad*, 1880; *Life on the Mississippi*, 1883; *Following the Equator*, 1897; *How to Tell a Story and Other Essays*, 1897; *My Debut as a Literary Person*, 1903; *Extracts from Adam's Diary*, 1904; *King Leopold's Soliloquy*, 1905; *Eve's Diary, Translated from the Original Ms*, 1906; *What Is Man?*, 1906; *Christian Science*, 1907; *Extract from Captain Stormfield's Visit to Heaven*, 1909; *Is Shakespeare Dead?*, 1909; *Mark Twain's Letters*, 1917 (Albert Bigelow Paine, editor, 2 volumes); *Europe and Elsewhere*, 1923 (Albert Bigelow Paine, editor); *Mark Twain's Autobiography*, 1924 (Albert Bigelow Paine, editor, 2 volumes); *Mark Twain's Notebook*, 1935 (Albert Bigelow Paine, editor); *Mark Twain Speaking*, 1976 (Paul Fatout, editor).

Bibliography

Brooks, Van Wyck. *The Ordeal of Mark Twain*, 1920.
De Voto, Bernard. *Mark Twain in Eruption*, 1940.
_____ . *Mark Twain's America*, 1932.
Geismar, Maxwell. *Mark Twain: An American Prophet*, 1970.
Howells, William Dean. *My Mark Twain: Reminiscences and Criticisms*, 1910.
Paine, Albert Bigelow. *Mark Twain: A Biography*, 1912, 1935 (3 volumes).
Wagenknecht, Edward. *Mark Twain: The Man and His Work*, 1935.

Lloyd N. Dendinger

ANNE TYLER

Born: Minneapolis, Minnesota; October 25, 1941

Principal long fiction

If Morning Ever Comes, 1964; *The Tin Can Tree*, 1965; *A Slipping-Down Life*, 1970; *The Clock Winder*, 1972; *Celestial Navigation*, 1974; *Searching for Caleb*, 1975; *Earthly Possessions*, 1977; *Morgan's Passing*, 1980; *Dinner at the Homesick Restaurant*, 1982.

Other literary forms

In addition to her nine novels, Anne Tyler has published more than forty short stories, including several in *Harper's*, *Mademoiselle*, *The New Yorker*, *Seventeen*, and the *Southern Review*. There is no collection to date, although two stories appeared in the O. Henry Prize volumes for 1969 and 1972 and others in the first edition of the Pushcart Prize anthology (1976), *Best American Short Stories* (1977), and *Stories of the Modern South* (1978, 1981). Tyler has also written several autobiographical and personal essays, one for the *Washington Post* in 1976 and another for *The Writer on Her Work* (1980), edited by Janet Sternburg. Since 1975, her reviews of current fiction, criticism, and biography have appeared in major newspapers and magazines, including the *Chicago Sun-Times*, the *Detroit News*, the *National Observer*, *The New Republic*, *The New York Times Book Review*, and the *Washington Post*.

Achievements

Despite praise for the truth of her characterizations and her eye for details, Tyler did not receive much national recognition for her fiction until the publication of her sixth novel, *Searching for Caleb*. The largest segment of her audience has been in the South, although her short stories appeared in prestigious national magazines throughout the 1960's and 1970's. All of her novels, except *A Slipping-Down Life*, have been published abroad. Besides English editions, translations into Danish, French, German, Italian, and Swedish have appeared. Still, the American academic and critical communities have been slow to appreciate Tyler's work. Her strong supporters include John Updike, who has favorably reviewed her novels for *The New Yorker*, beginning with *Searching for Caleb*, and Reynolds Price, Tyler's professor at Duke University, who has also reviewed her work.

Since 1976, Tyler has gained increasing recognition. In 1977, the American Academy and Institute of Arts and Letters cited her as a novelist of excellence and promise. *Earthly Possessions* and *Morgan's Passing* also received largely favorable national reviews. While a few critics, including Updike, expressed some disappointment in *Morgan's Passing*, the Writers Workshop of the University of Rochester awarded it the sixth annual Janet Heidinger Kafka prize for fiction by an American woman.

With the publication of *Dinner at the Homesick Restaurant*, her first novel to make the best-seller list, Tyler at last acquired full national stature. Benjamin DeMott's front-page notice in *The New York Times Book Review* pointed to the novel's wit and the depth of Tyler's psychological insight and characterizations. DeMott saw the book as clear evidence of Tyler's having joined the ranks of major novelists. Updike reiterated this praise, citing *Dinner at the Homesick Restaurant* as a work of considerable power. As a result of this increasing recognition and praise, scholarly studies of Tyler's work, including her early novels, will undoubtedly be forthcoming.

Biography

Anne Tyler was born in Minneapolis, Minnesota, on October 25, 1941, to Phyllis Mahon, a social worker, and Lloyd Parry Tyler, an industrial chemist. She was the oldest of four children, the only girl. Both parents were Quakers dedicated to finding an ideal community, a quest that produced the theme of frustrated idealism in Tyler's fiction. As a consequence of her parents' idealism, Tyler spent most of her early years from infancy until age eleven in various rural Quaker communes scattered throughout the Midwestern and Southern United States. When she was six, the family was settled in Celo, North Carolina—a large, isolated valley commune virtually independent of the outside world and unquestionably the setting for Tyler's short story "Outside," which appeared in the *Southern Review* in 1971.

Tyler has written of the impact of her early years on her fiction. Unable to sleep at night and needing to amuse herself, she began telling herself stories at age three. Her isolation in the rural communes in which she lived as a child contributed to the themes of isolation and community dominant in her novels. Additionally, growing up in North Carolina, where she spent summers tying tobacco, she listened carefully to the stories of the tobacco handlers and tenant farmers. Later, she was able to capture the cadences of everyday speech in her fiction, realizing that the stories these workers told could form the basis for literature. She was also to rely heavily on the North Carolina tobacco country as the setting for her early novels, especially *The Tin Can Tree* and *A Slipping-Down Life*.

When Tyler was eleven, she and her family moved to Raleigh, where they finally settled into an "ordinary" middle-class existence. There, Tyler attended Broughton High School and received encouragement in her writing. She also discovered the work of Eudora Welty, which was to have great influence on Tyler's own fiction.

In September, 1958, Tyler entered Duke University as an Angier Duke Scholar majoring in Russian. She was encouraged by Reynolds Price, who taught her freshman composition and later introduced her to his agent. At

Duke, Tyler helped edit the *Archive* (the student literary magazine), published three early stories there, acted in several productions of the Wesley Players, and learned a great deal about the craft of fiction from reading Leo Tolstoy and the other major Russian novelists. She twice received the Anne Flexner award for creative writing at Duke and was graduated Phi Beta Kappa, just three years after entering, in 1961.

In September, 1961, Tyler began work on a master's degree in Russian at Columbia University, an experience that provides some of the background for *If Morning Ever Comes*. She completed the coursework for the degree but quit before writing her thesis. The following summer she spent in Maine, supporting herself by working on a schooner and proofreading for a local newspaper.

In 1962, Tyler returned to Duke University as the library's Russian bibliographer. That fall, she met her future husband, Taghi Modarressi, an Iranian child psychiatry student at the Duke Medical Center. The couple married in May, 1963, three months after the publication of Tyler's first short story in a national magazine. They moved to Montreal, Canada, that spring; during their four years there, Tyler wrote her first novel, taught herself Persian in anticipation of living in Iran, and worked as a librarian at the McGill University law library. In September, 1965, she gave birth to her first child, Tezh, a girl. The publication of *The Tin Can Tree* followed the next month.

In June, 1967, the Modarressis moved to Baltimore, Maryland, where they have settled. While Tyler's short stories continued to appear frequently in national publications between 1965 and 1970, her third novel was not published until January, 1970, first in condensed form in *Redbook* and later that same year in its entirety by Alfred A. Knopf. Between *The Tin Can Tree* and *A Slipping-Down Life* came one other book—*Winter Birds, Winter Apples*—which remains unpublished. A second daughter, Mitra, was born in November, 1967, in Baltimore. Since then, the Modarressis have had no more children, and other novels have followed at one and two-year intervals. A dedicated mother and a productive organized writer, Tyler has managed her dual careers by writing almost daily while her children are at school.

Analysis

In *The Writer on Her Work*, Anne Tyler discusses the importance of her having lived as a child in "an experimental Quaker community in the wilderness." For her, this early experience of isolation and her later effort "to fit into the outside world" provided the "kind of setting-apart situation" the writer requires for aesthetic distancing. Tyler's early isolation and struggle to belong also provided both the style and material for her fiction: the ironic distance characteristic of her prose as well as the subject of the individual's relationship to the community, particularly to other members of one's own household and family. Most of Tyler's short fiction and all of her novels published to date, from *If Morning Ever Comes* to *Dinner at the Homesick Restaurant*, concern the intricacies of family relationships and the isolation of the individual within the family. For Tyler, families clearly provided not only her major source for learning about the world as a child, but also fertile ground for studying how people endure the pain of loss and disappointment of life, adjust to living with others, and yet continue to love. All of the major conflicts and central themes of her novels evolve from this concern with the family and the individual's relationship to the community.

In this regard, Tyler falls clearly within the Southern literary tradition with its emphasis on family life and history. As Paul Binding points out in *Separate Country: A Literary Journey Through the American South* (1979), Tyler, like her mentor Reynolds Price, relies on interaction and "badinage between members of a family or between people who know one another well in order to illuminate personality." Tyler does not, however, evoke nor write of a regional past. She focuses on the present, narrating the past to provide a personal or familial, not a regional history. Nor are her characters and families symbolic figures. They are, instead, idiosyncratic personalities, truthfully depicted, memorable yet atypical. In all but her first three novels, moreover, Tyler's setting is not the small towns and rural landscapes so often considered synonymous with Southern life. Rather, her terrain is the border city of Baltimore and the decay and transience of modern urban life. Price, in fact, has said that she is the closest thing the South has to an urban novelist, indicating Tyler's somewhat unusual position among late twentieth century American writers: a Southerner with a traditional interest in family, community, and the past; a modern woman fascinated with change and drawn to urban life; a writer with faith in man's ability to love and endure yet keenly aware of the difficulties of contemporary life, particularly the failure of communication within the family.

In her concern for familial relationships, Tyler's novels raise the existential issues of freedom and commitment. Significantly, hers is a compassionate art without explicit moral judgment—an absence of judgment for which some critics have faulted her. The effect of this gentle portrayal of serious themes is ironic: the disturbing failure of Tyler's characters to understand fully and to be understood by those they love is counterbalanced by a witty, carefully detailed style. Violence is usually absent from her work as well, and so are the grotesques found in the fiction of Flannery O'Connor and Carson McCullers. The most disfigured character in Tyler's work—Evie Decker, the fat teenager in *A Slipping-Down Life* who carves a local rock singer's name in her forehead—is compassionately portrayed. Like Eudora Welty, Tyler populates her novels with ordinary people, all of whom, she comments in *The Writer on Her Work*, are mildly ecccentric in some way and "have something unusual" at their centers, something "funny and strange" and "touching in unexpected ways." From Ben Joe Hawkes in *If Morning Ever Comes*, who reads upside down to relieve boredom, to the elusive and difficult black sheep of her fictional families—Caleb and Duncan Peck, Morgan Gower, and Cody Tull—Tyler warmly and humorously portrays a wide spectrum of fascinating yet ordinary human beings.

Tyler's view of human nature, her talent for realistically capturing generations of squabbling families, her keen ear for dialogue, and her interest in character and the isolation of the individual within the family derive from various sources. Her own "setting apart" experience in the North Carolina wilderness, her early childhood habit of telling herself bedtime stories for rest and amusement, and her long periods listening to tenant farmers' stories contributed substantially to her art. Shy, quiet, and keenly observant, she listened carefully to the stories the workers told. Later, she could call up the words of her own characters. "Having those voices in my ears all day," she has written, "helped me to summon up my own characters' voices." Additionally, with Reynolds Price as her teacher and Eudora Welty as a model, Tyler saw early in her career the rich source of literary materials offered by commonplace experience. Paul Binding also cites the influence of Tyler's study of the Russian masters, particularly Ivan Turgenev and Anton Chekhov, as a basis for her tolerant and warm portrayal of multiple generations of entangled and eccentric families. Finally, perhaps most prominent is Tyler's own witness to her parents' idealism, their quest for a perfect community throughout her youth, and later their apparently easy adjustment to an ordinary existence in a middle-sized Southern city. Like her own father, whom she describes in *The Writer on Her Work*, the heroes of Tyler's novels are those who are "infinitely adapting" and always "looking around . . . with a smile to say, 'Oh! So this is where I am!'" They are complex people, enriched and deepened by experience—Elizabeth Abbott in *The Clock Winder*, Justine Peck in *Searching for Caleb*, Charlotte Emory in *Earthly Possessions*, and Jenny Tull in *Dinner at the Homesick Restaurant* best represent the type—able to enjoy life because they view themselves and others with tolerance and wit.

In an interview with Clifford Ridley for the *National Observer*, Tyler commented that she did not particularly "like either" of her "first two books" because "they seem so bland." Ben Joe Hawkes, the hero of *If Morning Ever Comes*, is "a likable guy; that's all you can say about him." While it is true that Ben Joe lacks the zaniness and interest which some of Tyler's later characters exhibit, his struggle to deal with his family, to recognize both his own independence and theirs, and to come to terms with the past and the psychological distance that isolates people even within an intimate group, provides a basis for understanding Tyler's later work and her place within the Southern literary tradition. *If Morning Ever Comes* had its origins in two short stories: "I Never Saw Morning," which appeared in the April, 1961, *Archive* and was later collected in *Under Twenty-Five: Duke Narrative and*

Verse, 1945-1962 (1963), edited by William Blackburn; and "Nobody Answers the Door," which appeared in the fall, 1964, issue of the *Antioch Review*. Both involve incidents suggested by the novel but occurring prior to the time of its opening. With the novel, they indicate Tyler's strong sense of the continuity of her characters' lives.

As in later novels, the plot and subject of *If Morning Ever Comes*, Ben Joe's five-day journey home to Sandhill, North Carolina, from Columbia University where he is a law student, evolve from family conflict. The family of women Ben Joe has left behind—six strikingly independent sisters, a proud mother, and a spry, 78-year-old grandmother, the first of Tyler's zanies—fail to tell him what is happening at home. Jenny, the family letter-writer, is all business. No one mentions the illegitimate son that Ben Joe's father left behind with a mistress when he died, nor the support payments Ben Joe personally delivered for years before he left for New York. The family treats lightly even the fact that Ben Joe's oldest sister, Joanne, has taken her child, left her husband, and returned home after seven years. Their behavior and their failure to understand Ben Joe's concern and worry point clearly to the theme of the individual's isolation within the family, here a male in an entire family of women.

On the surface, *If Morning Ever Comes* is a simply structured novel covering less than a week in the life of its hero. As one critic has observed, however, going home is "only partly a spatial relocation." Ben Joe, like other Southern literary heroes, "from Quentin Compson to Jack Burden," must return home "to embrace the spiritual crisis" created by an unsettled past and attempt to forge a future shaped by that very past. In this regard, *If Morning Ever Comes* is clearly a Southern novel. That it draws on a sharp contrast between the peaceful North Carolina setting and the briskness of New York, as well as the hero's discomfort and sense of dislocation in the North, is also suggestive of Tyler's Southern literary roots.

Although not widely reviewed nor acclaimed, *The Tin Can Tree* is a moving novel which expands and deepens Tyler's treatment of family relationships and the individual's struggle to remain committed in the face of significant loss and change. Just as Ben Joe Hawkes in *If Morning Ever Comes* remained committed to his family despite their pride and reticence, and to his father's memory despite the elder Hawkes's unfaithfulness, so also the characters in *The Tin Can Tree*, the members of three separate families sharing one house—the Pikes, the Greens, and the Potters—must deal with the commonly experienced grief at the death of the Pikes's six-year-old daughter, Janie Rose, adjust, and resume the task of living. Tyler's achievement here is that she captures eight different characters' varying responses to grief while avoiding the sentimental and maudlin. She opens the novel with the close of the funeral service, thus deliberately focusing on life, rather than death, and the resumption of the tasks of everyday living.

In addition to this theme of grief, *The Tin Can Tree* explores the background and interactions of James and Ansel Green and Joan Pike, Janie Rose's cousin. The study of James's commitment to his ailing brother Ansel, the two brothers' alienation from their family, and Joan's distance from her own elderly parents as well as her unresolved romantic involvement with James, give the novel a depth lacking in *If Morning Ever Comes*, with its heavy focus on one central character. As one reviewer noted, *The Tin Can Tree* illustrates Tyler's talent for bringing "into focus a remarkable range of human traits and emotions." Lou Pike's depressive withdrawal and immobility after her daughter's death, her husband's worried yet practical concern, their son Simon's sense of rejection and neglect, Joan's uncertainty and anger at James and his brother Ansel—all acquire full portraiture. A love of detail permeates the book, from the Potter sisters' eccentric way of wearing hats and gloves even when visiting only at the other end of the porch to the details of Janie Rose's behavior, her "tin can tree" made in honor of God during a religious period and her wearing layer upon layer of underwear on "her bad days." Such details make the characters real and Janie Rose's death more immediate and painful.

The Tin Can Tree is also the first Tyler novel to draw explicitly on the author's tobacco-field experience. Joan Pike, a school secretary, spends part of her summers handing tobacco in the warehouses, as Tyler herself did as a teenager. Besides providing elements of plot and characterization, the Tobacco Road landscape mirrors the sterility of the characters' lives following Janie Rose's death and provides a spokesman for the novel's theme. "Bravest thing about people, Miss Joan," one of the tobacco tiers says, "is how they go on loving mortal beings after finding out there's such a thing as dying." Unlike Erskine Caldwell, whose stereotypical white trash characters are often farcical grotesques, Tyler deepens the Tobacco Road landscape by a compassionate, detailed account of the grief of several families at the death of a child. Hers is a fiction of psychological insight, not a document for social change. *The Tin Can Tree*, as one critic observed, is "a novel rich in incident that details the closing of a family wound and the resumption of life among people stunned by the proof of mortality."

In her third novel, *A Slipping-Down Life*, Tyler returned to the existential themes of the individual's isolation, his struggle for identity, and the lack of understanding and meaningful communication among people living closely together. Set in the fictional towns of Pulqua and Farinia, North Carolina—suspiciously similar to the actual town of Fuquay-Varina near Raleigh—it was the last of the Tyler's books set entirely in North Carolina but also the first to portray the barrenness of familial relationships in a clearly modern setting. While most of *If Morning Ever Comes* and all of *The Tin Can Tree* are set in peaceful, remote areas where family life, though troubled, seems unaffected by distinctly modern problems, *A Slipping-Down Life* draws heavily on the impact of modern American culture and media on family life. Also, where Tyler's first two novels covered only a few days in the lives of the principal characters, *A Slipping-Down Life* chronicles one full year in the life of its heroine—a fat, dowdy, teenage girl named Evie Decker—indicating a development in Tyler's ability to handle character over an extended period of time.

Originating in a "newspaper story about a 15-year-old girl in Texas who'd slashed 'Elvis' in her forehead," the novel traces Evie's barren interaction with her father, her only living relative, as well as the development and dissolution of a relationship with a local rock singer named Bertram "Drumstrings" Casey, the first of Tyler's unadmirable yet likable antiheroes—exploitative and selfish yet touchingly shy and dependent on his parents and Evie. Evie's entanglement with Drum, leading eventually to their marriage, is tragically initiated by her carving the name "Casey" in her forehead with a pair of nail scissors, and ends, equally as tragically, with the couple's separation, the death of Evie's family, and her discovery of Casey in bed with another woman. Throughout, Evie thinks of herself as though she were acting on a stage set, taking her cues from the soap operas she watches daily with Clotelia, the Deckers' sullen maid and Evie's sometime chiding surrogate mother. Like Joan Pike in *The Tin Can Tree* and later Tyler heroines—Justine Peck in *Searching for Caleb* and Charlotte Emory in *Earthly Possessions*—Evie is an only child faced with growing up alone in a dark, stifling household and creating an identity without the companionship and aid of siblings or understanding parents.

Besides its characterizations, *A Slipping-Down Life* is also noteworthy for capturing at least part of the American experience in the 1960's: the lonely world of teenagers, the generation gap, the high-school student's unending quest for popularity and romance, as well as a small town's tawdry local rock scene, featuring the chilled air in a roadside house, painfully loud music, necking couples, and the smell of stale beer. As one reviewer observed, *A Slipping-Down Life* captures "a *way* of life, a way that is tacked upon teenage bulletin boards, sewn to dresses 'decorated with poodles on loops of real chain,' enclosed in high-school notebooks containing *Silver Screen* magazine."

Tyler's first three novels all involve some type of journey home during which a central character confronts both the distance between himself and his family as well as the difficulties of unresolved past conflicts. Ben Joe's journey from New York to Sandhill in *If Morning Ever Comes* fits this pattern, as do James Green's trip to Caraway, North Carolina, in *The Tin Can Tree*, and, in *A Slipping-Down Life*, Evie Decker's return to her father's house following his death. A similar trip occurs in *The Clock Winder*. A novel characterized by Sarah Blackburn as having all the "virtues" of Southern writing—"an easy, almost confidential directness, fine skill at quick characterization, a sure eye for atmosphere, and a special nostalgic humor"—*The*

Clock Winder was at the time of its publication Tyler's most ambitious work, tracing the intricate relationships of a large cast of characters over an entire decade. It was also her first novel set in Baltimore.

The diverse, eccentric, eight-member Emerson family of Baltimore and their one adopted member, Elizabeth Abbott, clearly form one of those "huge," "loving-bickering" Southern families Tyler told Clifford Ridley she hoped to create in writing *If Morning Ever Comes*. Mrs. Emerson—a skinny, fragile widow—is unrelenting in nagging her children about their neglected duties to her. She is, consequently, estranged from all but one: Timothy, a pressured medical student who, with his twin Andrew, is one of the most neurotic disturbed characters in Tyler's novels. Into this entangled, crisis-prone family, Elizabeth Abbott brings the very skills she is unable to practice with her own family in Ellington, North Carolina. Tolerant, practical, dextrous, and witty—the first of Tyler's "infinitely adapting" heroines based on her own father—Elizabeth is a handyman and a godsend for the nervous Mrs. Emerson. In Ellington, she is a bumbler, a rebellious college dropout, and a painful reminder of failure to her minister father. Her life at home is bleak, ordinary, and restricted. Commitment to the Emersons, despite their family feuds, offers interest and freedom from the Abbott family's dicta, an opportunity to form a new identity and life free of reminders of past mistakes.

Besides expanding character, setting and time-frame, *The Clock Winder* is unusual among Tyler's first four works for its use of violence and its experimentation with point of view. Timothy Emerson commits suicide by shooting himself in Elizabeth's presence, sending her home to her family for several years. Later, after her return to Baltimore, his twin shoots her, though he causes only a flesh wound. Also, where earlier Tyler novels used omniscient point of view focusing largely on one major character—the exception is *The Tin Can Tree*, in which Joan Pike and James Green serve alternately as centers of consciousness—*The Clock Winder* shifts perspective among many characters, some of them minor. In one chapter, the reader witnesses the succession of disconnected thoughts, the confusion of physical sensations, and the temporal disorientation accompanying Mrs. Emerson's stroke. Another presents the views of the youngest Emerson, Peter, who appears only in the final chapter of the novel. These shifts in point of view result in an intimate portrait not only of the novel's central character, Elizabeth, but also of the Emersons— a varied, contrasting family of idiosyncratic individuals.

With *Celestial Navigation*, Tyler moved her novels to a totally urban landscape. Eight months after the novel's publication, she told a Duke University audience that she "could no longer write a Southern novel" since she had lived away from the South too long to capture realistically the "voices" and behavior of the people who live there. Set almost exclusively in a seedy Baltimore boardinghouse "smack in the middle" of a deteriorating inner-city neighborhood, *Celestial Navigation* is Tyler's portrait of the artist. It covers thirteen years in the central character's life, expanding the study of character development found in earlier novels and illustrating her increasing skill in handling point of view. The various boarders narrate firsthand their experiences and relationships to other residents. Additionally, since it focuses largely on boarders rather than kin, somewhat like *The Tin Can Tree* with its three families unrelated by blood, and since it includes the common-law marriage of its hero, *Celestial Navigation* redefines the meaning of family ties as characterized in Tyler's novels. It also intensifies the isolation of the protagonist. Jeremy Pauling, the artist-hero of the novel and the owner of the rooming house, is so reclusive that for years he has not left the city block where he lives. His principal ties are not with his two sisters in Richmond, neither very understanding of his peculiar artistic temperament, but with the boarders with whom he lives.

The caring family of boarders the novel studies, however, are essentially isolated strangers living in private rooms. They are mostly older people with severed family connections or no remaining kin. Ironically, they exhibit more tolerance and unquestioning respect for the peculiarities and privacy of one another than do many blood-related members. Mrs. Vinton, an aged spinster who works in a bookstore, stays on to care for Jeremy years after the others move or die, yet she never interrupts his trancelike states or work. With the other boarders—the elegant widow Mrs. Jarrett, the nubile Mary Tell, the young Olivia, and the fractious old Mrs. Somerset shuffling about in slippers—Mrs. Vinton is a testament to Tyler's talent for realistically capturing a gallery of idiosyncratic yet identifiably ordinary people.

The real achievement of *Celestial Navigation*, though, is Jeremy Pauling. He is one of Tyler's minor grotesques. A pale, pudgy sculptor, he rarely speaks and withdraws for days at a time to his secluded bedroom-studio. The novel works as Jeremy's story, however, partly because Tyler gives him a full range of emotions—including sexual attraction to several female boarders and a love for the children he has by his common-law marriage. She also views him with both compassion and humor and lets the reader see him from several points of view. Tyler shifts to third-person point of view to narrate Jeremy's chapters, since Jeremy himself is incapable of communicating his impressions in the coherent manner of the other characters. Tyler has said that the character of Jeremy is based in part on a shy, easily flustered little man she helped one day in the library where she worked, but she added several of her own traits to the character: a dread of telephones and doorbells (something retained from her isolated childhood) and, most important, her own artistic vision, an eye for the "smallest and most unnoticed scenes on earth," very much like those details Tyler captures in *Celestial Navigation*.

Searching for Caleb marked a turning point in Tyler's career. It was her first novel to receive national recognition, at a time when Tyler's own reviews began to appear in national publications. As Walter Sullivan commented in

1977 when reviewing *Searching for Caleb* for the *Sewanee Review*, Tyler "retained" in her work "a kind of innocence . . . a sense of wonder at all the crazy things in the world and an abiding affection for her own flaky characters." *Searching for Caleb* was also evidence that Tyler had retained her Southern literary roots and her delight in huge families and the range of human characters those families produce. Something of a combined family history and detective story, the novel is Tyler's most ambitious work to date, tracing five generations of one large, dichotomous, and extremely long-lived clan, the Pecks of Baltimore, from the 1880's through 1973. As in *The Clock Winder* and *Celestial Navigation*, Tyler shows her strong fascination with urban life, a result perhaps of her own early life in remote areas. She also returns to Roland Park, one of Baltimore's oldest residential neighborhoods and the main setting of *The Clock Winder*.

As the title suggests, *Searching for Caleb* involves a quest for the vanished Caleb, the great uncle of the novel's protagonists, Duncan and Justine Peck, and the half-brother of their grandfather, Daniel Peck. Representing one side of the family, Caleb, Justine, and Duncan are outcasts of a sort: spirited, talented, imaginative, and free individuals unable or unwilling to live as family rules dictate. Caleb becomes a musician, Justine a fortune-teller. Duncan, her husband and first cousin, leads an unsettled life as a mechanic and jack-of-all-trades, foreshadowing Morgan Gower, the hero of *Morgan's Passing*. Like Morgan, Duncan dismays his family.

The other side of the family, the Pecks of Roland Park, headed by Daniel, are uniformly humorless and restricted. The women, though educated, are unthreatening; the men, all attorneys educated at Johns Hopkins, drive black Fords and dress in Brooks Brothers suits. They are, above all, clannish, living side by side in similar Roland Park houses. For them, family tradition and training—in effect, the past—are inescapable. Even Daniel's late-life quest for his half-brother evolves from his ties to family and an unsettled conflict. It represents a delayed response to the question frequently asked in his childhood: "Daniel, have you seen Caleb?"

Searching for Caleb, like Tyler's earlier novels, also illustrates the author's belief in the need for human adaptability, tolerance, and love. Justine epitomizes the philosophy. She weathers a dark and uncertain childhood with a depressive mother, frequent moves with her restless husband, the death of both parents and her grandfather, and the loss of her one daughter in marriage to a Milquetoast minister. Yet, she remains spirited and continues to love her family. She insists on visiting Roland Park, a longing Duncan cannot understand, and she is committed to finding Caleb, not only out of a love of travel and adventure but also to share the experiences with her grandfather and to find her own roots. With its focus on community and family and its delineation of the unsettled conflicts of the past impacting on the present, *Searching for Caleb* indicates Tyler's own roots in the family of Southern literature.

When it appeared in 1977, *Earthly Possessions* was Tyler's most unfavorably received novel. Among disapproving reviewers, Roger Sale in *The New York Times Review of Books* saw the book as "a cartoon" of sorts, with the life of Charlotte Emory, the protagonist, "reduced . . . by her own hand" until all "possible anguish is . . . lost." The reason for this response is no doubt the sardonic nature of Charlotte herself, an entrapped housewife who sets out to leave her husband but gets kidnaped instead in a bungled bank robbery. Such reversals characterize Charlotte's life and have led her to "loosen" her hold so that she sees everything from an ironic distance. Charlotte, moreover, is the novel's only narrator, and she tells her life-story in chapters alternating perfectly with those narrating her experiences with Jake Simms, her kidnaper, on their trip south from Clarion, Maryland, Charlotte's hometown. Along the way, Tyler captures the fragmentation and transience of modern life, reflected in a string of drive-in restaurants, banks, and movies. The triumph of the novel is not, as in earlier Tyler works, characterization, but the panorama of contemporary American life that the book captures during this journey of hostage and kidnaper.

With its contrapuntal chapters, *Earthly Possessions* is Tyler's most highly structured novel, the first to be told entirely in the first person by one narrator. The result is an artificial temporal arrangement and a restricted focus, one lifetime as compared with those of eight or nine Emersons, five generations of Pecks. Also, the reader is always in the presence of two somewhat unsavory characters: a nail-biting, minor league criminal and a stoical, cynical woman. All might have come from the pen of Flannery O'Connor but for the touchingly human flaws Tyler draws. Neither Jake nor Charlotte, despite their failings, is morally culpable. What they share is a common, impractical desire for freedom from the entanglements of life: for Charlotte, marriage complete with a house full of relatives and in-laws, rooms of furniture (earthly possessions), even sinners from the mourner's bench at her husband's church; for Jake, jail for a petty crime and a pregnant girl friend. Heading south to rescue Mindy Callendar, Jake's Kewpie-doll girl friend, from a home for unwed mothers, Jake, Charlotte realizes, is like herself "criss-crossed by strings of love and need and worry." Even Charlotte and Jake's relationship grows into a type of commitment. Eventually the two share the driving as well as their troubles. Any "relationship," Tyler told Marguerite Michaels in an interview for *The New York Times Book Review*, even one "as bizarre as" that of "a bank robber and hostage could become . . . bickering [and] familiar . . . Anything done gradually enough becomes ordinary."

Earthly Possessions, despite its problems, shares with *The Tin Can Tree* and *Celestial Navigation*, a redefinition of family ties. With Tyler's other novels, it also illuminates the problems and conflicts of the individual within a close relationship, whether familial or not, and focuses on the eccentric nature of ordinary lives, the ordinariness of the bizarre.

In her eighth novel, Tyler returned to the heart of Baltimore for her setting and to a central character, Morgan Gower, who is strikingly eccentric. Reviewers compared him with Saul Bellow's Henderson and Joseph Heller's Major Major. He also resembles Duncan Peck as well as other Tyler protagonists. Like those heroes, Morgan is in conflict with his family: seven daughters who find him embarrassing, a slovenly though good-natured wife, a senile mother, and a depressed, inert sister. Like Ben Joe Hawkes, Morgan feels trapped and misunderstood in a house cluttered with "the particles of related people's unrelated worlds" and full of women with whom he is unable to communicate satisfactorily. While his family insists on going about life unconsciously, Morgan, spirited and highly inventive, faces a mid-life crisis that calls for a change. He must also come to terms with his past, the consequences of marrying Bonny for her money as well as his father's inexplicable suicide when Morgan was a teenager. Like Duncan Peck, Morgan is a kind of mechanical genius who takes up various projects, then drops them—"a tinkering, puttering, hardware sort of man." Like the renegade Pecks, he eventually abandons his Baltimore family to take up a new life and identity with a traveling amusement company.

Despite these resemblances to other Tyler heroes, Morgan is a unique creation, the product of Tyler's maturing vision of life. Her understanding of his sexual attraction to a young puppeteer and her portrayal of his frustration with his wife suggest a depth of insight into the problems of marriage, a depth lacking in the early *If Morning Ever Comes*. Morgan is also a complex character, a genuine impostor who tries on identities complete with appropriately matching costumes. At times he is "Father Morgan, the street priest of Baltimore"; at other times, he is an immigrant with family still abroad, a doctor who delivers a baby in the backseat of a car—any role in which people will accept him. Though most of this role-playing is harmless, Morgan is an anti-hero lacking a firm identity, a modern eccentric who revels in the anonymity and emptiness of decaying city neighborhoods and a man who assumes a false identity to take up life with another man's wife without benefit of divorce. Not surprisingly, reviewers found it difficult to like Morgan, but few found him unbelievable.

Tyler's increasing skill in capturing and making believable such a character testifies to her maturation as a writer. As John Leonard commented in *The New York Times* when reviewing the novel, readers "are obliged to care" about Tyler's "odd people" "because their oddities are what we see at an angle in the mirror in the middle of a bad night." Drawing from selected everyday scenes covering twelve years in Morgan's life, Tyler roots her novel firmly in the here and now. Morgan becomes believable because he is not always posing. He reads the morning paper over coffee, affectionately slaps his wife on her rear end, smokes too much, attends a daughter's wedding, despairs over a quarrel-filled family vacation, works in a hardware store, and comes down with a terrible cold. Tyler's is a realistic art illuminating family conflict and solidly based in the ordinary details of life.

Of all Tyler's novels, *Dinner at the Homesick Restaurant* most inspires comparison with the work of Flannery O'Connor. The title is reminiscent of O'Connor's wit and irony, and the mood of the novel, as one reviewer noted, is that of "O'Connor's Gothic South" with its "sullen, psychic menace." At her best, as in *Celestial Navigation*, Tyler captures the pain, anxiety, and isolation beneath the surface of ordinary lives. At times, however, particularly in *Earthly Possessions* but also *Morgan's Passing*, she treats this pain lightly, thus denying a sense of genuine struggle. In *Earthly Possessions*, Charlotte is flippant and ironic; in *Morgan's Passing*, Morgan is a zany, the mood quick and light. *Dinner at the Homesick Restaurant*, representing what John Updike called a "darkening" of Tyler's art, presents the other side of the coin from *Morgan's Passing*, not only in mood but also in story line. Its focus is not the husband who abandons his family to find a new life, but the family he left behind. It is a stunning psychological portrait of the Tulls, Pearl and her three children, and the anger, guilt, hurt, and anxiety they feel growing up in an uncertain world without a father. All carry their pain through life, illustrating more profoundly than any of Tyler's earlier books the past's haunting influence on the present.

Covering thirty-five years, three generations of Tulls, the novel opens with Pearl on her deathbed. This first chapter, reminiscent of Katherine Anne Porter's short story, "The Jilting of Granny Weatherall," depicts Pearl as a stoical, frightened woman who has weathered a youth filled with dread of being an old maid, a quick marriage, and a lonely struggle to rear three "flawed" children: Cody, the oldest boy, a troublemaker from childhood, "prone to unreasonable rages"; Jenny, the only girl, "flippant" and "opaque"; Ezra, his mother's favorite, a gentle man who has not "lived up to his potential," but instead has become the ambitionless owner of the Homesick Restaurant. Not one of Pearl's children has turned out as she wished. Consequently, she, like other Tyler characters, feels "closed off" from her family, the very children to whom she has devoted her life. Later chapters reveal why, focusing on each of the children in turn and tracing the evolution of their lives as well as their fear of their mother's rages. All, like their mother, end up in some way "destroyed by love."

Tyler's compassionate portrayal of her characters and her characteristic humor do mitigate the darkness of this novel. Although Pearl, her forehead permanently creased from worry, verbally and physically abuses her children, Tyler lets the reader understand the reasons for Pearl's behavior, even though he may not forgive her, and shows a far mellower Pearl in old age. Jenny, after struggling through medical school, two marriages, and a nervous breakdown, is nursed back to health by her mother. Cody spares no expense in caring for his family, even though he is unable to forgive Pearl for mistreating him as a child. The teenager Cody plays cruel but funny tricks on his brother Ezra—partly out of resentment of Ezra's being the favorite, but also from Cody's own pain and sense of rejection. Taking slats from Ezra's bed, Cody strews the floor with pornographic magazines so Pearl will think Ezra the kind of disappointment she finds Cody to be. Later, after stealing Ezra's sweetheart, he recognizes not only his guilt but also his love for his brother. These tales fill out the dark psychological portrait Tyler draws, making *Dinner at the Homesick Restaurant*, like many of Tyler's earlier books, a confirmation of life's difficulty as well as of the value of love.

Bibliography

Binding, Paul. *Separate Country: A Literary Journey through the American South*, 1979.

Michaels, Marguerite. "Anne Tyler, Writer 8:05 to 3:30," in *The New York Times Book Review*. LXXXII (May 8, 1977), pp. 13, 42-43.

Ridley, Clifford. "Anne Tyler: A Sense of Reticence Balanced by 'Oh, Well, Why Not?,'" in *National Observer*. XI (July 22, 1972), p. 23.

Tyler, Anne. "Because I Want More Than One Life," in *Washington Post*. August, 1976, pp. 1, 7.

_____ . "Olives Out of a Bottle," in *Archive*. LXXXVII (Spring, 1975), pp. 70-79.

_____ . "Still Just Writing," in *The Writer and Her Work*, 1980. Edited by Janet Sternburg.

Stella A. Nesanovich

JOHN UPDIKE

Born: Shillington, Pennsylvania; March 18, 1932

Principal long fiction
The Poorhouse Fair, 1959; *Rabbit, Run*, 1960; *The Centaur*, 1963; *Of the Farm*, 1965; *Couples*, 1968; *Rabbit Redux*, 1971; *A Month of Sundays*, 1975; *Marry Me, a Romance*, 1976; *The Coup*, 1978; *Rabbit Is Rich*, 1981; *Bech Is Back*, 1982.

Other literary forms
A prolific writer, John Updike has tried his hand at practically every literary form. During little more than a quarter of a century, Updike has published, in addition to his novels, two volumes of prose collected from his reviews, formal essays and addresses, autobiographical sketches; collections of poems; collections of short stories; and two plays.

The sheer mass of Updike's work is overwhelming, and it is tempting to take seriously his humorous confession in one of the appendices to his play *Buchanan Dying* (1974) that one of his youthful ambitions was to write twenty-six novels, each to be dominated by one letter of the alphabet. Impressive as the sheer quantity of Updike's work may be, it has been of consistently high quality, and he has met with critical as well as popular success as both a novelist and a short-story writer.

Achievements
Updike's career resembles that of F. Scott Fitzgerald in several important ways. Although enthusiastic reviewers have hailed him as the successor to Ernest Hemingway and William Faulkner, it is with Fitzgerald that the revealing comparisons are to be made. Each had the unusual fortune of appealing to both a popular and a critical audience and each is remembered as the chronicler of an era. In the future, Updike will be read for his definitive account of American life in the 1960's and the 1970's, just as Fitzgerald is now generally appreciated as the great interpreter of the Jazz Age. Both writers are also memorable as exceptional stylists, and it is occasionally said of each that he never found a subject adequate to the brilliance of his style. In neither case is this charge justified.

Unlike Fitzgerald, Updike has been a prolific novelist and short-story writer. Here he resembles Faulkner, both in the scope and variety of his work. Despite the fact that three of his novels are about the same group of characters, Updike's canon gives the impression that he never repeats himself. His first novel, *The Poorhouse Fair*, is—surprisingly, because the author was only twenty-six when he wrote it—a sensitive and compassionate work. It is the study of the crusty individuality and integrity of the indigent old people who are threatened by the regimentation and consequent loss of dignity imposed by the youthful administrator of the poorhouse in which they are destined to die. This administrator is not a villain, but representative of a modern trend toward statistical and antiseptic order. The author does not condemn him, but he clearly prefers the individualism represented by Hook, the aged antagonist of the young administrator. The three books about Harry Angstrom are, by contrast, deliberately cinematic in their composition, and each is narrated in the historical present.

The Centaur attempts to blend myth with present action, to associate the mythological centaur Chiron with the experiences of a contemporary high-school teacher, and the book even provides an index of the mythological characters associated with the contemporary ones. Like Charles Dickens' *Bleak House* (1852-1853), *The Centaur* is narrated from alternating points of view: in one sequence, the action is narrated by an omniscient observer who blends the contemporary with the mythic, while in the alternating sequence of chapters, Cauldwell's son Peter tells the story from the perspective of his manhood. *Of the Farm* is a low-key treatment of the themes of freedom and forgiveness. The plot centers on a three-day weekend during which the protagonist returns to the farm of his youth with his second wife and stepson, for the purpose of getting acquainted. At the obvious level, not much happens in the book; Updike has noted that he thought of it as "chamber music," in which the voices of protagonist, mother, wife, and stepson offer variations on the subjects of maturity and the roles of men and women in marriage and society at large. *Couples*, a best-seller and Updike's most notorious book, is a penetrating critique of sexual morality in modern suburbia. *A Month of Sundays* is set in a retreat for wayward ministers, where the randy Reverend Marshfield muses on the relationship between flesh and spirit and undergoes a rather unorthodox cure. *Marry Me* experiments with the device of multiple and mutually exclusive endings pioneered by John Fowles in *The French Lieutenant's Woman* (1969). *The Coup* is a startling experiment, a picaresque first-person account of the rise to power and subsequent fall of Colonel Ellelloû, an African dictator, sexual misadventurer, and fanatical hater of the United States.

Updike's novels exhibit an astonishing variety of thematic and technical interests; indeed, his versatility is in some ways itself his greatest achievement, for he never quite repeats his successes, even in the trilogy on Angstrom. His has been a restless imagination, one that seeks consistently to explore new and satisfactory ways to write a novel. In spite of, or perhaps because of, this versatility, he has emerged as one of the master stylists of the age.

Taken as a whole, Updike's work provides an impressive account of American life at mid-century. A hallmark of his style has been an emphasis on quotidian detail, from the catalog of radio broadcasts when Rabbit drives south in *Rabbit, Run*, to the television broadcast of the moon landing in *Rabbit Redux*, to the regular emphasis on the energy crisis and the adaptation this has imposed on modern American life in *Rabbit Is Rich*. Updike's instinct for the revealing detail has enabled him to compile an extraordinary chronicle of his time: Tony Tanner speaks of Updike's works as rendering a "compromised environment," a created world in which fidelity to the detail of experience evokes the power of that environment to impose mediocrity on his characters. By general consensus, Updike has been among the most acute and profound interpreters of American life in the second half of the twentieth century.

Biography

Like several of his characters, John Hoyer Updike was born during the Great Depression of the 1930's. The childhood of a sensitive and patriotic youth under the cloud of national economic crisis undoubtedly helped to shape Updike's interest in the relation between economic conditions and the quality of his characters' lives. His father, a schoolteacher, certainly inspired many of the father-teachers in the fiction. His mother was somewhat aristocratic by temperament, but her father lost most of his money when the banks failed. The family lived with Updike's maternal grandparents durng the Depression, moving to a farm outside Shillington during his adolescence.

Updike was a precocious student. He showed a special talent in art, and for some time aspired to be a cartoonist. From 1950 to 1954, Updike attended Harvard University on a full scholarship; he was graduated summa cum laude after having edited *The Harvard Lampoon*. He married Mary Pennington at the end of his junior year. The Updikes would have four children.

After leaving Harvard, Updike spent a year in Oxford, England, studying at the Ruskin School of Fine Arts and Drawing. He had a Knox Fellowship during this period, and several of these experiences contributed to the unpublished autobiographical novel *Home*, as well as to the short story of the same name. He returned to the United States and worked for two years as a "Talk of the Town" reporter for *The New Yorker*, thus fulfilling an ambition he had since he was twelve and shaping a literary style that is still occasionally derided as "cute" or "precious."

Fame as a fiction-writer came quickly, and Updike has been one of the most visible of the American novelists of the present century, often hailed as the successor to Hemingway and Faulkner. *The Poorhouse Fair* earned for him the Rosenthal Award of the National Institute of Arts and Letters in 1960; *The Centaur* won the National Book Award in 1964; "The Bulgarian Poetess" gained the O. Henry Award in 1966; *Rabbit Is Rich* was awarded both the Pulitzer Prize and the American Book Award in 1982. Updike was elected to membership in the National Institute of Arts and Letters in 1964. Shortly after that election, he was invited to participate in a cultural exchange program which took him to the Soviet Union, Rumania, Bulgaria, and Czechoslovakia. He has since traveled widely as a literary ambassador, with excursions ranging from Africa to Australia.

The Updike's separated in 1974 and were subsequently granted a no-fault divorce. In 1977, Updike married Martha Bernhard, and they now live in Georgetown, Massachusetts. In light of the volume and reputation of Updike's works, much more first-rate writing can be expected of him.

Analysis

In his Preface to the *Olinger Stories* (1964), John Updike sums up in a casual remark the world view which informs his fiction: "We are rewarded unexpectedly. The muddled and inconsequent surface of things now and then parts to yield us a gift." It is the muddle and inconsequence of life, rather than life's unexpected rewards, which are likely to strike the reader on his first approach to Updike's novels. *Rabbit, Run* ends with its hero in flight from his life. *Of the Farm* concludes with the mother of the main character accepting his desire to return to New York, while she, after her heart attack, prepares for loneliness and her impending death on the farm. She begs Joey not to sell the farm cheaply when she dies, and the only obvious consolation is that Joey tells her he considers it "our," not her, farm. *Couples* ends with a divorce between the two main characters, and the wife Angela is later seen in the company of the unpleasant, cynical, and lecherous Freddy Thorne. Piet, her husband, has married his mistress (who was divorced earlier in the novel) and is no longer a restless, Dionysian seeker for sexual harmony; he has become a bureaucrat, a construction inspector, rather than the conscientious builder he once was. Perhaps the most disturbing element of this ending is that Piet, once a seeker of a perfect order through sex and building well, has given up the search and allowed himself to become content with mediocrity. *The Coup* records the fall from power of Colonel Ellelloû, and at the end, he has been stripped of his power and is writing his memoirs in political exile.

These examples show that, at the level of plot, Updike's novels are records of the protagonists' failure to achieve their goals. Nevertheless, these same figures seek for and occasionally achieve glimpses of transcendence: a brief awareness of the richness and joy of earthly existence is afforded them. In *Rabbit, Run*, Harry works briefly for Mrs. Smith, a tough old widow, and while employed as her gardener, he feels a sense of peace and kinship with the cycles of nature, a wholeness of being, that is quite unlike his ordinary frustrations as a salesman and ex-athlete. He cannot maintain this state of serenity because he is compelled to return to the responsibility of a middle-class citizen, and his unexpected reward cannot protect him from the shocks life has in store for him, but he has experienced an intimation that a harmonious life is possible. In *Rabbit Is Rich*, the unexpected reward occurs at the very end, when Harry's infant granddaughter is placed in his arms, and he has a momentary realization of the meaning of his life.

Although these unexpected rewards are rare in the novels, they are important in the development of Updike's themes and his concept of life in general. Usually the rewards are associated with what he has called "The Three Great Secret Things: Sex, Religion and Art." These elements, in varying mixtures, constitute the unexpected rewards at the heart of the novels.

Sexual love is obviously at the heart of Updike's creative vision. He is often praised and occasionally condemned as a writer who has attempted to chronicle the ubiquity and variety of sexual impulses at the core of modern culture. Practically every conceivable form of heterosexual love has been described in at least one of his books, and in none save *The Poorhouse Fair* is there lacking at least one detailed erotic scene; in *Couples*, the number and variety approach exponential proportions. His characters not only have sexual experiences; they talk about them, think about them, dream about them, and even pray for them. So much energy is expended in contemplation of and engagement in sexual activities that one might be tempted to think his major theme is the post-Freudian cliché that all energy is essentially libidinal. Yet there is more to sex in Updike's fiction than biological function. While detractors such as Norman Podhoretz complain that this interest in the depiction of sexual behavior represents an adolescent compulsion, Richard Rupp has pointed out that sex is the only meaningful ceremony for many of Updike's characters; his theme, especially in *Couples*, is that sex means freedom, and as a character abuses his sexual nature, he loses freedom.

Most serious studies have agreed that sex represents a quest by the characters for some dimly intuited ideal. Tony Tanner, speaking about *Couples*, observes that sex represents a meeting of mind and matter for the characters. Joyce Markle labels Updike's heroes "fighters" and "lovers," persons dissatisfied with the drabness and weariness of modern life and willing to strike out for an alternative. They are also capable of giving, as well as receiving, love. Harry Angstrom, Piet Hanema, the Reverend Marshfield, and Colonel Ellelloû take pride in their capability to give of themselves as lovers. Many of the critics agree that Updike's interest in specifically detailed *eros* is in fact a vehicle for the study of more ideal love. The characters seek, through physical love, an expression of self adequate to their creator's conception of the human potential for other-directedness. In one of his essays, the author remarks, "Not to be in love, the capital N novel whispers to capital W western man, is to be dying." The sexual restlessness of Updike's characters is an index of their desire to live a meaningful life.

Religion is also at the heart of Updike's vision, and readers of the spicier passages from his books are sometimes surprised to learn that the author professes to be a Christian in an orthodox sense. Several of Updike's more interesting minor characters are ministers, from the formidable Kruppenbach and the do-gooder Eccles in *Rabbit, Run* to the homosexual Archie Campbell in *Rabbit Is Rich*. Two of Updike's ministers represent a precise connection between sensuous and religious values. The Reverend March in *The Centaur* becomes impatient with George Caldwell's questions about immortality because he is busy flirting with Vera Hummel. March therefore ignores his ministerial function because of his preoccupation with sex. Contrastingly, the Reverend Tom Marshfield, the main character of the technically brilliant *A Month of Sundays* with its touches of the playfulness of Vladimir Nabokov and James Joyce, is both minister and sexual athlete. The theme of this novel is the compatibility of the erotic with the spiritual impulse, for during his enforced retreat from the temptations of the flesh, Tom truly becomes a minister to his fellow, fallen clergymen. He never really renounces the flesh, but seeks to understand the relation between his love of the women in his congregation and the motives behind his becoming a minister. In his final sermon, he claims the necessity of a living faith, but he also insists that such faith must include our erotic selves: "For we do not want to live as angels, in ether; our bodies are us, us." Marshfield emphasizes the unity of sacred and sensuous experience, and his unexpected reward is that he is successful in his plan to seduce Ms. Prynne, the administrator of the retreat. The connection with Nathaniel Hawthorne's *The Scarlet Letter* (1850) is important. Tom's wife, the former Jane Chillingworth, believes that only good works prove grace. While she and her father are not evil in the sense that Hawthorne's Chillingworth was, they represent the incompleteness of living by intellect alone.

The main characters of the other major novels are, in Markle's phrase, "fighters" in the sense that they seek to understand the force that has created them and that sustains their existence; they seek a satisfactory answer to the question Updike poses in both "A Dogwood Tree" and *Midpoint*: "Why am I me?" They are usually unable to fulfill that quest by simply accepting the answers of traditional religious institutions. Still, the scene in *Couples* that most clearly emblematizes the entropic decline of social, spiritual, and even sexual values is the conflagration of a church: "God's own lightning had struck it," and the scene suggests a divine judgment on the morality of Tarbox. In a number of essay-reviews, Updike has demonstrated his familiarity with the most respected and complex modern theologians, and he has thus added intellectual structure and precision to his own attempt to understand the tension between the secular and the sacred. In one of his youthful, light verses, Updike wrote, "I flung myself on Kierkegaard to save my flagging soul," and he has stated that reading Karl Barth helped him through a religious crisis during the time he was writing *Rabbit, Run*.

Updike's three novels about Harry Angstrom constitute an unusual modern trilogy. Not systematically planned as were Frank Norris' three books on the production, distribution, and consumption of wheat, or John Dos Passos' chronologically sequential series of novels, *U.S.A.* (1937), Updike's trilogy, by contrast, seems to have evolved long after the first novel of the series had been written. The author has mentioned that he hit upon the idea of following up on his masterpiece because "the Sixties pressed heavily upon" him. His decision to "revisit my old friend" led to the unique inspiration to write a book about Rabbit every ten years in order to discover how such a character would react to the events and pressures of the recent decade, as well as to the universal burden of growing older and losing friends and relatives by death and distance. Updike has been true to this plan, and what is now a trilogy may well extend to at least one more volume. Although most critics consider both sequels inferior to *Rabbit, Run*, each of the three novels provides a remarkable insight into the impact of a changing society on an essentially ordinary man, a character who feels with some intensity but who is unable to think introspectively about the implications of his impulses.

Harry Angstrom has provided his creator with an admirable point of reference by which he can measure a pattern of deterioration in American society. In one way, Harry's progress from the failed basketball hero at twenty-six to the very successful partner in a Toyota agency at forty-six, does not seem at all like a pattern of deterioration. It is clearly the fulfillment of an American dream of wealth, power, and security. On the other hand, Harry's prosperity is earned almost in proportion to the loss of his instinct toward a meaningful life. As he becomes little more than a reflection of the values of the society around him, Rabbit prospers. It is in this progressive lethargy of spirit, that settling into the collective ideals of contemporary American society, that Updike articulates what has become a progressive indictment of the assumptions of that society.

Although the three novels differ in style, theme, and technique, each is narrated in the historical present and each employs the symbol of the journey, or the voyage out. These journeys form the literal as well as the figurative structure of the books. In *Rabbit, Run*, the journey is an attempt to escape the traps of an unwholesome and confining environment (the name of one of the towns, Mt. Judge, is revealing in itself), a dreary marriage, and a deadly job, but that literal journey quickly evolves into an exploration of alternative life-styles and eventually a quest for a religious dimension to Harry's experience. His return is an unfortunate capitulation before the pressures of the environment and an implicit recognition of his inability to accept responsibility for defining those values he might oppose to the prevailing system. By the end of the novel, freedom itself becomes a burden, for it brings as its consequence death, both in the drowning of the infant Becky and in the threat that his mistress Ruth will have an abortion. His attempt to return to the public morality is equally confining, for he cannot accept those constraints either, so he ends his quest in unstructured motion. He completes his self-serving quest for freedom by running away from all of his obligations, but now he is not running toward anything.

Updike opens the novel with one of the most memorable scenes in all of his fiction. Angstrom, now twenty-six and a former basketball star, pauses on the way home from work to watch, then, as an unwelcome intruder from the past, to join in a game of basketball. Now married and apparently adjusted to the life of husband and father, Harry is reminded of the deliberate pursuit of excellence his former role as an athlete demanded of him. As a result of this chance participation in the basketball game, Harry impulsively decides to take charge of his life, to return to and recover the perfection of his own lost past.

Harry initially represents an unwitting accommodation to mediocrity, some-one who has let his life drift into the acceptance of the norms of the times. He has apparently come to believe in his dreary job as a salesman of a kitchen device, the "MagiPeel"—so much so that, even while he is explaining his decision to change to his slightly drunk wife, he watches with appreciation the selling technique of a performer on the Mickey Mouse Club and wonders how he can apply the style to his own work. After the basketball game, Harry's drift into mediocrity comes, if not to a halt, to an incomplete rec-ognition, because he has recovered an essentially aesthetic feeling about the excellence toward which a human being can aspire. After he has abandoned his wife and son and has moved in with a prostitute, he will tell the Reverend Eccles that his rebellion against the prevailing norms of family life is justified because he once experienced a form of perfection on the basketball court: "I once did something right. I played first-rate basketball. I really did. And after you're first-rate at something, no matter what, it kind of takes the kick out of being second-rate."

Because he has discovered, through a momentary return to his past, the compromises he has made with mediocrity, Harry will embark on a journey to recover that excellence, and that voyage out will require that he attempt to redefine his personal standards. Robert Detweiler has called Angstrom's journey a "futile quest for the nonexistent Holy Grail," for he has only a dim intuition of what he wants from life, and is therefore subject to the promptings of his impulses. The futility of the quest is felt in the sheer nervous movement of the novel, in a ceaseless search for something Harry cannot identify. The voyage begins with an unplanned drive into the heart of America, toward the vague goal of sensuous freedom near the Gulf of Mexico, but ends in confusion in a lover's lane in West Virginia. This is followed by a metaphysical journey into the past, a return to his old coach for advice, but that trip also ends in disillusionment, for the coach has forgotten the exact nature of Harry's excel-lence. He attempts a new definition of love with the prostitute Ruth, and they temporarily bring some love and even beauty into each other's lives. She abandons the trade of the prostitute at Harry's insistence and recognizes that love is not a mere commodity. While looking for a perfection analogous to what he felt on the basketball court, he is overtly rejecting the pressures of contemporary society: family, home, job, success. His quest, however, proves entirely self-serving, for at one juncture he tells Ruth, "If you have the guts to be yourself . . . other people'll pay your price." The price is high indeed. His quest for personal satisfaction permanently scars his wife, his son, his parents, the minister who wants to help him, and finally his abandoned and pregnant mistress.

Although Updike is scrupulously honest about the injuries such a search for personal satisfaction can cause, at the heart of *Rabbit, Run* is the instinct that there must be a better life than the "lives of quiet desperation" most Americans lead. Harry's rejection of public values leads him to seek a religious dimension in his experience, an ideal form symbolized for him by an effortless basket in a game, a perfect golf drive, or a symmetrical church window. Here the search is again frustrated because he is surrounded by unbelievers and hypocrites. After his own disabling stroke and the death of Angstrom's daughter, his old coach pontificates that abstractions like right and wrong are human inventions, not the products of Divine Law. Ruth is an atheist who remembers the hypocrisy of a client who had to wake early to teach a Sunday-school class, and she is not persuaded by Rabbit's insistence that there is a divine presence behind visible events. Janice and her mother use religious institutions as a whip to punish Rabbit for his desertion. Lucy Eccles, the wife of the minister who undertakes to reform Rabbit, and who at the very least encourages him to believe that her interest in him is fundamentally sexual, is a disciple of Sigmund Freud; she mocks her husband's religion as a shelter from his own sexual nature. The Reverend Eccles, the spokesman for organized religion, is really a social worker in disguise, and he directs his effort at bringing Harry back to Janice and to an acceptance of the conditions at hand because his religion teaches the sanctity of marriage. After that goal has been achieved, and Harry's return has initiated the circumstances that lead to the death of Becky, Eccles confesses to his wife that his faith is empty, that he believes in nothing. The only real believer in the book is the formidable Reverend Kruppenbach, and his God is a stern, harsh and morally rigid figure. It is significant, however, that Rabbit never comes into direct contact with this single character who believes firmly in the divine.

In the final moments of the novel, Harry is confronted by Ruth's demand that he marry her and by Janice's demand that he forgive and return to her. Confused between his instinct for excellence with its attendant guilt and the social pull toward mediocrity, Rabbit invokes an image from his basketball days: when he was guarded by two men, he "passed and the ball belonged to others and your hands were empty and the men on you looked foolish because in effect there was nobody there." This may be the most revealing moment in *Rabbit, Run*; Harry feels double-teamed by the emptiness of the life around him and the guilt and responsibility that attend a search for an alternative set of values, so he chooses in essence to be "nobody." He elects merely to flee, not to conform and not to take responsibility for choosing alternatives to conformity. His flight is the confused reaction of an imagination capable of seeing the emptiness of the prevailing social customs, but insufficient to define viable alternatives.

The first of the Angstrom novels leaves its antihero at the birth of a decade; the second, *Rabbit, Redux*, picks up the story ten years after Rabbit's flight. With America, he has been through the tumultuous 1960's, and like many Americans, he has taken refuge from the culture-shock of the decade in extreme political conservatism. Updike glosses "redux" from the title as "indicating return to health after disease," and the recovery in this novel will be political, sexual, and sympathetic. Rabbit will recover from a decade of personal emptiness, but the recovery will be as painful as was his original quest.

This second Angstrom novel is even more thickly textured with quotidian detail than was its predecessor. The television is always on, and readers are reminded of the pervasive influence of this medium. Quiz and misery shows serve as emblems of a collective greed and voyeurism, whereas Rowan and Martin's *Laugh-In* represents the fabricated "media events" which characterized the decade. Most of the major characters see a new kind of film, Stanley Kubrick's *2001: A Space Odyssey* (1968), and the televised coverage of Neil Armstrong's and Buzz Aldrin's landing on the moon completes the fine first chapter while introducing the factual event that will serve as the unifying symbol for the entire novel.

Rich in references to the problems and issues of the decade, *Rabbit Redux* confirms that all that is potentially noble about Angstrom can be traced to his attempt to transcend the prevailing American system of values, whereas all that proves weak or contemptible about him is the result of his uncritical acceptance of those very values. In the second book, Harry has allowed himself to become completely identified with the prevailing cultural assumptions. He has become tired, fat, complacent, and conservative; he attaches a decal of the American flag to his station wagon to publicize his support of American involvement in Vietnam. He is a linotype operator, a position he will lose because this method of printing has become obsolete. It is revealing that he has become much closer to his father during the years they have worked together; in both books, his father Earl represents a durable but unthinking and moralistic traditionalism.

Harry has allowed himself to become as obsolete as his job. He has settled in, has given up on himself. After, and because of, the terrible events of ten years ago, he has ceased to question, and has even lost the will to act as a lover to his wife; in turn, this guilt-induced failure drives Janice into an affair.

Far more important than what Janice thinks of Harry's new state is what he himself thinks about it. Talking to his dying mother, he rates his life as "about a C minus," and when he does reflect on his life, he feels the despair of total moral paralysis: "He was lying down to die, had been lying down for years. His body had been telling him to. . . . No belief in an afterlife, no hope for it, too much more of the same thing, already it seems he's lived twice." This paralysis of will so permeates his character that he does not even mind that his wife has taken a lover. Although there is a scene of violent intimacy on the night of Jan's confession, she herself must make the decision to leave, in part because Harry proves too morally indifferent even to object to the new situation.

By the end of the 1960's, Rabbit has fallen victim to all of the pressures toward mediocrity with which he contended briefly at twenty-six. Like its predecessor, *Rabbit Redux* is organized around the symbol of the voyage out. Detweiler has argued in detail that the moon landing is the dominating symbol of the book, suggesting that Harry's reaction to his wife's departure is like a movement into a new kind of metaphysical space. The epigraph for the second chapter is Armstrong's transmission on the day of the landing: "It's different but it's very pretty out here." The new space Rabbit will have to learn to inhabit is certainly different—but not very pretty.

Being deserted by his former partner in guilt is the condition that forces Harry out of his passivity and into the space beyond his apathy. He will have to learn to deal with elements of American life which his complacency has allowed him to ignore. These forces are symbolized by the most important supporting characters: his mother, the flower-child Jill, and the black militant Skeeter. His very recovery will depend on his discovery of a capacity to care for them. His mother's impending death is a challenge with which he is ill-equipped to deal, for she has been the dominant force in the Angstrom home, but at the end of the book, when Harry and his son Nelson move in with the senior Angstroms, she is greatly comforted.

Jill, the second of his challenges, pushes Rabbit out of his sexual death, but his reaction to her is equivocal. She represents the culture that dropped out during the decade, and she therefore challenges all of the assumptions which Rabbit has come to accept. After his black coworker Buchanan has unloaded the politically inconvenient, rich flower-child on him, Rabbit feels a renewal of his sexual vigor, but more important, of his capacity to love. She brings love and life to Penn Villas, and even the food she prepares nourishes Harry and Nelson in ways Janice's cooking did not. She also shows Harry that there is an alternative to his materialism and insists that he is capable of rising beyond that creed. Updike expresses the total opposition of Harry and Jill in terms of the governing space image as Jill and Harry move toward each other, "crying over secrets far at their backs, moonchild and earthman."

She is, however, a moonchild with a past. Like many disaffected young people of the decade, she has been a drug addict, and she needs the earthman to protect her from the temptation to return to that refuge. She sees in him an inner beauty, and she feels that his paternal and erotic love may save her from the weakness that led her to drugs. His habit of indifference, compounded by her weakness, renders him incapable of protecting her; as Skeeter draws her back into the habit, she begs Rabbit to throw him out, but he believes that "He cannot help her." His failure to respond leads to the burden of guilt that fills the final episodes of *Rabbit Redux*. While he spends the night with Janice's best friend, irate vigilantes set fire to his house, and Jill, in a drug-induced stupor, is killed. Harry's failure is complete. He has not saved her from drugs: he was not there to rescue her; and his failure to send Skeeter away led his neighbors to set his house afire.

Harry's third challenge is Skeeter, who calls into question Harry's political and social creed in every conceivable way. Skeeter is black and militant, and Harry is a complacent product of white society; Skeeter is a fugitive, and Harry loves the law; Skeeter preaches a new form of social organization, and Harry supports the status quo at every opportunity; Skeeter claims to be the new Christ, and Harry distrusts any form of unorthodox thought. Yet, after a brutal confrontation in which Skeeter insults every value Harry holds sacred and forces Harry to beat him up, the two men begin to move toward each other like spacecraft docking. Harry never learns to like Skeeter, and the reader does not either, but he is fascinated by him.

Much has been written about Skeeter's role as blasphemer in *Rabbit Redux*, but perhaps the emphasis should be not on his perverse profession of divinity, but on the causes behind that profession. As his name implies, Skeeter too is a victim—of injustice, of prejudice, of the war, and of fear itself. He believes that fear is the universal condition: "Scared, *scared*. I'm scared of you, you scared of me, Nelson scared of both of us, and poor Jilly here so scared of everything she'll run and hide herself in dope again. . . ." Skeeter has been permanently affected by the horrors he experienced in Vietnam. Returning to a fearful white society resisting transition, he has confused the political and the religious dimensions of human experience, and therefore couches his demand for social change in the shocking rhetoric of the religious revolutionary. At the same time, his impact on the Angstroms is to bring an unfamiliar world to the sheltered conservatisim of Penn Villas. When he tells Harry, Jill, and Nelson about the absurdity, napalm, fragging, and unexpected heroism he saw in Asia, he uses language consistent with Updike's controlling symbol of space exploration, "It was like you learned there was life on another world." His war stories make Nelson want to turn the television on, to blot out the unthinkable, but some of Harry's mental rebirth is represented by his reaction; he makes Nelson listen, saying "it happened, so we got to take it in. We got to deal with it somehow." He is not persuaded that his conviction, that American involvement is justified, should be changed, but he has adapted to consider and reflect on views that contradict the ideas most dear to him.

Harry's new sympathy for Skeeter is the challenge that most alienates and disappoints him in the novel. He cannot like the young man, and he meets with pressures from the entire community to abandon Skeeter to his fate. The neighbors demand that Skeeter leave, and even Nelson and Jill beg that Rabbit throw him out. His loyalty to Skeeter cannot be traced to love or intellectual sympathy, but there is a fascination in Skeeter's presence that requires that Harry grow beyond his social and political prejudices. To a degree, this loyalty is reciprocated. Skeeter, the apostle of cynicism, the man who insists that no man is bound to another by any tie, gravitates toward his natural enemy. Although he deals in drugs and intends to make Jill dependent on dope, he demands that Harry not experiment with his wares: "Stay clean, you in deep trouble on account of me without being party to this, right? Split—I'm begging, man." The apostle of indifference has found someone worth protecting.

Rabbit's fascination with Skeeter leads to another disappointment. When the house is burned, Skeeter saves himself and his supply of drugs, but does nothing to save Jill. Believing that Skeeter's only crime was his failure to care enough to try to save her, Rabbit helps him to escape from the law. In a scene intense with religious imagery, Harry demands that Skeeter never return, and drops him near Galilee, Pennsylvania. Skeeter says he will return "only in glory" and spits in the hand Rabbit extends in friendship. He will hear of Skeeter again in *Rabbit is Rich*, when someone sends him a newspaper clipping that tells of the young man's death. His reflection at that time sheds light on what Skeeter meant to Harry: "Skeeter dead, a certain light was withdrawn from the world, a daring, a promise that all would be overturned."

Angstrom's voyage out has been into confusion, uncertainty, and the demand that he enlarge his sympathies and recover his capacity to love, but it has also brought him to face death and disappointment. His return is to forgive and reaffirm his life with Janice. She has lost her lover, but in the process has nursed him through a heart attack. Harry and Jan are reconciled at the symbolically named Safe Haven motel, which becomes "all interior space," and they become "radiant debris," but they can come to rest, partners in love and guilt. She tells him that the events are not his fault, and Harry comes as close to heroism as he does in all the Angstrom chronicles when he says, "I can't accept that." The two find not sex but rest in the Safe Haven; Updike requires the reader's acquiescence in their adjustment with his ambiguous ending: "He. She. Sleeps. O.K.?"

In *Rabbit Is Rich*, the voyage out is into affluence and the life-style of the 1970's. Harry prospers, reads *Consumer Reports*, covets his neighbors' wives, and supports the status quo. He is ten years fatter, richer, and more complacent than he was at thirty-six. He has ceased to question. Except for occasional moments of tenderness toward Nelson—not reciprocated, perhaps because of the shadow Jill's death cast between the two—Harry makes it a point to avoid reflection. Although he tells Nelson that he has avoided "the greatest sin," simply lying down to die, he avoids the kind of metaphysical questioning that got him into so much trouble in the earlier two novels. When he begins to reconsider the implications of the deaths of Skeeter and all the others, Harry realizes that he "doesn't want to think about the Invisible anyway, every time in his life he has made a move toward it somebody has gotten killed." He does make one voyage into the past. He seeks to discover whether a young woman he saw at his Toyota Agency is his daughter by Ruth, his mistress in *Rabbit, Run*. This search leads, after he has twice run away to avoid just such an encounter, to a painful meeting with Ruth, in which he reluctantly accepts her answer, that this daughter is not his own, and with it a feeling that the past cannot be recovered or forgiven. He later feels "amputated" by his encounter with Ruth.

A parallel voyage out is Nelson's, and herein the Angstrom novels again reveal a pattern of deterioration in American culture. Harry's son, Nelson now nearly as old as Harry was in the original novel, makes virtually the same journey his father made twenty years ago. The circle has come full, but Nelson is not the man his father was. Harry was a seeker, a stumbling and limited quester after a better, less secular, set of values. Nelson, the product of the generations Updike has explored in these chronicles (as well as of the repeated trauma in the Angstrom household), exhibits all the unpleasant qualities associated with Harry in the first novel—lust, selfishness, a willingness to ignore obligations to others in the search for self-fulfillment—but he has none of those redeeming qualities that made Harry admirable. The voyage out is not a voyage back this time. Nelson abandons his pregnant wife to join her best friend, his mistress. Harry was a seeker, but Nelson is a jerk. His actions do not lead to a search for redemption, but merely to revenge on his father, and the pointlessness of his violent motion can be symbolized in his wrecking five automobiles, two of them deliberately while his father watches in shock.

Harry, however, has a journey back. He and Jan, still together, spend a Caribbean holiday with two other couples, and while there experience a group sexual episode characteristic of the new values of the decade. When they return, Harry meets his infant granddaughter, the reincarnation of Becky, Jill, his lost sister Mim, and Ruth's daughter, all the sisters and daughters he has loved and lost: "Through all this she has pushed to be here, in his lap, his hands, a real presence hardly weighing anything but alive. Fortune's hostage, heart's desire, a granddaughter. His. Another nail in his coffin. His." All the voyages out have led to home, love, and mortality, and the perfection he has perversely sought throughout the decades has at last been granted him.

Shortly after completing the novel that would be acknowledged as his masterpiece, and that later would become the source for his continuing observation of American culture, Updike began work on a book that is as different from *Rabbit, Run* as it is possible to imagine. *The Centaur* departs radically from its predecessor in style, method, allusiveness, characterization, and theme, and in its general conception of the meaning of human behavior. It is Updike's most complex novel, especially in its insistence that the narrative operate on several simultaneous levels and yet not reduce to simple allegory. This superimposition of a story of contemporary, local life upon the background of a specific mythological narrative places the work deliberately in the tradition of Joyce's *Ulysses* (1922). Although homage to the modern masterwork seems intended, there is a counterpoint of playfulness when Updike appends, "at my wife's suggestion," an index by which the reader can sort out the more obscure mythological associations.

In addition to the problems presented by this remarkable experiment in double narration, any assessment of *The Centaur* is compounded by the obvious autobiographical element. Place-names and situations familiar to readers of Updike's autobiographical short stories form the milieu of the novel. These include the removal of the family from a small city to a farm that is feared and despised by the father and son, but revered by the mother; the presence with the family of one maternal grandparent; frantic motion of the father and son into town to escape the dread of the farm; the son's wish to escape spatially, to a place associated with culture, and spiritually, into an artistic or an academic setting; and the internal conflicts that occur when a young man is on the threshold of sexual but not social maturity. As in so many of the stories, the hero George Caldwell is modeled on Updike's father Wesley, from his vocation as schoolteacher to his lack of confidence in himself to his fussy and self-effacing ways. Although Peter, the son, is a painter rather than a writer, this does not minimize the autobiographical complication, for Updike aspired to become an artist and studied art in England; he still designs the covers for the hardbound editions of his novels. In his Preface to *Olinger Stories*, Updike reveals that he intended not only to write out of his own experiences, but also to make *The Centaur* his final attempt to convert autobiography to art: "by turning Olinger explicitly into Olympus, I intended to say the final word, and farewell."

These many and diverse elements in the novel have prevented anything like a uniform critical assessment. Some critics, such as Arthur Mizner, feel that the blend of mythic with the contemporary is artificial or unrealized artistically; others, such as Larry Taylor, find that the complex blend constitutes Updike's finest achievement. Among the sympathetic critics, there remain serious disagreements about the meaning of the book. Taylor sees it as a pastoral elegy in the tradition of John Milton's "Lycidas," and argues that the fusion of the classical with the contemporary is an appropriate way to realize the intentions of the traditional pastoral elegy. Detweiler observes that the structure of the novel is like that of a surrealist or cubist painting, and therefore maintains that Updike's artistic achievement lies precisely in this surrealistic use of simultaneous perspective with its attendant demand that the reader discover for himself the "*Gestalt* of the total scene in its equally significant multiple meanings and interrelations. . . ." Suzanne Uphaus argues that Updike's use of classical and contemporary narratives approximates the mock-epic, and that the theme therefore is the death of the heroic vision.

Although there is no critical consensus on the meaning or even the emphasis of this complex novel, one thing is clear: it is a book about love and sacrifice. The common denominator of the stories of Chiron, the immortal centaur who gave his life so that Prometheus could become immortal, and Caldwell, the teacher who exhausts himself in his love for his students and his family, is sacrifice. Even in this area, however, there is critical disagreement about exactly what happens in the closing episode. Caldwell goes out to dig the Buick out of a snowdrift; following the logic of the Caldwell-Chiron superimposition, one must conclude that the Buick, itself one of the crucial symbols of the novel, is in a way George's body. Its deterioration corresponds to George's own physical state; it was once an undertaker's car, and George has throughout the novel been, in John Keats's phrase, "half in love with easeful death." Thus, the automobile and the man are analogous to the combination of the body of man and horse that makes up the mythic centaur. The Buick is hopelessly stuck in a drift of snow, just as George feels helplessly caught in his job and his obligations. When he goes to free the Buick from its prison of snow, George yet again merges with Chiron going to the cave to die, and Updike quotes extensively from the Greek to emphasize the fact that Chiron "willingly went there to die." The episode ends with the declaration, "Chiron accepted death," and the parallel between Chiron and Caldwell admits the inference that George dies in this effort to free his metaphorical body. Rachel Burchard concludes poetically, "The earthly journey is over," and Detweiler suggests that Caldwell is "approaching death, and his apotheosis into the heavens."

Several kinds of evidence must be considered in determining whether Caldwell actually dies at the conclusion of the novel. First, all of Chapter Five is an obituary for Caldwell, written in a sentimental style by one of his former students. It would therefore seem logical that the actual death is intended by the author, especially because the age given in the obituary corresponds exactly with Caldwell's concern that he will not live beyond his present, fiftieth, year. In the next chapter, however, Peter, in the classical persona of Prometheus chained to the rock and mourning his father's death, is visited by his father, and he begs him not to die, not to rest: "Can't you forgive us and keep going?" Additionally, when the X-rays are read, they disclose that George's problem is not cancer but mucinous colitis, a treatable disease. The most important kind of evidence occurs when George, merging with Chiron and reflecting on how durable the old Buick really is, realizes that in "these last days he had been saying goodbye to everything. . . ." He discovers that he has been making himself ready for "a journey," but that there "would be none." Turning explicitly to another classical reference, Updike writes, "Atropos [the Fury or Fate that controls death] had opened her shears, thought twice, smiled, and permitted the thread to continue spinning." Caldwell, therefore, apparently feels that he must prepare for life, not death. In 1968, Updike revealed to an interviewer that he intended Caldwell's death to be metaphoric: "He dies in the sense of living, of going back to work, of being a shelter for his son." When George arrives at the snow-bound automobile, a "chariot Zimmerman had sent for him," it is not to die, but to return to the duties imposed on him by his love for others, and presumbly to discard the death wish he has used as a defense mechanism against the frustrations life imposes upon him.

The organizing symbol of *The Centaur* also supports the theme of the dignity of self-sacrifice. In a scene that has been widely and rightly praised for its style and its blend of the fantastic, the symbolic, and the experiental, Caldwell lectures his class on evolution. His pupils, unlike the heroes Chiron taught, are loud and unruly, and Zimmerman observes the class to make out his report on Caldwell's teaching effectiveness. While doing this, Zimmerman merges with Zeus in his sexual attraction to one of the pupils, Iris Osgood, whose "dull bovine beauty" allies her with Io; as the fantasy intensifies, Zeus seems well on the way to ravishing the girl, and Diefendorf (Achilles) has taken this as a clue to assault the Davis Girl. Chiron brings the chaos to a climax by striking the pupil, in part because he contributed so much to the chaos but was not as fearsome an adversary as its instigator, and in part because it was Diefendorf who broke the grille of Caldwell's car.

In the heart of this disorder, in which it is finally impossible to draw an exact line between actual event and fantasy, lies the organizing symbol of *The Centaur*. Lecturing his class on creation, George uses the analogy of the creation clock to make time comprehensible to them. He discusses the physiological theory that cells need not die, that their divisibility is a type of immortality. Then he tells the class about the volvox, which "interests us because he invented death." The volvox is critical because of its distinctive place in the evolutionary chain. The cells gave up their immortality to accept a specialized role in the life of the organism. The two issues central to the book, death and sacrifice, are thus traced to a common historical origin: "while each cell is potentially immortal, by volunteering for a specialized function within an organized society of cells it enters a compromised environment." The volvox thereby becomes the archetype of the being that sacrifices its life for the good of the community.

George Caldwell is of course the human equivalent of the volvox. He gives his life to a job in which he feels no fulfillment, to a farm with which he feels no kinship, for a son whose assumption of intellectual superiority must frighten him, and in fidelity to a wife he cannot hope to understand (he is tempted at least twice by Vera Hummel, or Venus). His sacrifice requires his acceptance of the specialized roles of husband, father, and teacher, so he is in direct contrast to Harry Angstrom, the seeker who insists on personal satisfaction within his compromised environment. George represents the paradox of the self-effacing hero and lover, who puts the interests of others above his own. His ultimate self-effacement requires not his death, but his acceptance of the continuing grind of frustration in the specialized roles he must play. He is therefore a centaur in the terms described by Karl Barth in the epigraph Updike selects for the novel: "the creature on the boundary between heaven and earth." What remains earthly about Caldwell is his hypochondria, self-loathing, and bumbling ineffectiveness; what approaches heaven is his transcendence of the personal to the sacrificial and other-directed.

Major publications other than long fiction

SHORT FICTION: *The Same Door*, 1959; *Pigeon Feathers and Other Stories*, 1962; *Olinger Stories*, 1964; *The Music School*, 1966; *Bech: A Book*, 1970; *Museums and Women and Other Stories*, 1972; *Warm Wine: An Idyll*, 1973; *Too Far to Go: The Maples Stories*, 1979; *Problems and Other Stories*, 1979.

PLAYS: *Three Texts from Early Ipswich: A Pageant*, 1968; *Buchanan Dying*, 1974.

POETRY: *The Carpentered Hen and Other Tame Creatures*, 1958; *Telephone Poles and Other Poems*, 1963; *Bath After Sailing*, 1968; *Midpoint and Other Poems*, 1969; *Seventy Poems*, 1972; *Six Poems*, 1973; *Tossing and Turning*, 1977.

NONFICTION: *Picked-Up Pieces*, 1975.

Bibliography

Buchard, Rachel C. *John Updike: Yea-Sayings*, 1971.

Detweiler, Robert. *John Updike*, 1972.

Galloway, David D. "The Absurd Man as Saint: The Novels of John Updike," in *The Absurd Hero in American Fiction: Updike, Styron, Bellow, Salinger*, 1966, 1970.

Hamilton, Alice, and Kenneth Hamilton. *The Elements of John Updike*, 1970.

Harper, Howard M., Jr. "John Updike: The Intrinsic Problem of Human Existence," in *Desperate Faith: A Study of Bellow, Salinger, Mailer, Baldwin, and Updike*, 1967.

Hunt, George W. *John Updike and the Three Great Secret Things: Sex, Religion and Art*, 1980.

Markle, Joyce B. *Fighters and Lovers: Theme in the Novels of John Updike*, 1973.

Podhoretz, Norman. "A Dissent on Updike," in *Doings and Undoings: The Fifties and After in American Writing*, 1964.

Rupp, Richard H. "John Updike: Style in Search of a Center," in *Celebration in Postwar American Ficiton, 1945-1967*, 1970.

Samuels, Charles Thomas. "The Art of Fiction LXIII," in *The Paris Review*. XL (Winter, 1968), pp. 84-117.

Tanner, Tony. "A Compromised Environment," in *City of Words: American Fiction 1950-1970*, 1971.

Taylor, Larry E. *Pastoral and Anti-Pastoral Patterns in John Updike's Fiction*, 1971.

Thorburn, David, and Howard Eiland, eds. *John Updike: A Collection of Critical Essays*, 1979.

Uphaus, Suzanne Henning. *John Updike*, 1980.

David C. Dougherty

CARL VAN VECHTEN

Born: Cedar Rapids, Iowa; June 17, 1880
Died: New York, New York; December 21, 1964

Principal long fiction

Peter Whiffle: His Life and Works, 1922; *The Blind Bow-Boy*, 1923; *The Tattooed Countess*, 1924; *Firecrackers*, 1925; *Nigger Heaven*, 1926; *Spider Boy*, 1928; *Parties*, 1930.

Other literary forms

Carl Van Vechten had three major careers in the arts; he was a critic, a novelist, and a photographer. His music criticism includes *Music After the Great War* (1915), *Music and Bad Manners* (1916), and *The Music of Spain* (1918). His involvement with major American and European writers and artists of the 1920's and 1930's is chronicled in his autobiographies, *Sacred and Profane Memories* (1932) and *Fragments from an Unwritten Autobiography* (1955).

Achievements

The spirit of the "jazz age," the "roaring twenties," and the "lost generation" is nowhere better depicted than in the saucy and irreverent novels of Van Vechten. Van Vechten moved deftly through three careers: he began as a music, dance, and drama critic, producing several volumes of wide-ranging, urbane essays; then, he devoted himself to fiction, writing seven well-received novels in a decade which saw the first publications of Ernest Hemingway, F. Scott Fitzgerald, and John Dos Passos; finally, he became a noted photographer, specializing in portraits of writers and artists. In all his diverse endeavors, Van Vechten was witty, cosmopolitan, and above all, unconventional. He publicized the work of such writers as William Faulkner, Ronald Firbank, and especially Gertrude Stein, who remained his close friend until her death, and who assigned him as her literary executor. He was among the first critics to recognize the exciting cultural renaissance flourishing in Harlem and devoted much effort to helping establish the careers of Countée Cullen, Langston Hughes, James Weldon Johnson, Bessie Smith, Ethel Waters, and other black artists. He saw himself as a popularizer and supporter of avant-garde artists, and with a clear eye and self-assurance, he brought to the attention of the American public exotic figures ranging from Waslaw Nijinsky to Erik Satie, from Mary Garden to Igor Stravinsky.

Van Vechten, more than many of his contemporaries, lived the literary life with seemingly boundless enthusiasm. His verve animates all of his writing, including the essays he frequently contributed to such trend-setting journals as *Trend*, *The Smart Set*, and *Vanity Fair*, and this effervescent spirit informs his novels as well. His wide interests, diverse friendships, and tireless pursuit of the new, the brilliant, and the innovative make Van Vechten a fascinating guide to America's cultural life in the first decades of the twentieth century.

Biography

Carl Van Vechten was born in Cedar Rapids, Iowa, on June 17, 1880. His father was a banker turned insurance company executive; his mother was a college graduate, suffragette, and for her time, a political and social activist. Born when his parents were in their forties, Van Vechten had two siblings much older than he and so spent his childhood surrounded by four adults. Predictably, this atmosphere nurtured a precocious child. By the time he was an adolescent, Van Vechten had thoroughly immersed himself in whatever cultural offerings could be found in Cedar Rapids—opera, theater, concerts which stopped in the city on tour—and began to apply his own talents to amateur theatrical productions and family piano recitals. Physically he was an awkward youth—too tall too early, with large buck teeth—and his omnivorous appetite for culture made him feel socially awkward among his peers. Longing to escape from the complacent bourgeois existence of Cedar Rapids, he enrolled at the University of Chicago and, in 1899, took his first steps East, a direction which would eventually lead to New York and then to Paris.

At college, Van Vechten studied with Robert Morss Lovett and William Vaughn Moody. He also began writing passionately and composing music. After he was graduated, he took a job on the *Chicago American*; he was assigned to write short news pieces and collect photographs to illustrate news stories. He soon decided, however, that, for his purposes, Chicago was little better than Cedar Rapids. In 1906, he left for New York.

Van Vechten's first writing assignment there was an opera review for Theodore Dreiser, then editor of *Broadway Magazine*. Soon, Van Vechten joined the staff of *The New York Times* as assistant to the music critic. From 1908 to 1909, he served as Paris correspondent for the *Times*, a post which brought him into close contact with leading European dancers, sculptors, artists, and writers. When he returned to New York in the spring of 1909, he resumed his job as music critic, but he longed to return to Europe. He was back in Paris in 1914.

By then, Van Vechten had, in many ways, left his Cedar Rapids days behind him. In 1912, he was divorced from Anna Elizabeth Snyder, a childhood sweetheart he had married just five years before. Shortly after the divorce, he met the Russian-Jewish actress Fania Marinoff, an attractive and exotic-looking woman whom he would soon marry. In 1913, he met Mabel Dodge, the irrepressible center of her own vibrant salon; in 1914, at the second performance of Stravinsky's *Sacre du Printemps* in Paris, he met Gertrude Stein, at whose rue de Fleurus home he would soon encounter the leading figures of Parisian cultural life.

From 1915 to 1932, Van Vechten wrote an astonishing number of books—first several volumes of essays on music and the arts, then seven novels. He preferred the experimental, the daring, the works of young artists being performed, written, and conducted in America and on the Continent, and the enthusiasm with which he greeted such works helped earn their acceptance by his readers. He predicted the enduring greatness of Stravinsky at a time when some wondered if what they were hearing was, indeed, music. He approached his task as critic with "curiosity and energy," he said, and his tastes, idiosyncratic as they were, reflected his certainty in empathizing with the aims of modern artists.

In 1928, his brother died, leaving Van Vechten a substantial bequest which allowed him financial independence. This event coincided with, and perhaps made possible, Van Vechten's new career, that of photographer. He had his first show in 1934, and became a portrait photographer of such writers and artists as Gertrude Stein, Truman Capote, George Gershwin, Leontyne Price, and William Faulkner.

Van Vechten was the founder of several libraries and archives, including the James Weldon Johnson Memorial Collection (black art and literature) at Yale, the George Gershwin Memorial Collection (music) at Fisk University, the Rose McClendon Memorial Collection (photographs of famous blacks) at Howard University, and the Florine Stettheimer Memorial Collection (fine arts) at Fisk.

Analysis

In *Peter Whiffle*, Carl Van Vechten's hero expounds upon the art of criticism, Van Vechten's vocation in the decade before he wrote fiction. Recalling Remy de Gourmont, Whiffle asserts: "Criticism is perhaps the most suggestive of literary forms; it is a perpetual confession; believing to analyze the works of others, the critic unveils and exposes himself to the public." So, he continues, one learns more about the critic than about the object of his observations. "Criticism should open channels of thought and not close them; it should stimulate the soul and not revolt it. And criticism can only be wholesome and sane and spiritually stimulating when it is contradictory." Van Vechten, above all, believed that life itself was contradictory, that appearances often deceived, that absurdity ruled more often than logic. Nevertheless, he exulted in strong, creative, exciting personalities, and believed that such strength could overcome the inherent absurdity of life. If there were no Truth, no unalterable Facts, there could at least be Style, Anecdote, Spirit—those qualities which Whiffle said readers looked for in "the old critics"—and there also could be enthusiasm and joy.

Given Van Vechten's notions about literary criticism, it is no wonder that he gravitated toward fiction, where characters might easily express contradictory ideas and where the writer's style, spirit, and personality are expected to pervade the text. In his novels, Van Vechten emerges as an observant and perceptive critic of his own society and his particular time. His novels, as Donald Pizer notes, "Chronicle either in authorial asides or miniature essays the taste and interests of the decade from the conventional to the avant garde." His friends and acquaintances often made appearances, sometimes under pseudonyms, and current music, books, and paintings are evoked vividly. Aiming to analyze his world, Van Vechten also reveals his own particular point of view: that of the tolerant but wiser and older participant (he was nearly forty-two when he published his first novel), one who looks with bemused sympathy on the antics around him. He accepts—as his characters often do not—that the world is absurd; he is not shocked or dismayed by the suffering, unhappiness, and anguish beneath the glittering life of cosmopolitan high society because he knows that life offers joy and satisfaction, if only one knows where to look. He is aware of the conflict between the sensitive artist and a world which would deny him, but he believes that strength of personality and self-assertion can overcome many obstacles. In his acceptance of absurdity and his belief in the capacity of the artist to survive emotionally and psychologically, he stands apart from some of the younger men writing at the same time: Sherwood Anderson, Hemingway, Fitzgerald, Sinclair Lewis. Though he shares many of their artistic problems, he does not share their anger, and this ability to delight and be delighted distinguishes Van Vechten's fiction.

Peter Whiffle, in this novel about writing a novel, is a would-be writer, searching for self and inspiration in a troubling world. He encounters Van Vechten, who reappears in the novel to meet Peter at several stages of his artistic development; Peter confides his theories of life and art to the patient older man, and reveals the confusions faced by the artist as a young man. At first, Peter announces that he plans to write a book, and Van Vechten asks him what it will be about. About three hundred pages, Peter replies. "That is what it is to be about, about three hundred pages, three hundred pages of colour and style and lists, lists of objects, all jumbled artfully. There isn't a moral, or an idea, or a plot, or even a character. There's to be no propaganda or preaching, or violence, or emotion, or even humour." Art, Peter says, is necessarily abstract—never concrete; art is the pattern which emerges from artful juxtaposition. Some sixty pages later, Peter has discarded these notions and come to another conclusion: art "has nothing to do with style or form or manner. . . . The *matter* is what counts. . . . No style, no form, just *subject.*"

Obsessed now with political and social revolution, Peter decides that he must opt for realism over expressionism; Theodore Dreiser—and not, for example, Georg Kaiser—must be his model. Again, some sixty pages later, Peter is thoroughly confused: "Never did I feel less sure of the meaning of art than I do here," he confesses. He has immersed himself in the world of literature, music, and painting, only to discover that no theory or formula will explain art. Finally, he decides that the personality of the artist and his ability to convey his impressions might yield a masterpiece of art. "I think a great book might be written if everything the hero thought and felt and observed could be put into it," he says. "These ideas, impressions, objects, should all be set down. Nothing should be omitted, nothing! One might write a whole book of two hundred thousand words about the events of an hour. And what a book! What a book!" That book will never be written by Peter Whiffle, however, nor would it be written by Van Vechten. Peter observes that one might be able to create a work of art from one's life, merely by living well. "I wanted to write a new Comedie Humaine," Peter says. "Instead, I have lived it. And now, I have come to the conclusion that that was all there was for me to do, just to live, as fully as possible. Sympathy and enthusiasm are something, after all. I must have communicated at least a shadow of these to the ideas and objects and people on whom I have bestowed them." He is disillusioned with the idea that the successful artist is a fulfilled human being. "All expression lifts us farther away from simplicity and causes unhappiness," he concludes. Of his own search for the meaning of art, he finds, "Everybody is striving to do something *new*, instead of writing or painting or composing what is natural. . . . The great secret is . . . to do what one *has* to do."

This paean to individuality and self-knowledge is the theme not only of *Peter Whiffle*, but also of many other Van Vechten novels. Indeed, *Peter Whiffle* is an example of what Van Vechten, in *Nigger Heaven*, calls a propaganda novel: his message is the celebration of self-awareness and a love of life.

Peter Whiffle leaves the provinciality of his native Toledo, Ohio, for the cultural capitals of the world. In *The Tattooed Countess*, Van Vechten reverses the process: Countess Ella Nattatorrini returns from an urbane European life to her childhood home, Maple Valley, Iowa. Maple Valley is as stifling as Carol Kennicott's Gopher Prairie, but unlike Carol, the Countess does not intend to enlighten the town. Instead, she decides to run from it, taking with her the only artist Maple Valley has spawned: Gareth Johns. Moreover, unlike Sinclair Lewis, Van Vechten does not depict small-town life with bitterness or rancor; instead, he is sympathetic toward the repressed characters of Maple Valley, just as he empathizes with the dreams of Ella and Gareth Johns.

The Countess, like Hester Prynne in *The Scarlet Letter* (1850), openly displays a symbol of nonconformity, of sexuality, of freedom: a tattoo on her arm. The "curious emblem" consists of a butterfly perched on a skull, with the phrase "*Que sais-je?*" beneath. Fragile, elusive beauty can distract humans from a preoccupation with their own mortality, but the butterfly must be taken for what it is, and not elevated into theories of art or into doctrines by which one decides to live. During a passionate love affair, Ella had the design tatooed on her arm, and it recalls for her not only her lost love—a sad reminder—but her ability to live fully, a notion she celebrates. Her sister is aghast: surely, even if one were foolhardy enough to be tattooed, one would do it in a discreet place. "That is the sort of thing we keep hidden here," she tells the Countess, but Ella Nattatorrini cannot live a hidden life. It is not Van Vechten's intention to flaunt Ella's quest for freedom and self-fulfillment, but only to allow her a world in which she, as well as the inhabitants of Maple Valley, can live as she must.

Nigger Heaven reflects Van Vechten's intense interest in black culture, an interest which went far beyond Pablo Picasso's fascination with African art or Gertrude Stein's interest in the Baltimore community upon which she drew for her story "Melanctha." Impressed with the vitality of the arts in Harlem, he befriended many black writers and musicians and brought them to the attention of important cultural leaders downtown. Without becoming political- ically or socially active in support of civil rights, Van Vechten managed to become a significant spokesman for an oppressed people through *Nigger Heaven*, a novel which, despite its blatant propaganda, is a vivid and sym- pathetic study of New York blacks of the 1920's.

The book centers on the relationship between Mary Love and yet another aspiring writer (surely Van Vechten had many models, black and white, from which to choose), Byron Kasson. Both are educated (Byron is a University of Pennsylvania graduate, Mary a librarian), articulate, sensitive young peo- ple, but their love and Byron's dreams are doomed to failure. Byron refuses to "see" Harlem and the real lives of blacks as suitable material for his stories; his insistence on his separateness leaves him isolated. Both the black and white communities look upon him as a misfit. Mary is willing to work within the limitations placed upon her and urges Byron to approach his own people with compassion and even humility. When he tells her he will use the prejudice against his people as a plot for a story, she cautions him against "becoming melodramatic, cheap even. Unless such a story is written with exquisite skill, it will read like a meretricious appeal to the emotions arising out of race prejudice." Ultimately Byron fails, not only in his story, but also in his effort to propel himself out of a culture which threatens to undermine all his hopes. Yet Van Vechten suggests that it is Byron himself—as Peter Whiffle had done before him—who causes his own downfall.

Van Vechten, like his writer-protagonist, faced the problem of seeming melodramatic in a novel which is in large part, as he put it, propaganda. He was, in 1926, anticipating the anger of James Baldwin and Richard Wright; for Van Vechten, "Nigger Heaven" (a black term, he explains, for the Harlem community) was ready to explode. Rarely is Van Vechten as sedate, con- trolled, and carefully paced as he is in this novel, and rarely is his authorial presence so discreet. *Nigger Heaven* is his most serious novel, his only attempt to deal with social issues in a culture and class different from his own; the book is a reflection of a deep commitment to social change.

Parties, Van Vechten's last novel, is an intense portrait of a dissolute and frenzied decade. David and Rilda Westlake, characters based on Van Vechten's friends Scott and Zelda Fitzgerald, move throughout the novel in a series of parties where they argue, drink, attempt seductions, gossip, toss off jaded remarks, and drink more, and still more. Vividly sketching his dissipated cast of characters, Van Vechten manages to portray their physical and emotional instability and the emptiness of their lives. Van Vechten's characters are often grotesque rather than enviably attractive. When the reader first meets David Westlake, he is a "distorted figure" with blood drying on his lips, crying "I've killed a man or a man has killed me." Rilda's entrance is by telephone: she claims to have committed suicide. An alleged murder victim appears alive, if not completely well, finally to be killed as the plot spirals. Among these living dead cavorts a sprightly seventy-year-old European aristocrat, the Grafin Adele von Pulmernl und Stilzernl, whose lively interest in parties places her in the company of the young Americans driven to drink and misery. She alone, unable to perceive the real meaning of the whirlwind social life, enjoys the parties and finds them amusing. "It is so funny," she tells David Westlake after he summarizes "the life of our times in words of two syllables. . . . We're here because we're here, and we should be extremely silly not to make the worst of it." The Grafin, delighted with David's pronouncement, has the last words of the book: "I love your country."

Though it was poorly received by critics, Van Vechten's novel succeeds in taking the prototypal Fitzgerald characters and spinning them in a mindless maelstrom. These are the damned, who spent a decade in drunken revelry, only to wake up, forced to confront a new decade and a new spirit. With *Parties*, Van Vechten's role as a social critic ended. He had chronicled an age, and written its epitaph.

Major publications other than long fiction

NONFICTION: *Music After the Great War*, 1915; *Music and Bad Manners*, 1916; *Interpreters and Interpretations*, 1917; *The Merry-Go-Round*, 1918; *The Music of Spain*, 1918; *In the Garret*, 1920; *Interpreters*, 1920; *The Tiger in the House*, 1920; *Red*, 1925; *Excavations*, 1926; *Sacred and Profane Memories*, 1932; *Fragments from an Unwritten Autobiography*, 1955.

Bibliography

Kellner, Bruce. *A Bibliography of the Work of Carl Van Vechten*, 1981.
_____ . *Carl Van Vechten and the Irreverent Decades*, 1968.
Lueders, Edward. *Carl Van Vechten*, 1965.
_____ . *Carl Van Vechten and the Twenties*, 1955.
Pizer, Donald. "The Novels of Carl Van Vechten and the Spirit of the Age," in *Toward a New American Literary History*, 1980.

Linda Simon

GORE VIDAL

Born: West Point, New York; October 3, 1925

Principal long fiction

Williwaw, 1946; *In a Yellow Wood*, 1947; *The City and the Pillar*, 1948, 1965; *The Season of Comfort*, 1949; *Dark Green, Bright Red*, 1950, 1968; *A Search for the King: A Twelfth Century Legend*, 1950; *The Judgment of Paris*, 1952, 1965; *Death in the Fifth Position*, 1952 (as Edgar Box); *Death Before Bedtime*, 1953 (as Edgar Box); *Death Likes it Hot*, 1954 (as Edgar Box); *Messiah*, 1954, 1965; *Three: Williwaw, A Thirsty Evil, Julian the Apostate*, 1962; *Julian, A Novel*, 1964; *Washington, D.C.: A Novel*, 1967; *Myra Breckinridge*, 1968; *Two Sisters: A Memoir in the Form of a Novel*, 1970; *Burr: A Novel*, 1973; *Myron: A Novel*, 1974; *1876: A Novel*, 1976; *Kalki: A Novel*, 1978; *Creation: A Novel*, 1981.

Other literary forms

In addition to his work in the novel form, Gore Vidal has made his major contributions in drama, writing both for the stage and for television, and in critical essays, both literary and otherwise. His more prominent teleplays were published in *Visit to a Small Planet and Other Television Plays* (1957). The title play was later produced successfully on Broadway. Vidal's works for the stage include *The Best Man* (1960), *On the March to the Sea* (1962), *Weekend* (1968), and *An Evening with Richard Nixon* (1972). He has also written or contributed to screenplays for such films as *Ben Hur*, *Suddenly, Last Summer*, and *Is Paris Burning?* Vidal's essays and reviews have appeared in a wide variety of magazines; his principal nonfiction is collected in *Rocking the Boat* (1962); *Reflections upon a Sinking Ship* (1969); *Homage to Daniel Shays: Collected Essays 1952-1972* (1972); *Matters of Fact and of Fiction: Essays 1973-1976* (1977); and *The Second American Revolution* (1982). His negligible contributions to the short story are represented in the rather dreary volume, *A Thirsty Evil: Seven Short Stories* (1956).

Achievements

Vidal has not received the badges by which artistic success is often measured—the Pulitzer Prize and the American Book Award—although his most recent collection of essays, *The Second American Revolution*, won the National Book Critics Circle Award. Certainly one of the greatest obstacles to an evaluation of Vidal's achievements is the enormous range of his work, the many roles he has played—novelist, playwright, screenwriter, literary critic, social critic, political commentator, television talk-show host, and occasional political candidate. He has expressed views on virtually everything from group sex to police brutality, from Eleanor Roosevelt to Alexander

Solzhenitsyn. Narrowing the focus to Vidal simply as novelist still presents a figure too various for those who, in Mitchell Ross's words, "like their art neat." On the contrary, says Ross in his 1978 book, *The Literary Politicians*, "Vidal has provided one of the best shows around . . . cashing in on the national predilection for preachers who combine entertainment with instruction." The confusion over Vidal, asserts Ross, is over his use of a "robust" first-person to personify here an eighteenth century American, there a fourth century Roman, here again a twentieth century denizen of Hollywood. Now and again, the "real" Vidal may peep out from behind that "I." Ross finds modern criticism largely "unprepared to handle a writer who speaks in the first person, but rarely about himself."

In all fairness, Vidal probably deserves a better assessment than he has generally received. His early novels—*Williwaw, In a Yellow Wood, The City and the Pillar*—are quite good for the work of an author in his early twenties. His novelistic production in the 1950's left a good deal to be desired, however, though his work in television drama during that period was, for the most part, excellent. Since the publication of *Julian* in 1964, Vidal's powers as a novelist have developed and strengthened, most notably in the companion pieces, *Burr* and *1876*. His satiric wit, his "auctorial audacity," as Robert F. Kiernan terms it, make his work, if not always profound, delightful to read.

As a cultural figure, Vidal would seem the very incarnation of the proverb, "Living well is the best revenge." He has managed to write well, too, well enough to allow him to live comfortably. Dr. Johnson once made the observation that those who live to please must please to live. Vidal has pleased enough readers to live very comfortably indeed. His critics would do well not to begrudge him that.

Biography

Gore Vidal was born Eugene Luther Vidal to Eugene and Nina Gore Vidal at the Cadet Hospital on the grounds of the United States Military Academy at West Point. Vidal's father, an instructor in aeronautics at the Academy, moved his family within a year of his son's birth to Washington, D.C., where he became successful in the growing aeronautics industry. As his fortunes improved, however, his marriage deteriorated; a divorce ensued in 1935. Young Vidal, in the meantime, spent more and more time with his maternal grandfather, the distinguished Oklahoma Senator Thomas P. Gore. It was in the Senator's extensive library that Vidal learned to love literature and history; when not reading on his own, he often read aloud to his blind grandfather. Under the Senator's tutelage, the boy gained an inside view of Washington politics. In retrospect, it was an auspicious beginning: literature, history, and politics would become the raw materials for Vidal's best work.

As the Depression took its numbing toll around him, Vidal attended exclusive private schools—St. Alban's in Washington, D.C., Los Alamos in New

Mexico, Phillips Exeter Academy in New Hampshire. He spent the summer of 1939 in England and on the Continent, studying briefly at Chateau de Mont Cel in France. By the time of his graduation from Phillips Exeter in 1943, he had changed his name to Gore Vidal and had pretty well decided to be a writer. He enlisted in the Army and was sent to Virginia Military Institute to study engineering. Perhaps as a result of his spending more time at work on a novel than at anything remotely related to engineering, Vidal was transferred to the Air Corps and stationed at Peterson Field, Colorado. His duties as a clerk gave him time to write, but he craved duty closer to the war. In 1944, he managed to pass an examination to become a Maritime Warrant Officer. Within a year, he was First Mate aboard a transport ship in the Aleutians; the climate did not at all agree with him, and he wound up in a military hospital in Van Nuys, California, for treatment of rheumatoid arthritis. He was subsequently transferred to Florida and thence to Mitchell Field, New York, where he sat out the war.

As military careers go, Vidal's had none of the glory befitting a young aristocrat. By the time of his discharge in 1946, however, he had completed his first two novels, *Williwaw* and *In a Yellow Wood*, published in 1946 and 1947, respectively. The success of these two novels gave Vidal the determination to leave an editorial position with E. P. Dutton and devote himself entirely to writing. From 1947 to 1949, he resided in Antigua, Guatemala; he was able to live cheaply there, and the surroundings provided plenty of material for his 1950 novel of Latin American revolution, *Dark Green, Bright Red*. In the meantime, he returned to Europe and made the acquaintance of a number of young literary figures—Paul Bowles, Christopher Isherwood, Tennessee Williams—as well as of the dying sage, George Santayana. Williams and Vidal became especially close, and spent a good deal of the spring and winter of 1948 touring Italy by jeep.

The same year, in the United States, Vidal's third novel, *The City and the Pillar*, was published. The book's frank treatment of homosexuality brought Vidal more notoriety than fame, but the novel was a considerable financial success. His next three novels, *The Season of Comfort*, *Dark Green, Bright Red*, and *A Search for the King*, did less well, complicating the author's life; on the strength of the success of his first three novels, Vidal had decided to return to the United States and bought a splendid house overlooking the Hudson River at Barrytown, New York. As the novels that followed *The City and the Pillar* failed to duplicate his earlier successes, Vidal slipped further and further into debt. In 1954, after attempting to satisfy a few of his creditors by writing a trio of detective novels under the pseudonym "Edgar Box," Vidal launched what he later termed "a kind of five-year plan: an all-out raid upon television, which could make me enough to live the rest of my life." The next two years were spent very productively. Television had not yet learned that it was not supposed to provide intelligent entertainment, and Vidal had the good fortune literally to cash in on this brief "Golden Age" of television drama, writing original plays and adaptations for such fine programs as *Studio One*, *Omnibus*, and *Philco Playhouse*. His original teleplays included *Visit to a Small Planet*, which later reappeared as a successful Broadway play, and, later still, as a motion picture. His adaptations of such works as Henry James's "The Turn of the Screw," William Faulkner's "Smoke" and "Barn Burning," and Ernest Hemingway's *A Farewell to Arms* (1929) were much acclaimed.

Vidal's television writing led to a 1956 contract with Metro-Goldwyn-Mayer to write scenarios and screenplays. In the next few years, he wrote screenplays for a number of films while gaining notice as a drama reviewer and playwright. In 1960, his political drama *The Best Man* began a long run on Broadway. Diversifying further, he somehow found the time to run, unsuccessfully, for Congress. Soon Vidal was offering his views on politics in articles in *Esquire*, and his views on the theater in *Partisan Review*.

In the midst of all the activity, Vidal did not entirely abandon the novel. In 1959, he began work on *Julian*, which he finally finished in 1963, along with the revision of *The City and the Pillar*. He spent a good deal of the next few years living in Paris and Rome, working on films, revising his earlier novels, *The Judgment of Paris* and *Messiah*, and, in 1966, finishing a new novel, *Washington, D.C.* In 1968, he published a revised version of *Dark Green, Bright Red*, along with the new novel, *Myra Breckinridge*. In the same year he campaigned vigorously for Democratic Presidential candidate Eugene McCarthy and won himself a place in television history when he and conservative columnist William F. Buckley nearly engaged in a fistfight during a national broadcast from the Republican Convention in Miami. This incident— Vidal referring repeatedly to Buckley as a "pro-crypto-Nazi" and Buckley threatening to "sock" this "queer" in his "goddamn face"—is the single most memorable public moment in Vidal's varied career. It is, in Robert F. Kiernan's words, "emblazoned on the public mind as a testament to high style run amok."

In the 1970's, Vidal turned his attention more fully back to the novel. Having sold his house on the Hudson in 1967, he continued to live primarily in Europe, purchasing a villa in Ravello, Italy, in 1972. Novels have appeared with great regularity since—*Burr* in 1973, *Myron*, a sequel to *Myra Breckinridge*, in 1974, and *1876*, a sequel to *Burr*, in 1976. When Italy revised its tax laws in 1976, Vidal was forced to spend a good part of the year away from Ravello; that year, he bought a home in Los Angeles, California. In 1978, *Kalki* was published, and in 1981, *Creation* appeared. Vidal currently lives in the Hollywood Hills of California, working at his accustomed variety of pursuits.

Analysis

In an essay for *The New York Times Book Review*, August 5, 1956, Gore

Vidal commented on the state of the novel: "After some three hundred years the novel in English has lost the general reader (or rather the general reader has lost the novel) and I propose that he will not again recover his old enthusiasm." Fortunately, this state of affairs did not dissuade Vidal from continuing as a novelist. Had he given up then, in 1956, he would be remembered as one more young writer who, discouraged by only a few initial successes, changed course and applied his energies elsewhere. In fact, he did continue, and, while many do not place him at the forefront of contemporary novelists, he has made a significant contribution to literature since 1956. Indeed, Vidal found during the 1960's the narrative voice that suits him best, and his work since then has been his best.

The diversity and range of Vidal's work make it difficult to present an analysis that is both brief and comprehensive. Perhaps the most profitable way to proceed is by looking first at the merits and flaws of his early novels, *Williwaw*, *In a Yellow Wood*, and *The City and the Pillar*, and then at Vidal's mature narrative skills as displayed in his first truly major novel, *Julian*, and in what is probably his most important novel to date, *Burr*.

Vidal's first novel, *Williwaw*, a tale of tedium and storms at sea along the Aleutian Chain during World War II, tersely interweaves the lives of seven men aboard a United States Army transport ship. The plot is connected to the actual fighting only by a thin line of military red tape; a smug West Pointer, Major Barkison, must deliver important papers to his superiors at Arunga and the ship must make the passage from its home base at Andrefski Bay under dangerous weather conditions, despite the objections of the skipper, Warrant Officer Evans. At the end of the voyage, the ship has narrowly escaped destruction in a violent storm (the *williwaw* of the title—"the Indian word for a big wind . . . that sweeps down suddenly from the mountains toward the sea") and a seaman has been drowned, knocked overboard during a quarrel with a rival for the affections of a certain prostitute. No one, however, cares enough about the dead man to make an inquiry, and he is simply reported as lost at sea; the documents the Major insisted on delivering to Arunga turn out to be typically trivial military paperwork.

It is commonplace to describe Vidal's flat, laconic style here as Hemingwayesque. Actually, Vidal achieves a prose that *looks* like Hemingway's, but that lacks Hemingway's close attention to rhythm and sound. For this reason, parts of *Williwaw* read too flatly. Vidal fares better in his decision to tell the story from the perspective of successive characters; he keeps the narrative third-person, but from chapter to chapter "looks over the shoulder" of different characters. His vivid description of the dreaded, inevitable storm is a high point, and it achieves even greater power through its juxtaposition with the jaded routines of military life with which the book opens and to which the action descends in the end. Not one of the great novels of men and the sea, *Williwaw* was nevertheless no mean achievement for a nineteen-year-old.

Vidal's second novel, *In a Yellow Wood*, takes its title from the Robert Frost lyric: "Two roads diverged in a yellow wood,/ And sorry I could not travel both/ And be one traveller. . . ." It is a novel about choice, about direction. Vidal's "traveller" is Robert Holton, a veteran of World War II working for a prominent New York brokerage firm. He is a young man on the threshold of a successful, if drab, career, and the choice that faces him in the "yellow wood" of one ordinary autumn day is whether to seek a secure career in the stock exchange or to pursue something better, something more adventurous.

The choice is presented at a routine late afternoon cocktail party. Holton's boss, Lawrence Heywood, offers Holton a promotion. The other "road" appears in the form of an unexpected meeting with Carla Bankton, a sensuous, beautiful woman with whom Holton had had a brief affair in Italy during the war; she has never quite forgotten him, and, the old flame rekindled, offers him an escape from the colorless life that is taking hold of him. They spend the night together, make passionate love, and Holton feels a peace, a security he has never known. It is not enough, though, to move him to take the risk of loving Carla, of going with her to Europe to begin a new life. The novel ends where it began; Robert Holton begins another day, only this time he has resolved the uneasiness that plagued him the previous day. "Everything had worked out nicely and soon he would be making more money and everyone he knew was happy."

In this tale of a sort of "Babbitt-Before-the-Fall," Vidal displays his ability to get below the surface of his characters, revealing the motivations of Holton, Carla, and the various supporting figures. The novel achieves a sharper focus through Vidal's observance of the classic unity of time—the action of the novel is compressed into the space of one day in the characters' interconnected lives. Additional unity derives from the controlling metaphor of the Frost poem. Vidal's art has its limits, however, and there are times when the third-person point of view fails to convince the reader that these are real human beings, not characters mechanically set in motion in the service of a metaphor. A certain amount of mechanical treatment is perhaps appropriate for those characters caught up in their varying degrees of business routine. It becomes bothersome in the case of Carla, who, in Vidal's attempt to counter the ennui of corporate existence, is revealed as too methodically bohemian.

Still, the novel was rather successful, and it establishes a theme—choice—to which Vidal would return more fully (and more successfully) in the delightfully inventive novel, *The Judgment of Paris*. Unlike Holton, the protagonist of the later book, Phillip Warren, chooses love over riches or power. In Robert Holton's defense, however, it is clear by the end of *In a Yellow Wood* that he was never so free to choose as Vidal may have led the reader to believe in the beginning. His final choice is less a product of free will than it is the avoidance of real choice in following the path of least resistance. He takes the well-worn path, not the one that for Frost's traveler had "the better claim/ Because it was grassy and wanted wear. . . ." In this light, Holton's choice, eminently practical though it is, is really a non-choice; love and happiness become "The Road Not Taken."

Vidal's third novel, *The City and the Pillar*, was even more successful than his first two, though it won him a good deal of notoriety, dealing as explicitly as it does with what was then a taboo subject: homosexuality. *The City and the Pillar* is the story of Jim Willard, a young man whose life has been shattered by his inability to reconcile his ideal of true human love with the real, earthly article. (There is much more at stake here than mere sexual preference.) His first sexual experience is with Bob Ford, a boyhood friend. In the years that follow, Jim comes to terms with his homosexuality and experiences more than one satisfying homosexual relationship as he drifts from job to job, from one town to another. His encounter with Bob—free, uninhibited, completely natural—remains his ideal, however, and all other relationships fall short of it. Finally, his and Bob's paths cross again in New York, but with disastrous consequences. Bob, married now to his high school sweetheart, has never considered his sexual experience with Jim to be more than a chance, youthful encounter, and he reacts with anger and disgust to Jim's attempt to seduce him. In a fit of frustration, Jim strangles his ideal lover, then makes his way to a bar, where he sits, drinking, mourning the death of his one and only dream. Vidal later revised this novel (a common practice with him); in the revision, Jim rapes Bob, a more satisfying conclusion that leaves the dream just as dead.

Aside from glimpses into the peculiarities of the homosexual subculture—the inevitable "types" of homosexuals, their haunts, their feelings about themselves—Vidal affords his readers the opportunity, rare in 1948, to see not only the abnormality of the homosexual but also his normalcy. Jim Willard is, in Robert F. Kiernan's words, "a mainstream character. . . . Willard is Everyman and yet he is *l' étranger*." He is likeable and recognizable. His crime is a crime of passion, and his tragedy, as the title suggests, is in looking back, as Lot's wife did. Jim is, in the end, little more than a pillar of salt, drunk, no longer able to feel, dead at the core. The narrative is packaged neatly, beginning as it does at the end, opening with Jim drinking in the bar and returning to that scene by way of a life's story not so much sordid as sad, not so much sad as gnawingly incomplete. *The City and the Pillar*, in spite of the criticism it has received for waxing too heavy-handedly symbolic, too moralistic, constitutes a more ambitious excursion into character than either of the previous books. For the first time, the reader has come to know Vidal's protagonist. It seems ironic that a novel about individuals whom many profess not to know, or even want to know, should succeed in this regard. Vidal makes Willard's life more a matter of broken dreams than of sexual peculiarity, and his strategy works, both in the original and the revised versions of the novel, though more persuasively in the latter.

In 1964, Vidal, after a six-novel apprenticeship, several years of television writing, and some initial success as a cultural commentator, published what is widely considered to be his first major novel and what remains perhaps his most ambitious study of character. *Julian* is the story of the fourth century Roman emperor, Julian the Apostate, so called because he attempted to replace Constantine's establishment of Christianity as the one true religion with a policy of tolerance for all religions, especially for the rites of the old Hellenistic gods whose place "the Galilean" had usurped.

The novel makes use of Vidal's most complex narrative framework; gone are the flat third-person narrations and simple framing devices of the early novels. Julian's story is told by means of a memoir in the Emperor's own hand, and commentary on the memoir in the form of letters between two shrewd old scholars, Priscus of Athens and Libanius of Antioch. No such documents exist, in fact, but all three narrators are historical figures, and Vidal carefully researched his characters and their time. The result was a tremendously vivid portrait of a period that saw the politics of the early Church in close, at times violent, competition with the politics of Caesar. Christianity won, but Vidal wants his readers to see that it need not have been that way. As he himself stated, "Just because the Church has endured such a long time does not mean that it was inevitable. Nothing is."

In *Julian*, Vidal exploits fully the potential of the first-person narrator. By adopting the seemingly more intimate "I," he is much better able to evoke another time and make it live. He shows that he can work with a much larger canvas than in any of his earlier works, giving his powers of invention free rein within a context that retains great respect for historical fact. Thus, Julian's youth, the taste for philosophy that led him to a scholarly life in contrast to the military career of his brother, Gallus, the events beyond his ambitions that thrust him to political prominence, his short reign as emperor before accepting bad advice to pursue a disastrous invasion of Persia, Julian's death at the hands of one of his own soldiers—all this is presented with great fidelity to history.

The modern reader should not be surprised that Vidal is concerned with more than the fourth century. What brings Julian to life, finally, is a firm insistence on the presence of the past. "We should never forget," observes Vidal, "that we are the descendants of the barbarians."

After *Julian*, Vidal's serious contributions to the novel have continued to develop the possibilities of the historical novel, and it is with his most impor-tant subsequent attempts in this form that any analysis of his work comes to rest. After his 1967 novel, *Washington, D.C.*, in which Vidal at last brought to the novel the inside angle on American politics that had been his legacy from his grandfather, Senator Gore, he combined his firsthand knowledge of contemporary politics with his fascination with the idiosyncracies of history. The result was *Burr*, probably his most significant achievement to date.

"It was typically perverse of Vidal," remarks Mitchell Ross, "to choose the least admired early American celebrity and present him as the central figure of the Founding Fathers' world." It is also typical of Vidal that his strategy works. Indeed, Aaron Burr, who killed Alexander Hamilton in a duel and who a few years later became involved in a secessionist plot, was an immensely unpopular figure in his day. Yet, as Vidal portrays him, through Burr's own memoirs and through the eyes of Charlie Schuyler, a clerk in Burr's New York law firm, he is a fascinating figure, comparable within Vidal's fiction only to the doomed Julian. Shrewd and adventurous, even at the age of seventy-seven, Burr has not been defeated by his reputation. The novel opens in 1833 with his marriage to the wealthy widow, Eliza Bowen Jumel. His motive is to raise enough money to buy a large part of the Texas territory and settle it. It is not an overly ambitious scheme for a man who shared the world not only with Hamilton and Thomas Jefferson, but also with the legendary figures such as Napoleon and Talleyrand. Typically, he quotes Talleyrand to make a point against the hopelessly dull General himself, George Washington: "Despite his [Washington's] incompetence, the gods always supported him in the end. I suspect Cromwell was right: the man who does not know where he is going goes farthest. Talleyrand used to tell me that for the great man all is accident." This is name-dropping of the first order.

The premise of *Burr*, like that of *Julian* and *Creation*, allows Vidal to introduce pseudohistorical material into his narrative in a brilliant blending of fact and fiction. Charlie Schuyler, his eye on a journalistic career, undertakes to write a political pamphlet proving that President Jackson's Vice President, Martin Van Buren, is Burr's bastard son. His purpose is not to harm Burr; in fact, he consoles himself with the fact that the pamphlet will be anonymous, and that the Colonel is well conditioned to bad press. The point is to discredit Van Buren and rob him of the chance to be President. In the course of this "undercover" assignment, Charlie manages to learn a great deal about Burr's life, both in conversation and in the form of a memoir that Burr, thinking his clerk is preparing a biography, gives him to read. The novel, then, is an interweaving of Charlie's narration and notes with Burr's own account of his career. In the course of his research, Charlie discovers that Van Buren is, indeed, Burr's illegitimate offspring, but is startled to learn after the Colonel's death that he is himself a son of Aaron Burr.

The plot, however, really is secondary to the enormous presence of Aaron Burr; the novel is distinguished by the vitality which Vidal is able to breathe into his portrait of the man, and by the new light he throws upon the storied fathers of the Republic. In an afterword to *Burr*, the author poses the question, "Why a historical novel and not history?" His answer is that the form allows one to be "as meticulous (or as careless!) as the historian and yet reserve the right not only to rearrange events but, most important, to attribute motive." There is, one suspects, more to it. Because the larger plot is already provided for him by history, Vidal is free to work at what he does best— delightful dialogue, ironic observation, the well-wrought detail. Then, too, there is the wide and careful reading that Vidal's brand of historical fiction demands, a task the author seems to enjoy as much as what he terms "the sullen, solitary joys of prose." Vidal has done his best work in the genre of the historical novel; it is for his work in this form that he is likely to be remembered if his fiction endures.

Major publications other than long fiction

SHORT FICTION: *A Thirsty Evil: Seven Short Stories*, 1956.

PLAYS: *Best Television Plays*, 1956 (edited); *Visit to a Small Planet and Other Television Plays*, 1957; *The Best Man: A Play About Politics*, 1960; *On the March to the Sea: A Southron Tragedy*, 1962 (also known as *Honor*); *Romulus: A New Comedy*, 1962; *Weekend: A Comedy in Two Acts*, 1968; *An Evening with Richard Nixon*, 1972.

NONFICTION: *Rocking the Boat*, 1962; *Reflections upon a Sinking Ship*, 1969; *Homage to Daniel Shays: Collected Essays 1952-1972*, 1972; *Matters of Fact and of Fiction: Essays 1973-1976*, 1977; *The Second American Revolution*, 1982.

Bibliography

Dick, Bernard F. *The Apostate Angel: A Critical Study of Gore Vidal*, 1974.
Kiernan, Robert F. *Gore Vidal*, 1982.
Ross, Mitchell S. *The Literary Politicians*, 1978.
Stanton, Robert J. *Gore Vidal: A Primary and Secondary Bibliography*, 1980.
_____ and Gore Vidal. *Views from a Window: Conversations with Gore Vidal*, 1980.
White, Ray Lewis. *Gore Vidal*, 1968.

Richard A. Eichwald

KURT VONNEGUT, JR.

Born: Indianapolis, Indiana; November 11, 1922

Principal long fiction

Player Piano, 1952; *The Sirens of Titan*, 1959; *Mother Night*, 1961; *Cat's Cradle*, 1963; *God Bless You, Mr. Rosewater*, 1965; *Slaughterhouse-Five*, 1969; *Breakfast of Champions*, 1973; *Slapstick*, 1976; *Jailbird*, 1979; *Deadeye Dick*, 1982.

Other literary forms

Although Kurt Vonnegut has published no lasting work outside the novel, his work in other forms may shed light on his recurring themes and preoccupations as a novelist. *Canary in a Cat House* (1961, reissued in 1968 as *Welcome to the Monkey House* with a small number of additions and deletions) is a collection of early short stories, most of them published originally in slick magazines. *Happy Birthday, Wanda June* (1970), a play, opened on Broadway in October, 1970; Vonnegut has also written a play for television, *Between Time and Timbuktu* (1972). *Wampeters, Foma, and Granfalloons* (1974) is a collection of essays, speeches, and reminiscences; in *Palm Sunday: An Autobiographial Collage* (1981), Vonnegut again gathered the fragments of his industry: letters, songs, funeral orations, plays, and short stories.

Achievements

All of Vonnegut's novels in some fashion address the question of how mankind can live in a world without God, a world in which man faces imminent apocalypse because his technology finally allows full range to his capacity for cruelty. Vonnegut looks at this fearful world view squarely and with humor; with laughter and hope, he satirizes the insecurities which feed such awful fear, because he sees how they might lead instead to kindliness, affection, love, faith (however half-cocked), and to a generally supportive family of man. Seen in the light of most postmodern fiction, Vonnegut's work thinly conceals a sustained, old-fashioned, and continually frustrated faith in the potential goodness of humanity.

Biography

Kurt Vonnegut, Jr. is a Midwesterner from Indiana, the descendant of German-Americans who came to the United States just before the Civil War and from whom he inherited his atheism, pacifism, and humor. His father was a well-known architect in Indiana, as was his grandfather; the elder Vonnegut held the distinction of being the first licensed architect in Indiana. Vonnegut's Midwestern family background left him a legacy of middle-class values that underlie many of the absurd fantasies he has created. Idealism striates his often pessimistic irony; a solid respect for family and individualism provides the basis for an advocacy of values which Benjamin Franklin could have endorsed: self-reliance, common sense, simplicity, and practicality.

The American dream came true for the Vonnegut family and then disappeared after World War I and the Depression. His father and mother lived well in a spacious house in the early phase of their marriage. On his mother's side, the Liebers ran a prosperous brewery, and on his father's side, an established architecture practice meant nannies, private schools, and eastern universities for the children. The war and the economy changed those patterns drastically. Prohibition ended profits for the brewery business, and a depressed economy crippled the building industry. The family's fortunes were never the same again. They moved to a smaller home, and Kurt, the youngest of the three children, went to public schools. A ruined career permanently saddened Vonnegut's father, and his mother took an overdose of sleeping tablets the night before Mother's Day in 1944; Vonnegut returned home on special leave from the army to find her dead. The combination of sardonic humor and depression was no stranger to the Vonnegut household in the years following World War I. Not surprisingly, the failure of the American dream is a recurring theme in Vonnegut's work.

Vonnegut's writing career began on the Shortbridge High School *Echo*, a daily secondary school paper. He found that he wrote easily and had his initial experience with a live and critical audience. Heading east, like many Midwestern writers, Vonnegut majored in biochemistry at Cornell University. There he worked on the university newspaper, the *Cornell Sun*, where his column "Well All Right" appeared regularly on the editorial page.

Satirical targets such as the Nazis, ROTC programs, and Charles A. Lindbergh lost their appeal after Pearl Harbor, and Vonnegut enlisted in the Army in 1942. He was taken prisoner in the Battle of the Bulge and ended up in Dresden making a diet supplement for pregnant women. Later—after the British and American bombings leveled the city—Vonnegut emerged from the safety of an underground meat storage cellar to dig for the charred and mutilated corpses. Because of Billy Pilgrim's similar experience in *Slaughterhouse-Five*, a number of critics have pointed to this experience as central to Vonnegut's development as an artist; Vonnegut, however, denies that this experience had the formative influence often attributed to it, although its impact was terrible and unforgettable.

Liberated by the Russians and awarded a Purple Heart, Vonnegut took leave of Europe in the spring of 1945 and married Jane Marie Cox, whom he had met originally in kindergarten in Indianapolis. He then began to study anthropology at the University of Chicago. His M.A. thesis, "Fluctuations Between Good and Evil in Simple Tales," struck his committee (unanimously) as less than scientific, and he left without a degree. Vonnegut saw more than the academic side of Chicago during this period, working as a police reporter in 1946 for the Chicago City News Bureau.

In 1947, Vonnegut found a job as research-laboratory publicist with the General Electric Corporation in Schenectady, New York, a job he was to hold until 1950. His experience at General Electric provided him with a perspective on technology and corporations that would appear again and again in his fiction, most notably in his first novel, *Player Piano*. The new world promised by corporate life symbolized for Vonnegut the antithesis of the middle-class, Midwestern, and family-centered world in which his values were rooted.

Leaving General Electric in 1950, Vonnegut moved to Provincetown, Massachusetts, to write full time. Here and in West Barnstable, he began writing commercially successful short stories for the *Saturday Evening Post, Ladies' Home Journal, Cosmopolitan, Collier's*, and other popular magazines. During this period, Vonnegut acquired a reputation as a science-fiction writer; the conventions of this genre were employed in a number of his early works, but his main emphasis was on the impact of science and technology on the lives of ordinary people. (Vonnegut has resisted being called a "science-fiction writer" even more forcefully than he has objected to the label "black humorist.") The majority of these early narratives are conventional in plot and point of view, and surprisingly traditional values underlie their satiric intent.

Despite his growing popularity, Vonnegut remained a minor paperback writer until the ferment of the 1960's. Almost overnight, he became a guru to worshipful readers on campuses all over America, who took to heart his combination of irony, hope, and a belief in man's basic innocence in the era of Vietnam, riots, and assassinations. Academic acknowledgement followed in the form of *The Vonnegut Statement* (1973), a series of essays on Vonnegut and his work. This collection included an interview with Robert Scholes, whose consideration of Vonnegut in his influential critical study, *The Fabulators* (1967), granted academic respectability not only to Vonnegut but also to a whole subgenre of contemporary fiction.

Recognition for Vonnegut's achievements has since proceeded at a rapid pace—Iowa Writer's Workshop, Guggenheim Fellowship, honorary degrees, lecture circuit, Harvard teaching. At present, he lives in New York City with his second wife, professional photographer Jill Krementz.

Analysis

Kurt Vonnegut's first novel, *Player Piano*, relates somewhat predictably a stock middle-class fable: man versus the machine and the work-success ethic. Paul Proteus, up-and-coming businessman at the Illium Works, glimpses the top of the executive ladder only to shudder in disgust. His old friend, Ed Finnerty, has already dropped out of the money-status-power world of technologyland. Also an engineer-manager, Finnerty has become an outlaw, and his visit turns Paul into a revolutionary. Proteus rejects the Fascist brave new world of automation and depersonalization and joins the Ghost Shirt Society. He leads a neo-Luddite armed rebellion against the system responsible for the indignity of labor and the individual's loss of autonomy and independence. Retelling this derivative tale of social determinism, Vonnegut openly acknowledged his debt to Aldous Huxley, yet the tone of this novel is distinctively Vonnegut's own: one can already find in *Player Piano* the narrative voice which later became famous.

Paul fails, of course, smashing the machines is a marvelous display of will and commitment, but it has virtually no effect on those whom it was meant to rescue from servitude. There will be no return to some preindustrial, agrarian golden age. Instead, the narrative voice directs the reader to love and laugh at Paul Proteus and his fruitless and naïve idealism. A mood of romantic nostalgia plays over Paul's efforts like the flute music in Arthur Miller's *Death of a Salesman* (1949). The description of his world and activity takes on the aspect of an extended joke, the mockery of nostalgia for a golden age characteristic of Vonnegut's fiction, in which the wish for a return to a prelapsarian innocence appears again and again, only to be laughed back into the unconscious as an attractive but outrageous illusion.

While Paul's passionate activity ultimately leads to the people's rebuilding the oppressive machines he has smashed in their behalf, the visiting Shah of Bratpur offers comic relief. The Shah's American interviews and commentary on technological advancement point out that the world Paul cannot save from itself is genuinely crazy. The cycle of romantic illusion leading to revolution, which in turn leads, once again, to the same depressing conditions that create romantic illusion in the first place, is a comic merry-go-round. Nothing, the novel argues, can save man from himself. Even so, man is both humorous and lovable in his bungling attempts to create a decent middle-class world. Society may be a huge player piano repeating mechanically the same tune, but the protean nature of human beings makes their strivings as heroic in Schenectady as in Troy.

Player Piano never achieved the popular or critical acclaim of Vonnegut's *Cat's Cradle* or *Slaughterhouse-Five*, but it expresses Vonnegut's humorous fatalism and middle-class morality in the form of a satiric fable which anticipates his later works both in style and in outlook. The authorial voice is kind, compassionate, and involved, but brutally honest. An ironic humor sustains stock characters and a deterministic perspective in an extended verbal cartoon which makes the reader laugh at the absurd without losing hope.

Vonnegut's second novel, *The Sirens of Titan*, was largely responsible for the misleading categorization of his work as "science fiction" which bedevils him to this day. After its entertaining parody of science fiction has delighted the reader, *The Sirens of Titan* has another level of meaning to yield. Winston

Niles Rumfoord, agent of the extraterrestrial Tralfamadorians, appears from the "chronosynclastic infundibulum" where he has seen the future. He summons to his estate Malachi Constant, the richest man in the United States, and tells him his future. Despite Constant's resistance, everything predicted comes true. He marries Rumfoord's wife, Beatrice, has a child, and survives a whirlwind of space adventures.

In *The Sirens of Titan*, Vonnegut's use of standard motifs from science fiction reflects his own interpretation of the role of the artist: "Writers are a means of introducing new ideas into the society, and also a means of responding symbolically to life." The world he creates in *The Sirens of Titan*, with its time and space travel, thought control, extraterrestrial creatures, and new religions (such as the Church of God the Utterly Indifferent) all serve to support Vonnegut's vision of a relativistic world. There is no providential design, no absolute answer to those searching for the meaning of life—nor is there any real need of them, either. Man looks outward when he should look inside. Thus, Vonnegut implies the world of Malachi and Beatrice is not categorically absurd: instead, it is their acceptance of Rumfoordian and Tralfamadorian interpretations of the meaning of their existence that distorts their lives and values. Once they see that, they are free of externally imposed ideologies.

Vonnegut's ethical prejudices are, once again, traditionally middle-class and sentimental. Beatrice and Constant eventually learn to live together and to love each other because they are there to be loved. Just being and loving whomever or whatever is there to be loved is preferable to finding solutions to the riddle of existence outside oneself in absurd and alien worlds and systems of belief.

In his next novel, *Mother Night*, Vonnegut once again focused on social determinism. *Mother Night* recounts the confessions of an American double agent, Howard W. Campbell, who masquerades as a Nazi during World War II. As an American writer married to a German woman, he is recruited by the Allies to help the war effort. Howard—a writer of modernized medieval romances—turns out to be more effective at simulating German partisanship than he is gratified by the encoded messages that he sends simultaneously to the Allies along with his anti-Semitic propaganda. He does not even know what valuable information he may be passing on. On the other hand, the compliments he receives for his passionate nationalism convince him that he is a master at creating hateful, militant enthusiasm. They also cause him to wonder about his own values and personality.

The vision in this confessional novel is much darker than the one in the earlier short stories and novels. It accents the vulnerability of individuals once they venture outside the inner circle of monogamous romantic love. (Campbell is working on a play called *Nation of Two* as the war breaks out, a story about a couple whose exclusive love insulates them from the insane world outside.)

Not even Vonnegut's standard sentimental, middle-class epigrams advocating love can rescue the dark vision of the fragility of selfhood in *Mother Night*. The confusion between authentic and false selves as well as between truth and lies remains despite his humor and usually benign vision. Vonnegut suggests that "We are what we pretend to be, so we must be careful about what we pretend to be." Exploring the borderlines between reality and fantasy, inauthenticity and genuineness, *Mother Night* is an unsettling, almost Manichaean vision of the contemporary world.

Vonnegut's fourth novel, and perhaps his finest, begins with a parody of the famous opening sentence of Herman Melville's *Moby Dick* (1851). "Call me Jonah," says John, the free-lance journalist and narrator of *Cat's Cradle*. Vonnegut's tone here is characteristically double-edged: he is both mocking the pretensions of any metaphysical quest and acknowledging that, like Melville, he is nevertheless searching for God, for meaning in the chaos of experience. Jonah is writing a book to be titled *The Day the World Ended*, and he lives to experience and survive Earth's destruction. His research takes him to the laboratory of the late Dr. Felix Hoenikker, where he uncovers the source of its ruination—inhuman science.

Hoenikker lays claim to the title of father of nuclear weapons. He is dangerously innocent, as well as being a bad father and an insensitive husband who leaves a tip for his wife under his breakfast plate. His brilliant search for scientific truth is untainted by any sense of the consequences of his discoveries. Before his death, Hoenikker invented *ice-nine*, a substance that could make water freeze at a higher temperature. One of his sons brings this discovery to Papa Monzano, the dictator of a Caribbean island, San Lorenzo, and it eventually destroys the world as well as the chief of state. The narrator and a character named Bokonon survive the holocaust of tornadoes and frozen oceans. In their good fortune lies the substance of Vonnegut's antiscientific hopeful vision. The narrator lives to do what Bokonon (the founder of a new religion on San Lorenzo) wished to do were he a younger man—to "write a history of human stupidity."

When Newt, the midget son of the mad scientist in the novel, complains of centuries of parental deception and laments: "'*No damn cat, and no damn cradle*,'" he has missed the point of the novel. Life is a complex web of serious games and elaborate fictions. People have to lie about reality in order to be able to live with it; people have to pretend to understand life, even when they do not.

The religion of Bokonon provides the moral center for Vonnegut's expression of faith in *Cat's Cradle*. The title page of the first of the *Books of Bokonon* cautions the potential believer: "Don't be a fool! Close this book at once! It is nothing but *foma*!" ("harmless untruths"). Bokononism is the invention of Lionel Boyd Johnson, a black Caribbean islander, with the help of his friend

Earl McCabe, a Marine Corps deserter. Together they arrange for the religion to be outlawed and for McCabe to play the role of evil dictator. The resulting persecution creates a tension that reinforces the people's faith and obscures their miserable poverty. They struggle with Bokonon for the good of their religion against the evil of political oppression. Out of potential chaos (a riot of limp string) a meaningful structure (a cat's cradle) is formed.

Followers of Bokononism believe in a deterministic world guided by the mysterious will of God. He organizes humanity into teams—*krass*—which do his will, yet never discover what they are doing. After surviving the destruction of San Lorenzo brought on by *ice-nine*, Bokonon himself considers taking these crystals, turning himself into a statue lying prone on a mountaintop and thumbing his nose at "You Know Who." However irreverent this gesture, it nevertheless acknowledges an inscrutable God in charge of the universe. Of the two kinds of cat's cradles—the scientific and the religious—Vonnegut admits a prejudice for the latter because it promotes love and commmunity rather than hate and destruction.

Next to *Slaughterhouse-Five*, *Cat's Cradle* is perhaps Vonnegut's most popular novel. It exposes the infantile nature of most human behavior without bitterness. Rather than creating the uneasy schizophrenic darkness evident in *Mother Night*, *Cat's Cradle* destroys the world yet sees in the survivors a capacity for humor, fellowship, and hope that gives Vonnegut's deterministic vision a benign hue. The satirist and the sentimental middle-class humanist are in finely tuned equilibrium in this novel.

God Bless You, Mr. Rosewater develops an extended (and comic) wish-fulfillment-fantasy of generosity—the other side of capitalist greed, the way a good (and poor) Christian knows he would act if *he* were wealthy. A visit to a science-fiction writer's convention reforms Eliot Rosewater; from the model president of a fabulously wealthy charitable foundation, Rosewater turns into an American missionary to the poor, the rejected, and the downtrodden. At times, as in the conclusion, *God Bless You, Mr. Rosewater* puts a white collar on the narrative voice in the guise of "Kilgore Trout," a science-fiction writer who frequently appears in Vonnegut's work: "Thanks to the example of Eliot Rosewater, millions upon millions of people may learn to love and help whomever they see." Like a 1930's movie, yet with an exceptionally elaborate plot, *God Bless You, Mr. Rosewater* follows Rosewater's development as the guardian angel of the poor: in the novel, Vonnegut's sentimentality runs out of control.

Eliot's father, Senator Rosewater, plays the selfish, laissez-faire villain to his son's mad frenzy of universal love. His arguments erode confidence in Eliot's starry-eyed kindness. When a plot involving fifty-seven fraudulent paternity suits against Eliot fails to strip him of the family fortune, Eliot turns it to his advantage with a magnanimous gesture worthy of a saint. He has papers drawn up that admit not only the children named in the paternity suit but also all the other children in Rosewater County are his. The inheritance is thus subdivided as Eliot proclaims: "Let their names be Rosewater from this moment on. And tell them that their father loves them no matter what they may turn out to be. And tell them . . . to be fruitful and multiply."

God Bless You, Mr. Rosewater is a humorous tour de force about the messianic madness inherent in generosity run amok. In it, Vonnegut reaches giddy heights of ironic doubt as he stretches the reader's belief in the gentler emotions to the breaking point of a sobering chuckle. Dancing precariously on the point of farce, the novel somehow manages to be more than indulgent—and uproariously funny—yet less effective than *Cat's Cradle* in artistic design. Despite it all, Vonnegut's message is clear: "God damn it, you've got to be kind."

Apocalypse appears, explicitly or otherwise, in most of Vonnegut's works. Some critics argue that in *Slaughterhouse-Five*, he was able at last to face and work through his traumatic experience of the senseless firebombing of Dresden, in which 135,000 to 200,000 innocent people were incinerated in a conflagration that destroyed a target of virtually no military value. Certainly for Vonnegut it provided an indelible image of annihilation. Perhaps the most effective way to read *Slaughterhouse-Five* is as an answer to the question: How can a human being live with imminent apocalypse?

To answer the question, Vonnegut creates Billy Pilgrim, the main character and *Doppelgänger* whom he claims was in Dresden with him. Billy's response to the holocaust is to escape into an imaginary kidnaping at the hands of the Tralfamadorians of *The Sirens of Titan*. There he finds a way to become "unstuck in time." From his captors, he learns how to see life as a continual present, one with neither past nor future. This existential determinism enables Billy to endure the trauma of Dresden and to live with the threat of apocalypse; it also makes him an ethical basket case (not necessarily a bad thing in Vonnegut's fiction, which sees purpose and meaning so often twisted into justification for cruelty). Still, Billy drifts off into a world outside of time, without values or reason, a condition in which things just are and nothing can be done about them. The Tralfamadorians teach him that there is no free will and that to behave as if there were is absurd. This trick of the imagination works reasonably well for Billy, even though he spends his life on the verge of tears and potential breakdown.

The implications of this escapist philosophy are as discomforting as they are comfortable for Billy, especially since he, a Christ-figure, attempts to communicate his visions publicly. Like Eliot Rosewater before him—whom he meets in a mental institution in *Slaughterhouse-Five*—Billy is considered insane. Mad or not, he preaches a disquieting indifference, a chilling form of psychic withdrawal. Vonnegut's point in this escapist fantasy may lie in what Eliot Rosewater tells the psychiatrist in *Slaughterhouse-Five*: "I think you are going to have to come up with a lot of wonderful lies, or people just aren't going to want to go on living." Billy reflects man's infinite capacity for imaginative lying, a gift some writers use to keep characters such as Eliot Rosewater alive and functioning. Their fictions, like Pilgrim's, can mute the terror of apocalypse, preserving and even creating happy moments, at least until something better comes along. Both Bokonon's final gesture and the Alcoholics Anonymous pledge in *Slaughterhouse-Five* (which does not work for Billy) argue that Vonnegut is not ruling out any possibilities.

After *Slaughterhouse-Five*, Vonnegut began a period in which he seemed to be searching for direction; frequently, he merely repeated himself. *Breakfast of Champions*, perhaps his weakest novel, is marred not only by overfamiliarity but also by the author's cynical attitude toward his own work, a new note in Vonnegut's fiction. *Slapstick*, although it covers familiar Vonnegut territory, has more to offer. The novel begins as the last president of the United States, sitting in a jungle clearing on Manhattan Island, adds pomp to his garb (a purple toga made from the Americana Hotel draperies) despite his imminent unemployment). An incurably optimistic genetic mutation ("Neanderthaloid"), Dr. Wilber Daffodil-11 Swain has become president with his "Lonesome No More" campaign. He would change a nation of schizoid isolatoes back into a tribal society of artificially extended families arranged by a computer.

The United States has managed to deplete its own resources with an all-consuming greed. America is reduced to a state of feudal renaissance ("Kingdom of Michigan" and "Duke of Oklahoma"), a hopeless paranoia (the Chinese "Green Death"), and crackbrained hope (the Church of Jesus Christ the Kidnapped). A more hilarious variation on the determinism of *Player Piano*, *The Sirens of Titan*, and *Mother Night*, *Slapstick* tells many of the familiar jokes again as an encore for Vonnegut aficionados.

Vonnegut has said that *Slapstick* was "the closest I will ever come to writing an autobiography." It is in fact a kind of autobiographical fantasy. Like the clown prince recently ascended to the throne, Vonnegut identifies with President Daffodil-11 Swain. He, too, has achieved a variation on the American dream: he is another kind of monarch in the shadow kingdom of popular culture. His success makes him the last of the line, and he faces death before he completes his story. The tale of the cockeyed, optimistic, middle-class king whose sentimental "Lonesome No More" platform will surely fail is a way of freeing himself of the moral responsibility which the popularity of his fiction has thrust upon him. He leaves the lecture circuit, frees his characters, and mocks and dismisses himself. So much for the family of Vonnegut freaks. As slapstick, the comic exaggerations are delightful, but as autobiography, they are chilling indeed.

Jailbird departs very little from Vonnegut's established style and values, although fantasy is fused more explicitly with American social reality. Like all Vonnegut plots, that of *Jailbird* has enough convolutions to suggest the arabesque design of an eastern temple. Equally characteristic is the tight hold on plot and the underlying division of beginning, middle, and end.

Walter Starbuck, the son of a chauffeur, is the recipient of a Harvard education after his father's guilty millionaire boss launders his name from Stankiewicz to a WASP moniker which suggests the preeminent value of money. Walter manages to alienate accidentally his benefactor during a brief flirtation with Communism, ruin the careers of friends whom he naïvely betrays to pre-McCarthyite Red-scare investigators, and serve two jail terms as unwitting accessory to treasonous and illegal activity (Watergate money is found in the office which President Richard Nixon assigned to him).

While his bumbling ineptitude is being established, a grab bag of American injustices trail at his side: Nixon, Watergate, Nicola Sacco and Bartolomeo Vanzetti, Alger Hiss, violent labor disputes, and Kent State. Should the reader fail to connect the fiction to life, Vonnegut includes an index of more than two hundred names, including Adam and Eve as well as Jesus Christ, Joan of Arc, Robert Redford, and Jane Fonda. So much for the American dream. After Walter trades places with his father's boss (in the back of Heinrich Himmler's chauffeur-driven Mercedes in occupied Germany), he fumbles away his life until his second release from prison at age sixty-four.

Vonnegut then allows his hero to take part in a fantasy of social justice. Walter is finally reunited with his first lover, Mary Kathleen O'Looney, once an eighteen-year-old volunteer on his radical newspaper at Harvard. Mary Kathleen has never given up her romantic dream of warmhearted socialism. She is busily acquiring control of corporate America with capital from an inherited fortune: RAMJAC is her metacorporation. Disguised as a ragged baglady, O'Looney plans to give the corporations she has acquired back to "the people," to whom she claims, they rightfully belong. Her plan fails, as any Vonnegut reader might have guessed. She dies unknown in her tawdry disguise, and Walter covers up her departure in order to keep the dream going, and to have some fun of his own. Turning a profit with his share of the RAMJAC empire with the pride of a capitalist child playing the board game Monopoly, Walter is discovered and jailed once again. RAMJAC goes on the auction bloc, and corporate America proceeds with business as usual.

In *Deadeye Dick*, published in 1982, Vonnegut resorts once again to clever storytelling in spinning the tale of Rudolph Waltz, born in Midland City, Ohio, to a wealthy and eccentric father, Otto, who teaches classes in gun safety to Midland City's youth. Rudy, at the age of 12, fires a round from one of his father's rifles and accidentally kills a pregnant woman living several blocks away. He is jailed and the ensuing lawsuits financially ruin his father.

Rudy, who has come to be known by the mocking nickname that gives the book its title, emerges from prison in late adolescence. Torn between professional writing and business (Otto's choice of career for him), he earns a degree in pharmacology while living at home and cooking for his parents, then goes to work at Schramm's Drugstore. He also writes a play, which flops on Broadway. His culinary interests lead him to move to Port-au-Prince, Haiti, where he becomes chef and co-owner of a prestigious hotel. From this distant haven, he learns of his parents' death in an Ohio snowstorm. Not long after, an exploding neutron bomb destroys the entire population of his hometown.

Deadeye Dick is vintage Vonnegut—comic, clever, original. Yet Vonnegut seems to have drifted into the role of stand-up comedian, circling rather than going in a new direction. In spite of the fundamental optimism and hope for humanity that underlies his work, he continues to make fun of things. *Deadeye Dick*, like other Vonnegut novels, too often merely seems to echo his earlier works.

In this naturalistic fabulation, Vonnegut joins the tradition of Stephen Crane, Frank Norris, and Theodore Dreiser, indicting capitalist greed in his own tale of Horatio Alger as a naïve ex-con, of the American dream with its heart in the right place, but its body too often in prison. "The economy is a thoughtless weather system—and nothing more. Some joke on the people, to give them such a thing." *Jailbird*, the best of Vonnegut's later fiction, lacks the complex ironic tension of *The Sirens of Titan*, *Cat's Cradle*, and *Slaughterhouse-Five*, but in it the writer reshuffles his plots with engaging verve.

Major publications other than long fiction
SHORT FICTION: *Canary in a Cat House*, 1961; *Welcome to the Monkey House*, 1968.
PLAYS: *Happy Birthday, Wanda June*, 1970; *Between Time and Timbuktu*, 1972.
NONFICTION: *Wampeters, Foma, and Granfalloons*, 1974; *Palm Sunday: An Autobiographical Collage*, 1981.

Bibliography
Hudgens, Betty L. *Kurt Vonnegut, Jr.: A Checklist*, 1972.
Klinkowitz, Jerome, and Donald Lawler, eds. *Vonnegut in America*, 1977.
Klinkowitz, Jerome, and John Somer, eds. *The Vonnegut Statement*, 1973.
Lundquist, James. *Kurt Vonnegut*, 1977.
Olderman, Raymond M. *Beyond the Waste Land*, 1972.
Pieratt, Asa B., and Jerome Klinkowitz. *Kurt Vonnegut, Jr.: A Descriptive Bibliography and Annotated Secondary Checklist*, 1974.
Reed, Peter J. *Kurt Vonnegut, Jr.*, 1972.
Schatt, Stanley. *Kurt Vonnegut, Jr.*, 1976.
Scholes, Robert. *The Fabulators*, 1967.
Tanner, Tony. *City of Words*, 1971.

Ronald T. Curran

JOHN WAIN

Born: Stoke-on-Trent, England; March 14, 1925

Principal long fiction

Hurry on Down, 1953; *Living in the Present*, 1955; *The Contenders*, 1958; *A Travelling Woman*, 1959; *Strike the Father Dead*, 1962; *The Young Visitors*, 1965; *The Smaller Sky*, 1967; *A Winter in the Hills*, 1970; *The Pardoner's Tale*, 1979.

Other literary forms

A complete man of letters, John Wain has published short stories, poetry, drama, many scholarly essays, and a highly respected biography in addition to his novels. Wain's writing reflects his determination to speak to a wider range of readers than that addressed by many of his modernist predecessors; it reflects his faith in the common reader to recognize and respond to abiding philosophical concerns. These concerns include his sense of the dignity of human beings in the midst of an oftentimes cruel, indifferent, cynical world. His concern is with a world caught up in time, desire, and disappointment.

Most significant among Wain's writings other than novels are three collections of short stories—*Nuncle and Other Stories* (1960); *Death of the Hind Legs and Other Stories* (1966); and *The Life Guard* (1971)—and eight volumes of poetry: *Mixed Feelings* (1951); *A Word Carved on a Sill* (1956); *Weep Before God: Poems* (1961); *Wildtrack: A Poem* (1965); *Letters to Five Artists* (1969); *The Shape of Feng* (1972); *Feng: A Poem* (1975); and *Poems: 1949-1979* (1981). Wain has also published criticisms which communicates a sensitive and scholarly appreciation of good books. Readers should pay particular attention to *Preliminary Essays* (1957); *Essays on Literature and Ideas* (1963); *A House for the Truth: Critical Essays* (1972); *Professing Poetry* (1977); and his autobiography, *Sprightly Running: Part of an Autobiography* (1962). Of all his nonfiction, however, most readers believe that *Samuel Johnson: A Biography* (1974) is his best and most lasting work. In this monumental biography, many of the commitments reflected in Wain's other writings come through clearly and forcefully.

Achievements

To understand something of Wain's uniqueness as a novelist, the reader must look back at least to the end of World War II. For about ten years after the war, established writers continued to produce successfully. Men such as Aldous Huxley, Graham Greene, Evelyn Waugh, C. P. Snow, and Anthony Powell had made their reputations before the war and continued to be the major literary voices at that time. Most of them had been educated in public schools, then at Oxford or Cambridge, and were from upper- or upper-middle-class origins. Their novels were likely to center around fashionable London or some country estate. Often they confined their satire to the intellectual life and the cultural as well as social predicaments of the upper-middle class.

A combination of events in postwar England led to the appearance of another group of writers, soon referred to by literary journalists as the "Angry Young Men." Among these writers was John Wain, who, along with Kingsley Amis, John Braine, John Osborne, Angus Wilson, Alan Sillitoe, and others, turned away from technical innovations, complexity, and the sensitive, introspective protagonist to concentrate on concrete problems of current society. Thus, in the tradition of the eighteenth century novel, Wain fulfills most effectively the novelist's basic task of telling a good story. His novels move along at an even pace; he relies upon a simple, tightly constructed, and straightforward plot; clarity; good and bad characters; and a controlled point of view. The reader need only think of James Joyce and Franz Kafka, and the contrast is clear. What most of Wain's novels ask from the reader is not some feat of analysis, but a considered fullness of response, a readiness to acknowledge, even in disagreement, his vision of defeat.

Wain's typical protagonist is essentially an "antihero," a man at the mercy of life. Although sometimes capable of aspiration and thought, he is not strong enough to carve out his destiny in the way he wishes. Frequently, he is something of a dreamer, tossed about by life, and also pushed about, or at least overshadowed, by the threats in his life. Wain's Charles Lumley (*Hurry on Down*) and Edgar Banks (*Living in the Present*) bear the marks of this type. Often there is discernible in his characters a modern malaise, a vague discontent, and a yearning for some person or set of circumstances beyond their reach. Sometimes, this sense of disenchantment with life as it is becomes so great that the individual expresses a desire not to live at all, as Edgar Banks asserts in *Living in the Present* and as Gus Howkins declares in *The Pardoner's Tale*.

Wain is also accomplished in his creation of place and atmosphere. In *Strike the Father Dead*, he fully captures the grayness of a London day, the grayness of lives spent under its pall, the grayness of the people who wander its streets. When Wain describes an afternoon in which Giles Hermitage (*The Pardoner's Tale*) forces himself to work in the subdued light at home; when Arthur Geary (*The Smaller Sky*) walks the platforms at Paddington Station; when Charles Lumley walks in on a literary gathering; when Roger Furnivall (*A Winter in the Hills*) makes his way home through the Welsh countryside—at such moments the reader encounters Wain's mastery of setting and atmosphere.

The themes communicated through Wain's novels are, like his method, consistent. It is clear that he sees the eighteenth century as a time of dignity, pride, and self-sufficiency—qualities lacking in the twentieth century. Like Samuel Johnson, Wain defends the value of reason, moderation, common sense, moral courage, and intellectual self-respect. Moreover, his fictional themes of the dignity of the human being, the difficulty of survival in the modern world, and the perils of success have established him principally as a moralist concerned with ethical issues. In later works, the value of tradition, the notion of human understanding, and the ability to love and suffer become the chief moral values. In all his novels, he is primarily concerned with the problem of defining the moral worth of the individual. For all these reasons, Wain is recognized as a penetrating observer of the human scene.

One final point should be noted about Wain's capacities as a novelist. Clearly, the spiritual dimension is missing in the world he describes; and yet, there is frequently the hint or at least the possibility of renewal, which is the closest Wain comes to any sort of recognized affirmation. Charles Lumley, Joe Shaw, Jeremy Coleman, and Roger Furnivall are all characters who seem to be, by the end of their respective stories, on the verge of rebirth of a sort, on the threshold of reintegration and consequent regeneration. In each case, this renewal depends on the ability of the individual to come to terms with himself and his situation, to confront and accept at a stroke past, present, and future, and to accept and tolerate the contradictions inherent in all three. Wain's sensitive response to the tragic aspects of life is hardly novel, but his deep compassion for human suffering and his tenderness for the unfortunate are more needed than ever in an age when violence, brutality, and cynicism are all too prevalent.

Biography

Although his world is that of the twentieth century, John Wain is very much an eighteenth century man. He delights in pointing out that he and Samuel Johnson were born in the same district ("The Potteries") and in much the same social milieu; that he attended the same university as Johnson (Oxford, where he served from 1973-1978 as Professor of Poetry); that he has known, like Johnson, the Grub Street experiences and "the unremitting struggle to write enduring books against the background of an unstable existence." What chiefly interests the critic in surveying Wain's formative years are the reasons for his increasingly sober outlook. Wain's autobiography, *Sprightly Running*, remains the best account of his formative years as well as offering engaging statements of many of his opinions. In it, the reader finds some of the profound and lasting effects on Wain's writing of his childhood, his adolescence, and his years at Oxford.

John Barrington Wain was born on March 14, 1925, in Stoke-on-Trent, Staffordshire, an industrial city given over to pottery and coal mining. Here, as in other English cities, a move upward in social status is signaled by a move up in geographical terms. Therefore, the Wain family's move three years later to Penkhull—a manufacturing complex of kilns and factories and, incidentally, the setting for Wain's third novel, *The Contenders*—marked a step up into the middle-class district.

From infancy, Wain had a genuine fondness for the countryside. He immersed himself in the sights and sounds and colors of rural nature, all of which made an impression on him that was distinctive as well as deep. This impression developed into an "unargued reverence for all created life, almost a pantheism." On holidays, he and his family traveled to the coast and hills of North Wales—an association which carried over into his adult years, when, at thirty-four, he married a Welsh woman. His feeling for Wales—for the independent life of the people, the landscape and mountains, the sea, the special light of the sun—is recorded in *A Winter in the Hills*. Here and elsewhere is the idea that nature is the embodiment of order, permanence, and life. Indeed, the tension between the nightmare of repression in society and the dream of liberation in the natural world is an important unifying theme throughout Wain's work.

The experience of living in an industrial town also left an indelible imprint upon Wain's mind and art. His exposure to the lives of the working class and to the advance of industrialism gave him a profound knowledge of working people and their problems, which he depicts with sympathy and humanity in his fiction. Moreover, Wain's experiences at Froebel's Preparatory School and at Newcastle-under-Lyme High School impressed on him the idea that life was competitive and "a perpetual effort to survive." He found himself surrounded and outnumbered by people who resented him for being different from themselves. His contact with older children, schoolboy bullies, and authoritative schoolmasters taught Wain that the world is a dangerous place. These "lessons of life" were carried into his work. The reader finds in Wain's fiction a sense of the difficulty of survival in an intrusive and demanding world. The worst of characters is always the bully, and the worst of societies is always totalitarian. Beginning with *Hurry on Down*, each of Wain's published novels and stories is concerned in some way with the power and control that some people seek to exercise over others.

To cope with these injustices as well as with his own fears and inadequacies during his early years, Wain turned to humor, debate, and music. For Wain, the humorist is above all a moralist, in whose hands the ultimate weapon of laughter might conceivably become the means of liberating mankind from its enslavement to false ideals. Thus, his mimicry of both authorities and students was used as the quickest way to illustrate that something was horrible or boring or absurd. In both *Hurry on Down* and *The Contenders*, the heroes use mockery and ridicule to cope with their unjust world.

Wain's interest in jazz has also influenced his personal and literary development. He has spoken and written often of his lifelong enthusiasm for the trumpet playing of Bill Coleman; and he admits that Percy Brett, the black jazz musician in *Strike the Father Dead*, was created with Coleman in mind. Accompanying this interest was a growing interest in serious writing and reading. Unlike many youths, Wain did not have to endure the agonizing doubt and indecision of trying to decide what he wanted to do in life. By the age of nine, he knew: he wanted to be an author. He began as a critically conscious writer who delighted in "pastiche and parody for their own sake." Then, as now, he found most difficult the task of maintaining a steady plot line. Wain matched his writing with voracious reading. His early interest in the novels of Charles Dickens, Tobias Smollett, Daniel Defoe, and others in the tradition of the English novel influenced his later literary style. Like these predecessors, Wain approaches his characters through the conventional narration of the realist, and his concerns are social and moral.

The second major period in Wain's life occurred between 1943, when he entered St. John's College, Oxford, and 1955, when he resigned his post as lecturer in English at Reading University to become a full-time writer. Two friends made in his Oxford period especially influenced his writing. One was Philip Larkin, whose "rock-like determination" continues to be an inspiring example to Wain. The other friend was Kingsley Amis, whose work on a first novel inspired Wain to attempt writing a novel in his spare time. Wain wrote his first novel, not particularly because he wished to be a novelist, but to see if he could write one that would get into print. In 1953, Frederick Warburg accepted *Hurry on Down*, and its unexpected success quickly established Wain as one of Britain's promising new writers.

Wain's exhilarating experience with his first book was, however, poor preparation for the sobering slump that followed. Ill-health, divorce proceedings, and the drudgery of a scholar's life pushed him into a crisis of depression and discouragement. He tried to climb out of this crisis by leaving the university for a year and retreating to the Swiss Alps. There, he let his imagination loose on his own problems. The result was *Living in the Present*, a depressing book of manifest despair and disgust. Out of this period in his life, Wain developed a profound awareness of love and loneliness, union and estrangement. The essential loneliness of human beings, and their more or less successful attempts to overcome their loneliness by love, become major themes in his later fiction.

Analysis

As a novelist, John Wain has been described as a "painfully honest" writer who is always, to an unusual degree, writing autobiography. His own fortunes and his emotional reactions to these fortunes are, of course, transformed in various ways. His purpose is artistic, not confessional, and he shapes his material accordingly. As Wain himself states, this intention is both pure and simple: to express his own feelings honestly and to tell the truth about the world he knows. At his best—in *Hurry on Down*, *Strike the Father Dead*, *A Winter in the Hills*, and *The Pardoner's Tale*—Wain finds a great many ways to convey the message that life is ultimately tragic. Human beings suffer; life is difficult; the comic mask conceals anguish. Only occasionally is this grim picture relieved by some sort of idealism, some unexpected attitude of unselfishness or tenderness. What is more, in all of his writings Wain is a thoughtful, literate man coming to terms with these truths in a sincere and forthright manner.

In his first novel, *Hurry on Down*, Wain comically perceives the difficulties of surviving in a demanding, sometimes fearful world. Detached from political causes and progress of his own life, the hero is a drifter, seeking to compromise with or to escape from such "evils" as class lines, boredom, hypocrisy, and the conventional perils of success. Although the novel carries a serious moral interest, Wain's wit, sharp observations, and inventiveness keep the plot moving. His comedy exaggerates, reforms, and criticizes to advocate the reasonable in social behavior and to promote the value and dignity of the individual.

In *Strike the Father Dead*, Wain further extends himself with a work more penetrating than anything he has written before. Not only is it, as Walter Allen said, a "deeply pondered novel," but it is also a culmination of the promises inherent in Wain's earlier works. Plot, theme, character, and setting are integrated to tell the story of a son who breaks parental ties, thereby freeing himself to make his own way in life as a jazz pianist. Pointing to the foibles of his fellow man and probing the motives of an indignant parent, Wain's wit and sarcastic humor lighten this uncompromising study of the nonconformist's right to assert his nonconformity.

Finally, Wain's most recent novels—*A Winter in the Hills* and *The Pardoner's Tale*—continue and elaborate upon many of the central themes of his fiction, but they surpass the earlier novels in richness and complexity. Both novels exhibit, far more than do his earlier writings, an interest in the tragic implications of romantic love; a greater complexity in character development allows Wain to portray convincingly men whose loneliness borders on self-destruction. Each novel is not simply another story of isolation or spiritual desolation, although it is that. Each hero is cast into a wasteland, and the novel in a sense is the story of his attempts to find the river of life again, or possibly for the first time. One of the themes that develops from this period in Wain's career is that personal relationships are the most important and yet most elusive forces in society.

Like Kingsley Amis's *Lucky Jim* (1954), John Braine's *Room at the Top* (1957), and Alan Sillitoe's *Saturday Night and Sunday Morning* (1958), Wain's first novel probes tellingly into a central problem of the 1950's. Its hero—Charles Lumley—is a creation of the postwar British Welfare State. As a disconnected youth on his own for the first time, he feels that neither his upbringing nor his university education has prepared him for making a satisfactory living. Because he has a driving obsession to avoid the phony in life, he detests the world he sees and rebels against whatever is bourgeois and commonplace.

Hurry on Down has the characteristic features of the picaresque novel: A series of short and often comic adventures loosely strung together; an opportunistic and pragmatic hero who seeks to make a living through his wits; and satirical characterization of stock figures rather than individualized portraits. Unlike the eighteenth century picaro, however, who is often hardhearted, cruel, and selfish, Wain's central character is a well-intentioned drifter who compromises enough to live comfortably. His standby and salvation is a strong sense of humor that enables him to make light of much distress and disaster. Lumley's character is revealed against the shifting setting of the picaresque world and in his characteristic response to repeated assaults on his fundamental decency and sympathy for others. He remains substantially the same throughout the novel; his many roles—as window cleaner, delivery driver, chauffeur, and the like—place him firmly in the picaresque tradition. Lumley's versatility and adaptability permit Wain to show his character under a variety of circumstances and in a multiplicity of situations.

Lumley's character is established almost immediately with the description of his conflict with the landlady in the first chapter. The reader sees him as the adaptable antihero who tries to control his own fate, as a jack of all trades, a skilled manipulator, an adept deceiver, an artist of disguises. Wain stresses Lumley's ingenuity rather than his mere struggle for survival; at the same time, he develops Lumley's individual personality, emphasizing the man and his adventures. The role that Lumley plays in the very first scene is one in which he will be cast throughout the story—that of a put-upon young man engaged in an attempt to cope with and outwit the workaday world.

The satire is developed through the characterization. Those who commit themselves to class—who judge others and define themselves by the class structure—are satirized throughout the novel. Surrounding the hero is a host of lightly sketched, "flat," stock figures, all of whom play their predictable roles. These characters include the proletarian girl, the American, the landlady, the entrepreneur, the middle-class couple, and the artist. In this first novel, Wain's resources in characterization are limited primarily to caricature. The comedy functions to instruct and entertain. Beneath the horseplay and high spirits, Wain rhetorically manipulates the reader's moral judgment so that he sympathizes with the hero. In the tradition of Tobias Smollett and Charles Dickens, Wain gives life to the grotesque by emphasizing details of his eccentric characters and by indicating his attitude toward them through the selection of specific bodily and facial characteristics.

Wain has also adopted another convention of eighteenth century fiction: the intrusive author. The active role of this authorial impresario accounts for the distance between the reader and the events of the novel; his exaggerations, his jokes, and his philosophizing prevent the reader from taking Lumley's fate too seriously. In later novels, Wain's authorial stance changes as his vision deepens.

Any discussion of comic technique in *Hurry on Down* leads inevitably to the novel's resolution. Ordinarily, a reader does not like to encounter "perfect" endings to novels; nevertheless, he is not put off by the unrealistic ending to this novel because he knows from the beginning that he is reading a comic novel which depends upon unrealistic exaggeration of various kinds. Elgin W. Mellown was correct when he called the novel "a pastiche: Walter Mitty's desire expressed through the actions of the Three Stooges—wish fulfillment carried out through outrageous actions and uncharacteristic behavior." The reader feels secure in the rightness of the ending as a conclusion to all of the comic wrongness that has gone on before.

The plot of Wain's fifth novel, *Strike the Father Dead*, is arranged in an elaborate, seven-part time-scheme. Parts 1 and 6 occur sometime late in 1957 or early in 1958; Part 2 takes place in the immediate prewar years; and the other divisions follow chronologically up to the last, which is set in 1958. The scene shifts back and forth between a provincial university town and the darker, black-market-and-jazz side of London, with a side trip to Paris.

Wain narrates the story from the points of view of four characters. The central figure, Jeremy Coleman, revolts against his father and the academic establishment in search of self-expression as a jazz pianist. Alfred Coleman, Jeremy's father and a professor of classics, is an atheist devoted to duty and hard work. Eleanor, Alfred's sister and foster mother to Jeremy, is devoted to Jeremy and finds comfort in innocent religiosity. Percy Brett, a black American jazz musician, offers Jeremy his first real parental leadership. Like Ernest Pontifex, in Samuel Butler's *The Way of All Flesh* (1903), Jeremy escapes from an oppressive existence; he has a passion for music, and once he has the opportunity to develop, his shrinking personality changes.

Strike the Father Dead marks a considerable advance over *Hurry on Down* in the thorough rendering of each character and each scene. By employing a succession of first-person narrators, Wain focuses attention more evenly on each of the figures. The result is that the reader comes away knowing Jeremy even better, because what he learns about him comes not only from his own narration, but also from other sources as well. Inasmuch as there are three central characters, *Strike the Father Dead* represents a larger range for Wain. Each interior monologue is a revelation; the language is personal, distinctive, and descriptive of character.

In the manner of a *Bildungsroman*, *Strike the Father Dead* is also a novel which recounts the youth and young manhood of a sensitive protagonist who is attempting to learn the nature of the world, discover its meaning and pattern, and acquire a philosophy of life. Setting plays a vital role in this odyssey. The provincial and London backgrounds and the accurate rendering of the language make the novel come alive. *Strike the Father Dead* moves between two contemporary worlds—a world of rigidity and repression, represented by Alfred, and a world of creativity, international and free, represented by London and Paris. The first world oppresses Jeremy; the second attracts and draws him. He dreams about it and invents fictions about it. Central to this new world is Jeremy's love of jazz. For him, the experience of jazz means beauty, love, life, growth, freedom, ecstasy—the very qualities he finds missing in the routine, disciplined life of Alfred.

Although *Strike the Father Dead* tells the story of a British young man who becomes successful, the success is to a certain extent bittersweet. In his triumphs over his home circumstances, Jeremy loses something as well. There are various names given to it: innocence; boyhood; nature; the secure, predictable life at home. The world beyond the academic life waits for Jeremy, and he, unknowingly, does his best to bring it onstage. With such a life comes a developing sense of injustice, deprivation, and suffering. These concerns become focal points in Wain's subsequent novels, as he turns toward the impulse to define character and dilemma much more objectively and with greater moral responsibility.

With its setting in Wales, *A Winter in the Hills* marked a departure from Wain's first six novels, all of which were centered in England. The story expresses, perhaps more comprehensively than any other, Wain's feelings for the provincial world, its cohesion and deep loyalties, and its resistance to innovation from outside. Furthermore, it is Wain's most ambitious presentation of the sadness of contemporary alienation. Here the reader finds Wain's sympathy for the underdog, his respect for decency and the dignity of man, his affirmation of life; here, too, is expressed Wain's deep interest in the causes and effects of loneliness and alienation.

The reader's first inclination is to approach the novel as primarily a novel of character, the major interest and emphasis of which is the constantly developing character of Roger Furnivall himself. Using third-person narration, Wain keeps the focus steadily on his main character as he progresses straight through several months that constitute a time of crisis in his life. Through most of the novel, Roger struggles doggedly against a combination of adverse circumstances, always in search of a purpose. Outwardly, he forces himself on Gareth, for example, as a way of improving his idiomatic Welsh. Inwardly, he "needed involvement, needed a human reason for being in the district." The guilt he carries because of his brother's suffering and death helps to propel him into a more active engagement with contemporary life. His conflict with Dic Sharp draws him out of his own private grief because he is helping not only Gareth, but also an entire community of people.

The reader learns about Roger in another way, too: Wain uses setting to reveal and reflect the protagonist's emotions and mental states. Roger's walk in the rain down the country roads, as he attempts to resolve his bitterness and disappointment at Beverley's rejection of him, is vividly depicted. It carries conviction because Roger's anxiety has been built up gradually and artistically. The pastoral world is a perpetually shifting landscape, and Wain depicts its shifts and contrasts with an acute eye for telling detail. Especially striking are the sketches of evening coming on in the Welsh hills, with their rocks and timber and vast expanses of green. Such descriptions help to convey Roger's yearning for happiness in a world which seems bent on denying it to him.

One major theme of the book is the invasion of the peaceful, conservative world of Wales by outsiders who have no roots in the region, and therefore no real concern for its inhabitants. These invaders are characterized by a sophisticated corruption that contrasts sharply with the unspoiled simplicity and honesty of the best of the natives. A related theme is the decline of the town: its economic insecurity, its struggle to resist the progressive and materialistic "cruelty, greed, tyranny, the power of the rich to drive the poor to the wall." Through Roger's point of view, Wain expresses his opposition to the pressures—economic, political, cultural—that seek to destroy the Welsh and, by implication, all minority enclaves. Thus, *A Winter in the Hills* is more than a novel about the growth of one human being from loneliness and alienation to mature and selfless love; it is also a powerful study of the quality of life in the contemporary world, threatened by the encroachments of bureaucracy, greed, and materialism.

The somewhat optimistic resolution of *A Winter in the Hills* stands in stark contrast to that of *The Pardoner's Tale*, Wain's most somber novel. In no other work by Wain are the characters so lonely, so frustrated, or so obsessed with thoughts of mutability, lost opportunities, and death. The novel is really two stories: a first-person tale about Gus Howkins, an aging Londoner contemplating divorce, and a third-person narrative (the framing narrative) about Giles Hermitage, an established novelist and bachelor living in an unnamed cathedral town, who gets involved with the Chichester-Redferns, a woman and her daughter, while he is working out the story of Howkins. It is the interplay between these two stories which constitutes the plot of *The Pardoner's Tale*.

Giles Hermitage is obviously the figure with whom Wain is the most intimately involved. He is a highly idiosyncratic figure with very recognizable weaknesses; he is easily discouraged (there is an early thought of suicide), and he resorts to excessive drinking. The root cause of his death wish and of his drinking is loneliness. Like Wain's earlier heroes, he is very much a modern man: vague in his religious and humanitarian aspirations; rootless and alienated from the social life of the community in which he lives; and initially weak and confused in his relationships with women. Plagued by anxiety, depression, vague discontent, and a sense of inner emptiness, he seeks peace of mind under conditions that increasingly militate against it. Add to his problems the ever-growing urge toward self-destruction, and the reader begins to recognize in this novel a truly contemporary pulsebeat. Hermitage is a stranger in a world that does not make sense.

Unlike Wain's earlier heroes, however, Hermitage tries to make sense of the world through the medium of his writing by stepping back into what he calls "the protecting circle of art." His approach to writing is autobiographical, personal, even subjective. The hero of his novel is a mask for himself. The author is creating a character who is in his own predicament, and the agonies he endures enable him to express his deepest feelings about life. In Hermitage, Wain presents a character who tries to create, as artists do, a new existence out of the chaos of his life.

The remaining major characters in *The Pardoner's Tale* bear family resemblances to those in other of Wain's novels. If the part of the lonely, alienated hero so effectively carried in *A Winter in the Hills* by Roger Furnivall is here assigned to Giles Hermitage, then the role of the manipulator is assigned in this novel to Mrs. Chichester-Redfern. Although a good deal less ruthless than Dic Sharp, she nevertheless seeks to exploit the hero.

The process by which Mrs. Chichester-Redfern is gradually revealed through the eyes of Hermitage is subtle and delicate. At first merely a stranger, she comes to seem in time a calculating and educated woman, the innocent victim of a man who deserted her, a seventy-year-old woman grasping for answers to some vital questions about her own life. She summons Hermitage under the pretense of wanting to gain insight into her life. From these conversations, the reader learns that she, like Hermitage, is confronted and dislocated by external reality in the form of a personal loss. Also like the hero, she desires to come to some understanding of her unhappy life through the medium of art. Her true motive is revenge, however, and she wants Hermitage to write a novel with her husband in it as a character who suffers pain. Then, she says, "there will be that much justice done in the world."

In addition to the alienated, lonely hero and the manipulator, most of Wain's fiction portrays a comforter. In his latest novel, the comforter is embodied in Diana Chichester-Redfern, but the happiness Diana offers is only temporary. In this novel, love is reduced to a meaningless mechanical act: Diana, also, is living in a wasteland.

The basic tension of this novel is a simple and classic one—the life-force confronting the death-force. As surely as Mrs. Chichester-Redfern is the death-force in the novel, Diana is the active and life-giving presence. She is depicted as an abrasive, liberated, sensual, innately selfish modern young woman who stands in positive contrast to the deathlike grayness of her mother. She is earthy and fulfilled, accepting and content with her music (playing the guitar satisfies her need for proficiency), her faith (which takes care of "all the moral issues") and her sexuality (which she enjoys because she has no choice). Diana goes from one affair to another, not in search of love (she claims she "can't love anybody") but out of a need for repetition. Diana defines love and meaning as the fulfillment of a man or woman's emotional requirements. To her, love does not mean self-sacrifice; rather, love is synonymous with need.

The world of *The Pardoner's Tale* is thus the archetypal world of all Wain's fiction: random, fragmented, lonely, contradictory. It is a world in which wasted lives, debased sexual encounters, and destroyed moral intelligences yield a tragic vision of futility and sterility, of isolation from the community, estrangement from those who used to be closest to one, and loneliness in the midst of the universe itself.

In retrospect, Wain's insistence on the contradictions of life is at the very center of his works, and is itself a tacit recommendation to the reader to look with honesty at the reality around him. For Wain, writing seems almost a test of his own honesty, reminding himself that, for the most part, he can look at things squarely, without flinching and without telling lies. This sense of stoic honesty is the single most dominant impression emerging from his work. Add to that a gentleness in his treatment of people, and there emerges the portrait of a man who from the 1950's has become more seriously, deeply, and intelligently the critic of contemporary English society. "I hope my work is taking on a deeper note," he commented once; "otherwise there's no point in going on."

Major publications other than long fiction

SHORT FICTION: *Nuncle and Other Stories*, 1960; *Death of the Hind Legs and Other Stories*, 1966; *Selected Shorter Stories of Thomas Hardy*, 1966 (edited); *The Life Guard*, 1971.

POETRY: *Mixed Feelings*, 1951; *A Word Carved on a Sill*, 1956; *Weep Before God: Poems*, 1961; *Wildtrack: A Poem*, 1965; *Selected Shorter Poems of Thomas Hardy*, 1966 (edited); *Letters to Five Artists*, 1969; *The Shape of Feng*, 1972; *Feng: A Poem*, 1975; *Poems, 1949-1979*, 1981.

NONFICTION: *Contemporary Reviews of Romantic Poetry*, 1953 (edited); *Interpretations: Essays on Twelve English Poems*, 1955 (edited); *Preliminary Essays*, 1957; *Gerard Manley Hopkins: An Idiom of Desperation*, 1959; *International Literary Annual*, 1959, 1960 (edited); *Fanny Burney's Diary*, 1960 (edited); *Sprightly Running: Part of an Autobiography*, 1962; *Essays on Literature and Ideas*, 1963; *The Living World of Shakespeare: A Playgoer's Guide*, 1964; *Arnold Bennett*, 1967; *Shakespeare: Macbeth, a Casebook*, 1968 (edited); *Shakespeare: Othello, a Casebook*, 1971 (edited); *A House for the Truth: Critical Essays*, 1972; *Johnson as Critic*, 1973 (edited); *Samuel Johnson: A Biography*, 1974; *Professing Poetry*, 1977.

ANTHOLOGY: *Anthology of Modern Poetry*, 1963.

MISCELLANEOUS: Thomas Hardy's *The Dynasts*, 1966 (edited).

Bibliography

Bode, Carl. "The Redbrick Cinderellas," in *College English*. XX (April,

1959), pp. 332, 334-337.

Burgess, Anthony. *The Novel Now: A Guide to Contemporary Fiction*, 1967.

Mellown, Elgin W. "Steps Toward Vision: The Development of Technique in John Wain's First Seven Novels," in *South Atlantic Quarterly*. XVII (Summer, 1969), pp. 330-342.

O'Connor, William Van. "John Wain: The Will to Write," in *Wisconsin Studies in Contemporary Literature*. I (Winter, 1960), pp. 35-49.

Salwak, Dale. *John Braine and John Wain: A Reference Guide*, 1980.

Walzer, Michael. "John Wain: The Hero in Limbo," in *Perspective*. X (Summer-Autumn, 1958), pp. 137-145.

Wilson, Colin. "The Writer and Publicity," in *Encounter*. XIII (November, 1959), p. 9.

Dale Salwak

ALICE WALKER

Born: Eatonton, Georgia; February 9, 1944

Principal long fiction
The Third Life of Grange Copeland, 1970; *Meridian*, 1976, *The Color Purple*, 1982.

Other literary forms
Alice Walker is well on her way to establishing herself as a major contemporary American writer. At age thirty-nine, she had already published, in addition to her three novels, three books of poetry and two collections of short stories. Walker is also an accomplished writer of nonfiction, having produced essays on Zora Neale Hurston, Ida B. Wells, Flannery O'Connor, feminism, pornography, life in the South, and motherhood, as well as a number of book reviews. Her essays are being collected for a forthcoming volume called *In Search of Our Mothers' Gardens: A Collection of Womanist Prose*. Walker was an early editor at *Ms.*, in which many of her essays first appeared. Her interest in the then little-known writer Zora Neale Hurston led to her pilgrimage to Florida to place a tombstone on Hurston's unmarked grave, to Walker's editing of *I Love Myself When I Am Laughing . . . And Then Again When I Am Looking Mean and Impressive: A Zora Neale Hurston Reader* (1979), and to her introduction to Robert Hemenway's *Zora Neale Hurston: A Literary Biography* (1977). Walker has also published a children's book, *Langston Hughes: American Poet* (1973).

Achievements
Walker's literary reputation is based primarily on her fiction, although her second book of poetry, *Revolutionary Petunias and Other Poems* (1973), received the Lillian Smith Award and a nomination for a National Book Award. Her first short-story collection, *In Love and Trouble*, won the Rosenthal Award of the National Institute of Arts and Letters. In addition, she has received a Charles Merrill writing fellowship, an award for fiction from the National Endowment for the Arts, and a Guggenheim Fellowship. She has also been a Bread Loaf Scholar and a fellow at the Radcliffe Institute. *The Third Life of Grange Copeland* was widely and enthusiastically reviewed in journals as varied as *The New Yorker*, *The New Republic*, and *The New York Times Book Review*, although journals aimed primarily at a black readership were often silent or critical of the violence and graphic depiction of rural black life. With the publication of *Meridian*, Walker's second novel, her work as a poet, novelist, essayist, editor, teacher, scholar, and political activist came together. *Meridian* was universally praised in scholarly journals, literary mag-

azines, popular magazines, and black-oriented journals. Some critics, mainly black male reviewers, objected again to the honest, straightforward portrayals of black life in the South and to Walker's growing feminism, which they saw in conflict with her commitment to her race. Walker's third novel, *The Color Purple,* has been widely praised: Gloria Steinem has written that this novel "could be the kind of popular and literary event that transforms an intense reputation into a national one," and Peter Prescott's review in *Newsweek* begins by saying "I want to say at once that *The Color Purple* is an American novel of permanent importance." These accolades were substantiated by receiving the 1983 Pulitzer Prize in Literature.

Biography

Alice Walker was born in Eatonton, Georgia, on February 9, 1944, the last of eight children of Willie Lee and Minnie Lou Grant Walker, share-croppers in rural Georgia. Her relationship with her father, at first strong and valuable, became strained as she became involved in the civil rights and feminist movements. A moving depiction of her estrangement from her father occurs in her essay "My Father's Country Is the Poor," which appeared in *The New York Times* in 1977. For Walker, a loving and healthy mother-daughter relationship has endured over the years. An account of that relationship is central to her essays "In Search of Our Mothers' Gardens" and "Lulls—A Native Daughter Returns to the Black South" and in Mary Helen Washington's article "Her Mother's Gifts," in which Walker acknowledges that she often writes with her mother's voice—"Just as you have certain physical characteristics of your mother . . . when you're compelled to write her stories, it's because you recognize and prize those qualities of her in yourself."

One of the central events in Walker's childhood was a BB gun accident which left her, at age eight, blind in one eye. Scar tissue from that wound, both physical and psychological, seems to have left her with a compensating acuteness of vision, despite the conviction that she was permanently disfig-ured. Walker was affected enough by the accident to say in a 1974 interview with John O'Brien, "I have always been a solitary person, and since I was eight years old (and the recipient of a disfiguring scar, since corrected, some-what), I have daydreamed—not of fairytales—but of falling on swords, of putting guns to my heart or head, and of slashing my wrists with a razor." Walker's partial blindness allowed her to attend Spelman College in Atlanta on a scholarship for the handicapped, following her graduation from Butler-Baker High School in 1961. She left Spelman after two years—which included summer trips to the Soviet Union and to Africa as part of a group called Experiment in International Living—for Sarah Lawrence College, where she was graduated in 1965.

Walker's political activity controlled her movements during the years immediately following her college graduation: she spent the summer of 1965 in the Soviet Union and also worked for civil rights in Liberty County, Georgia. The next year she was a case worker for New York City's Department of Social Services, and then a voter-registration worker in Mississippi. In 1967, she married Melvyn Leventhal, a civil rights lawyer, and moved to Jackson, Mississippi, where she continued her civil rights work, lived in the heart of the South as part of an interracial couple, and taught at Jackson State University, while continuing to write stories, poems, and essays. She taught at Tougaloo College in Mississippi for a year before returning to the East, where she was a lecturer in writing and literature at Wellesley College, an editor at *Ms.* magazine, and an instructor at the University of Massachusetts at Boston. By 1977, she had divorced her husband, accepted a position as Associate Professor of English at Yale University, and written six books.

Throughout the 1970's, Walker continued to write, teach, edit, lecture, and read poetry across the nation. She now lives with her twelve-year-old daughter, Rebecca, in San Francisco, California, where she is Distinguished Writer in the Afro-American Studies department at the University of California at Berkeley.

Analysis

The story of Alice Walker's childhood scar provides the most basic metaphor of her novels: the idea that radical change is possible even under the worst conditions. Although she was never able to regain the sight in one eye, Walker's disfigurement was considerably lessened:

> I used to pray every night that I would wake up and somehow it would be gone. I couldn't look at people directly because I thought I was ugly. . . . Then when I was fourteen, I visited my brother Bill [who] took me to a hospital where they removed most of the scar tissue—and I was a *changed person.* I promptly went home, scooped up the best-looking guy, and by the time I graduated from high school, I was valedictorian, voted 'Most Popular,' and crowned queen!

That change and personal triumph is possible, despite the odds, is central to all of Walker's writing. Her work focuses directly or indirectly on the ways of survival adopted by black women, usually in the South, and is presented in a prose style characterized by a distinctive combination of lyricism and unflinching realism. Walker's women attempt not merely to survive, but to survive completely with some sense of stability, despite the constant thread of family violence, physical and mental abuse, and a lack of responsibility on the part of the men in their lives. Walker is simultaneously a feminist and a supporter of civil rights, not only for black Americans, but also for minorities everywhere.

Walker's vision has been shaped in part by a work from the first flowering of black writing in America: Jean Toomer's *Cane* (1923). She said in 1974 about Toomer's book, "it has been reverberating in me to an astonishing degree. *I love it passionately*; could not possibly exist without it." Like *Cane*, the first part of which centers mainly on women in the South, Walker's novels are made up of nearly equal parts of poetry, portraiture, and drama, broken up into a series of sections and subsections. Other important literary influences on Walker include Zora Neale Hurston, from whom she inherited a love of black folklore; Flannery O'Connor, who wrote of Southern violence and grotesqueries from her home in Milledgeville, Georgia, less than ten miles from Walker's childhood home; and Albert Camus, whose existentialism speaks to the struggle for survival and dignity in which Walker's characters are engaged. Walker herself has defined her "preoccupations" as a novelist: "The survival, the survival *whole* of my people. But beyond that I am committed to exploring the oppressions, the insanities, the loyalties, and the triumphs of black women." *The Third Life of Grange Copeland*, on the surface a novel about the cycle of rage and violence torturing the lives of a father and his son, is as much about the recipients of that rage—the women and children whose lives are directly affected. Although the novel is unremitting in its picture of desperate poverty's legacy of hatred, hopelessness, and cruelty, it concludes optimistically with Ruth Copeland's hope for a release from sorrow through the redemption promised by the early days of the civil rights movement and by the knowledge and love inherited at the sacrificial death of her grandfather.

Walker's second novel, *Meridian*, picks up chronologically and thematically at the point where her first novel ended. *Meridian* describes the struggles of a young black woman, Meridian Hill, about the same age as Ruth Copeland, who comes to an awareness of power and feminism during the civil rights movement, and whose whole life's meaning is centered in the cycles of guilt, violence, hope, and change characteristic of that dramatic time. Thematically, *Meridian* picks up the first novel's theme of self-sacrificial murder as a way out of desperate political oppression in the form of the constant question that drives Meridian Hill—"Will you kill for the Revolution?" Meridian's lifelong attempt to answer that question affirmatively (as her college friends so easily do) while remaining true to her sense of responsibility to the past, her sense of ethics, and her sense of guilt of having given to her mother the child of her teenage pregnancy, constitutes the section of the novel entitled "Meridian." The second third of the novel, "Truman Held," is named for the major male character in the narrative. At one time, Meridian loves Truman, but his callous treatment of her and his desertion of her for Lynne Rabinowitz, a white civil rights volunteer from the North, causes their relationship to change. By the novel's end, Meridian has become teacher, confidante, and savior to both Truman and Lynne, whose eventual marriage is destroyed by the pressures of interracial tensions. The third major section of the novel, "Ending," looks back at the turmoil of the movement from the perspective of the 1970's. Long after others have given up intellectual arguments about the morality of killing for revolution, Meridian is still debating the question, still actively involved in voter registration, political activism, and civil rights organization, as though the movement had never lost momentum. Worrying that her actions, now seen as eccentric rather than revolutionary, will cause her "to be left, listening to the old music, beside the highway," Meridian achieves release and atonement through the realization that her role will be to "come forward and sing from memory songs they will need once more to hear. For it is the song of the people, transformed by the experiences of each generation, that holds them together."

Like her first two novels, Walker's most recent novel has an unusual form. *The Color Purple* presents the author's familiar and yet fresh themes—survival and redemption—in epistolary from. Most of the novel's letters are written by Celie, an uneducated, unloved, black woman living in rural Georgia in the 1920's; Celie's letters are written in what Walker calls "black folk English," a language of wit, strength, and natural humor. Ashamed of having been raped by her stepfather, a man whom Celie thinks at the time is her father, she begins to send letters to God, in the way that children send letters to Santa Claus, because her rapist told her to tell nobody but God. Although her early letters tell of rape, degradation, and pain, of her stepfather's getting rid of the two children born of his cruelty, the tone is nevertheless captivating, ironic, and even humorous. Soon the despair turns into acceptance, then into understanding, anger, rebellion, and finally triumph and loving forgiveness as the fourteen-year-old Celie continues to write until she reaches an audience, some thirty years later. Like the author, who began writing at the age of eight, and who has turned her childhood experience in rural Georgia into three novels of violence, hatred, understanding, love, and profound hope for the future, Celie is a writer, a listener, a thinker, and a promoter of Walker's constant theme: "Love redeems, meanness kills."

Writing in 1973, Walker observed that her first novel, *The Third Life of Grange Copeland*, "though sometimes humorous and celebrative of life, is a grave book in which the characters see the world as almost entirely menacing." This dark view of life is common to Grange Copeland, the patriarch of a family farming on shares in rural Georgia, his son Brownfield, and the wives and daughters of both men. For all these characters, the world is menacing because of the socioeconomic position they occupy at the bottom of the scale of the sharecropping system. Father and son menace each other in this novel because they are in turn menaced by rage born out of the frustration of the system. Although the white people of the book are nearly always vague, nameless, and impersonal, they and the system they represent have the ability to render both Grange and Brownfield powerless.

It is not accidental that these characters' names have agricultural connotations. "Grange" suggests a late nineteenth century association of farmers, a feudal farm and grain storage building, and a combination of graze and range, while "Brownfield" and "Cope*land*" are self-explanatory—for the inability to cope with the land is what leads both male characters along virtually parallel paths. For the father, the mere appearance of the white farm boss's truck is enough to turn his face "into a unnaturally bland mask, curious and unsettling to see." The appearance of the truck causes the son to be "filled with terror of this man who could, by his presence alone, turn his father into something that might as well have been a pebble or a post or a piece of dirt. . . ." Although Grange is, in this same image, literally a piece of land, he eventually returns to the South and learns to live self-sufficiently, farming a section of soil he tricked his second wife into giving to him. Brownfield, in contrast, is never able to escape from the sharecropping system, although he sees that, like his father, he is "destined to be no more than overseer, on the white man's plantation, of his own children." Brownfield is able to live obliviously on a farm in Georgia, content to blame all of his problems on others. The poor rural black workers of this novel are themselves little more than a crop, rotated from farm to farm, and producing a harvest of shame and hunger, cruelty and violence.

Unlike the men of the novel, the women are menaced by both blacks and whites, by both the agricultural system and the "strange fruit" it produces. Margaret, Grange's first wife, is both physically and mentally degraded by her husband and then sexually exploited by a white truck driver, resulting in her second pregnancy. Unable to cope with this situation, Grange deserts his family, after which his wife poisons both her child and herself. Following his father's pattern, Brownfield marries and begins to work the land, but after "a year when endless sunup to sundown work on fifty rich bottom acres of cotton land and a good crop brought them two diseased shoats for winter meat. . . ." he too begins to abuse his wife. Although Brownfield's wife, Mem, is a schoolteacher intelligent enough to try to break the cycle of raising others people's crops, her brief rebellion against her husband's malevolent beatings and mental tortures is a failure: he is able to subjugate her through repeated pregnancies that sap her rebellion as they turn her once rich and strong body into a virtual wasteland of emaciation. Because her body, which represents the land of the South, is still able to produce children despite its depleted condition, Brownfield is enraged enough to murder her in retaliation for her physical shape: "he had murdered his wife because she had become skinny and had not, with much irritation to him, reverted, even when well-fed, to her former plumpness. . . . Plumpness and freedom from the land, from cows and skinniness, went all together in his mind." Despite his irrational abuse of her, Mem is not ashamed "of being black though, no matter what he said. . . . Color was something the ground did to the flowers, and that was an end to it."

What the ground did to these generations of Southern black people is the subject of Walker's novel—the whole lurid history of violence, hatred, and guilt that she chronicles in this story of one family's griefs. By the book's end, Brownfield Copeland has murdered his wife and an unnamed albino baby, while Grange Copeland has murdered his son Brownfield—first spiritually, then physically—and indirectly has killed his first wife and her infant.

Walker's characters are allegorical representations of the classic modes of survival historically adopted by black Americans in dealing with their oppression. Brownfield identifies with whites by daydreaming of himself on a Southern plantation, sipping mint juleps, and then by bargaining for his freedom with the sexual favors of black women. Both of Grange's wives attempt to live up to the white stereotype of black women as promiscuous sexual beings, free of any moral restraints. Brownfield's wife, Mem, attempts the passive resistance advocated by Martin Luther King, but she is destroyed by what her husband calls "her weakness . . . forgiveness, a stupid belief that kindness can convert the enemy." Brownfield's daughter, Daphne, who calls herself the Copeland Family Secret Keeper, tries the strategy of inventing a falsely romantic history of the past, of the good old days when her father was kind, echoing those historical revisionists who try to argue that slavery was not that bad. Brownfield's other daughters try to stay away from their father altogether, regarding him "as a human devil" of whom they were afraid "in a more distant, impersonal way. He was like bad weather, a toothache, daily bad news," a description that suggests that traditional black view that white people are blue-eyed devils, impossible to understand, and to be avoided at all costs, rather than confronted.

Each of the title character's three lives (at home in the South as a sharecropper married to Margaret; in the North as a hustler of alcohol, drugs, and women; and finally back in the South as a farmer married to Josie and rearing his granddaughter Ruth) parallels a traditional survival strategy, which Grange summarizes as follows, "The white folks hated me and I hated myself until I started hating them in return and loving myself. Then I tried just loving me, and then you, and *ignoring* them much as I could." To put it another way, Grange tries at first to adapt to the system by believing what whites say about blacks; then he turns to the classic escape of the runaway slave—heading North to freedom; finally, he tries the technique of praising black life while ignoring whites altogether. A large part of the novel's devastation is caused by the repeated use of these techniques, not against whites, but against other members of the Copeland family. Only Ruth, the granddaughter through whom Grange seeks redemption, is able to deal with whites in an intelligent, balanced, nondestructive yet independent way. She has learned from her grandfather, and from her family history, that pure hatred becomes self-hatred, violence begets self-violence, and she therefore becomes the novel's symbol of the new black woman, ready to assume her place in black history as a courageous worker in the civil rights movement which the rest of her family has been groping to discover.

In 1978, Walker described her second novel, *Meridian*, as "a book 'about' the civil rights movement, feminism, socialism, the shakiness of revolutionaries and the radicalization of saints. . . ." Her word "about" is exact, for all of these topics revolve not chronologically but thematically around a central point—the protagonist, Meridian Hill. In some ways, Meridian *is* a saint; by the book's end she has sustained her belief in the civil rights movement without losing faith in feminism and socialism, despite family pressures, guilt, literally paralyzing self-doubts, the history of the movement, and the sexism of many of its leaders. In contrast, Truman Held represents those males who were reported to have said that "the only position for a woman in the movement is prone." Although Truman Held is Meridian's initial teacher in the movement, she eventually leaves him behind because of his inability to sustain his initial revolutionary fervor, and because of his misogyny. Unlike Brownfield Copeland, Truman argues that women are of less value than they should be, not because of skinniness, but because "Black women let themselves go . . . they are so fat." Later in the novel, Truman marries a white civil rights worker, whose rape by another black man produces disgust in him, as much at his wife as at his friend. When Truman seeks Meridian out in a series of small Southern hamlets where she continues to persuade black people to register to vote and to struggle for civil rights, he tells her that the movement is ended and that he grieves in a different way than she. Meridian answers, "I know how you grieve by running away. By pretending you were never there." Like Grange Copeland, Truman Held refuses to take responsibility for his own problems, preferring to run away to the North.

Meridian's sacrificial dedication to the movement becomes a model for atonement and release, words that once formed the working title of the book. *Meridian* could also have been called "The Third Life of Meridian Hill" because of similarities between Meridian's life and Grange Copeland's. Meridian leads three lives: as an uneducated child in rural Georgia who follows the traditional pattern of early pregnancy and aimless marriage; as a college student actively participating in political demonstrations; and as an eccentric agitator—a performer, she calls herself—unaware that the movement is ended. Like Grange Copeland in another sense, Meridian Hill is solid proof of the ability of any human to change dramatically by sheer will and desire.

Meridian is always different from her friends, who, filled with angry rhetoric, ask her repeatedly if she is willing to kill for the revolution, the same question that Grange asked himself when he lived in the North. This question haunts Meridian, because she does not know if she can or if she should kill, and because it reminds her of a similar request, posed in a similar way by her mother: "Say it now, Meridian, and be saved. All He asks is that we acknowledge Him as our Master. Say you believe in Him . . . don't go against your heart." In neither case is Meridian able to answer yes without going against her heart. Unlike her college friends and Truman Held, who see the movement only in terms of future gains for themselves, Meridian is involved with militancy because of her past: "But what none of them seemed to understand was that she felt herself to be, not holding on to something from the past, but *held* by something in the past."

Part of the past's hold on her is the sense of guilt she feels about her relationships with her parents. Although her father taught her the nature of the oppression of minorities through his knowledge of American Indians, her strongest source of guilt comes from her mother, who argues, like Brownfield Copeland, that the responsibility for *all* problems stems from outside oneself: "The answer to everything," said Meridian's mother, "is we live in America and we're not rich." Meridian's strongest sense of past guilt comes from the knowledge she gains when she becomes pregnant: "it was for stealing her mother's serenity, for shattering her mother's emerging self, that Meridian felt guilty from the very first, though she was unable to understand how this could possibly be her fault."

Meridian takes the form of a series of nonchronological sections, some consisting of only a paragraph, some four or five pages long, that circle around the events of Meridian's life. The writing is clear, powerful, violent, lyrical, and often symbolic. Spelman College, for example, is here called Saxon College. The large magnolia tree in the center of the campus, described with specific folkloric detail, is destroyed by angry students during a demonstration: "Though Meridian begged them to dismantle the president's house instead, in a fury of confusion and frustration they worked all night, and chopped and sawed down, level to the ground, that mighty, ancient, sheltering music tree." This tree (named The Sojourner, perhaps for Sojourner Truth) expands symbolically to suggest both the senseless destruction of black ghettos by blacks during the turmoil of the 1960's, and also Meridian Hill herself, who receives a photograph years later of The Sojourner, now "a gigantic tree stump" with "a tiny branch, no larger than a finger, growing out of one side." That picture, suggesting as it does the rebirth of hope despite despair, also evokes the last vision of Meridian expressed by the now-shamed Truman Held: "He would never see 'his' Meridian again. The new part had grown out of the old, though, and that was reassuring. This part of her, new, sure and ready, even eager, for the world, he knew he must meet again and recognize for its true value at some future time."

Like Meridian Hill, Celie, the main character in Walker's third novel, *The Color Purple*, compares herself to a tree. Repeatedly raped by her stepfather, Celie is then sold into a virtual state of slavery to a man who beats her, a man she neither knows, loves, nor talks to, a man she can never call anything but Mr. _____ , an ironic throwback to the eighteenth century English epistolary novel. Celie tries to endure by withholding all emotion: "I make myself wood. I say to myself, Celie, you a tree. That's how come I know trees fear man." Like The Sojourner, or like the kudzu vine of the deep South that thrives despite repeated attempts to beat it back, Celie continues to express her fears and hopes in a series of letters written in a form of black English that is anything but wooden. The contrast between the richly eccentric prose of Celie's letters and the educated yet often lifeless sentences of her sister Nettie's return letters supports Walker's statement that "writing *The Color Purple* was writing in my first language. . . ." The language of the letters is at first awkward, but never difficult to follow. As Celie grows in experience, in contact with the outside world, and in confidence, her writing gradually becomes more sophisticated and more like standard written English, but it never loses its originality of rhythm and phrase.

Based on Walker's great grandmother, a slave who was raped at twelve by her owner, Celie works her way from ignorance about her body and her living situation all the way through to an awakening of her self-worth, as well as to an understanding of the existence of God, the relations between men and women, and the power of forgiveness in uniting family and friends. Much of this transformation is brought about through the magic of a blues singer named Shug Avery, who guides Celie in understanding sexuality, men, and religion without causing her to lose her own fresh insights, naïve though they are.

The letters that make up the novel are something like the missives that the protagonist of Saul Bellow's novel *Herzog* (1964) writes but never sends, in that they are often addressed to God and written in an ironic but not self-conscious manner. Because of the combination of dark humor and despair, the letters also evoke memories of the desperate letters from the physically and spiritually maimed addressed to the hero of Nathanael West's *Miss Lonelyhearts* (1933). Although Celie is unlettered in a traditional sense, her ability to carry the complicated plot forward and to continue to write—first without an earthly audience, and then to her sister, whom she has not seen for more than twenty years—testify to the human potential for self-transformation.

Discussing Celie's attempts to confirm her existence by writing to someone she is not certain exists, Gloria Steinem says "Clearly, the author is telling us something about the origin of Gods: about when we need to invent them and when we don't." In a sense, Shug Avery becomes a god for Celie because of her ability to control the evil in the world and her power to change the sordid conditions of Celie's life. Early in the book, when Celie is worrying about survival, about rape, incest, beatings, and the murder of her children, her only source of hope is the name "Shug Avery," a name with a magical power to control her husband. Not even aware that Shug is a person, Celie writes "I ast our new mammy bout Shug Avery. What it is?" Finding a picture of Shug, Celie transfers her prayers to what is at that point only an image: "I see her there in furs. Her face rouge. Her hair like somethin tail. She grinning with her foot up on somebody motocar. Her eyes serious tho. Sad some. . . . An all night long I stare at it. An now when I dream, I dream of

Shug Avery. She be dress to kill, whirling an laughing." Shug Avery becomes a god to Celie not only because she is pictured in the first photograph Celie has ever seen, but also because she is dressed in a style that shows a sense of pride and freedom.

Once Celie's sister's letters begin to appear, mailed from Africa, where Nettie is a missionary, the ironic connection between the primitive animism of the Africans and Celie's equally primitive reaction to Shug's picture becomes clear. Although Nettie has crossed the ocean to minister to a tribe of primitive people, her own sister is living in inhuman conditions in Georgia: ignorance, disease, sexism, lack of control of the environment, and the ever-increasing march of white people. When Shug explains her own animistic religious beliefs—which include the notion that God is not a he or a she, but an it (just as Celie once thought Shug Avery was an it)—Celie is converted to a pantheistic worship that makes her early identification with trees seem less naïve.

When the narrator of Herman Melville's "Bartleby the Scrivener" tries to explain Bartleby's withdrawal from life, he thinks of the dead letter office in which the scrivener was rumored to have worked, and says, "On errands of life, these letters speed to death." In contrast, Celie's and Nettie's letters, ostensibly written to people long thought to be dead, speed across the ocean on errands of life, where they grow to sustain, not merely the sisters in the book, but all those lucky enough to read them. As the author says of *The Color Purple*, "It's my happiest book . . . I had to do all the other writing to get to this point." For the reader who has gotten to this point in Walker's career by reading all of her other books, there is no question that Alice Walker's name could be substituted for Celie's in the author's statement about her most recent novel: "Let's hope people can hear Celie's voice. There are so many people like Celie who make it, who come out of nothing. People who triumph."

Major publications other than long fiction

SHORT FICTION: *In Love and Trouble: Stories of Black Women*, 1973; *You Can't Keep a Good Woman Down*, 1981.

POETRY: *Once: Poems*, 1968; *Revolutionary Petunias and Other Poems*, 1973; *Goodnight, Willie Lee, I'll See You in the Morning: Poems*, 1979.

NONFICTION: *I Love Myself When I Am Laughing . . . And Then Again When I Am Looking Mean and Impressive: A Zora Neale Hurston Reader*, 1979 (edited).

CHILDREN'S LITERATURE: *Langston Hughes: American Poet*, 1973.

Bibliography

Christian, Barbara. "Novels for Everyday Use: The Novels of Alice Walker," in *Black Women Novelists: The Development of a Tradition, 1892-1976*,

1980, pp. 180-238.

McGowan, Martha J. "Atonement and Release in Alice Walker's *Meridian*," in *Critique*. XXIII (1981), pp. 25-36.

O'Brien, John. *Interviews with Black Writers*, 1973.

Steinem, Gloria. "Do You Know This Woman? She Knows You: A Profile of Alice Walker," in *Ms*. X (June, 1982), pp. 36-37, 89-94.

Walker, Alice. "*One* Child of One's Own: A Meaningful Digression Within the Work(s)," in *The Writer on Her Work*, 1980. Edited by Janet Steinburg.

Timothy Dow Adams

EDWARD LEWIS WALLANT

Born: New Haven, Connecticut; October 19, 1926
Died: Norwalk, Connecticut; December 5, 1962

Principal long fiction

The Human Season, 1960; *The Pawnbroker*, 1961; *The Tenants of Moon-bloom*, 1963; *The Children at the Gate*, 1964.

Other literary forms

The brevity of Edward Lewis Wallant's literary career did not allow for a long list of publications. He did contribute three short stories to the *New Voices* series: "I Held Back My Hand," appeared in *New Voices 2* (1955); "The Man Who Made a Nice Appearance," in *New Voices 3* (1958), and the posthumously published "When Ben Awakened," in *American Scene: New Voices* (1963). Wallant also wrote an essay on the art of fiction which was published posthumously in the *Teacher's Notebook in English* (1963). In addition, there is a sizable collection which includes unpublished manuscripts, the final drafts of his first two unpublished novels, some half-dozen short stories, various drafts of his published novels, the first act of a play, his journal and his notebooks, and miscellaneous loose notes and fragments. All of these papers are on deposit at the Beinecke Library at Yale University.

Achievements

Wallant's literary output was so small and his career so short that it is difficult to assess his place in postwar American fiction. Wallant's work is best seen in its relationship to kindred works in the late 1950's and early 1960's. Although he is still little known to the public, Wallant's four novels rank with J. D. Salinger's *Franny and Zooey* (1961), Saul Bellow's *Henderson the Rain King* (1959), Bernard Malamud's *A New Life* (1963), and Ken Kesey's *One Flew over the Cuckoo's Nest* (1962) as examples of what has been described as the "New Romanticism." Wallant's novels reflect an outlook on life that led him to write about the unfortunate, the outcast, and the common man, whom he portrayed with compassion and dignity. His unwaveringly realistic perception of life and its often painful demands leaven his general optimism. In each of his fictions, Wallant's central character is shocked out of a moral lethargy and into action on behalf of his fellow human beings. This shock is preceded by a submersion into the contemporary human condition, which provides Wallant the opportunity to explore the interconnections and disconnections of modern urban life. He was a committed writer whose commitment acknowledged the darker side of the lives of his characters. It is not surprising, then, that while some critics should emphasize the positive nature of Wallant's work, his "happy endings" and his optimism, there should also be those who find in his work a note of despair and a presentiment of his own early death. It was Wallant's achievement to fuse the qualities of an old-fashioned novelist with the perceptions of a modern urban realist. The combination resulted in novels which offer a particularly clear view of the 1960's.

Biography

Edward Lewis Wallant was born in New Haven, Connecticut, on October 19, 1926. His father, who was invalided by mustard gas during World War I, was almost continuously hospitalized during Wallant's early years, and he died when his son was six. Wallant, an only child, was reared in a shabby although respectable middle-class neighborhood by his mother, Anna, and two aunts. Except for his Russian-born grandfather, who told him stories of the old country, it was a household without males. During his years at New Haven High School, Wallant held a number of jobs including plumber's assistant, delivery boy for a drugstore across the street from a Catholic hospital, and hot-dog hawker at Yale football games. Although his academic career in high school was not remarkable, he did attend briefly the University of Connecticut. He soon left, however, to join the navy.

The final months of World War II found Wallant serving as a gunner's mate in the European Theater of Operations; after his discharge from the navy in 1946, he enrolled in Pratt Institute to prepare for a career as an artist. In 1947, he married Joyce Fromkin, a girl he had known since childhood; in 1948, they moved to Brooklyn. After his graduation from Pratt in 1950, he was hired by the L. W. Frohlich advertising agency, where he became art director for the Westinghouse account. In the same year, he also enrolled in creative writing courses at the New School for Social Research, where he studied with Harold Glicksberg and Don Wolfe. Under their guidance, Wallant wrote a group of short stories and a novel, *Tarzan's Cottage*, which was never published.

In 1953, Wallant moved to the advertising agency of Doyle, Kitchen, and McCormick. He also moved his family from New Rochelle, New York, where a son, Scott, had been born in 1952, to Norwalk, Connecticut, where, in 1954, his daughter Leslie was born. In 1955, his short story "I Held Back My Hand" appeared in *New Voices 2: American Writing Today*, edited by his writing instructor, Don Wolfe. It was his first publication. During the late 1950's, Wallant submitted to various publishers his early novels *Tarzan's Cottage* and *The Odyssey of a Middleman*, but neither met with any success. Wallant changed jobs a third time in 1957, moving to McCann Erikson as an art director, a position he was to hold until shortly before his death. His second daughter, Kim, was also born the same year. Another story, "The Man Who Made a Nice Appearance," was published in 1958 in *New Voices 3*, edited by Charles Glicksberg.

Wallant's third novel was accepted within twenty-four hours of its submis-

sion to Harcourt, Brace. Originally entitled *A Scattering in the Dark*, it
appeared in 1960 retitled as *The Human Season*. Although it received few
reviews, some were enthusiastic and helped to create a small, underground
reputation for his work. In spite of its limited commercial success, the novel
received the Harry and Ethel Daroff Memorial Fiction Award from the Jewish
Book Council for the best novel on a Jewish theme. The publication of *The
Pawnbroker* in 1961, also by Harcourt, Brace, established Wallant's reputation
as a novelist. The book was nominated for a National Book Award, and the
screen rights were sold to Sidney Lumet, who in 1965 made a critically
acclaimed film starring Rod Steiger.

The modest success of *The Pawnbroker* came at a crucial period in Wallant's
life. For years, he had balanced his work as an advertising art director with
his after-hours vocation of writing, and he was having increasing difficulty in
reconciling his two lives. A resolution of sorts seemed imminent when he
received a Guggenheim fellowship in 1962, which allowed him to travel in
Europe and to write full time. For three months, he traveled abroad. Joyce
joined him briefly in Italy, and then Wallant went on to Spain. He returned
home with the idea for a comic novel, to be called *Tannenbaum's Journey*,
based on his travels. He also resolved to devote his life to full-time writing
and resigned his position with McCann Erikson. He took a small room in
New York to use as a retreat for his work. In spite of feeling tired, Wallant
was excited by his prospects; the European trip had given him inspiration.
Then, quite suddenly, he was stricken by a viral infection and lapsed into a
coma. He died of an aneurysm of the brain a week later on December 5,
1962.

At the time of his death, Wallant had two novels, *The Tenants of Moonbloom* and *The Children at the Gate*, under consideration by Harcourt, Brace,
and it fell to his editor, Dan Wickenden, to see these projects through the
press. *The Tenants of Moonbloom* was published in 1963, as were two other
pieces: a story, "When Ben Awakened," in *American Scene: New Voices*,
again edited by Don Wolfe, and an essay, "The Artist's Eye," for the *Teacher's
Notebook in English*. *The Children at the Gate*, although written before *The
Tenants of Moonbloom*, was not published until 1964.

Analysis

Just before his death, Edward Lewis Wallant wrote: "I suggest that most
people are nearsighted, myopic in their inability to perceive the details of
human experience." It was a condition he found perfectly normal; there is
simply too much energy used up in everyday life, having families, supporting
oneself, and living in a community, for much insight into the lives of fellow
human beings, except as they relate to one's own immediate needs. Yet there
are times, Wallant noted, when people experience an unrecognized yearning
to "know what lies in the hearts of others." "It is then," he wrote, "that we

turn to the artist, because only he can reveal even the little corners of the things beyond bread alone." It is revealing that Wallant, first trained as a graphic artist, should title the one essay in which he set forth his artistic credo "The Artist's Eye." In this essay, Wallant explores the relationship between the observable, everyday world and the interpretation of that world through the writer's heightened sense of awareness.

In all four of Wallant's published novels, this theme of heightened perception is central. The protagonist, who has become emotionally insulated from life, experiences a reawakening of feelings and rejoins the world around him. This spiritual and emotional rebirth comes as the result of the death of someone who has become close to the protagonist. The impact of this death, which often happens in a shocking way and with suddenness, penetrates the emotional barriers Wallant's characters erect against the onslaught of modern, urban life: Joe Berman escapes the past, Sol Nazerman is rescued from both the past and the dim recesses of his pawnshop, Angelo DeMarco gets beyond his streetwise sassiness, and Norman Moonbloom overcomes his inertia and learns to act. In each case and with each novel, Wallant takes his readers into the lives of his characters and reveals the little corners of the human heart.

Wallant's first novel, *The Human Season*, is the story of a middle-aged, middle-class man who must come to grips with himself following the death of his wife. Joe Berman is recognizably a twentieth century Everyman who lives a life barely distinguishable from that of his neighbors. He is a Russian Jew who immigrated to America when he was a little boy, and he seemingly has attained the American dream, founding his own plumbing business, owning his own modest home, marrying, and fathering three children. His wife, Mary, of "obligatory blonde, American prettiness," as one critic has described her, dies prior to the beginning of the novel, leaving him alone to face life and his largely unrecognized emotions. The structure of the novel intensifies the tension between past and present by alternating scenes from the present, in which Wallant skillfully renders Berman's daily life through a series of highly detailed episodes, with incidents from the past, each of them exposing some traumatic memory. In their reverse progression into the earlier years of Berman's life, these dreams deepen one's understanding not only of Berman's character but also of the formation of his emotional paralysis. Beginning on April 30, 1956, the day of Mary's fatal stroke, they recede back to September, 1907, when Berman was a little boy of nine living in Russia. The dreams contrast sharply in their emotional vividness with the increasingly comatose quality of Berman's present life. He has become an automaton, living without connection in an environment increasingly alien to him. He lashes out at the objects which remind him of his wife's delicacy and sensitivity as he succumbs to his "numbing, disorienting grief." Finally, Berman tries to kill himself.

As he becomes more and more blind to the real world, the world of his dreams, his past, becomes more vivid until it begins to intrude into his present, waking life. Increasingly, Wallant returns to images of the natural sources of Berman's earlier feelings in his memories of his father and of his life in Russia. Although there is a pastoral quality to these memories, Wallant does not suggest a return to some agrarian ideal. Berman's dreams remind him of his human capacities and inaugurate his search for something which will approximate the bond with the nature of his youth. Among the dreams are recollections of his father and Judaism. Berman realizes how neglectful he was of his own son, who was killed in the war, and how estranged from the healing qualities of his Jewishness he had become. The death of his wife, after all, merely provides a catalyst for his sickness, causing his self-doubt and sense of alienation to surface. The initial moment of his illumination quite literally comes as a shock: in an attempt to fix a faulty television set, Berman is thrown across the room, and in his fear and astonishment, he begins to pray in a jumble of English, Yiddish, and Russian. In that moment, he discovers the meaning of all of the months of his suffering. He is alone.

It is from this revelation that he begins to reconstruct his life, one which will be authentic and will result in a new self. He discovers a craving for people; his dreams no longer haunt him but provide him with soothing images which strengthen his zest for self-renewal. In a scene that elevates the fiction to a mythical dimension, Berman is born again as he walks home in the rain after having "witnessed" the life around him. As the novel ends, Berman is waiting in his empty house for his son-in-law to take him home for a family dinner. In this final chapter, Wallant convincingly depicts a poignant example of man's infinite capacity for self-renewal.

Wallant abandoned work on a comic fiction, *Gimple the Beast*, to write his second novel, *The Pawnbroker*. As in his first novel, the central character is a middle-aged, Jewish immigrant. Sol Nazerman, however, did not arrive in America as a youth; instead, the forty-five-year-old ex-professor from the University of Krakow fled Europe and the death camps in which he had been a prisoner during World War II. Now he is the operator of a pawnshop in a black ghetto in New York City. The shop is owned by a minor underworld figure who uses it as a drop point for the transferral of illegal money. Nazerman is aware of the criminality of the operation but does not protest. He uses his income to support his sister and her family, who live in the suburbs. He also contributes to the support of his mistress, Tessie Rubin, who lives with her dying father. The novel brings together the nightmare world of the concentration camp as Nazerman remembers it with the corrupt urban world of the pawnshop.

As in *The Human Season*, the central character has walled himself off from the pain and suffering of the world around him. Amid the grotesques who visit his shop, Nazerman remains a private, isolated man. The novel is the story of his spiritual reawakening, which is largely brought about through the intervention of Jesus Ortiz, the black, Catholic assistant who works in the business, and whose energy and ambition awaken sympathy from Nazerman. The death of Ortiz during an attempted robbery of the shop, which occurs on the fifteenth anniversary of the destruction of Nazerman's family in the death camps, provides the shock that penetrates the insulation with which Nazerman has wrapped his feelings in order to maintain his delicate sense of survival. He recognizes the part he willingly plays in the chain of human exploitation of which his pawnshop is a microcosm, and he is forced to acknowledge the community of grief to which he belongs and from which he has so long isolated himself. The novel concludes with three acts of atonement for Nazerman as he rejoins the world. He telephones his nephew, Morton, and asks him to become his new assistant, thereby opening a father-son relationship with the young man who has been wanting it for so long. After the phone call, Nazerman sleeps and dreams, not a nightmare as he usually does, but a dream in which he is able to lay the dead past to rest. Finally, he, like Berman, learns to mourn and goes to Tessie to help her grieve over the death of her father. As in the previous novel, this act is an important sign of his rebirth.

The connections between Wallant's first two novels are more than superficial. The two protagonists, who have much in common, experience similar awakenings. Both novels interweave dreams with the narrative thread. Both men must expiate their guilt over the death of their sons. Berman never did respond to his son, who died in the war unaware of his father's love; Nazerman must seek forgiveness for the guilt he feels for the death of his son, who slipped out of his grasp and suffocated on the floor of a cattlecar on their way to the death camp. Both men are finally free from their past when they can fully and properly mourn the dead; then they can rebuild their lives again in the present. *The Pawnbroker* is the darkest of Wallant's books and seems to have provided a release for the marvelously comic voice of the last two novels.

During the summer of 1961 while he was awaiting the outcome of his Guggenheim application, Wallant underwent a radical shift in attitude concerning his vocation as a writer. In the little more than six months he took to complete the manuscript of *The Pawnbroker*, he drafted the first version of *The Children at the Gate*, a completed version of which was left with his editor before he began his European travels with the fellowship money.

The novel concerns the relationship between the literal-minded, nineteen-year-old Angelo DeMarco, who makes the rounds of a Catholic hospital to take orders among the patients for the pharmacy where he works, and Sammy Cahan, a clownish Jew who is an orderly in the hospital. DeMarco, who clings to a rationalism as a defense against the horrors of his life—his idiot sister, his fatherless home, his obsessively religious mother, and the dying patients among whom he must spend his days—is redeemed by the antics of Cahan, whose essentially emotional view of life provides DeMarco with his spiritual change. Unlike Berman and Nazerman, Cahan seems to have inherited his life-giving vision, which he is able to spread throughout the hospital. As with the pawnshop and later the apartment houses of *The Tenants of Moonbloom*, the hospital setting provides a microcosm for the world's suffering humanity against which the drama of the central character's spiritual growth can take place. Once again, it is a death, Cahan's, which shocks DeMarco awake to the final recognition of his stifling life and the possibility of rebirth, a recognition which is made concrete in DeMarco's ministrations to his retarded, childlike sister, who has been raped by their father. Like Berman and Nazerman before him, DeMarco reveals his growing humanity through his acts of kindness and tenderness.

The centrality of the dream-world which played so important a part in the previous novels is replaced here by a living world of dreams which DeMarco must shatter before abandoning his barricade of toughness. It is no coincidence that he first discovers Cahan in the children's ward at the hospital, for it is the childlike simplicity of the orderly, his trust and innocence, which DeMarco must rediscover in order to be reborn. *The Children at the Gate* reveals the intermingling of Christian and Jewish myths which Wallant used to such great effect in all of his novels. It is not only the accumulation of religious artifacts or references in the novel, but also Cahan's portrayal as the religious fool and his martyrdom in the Christlike crucifixion on the hospital gates which sets the tone. Just as the death of the assistant, Ortiz, in *The Pawnbroker*, precipitated Nazerman's rebirth, so here Cahan's death reveals to DeMarco the path he must follow. The roles of teacher and priest, the relationship between suffering and redemption, the confluence of death and rebirth form a religious nexus which gives this book its especially powerful message of commitment, community, and love.

Although there were comic elements in *The Children at the Gate*, it was only in *The Tenants of Moonbloom* that Wallant's comic genius flowered. His last novel exhibits a certainty of handling and a smoothness of execution which were the results of his growing confidence as a writer. Wallant had thrown over his job as an advertising man and had made a commitment to literature.

The Tenants of Moonbloom traces the emergence of Norman Moonbloom, an introverted rent collector who manages four decrepit apartment buildings for his brother, and who emerges from his passivity as the result of his contact with the urban flotsam and jetsam who inhabit his apartments. Moonbloom, who is thirty-three at the time of the story, has finally settled down after years of college and a number of majors. He is a rather average young man who has spent his life retreating from people, and although he would prefer to hide in the womblike security of his apartment, his tenants persistently intrude on his consciousness. Finally unable any longer to retreat from the world, Moonbloom plunges into his past, like Berman and Nazerman, to search for a base upon which he can build a relationship with life. Through a series of seemingly disconnected visions, Moonbloom awakens to an understanding of the humanity which he shares with even the most bizarre of his tenants. He launches a "holy war" of rehabilitation in order to try to respond to the needs of those human beings placed into his trust.

Through a series of jolts, not unlike the ones received by Wallant's other anti-heroes, delivered by the various inhabitants of Moonbloom's apartments, he is transformed. This is accomplished during three visits he makes to his tenants. Each successive visit further shocks him into responding. His reaction culminates in the frenzy of activity in which he engages to bring the buildings and by extension the lives of his tenants up to some sort of standard. Although Moonbloom, a former rabbinical student, is Wallant's final Christ-figure, this novel relies far less than its predecessors, most notably *The Children at the Gate*, on biblical imagery and allusions, despite Moonbloom's messianic zeal to convert his tenants into full-blown human beings. In his last novel, Wallant was to integrate the comic and the tragic. As one critic has written, Wallant moved from being a cautious optimist to become "the comic celebrant of man's capacity to live an energetic, courageous, and spiritually dedicated existence."

Wallant's reputation rests firmly on a small body of fiction which he wrote with much passion and energy. Necessarily, this reputation has been enhanced by the tragedy of his untimely death and the unfulfilled promise of his career. His prose reflects a joyful celebration of life, life in all of its manifest complexities. Although he has often been compared to two other Jewish writers, Bruce Jay Friedman and Nathanael West, Wallant did not succumb to the absurd fantasies of the first nor to the despair of the second. Perhaps his importance as a modern novelist is best summarized by a critic who wrote that it was his cautious refusal to accept "the existential despair and the universal isolation of modern man" which distinguished him from his contemporaries and led him to affirm quietly the worth and joy of life. Wallant's novels are a testament to the continuing resilience of the human spirit.

Bibliography
Ayo, Nicholas. "Secular Heart: The Achievement of Edward Lewis Wallant," in *Critique*. XII (1970), pp. 86-94.
Baumbach, Jonathan. *The Landscape of Nightmare: Studies in the Contemporary Novel*, 1965.
Galloway, David D. *Edward Lewis Wallant*, 1979.
Gurko, Leo. "Edward Lewis Wallant as Urban Novelist," in *Twentieth Century Literature*. XX (October, 1974), pp. 252-261.
Lewis, Robert W. "The Hung-Up Heroes of Edward Lewis Wallant," in

Renascence. XXIV (1972), pp. 70-84.
Stanford, Raney. "The Novels of Edward Wallant," in *Colorado Quarterly.* XVII (1969), pp. 393-405.

Charles L. P. Silet

ROBERT PENN WARREN

Born: Guthrie, Kentucky; April 24, 1905

Principal long fiction

Night Rider, 1939; *At Heaven's Gate*, 1943; *All the King's Men*, 1946; *World Enough and Time*, 1950; *Band of Angels*, 1955; *The Cave*, 1959; *Wilderness: A Tale of the Civil War*, 1961; *Flood: A Romance of Our Times*, 1964; *Meet Me in the Green Glen*, 1971; *A Place to Come To*, 1977.

Other literary forms

Robert Penn Warren has written successfully in so many genres that Charles Bohner has called him "the pentathlon champion of American literature." In addition to his novels, he has published short stories, numerous volumes of poetry, and a considerable amount of nonfiction. Warren's fiction and his poetry often consider the same philosophical themes: the meaning of history, the loss of innocence and the recognition of evil in the fallen world, and the difficulty of finding a moral balance in a world in which traditional Christian values seem to be faltering. For example, in his book-length poem, *Brother to Dragons: A Tale in Verse and Voices* (1953), Warren begins with a historical event—a brutal murder of a slave by Thomas Jefferson's nephew, Lilburne Lewis—and creates a philosophical examination of man's fallen nature. Warren does something very similar in his novel *World Enough and Time*. The story is based on a murder which occurred in 1825, but the novel, like the poem, becomes an examination of man's fall from innocence and the difficulty of establishing moral ideals in a fallen world.

Warren's concerns over history and morality are also evident in his earliest, nonfiction works. In his first book, a biography, *John Brown: The Making of a Martyr* (1929), Warren contends that Brown did not tread the path of morality quite so righteously as Ralph Waldo Emerson had thought he had; in his fallen condition, Brown mistook his own egotism for pure idealism. Warren's neoorthodox insistence on man's fallen nature and his skepticism about the possibilities of pure idealism, both of which are reflected in his novels, led him to accept the traditionalist attitudes of the Southern intellectuals who made up the "Fugitive Group," and he contributed to the Agrarian Manifesto, *I'll Take My Stand* (1930). Warren did, however, espouse a more liberal attitude toward racial matters in his later nonfiction works, *Segregation: The Inner Conflict in the South* (1956) and *Who Speaks for the Negro?* (1965).

Warren's social criticism has ultimately proved less influential than his literary criticism. His *Selected Essays* (1958) contains perceptive studies of Samuel Taylor Coleridge's *The Rime of the Ancient Mariner*, Joseph Conrad's *Nostromo* (1904), William Faulkner, Ernest Hemingway, and Katherine Anne

Porter. These essays are important not only for what they say about these authors, but also for what they reveal about Warren's own work. Even more important than these essays, however, has been Warren's collaboration with Cleanth Brooks. Their textbooks, *Understanding Fiction* (1943, 1959) and *Understanding Poetry*, (1938, 1950, 1960) helped to change substantially the way literature was taught in the United States.

Achievements

For most readers Warren's name is probably most associated with his novel *All the King's Men*, for which he won both the Pulitzer Prize for Fiction and the National Book Award. He also won the Robert Meltzer Award from the Screen Writer's Guild for the play based on that novel. Warren's short story "Blackberry Winter" has also been highly acclaimed and widely anthologized. Other readers think of Warren primarily as a poet, and with good reason; he has won the Pulitzer Prize for Poetry twice, first for *Promises: Poems 1954-1956* (1957), which also won the Edna St. Vincent Millay Prize and the National Book Award for Poetry, and a second time for *Now and Then: Poems 1976-1978* (1978). *Selected Poems: New and Old, 1923-1966* (1966) won the Bollingen Prize from Yale University, and *Audubon: A Vision* won the Van Wyck Brooks Award and the National Medal for Literature. Warren was elected to the American Philosophical Society in 1952 and to the American Academy of Arts and Sciences in 1959. When all of his activities are taken together, he well may be considered as Marshall Walker claims, "America's most distinguished living man of letters."

Biography

Robert Penn Warren's background and experience have had a tremendous impact upon the thematic concerns of his fiction. He demonstrates the need, common to so many Southern writers, to cope with the burden of the past. He also writes out of a scholar's familiarity with and devotion to certain prominent literary artists, past and present, particularly the Elizabethan and Jacobean dramatists, Joseph Conrad, William Faulkner, and T. S. Eliot. His academic studies, pursued in a long career as an English professor, may have a great deal to do with the structure of his works and their typically tragic mode. His recurring subject, however, is the peculiar experience of the South; a love-hate relationship with a dying heritage runs throughout his work.

Born to Robert Franklin and Anna Ruth Penn Warren on April 24, 1905, in the tiny Kentucky town of Guthrie, Warren grew up in an almost classic Southern situation. His father, a banker and businessman struggling to support a large family, did not initially fire the young Warren's imagination as his grandfather did. The emotional bond between Warren and his maternal grandfather, Thomas Gabriel Penn, ripened during long summers spent on his grandfather's tobacco farm. Here, Warren experienced the pastoral charms of agrarian life, soaked up the nostalgic glow of the American Civil War from his grandfather, and absorbed the rhetoric and humor that permeates the Southern storytelling.

Thomas Gabriel Penn had been a cavalryman during the Civil War, and many an afternoon with his grandson was spent reliving the legendary time. It is not surprising that the boy looked upon the Civil War as America's great epic, as imbued with nobility and tragedy as Homer's *Iliad* (c. 800 B.C.). He was not blind, however, to the irony and ambiguity of his grandfather, as representative of the values of the aristocratic horse soldier. Warren has commemorated his realization that the romantic image of the Confederate cavalryman had its darker side in the poem "Court Martial" in *Promises: Poems 1954-1956*, which is about his grandfather's hanging of bushwhackers without benefit of legal trial. Since this poem was written much later, however, it is possible that the ambiguous view of the grandfather was partially constructed from a more mature understanding. The event, however, was a true one that evidently made a deep impression on the young Warren. In any case, Warren was absorbing background for a number of later novels, such as *Wilderness: A Tale of the Civil War* and *Band of Angels*. In neither of these does he write as an apologist for the Old South, but he does expose the moral shortcomings of Northerners, much as he does in his early biography of John Brown.

Warren was also absorbing the local tales of tobacco war, when the growers of dark-fired tobacco banded together to boycott the tobacco company that regulated prices. Warren's first novel, *Night Rider*, was written from childhood memories of such local stories. Warren's brother Thomas, who became a grain dealer, knew all the farmers of the region and was adept at repeating such tales.

The young Warren loved nature, collected butterflies, snakes, rocks, leaves, and aspired to paint animals (an interest reflected in his poem about John Audubon). Later, he hunted with his brother and learned taxidermy. These experiences were more important, perhaps, to the content of his poetry than to his fiction. In spite of his persistent affinity for nature, he has usually recognized in his fiction its essential amorality: "The blank cup of nature," he calls it in *World Enough and Time*.

In spite of the contribution to his early imaginative development by his grandfather and his agrarian milieu, the influence of Warren's father was subtle and pervasive, perhaps more significant in the long run to the human relationships explored in his novels. Ambiguous father-son relationships appear over and over in such novels as *All the King's Men*, *The Cave*, *At Heaven's Gate*, and *A Place to Come To*. None is modeled after Warren's actual relationship to his own father, but they reflect a combination of admiration, guilt, and mystery that suggests some deep personal involvement in the issues they raise.

Warren has often admitted to an odd sense of guilt about "stealing his father's life." Robert Franklin Warren had wanted to be a lawyer and a poet, but had become a businessman instead, because of financial responsibilities not only to his own family, but also to a family of half brothers and sisters left without a provider when his father died. One of Warren's favorite reminiscences is about finding a book with some poems written by his father in it and carrying it with delight to him. His father summarily confiscated the book, and his son never saw it again. Warren thought perhaps his father had been embarrassed or pained at this reminder of a goal long since set aside. According to Warren, his father never regretted the obligations that dictated the terms of his life. Indeed, he took joy in them. Warren speaks with an admiration bordering an awe of the seemingly effortless rectitude of his father, and the ideal relationship between his father and mother.

As the result of an accident when he was fifteen years old, Warren lost the sight of one eye and was thus prevented from pursuing a career as a naval officer, as he had planned. Warren went, instead, to Vanderbilt University and came under the influence of John Crowe Ransom and the Fugitives, a group of academics and townspeople who met regularly to discuss philosophy and poetry. Ransom soon recognized Warren's unusual ability and encouraged him to write poetry.

Warren was graduated summa cum laude from Vanderbilt in 1926 and pursued an M.A. at the University of California at Berkeley. While there, he became an ardent student of Elizabethan and Jacobean drama, which perhaps struck a responsive chord in an imagination already steeped in the violence and melodrama of Southern history. He started to work on a doctorate at Yale University, but left for Oxford, England, as a Rhodes scholar, where he received a Bachelor of Letters Degree in 1930.

During this period, Warren wrote his first book *John Brown: The Making of a Martyr*. To some extent, this book grew out of an impulse shared with a number of his Vanderbilt friends and other writers of the so-called Southern Renaissance. They were concerned about the exclusively Northern bias of most historians dealing with events leading up to and during the Civil War and its aftermath. Certainly, Warren presents a jaundiced view of the radical abolitionist. Brown seems to have provided a nucleus for Warren's meditations about the effects of power and the misuses of altruism which were to be explored in a number of later novels, especially *Night Rider* and *All the King's Men*. He also wrote his first fiction while at Oxford, a short story called "Prime Leaf," about the impact of the Kentucky tobacco war on an old man, his son, and his grandson. The old man has a role similar to that of the elder Todd in *Night Rider*, the wise man who bows out of the organization when it resorts to vigilante tactics.

Warren taught at a number of universities, including Louisiana State, where he lived in the legendary ambience of the Southern demogogue, Huey Long, whose presence lies behind the fictional Willie Stark of *All the King's Men*. Warren says he knew nothing about the real Huey Long, but the mythical Huey was on everyone's lips. Even casual conversations often dwelt upon questions of power and ethics, of means and ends, of "historical costs." In an essay entitled "All the King's Men: The Matrix of Experience," in John Lewis Longley's *Robert Penn Warren: A Collection of Critical Essays* (1965), Warren writes:

> Melodrama was the breath of life. There had been melodrama in the life I had known in Tennessee, but with a difference; in Tennessee the melodrama seemed to be different from the stuff of life, something superimposed upon life, but in Louisiana people lived melodrama, seemed to live, in fact, for it, for this strange combination of philosophy, humor and violence. Life was a tale that you happened to be living—and that "Huey" happened to be living before your eyes.

These remarks demonstrate that Warren is not primarily a historical novelist, but rather a classicist, fascinated with the universal patterns in particular experience. Thus, he discourages close comparisons between Willie Stark and Huey Long, pointing out that he wrote the first version of the story as a verse drama in Italy, as he watched Benito Mussolini, another man of the people, consolidate his power.

In Warren's writing career, the years from 1944 to 1950, though a dry period for poetry, were productive ones for fiction and literary criticism. Besides *All the King's Men*, he produced *At Heaven's Gate*, about the unscrupulous liaison between government and industry, and *World Enough and Time*, about a nineteenth century murder case. When Warren was poetry consultant for the Library of Congress in 1944-1945, Katherine Anne Porter, who was fiction consultant that year, threw on his desk the confession of Jeroboam Beauchamp, hanged for murder in Kentucky in 1826. Porter announced cryptically that she was giving him a novel. This was, indeed, the germ for his most complex novel, *World Enough and Time*.

Warren's dry period in poetry eventually ended after he divorced his first wife, Emma Brescia, married the writer Eleanor Clark, and fathered two children. He has been writing excellent poetry ever since and has produced several more novels. The melodramatic *Band of Angels*, about a young woman brought up by a doting white father in ignorance of her slave status, is one of Warren's least successful achievements. Perhaps its shortcomings simply reflect the fact that Warren was not reared in the Deep South. His blacks do not have the same authenticity as his hill people. In fact, none of his later novels have equaled his early *Night Rider*, *All the King's Men*, and *World Enough and Time*.

Analysis

What Robert Penn Warren says about other writers often provides an important insight into his own works. This is especially true of Warren's perceptive essay on "The Great Mirage: Conrad and *Nostromo*" in *Selected Essays*, in which he discusses the enigmatic speech of Stein in Joseph Conrad's *Lord Jim* (1900):

> A man that is born falls into a dream like a man who falls into the sea. If he tries to climb out into the air as inexperienced people endeavor to do, he drowns—*nicht wahr?* . . . No! I tell you! The way is to the destructive element submit yourself, and with the exertions of your hands and feet in the water make the deep, deep sea keep you up.

Warren interprets the dream here as "man's necessity to justify himself and his actions into moral significance of some order, to find sanctions." The destructiveness of the dream arises from man's nature as an egotistical animal with savage impulses, not completely adapted to the dream-sea of ideas. The one who learns to swim instead of drowning in the unnatural sea of ideas is he who realizes that the values he creates are illusion, but that "the illusion is necessary, is infinitely precious, is the mark of his human achievement, and is, in the end, his only truth." Warren calls *Nostromo* "a study in the definition and necessity of illusion." This phrase could also describe most of Warren's works of fiction.

Warren's classification of thematic elements in Conrad's stories could also be applied to his own. Warren writes that Conrad is concerned with the man who lacks imagination, but clings to fidelity and duty (like the old captain in *Youth*, 1902); the sinner against human solidarity and the human mission (like Kurtz in *Heart of Darkness*, 1902, and Decoud in *Nostromo*); and the redeemed man (Jim in *Lord Jim* and Dr. Monygham in *Nostromo*). Warren says that Conrad is most interested in the latter—"the crisis of this story comes when the hero recognizes the terms on which he may be saved, the moment, to take Morton Zabel's phrase, of the 'terror of the awakening.'"

One might note that in Warren's novel *At Heaven's Gate*, Jerry's dirt farmer father fits the pattern of natural rectitude, while Slim Sarrett, the nihilistic, cynical artist, is certainly the sinner against human solidarity. No one seems to be redeemed in *At Heaven's Gate*, though Jerry might have a chance in a hypothetical future, since he has acquired considerable self-knowledge. Mr. Munn in *Night Rider* has also stripped away his own illusions, but he dies, like William Shakespeare's Macbeth, without redemption. In other novels of this period, however, Burden in *All the King's Men*, and perhaps even the murderer in *World Enough and Time*, achieve some kind of absolution. Warren and Conrad share this deep obsession with the need for redemption, and though the sentiment is religious and may be expressed in Christian imagery, it is consistently humanistic in emphasis. The world they both recognize is a naturalistic one, but man must live in two worlds, the world of facts and the world of ideas, which he creates himself. Warren's notion of submission to the realm of ideas is analogous, perhaps, to Ernest Hemingway's code of the hunter, the fisherman, the bullfighter, or the soldier, which provides existential meaning in a meaningless world.

Warren's early novels, particularly *Night Rider*, *All the King's Men*, and *World Enough and Time*, which critics generally agree are his best, trace a pattern of increasing complexity in the theme of man's vacillation between the fantasy of dreams and the reality of facts. After *World Enough and Time*, which is almost too densely packed and convoluted in theme, Warren relaxed his insistence that everything must be said on the subject of illusion and reality in one novel. Later works, such as *Meet Me in the Green Glen* and *Wilderness: A Tale of the Civil War*, though not conspicuously different in theme, concentrate on a particular manifestation of the problem—on the nature of love in *Meet Me in the Green Glen*, and on the nature of altruism in *Wilderness*.

Actually, Warren's examination of the apposition between the world of ideas and the world of facts begins in his first book, *John Brown: The Making of a Martyr*. Warren portrays the militant abolitionist as not so much obsessed with freeing slaves as with starring in his own myth. Brown is encouraged in this role by the unqualified praise of Ralph Waldo Emerson, whom Warren believes is a writer of empty words, with little perception of the real world; Warren quotes Emerson as saying of Brown, "He is a man to make friends wherever on earth courage and integrity are esteemed—the rarest of heroes, a pure idealist, with no by-ends of his own." Warren does not for a moment believe that Brown was a "pure idealist"; moreover, Warren has a continuing distrust of "pure idealists," whoever they may be. In his fiction, Warren is inclined to show abstract idealists as lacking in self-knowledge, capable of self-righteous violence because they refuse to acknowledge their own irrational impulses. The best example of this personality-type in Warren's fiction is Adam Stanton, in *All the King's Men*, who assassinates Willie Stark because Willie, the man of fact, seduced Adam's sister.

John Brown, however, as a man who uses exalted ideas to inflate his own self-image, is more akin to Warren's Professor Ball, Dr. MacDonald, and Mr. Munn of *Night Rider*; Bogan Murdock, the industrialist, and Slim Sarett, of *At Heaven's Gate*; and Wilkie Barron, the manipulative false friend of Jeremiah Beaumont, in *World Enough and Time*. Willie Stark, though categorized by Jack Burden as the "man of fact," in contrast to Adam Stanton, the "man of idea," has his own idealistic dream of the people's hospital, free to anyone who needs it. Whether that dream was truly altruistic, however, or tinged by the secret need for a personal monument to his existence, is ambiguous.

Thus, Warren suggests that the self is itself part of the dream-sea of ideas. Warren's protagonists are often initially passive persons whose emptiness is filled by other more dynamic personalities. Having acquired a somewhat fictitious self under such influence, they proceed to act in the real world as though that dream were true—often with tragic results. Thus, Mr. Munn seems an innocuous, ordinary young lawyer when he first appears in *Night*

Rider, but he is drawn irresistibly to his more dynamic friend, Mr. Christian, who has a legitimate concern for the plight of the tobacco growers at the mercy of the price-controlling tobacco company. Munn learns to savor his new role as labor leader. He is ripe, then, for indoctrination by more conniving, professional agitators, Professor Ball and Dr. MacDonald, who preach a secret society that will scrape the fields of uncooperative growers and punish backsliders who dare to violate the embargo. What begins as a lawful strike by the downtrodden majority becomes a lawless vigilante group that destroys crops, burns warehouses, and commits murder. In the case of Munn, the crisis of this psychic change in direction comes when he realizes that his assigned task to assassinate the tobacco farmer Bunk Trevelyon, whom he once defended in court on a murder charge, is not only his "duty" to the group; it satisfies something very personal in himself that he has not yet recognized. Trevelyon had committed the murder of which he was once accused, and the black who was hanged for that murder was innocent. Trevelyon thus becomes the symbol for Munn's half-conscious cooperation in framing the black, or, to use another favorite term of Warren, Munn's original sin. In this ritual of retribution, the shared myth of community justice fuses with Munn's private myth of killing the shadow-self, an act of both self-condemnation and deliberate concealment of a secret crime.

After this private confrontation and ritual killing of his shadow-self, Munn makes no more moral objections to anything Ball and MacDonald want to do. The three lead a concerted assault on the company warehouses, which results in a number of casualties. One person who dies is young Benton Todd, who had been an ardent admirer of Munn. Moreover, Todd hoped to marry Mr. Christian's daughter, Lucille, who has been having a secret affair with Munn. If Trevelyon symbolizes the murderous shadow-self that Munn has hated to acknowledge, Benton Todd suggests the lost idealism, the better dream that Munn has betrayed.

Munn's subsequent flight to the West to escape prosecution for a murder he did not commit might have resulted in redemption, but it does not. The pattern of redemption is presented to him obliquely by the story of Proudfit, the impoverished farmer who is sheltering Munn. Proudfit tells of his own checkered career in the West, as a buffalo hunter and hide-tanner, with companions as rough and wild as himself. Eventually, however, he lives in peace among Indians. When he becomes ill, the Indians care for him, using all their resources of natural healing and religious ritual. In his fever, he eventually has a vision of Kentucky, where he was reared, and a young woman waiting beside a stream. His strength then begins to return, so he leaves the Indian friends and goes back to find the very woman he saw in his vision, now his wife, and the very hill he saw, which is now his farm.

Proudfit's story is both an engrossing dialect narrative and a unique version of the underlying myth of death and resurrection. Proudfit's humble redemption contrasts with the myth of sin and damnation implied in Munn's career. Both Proudfit and Munn have a period of withdrawal (Proudfit, among the Indians; Munn, on Proudfit's remote farm), time to rethink their past lives and future goals. This experience is analogous, perhaps, to the withdrawal and contemplation that the mythic hero undergoes before he returns to his homeland as a new man. Munn, however, is not transformed. He does become mildly obsessed with the innocent black who died in Trevelyon's stead, but he cannot even remember the man's name. Perhaps his inability to name the scapegoat is intended to suggest Munn's distance from the redemption offered by Christ's sacrifice. This does not mean that Warren was advocating Christianity; he was admitting, at least, a moral vacuum where traditional values have been eliminated in a society concerned primarily with power and wealth.

The polarity of idea and fact receives more explicit development in *All the King's Men*. Again, an essentially passive person, Jack Burden, feeds emotionally on a more dynamic personality, Willie Stark. Burden calls himself—somewhat cynically—an idealist, but his idealism consists mostly of a fastidious preference for not getting his hands dirty with some of Stark's more questionable political manuevers. Willie is good-naturedly tolerant of Jack's moral preferences, since he has Tiny Duffy to do his dirty work.

Jack considers himself a good judge of character and motives, but when a cherished image about the purity and goodness of his old girl friend, Anne Stanton, is proven to be false, he is devasted and lost in self-doubt. Anne, who is quite a passive, unfulfilled person herself, has become Stark's mistress. Jack's first impulse is to flee, to escape, to drown, to fall into what he calls the Great Sleep. From this symbolic death, Burden is born again into a bleak but emotionally insulating belief in the Great Twitch—an understanding of the world as completely amoral and mechanistic, wherein no one has any responsibility for what happens. Here, indeed, Burden has stepped out of the fantasy of dreams into the reality of facts.

Burden can now consent to let Stark use the information he has uncovered concerning Judge Irwin's long-forgotten political crime. Burden soon discovers how brutal the world of fact can be, when Judge Irwin's suicide reveals that the judge was actually Jacks' father. Hardly recovered from this blow, Burden recognizes a measure of responsibility for the deaths of Willie Stark and his best friend, Adam Stanton, who is shot by Willie's bodyguard after the assassination. Though his passivity and noninvolvement, Jack Burden had virtually handed over Anne Stanton to his more dynamic boss, and thus set the stage for assassination.

The novel is a fascinating study of symbiotic relationships, of which the most striking is that between Willie Stark, the practical politician, and Adam Stanton, the puritanical idealist and perfectionist. Warren also suggests a politically symbiotic relationship between the demagogue and the people he represents. In social terms, the world of *All the King's Men* is more complex than that of *Night Rider*. Munn's career is essentially that of the tragic hero, the good but not exclusively good man who is corrupted by power. Willie Stark, however, is sustained not only by his own drive for power, but also by the concerted will of his constituency, who feel themselves to be socially and politically helpless. He is probably more significant as an antidote to their depression than as an answer to their physical needs. Even though Willie wants to change the world of facts for their benefit—build roads, bridges, a free hospital—it is for his psychological impact, exemplifying the triumph of the common man over the privileged elite, that he is beloved. Thus, even the man of facts floats in the symbolic sea of ideas.

If the relationship between dream and reality is complicated in *All the King's Men*, in *World Enough and Time* it becomes intricately complex. Seldom have human aspirations been so relentlessly exposed, one after another, as frail illusions. Though it might be termed a historical novel, since it is based loosely on an actual event, or a philosophical novel, since it comments repeatedly on the abstract meaning of human behavior and aspiration, *World Enough and Time* is better termed a psychological novel, or more precisely, perhaps, an examination of the psychological motivations for philosophizing. It is certainly not, like Andrew Marvell's poem, "To His Coy Mistress," to which the title ironically alludes, a neat argument for seizing pleasures while one may. It is not a neat argument for any philosophical position, but it illuminates the sequential confusion of a reasonably thoughful, well-meaning person trying to identify himself and justify his actions.

Jeremiah Beaumont, the orphaned son of an unsuccessful Kentucky farmer in the early nineteenth century, becomes the loved protégé of Colonel Cassius Fort, a well-known lawyer and statesman of the region. Beaumont's exalted view of Colonel Fort receives a cruel blow from his dashing friend, Wilkie Barron, a popular man-about-town and dabbler in politics. Wilkie tells Jerry of a beautiful woman he once loved in vain, who was seduced by an older man who had come to console her when her father died. When the young woman, Rachel Jordan, had a stillborn child, the older man abandoned her. The knave who wronged her was the unimpeachable Colonel Fort.

The persuasive Wilkie succeeds in promoting in a somewhat passive Jerry a romantic vision of wronged womanhood. From this point on, Jerry creates his own drama of love and revenge, though Wilkie continues to manipulate him in ways he never understands until near the end of his life. Jeremiah repudiates Colonel Fort, his surrogate father, and woos and eventually wins the lovely Rachel, who is in a neurotic state of depression, not because of the supposed perfidy of Colonel Fort, but because of her baby's death. Jeremiah, blind to the real source of her despondency, hounds her into commanding him to defend her honor. Fort refuses a duel with Jerry, however, and the honorable vengeance seems destined to fizzle. Rachel is again pregnant and Jerry is fitting into the comfortable role of country squire. An unknown messenger brings to Rachel a slanderous handbill in which Colonel Fort, presumably denying to his political opponents his affair with Rachel, claims that Rachel had slept with a slave. Fort had gallantly claimed paternity of the child as a chivalric gesture. This shocking document, which is actually a forgery written by Wilkie Barron, precipitates Rachel's labor, and Jeremiah's child is also born dead. Jerry, in remorse, kills Fort—not openly in a duel, as he had planned, but secretly, letting it appear to be a political assassination.

Beaumont's trial is a bewildering process where deceit and truth become inextricably mixed. Wilkie Barron appears, however, and reveals Beaumont's vow to kill Fort, the reaction Wilkie had himself orchestrated even before Jeremiah had met the wronged lady. All is lost, and Beaumont is sentenced to hang. Rachel comes and stays with him in his basement jail cell, where they indulge in a passionate interlude—a veritable frenzy of love in the face of imminent death.

The unpredictable Wilkie appears at the last minute, after the lovers have unsuccessfully tried to commit suicide by drinking laudanum. Wilkie rescues them and sends them West to live in the desolate island refuge of a notorious bandit. This is a return to nature, but a nature devoid of its original innocence, incapable of healing the scars of "civilization." Jerry sinks into a bestial pattern and Rachel into insanity, eventually killing herself. Beaumont, who finds out that the slanderous handbill came from Wilkie Barron, is himself murdered as he seeks to find his way back to the hangman, resigned now to the most austere prize of all—neither love nor honor, but simply knowledge.

The flight to the West seems an almost gratuitous extension of suffering, especially since the real Jereboam Beauchamp, who murdered Colonel Solomon Sharp in 1825, did hang for his crime. The real trial and death of Beauchamp and his wife, Ann Cook, were only slightly less miserable, however, than Warren's fictional account.

Warren's extension to allow further demoralization of the lovers does help to explore all possible approaches to the problem of reconciling the ideal and the real. At first, Jeremiah believes that the idea must redeem the world: the mental context defines the object. Unfortunately, this route leads to an idealism divorced from action and allows a further evil to develop in the world— the death of his child. Then he believes that the world will redeem the idea— that is, the act of killing Fort will vindicate the idea of honor. In his flight to the West, he commits a third error, the opposite to his first: to deny the idea completely and embrace the physical world—"to seek communion only in the blank cup of nature."

Perhaps this tortured journey through innocence and experience should arrive at some reconciliation of opposites, but, if so, that too seems more dream than reality. "There must be a way whereby the word becomes flesh," muses Jeremiah in his last days. Even so, "I no longer seek to justify. I seek only to suffer." If this is not a particularly lucid analysis of philosophical possibilities, it may nevertheless by true psychologically to the mental and moral confusion in which men live. Perhaps it is intended to represent that "terror of the awakening" which Warren remarks in Conrad's *Lord Jim* when the "hero recognizes the terms on which he may be saved. . . ."

In his later novels, Warren continued to deal with the tension between the ideal and the real. The central mystery is usually the self, which the protagonist does not know except through a painful dialectic between exalted idea and gross fact. The protagonist also suffers from an inability to identify his real father or the real home where he belongs. Jack Burden and Jeremiah Beaumont both have several surrogate fathers, but they are responsible for the deaths of those to whom they owe the greatest filial loyalty. In *At Heaven's Gate*, Jerry Calhoun rejects his real father, the man of natural rectitude and love, and gives his devotion to Bogan Murdock, who, in Conrad's phrase, is hollow at the core.

Even in Warren's latest novel, *A Place to Come To*, the protagonist's first act is to despise his father and flee from his homeland; his last is to return to his hometown and make peace with the gentle stepfather he had never wanted to meet and the deaf father who had humiliated him as a child. As Warren wrote in "The Ballad of Billie Potts," the son must always return to the father, who often represents the flawed and fallen world which is our heritage.

The struggle between the ideal and the real in Warren's later novels is most explicit in *Wilderness: A Tale of the Civil War*, about an idealistic young Jew from Bavaria who comes to the United States to fight for the freedom of the slaves. When his father, a political prisoner in Berlin, dies, Adam Rosenzweig realizes that he has "lived only in the dream of his father's life, the father's manhood, the father's heroism." The trip to America is a way to star in his own heroic story. Adam's career in America is a progress in disillusionment; the telltale symbol of the compromising world of physical fact is his clubfoot, which he has desperately sought to hide in a specially constructed boot. If *World Enough and Time* is Warren's most complex treatment of idealism, *Wilderness* is his most direct treatment of this recurring subject, uncluttered by secondary themes or plots. Some critics prefer it for that reason, though it lacks the depth and humanity of Warren's earlier epic treatment of romantic idealism.

Meet Me in the Green Glen, is a pastoral novel about the nature of love. The love of a homeless young Italian immigrant for a dowdy country wife begins with carnal passion devoid of any attempt to idealize sexual attraction. The ironically named Angelo has distinct similarities to Conrad's "natural man," Nostromo, who lives in the physical world with little thought of any other. In fact, Angelo protects himself from any really serious bond with Cassie, the frustrated wife of a paralyzed man, casting her in the more tawdry dream of "scarlet woman" with gifts of a tight red dress and cosmetics. Only at the last, when she pleads for his life in court by confessing to the murder of her husband, of which Angelo is accused, does he recognize a love that transcends the merely physical. Just as Adam in *Wilderness* becomes more human when he admits the strength of flawed reality, so Angelo becomes more human when he recognizes the strength of dreams. In spite of Cassie's confession, Angelo is condemned to die, because, in his ignorance of the racial situation, he violates the mores of the community. Cassie, unable to save her lover, drifts off in the dream-sea of ideas, forgetting the sordid elements of their affair and only retaining the dream that transcends the body's need.

In these and other episodes in his fiction, Warren shows his fascination with what he called, in his Conrad essay, "the Great Mirage." It is a dark vision which sees all human values as illusions, yet insists—with the passion which has fueled five decades of creative work—that such illusions are necessary, and that man must continue to invent himself.

Major publications other than long fiction

SHORT FICTION: *Blackberry Winter*, 1946; *The Circus in the Attic and Other Stories*, 1947.

PLAY: *All the King's Men*, 1960.

POETRY: *Thirty-Six Poems*, 1935; *Eleven Poems on the Same Theme*, 1942; *Selected Poems 1923-1943*, 1944; *Brother to Dragons: A Tale in Verse and Voices*, 1953; *Promises: Poems 1954-1956*, 1957; *You, Emperors, and Others: Poems 1957-1960*, 1960; *Selected Poems: New and Old, 1923-1966*, 1966; *Incarnations: Poems 1966-1968*, 1968; *Audubon: A Vision*, 1969; *Homage to Theodore Dreiser on the Centennial of His Birth*, 1971; *Or Else—Poem/Poems 1968-1974*, 1974; *Selected Poems: 1923-1975*, 1976; *Now and Then: Poems 1976-1978*, 1978; *Brother to Dragons: A New Version*, 1979; *Being Here: Poetry 1977-1980*, 1980; *Ballad of a Deep Dream of Peace*, 1981 (with Bill Komodore); *Rumor Verified: Poems 1979-1980*, 1981.

NONFICTION: *John Brown: The Making of a Martyr*, 1929; *Understanding Poetry: An Anthology for College Students*, 1938, 1950, 1960 (with Cleanth Brooks); *Understanding Fiction*, 1943, 1959 (with Cleanth Brooks); *Segregation: The Inner Conflict in the South*, 1956; *Selected Essays*, 1958; *The Legacy of the Civil War: Meditations on the Centennial*, 1961; *Who Speaks for the Negro?*, 1965.

Bibliography

Bohner, Charles H. *Robert Penn Warren*, 1964.
Casper, Leonard. *Robert Penn Warren: The Dark and Bloody Ground*, 1960.
Guttenberg, Barnett. *Web of Being: The Novels of Robert Penn Warren*, 1975.
Huff, Mary Nance. *Robert Penn Warren. A Bibliography*, 1968.
Justus, James H. *The Achievement of Robert Penn Warren*, 1981.

Longley, John Lewis, Jr., ed. *Robert Penn Warren: Collection of Critical Essays*, 1965.
Walker, Marshall. *Robert Penn Warren: A Vision Earned*, 1979.

Katherine Snipes

FRANK WATERS

Born: Colorado Springs, Colorado; July 25, 1902

Principal long fiction

The Wild Earth's Nobility, 1935; *Below Grass Roots*, 1937; *The Dust Within the Rock*, 1940; *People of the Valley*, 1941; *River Lady*, 1942 (with Houston Branch); *The Man Who Killed the Deer*, 1942; *The Yogi of Cockroach Court*, 1947; *Diamond Head*, 1948 (with Houston Branch); *The Woman at Otowi Crossing: A Novel*, 1966; *Pikes Peak: A Family Saga*, 1971 (completely re-written, one-volume novel based on *The Wild Earth's Nobility*, *Below Grass Roots*, and *The Dust Within the Rock*).

Other literary forms

In addition to his long fiction, Frank Waters has written a number of books which combine history, enthnography, mythology, and speculative essay. All of these are centered in the American Southwest, and all deal, in whole or in part, with American Indian subjects. Of these, *Book of the Hopi* (1963) comes closest to ethnography in the strict sense, being the actual Hopi versions of their mythology, ritual, and belief, which Waters recorded from the words of tribal spokesmen. *Masked Gods: Navaho and Pueblo Ceremonialism* (1950) covers analagous material in relation to the Navaho and Pueblo tribes, and contains substantial sections in which these traditional beliefs are compared to the teachings of the Far East (particularly Tibetan Buddhism) and with the findings of nuclear scientists. *Pumpkin Seed Point: Being Within the Hopi* (1969) is a personal account of Waters' three-year residence among the Hopi, while he was compiling material for *Book of the Hopi*. *Mexico Mystique: The Coming Sixth World of Consciousness* (1975) treats the history, myth, and science (particularly calendrical) of Mexico. *Mountain Dialogues* (1981) is more eclectic in style, a series of essays ranging in subject matter from the relation of mind and matter to the bipolar symbolism reflected in the land around Waters' New Mexico home.

Waters' three biographies all deal with Western subjects: *Midas of the Rockies: The Story of Stratton and Cripple Creek* (1937) is the biography of Winfield Scott Stratton; *To Possess the Land* (1973) is the biography of Arthur Rochford Manby. *The Earp Brothers of Tombstone* (1937) is based on the recollections of Mrs. Virgil Earp, and amplified by material from Waters' own research.

In 1946, Waters published *The Colorado* as part of the "Rivers of America Series" (Farrar and Rinehart), and in 1964, an art monograph, *Leon Gaspard*. From 1950 to 1956, he was a regular contributor to the *Saturday Review* with reviews on books about the West. Numerous periodicals contain his essays on ethnography, history, and literary criticism, as well as a few short stories. These have not yet been collected into a book.

Achievements

Waters has given the American Southwest its finest and most complete literary rendering. In both his fiction and his nonfiction, he has sought to give literary vitality to the "spirit of place" imbuing that section of the American continent, and to show how this spirit variously affects the different races who live there, finding its expression in mythology, life-style, architecture, and ritual, all reflecting, in their different ways, the "vibratory quality of the land itself." Whether he portrays life by presenting the facts of history (as in his nonfiction), or in the symbols of his novels, or whether he writes about the mythological realm which occupies the zone between the two, his work captures the deep resonance of his locale, and thus the significance of place, per se, to man's development.

Waters is probably best known for his work on and about American Indians, and he is one of the few writers whose work has earned the respect of both the literary establishment and the American Indian communities. He is also one of the few writers who has worked successfully both in ethnography and in prose fiction. His firsthand knowledge of the Indian tribes of the Southwest, and his deep respect for their traditions and their instinctual attunement to their locale, have made it possible for Waters to write about these matters without romanticism, and thus to reveal not only the rugged dignity of their lives, but also the value of their wisdom.

Thus, *The Man Who Killed the Deer*, Waters' most popular novel, has long been recognized as a classic in the literature on the American Indian, just as *Book of the Hopi* is a landmark in ethnography. Recently, the relevance and quality of his other work has resulted in a greater degree of recognition, made tangible by the republication of much of his fiction.

Biography

Frank Waters was born on July 25, 1902, and spent most of his childhood and youth in Colorado Springs. These years provided much of the material for his first three novels (*The Wild Earth's Nobility*, *Below Grass Roots*, and *The Dust Within the Rock*) and consequently for their revised version, *Pikes Peak*. Waters' grandfather became the model for Joseph Rogier, the main character of these books, and Waters' boyhood experience in the Cripple Creek mining camps provided much of the background. His experience as an engineering student at Colorado College (from 1922 to 1925) and as a day-laborer in the Salt Creek oilfields are also incorporated into these early novels.

After his work at Salt Creek, Waters traveled to California, where he was employed by the telephone company in the border town of Calexico-Mexicali. It was there, among imported Chinese laborers, opium dens, and general degradation, that he came across Tai Ling, who became the protagonist of *The Yogi of Cockroach Court*. This novel was actually drafted before the above-mentioned Colorado novels, but technical problems prevented its completion until some years later.

The move to California marks a dividing line in Waters' treatment of his material. The personal experiences from before the move went into novels of a semiautobiographical nature. Those which drew their material from after the move were not autobiographical, though they continued to draw their characters from people Waters knew, their settings from places he had lived, and even their incidents from actual events. (The ending of *The Yogi of Cockroach Court*, for example, was taken directly from newspaper accounts.)

From the Mexican-American border, Waters moved to the town of Mora in the Sangre de Cristo Mountains of New Mexico. There he wrote *The Dust Within the Rock* and planned *People of the Valley*, drawing again on his youth in Colorado. The latter novel takes its material from the Mora locale, an isolated valley that is inaccessible for most of the year and was settled by Spanish-speaking people from Mexico. It was in Mora, too, that Waters witnessed the rituals of the Penitente cult, which he incorporated into the novel.

After leaving Mora, Waters moved to Taos. From there, in the mid-1930's, he drew the material (again, based on actual events) for *The Man Who Killed the Deer*, and later for two nonfiction works, *Masked Gods* and *Mountain Dialogues*. He has continued to make Taos his home, returning there after the war and working as editor for *El Crepusculo*, a local Spanish-English newspaper; he also worked from 1953 to 1956 as an information consultant at the Los Alamos Scientific Laboratory. These latter two positions are reflected in *The Woman at Otowi Crossing*, though it is evident from *Masked Gods*, published sixteen years earlier, that Waters had long been concerned with the curious juxtaposition of atomic research facilities and Indian kivas in the Four Corners area. At present, Waters lives in the village of Arroyo Seco, near Taos in northern New Mexico.

Analysis

The writing of Frank Waters is always concerned with the bipolar tensions which underlie human existence: male and female, reason and instinct, conscious and unconscious, progress and tradition, linear and nonlinear, matter and energy (or spirit). His fictional characters are involved in efforts to reconcile these polarities, either within themselves, or in the world of events. The search for reconciliation is inseparable from what Waters has called "the spirit of place," for once one is able to embody the unconscious rhythms of one's locale, one may move more completely toward the reconciliation of bipolar tensions.

In another sense, his work is a continuing attempt to give literary expression to this spirit of place. Viewed sociologically, his novels show how this spirit imbues the various racial types of the Southwest. The spirit of place is found in the blood, is experienced as a "blood-power" from which one can never quite break free. Because of these instinctual or biological ramifications, the novels about "racial types" are not mere sociological studies, but expressions of a spiritual search.

Waters has said that the three novels, *People of the Valley*, *The Man Who Killed the Deer*, and *The Yogi of Cockroach Court*, express his interest in the racial types of the West: the Spanish or Mexican, the Indian, and the Mestizos, or those of mixed blood. *The Woman at Otowi Crossing: A Novel* which deals primarily with whites, completes this study of racial types. *Pikes Peak: A Family Saga*, Waters' most recent novel, portrays the mingling of various racial types; but here, Pikes Peak itself is portrayed as an active agent.

Thus, the final novel makes graphic what in the previous novels was a subtle but powerful undercurrent: in all of Waters' work, the Earth itself plays a dominant role. It is the matrix which reconciles polarity. Fruitful and destructive by turns, benevolent or menacing, it resists man's efforts at domination or comprehension, yet demands of him that continuing process of individuation which is inseparable from the reconciliation of polarity. The Earth, the source of life, embodies a mystery which cannot be overcome but must be understood through faith. As the beginning and end of man's essential polarities (such as life and death, summer and winter), it is both a material fact and a rhythmic energy with which one must be in harmony.

Harmony, however, does not indicate a static equilibrium. Waters' novels end with reconciliation, yet the reconciliation leads to ongoing movement. As Waters points out in an explication of the Nahuatl hieroglyph "Ollin" ("Movement"), the tension between dualities results in movement. This movement is found not only in the processes of the natural world, but also inside the heart of man. This ancient Nahuatl concept is reflected in all of Waters' novels. The central reconciliation is in the human heart, as the characters attempt to find that harmony in movement that enables them to be part of the great pattern of Creation.

People of the Valley was Waters' first nonautobiographical novel to be published. The most obvious social polarity—progress and tradition—is the main impetus of the plot. The government is going to build a dam which will uproot all the people of the Beautiful Blue Valley. The name is significant: the color blue symbolizes the abiding faith of the people in their traditional ways, and in the faithful fruitfulness of the valley itself. (This symbolic use of the color blue returns in other novels, most notably *The Man Who Killed the Deer*, where Dawn Lake, the center of the Pueblo religious life, is referred to as the "Blue Eye of Faith.") In this period, when their faith is threatened, the people of the valley look to Maria, a local bruja, for her reaction and her strength, her wisdom and her faith.

Maria has been in the Beautiful Blue Valley for as long as anyone can remember, and has become, in the minds of its inhabitants, synonomous with the valley itself. She knows its secrets and its cures and has lived through its periods of fruitfulness and flood. She is, then, an embodiment of the spirit of place; by turns, she is a goad and a comfort, a shrewd businesswoman and a prophet. As the story progresses (a chapter is devoted to each period of her life), it becomes clear why she is the repository of the implicit faith of the people: she is trusted because of her own implicit trust in the Earth, in the essential trustworthiness of its rhythms, even of its floods. Because she accepts the Earth in all of its many moods, she is the spokesperson for its wisdom. Like the Earth, she can be sharp and repelling, or healing and comforting. Like the Earth, she accepts all who come to her, whether as lovers, questioners, or even husbands. Within change, however, she abides in a faith that grows, year by year.

In addition, Maria makes the welfare of the Earth—of the valley—synonomous with her own welfare. She has reconciled the duality of self and other by making her own wealth inseparable from that of the valley, and hence of its people. The clearest example of this comes from her early life, when, destitute, she survived by gathering discarded wheat-seed from the local fields. This seed she divided into superior and inferior. The latter she used for food; the former she kept until spring, when she would trade it for a double measure to be collected at the next harvest. This process she repeated yearly. Because she kept the best seed for replanting, the wealth of the valley's wheat increased; because she received a double measure at harvest, her own wealth increased as well. Her wealth, however, was never monetary; rather, it was in the natural yield of the Earth, and in the faith that such a yield is sufficient for all purposes.

In the end, it is this faith that makes Maria significant. Faith, too, is the essence of the people of the valley, and of their traditions. Without such faith, life there is not possible. This faith, as she points out, is not a concept, but a baptism into life itself, into the rhythmic experience of harmony, which comes from giving oneself wholly to the spirit and energy of one's locale, the spirit of place. The significance of the dam is that it stops the flow of faith, which is likened to water. Faith refreshes life and gives it meaning; the dam causes stagnation, a break in natural rhythms. The example of Maria shows, however, that if one's faith is deep enough, it will not be disrupted by surface events. In the end, this faith is in the heart, and what one sees in the external world corresponds to one's inner nature.

The idea of faith carries over into Waters' next novel, *The Man Who Killed the Deer*. Whereas Maria had grown slowly into her faith, and had never been torn from it, Martiniano must find a faith within the exacerbated polarities of his nature. The disruptions of progress had not come to Maria until she was an old woman; they come to Martiniano during his formative years.

Because of this, his search is one of finding what he has lost, not simply deepening what he already knows.

Half Apache and half Pueblo, Martiniano's mixed blood indicates the duality of his nature, the spirit of independence and rebellion opposed to the spirit of acceptance and harmony. Sent away to a government school at an early age and thus deprived of his initiation into the kiva at the proper age, Martiniano must be taught to find harmony, not only with his world but also within himself, where the pole of masculine independence has not recognized the pole of the female imperative.

The story of the novel is, on the surface, a simple one. Martiniano has killed a deer out of season, against the regulations of the United States government as it is against those of the pueblo. The matter seems simple, but as the story unfolds, it becomes clear that the apparently simple event has many layers. It is not so much that Martiniano has broken the white man's law, but that his insistence on his own independence of action indicates an inner disharmony and a lack of wisdom. It indicates, finally, a lack of connection with the mystery of life itself. In place of this connection is a belief that a person can be free when alone, when cut off from society or the Earth, from the source of faith, symbolized by the Blue Lake in the mountains above the pueblo, "The Blue Eye of Faith," the center of the pueblo's religious-ceremonial life.

The deer that Martiniano has killed becomes for him a totem, appearing to him in various places and guises to demonstrate that there is something in his situation that he cannot defeat by confrontation, something that he first must understand, to which he must submit. Eventually, the deer appears in his wife, Flowers Playing; as she grows with child, with the mystery of life, Martiniano begins to lose connection with her.

Martiniano learns, slowly, that even his own sense of manhood is held in bondage to the feminine part of his being, and that until he reconciles this polarity, he will never feel fully alive. This is best symbolized by the description of the Deer Dance (in a passage found in both *The Man Who Killed the Deer* and *Masked Gods: Navaho and Pueblo Ceremonialism*). Flower Playing is one of the Deer Mothers in the ceremony, the embodiment of the mystery of organic life. The Deer Dance symbolizes how the male force of independence and escape is held bondage, unwillingly but necessarily, by "the female imperative," the rhythms of Earth that are deeper than the ego. The dance offers another vantage on the spirit of place, here appearing as the "blood power" from which man can never break free, and upon which he is dependent for the development of wisdom.

There is another sense in which Martiniano's action was not done in isolation: his killing of the deer has repercussions that are felt in the wider sphere of politics. It has made more difficult the pueblo's case for restoration of Dawn Lake. As the pueblo elders point out again and again, one man's action is like a pebble dropped into a pool; the ripples extend far beyond the action itself. The effort of the elders enables Martiniano to see that much wider whole, of which he is an integral part, and without which he is an incomplete human being.

The pueblo elders embody a different way of knowing than that of the white race which has control of the lake. The polarity is rational-linear opposing nonrational, nonlinear. The method of the elders is intuitive, and, while it does not deny the validity of rational methods (any more than the female imperative denies the validity of the male drive for independence), it does indicate a deeper level of wisdom. The elders know the eventual result of their legal disputes over Dawn Lake far before these results come over the telegraph, even when all indications (relayed, of course, over the telegraph) point to the futility of their case.

To the elders—as, it seems, to Waters himself—linear or rational knowledge is not as encompassing or effective as the more intuitive method which comes so naturally to the Indians. The difference between these two methods of knowing is a duality to which Waters returns in later books, particularly *The Woman at Otowi Crossing*. It is interesting to note, in this context, that just as the pueblo elders correctly predicted that they would regain their Dawn Lake, so Waters himself, in his novel, predicted the actual political event; for just as in the novel the Indians regain rights to their lake, so, thirty years later, did they do so in fact, through a congressional decision in December of 1970.

Waters' next novel, *The Yogi of Cockroach Court*, takes the working of polarities one step further to juxtapose Eastern mysticism (particularly Buddhist) with life in a Mexican border town. Sociologically, Waters is here concerned with the Mestizo culture. Barby is an example of this type. Orphaned as a child, he is brought up by Tai Ling, who runs a small shop, The Lamp Awake, beside the prostitute district, Cockroach Court. The name of the shop itself introduces the duality of light and dark, associated respectively with the clarity of the mind and the darkness of the senses. Tai Ling is repeatedly pictured meditating by his lamp, amid the swirl of a violent, dark world.

Barby and Guadalupe (Barby's lover, and another person of mixed blood) cannot detach themselves from that dark world, which to Tai Ling is the result of blindness, the working out of karma. Their relationship is a tempestuous one, fueled by Barby's impotent desire for control. This impotence results from Barby's rootless feeling of inferiority, from his inner division. Where Barby is at the mercy of his internal division, Guadalupe is at the mercy of external ones. In the daytime, she is alive in the absorption in her own physical vitality; at night, she comes under the domination of Barby.

These complexities are interwoven with the life of Tai Ling, whose lamp illumines the darkness of the physical world in which he sits, even as his search for a way to transcend the play of polarities illumines the darkness of his mind. Inherent in Tai Ling's search for transcendence, however, is yet another polarity: The life of transcendence is itself polarized with life in a physical body. In this way, Tai Ling is still involved in duality, or karma, and in the end, just as Barby cannot dominate Guadalupe except in darkness, so Tai Ling cannot subdue the ongoing karma of the physical world until the darkness of death surrounds him.

Both Barby and Tai Ling bring about their own deaths by attempts to conquer the physical world. The difference between them is nevertheless a significant one: Barby dies while blinded by passion, aggression, and ignorance; Tai Ling, whose mind is clearer, finally sees and accepts his inner polarity, accepts his karma and his situation, and sees the folly of trying to transcend the world by separating oneself from it. Tai Ling, therefore, achieves a reconciliation, and though it comes at the moment of death, there is great hope in it, as Tai Ling finally comes to a unity with his world, comes to true knowledge.

Tai Ling's realization is not a rational one. He uses rationality to dissect his ego, but his realization is intuitive. He speaks of the difference between those who see that life's journey is a spiral, and those whose vision is so limited that the curve of the spiral seems a straight line. To men of unconsidered action, whose vision is limited to the rational, horizontal plane, all seems linear, not cyclic. The man of contemplation, however, sees the nonlinear nature of things which underlies the linear but does not negate it. Thus, the treatment of two ways of knowing is here given an additional perspective.

The Yogi of Cockroach Court was published in 1947. *The Woman at Otowi Crossing*, Waters' next novel, was published in 1966. The intervening years saw the publication of *Masked Gods*, *The Earp Brothers of Tombstone: The Story of Mrs. Virgil Earp*, *Leon Gaspard*, and *Book of the Hopi*. In addition, Waters had worked as the editor of a local newspaper and at the Los Alamos Scientific Laboratory as a consultant. His deepening knowledge of and feeling for Pueblo traditions, as well as his firsthand knowledge of the activities at Los Alamos, are both brought to expression in the later novel.

The Woman at Otowi Crossing deals primarily with Anglos and thus completes the cycle of novels dealing with racial types. It also brings many of Waters' concerns into a contemporary focus. As in previous books, the action develops out of the tension between polarities. The developing, intuitive awareness of Helen Chalmers is juxtaposed with the development of the atomic bomb on the mesa above her. Both developments signal man's evolutionary potential, and both involve the unification of matter and energy.

Helen Chalmers has come from a broken marriage to operate a small teahouse at the edge of Pueblo Indian land. Coincident with the beginning of the Los Alamos Research Laboratory—called "The Project"—she discovers a growth on her breast. Her assumption that it is cancerous, and the resultant immediacy of death, triggers in her a chain reaction of explosively expanding awareness, an explosion which radically alters her view of the world around her and her relationship with it.

The scene of Helen's discovery ends with Facundo, a member of the pueblo kiva, tossing pebbles against her window. The moment is significant, for in the kiva, the Indians continue their attempt to understand and ensure the unity of matter with energy, or spirit. Facundo's response to Helen's condition is one of immediate comprehension, but his response is undramatic. He simply points to the sun, the source of life, empowered by the same unity of energy and matter that the men of the project seek to harness. Facundo's emphasis, however, is on the presence of that process, that reality, in each moment.

Thus, Helen's task becomes what will eventually become the task of everyone: to integrate her newfound knowledge with the tangible events of her life. The discovery of the bomb requires the same integration; the two discoveries together create a new world order in which one must learn to live. Again, the methods of the Indians point the way to reconciliation, for they have shown how the development of insight and the knowledge of the unity of matter and spirit can be integrated into, and are in fact a necessary part of, a stable, viable society.

Waters draws a number of additional parallels between the activities of the Pueblo kiva and those of the project. Both are shrouded in secrecy, and both have their selected initiates who take on new identities vis à vis the rest of their society. (Members of the kiva take on the identity of cosmic forces; men of the project take on new, common names: Niels Bohr becomes Nicholas Baker.) Both kiva and project exclude women, and in both there is an attempt to empower the mystery of life, to make use of the unity within duality represented by matter and energy, matter and spirit. (These parallels echo Waters' speculations in *Masked Gods*, where he writes of the common search of all people, whether in a Tibetan monastery, an Indian kiva, or an atomic research laboratory.)

Along with these parallels, however, the book demonstrates obvious differences as well. Primary among these is that the rituals of the Pueblo are to ensure the ongoing life of all creatures, whereas the activity of the project is directed toward death. The method of the kiva, being intuitive and nonrational, includes and embraces polarity, whereas the method of the project, being rational, divides one entity from another. Even this polarity, however, can result in a reconciliation, not in the external world, necessarily, but within the individual heart. The scientists involved in creating the bomb are presented in warm, human terms. Gaylord, a young scientist and the lover of Helen Chalmers' daughter, comes to a more intuitive, even mystical awareness as a result of his overexposure to radiation.

Waters' most recent novel, *Pikes Peak*, is a kind of summing up of his work. This may be understood literally, because the novel is a rewritten and shortened version of his first three novels the titles of which are retained as major divisions of the new novel. It may also be understood symbolically, because in its panoramic scope, *Pikes Peak* encompasses many of Waters' lifelong concerns.

Joseph Rogier, the protagonist, is largely a fictionalized version of Waters' grandfather; Waters himself, like the character March (grandson of Rogier, and part Indian) spent much of his youth in the mining camps of Cripple Creek, went to college as an engineering student, and worked in the Salt Creek oil fields. The novel transcends the category of autobiographical fiction, however, because of Waters' use of symbolism, in particular that of Pikes Peak itself, which stands as both tangible fact and intangible symbol. A mystery to be understood, an ungraspable meaning which one feels impelled to grasp, it stands at the borderline between the conscious and the unconscious, at once numinous and tangible.

The peak both draws and repels Rogier, who seeks within it for its golden heart. The pull is irresistible, and in his effort to plumb the peak, Rogier slowly lets go of all his social responsibilities. His building firm deteriorates; his family becomes near destitute; he loses the respect of the community and becomes an object of mockery. His search is an obsession, not for mere gold, and not for riches (though he is not above their temptation), but for the symbolic golden heart, within himself as it is within Pikes Peak, shining in the center of the dense granite, or in the center of the flesh.

The method of his search combines the rational and the irrational. The obsession is irrational, and at its service he places his considerable rational gifts and material wealth. Yet, despite his knowledge of engineering and geology, he cannot strike a significant vein, while men of lesser knowledge, and without his material resources, make seemingly lucky strikes, literally at the drop of a hat. Rogier's situation has parallels to that of Martiniano, for he, like Rogier, finds something in his search that he cannot conquer by rational means or external manipulation. Rogier's attempts to find gold— symbolic or literal—lead him increasingly deeper into darkness and isolation. Like the deer for Martiniano, the peak for Rogier becomes a sort of totem, appearing as a lure, as a guide, or as an obstacle; a truth he cannot grasp, but which is constantly within his sight.

The tragedy of Rogier is that his view of the world is linear. As a miner, he has literal and symbolic tunnel vision. By going straight ahead, mining a vertical shaft, he hopes to find the essence of the mystery symbolized by the mountain itself. Its apparent tangibility as real gold draws him irresistibly, but Rogier's linear viewpoint blinds him to the world around him, isolating him from the sympathies and understanding of his family. His search for truth takes place at the expense of human warmth and community, and he finds, as does Martiniano, that such obsessive pride—even if it seems to be a search for truth—is doomed to futility. Where Martiniano is finally able to understand his folly and arrange for his son to enter the kiva and so live in the harmony it had taken him so long to achieve, Rogier dies in psychological isolation, unable to release his passion into genuine human community.

For all that, however, the tragedy contains a triumph. March, Rogier's grandson, carries on a search encompassing many of Rogier's ideals. Of mixed blood, March shows promise of reconciling the intuitive ways of his Indian blood with the rational methods of his grandfather. Despite himself, Rogier has passed on to March a profound respect for depth and knowledge; one feels for him a deep sympathy, because for all his gruffness, even his selfishness, he has somehow managed to give March a profound respect for enduring value, and the determination to search for it, for the enduring gold within the dense rock of material being.

The search for eternal value in the midst of flux is a final polarity. Tai Ling sought it in his meditation, Maria found it in her inseparability from natural cycles; even Martiniano found it by acquiescing to the Pueblo's ways. For Helen Chalmers, the search was for a way to integrate eternal value into the apparently mundane particulars of everyday living. Thus, even the discovery of eternal verities is not a final resting point. The eternal is continually juxtaposed and interwoven with the mundane, and just as the action of the novels is given impetus by this polarity, so the movement of the world both rises from it and expresses it. As each new layer is peeled off, new polarities emerge.

Waters' writing is a continuing attempt to penetrate and illuminate these symbolic and literal layers, and to find within movement the enduring values of human life. His characters seek these values within the temporal, within enduring change, the first cause and final truth. Thus, in Waters' novels, the Nahuatl hieroglyph "Ollin" comes to literary expression: that eternal movement comes from the tension between polarities. The reconciliation between polarities is found in the movement of tangible existence—in concrete substance, not abstract form; in the harmony within activity that expresses harmony with greater cycles, such as those of society, of one's locale, or of the Earth. In this sense, the expression of the spirit of place is an expression of the unity of mankind, for all are subject to the same enduring, cyclic existence. In a wider sense, Waters' writing is rightly considered mystical, concerned with the oneness of man with others, with the Earth, with all that exists.

Major publications other than long fiction
NONFICTION: *Midas of the Rockies: The Story of Stratton and Cripple Creek*, 1937; *The Earp Brothers of Tombstone: The Story of Mrs. Virgil Earp*, 1937; *The Colorado*, 1946; *Masked Gods: Navaho and Pueblo Ceremonialism*, 1950; *Book of the Hopi*, 1963; *Leon Gaspard*, 1964; *Pumpkin Seed Point: Being Within the Hopi*, 1969; *To Possess the Land: A Biography of Arthur Rochford Manby*, 1973; *Mexico Mystique: The Coming Sixth World of Consciousness*,

1975; *Mountain Dialogues*, 1981.

Bibliography

Hoy, Christopher. "The Archetypal Transformation of Martiniano in *The Man Who Killed the Deer*," in *South Dakota Review*. Winter, 1975.
Lyon, Thomas. *Frank Waters*, 1973.
Milton, John. *Conversations with Frank Waters*, 1971.
_____ . "The Land as Form in Frank Waters and William Eastlake," in *Kansas Quarterly*. Spring, 1970.
South Dakota Review. Autumn, 1977, special Frank Waters issue.

Tim Lyons

EVELYN WAUGH

Born: London, England; October 28, 1903
Died: Combe Florey, England; April 10, 1966

Principal long fiction

Decline and Fall, 1928; *Vile Bodies*, 1930; *Black Mischief*, 1932; *A Handful of Dust*, 1934; *Scoop*, 1938; *Put Out More Flags*, 1942; *Brideshead Revisited*, 1945, 1959; *Scott-King's Modern Europe*, 1947; *The Loved One*, 1948; *Helena*, 1950; *Men at Arms*, 1952; *Officers and Gentlemen*, 1955; *The Ordeal of Gilbert Pinfold*, 1957; *The End of the Battle* 1962 (also known as *Unconditional Surrender*); *Sword of Honour*, 1965 (includes *Men at Arms*, *Officers and Gentlemen*, and *The End of the Battle*).

Other literary forms

Evelyn Waugh wrote seven travel books, three biographies, an autobiography, and numerous articles and reviews. The only completed section of Waugh's planned three-volume autobiography, *A Little Learning* (1964), discusses his life at Oxford and his employment as a schoolmaster in Wales—subjects fictionalized in *Brideshead Revisited* and *Decline and Fall*. The autobiographical background for virtually all of Waugh's novels is evident in his travel books, his diaries, and his letters. His articles and reviews for English and American periodicals include a wide range of topics—politics, religion, and art—and contribute to his reputation as a literary snob, an attitude Waugh himself affected especially in the 1940's and 1950's.

Achievements

Waugh was esteemed primarily as a satirist, especially for his satires on the absurdly chaotic world of the 1920's and 1930's. His ability to make darkly humorous the activities of the British upper class, his comic distance, and his vivid, at times brutal satire made his early novels very popular among British and American literary circles. His shift to a more sentimental theme in *Brideshead Revisited* gave Waugh his first real taste of broad popular approval—especially in America—to which he reacted with sometime real, sometime exaggerated snobbishness. Waugh's conservative bias after the war, his preoccupation with religious themes, and his expressed distaste for the "age of the common man" suggested to a number of critics that he had lost his satiric touch. Although his postwar novels lack the anarchic spirit of his earliest works, he is still regarded, even by those who reject his political attitudes, as a first-rate craftsman of the comic novel.

Biography

Evelyn Arthur St. John Waugh was born in Hampstead, a suburb of London, in 1903 to Arthur and Catherine Waugh. He attended Lancing College from 1917 to 1924 and Hertford College, Oxford from 1921 to 1924, from which he left without taking a degree. Although Waugh turned to writing novels only after aborted careers as a draftsman, a schoolmaster, and a journalist, his family background was literary; his father directed Chapman and Hall publishers until 1929, and his older brother Alec published his first novel, *The Loom of Youth*, in 1917.

Waugh's years at Oxford and his restless search for employment during the 1920's brought him experiences which were later fictionalized in several of his novels. After leaving Oxford in 1924, he enrolled in the Heatherley School of Fine Art, where he aspired to be a draftsman; later in that year, he was apprenticed to a printer for a brief period. His employment as a schoolmaster in Wales in 1925 and in Buckinghamshire in 1926 formed the background for his first novel, *Decline and Fall*. His struggle to establish himself as a writer and his participation in the endless parties of London's aristocratic youth during the last years of the 1920's are fictionalized in his second novel, *Vile Bodies*.

In 1927, Waugh was engaged to Evelyn Gardner and, despite the objections of her family, married her in 1928 when his financial prospects seemed more secure after the publication of his life of Dante Gabriel Rossetti and his first novel. In 1929, while Waugh was working in seclusion on *Vile Bodies*, his wife announced that she was having an affair; the couple, temperamentally unsuited to each other, were divorced that year.

The next seven years of Waugh's life were a period of activity and travel. Two trips to Africa in 1930 and 1931 resulted in a travel book and provided Waugh with the background of *Black Mischief*. A journey through Brazil and British Guiana in 1932 resulted in another travel book and his fourth novel, *A Handful of Dust*. In addition, Waugh traveled to the Artic and once more to Africa; he was a correspondent for the London *Times*, reviewed books for *The Spectator*, and wrote a biography of Edmund Campion, a British-Catholic martyr. During this unsettled period, Waugh converted to Roman Catholicism in 1930, an event which provided much of the stability of his later life. In 1933, he met Laura Herbert, a Catholic, whom he married in 1937, after securing an annulment of his previous marriage from the Catholic Church.

Waugh's experiences during World War II are fictionalized in *Put Out More Flags* and the *Sword of Honour* trilogy. After several months unsuccessfully seeking military employment, Waugh joined the Royal Marines in 1939 and was part of an ineffectual assault on Dakar in 1940. Later in 1940, Waugh joined a commando unit with which he served in the Middle East, taking part in the battle of Crete in 1942. In 1943, after an injury in parachute training, Waugh was forced to resign from the commandos and, in 1944, he was granted military leave to write *Brideshead Revisited*. In the last year of the war, he served as a liaison officer with the British Military Mission in Yugoslavia, where he struggled against the persecution of Roman Catholics by the partisan government.

Waugh's life from 1945 to 1954 was relatively stable. The success of *Brideshead Revisited*, a Book-of-the-Month-Club selection in America, brought him moderate financial security and several offers from filmmakers. Although none of these film offers materialized, they resulted in the trip to Hollywood in 1947 that inspired *The Loved One*, and in several commissioned articles for *Life*. During this nine-year period, Waugh published four short novels and the first volume of the World War II trilogy. In the first three months of 1954, on a voyage to Ceylon, Waugh suffered the mental breakdown that he later fictionalized in *The Ordeal of Gilbert Pinfold*.

Waugh led a relatively reclusive life during the last ten years, avoiding the public contact that had made him notorious earlier. In this period, he finished the war trilogy, published a biography of Ronald Knox, another travel book on Africa, the first volume of his autobiography, a revision of *Brideshead Revisited*, and the recension of the war trilogy into a single volume; he also began several other projects which were never completed. Waugh died on Easter Day in 1966.

Analysis

Evelyn Waugh's novels are distinguished by the narrative detachment with which they survey the madness and chaos of the modern age. His characters participate in a hopeless, often brutal struggle for stability which hardens them to the absurdities of civilization and leads them, ultimately, to an unheroic retreat from the battle of life. Ironic detachment, thus, is Waugh's principal comic technique and his principal theme as well.

Because each of Waugh's novels reflects actual experiences, the nature of this detachment changes through the course of his career. In his early works, which satirize the havoc and instability of the 1920's and 1930's, he achieves comic detachment by splicing together the savage and the settled, the careless and the care-ridden, the comic and the tragic. Victims and victimizers alike are caught in the whirlwind of madness. Waugh's satiric method changes in his postwar novels: comically ineffectual characters still wage battle against the absurdities of life, but one is more aware of their struggle to maintain or recapture spiritual and moral values amid the absurdity. Waugh maintains comic distance in these novels by recommending a quiet sort of spiritual heroism as the only source of man's happiness in the uncertain postwar world.

Waugh's first novel, *Decline and Fall*, traces the misadventures of Paul Pennyfeather, a temperate, unassuming student of theology at Scone College, Oxford. He is "sent down" for indecent behavior when drunken members of the university's most riotous (and, ironically, most aristocratic) club assault him, forcing him to run the length of the quadrangle without his trousers. Like Voltaire's Candide, Pennyfeather is an innocent victim temperamentally ill-suited for the world into which he is thrust. Indeed, *Decline and Fall* owes much to *Candide* (1759): its Menippean satire, its cyclical "resurrection" of secondary characters, and the hero's ultimate resignation from life.

The action itself provides a thin framework for Waugh's satire on modern life. Pennyfeather finds employment, as Waugh himself did, as a schoolmaster in Wales—the only occupation, Pennyfeather is told, for a young man dismissed from the university for indecent behavior. At Llanabba Castle, he meets three characters with whose stories his own is interlaced: Grimes, a pederast and bigamist who pulls himself out of the continual "soup" he gets into by feigning suicide; Prendergast, a doubting cleric who becomes a "modern churchman" and is eventually murdered by a religious fanatic; and Philbrick, the school butler, a professed imposter, jewel-thief, and arsonist who manages to secure a continual life of luxury by his preposterous stories about his criminal life. At Llanabba, Pennyfeather also meets Margot Beste-Chetwynde, a rich socialite to whom he becomes engaged; he is arrested the afternoon of their wedding for unknowingly transporting girls to France for her international prostitution ring. His innocent association with Margot thus leads to his conviction for another act of "indecent behavior," this time leading to a prison sentence in Blackstone Gaol—a "modern" penal institution.

What strikes one about the novel is not the injustices served Pennyfeather, but the very madness of the world with which his innocence contrasts. Characters with criminal designs—Margot, Philbrick, and Grimes—are unaffected by changes in fortune; those in charge of social institutions—Dr. Fagan of Llanabba Castle, and Sir Lucas-Dockery of the experimental prison—are eccentrically out of touch with reality. Their absurdity, when contrasted with Pennyfeather's naïve struggle, defines Waugh's theme: the only sanity is to become cautiously indifferent to the chaos of modernism. At the end of the novel, when Pennyfeather returns to Oxford under a new identity and continues his study of the Early Church, he assumes the role of a spectator, not a participant, in the madness of life.

Although *Decline and Fall*'s narrative structure is more derivative and its characters less fully rounded than those of Waugh's later novels, it displays techniques typical of his fiction at its best. The callous descriptions of the tragic—little Lord Tangent's death from Grimes's racing pistol or Prendergast's decapitation at Blackstone Gaol—and their fragmented interlacement into the plot are hallmarks of Waugh's comic detachment. Tangent's slow death from gangrene is presented through a series of casual offstage reports; the report of Prendergast's murder is incongruously worked into verses of a hymn sung in the prison chapel, "O God, our Help in Ages Past." The tragic and the savage are always sifted through an ironic filter in Waugh's novels, creating a brutal sort of pathos.

Waugh's fourth novel, *A Handful of Dust*, was his first to present a dynamically sympathetic protagonist. Pennyfeather, from *Decline and Fall*, and

Adam Symes, from *Vile Bodies*, attract one's interest largely because they provide a detached perspective from which one can observe the chaos of modern civilization. Basil Seal in *Black Mischief*, although a participating rogue, is amiable largely because of his comic disregard for the mischief he makes. Tony Last of *A Handful of Dust*, however, is a fully sympathetic character as well as a pathetic victim of the modern wasteland to which the title alludes. Unlike Paul Pennyfeather, Tony is not simply an observer of social chaos: his internal turmoil is set against the absurdity of external events, and in that respect, his quest for lost values anticipates that of Charles Ryder in *Brideshead Revisited* and of Guy Crouchback in *Sword of Honour*.

Waugh's theme is the decadence of tradition, emblematized, as it is in many of Waugh's novels, by the crumbling estates of the aristocracy. Tony's futile effort to maintain his Victorian Gothic estate, Hetton Abbey, thus symbolizes his struggle throughout the plot. He is wedded to the outmoded tradition of Victorian country gentlemen, while his wife, Brenda, embraces the social life of London. She eventually cuckolds Tony by having an affair with the parasitic John Beaver, whose mother, an interior decorator, sees in her son's affair an opportunity to "modernize" Hetton with chromium plating and sheepskin carpeting.

The pathos one feels for Tony is ultimately controlled by the absurd contexts into which Waugh sets the pathetic scenes. When his son, John Andrew, dies in a riding accident, Tony is left emotionally desolate, yet the cause of the accident is ironic; John Andrew's horse is startled by a backfiring motorcycle, a modern "horse." Later, one is made brutally aware of the irony of Tony's grief when one learns of Brenda's initial rection to the news of her son's death: she assumes it was John Beaver, her lover, not John Andrew, her son, who died. In the same way, Tony's later divorce from Brenda empties him of values he traditionally respected. He consents to the legal convention that he should give evidence of his infidelity, even if his wife has been the unfaithful partner. His evidence incongruously turns into an uncomfortable weekend with a prostitute and her daughter at Brighton, and the absurdity of this forced and inconsummate infidelity further defines Tony's loneliness. Ironically, it provides him with a means to deny an exorbitant divorce settlement that would force him to sell Hetton Abbey.

In the end, Tony searches for his Victorian Gothic City in the jungles of South America and suffers a delirium in which his civilized life at Hetton Abbey is distorted; these are made comically pathetic by interlaced scenes of Brenda in London trying to regain the civilized life she lost in her estrangement from Tony. Ultimately, she does not find in London the city she sought, nor does Tony in South America. Tony does find, instead, an aberration of his vision; he is held captive by an illiterate who forces him to read aloud from Charles Dickens's novels in perpetuity.

Perhaps Waugh's emotional reaction to his own divorce from Evelyn Gardner prior to the publication of the novel accounts for the increase of pathos in *A Handful of Dust*. Perhaps Waugh realized that thinness of characterization in his earlier novels could lead only to stylistic repetition without stylistic development. Whatever the reason, this novel depicts characters struggling for moral equilibrium in a way that no previous Waugh novel had done.

Brideshead Revisited is different from Waugh's earlier novels in two important ways. First, it is the only novel Waugh finished which employs the first-person point of view. (He had attempted the first person in *Work Suspended* in 1942, but either the story itself faltered, or Waugh could not achieve a sufficient narrative detachment to complete it.) Second, *Brideshead Revisited* was the first novel in which Waugh explicitly addressed a Roman Catholic theme: the mysterious workings of divine grace in a small aristocratic Catholic family. As a result, it is Waugh's most sentimental and least funny novel. Although it departed radically from his earlier satires, it was Waugh's most popular and financially successful work.

The narrative frame creates much of what is sentimental in the novel but also provides a built-in detachment. Charles Ryder's love for Sebastian Flyte during his years at Oxford in the 1920's and for Julia Mottram, Sebastian's sister, a decade later, live vividly in Ryder's memories when he revisits the Brideshead estate during a wartime bivouac. His memories tell the story of Sebastian's and Julia's search for happiness, but because they are remembered by an emotionally desolate Ryder, the novel is a study of his spiritual change as well.

Before he meets Sebastian, Ryder is a serious-minded Oxford undergraduate, not unlike Paul Pennyfeather at the end of *Decline and Fall*. Like Pennyfeather, he is drawn into a world for which he is unprepared, yet, unlike Waugh's earlier protagonist, Ryder is enthralled by a make-believe world of beauty and art. The Arcadian summer Ryder spends with Sebastian at Brideshead and in Venice are the most sumptuously written passages in any of Waugh's novels, reflecting—as Waugh admitted in his 1959 revision of the novel—the dearth of sensual pleasures available at the time of its composition. The change in style also reflects a change in theme. Sebastian's eccentricities about his stuffed bear, his coterie of homosexual "aesthetes," and his refusal to take anything seriously would have been the object of satire in Waugh's earlier novels. In *Brideshead Revisited*, however, the absurdities are sifted through the perspective of a narrator aware of his own desperate search for love. When Sebstian's make-believe turns to alcoholism, the narrator himself becomes cynically indifferent.

Ryder's love for Julia ten years after he has left Brideshead is an attempt to rediscover the happiness he lost with Sebastian. One is more aware, in this second half of the narration, of Ryder's cynicism and of the discontentment which that cynicism hides. When he and Julia fall in love on a transatlantic voyage back to England, they are both escaping marriages to spouses whose worldly ambitions offer no nourishment for the spiritual emptiness each feels. Julia's return to the Church after the deathbed repentance of her father causes Ryder to realize that he has fathomed as little about Julia's faith as he had about Sebastian's. The narration itself thus ends on a note of unhappiness which recalls the separtion of Ryder and Sebastian. In the epilogue following Ryder's memories, however, Waugh makes it clear that the narrator himself has converted to Catholicism in the intervening years. Ryder sees in the sanctuary light of the chapel at Brideshead the permanence he sought with Sebastian and Julia and finds contentment, if not hope for the future.

It is easy to overstress the religious implications of the novel. Indeed, many critics find Julia's hysteria about sin, Lord Marchmain's return to the Church, and Ryder's conversion strained. Some, such as Edmund Wilson, see the novel as an adulation of the British upper classes. *Brideshead Revisited*, however, is less a Roman Catholic novel than it is a lament for the past and a study in spiritual and artistic awakening. It was a turning point in Waugh's fiction: his novels after *Brideshead Revisited* dealt less with the absurdity of life and more with the spiritual values that have disappeared as a result of the war.

Perhaps the grimmest of Waugh's satires, *The Loved One* presents a sardonic vision of American culture. Its principal satiric target is Forest Lawn Memorial Park—a place that in many ways served for Waugh as the epitome of American pretensions to civilization. In "Half in Love with Easeful Death," an essay Waugh wrote for *Life* in 1947 after his visit to Hollywood, Waugh describes Forest Lawn as it would appear to archaeologists in the next millennium: a burlesque necropolis, like the tombs of the Pharoahs in its aspirations, but, in fact, the product of a borrowed, devalued culture. His version of Forest Lawn, Whispering Glades, is a distorted wonderland in which the cosmetic and the artifical substitute for beauty and in which banality is glorified and substitutes for the poetic vision.

It is fitting that the protagonist, Dennis Barlow, be a poet—even though an unproductive one who has been seduced to Hollywood by a consultantship with Megalo Studios. Like many of Waugh's other protagonists, he is the filter through whom one sees absurdities satirized. Like Basil Seal in *Black Mischief* and *Put Out More Flags*, he is an opportunist, flexible enough to engineer a profit for himself out of the chaotic world into which he is thrust. His vision is grimly sardonic, however, in a way that even Seal's is not.

When he first enters Whispering Glades, he is intrigued, as Seal would be, by its absurd glamour and by the potential of using that glamour to improve his own position at The Happier Hunting Grounds, a pet mortuary where he is employed. Whispering Glades, however, has a far deeper attraction; it would be the kind of place, if it were real, that would appeal to any poet, but Barlow is enchanted by its very fraudulence. At the man-made Lake Isle of Innisfree (complete with mechanized humming bees), Barlow falls in love with a mortuary cosmetician and enchants her by the very fact that he is a poet. The enchantment is false, just as everything is at Whispering Glades; he sends her plagarized verses from *The Oxford Book of English Verse* and pledges his troth to her by reciting a stanza from Robert Burns's "A Red, Red Rose" at The Lover's Nook near the Wee Kirk o' Auld Lang Syne.

If plagarism lies at the heart of Barlow's involvement at Whispering Glades, it also lies at the heart of Whispering Glades itself and the characters who work there—even though the place and the people are possessed by the utmost seriousness. The girl with whom Barlow falls in love is named Aimee Thanatogenos. Although she professes to be named after Aimee McPherson—the American huckster of religion whom Waugh satirized in *Vile Bodies*—her given name and her surname both translate into the euphemism that embodies all of Whispering Glades's false coating: "The loved one." Her enchantment with Barlow eventually takes the form of a burlesque tragedy. She is torn between Barlow and the head mortician, Mr. Joyboy—a poet of a different sort, whose special art is preparing infant corpses.

Aimee's tragedy results from a bizarre sequence of events, comic in its effects. When she discovers Joyboy's mother-fixation and Barlow's fraudulence, she seeks advice from her oracle, the Guru Brahmin, an advice columnist. When the Guru, Mr. Slump—fired from his job and in an alcoholic funk—advises Aimee to jump off a roof, she kills herself in the more poetic environment of Whispering Glades. Her suicide by drinking embalming fluid gives a doubly ironic force to her name and to the title of the novel. The tragedy ends with a darkly humorous catharsis. Joyboy, fearful that Aimee's death on his table might mar his lofty position at Whispering Glades, consents to Barlow's extortion and to Barlow's plan to cremate their beloved Aimee at The Happier Hunting Grounds. The novel's conclusion, thus, strikes the grimmest note of all: Barlow sits idly by, reading a cheap novel, while the heroine—a burlesque Dido—burns in the furnace.

In some ways, *The Loved One* is atypical of Waugh's postwar novels. In *Scott-King's Modern Europe*, and the *Sword of Honour* trilogy, Waugh turns his satiric eye on political issues. *The Loved One*, however much it satirizes American values, transcends topical satire. Barlow lacks the spiritual potential of Charles Ryder in *Brideshead Revisited*, even though he displays Ryder's callousness. Barlow is an artist in search of beauty, but he leaves California, ironically, with an artist's load far different from what he expected. It is the view of an ironist, like Waugh himself, who could hardly make a better travesty of Whispering Glades than it makes of itself.

The *Sword of Honour* trilogy, like *Brideshead Revisited*, is infused with a predominantly religious theme; it traces Guy Crouchback's awakening to spiritual honor—a more active form of spiritual growth than Charles Ryder experienced. Like *Brideshead Revisited*, *Sword of Honour* is more somber and more deliberately paced than Waugh's satires in the 1920's and 1930's, but it shares with his early works a detached satiric framework. Each volume is composed at a distance of ten or more years from its historical occurrence and, as a result, reflects a greater consciousness of the long-range implications of the absurdities presented.

Men at Arms concerns the chaos of Britain's first entry into the war, much like Waugh's wartime satire *Put Out More Flags*. One is immediately aware, however, of the difference in Waugh's detachment. *Put Out More Flags* was the product of a writer in his mid-thirties looking wryly at the days of peace from the middle of the war. Its protagonist, Basil Seal, is a mischief-making opportunist for whom greater chaos means greater fun and profit; the novel satirizes the madness of a world which leaves the characters trapped in the ever-changing insanity of war. *Men at Arms*, however, and, indeed, the entire trilogy, looks back from the perspective of the author's later middle age, with a sense of disappointment at the final results of the war. Appropriately enough, Guy is an innocent at the outset of the war, not a mischief-maker like Basil Seal. He is a middle-aged victim who is literally and figuratively cast into a battle for which he is ill-prepared.

Guy's heroic illusions are shattered in three successive stages through the separate volumes of the trilogy. *Men at Arms* concerns Guy's search for the self-esteem he lost eight years earlier after his divorce from his wife. As an officer-trainee in the Royal Corps of Halberdiers, Guy temporarily finds self-respect, but the elaborate traditions of the Halberdiers and his traineeship at commandeered prepatory schools causes Guy to revert to adolescence. His physical awkwardness, his jealousy of fellow trainees, his vanity about growing a mustache, his ineffectual attempt to seduce his former wife on Saint Valentine's Day, and the blot he receives on his military record at the end of the novel all seem more appropriate for a schoolboy than for an officer preparing to lead men into battle.

As in Waugh's earlier novels, the comedy of *Men at Arms* depends, not on the protagonist, but on the events and characters whom he encounters. Apthorpe, a middle-aged *miles gloriosus*, and Ben Ritchie-Hook, Guy's brigadier, represent two forms of the military insanity for which Guy trains. Apthorpe's preoccupation with boots, salutes, and his portable field latrine, the "Box," makes him an unlikely candidate for leading men into battle; Ritchie-Hook, whose only notion of military strategy is to attack, makes an elaborate game out of officer-training by booby-trapping Apthorpe's "Box"— a prank which causes Apthorpe to sink deeper into his madness. The confrontation between Apthorpe and Ritchie-Hook defines an absurd pattern which recurs later in the trilogy. Seeming madmen control the positions of power, and the protagonist is unwittingly drawn into their absurd worlds.

Officers and Gentlemen further trains Guy in the illogic of military life, this time focusing on the efforts of gentlemen soldiers to re-create the comforts of their London clubs during the war. The novel ends on a more somber note, however, than did *Men at Arms*. Guy finds temporary solace in the commando unit to which he is transferred after his disgrace as a Halberdier and believes again that he will find some honorable role to play in the war, but the British defeat at Crete at the end of this volume negates whatever notions of honor he entertained.

Even more than *Men at Arms*, *Officers and Gentlemen* relentlessly travesties espirit de corps and pretentions to heroism. Ian Kilbannock's gentlemanly service as a military journalist, for example, is to transform the ineffectual Trimmer into a propaganda hero for the common man. Julia Stitch's yacht, the *Cleopatra*, brings the comforts of the English social world to the Mediterranean war. The burrowing Grace-Groundling-Marchpole absurdly continues the secret file he began in *Men at Arms* about Guy's supposed counterintelligence activities. All of these events occur while England is suffering the first effects of German bombing and while the British disgrace at Crete looms ahead.

For a time, Guy imagines that the commandos are the "flower of England"; he even sees Ivor Claire as the ideal soldier, the kind of Englishman whom Hitler had not taken into account. The flower withers, however, in the chaotic retreat of British forces from Crete. Although Guy himself manages to maintain an even keel through most of the ordeal, the officers with whom he serves prove unheroic. His commander, "Fido" Hound, suffers a complete mental collapse in the face of the retreating troops; Ivor Claire, unable to face the prospect of surrendering, deserts his men and flees to India, where he is protected by his genteel birth. Eventually, Guy unheroically joins a boat escaping from the island and, exhausted, suffers a mental collapse. Guy initially resists Julia Stitch's efforts to cover up Claire's disgrace, but eventually destroys his own diary recording the orders to surrender when he learns that nothing will be done about Claire's desertion and when he learns of England's alliance with Russia. Unlike the first volume, the second volume ends with Guy's realization that he is an ineffectual player in a war that has lost a sense of honor.

It is curious to note that Waugh announced in the dust-jacket blurb for *Officers and Gentlemen* that, although he had planned the series for three volumes, he wanted his readers to regard it as finished with this second volume. The grimness of Guy's disillusionment thus sheds a somber light on Waugh's personal dilemma during the mid-1950's. After completing about a third of the draft of this second volume, Waugh suffered the mental collapse fictionalized in *The Ordeal of Gilbert Pinfold*. Guy's hallucination at the end of *Officers and Gentlemen* probably owes some of its vividness to the madness Waugh himself endured in 1954, and perhaps the numbness that affects Guy at the end of the novel reflects Waugh's own consciousness of his failing physical and mental powers.

Men at Arms and *Officers and Gentlemen* each deflate Guy's illusions about honor. *The End of the Battle* follows the same pattern in terms of wartime politics and in terms of Guy's military life, but in personal terms, Guy achieves a kind of unheroic, unselfish honor by the end of the novel. As a soldier, Guy accomplishes nothing heroic; even his efforts to liberate the Jewish refugees from partisan Yugoslavia is unsatisfying. Although most of the refugees are liberated, the leaders of the group—the Kanyis—are imprisoned and presumably executed. Guy's struggle with the Yugoslavian partisans and his disgust at Britain's alliance with the Communist-bloc countries further defines the dishonorable end that Guy and Waugh see in the war.

Unlike the two previous volumes, however, *The End of The Battle* ends on a note of tentative personal hopefulness, effected by Guy's renewed Roman Catholic faith. In the first two novels of the trilogy, Guy's religion lay dormant—a part of his life made purposeless since his divorce from Virginia. In *The End of The Battle*, the death of Guy's piously religious father causes Guy to realize that honor lies not in the "quantitative judgments" of military strategy, but in the spiritual salvation of individual souls. Guy's efforts to rescue the Yugoslavian Jews is selflessly honorable, even if ultimately futile. His remarriage to Virginia, who is pregnant with Trimmer's baby, is directed by the same sense of honor. Guy has little to gain emotionally from his remarriage; he does it for the preservation of the child's life and, implicitly, for the salvation of its soul. It is a different sort of heroism than he sought at the beginning of the war, possible only because Virginia has died.

Sword of Honour is, in many ways, a fitting climax to Waugh's literary career. It poignantly expresses his reverence for religious values yet recognizes the anomalous existence of those values in the modern world. It burlesques the eccentric and the absurd, yet moves beyond superficial satire to a more deeply rooted criticism of postwar politics. It displays Waugh's masterful ability to capture minor characters in brisk, economical strokes while working them thematically into the emotional composition of the protagonist. Waugh's importance as a novelist lay in his ability to achieve this kind of economy in a traditional form. He kept alive, in short, a tradition of the comic novel that reaches back to the eighteenth century.

Major publications other than long fiction
SHORT FICTION: *Mr. Loveday's Little Outing*, 1936; *Tactical Exercise*, 1954.
NONFICTION: *Rossetti: His Life and Works*, 1928; *Labels*, 1930; *Remote People*, 1931; *Ninety-Two Days*, 1934; *Edmund Campion: Jesuit and Martyr*, 1935; *Waugh in Abyssinia*, 1936; *Robbery Under the Law*, 1939; *The Holy Places*, 1952; *The Life of the Right Reverend Ronald Knox*, 1959; *Tourist in Africa*, 1960; *A Little Learning*, 1964; *The Diaries of Evelyn Waugh*, 1975 (Christopher Sykes, editor); *The Letters of Evelyn Waugh*, 1980 (Mark Amory, editor).

Bibliography

Carens, James F. *The Satiric Art of Evelyn Waugh*, 1966.

Cook, William J. *Masks, Modes, and Morals*, 1971.

Davis, Robert M., ed. *Evelyn Waugh: A Checklist of Primary and Secondary Sources*, 1972.

_____ . *Evelyn Waugh, Writer*, 1981.

Doyle, Paul. *Evelyn Waugh: A Critical Essay*, 1969.

Stopp, Frederick J. *Evelyn Waugh: Portrait of an Artist*, 1958.

Sykes, Christopher. *Evelyn Waugh: A Biography*, 1975.

James J. Lynch

H. G. WELLS

Born: Bromley, England; September 21, 1866
Died: London, England; August 13, 1946

Principal long fiction

The Time Machine, 1895; *The Wonderful Visit*, 1895; *The Island of Dr. Moreau*, 1896; *The Wheels of Chance*, 1896; *The Invisible Man*, 1897; *The War of the Worlds*, 1898; *The Sleeper Wakes*, 1899; *Love and Mr. Lewisham*, 1900; *The First Men in the Moon*, 1901; *The Sea Lady*, 1902; *The Food of the Gods*, 1904; *Kipps*, 1905; *In the Days of the Comet*, 1906; *The War in the Air*, 1908; *Tono-Bungay*, 1909; *Ann Veronica: A Modern Love Story*, 1909; *The History of Mr. Polly*, 1910; *The New Machiavelli*, 1911; *Marriage*, 1912; *The Passionate Friends*, 1913; *The Wife of Sir Isaac Harman*, 1914; *The World Set Free*, 1914; *The Research Magnificent*, 1915; *Bealby*, 1915; *Mr. Britling Sees It Through*, 1916; *The Soul of a Bishop*, 1917; *Joan and Peter*, 1918; *The Undying Fire*, 1919; *The Secret Places of the Heart*, 1922; *Men Like Gods*, 1923; *The Dream*, 1924; *Christina Alberta's Father*, 1925; *The World of William Clissold*, 1926; *Meanwhile*, 1927; *Mr. Blettsworthy on Rample Island*, 1928; *The Treasure in the Forest*, 1929; *The King Who Was a King*, 1929; *The Autocracy of Mr. Parham*, 1930; *The Bulpington of Blup*, 1933; *The Shape of Things to Come*, 1933; *The Croquet Player*, 1937; *Star-Begotten*, 1937; *The Camford Visitation*, 1937; *Brynhild*, 1937; *Apropos of Dolores*, 1938; *The Brothers*, 1938; *The Holy Terror*, 1939; *Babes in the Darkling Wood*, 1940; *All Aboard for Ararat*, 1941; *You Can't Be Too Careful*, 1942.

Other literary forms

Despite the number of full-length, fully developed novels written by H. G. Wells, his reputation rests on more than a dozen pieces of fiction that he termed, variously, fantastic romance and scientific romance. The works themselves focused upon a number of completely familiar Wellsian themes: space travel, interplanetary war, space and time machines, seemingly improbable (at least during the time he wrote about them) scientific experiments. The titles of those pieces are equally familiar, even to those who never got beyond their opening pages or came to know them through a number and variety of film adaptations, among them: *The Time Machine*, *The Island of Dr. Moreau*, *The Invisible Man*, and *The War of the Worlds*.

Wells's nonfiction scientific projects, most of which he wrote prior to the twentieth century, include the two-volume *Text Book of Biology* (1893), *Honors Physiography* (1893, with Sir Richard Gregory), *A Text Book of Zoology* (1898, with A. M. Davis), *The Science of Life* (1931, with Julian Huxley and G. P. Wells), and *Science and the World Mind* (1942).

Last, there exists a large number of sociological/political/historical tracts that remain not only important items within the Wells canon but also reflect both the writer's fear of and idealism about the present and the future. These include *A Modern Utopia* (1905) and *The Outline of History* (1920), which went through five revisions through 1930. The two-volume *An Experiment in Autobiography* (1934) remains as the best means by which to view Wells's own insights into his life and his work.

Achievements

The achievement of Wells, both as person and as artist, exists as a series of extremes. He held an honorary D.Litt. from London University and stood as an honorary fellow of the Imperial College of Science and Technology; yet, the Royal Society would never grant him a fellowship, even after, at age seventy-eight, he submitted a doctoral thesis to the University of London and earned the degree of Doctor of Science. His very name held a prominent position in contemporary letters for half a century, and he gave to the world approximately 120 volumes of social and scientific fiction, political and scientific prophecy, education, and history. A large, worldwide audience praised him for the genius, foresight, and originality reflected in his scientific romances that children and adults continue to read. An equally large audience condemned his "Wellsian" inventions and conventions as the work of a childish fancy and preposterous pseudoscience.

Although literary history clearly identifies Wells as a novelist, the writer himself preferred to be known as a journalist or as a generalist whose prose would be limited to the events of the moment. Indeed, he seemed obsessed with the need to react to each moment as though it would be the last for Earth and man, and he seemed to feel the need to record each reaction. For example, his three major encyclopedic projects—*The Outline of History*, *The Science of Life*, and *The Work, Wealth, and Happiness of Mankind* (1931)— by themselves would have been sufficient productions for anyone trying to carve a niche for himself in the intellectual history of mankind; yet, those volumes constitute but a minute percentage of the Wellsian canon. Unfortunately, the sheer size of his collective effort probably did more to negate Wells's overall literary reputation than to advance it.

Wells, however, will always rank as a major novelist; even such contemporaries as Henry James and Ford Madox Ford clearly recognized that achievement. He combined comedy with an astute sense of prophecy, anticipation, and pure sociological guesswork to produce a form of fiction that was, simultaneously, negative, gloomy, and satirical. For example, Wells's characters futiley try to search for, to discover, or to invent variations on the Utopian ideal, yet they never are able to create or to achieve such a state. Wells, of course, had no intention of having his fictional characters create or achieve something in which he, himself, did not always believe.

In the final analysis, Wells's achievement as a novelist may be said to have derived from the very breadth of his creative range. Few writers have equaled him in versatility, ingenuity, or even credibility. There are those who maintain that in *Kipps*, *Tono-Bungay*, and *The History of Mr. Polly*, Wells achieved greatness as a comic novelist; others claim that *Mr. Blettsworthy on Rampole Island* constitutes the best example of anti-Utopian fiction written in the twentieth century; still others praise him for having shaped, in *The Bulpington of Blup*, a truly significant contribution to the psychological novel. Wells responded to the human urge, to a lust for fantasy and wonder; he gave light—to some it was the light of hope, to others it was simply escape—to a large number of people living in what they believed to be an exceedingly dull world. Certainly, there may be justification in the criticism that he never cared to assist in the struggle of mind over imagination; however, despite that lack of intellectual depth, Wells's fiction still managed to breathe life into a post-Victorian world suffocating under the weight of its own pessimism and skepticism, yet keenly alert to the prospect of a twentieth century promised land.

Biography

The briefest of glances at Herbert George Wells's background, especially at the early and formative years, reveals clearly the extent of the relationship between biography and fiction. The writer's father, Joseph Wells, was the son of a Kentish gardener, while his mother, Sarah Neal, came from Sussex, where her father served as an innkeeper and she had worked as a serving maid. H. G. Wells was his parents' fourth child and third son. Joseph Wells had been at one time a gardener, but he abandoned that ancient vocation for the cricket fields of provincial England. To supplement his seasonal earnings, the elder Wells operated a variety shop in Bromley, but generally he had little success in keeping his family much beyond the poverty level. It is not surprising then, that the seeds of socialism, republicanism, atheism, and anti-intellectualism found fertile ground in the mind of the youngest of Joseph Wells's children.

H. G. Wells's education appeared, at the outset, to be as grim a prospect as his family surroundings. He began at a "dame school" in Bromley then moved to Thomas Morley's Commercial Academy for Young Gentlemen. The latter institution proved to be a single room built over a scullery and specializing in the education of tradesmen's sons destined to follow the lots of their fathers. Thus, the "young gentlemen" mastered addition, bookkeeping, and penmanship. Anything else had to be learned independent of Mr. Morley. The decline in the family's already fragile fortunes, however, interrupted further thoughts of education and learning; in 1870, the family virtually dissolved: Young Herbert eventually became a probationary draper's apprentice with the firm of Rogers and Denyer, at Windsor. Although his brothers Frank and Fred were working as journeymen drapers, Herbert (or "Bertie," as he was called) resisted any movement in that direction. Fortunately, he was offered a position as a student teacher in a national school at Wookey, Somerset, where he learned to defend himself against the more irreverent among his pupils. Nevertheless, his career came to an end when local authorities discovered that the headmaster had obtained his post under false pretense.

Wells then returned to his mother at Up Park and took advantage of the large and varied library there. The stay proved short lived, as he ventured to Midhurst to learn about being a pharmaceutical chemist. The young Wells, however, lacked both finances and a knowledge of Latin, causing him to attend Horace Byatt's grammar school at Midhurst; again, however, expenses proved a problem as he simply could not raise enough money for the apprenticeship in pharmacy.

Thus, at the age of fifteen, Wells went back to the drapery trade; but, in 1883, he returned to Midhurst and Byatt's school, where he both taught and studied. He crammed for and then passed his examinations with an advanced first class, which resulted in a scholarship (plus a one pound per week stipend) at the Normal School of Science at South Kensington.

At Kensington, he came under the direct tutelage of Thomas Henry Huxley and proceeded to distinguish himself in biology; but away from Huxley he performed miserably and, as a result, failed his third year examinations. Literature and socialism became substitutes for science. He then drifted to Holt Academy, Wrexham, where a soccer injury permanently damaged a kidney, which in turn led to tuberculosis, hemorrhages, and early retirement to Up Park and the large library of his mother's employer.

In 1889, Wells accepted a teaching post at Henley House School, Kilburn. A year later, he managed to earn the B.S. with a first class in zoology and a second in geology, which in turn earned for him, in 1891, a position as tutor at the University Tutorial College. By 1895, after marriage, divorce, and remarriage, Wells determined to devote himself almost entirely to the profession of letters.

He began with the short story, moved on to the social fable, and launched his literary career with a long series of fantastic and imaginative romances, beginning in 1897 with *The Invisible Man* and terminating in 1933 with *The Shape of Things to Come*. Indeed, those pieces established his reputation, not so much as an artist or a creator of exemplary literature, but as a scientific and political prophet who told of a war in the air, of tanks, of atomic weapons, of a second world war, and all well in advance of their actual occurrences or developments. He would take hold of an emerging scientific fact (radium, for example) and then forecast, in his fiction, the application of that fact to a larger phenomenon (the atomic bomb). If a certain problem arose about which he might plead ignorance, he would simply invent a shortcut around the obstacle (as with *cavorite* and *quap*), leaving his readers with at least some basis for scientific fact.

After World World I, Wells shifted his emphasis from science to education. The disappointments of his youth caused him to view the system as responsible for much of mankind's misery. From education he seized upon history, entering an encyclopedic phase of his work with such projects as *The Outline of History*, *The Science of Life*, and *The Work, Wealth, and Happiness of Mankind*. Those pieces earned both wealth and reputation for Wells, but he thought of them really as public-spirited attempts to discover common origins for world education. The attempts were necessary, Wells maintained, because civilization had found itself (on the eve of World War II) in a race between education and catastrophe.

Wells's political leanings seemed to fluctuate at the same rate as his scientific and historical interests. He continued his interest in Socialism but had difficulty choosing between the Fabians and the Laborites. Simply, he had not the patience to allow personalities and procedures to catch up with principles; he refused to come to grips with details and programs. Thus, his tendency toward sweeping generalizations, his almost total disregard for tact in dealing with small groups and in committees, and his inability to speak well in public (he had a small, piping voice) made him a poor politician and an even worse candidate for public office. Indeed, he recognized his own inadequacies, and so he sought other means for expression and action. Two visits to Russia (fourteen years apart) and interviews with Vladimir Lenin and Joseph Stalin demonstrated the range and the depth of his political intellect, but the controversies that followed his return to England detracted from the honest intentions of those adventures into the heartland of twentieth century Communism. A visit to the United States to see Franklin D. Roosevelt did even less to advance his influence upon the politics of the world.

To his credit, toward the end of his long life, Wells wrote two film scripts: *The Man Who Could Work Miracles* and *Things to Come*. Almost to the very end of his days, he continued to be involved with the struggle for human rights on a world level, but again, he despaired of the process and the inabilities of people and groups to respond to the letter of a particular principle. The tragedy of that experience was that his death, on August 13, 1946, prevented him from seeing most of what he had already said about human rights embodied in the United Nations' Convention of Human Rights.

Analysis

Writing from behind the mask of one of the central characters in *Tono-Bungay*, H. G. Wells maintained that although he enjoyed writing novels, he could rate himself no higher than an undisciplined storyteller who had to "sprawl and flounder, comment and theorize" to convey exactly what he intended. Certainly, without giving himself full credit, he nevertheless overwhelmed his readers with the full force of those sometimes preposterous ideas that he continued to advance. In other words, he wrote novels principally to discuss that which he believed relevant to society at a particular moment in history. Naturally, he had to pay the consequences for such practice; novels such as *Joan and Peter, Babes in the Darkling Wood*, and *The Autocracy of Mr. Parham* declined in literary significance once they lost their social relevance. In his defense, however, Wells never intended that everything he wrote should transcend the moments for which they were written; thus, few readers remember *The Holy Terror*. Few can forget, however, such timeless social documents as *Tono-Bungay, The New Machiavelli, The Dream,* and *The Time Machine*. In a sense, Wells saw the novel as a way to present ideas and to criticize life. As Samuel Johnson was quick to perceive eighteenth century London as "all that life could afford," so did Wells look upon the novel as the grand receptacle for the politics, religion, philosophy, and sexual morality of the world.

Ann Veronica gained a degree of notoriety for its advocacy of women's rights. The novel led to scandalized reviews and tirades from many parish pulpits, all because the novelist had allowed his youthful heroine to express her desires and to partake in sexual adventures—none of which, supposedly, had previously been explored in English fiction. Wells reeled from the effects of such negative criticism, horrified that his detractors could be so insensitive to his real purpose: to inject life and dimension into a character made flat and almost lifeless by the repressive mores of the times during which she lived. His principal instrument is Ann's defiance, through which she attends a science school in London and falls in love with a teacher, who is separated from his wife. The reader here observes the extent to which, fairly early in his career as a novelist, Wells relied on his own experiences to give fictional support to his ideas and to maintain a sense of reality throughout his novel. In this case, Wells left his first wife for a student, whom he married in 1895. Then, in 1906, Wells met Amber Pember Reeves, with whom he had an affair for almost two years.

The autobiographical elements aside, *Ann Veronica*, subtitled "A Modern Love Story," may have been the first Edwardian novel in which the heroine dared to demonstrate the meaning of "modern" love. For twenty-one-year-old Veronica Stanley, action seemed more important than superficial definition. Essentially, she determined to select her own partner and to marry only for love, an exceptional course of action at the dawn of the twentieth century. What set her apart from her fictional predecessors were her youth, her open defiance, and, perhaps most important, the obvious approval of the novelist. Wells not only created Ann Veronica Stanley, but he also knew her and had played a principal role in her rebellion.

Wells viewed *Tono-Bungay* as "his" novel, his masterpiece, his serious and concentrated effort to fit comfortably into the mold of Charles Dickens and William Makepeace Thackeray. Those who have carefully studied his fiction will agree, for it stands apart from the remainder of his fiction because of its unity and its consistency. In *The Time Machine, The Wheels of Chance, Love and Mr. Lewisham,* and even *Kipps,* Wells had divided his attention among narrative tale, novel, scientific romance, social criticism, and humor; in *Tono-Bungay,* he managed to focus that attention onto the highest of all Dickensian planes. Again, however, the autobiographical elements are most prominent, borrowed heavily from Wells's impressionable years: the miserable shop at Bromley, Midhurst, the drapers' and chemists' shops, Up Park, the love affairs and marriages, the attempts at formal and self-education.

The characters are well conceived and fully developed: the delightful and attractive Aunt Susan Ponderevo, with her playful bantering, lively sense of humor, keen interest in her husband's often fantastic ideas, and a genuine concern for her husband's personal happiness; Edward Ponderevo, the Wimblehurst chemist who rises to become a wealthy financier and then falls into financial and spiritual collapse, but not before he invents "tono-bungay." Uncle Edward is a biographical hybrid, a character drawn from a score of late Victorian Dickensian types who actually crossed Wells's path. Perhaps the most fascinating of the *Tono-Bungay* characters is the hero, George Ponderevo, an accurate description and characterization of Wells himself. George narrates the novel, and the reader learns of how, after serving an apprenticeship in his uncle's chemist shop, he receives a principal role in the tono-bungay scheme, promotes that fantastic product, and then withdraws to involve himself in a series of aeronautical experiments. As his marriage to Marion Ramboat (whom he met as a science student in London) declines, his skepticism and frustration rise, and the autobiographical model becomes all too evident. Still, George Ponderevo clings to his ideals, "a spiritual guttersnipe in love with unimaginable goddesses."

The success of *Tono-Bungay* as a novel springs from its epic sense of journey; a quest for an illusive idea that is, essentially, a realistic and continuing experience. Wells's ability to adapt the specifics of his narrative to the generalities surrounding his own world allowed the work to gain credibility as an accurate commentary on the social milieu. Wells revealed to the young reader his own world; he threw down before them, by way of George Ponderevo, the realities of the social and political order that had obscured the Victorian/Edwardian establishment. Yet, in *Tono-Bungay* and through George Ponderevo, Wells did more than describe and reveal, he prophesied the end of the world into which he had been born and against which he had struggled, and he announced the beginning of a new order, one dominated by a coalition of science and the young. At the end of the novel, George Ponderevo sails down the Thames River and into the open sea, into a new world of cautious optimism. It may well be an unknown world, but at least it appears to George (and Wells) to be a better one than its predecessor.

Although *The History of Mr. Polly* contains its share of autobiographical elements, those elements seem less graphic, receive less overstatement and emphasis, than in either *Ann Veronica* or *Tono-Bungay*. That does not mean, however, that the novelist departed from his usual themes. On the contrary, Wells launches Alfred Polly forward upon the recognizable vehicles of frustration and defeat, and in the end, he emerges to engage in a magnificent rebellion.

After six years as an apprentice in a drapery emporium at Port Burdock, Polly establishes his own haberdashery shop at Fishbourne. There, he marries his cousin, Miriam Larkins; after fifteen years of unhappiness, he leaves her for the life of a general handyman at a country inn. He achieves, at least, a significant degree of spiritual independence.

Polly represents Wells's view of a diseased society brought about by that same social disorder apparent in *Tono-Bungay*. Wells deftly obscures that disorder behind a thin veil of comedy—particularly Alfred Polly's upset stomach. The intestinal disorder originated from unwise feeding habits during Polly's childhood; his wife's incompetence as a cook simply provokes the disorder. Polly's stomach thus becomes the metaphor for the ills of the world, and that metaphor weaves its way throughout the novel upon the spasms of the hero's indigestion. Only drastic change—a simple purge or outright revolution—can bring about a positive change in his physical condition.

At the novel's conclusion, Wells portrays Polly as an untrained, undisciplined, and utterly spontaneous savage; however, both Wells and his readers know that Polly has successfully transformed his life by escaping from an intolerable environment. The death of his father allows him to escape from his apprenticeship, while the decision to burn his own shop sets the stage for his escape from his wife; Wells chooses not to judge either situation. Nevertheless, the novel's message stems from its author's conviction that, in the end, only the individual can generate the power to transform his life to a positive or a negative condition. In the end, only the individual can be held responsible for his actions.

If *Tono-Bungay* directs itself toward social and economic issues, *The New Machiavelli* according to Wells's assessment of the two novels, focuses upon political matters. The central theme of the piece can best be appreciated from the perspective of the main character, Richard Remington. The only son of Arthur Remington, a science teacher at the Bromstead Institute, Richard wins a scholarship to the City Merchants School, then moves on to Cambridge. He marries Margaret Seddon, a quiet, graceful, and studious woman, five years after their initial meeting; but a combination of Richard's infidelity and fluctuating political views puts an end to that union. In a sense, the marriage neatly identifies Remington's function in *The New Machiavelli*: the politician torn between the mind and the heart, the intellectual in pursuit of constructive statesmanship and the satisfaction of the passions. Richard Remington, however, cannot find the middle ground; he elopes with Isabel Rivers to Italy, thus putting an end to his political career.

As Alfred Polly engaged in constant warfare with the conflicting disorders of his stomach, Richard Remington does battle with the forces of passion and of order. On the surface, he speaks out for order and for system, but in terms of his own moral actions, he breaks the very laws that he defends. At one moment he seems to be trying to create his world, but at another, he wishes either to destroy it or to rebel against its values. His wife accuses both him and Isabel of being bad, of actually being criminal in their conduct; yet, she also identifies both as being "full of something the world must have." Perhaps, she reasons, nothing can be constructed without its first being destroyed.

Upon closer examination, however, Richard Remington proves to be no one unusual. Wells did not, in *The New Machiavelli*, set out to create a utopian political ideal or even a utopian politician. Indeed, Remington forces the reader closer to the realities of politics, a situation in which there exist no perfect creatures. Instead, the world of *The New Machiavelli* is inhabited by people prone to err, by people unable to control their jealousies. As weak and disorderly as the system appeared, Wells knew that it could not be changed by shaping some fantastic sphere of political perfection. Instead, as Remington recognizes, men must be made to see the lights of construction and selectivity. Men must look less to the past and more to the future, and those who will govern must do so beyond the limitations of their schools, their colleges, and their home counties.

Wells did not enjoy the years of England's involvement in World War I. Emotionally, it caused him to turn his heart and mind on the true state of the world; professionally, he spent time at Crewe House, writing government propaganda. In 1914, he produced two volumes of essays, *The War That Will End War* and *An Englishman Looks at the World*; two years later, he wrote *Mr. Britling Sees It Through*, a powerful yet conventional novel in which he related the impact of war upon a sensitive mind. After the end of hostilities, Wells apologized for his dramatic and vituperative attacks on those who had not wholeheartedly supported the war, and he embraced with enthusiasm the idea of the League of Nations (an organization that he attacked later because he believed it only thwarted his pursuit of the World State concept). *Mr. Britling Sees It Through* demands recognition within the context of Wells's "war and peace" period.

In *Mr. Britling Sees It Through*, Wells takes a long, careful look at himself as a mature individual approaching fifty years of age who must, politically and intellectually, come to grips with the present chaos of the world. Hugh Britling the elder possesses a naturally irritable mind, seasoned with obstinate originality and a generous disposition. Above all, Britling is a man with ideas about everything, but he has no control over their origins. The novelist not only looks into himself but also focuses with equal clarity upon his surroundings; his home, neighbors, and friends appear in this novel with little fictional disguise. Furthermore, Wells wrote *Mr. Britling Sees It Through* in the third person rather than in the first, allowing a strong degree of objectivity to control so highly personal a work.

Unfortunately, in his serious attempts at self-analysis, the spark and vitality of characterization is missing. Instead, he created a totally realistic novel, trying hard to contrast the static order of prewar England (and the world) to the chaos that peace must necessarily bring. Indeed, the novel exists almost as a grand discourse, wherein fictional but obviously representative characters reflect the disillusionment of worldwide warfare closing in upon all peoples. Republicans battle aristocrats and defenders of the Empire grapple with the likes of suffragettes and advocates of Irish home rule. Above it all, but certainly not removed or aloof, Hugh Britling records, comments, and analyzes the British conscience as it seeks to understand the catastrophe of world war.

The novel moves forward in a series of war-related events that, in the end, prove tragic. Hugh Britling, the central character's eldest son, is killed in France; instead of suffering the usual anger and depression, the elder Britling turns to and finds God. The hope is that some day God will triumph over the horrors of life and that kindness, goodness, and love will put an end to cruelty, injustice, and aggression. Because of such a positive ending in the face of tragedy—because so many British mothers and fathers had received the same telegram from the war office as had Mr. Britling—the novel achieved a high level of popularity in both England and America. The mere idea of Wells relying upon God as a means out of the recent chaos and into a world of order became too grand a vision for people to ignore. He seemed to have expressed the grief and the trauma of an entire generation.

If *Mr. Britling Sees It Through* revealed Wells looking hard and long into his own moral and religious conscience, *The World of William Clissold* served as his opportunity to reach outward and address the world. Thus, his 1926 effort exists almost as a pseudonovel in which the author disguised himself as a retired industrialist to demonstrate to his readers the chaotic state of the world and to suggest some cures for a number of universal ills. The retirement to the Villa Jasmin, near Grasse, allows Clissold to gather his thoughts for inclusion into his memoirs; in the end, Wells, through his titled character, announces his sponsorship of an open conspiracy of intelligent men and women throughout the world—an idea that appealed to the postwar generation, to those who sought something more intellectually stimulating than what Wells had suggested in *Ann Veronica* and *The New Machiavelli*.

Wells gave his readers ample room through which to wander and to consider the world: three volumes that he likened to "a vast three decker . . . which broke down the endurance of readers and book-sellers alike." He also, at age sixty, gave himself plenty of room and time to reminisce: childhood at Up Park, the houses in which he had lived and written, reflections upon his own political, philosophical, and economic theories. In writing both honestly and emotionally about real people and real events, Wells (as Clissold) carries the reader off into a series of digressions that have been identified as essays rather than fictional interludes. In other words, the discussion of such issues as the psychoanalysis of Karl Marx, the reincarnation of socialism, or the rise of patent medicine and drug companies may have sacrificed the artistic aim of fiction for the more practical purpose of political argument or journalism.

Nevertheless, Wells's rhetorical ramblings are not very disruptive, especially when the novelist unveils, in *The World of William Clissold*, his grand scheme of world revolution by the highest levels of intelligent men and women. His intelligentsia, however, are also practical people, a new functional class of managers, engineers, and educators, a scientifically trained class that would unite for the formation of a new social order. Furthermore, the revolution must come as the result of new influence and vitality replacing the worn-out mechanism of existing states and institutions. Naturally, the revolution is not an uprising of the masses, but a careful strategy worked out by the leadership of the intellectual and intelligent minority—a new managerial class of technocrats and artisans who would seize power toward the end of the century, immediately prior to or during a world war. Again, Wells as prophet attracted a number of readers: individuals who could easily commit themselves to a strong ray of positivism, to an idea seething with intellectual promise, to a world that could simultaneously think and act.

The real force behind Wells as novelist may be appreciated in terms of his ability to stimulate his readers' imaginations and to appraise people of the various possibilities for the world in which they lived. Toward that end, he advanced his own materialistic interpretation of life, although (both in and outside of his fiction) he despaired of human inadequacies that prevented the shaping of a higher human species. Although not an intellectual snob, Wells nevertheless sought the highest possible goals for mankind, trying to find the right ground upon which science and education could operate for the betterment of the entire world. Unfortunately for Wells the novelist, the educational and scientific theories of Wells the social schemer detracted from the art and the craft of his fiction. He recognized clearly those problems and weaknesses and, although he disliked being reminded of them, he stood ready to accept full responsibility. "I shall die," he once remarked, "as I have lived, the responsible centre of my world."

Major publications other than long fiction

SHORT FICTION: *The Stolen Bacillus and Other Incidents*, 1895; *Thirty Strange Stories*, 1897; *The Plattner Story and Others*, 1897; *The Vacant Country*, 1899; *Tales of Space and Time*, 1899; *Twelve Stories and a Dream*, 1903; *The Country of the Blind*, 1911; *The Short Stories of H. G. Wells*, 1927; *The Favourite Short Stories*, 1937; *The Complete Short Stories*, 1971.

NONFICTION: *Text Book of Biology*, 1893 (2 volumes); *Honors Physiogra-*

phy, 1893 (with Sir Richard Gregory); *Certain Personal Matters*, 1897; *A Text Book of Zoology*, 1898 (with A. M. Davis); *Anticipations*, 1902; *The Discovery of the Future*, 1902; *Mankind in the Making*, 1903; *A Modern Utopia*, 1905; *Socialism and the Family*, 1906; *The Future in America*, 1906; *The Misery of Boots*, 1907; *Socialism and Marriage*, 1908; *New Worlds for Old*, 1908; *First and Last Things*, 1908; *Socialism and the Great State*, 1912; *The War That Will End War*, 1914; *An Englishman Looks at the World*, 1914; *God, the Invisible King*, 1917; *The Outline of History*, 1920; *The Salvaging of Civilization*, 1921; *Russia in the Shadows*, 1921; *A Short History of the World*, 1922; *Socialism and the Scientific Motive*, 1923; *The Open Conspiracy*, 1928; *The Book of Catherine Wells*, 1928; *After Democracy*, 1929; *Imperialism and the Open Conspiracy*, 1929; *The Way to World Peace*, 1930; *The Work, Wealth, and Happiness of Mankind*, 1931; *The Science of Life*, 1931 (with Julian Huxley and G. P. Wells); *What Are We to Do with Our Lives?*, 1931; *Evolution, Fact and Theory*, 1932 (with Julian Huxley); *An Experiment in Autobiography*, 1934 (2 volumes); *The New America*, 1935; *The Anatomy of Frustration*, 1936; *World Encyclopedia*, 1936; *World Brain*, 1938; *The Fate of Homo Sapiens*, 1939; *Fate of Man*, 1939; *The New World Order*, 1940; *The Common Sense of War and Peace*, 1940; *The Conquest of Time*, 1942; *Phoenix*, 1942; *Science and the World Mind*, 1942; *'42 to '44: A Contemporary Memoir*, 1944; *Ansata: An Indictment of the Roman Catholic Church*, 1944; *Mind at the End of Its Tether*, 1946.

Bibliography

Bergonzi, Bernard. *The Early H. G. Wells*, 1961.
Bloom, Robert. *Anatomies of Egotism: A Reading of the Last Novels of H. G. Wells*, 1977.
Costa, Richard Hauer. *H. G. Wells*, 1967.
Dickson, Lovat. *H. G. Wells: His Turbulent Life and Times*, 1969.
Hammond, J. R. *Herbert George Wells: An Annotated Bibliography of His Works*, 1977.
_____ . *An H. G. Wells Companion*, 1979.
Hillegas, Mark R. *The Future as Nightmare: H. G. Wells and the Anti-Utopians*, 1967.
Nicholson, Norman. *H. G. Wells*, 1950.
Parrinder, Patrick. *H. G. Wells*, 1970.
Raknem, Ingvald. *H. G. Wells and His Critics*, 1962.
Wager, W. Warren. *H. G. Wells and the World State*, 1961.
West, Geoffrey. *H. G. Wells: A Sketch for a Portrait*, 1930.

Samuel J. Rogal

EUDORA WELTY

Born: Jackson, Mississippi; April 13, 1909

Principal long fiction

The Robber Bridegroom, 1942; *Delta Wedding*, 1946; *The Ponder Heart*, 1954; *Losing Battles*, 1970; *The Optimist's Daughter*, 1972.

Other literary forms

In spite of her success and acclaim as a novelist, Eudora Welty regards herself as essentially a writer of short stories. In an interview that appeared in the fall, 1972, issue of the *Paris Review*, she says, "I'm a short-story writer who writes novels the hard way, and by accident." It is interesting to note, however, that her last collection of new stories appeared in 1955, and that her last two books of new fiction have been novels. In 1980, all of her previously collected short fiction and two uncollected stories were published in one volume, *The Collected Stories of Eudora Welty*. Prior to that, some had appeared in *Short Stories* (1950) and in *Selected Stories of Eudora Welty*, (1954). The original short story collections are *A Curtain of Green and Other Stories* (1941); *The Wide Net and Other Stories* (1943); *The Golden Apples* (1949), regarded by some as a loosely structured novel, but considered by Welty to be a group of interconnected stories; and *The Bride of the Innisfallen* (1955). Welty has also published numerous essays and reviews, some of which have been collected in *The Eye of the Story: Selected Essays and Reviews* (1978). In addition, she has published a book for children, *The Shoe Bird* (1964), and a book of her own photographs, *One Time, One Place* (1971).

Achievements

Although it was not until she wrote *Losing Battles* and *The Optimist's Daughter* that Welty's name began to appear on the best-seller lists, her work had long been recognized and appreciated by discerning readers. In four decades of writing and publishing, she has received nearly every major award for fiction offered in the United States. Among them are the prestigious William Dean Howells Medal of the Academy of Arts and Letters for "the most distinguished work of American fiction" for the years 1950 through 1955, the National Institute of Arts and Letters Gold Medal for the Novel in 1972, the Pulitzer Prize for Fiction in 1973, and the National Medal for Literature at the American Book Awards ceremony in 1980. In addition, she has been awarded several honorary doctorates, Guggenheim Fellowships, special professorships, and membership in the National Institute of Arts and Letters.

Disinterested in either fame or fortune, Welty has simply wanted the opportunity to write and the assurance that there are readers who enjoy her work. She repeatedly expresses gratitude to such writers and editors as Robert Penn

Warren, Cleanth Brooks, Albert Erskine, Ford Madox Ford, and Katherine Anne Porter, who were among the first persons of influence to recognize her ability and to promote interest in her early stories. Warren, Brooks, and Erskine accepted some of her first stories for *The Southern Review* and thus opened the door for subsequent publication in such magazines as *The Atlantic*, *Harper's Bazaar*, and *The New Yorker*. This exposure to a national audience also facilitated the publication of her first volume of stories.

Regarded by Reynolds Price, Guy Davenport, and other distinguished readers as America's greatest living writer, Welty has only recently begun to receive critical attention commensurate with her achievements.

Biography

Eudora Alice Welty was born in Jackson, Mississippi, on April 13, 1909. She has lived there most of her life, and still lives in the family home in which she was reared. She was the only daughter of Christian Webb Welty and Mary Chestina Andrews Welty; she had two younger brothers. Soon after their marriage in 1904, Welty's parents moved to Jackson. Her father, who came from Ohio, where his father owned a farm, was president of the well-established Lamar Life Insurance Company. Her mother, a West Virginian, was descended from pre-Revolutionary War Virginia stock, engendered by country preachers, teachers, and lawyers. Welty, who claims that she would feel "shy, and discouraged at the very thought" of a biography about her, feels that a "private life should be kept private." Hence, biographical data on her is sketchy at best. She admits, "They'd have a hard time trying to find something about me." At any rate, she insists that it is the writer's work, not his or her life, that is important.

Perhaps one reason why she suggests that her own biography would not "particularly interest anybody" is that she has lived for the most part in the mainstream of American society. As Katherine Anne Porter aptly observes in her introduction to *A Curtain of Green*, Welty is not the "spiritual and intellectual exile" that typifies the modern artist. She attended Central High School in Jackson, then went for two years to Mississippi State College for Women, in Columbus, before transferring to the University of Wisconsin in 1927. After graduating with a bachelor of arts degree in English in 1929, she enrolled in the School of Business at Columbia University, where she studied advertising for a year. By then, the country was in the throes of the Depression, and she returned to Jackson to seek work. During the next several years, she held a variety of jobs in advertising, radio scriptwriting, and part-time newspaper work. She also began writing stories. Possibly the most important of those early jobs was the position of "Junior Publicity Agent" with the Works Project Administration from 1933 to 1936. In this position, Welty was required to travel extensively through Mississippi doing newspaper stories on various WPA projects. Her work involved taking photographs, talking with a great variety of people, and—perhaps most important—listening to them. As Welty herself confesses, she has a "good ear" and a visual imagination, qualities that enabled her to hear and observe things and people during those three years that she would use in her fiction throughout her life.

A number of the photographs she took while on her WPA assignment were displayed for a month in the Lugene Gallery in New York, a small camera shop. Later, some of them appeared in her published collection of photographs, *One Time, One Place*. Only after several years of discouraging rejection slips did Welty finally publish a story, "Death of a Traveling Salesman," in a small magazine called *Manuscript* in 1936. Soon after that, her talent was discovered by Robert Penn Warren, Albert Erskine, and Cleanth Brooks. Then, John Woodbury of Doubleday, Doran, and Company became interested in her work, and with his support, her first collection of short stories, *A Curtain of Green and Other Stories*, was published in 1941. The next year, her first novel, *The Robber Bridegroom*, appeared. Two of her books have been successfully adapted for the stage, *The Robber Bridegroom* as a Broadway musical in 1974 and *The Ponder Heart* as a New York stage play in 1956.

Humane, thoughtful, and generous, Welty has modestly accepted the many honors that have come to her. Scarcely a year has passed since 1940 in which she has not received a major award of some kind. At the same time, she has given abundantly of her time to school children, scholars, interviewers, and aspiring writers. She has been active in community causes in Jackson, given scores of lectures and readings, assisted numerous charities, and even provided recipes for cookbooks. During the years of severe unrest over civil rights issues, her critics blasted her for not actively taking up that cause in her fiction. She answered those critics eloquently in a 1965, *The Atlantic* essay entitled "Must the Novelist Crusade?"

In her Introduction to *The Collected Stories of Eudora Welty*, Welty expresses characteristic gratitude for the help and encouragement she received along the way. In other places she speaks of her good fortune in being reared in a family that encouraged the reading of books. She has a particular love for myths, fairy tales, and legends, and she counts it her good fortune to have grown up in a region where, as she says, people love talking and delight in a good yarn. Even though she was teased as a child for having a "Yankee" father, her work is deeply rooted, like its creator, in the South as a place. Still, neither she nor her fiction could be called "regional" in any narrow sense of the term. In fact, she balks at the regionalist title. Her work, for all its down-home Southern flavor, attests the universality of her vision and the capacity of her art to elude easy labels. Her subject is not the South, but humanity.

Analysis

Paramount in Eudora Welty's work is the sense of what "community," or group membership, means in the South and how it is expressed through manners, attitudes, and dialogue. Clearly, it provides a special way of seeing and responding. In Welty's published essays and interviews, certain concerns keep surfacing—the relationship between time and place and the artistic endeavor; the importance of human relationships in a work of fiction; the necessity for the artist to be grounded in real life and yet be aware of life's "mystery"; the value of the imagination; and the function of memory. These concerns find expression in her work principally in the tension between what is actual, what is seen and heard in a specific time and place, and what is felt or known intuitively. Welty uses the sometimes conflicting demands of the community and the self, the surface life and the interior life, to describe this tension in her novels. On the one hand is the need for community and order; on the other is the need for the separate individual life which often works against community and order.

Typically, a Welty novel swings between overt action, including dialogue, and individual contemplation. This is especially evident in *Delta Wedding*, where Welty almost rhythmically alternates dialogue and action with the inner musings of her principal female characters. In *The Optimist's Daughter*, only Laurel Hand's thoughts are set against the exterior action, but it becomes apparent that her father, as he lies unmoving on his hospital bed, is silently contemplating the mystery of life and human relationships for perhaps the first time in his life. Her mother, too, near the end of her life, had begun speaking out the painful things she must have harbored for many years in her dark soul. Even Edna Earle Ponder in *The Ponder Heart* seems to talk incessantly to keep the inner life from raising itself into consciousness. In *Losing Battles*, where Welty says she consciously tried to tell everything through speech and action—she had been accused of obscurantism in previous works—the pattern still emerges. Instead of swinging between action and cerebration, however, this novel swings between action and description. Still, the effect is surprisingly similar, though the pages of action and dialogue far outnumber the pages of description, and the transitions between the two modes of narration are very abrupt. Even so, the young schoolteacher who chooses love and marriage against her mentor's advice slips occasionally into Welty's meditative mode. The alternation of thought and action is also the basic structural pattern of the stories in *The Golden Apples*.

Thus, in Welty's novels, external order is established through speech and action that sustain community, either the social or family group. In fact, the novels are often structured around community rituals that reinforce the group entity against outside intrusions and shore up its defenses against its most insidious foe, the impulse to separateness in its individual members. *Delta Wedding* is set entirely in the framework of one of these community-perpetuating rituals. For the moment, the wedding is everything, and members of the group pay it homage by gathering, giving gifts, feasting, and burying their individual lives in its demands. *Losing Battles* is also framed by a community ritual, the family reunion. The threat from individual outsiders is felt constantly, and the family takes sometimes extreme measures to ward off influences that might undermine its solidarity. There are at least two rituals that provide structure for *The Ponder Heart*, the funeral and the courtroom trial. The first of these is conducted in enemy territory, outside the acceptable group domain; the second is conducted in home territory, and acquittal for the accused member of the group is a foregone conclusion. A funeral is also the major external event of *The Optimist's Daughter* and becomes the battleground in a contest for supremacy between two opposing groups or communities. Several of the stories or chapters in *The Golden Apples* are also structured around community rituals, including the June piano recital, the girls' summer camp, and the funeral.

In addition to these large, highly structured observances, there are the multitude of unwritten laws that govern the group. Welty's community members attach great importance to certain objects and practices: a treasured lamp given to the bride, a hand-crafted breadboard made for a mother-in-law, the establishment of family pedigrees, the selection of one male member of the community for special reverence and heroic expectation, the protection of the past from intrusion or reassessment, and, perhaps most important of all, the telling of stories as an attestation of the vitality and endurance of the group.

Underlying all of this attention to ritual and group expectation, however, is the unspoken acknowledgment that much of it is a game the participants have agreed to play, for their own sake and for the sake of the community. Some of the participants may be fooled, but many are not. Aware but fearful, they go through the motions of fulfilling community requirements in an effort to hold back the dark, to avoid facing the mystery, to keep their individual selves from emerging and crying for existence. They sense themselves to be at what Welty calls "the jumping off place," and are afraid to make the leap in the dark. They agree to pretend to be fooled. They tell stories instead of rehearsing their fears and uncertainties. The bolder ones defy the group and either leave it or live on its periphery. In every book, there are moments when a character confronts or consciously evades the dark underside of human personality and experience, and memory becomes a device for dealing with the effects of that confrontation or for evading it.

Paradoxically, storytelling, an important ritual for securing the past and bolstering community against passion, disorder, the intimations of mystery, and the erosive effects of individual impulses and yearnings, assists in the breakdown of the very group it was intended to support. The risk of indulging in rituals is that they sometimes set people to thinking and reevaluating their own individual lives and the lives of others close to them. The ritual is performed by the group, but it may stir the solitary inner being to life and to the kind of probing contemplation that jeopardizes the group's authority. Such a countereffect may be triggered by the storytelling ritual even though that ritual is meant to seal up the past for ready reference whenever the group needs reinforcement. Because storytelling relies on memory, it can become an exercise of the individual imagination. It tends to lapse, as one commentator observes, "into the memory of a memory" and thus shifts sides from the group's activities into the realm of mystery. The community's habit of setting up straw men for heroes can similarly erode community solidarity because it too relies upon imagination and memory. It glorifies the individual rather than the group spirit.

As Welty presents this conflict, then, between the self and the group, and between the intuitive and the actual, she writes into her work a sense of foreboding. The community, especially the traditional Southern community, is doomed. It cannot forever maintain itself on the old terms, for it is dependent upon the acquiescence of separate individuals who seem increasingly impervious to the efforts of the group to contain them. Welty's work also suggests that some of the things the community prizes and perpetuates are merely gestures and artifacts with little intrinsic value or meaning. When the meanings behind what a community treasures have been lost or forgotten, that community cannot long endure. In actively laboring to exclude others, the group works against its own best nature, its capacity for loving and caring. Threats to order and community may indeed come from the outside, but Welty insists that the more serious threats come from the inside, from that part of the human heart and mind that seeks to go its own way.

Welty's first novel, *The Robber Bridegroom*, is quite unlike her others. Its most noticeable differences are its setting in a much older South, on the old Natchez Trace in the days of bandits and Indians, and its fairy-tale style and manner. Even with these differences, Welty establishes what becomes her basic fictional stance. She achieves tension between the actual and the imaginary by freighting this very real setting with fabulous characters and events. The legendary characters are transformed by Welty's imagination and deftly made to share the territory with figures from the Brothers Grimm. Welty indicated the double nature of her novel, or novella, when in an address to the Mississippi Historical Society she called it a "Fairy Tale of the Natchez Trace." A favorite of William Faulkner, the book is a masterpiece, a delightful blend of legend, myth, folklore, and fairy tale that swings from rollicking surface comedy and lyrical style to painful, soul-searching explorations of the ambiguities of human experience. Although it deals with love and separateness—Robert Penn Warren's terms for the conflicting needs of communities and individuals in Welty's work—it does not deal with them in the same way that the later novels do. Clement Musgrove, a planter whose innocence leads him into marriage with the greedy Salome and an excursion into humanity's heart of darkness, learns what it is like to face the cold, dark nights of despair comfortless and alone. His daughter, Rosamond, is beautiful and loving, but she is also an inveterate liar who betrays her husband's trust in order to learn his "real" identity. Jamie Lockhart, who leads a double life as both bandit and gentleman, keeps his true identity hidden even from her whom he loves. Thus, like so many Welty characters, the principal actors in *The Robber Bridegroom* have interior lives that threaten the equilibrium of their exterior worlds.

In another sense, too, *The Robber Bridegroom* is closely linked with Welty's other novels. In writing the book, Welty testifies to the value of stories and the storytelling ritual that buttresses community, a theme that reappears in all her novels. She finds common ground with her readers in this novel by spinning a yarn full of their favorite childhood fairy tales. Then, too, fairy-tale worlds, imaginative though they are, sustain surface order, for they are worlds of sure answers, of clear good and evil, of one-dimensional characters, and of predictable rewards and punishments. As such, they confirm what the community collectively believes and perpetuates. Just as imagination, intuition, and the ponderings of the individual human soul jeopardize the codes a community lives by in other Welty novels, so do they undercut the basic assumptions of the fairy tale in this novel. Here, answers are sometimes permanently withheld, people are complex and unpredictable, the richest prize is found in human relationships rather than in kingdoms and gold, appearances are deceiving, and evil may lie in unexpected places. It is worthy of note that Welty begins her novel-writing career with a book that delights in the fairy tale at the same time that it questions community assumptions about fairy-tale morality.

The tension between community expectations and individual yearnings and apprehensions is central to *Delta Wedding*. The narrative takes place in the Mississippi delta country, during the week of Dabney Fairchild's wedding. The Fairchild family, after whom the nearby town is named, is of the social elite and has moderate wealth, mostly in property. The wedding provides an occasion for the family to gather and exercise the rituals and traditions that bind them together and strengthen their sense of community. The wedding itself is the principal ritual, of course, with its attendant food preparation, dressmaking, rehearsal, and home and yard decorating. Welty's eye for manners and ear for speech are flawless as the Fairchilds deliberate over the consequences of George Fairchild's having married beneath him and Dabney's seemingly unfortunate repetition of her father's mistake. The Fairchilds still claim George, however, even though they have little use for his wife, Robbie Reid; and they will continue to embrace Dabney in spite of her choosing to marry an outsider, Troy Flavin. It is the habit of community to maintain order by defining and placing people and things in relation to itself. A person either does or does not have legitimate ties to the group.

The Fairchilds also repeat family stories in order to keep the past secure and give stability to the present. Their current favorite story is also one that makes a hero out of the male heir-apparent. George's dead brother was apparently more remarkable than he, but George is the one survivor, and the family's hopes rest with him. At least a dozen times in the book, some version is told of George's staying on the railroad track with his mentally retarded niece whose foot was caught in the rails. Instead of leaping to safety with the others, he stayed to face the oncoming train. Luckily, the engineer of the Yellow Dog was able to stop the train in time. By choosing to stay with Maureen instead of answering his wife's plea to save himself, George made a reflexive choice for honor and blood over marital obligation. Later, he again chooses family over wife when he comes for the pre-wedding activities instead of looking for his absent, heartbroken wife.

Running counter to the speech and actions that affirm order and community, however, is an undercurrent of threat to that order. Welty intersperses the overt actions and attitudes of the family, especially of the aunts, whose sole desire is to perpetuate the clan structure, with individual ruminations of other female characters who are part of that structure and yet somewhat peripheral to it. Ellen, who married into the Fairchilds and has never dared resist them, has moments of personal doubt that would be regarded as treasonous were they known by her aunts. Dabney also wonders, in a brief honest moment, about the homage paid to the wedding ritual for its own sake. Further, she accidentally breaks a treasured lamp, a family heirloom given her by the aunts as a wedding present. Little Laura, having lost her mother, has also lost her basic tie to the family. From her position on the edge of the Fairchild clan, she questions the community tenets that exclude her. Even George seems ready to violate community expectations by his apparent willingness to deprive two of the aunts of their home.

The novel's essential statement, then, is that the community is losing its hold. In an interview published in 1972 by *The Southern Review*, Welty is asked the question: "Is Shellmound [the home of the Fairchilds] with its way of life and its values doomed?" She replies, "Oh, yes. I think that was implicit in the novel: that this was all such a fragile, temporary thing. At least I hope it was." She adds that: "Well, you're living in a very precarious world without knowing it, always." The community's position is inexorably altered in the face of individual yearning and independent action.

There are two large community rituals in *The Ponder Heart*: the funeral of Bonnie Dee Peacock and the trial of Uncle Daniel Ponder for her murder. Such narrative matter sounds ominous enough to one unfamiliar with Welty's capacity for comedy, but to the initiated, it promises a hilarious display of Southern talk and manners. Still, *The Ponder Heart* is troubled, as Welty's other novels are, by an ominous current running beneath its surface action. Like the Fairchilds of *Delta Wedding*, the Ponders have social position and wealth—perhaps greater than that of the Fairchilds. They are on the decline, however, in spite of the efforts of Edna Earle Ponder, Welty's first-person narrator, to maintain the family and its image. Symbolic of the failing family or community image that Edna Earle seeks to perpetuate and protect are two buildings which the family owns, the Beulah Hotel, run by Edna Earle, and the Ponder home a few miles out of town. In the end, both buildings are virtually empty. The family has shrunk to two members and the future holds no promise.

The storyline tells of middle-aged Uncle Daniel's taking to wife young Bonnie Dee Peacock, losing her, regaining her, losing her again, reclaiming her, and then finally losing her by tickling her to death in the aftermath of an electric storm. Uncle Daniel's mental age is considerably lower than his chronological age, but he is blessed with a generous nature. He gives away everything he can get his hands on, and has to be watched continually. Not that Edna Earle cares to restrain him very much, for he is the revered scion, like George, in *Delta Wedding*, without whose approbation and presence the community would totter. Her duty is to protect and sustain Daniel, and she will not even permit herself private doubts over what that duty requires. The entire novel is the report of her conversation about Uncle Daniel with a visitor who is stranded at the Beulah. Clearly, Edna Earle's talk and actions are designed to maintain order and community as she has known them all her life. She believes that if she relaxes her vigil, the structure will collapse.

The ritual of the Peacock funeral is important because it is grossly inferior to the Ponder notion of what constitutes a funeral. The Peacocks are what the Ponders (except Daniel, who in his innocence would not know the difference) would call "country"; in other words, they are regarded as comically inferior beings who have no business marrying into the Ponder family. The trial is more to Edna Earle's liking, though it is threatened by the presence of the low-bred Peacocks and a prosecuting shyster lawyer who is an outsider. Edna Earle gets caught in a lie designed to protect Daniel, but the day is saved when Daniel begins passing out greenbacks in the courtroom. The jury votes for acquittal in record time, and Daniel cheerily dispenses the whole family fortune. He discovers to his sorrow afterward, however, that people who have taken his money can no longer face him. Thus, in the end, Daniel, who wanted nothing more than company and an audience for his stories, is left lonely and friendless. Though Edna Earle tries to inject new hope through the promise of a new audience—her captive guest at the Beulah—doom is on the horizon for the Ponders even more surely than it was for the Fairchilds. The collapse of community structure in this novel, as in *Delta Wedding*, can be laid partly to the failure of the community's rather artificial system of supports—rituals, traditions, family stories, pedigrees, and a family "hero." It must also be laid, however, to the fact that Uncle Daniel, in his innocence, breaks away and acts as an individual. He is not capable of the contemplation that undermines community in *Delta Wedding*, but neither can he be restrained to act as a member of the group instead of as himself.

In *Losing Battles*, Welty partially turns the tables on what she had done with the conflict between community and self in her previous two novels and in *The Golden Apples*. Here, she shows that community, though mildly ruffled by individual needs and doubts, can prevail when it is sustained by strong individuals who are also loyal group members. Welty indicates in a *Southern Review* interview that she deliberately chose as her setting the poorest section of Mississippi during the time of the Depression, so that her characters would be shown on a bare stage with themselves as their only resource, without "props to their lives." Thus, the artificial structures built of money and status that support community in *Delta Wedding* and *The Ponder Heart* are not available to the Vaughn-Beecham-Renfro clan in *Losing Battles*. Perhaps that is one reason for their greater durability.

The story is told almost entirely through dialogue and action, interlaced with occasional lyrical descriptions of setting and even less frequent ruminations of the story's principal outsider, Gloria Renfro, the hero's wife. The action takes place entirely in one day and the following morning, with details of the past filled in through family storytelling. Jack Renfro, the young grandson who has been exalted by family hope and expectations, bears some resemblance to George Fairchild and Daniel Ponder. On him lies the chief burden of sustaining the family, of guaranteeing its survival as a unit. He returns home from the state penitentiary to the waiting family reunion that is celebrating old Granny Vaughn's birthday. He finds there not only his bride, but a baby daughter he has never seen. The family has believed, has had to believe, that things will be better once Jack has returned home. Jack himself believes it and, as Welty indicates, the others take their faith from his. Through a series of wild, funny episodes—and more than a few tender moments—the family prevails. Welty says that in this comic novel she intended to portray the indomitability, the unquenchable spirit of human beings. Folks such as these may be losing the battles, but they are still fighting them, and that is what counts.

Welty describes "the solidity of the family" as "the strongest thing in the book." She also recognizes that, in a clan such as this, a character sometimes has to be himself before he can reinforce the unity of the group. Welty says that such a "sticking together" as is seen in *Losing Battles* "involves both a submerging and a triumph of the individual, because you can't really conceive of the whole unless you *are* an identity." The extended family of *Losing Battles* engages in rituals to maintain itself just as the Fairchild family does in *Delta Wedding*. It acknowledges milestones reached by its members, milestones such as weddings and ninetieth birthdays; it tells stories; it creates a hero; and it works painstakingly to establish and affirm blood relationships with any who might seek entrance into the group. All is done with the honor of the clan—or the individual as member of the clan—in mind, whether it is going to jail or rescuing a car from a cliff on Banner Top.

In spite of the prevailing unity and the optimistic conclusion to the novel's events, there are small rumblings of individual assertion against community. Gloria loves Jack, but she does not want to be a member of his family. She envisions a smaller community, made up of just her, Jack, and their baby, Lady May. The group, however, will not allow her to build a community of her own. Against her will, it tries to reconstruct a parentage for her that would make her a blood relation. The relatives perform a rather cruel ritual of pouncing on her and forcing her to eat watermelon, but she remains adamant. She also remains steadfast in her admiration for Miss Julia Mortimer, the schoolteacher who picked Gloria as her successor and who fought a losing battle all her life against the joyful ignorance of the likes of Jack's family.

Thus, there are several influences in the book that threaten, though not seriously, the sense of community. Gloria and her child, and Miss Julia, are the most obvious ones. It becomes apparent, though, in the very style of the narration, which repeatedly turns from family action and talk to brief imaginative description, that the ordering of the actual and the real according to community necessity does not entirely carry the day. There is another side to experience, the imaginative, the intuitive—a part of the individual soul that resists allegiance.

In *The Optimist's Daughter*, Welty returns to a more balanced combination of action and contemplation. The book's perceiving eye is Laurel Hand, daughter of Becky and Judge McKelva. The abiding question for Laurel is why, after the death of the intelligent, sensitive Becky, the Judge took for a wife a crass, tasteless woman half his age. Laurel helplessly watches her father's still form as he silently reviews his life in a hospital room, ironically set against the backdrop of the Mardi Gras festival. She repeats her helpless watch as he lies in his coffin at Mount Salus while his wife, Wanda Fay Chisom, performs her gnashing, wailing ritual of bereavement and his old friends perform their ritual of eulogy. The Chisom family, who nod appreciatively as Fay grossly mourns, are the same breed as the Peacocks in *The Ponder Heart*, entirely out of context in the McKelva home. Laurel, however, is equally uncomfortable with her own group's rites of community preservation—telling stories about the Judge that make a hero of him, despising the intrusive outsider, urging Laurel to stay and bolster the old relationship. Laurel's husband Phil was killed in military service many years ago and Laurel herself is working in Chicago, but the women who were bridesmaids at her wedding have kept that group intact and still refer to themselves as "the bridesmaids."

Laurel's last night at home is spent in anguish. Trapped by an invading chimney swift in rooms full of memories, she is caught hopelessly in the past. In the course of the night, she is forced to examine the protective structure she had built around her parents' marriage and her own. In doing so, she must allow memory and imagination to reinterpret the past which she had wanted to keep sealed away in the perfection of her own making, and she must relinquish her old idea of what constitutes group unity and loyalty. The Wanda Fays of the world will always claim their space, will always intrude. The secret for surviving their intrusion, Laurel discovers, is to withdraw one's protective walls so that the Fays have nothing to knock down. Laurel at last allows truth to dismantle the edifice of community as she had conceived it, and she finds, through the imagination and the heart, a new source of strength in watching the artificial construct tumble. Thus, the foreboding and pessimism arising from the impending doom of community in *Delta Wedding* and *The Ponder Heart*, diverted for a time in the paradoxical optimism of *Losing Battles*, are to some extent reversed in Laurel's final acceptance in *The Optimist's Daughter*. *The Golden Apples* had foretold such an outcome, for a number of its characters must also deal with the relationship between their individual lives and the group life.

The miracle of Welty's work is the skill with which she has brought her imagination to bear on the actual and made a reconciliation out of the conflicting demands of the community and the private life, out of that which can be perceived by the senses and that which can be known only intuitively. For Welty, the actual is mainly the realities of Mississippi life. In her work, however, the reality of Mississippi becomes a springboard rich with possibilities for an imagination that knows how to use time and place as doorways to the human heart.

Major publications other than long fiction
SHORT FICTION: *A Curtain of Green and Other Stories*, 1941; *The Wide Net and Other Stories*, 1943; *The Golden Apples*, 1949; *Short Stories*, 1950; *Selected Stories of Eudora Welty*, 1954; *The Bride of the Innisfallen*, 1955; *A Sweet Devouring*, 1969; *The Collected Stories of Eudora Welty*, 1980.
NONFICTION: *Music from Spain*, 1948; *Place in Fiction*, 1957; *Three Papers on Fiction*, 1962; *One Time, One Place: Mississippi in the Depression, A Snapshot Album*, 1971; *A Pageant of Birds*, 1974; *The Eye of the Story: Selected Essays and Reviews*, 1978.
CHILDREN'S LITERATURE: *The Shoe Bird*, 1964.

Bibliography
Appel, Alfred, Jr. *A Season of Dreams: The Fiction of Eudora Welty*, 1965.
Bryant, J. A., Jr. *Eudora Welty*, 1968.
Desmond, John F. *A Still Moment: Essays on the Art of Eudora Welty*, 1978.
Dollarhide, Louis, and Ann J. Abadie, eds. *Eudora Welty: A Form of Thanks*, 1979.
Howard, Zelma Turner. *The Rhetoric of Eudora Welty's Short Stories*, 1973.

Isaacs, Neil D. *Eudora Welty*, 1969.
Kreyling, Michael. *Eudora Welty's Achievement of Order*, 1980.
Prenshaw, Peggy Whitman, ed. *Eudora Welty: Critical Essays*, 1979.
Thompson, Victor H. *Eudora Welty: A Reference Guide*, 1976.
Vande Kieft, Ruth M. *Eudora Welty*, 1962.

Marilyn Arnold

GLENWAY WESCOTT

Born: Kewaskum, Wisconsin; April 11, 1901

Principal long fiction

The Apple of the Eye, 1924; *The Grandmothers: A Family Portrait*, 1927; *The Pilgrim Hawk: A Love Story*, 1940; *Apartment in Athens*, 1945.

Other literary forms

Glenway Wescott's first published work was *The Bitterns: A Book of Twelve Poems* (1920); another volume of poetry, *Natives of Rock: XX Poems, 1921-1922* appeared in 1925. Two of his short stories were privately published in France by friends as separate books: . . . *Like a Lover* (1926) and *The Babe's Bed* (1930). A collection of stories with a long title essay, *Good-bye, Wisconsin*, was published in 1928. Other books include a variety of forms: *Fear and Trembling*, a collection of essays (1932); *Twelve Fables of Aesop, Newly Narrated* (1954); and *Images of Truth: Remembrances and Criticism* (1962). Several uncollected poems and stories appeared in literary journals over the years, along with a number of personal and critical essays. Perhaps Wescott's most imaginative work is "The Dream of Audubon, Libretto of a Ballet in Three Scenes," in *The Best One-Act Plays of 1940* (1941), which holds the key to Wescott's extensive use of bird imagery and symbolism.

Achievements

After his beginnings as a published poet, Wescott often reviewed books of poetry and fiction. His critical pieces reveal that from the time of his earliest experiments in prose fiction, he was forming his idea of the novel and the aims of the art that it best embodied: To present images of reality and the truth of experience.

Even after his first two novels were published, critics disagreed as to whether Wescott *was* a novelist. The skepticism had several causes, mostly related to form. The first section of his first novel, *The Apple of the Eye*, was published separately as the story, "Bad Han," in two parts in *The Dial*. Wescott then expanded it with two more parts to make a novel. *The Grandmothers*, accepted as a novel by the Harper's Prize judges, was a series of portraits of individual characters. Today, these books are recognized as formally innovative: they focus on the process of self-discovery, and they are unified by the relation of the parts to the experience of the protagonist.

The short stories in *Good-bye, Wisconsin* seemed to support the critics' judgment that Wescott was essentially a short-story writer and their further pigeonholing of him as a regional realist attacking the narrowness of culture in the Midwest and as a typical expatriate writer. Doubts about Wescott's capacities as a novelist were permanently laid to rest, however, with the triumph of *The Pilgrim Hawk* which was hailed as a masterpiece of its genre and later reprinted in two anthologies of great short novels. *The Pilgrim Hawk*, set in France, and the next novel, *Apartment in Athens*, showed that Wescott could go beyond regional materials. The latter, however, although chosen by the Book-of-the-Month Club, was not a critical success, probably because its propagandistic aims were too obvious.

Wescott spent many years in service to literature. He was president of the National Institute of Arts and Letters, 1958-1961. He wrote and delivered a number of introductory and presentation speeches, later published in the Proceedings of the American Academy of Arts and Letters. He also became a member of the National Commission for the United Nations Educational, Scientific, and Cultural Organization (UNESCO). As a public man of letters, he gave many talks and readings, appeared on radio and television, participated in symposia and writers' conferences, and served on various committees for the Institute and the Authors' Guild. He edited *The Maugham Reader* (1950) and *Short Novels of Colette* (1951), writing the Introduction for the latter.

Currently an unfashionable writer, Wescott should be read in any survey of the great decades of the American novel from 1920 to 1940. A revival of critical interest in his work is long overdue.

Biography

Glenway Wescott was born in Kewaskum, Wisconsin, on April 11, 1901, the first of six children. According to the autobiographical portrait of Alwyn Tower in *The Grandmothers*, he was a sensitive, imaginative, and solitary child. His nature was antipathetic to the physical and cultural poverty of the farm life in which he spent his boyhood. At age thirteen, because of difficulties with his father, he left home and lived with an uncle and others while going to high school.

In 1917, Wescott entered the University of Chicago, began writing poetry, and soon joined the Poetry Club. The following year, he became engaged, but he did not marry then or later; the engagement was broken in 1921. During this period, Wescott tried fiction, beginning the story "Bad Han," which became part of his first novel.

Because of ill-health, Wescott withdrew from the University of Chicago after a year and a half, thus ending his formal education. Shortly thereafter, he went to New Mexico for an extended visit with Yvor Winters, a period which he referred to as one of the happiest of his life.

In 1920, after a visit to his family, Wescott went to Chicago to stay with Monroe Wheeler, with whom he was to share his travels abroad and much of his life in the United States and to whom he dedicated his 1962 volume of essays. He traveled with Wheeler to New York City, then to England and

Germany, before returning to the United States and embarking on a career of serious writing.

In 1925, Wescott moved to France, beginning eight years as an expatriate but returning yearly for a visit to his family. He used the experience of an expatriate looking back at his pioneer family in Wisconsin as the framework for *The Grandmothers*, which was written during the first year of his stay abroad. Winning the prestigious Harper's Prize, the book was a critical and popular success. With the publication of a volume of short stories the following year, Wescott's position in the forefront of talented young writers seemed assured.

During his stay abroad, Wescott spent extended periods in Germany, leading him to write the essays in *Fear and Trembling*, and later during wartime to try to explain the German character in the novel, *Apartment in Athens*. In 1933, Wescott moved back to the United States, dividing his time between New York City and the farm in New Jersey where his family had moved. He went to Europe with his brother and the latter's bride, Barbara Harrison, in 1935 and again traveled abroad in 1938, before finally settling in America.

The year 1940 marked a period of renewed creativity for Wescott with the appearance of his acclaimed short novel, *The Pilgrim Hawk*, a ballet libretto, several lyrical essays, and, in 1945, *Apartment in Athens*, a war novel set in Greece (which Wescott had never visited). Thereafter, he produced less, leading the life of a public man of letters. Besides the distractions of that role, he suggested another reason for his diminished literary output in later life, saying, "I am an incorrigibly copious letter-writer, and doubtless have wasted time in that way."

His father, with whom he eventually became reconciled, died in 1953, and his mother, to whom he was extremely devoted, died in 1960. Wescott still lives on the family farm in rural New Jersey.

Analysis

When Glenway Wescott left his native Wisconsin, returned and left again, each time it was to move farther east, first to Chicago, then New York, then Europe. It was also to plunge into the major literary currents of the day: imagism in poetry, regionalism in fiction, criticism of American culture and society by the expatriates, focus on the self as a major theme, revolt against traditional forms and experiments with new ones. If he was typical of the young writers of the 1920's, then he was also—like F. Scott Fitzgerald, Ernest Hemingway, and William Faulkner—a distinctive voice whose contributions to this innovative period of American fiction should be studied along with those of his greater contempories.

Published when Wescott was twenty-three, *The Apple of the Eye* was considered an impressive, although not faultless, first novel by such reviewers as Kenneth Burke and Ruth Suckow. In content, it is a typical initiation story, following the self-discovery of the hero, Dan Strane, as he rebels against Midwestern puritanism, finds an affirmative meaning in life, and departs to live it his own way. In form, the novel is more original, with its tripartite structure. Its style reveals, even this early, the author's mastery of what Ira Johnson calls the "lyric, disciplined, imagistic prose of sensibility."

Book I elaborates on a sort of legend that Wescott's mother once told him about an old servant. Hannah Madoc, called "Bad Han," is a "secular saint" who accepts love and lives life as it comes, without the common tortures of guilt. Han's lover, Jules Bier, influenced by his father, leaves her to marry Selma Duncan, who represents puritanism, the "evasion of experience." Book II introduces Rosalia and tells of her love affair with Dan's new friend, Mike Byron. Mike begins Dan's initiation by explaining that while puritanism appeals to the imagination, it is unhealthy in its division of the flesh from the spirit. Dan turns away from his beloved mother and her religion, while Mike initiates in him an awareness of the pleasures of sensuality. Meanwhile, Mike's and Rosalia's affair gains momentum, then dies, and Rosalia is deserted by Mike. Maddened by sorrow and guilt, she dies in the marsh.

In Book III, Dan's uncle, Jules Bier, retells the story of Bad Han as an object lesson in what is wrong with the local religious views, which have brought Rosalia and others tragedy. Bad Han becomes a powerful symbol, leading Dan to feel he is her spiritual son. Completing his separation from the sterile, frustrating environment, he departs for college, at the same time realizing that he has been blessed by experiencing several kinds of love and has felt a "sense of awakening."

Dan Strane is the first of Wescott's several autobiographical portraits. The natural setting, the rural poverty, the roughness of farm life, the puritanism, all were elements of the author's boyhood against which he rebelled. Even some of the most intimate aspects of Dan are tied to Wescott's life: the devotion to the mother, the conflict with the father, the despair and thoughts of suicide (Wescott had attempted suicide when he was eighteen), the implied homosexual attachment.

Most striking for a first novel is Wescott's lyrical style, with its piling of images into central symbols with many facets. The meaning of a symbol such as the marsh changes with the season of the year and the perception of it by a character or the omniscient narrator. It appears variously fecund, barren, ominous, even sexual. Bad Han, herself a creature of the marsh, also assumes symbolic import. A natural symbolist from the beginning, Wescott grew ever more powerful in his control of this tool of meaning, reaching finally its near-perfect use in *The Pilgrim Hawk*.

Even in this first novel, bird imagery and symbolism are pervasive, with passages about bitterns, turkeys, pigeons, wild geese, and crows. Later, in his ballet libretto, "The Dream of Audubon," Wescott sums up the key to his bird symbolism: "We are all hunters; and our heart's desire, whatever it may be, is always somehow a thing of air and wilderness, flying away from us, subject to extinction in one way or another."

In addition to the search for self-knowledge, Wescott was preoccupied with the search for an organic form to fit his materials; in his second novel, *The Grandmothers* he found one of great originality. An expatriate poet, Alwyn Tower, puts together a series of individual histories to create a family portrait. As a third-person participant-narrator, looking back from the "tower" of Europe at his origins, Alwyn treats time as fluid, moving from the self-present to the self-past when as a child he heard fragments of stories from his paternal grandmother. His curiosity roused, he watched his grandparents' life, caught glimpses of their past life, and now as an adult is able imaginatively to re-create it, as he does the lives of his parents and of other relatives. The task the adult Alwyn sets himself, at his desk in a Riviera hotel, is a purposeful search for usable knowledge needed by the self, the "all" that he will "win": "For the personages in rocking-chairs, the questionable spirits leaning over his cradle, had embodied not only the past, but the future—his own wishes and fears; and he was not to be content until an everyday light had unveiled all their faces."

Devoting himself to the acceptance of life and the creation of art, once he has exorcised their spirits, Alwyn can find meaning where they failed. His close examination of the family, and all the misguided ambition, anxiety, pride, and stubbornness of its members, remembered and imagined with compassion, will result finally in the detachment needed for the full creation of the self.

The first chapter shows Alwyn as a small boy in Wisconsin, remembered by the adult Alwyn in Europe, sensing the rich, mysterious layers of family history in his grandmother's rooms, hearing hints and half-explanations, and being tantalized by curiosity about the whole of the stories. In the second chapter he sees the Towers as making up a "composite character, the soul of a race; something so valuable that one recognized it only as an atmosphere, a special brightness, or a peculiar quality of the temperaments and customs and fortunes of Americans; as if it were the god of place." Despite his affinity for Europe, Alwyn loves his country and his family; in fact, he feels they are one and the same.

In the next twelve chapters, the narrator reconstructs and reflects on the lives of family members in the two preceding generations. The reader learns snatches of their stories as the boy learns them. Such suspense as there is in the essentially plotless book comes from waiting with him to get the answers: Why did his grandmother Rose marry Henry Tower instead of his brother Leander, who was her sweetheart before he went off to war? What happened to their brother Hilary, who went with Leander and never came home? Why did his Aunt Flora look like "a girl of thirty" and die early? These questions and more are answered in relation to love, family, religion, and historical context, although whether the answers are actually remembered or are imagined is always a guess.

Through this one family, Wescott explores the many ways of love and how it makes the Towers its victims. Henry and Rose, the grandparents, each lose their first, romantic love: Henry, when his first wife, Serena, dies; Rose, when Leander will not marry her and she has to settle for his brother. Rose marries her second choice, Henry, because she wants to escape from her own family of rough boys, and she wants "nothing in the world . . . but to be acceptable" to the Towers. Throughout the novel, events and their interpretation hinge on the family—its honor (the boys go to fight in the Civil War); its pride (the one who deserts cannot come home); its narrowness (James cannot choose a career in music); its prejudices (the spinster cannot marry a Catholic). For its members, love of family and of place are all-important and almost identical. Even though it means facing Rose, whom he jilted, Leander decides to return to Hope's Corner from California. The deserter, Evan, returns for visits, even though he knows his father will spurn him. Hope's Corner, poor as it is, symbolizes what has been the dream of the American pioneers, now changed: "The West, that point of the compass which had glittered with hope like a star, came to resemble the East—the light went out of it. . . . Every hope had a rendezvous with disappointment."

"Mother" and "home" are important themes in the novel. In its beginning, the author protagonist hears a drunken sailor on the quay below crying, "I want my mother!" While exploring memory, Alwyn discovers that, beginning with Rose and certainly including his own mother, the strong women who have married the Tower men been their salvation, and he proclaims America a matriarchy. He finds in himself some of the characteristics of the Tower men and realizes that he will have to accommodate them somehow in his artist self.

Many kinds of love abound in these portraits, but in the conclusion, Wescott develops the theme of incest, making of it a complex metaphor for what Alwyn is doing. He looks back from the "tower" of Europe at his nineteenth year, when he spent many nights watching by the bed of his dying grandmother, Rose Tower. His other grandmother, Ursula Duff, in the confusion of age has called him by the name of her eldest son and also called him her sweetheart. He thinks of this as oracular, "a menace or a promise" that must be interpreted. In the effort, he meditates on the incest taboo, and he also recalls the tradition that the breaking of that law may sometimes create a legendary hero—or god. This idea, in turn, symbolizes his way of becoming self-created: "Memory was incest. . . . The desire to understand was, after all, desire." If the word *mother* "meant that which had produced one," then it included the wilderness, Wisconsin, the family, its "squalor, ideals, manias, regrets, sensuality, what consolations there had been." He had broken the law by going back to what had produced him, going back in imagination and going forward again: "Alwyn thought with rather unreasonable pride that he had become a man in as nearly as possible the way that men had become heroes or gods."

In his third autobiographical novel, *The Pilgrim Hawk*, Wescott again treats the themes of the self and love, again evokes their essences through symbolism, and for the second time places the development of the story inside the consciousness of a narrator, this one with a first-person viewpoint. Here the self is not, as in *The Grandmothers*, primarily a member of a family or an evolving artist but a practicing artist exploring the difficulties of his vocation and probing the extent of his talent as well as his own problems of love.

Geographically, there is a reversal: the narrator, Alwyn Tower, the protagonist of *The Grandmothers*, has been an expatriate in France but is now in America about ten years later, looking back at that other place and time. The historical context is the world on the verge of war; he visualizes gun emplacement in the idyllic countryside he once visited. Again, the structural framework makes possible a double layering of time. Tower remembers what happened on one May afternoon and how he speculated on the meaning of the events; in present time, he mediates and elaborates still further on those meanings.

On that day, Alwyn Tower is at the home of his friend, Alexandra Henry (who later meets and marries his brother), when the Irish Cullens arrive. From the beginning, all attention is centered on Lucy, the pilgrim hawk Madeleine Cullen carries on her leather-encased wrist. The bird, along with the lore of falconry, is fascinating to Tower. Even more so is the conundrum of the triangular relationship of the two Cullens and the hawk. Tower sees the hawk, its needs and activities, as vastly symbolic, even of certain aspects of himself.

The events of that day, presented chronologically, can be summarized briefly as following the patterns established by the hawk. The account is interspersed with the reflective analogies drawn by the narrator. He first notes Lucy's "hunger," which can be a "painful greed, sick singlemindedness," it reminds Tower of "human hungers, mental and sentimental," for example, his own hunger to be a literary artist, which, because no one warned him that he did not have enough talent, "turned bitter, hot and nerveracking." Then, because his work has not been going well, he thinks of her as "an image of amorous desire," which would be a "natural consolation" to the weary artist.

The hawk bates—that is, throws herself headlong off her perch on the wrist and hangs helpless, upside down. While Mrs. Cullen brings her under control and soothes her, the narrator meditates on the woman's apparent need to dominate, and the group debates the value of independence. Larry Cullen, who is tethered to his wife as firmly as Lucy is, says that such yearning for freedom is the only human characteristic of hawks.

Later in the novel, Tower hears Cullen express embarrassingly frank sexual feelings toward his wife, as well as resentment at the way Lucy, constantly on his wife's arm, interferes with his embraces while traveling. These comments about sexual desire continue the hunger-imagery. Tower, also, has been thinking of his own need for love: "Old bachelor hungry bird, aging-hungry-man-bird, and how I hate desire, how I need pleasure, how I adore love, how difficult middle age must be!"

With his jealousy fully roused, Cullen goes to free Lucy, who has been left weathering in the garden. Thus he, in his own way, bates. Having observed the act, Tower quietly informs Madeleine, and she is able to recapture the bird.

Jealousy also erupts in a subtriangle: Jean, the cook, is enraged by the flirtation of his wife, Eva, with Ricketts, the Cullens' chauffeur. Disturbed by both episodes, the Cullens leave early, only to return immediately. Madeleine enters the house with the news that her husband has tried to shoot someone, whether the chauffeur—of whom he is also jealous—or himself is not clear. In other words, he has bated again. She goes to toss the gun into the pond in the garden and returns to make a final farewell. Alwyn and Alexandra linger on the scene, discussing what it all has meant, at the same time concluding from sounds in the garden that Jean and Eva have been reconciled.

The ridiculousness of Mrs. Cullen's appearance while she enacts this drama with Lucy still clutching her wrist makes the bird, too, seem funny to Tower; he begins to unload all the symbols he has piled on her and to see more realistically. The narrator is amused at "how often the great issues which I had taken this bird to augur come down in fact to undignified appearance, petty neurasthenic anecdote." The bird's—and Cullen's—"poor domestication" reminds him of "the absurd position of the artist in the midst of the disorders of those who honor and support him, but who can scarcely be expected to keep quiet around him for art's sake." So it goes, while brick after brick of the carefully built, towering symbol is pulled down.

In his final meditations, the narrator becomes ashamed of the intricate theories he has spun during the afternoon and dubious about their validity. They may be only projections of the artist's self. He calls them "guessing," "cartooning," "inexact and vengeful lyricisms," and says, "Sometimes I entirely doubt my judgment in moral matters; and so long as I propose to be a story-teller, that is the whisper of the devil for me." While Alex absents herself on household duties, he tries to "compress the excessive details of the afternoon into an abstraction or two," even though he knows that "abstraction is a bad thing, innumerable and infinitesimal and tiresome."

Abstraction—that is, the expression of truth in statement rather than in images—is what Wescott could not or would not give up. In William H. Rueckert's opinion, "Without absurdity, it can be said that Wescott slays himself as an artist in this work." The work itself remains a jewel of art.

Wescott, through the persona of Alwyn Tower in *The Pilgrim Hawk*, appeared to reject further attempts at the art of fiction. Meanwhile, however, he had thought about what the ideal novel should be like: objective, written "with precise equivalents instead of idioms, a style of rapid grace for the eye rather than sonority for the ear," one out of which the self, its prejudices, and its parochial origins "will seem to have disappeared." His next book, *Apartment in Athens*, is a traditional novel, and it suffers by comparison with his more original works.

The chief problem with the novel is its didacticism, arising from its design as propaganda. Since he was ineligible for the draft, Wescott has said, he wanted to contribute to the war effort by embodying in a novel his understanding of the German mentality gained on several visits to Germany. He got the idea of setting the story in Athens in meetings with a hero of the Greek underground who was visiting in the United States.

When a Nazi officer, Captain Kalter, is billeted in the apartment of the Helianoses, a Greek family of four, they become his "slaves," constantly harassed and abused. Somehow, though, the parents, an aging couple, find their love renewed by the experience. After leave in Germany, Kalter comes back a changed man, and the Helianoses are baffled by his kindness. When he reveals that he has lost his whole family in the war, Mr. Helianos offers sympathy and blames Hitler, whereupon the Nazi flies into a rage, beats him, and has him arrested. With her husband in jail, Mrs. Helianos and her children, Alex and Leda, expect more abuse, but Kalter, although obviously declining in health, continues to be kind. When he commits suicide, he leaves a note to a friend in the military suggesting that his death may be charged against this Greek family and used to get information from them about the underground. His friend declines to pursue the suggestion. Helianos is executed anyway. His wife, who has refused to become involved in the Resistance, now joins it and resolves to dedicate her children also to the eventual freedom of Greece.

Told in plain style, from the omniscient point of view, thus without the voice and play of intellect of a participating narrator, *Apartment in Athens* is not an artistic success. Although Edmund Wilson praised this novel, and it was a Book-of-the-Month-Club selection, it lacks the rich imagery and symbolism of Wescott's previous novels, and it is also marred by long stretches of exposition and argument. One chapter amounts to a lecture by Kalter on the Nazi view of German superiority in all things; another is mostly given over to a letter from prison expressing the views of Helianos on the threat of Germany and the prospects of Greece.

Wescott found his materials in his own life, primarily among the people of the farms and small towns of Wisconsin, with their hard work, cultural poverty, and puritanical outlook, but he wrote of them with nostalgia and compassion rather than with the satiric venom of many Midwestern writers of the period. He dwelt on the themes of self, love, family, and home, showing how they interacted with one another and the environment to determine the fate of his characters. His major theme was the self-discovery of the artist, a participant-narrator in his two best novels who is also an expatriate. Because of the established distance in time and place, the narrator is able to reflect not only on the events he is recounting but also on himself as an artist. The memories are laden with rich imagery, often linked in a matrix of symbols in the narrator's mind. When Wescott abandoned his distinctively subjective, symbolic style, he seemed to have lost his impulse as a storyteller, although he continued to be active as a man of letters.

Major publications other than long fiction
SHORT FICTION: . . . *Like a Lover*, 1926; *Good-bye, Wisconsin*, 1928; *The Babe's Bed*, 1930.
POETRY: *The Bitterns: A Book of Twelve Poems*, 1920; *Natives of Rock: XX Poems, 1921-1922*, 1925.
NONFICTION: *Elizabeth Madox Roberts: A Personal Note*, 1930; *Fear and Trembling*, 1932; *A Calendar of Saints for Unbelievers*, 1932; *Images of Truth: Remembrances and Criticism*, 1962.
MISCELLANEOUS: *The Maugham Reader*, 1950 (edited); *Short Novels of Colette*, 1951 (edited); *Twelve Fables of Aesop, Newly Narrated*, 1954.

Bibliography
Johnson, Ira. *Glenway Wescott: The Paradox of Voice*, 1971.
Kahn, Sy Myron. *Glenway Wescott: A Critical and Biographical Study*, 1957.
Rueckert, William H. *Glenway Wescott*, 1965.
Schorer, E. E. "The Maturing of Glenway Wescott," in *College English*. XVIII (1957), pp. 320-326.

Eileen Tarcay

NATHANAEL WEST

Born: New York, New York; October 17, 1903
Died: El Centro, California; December 22, 1940

Principal long fiction

The Dream Life of Balso Snell, 1931; *Miss Lonelyhearts*, 1933; *A Cool Million: Or, The Dismantling of Lemuel Pitkin*, 1934; *The Day of the Locust*, 1939.

Other literary forms

Nathanael West often used the short-story form for preliminary sketches of characters and themes that later appeared in his novels. Between 1930 and 1933 especially, he wrote stories with a broader focus and in a more sophisticated style than his first work, *The Dream Life of Balso Snell*. The stories include "The Adventurer," "Mr. Potts of Pottstown," "Tibetan Night," and "The Sun, the Lady, and the Gas Station," all unpublished. After the publication of *Miss Lonelyhearts* in 1933, West also worked as a scriptwriter in Hollywood for several years.

Achievements

Since West's death in a automobile accident in 1940, his work has steadily gained critical attention. His characters' hysterical pitch of loneliness, their frustration, and their inability to find a source of relief have gradually interested a wide audience, especially since World War II. Stripped of their professional masks, the people in West's novels reveal a talent for cruelty. They tease, exploit, or murder to ensure their own survival in a world reminiscent of T. S. Eliot's *The Waste Land* (1922), but their world is without Eliot's hint of redemption or spirituality. In *Miss Lonelyhearts*, the world is dead; in *The Day of the Locust*, it is corrupt and jaded, a modern Sodom which West symbolically destroys. This last novel was made into a film in the 1970's; although it never became a box-office hit, West would have approved of its powerful treatment of dreamers and misfits.

Biography

Nathanael West was born Nathan Weinstein in New York City on October 17, 1903. His father's and mother's families had known one another before they immigrated to the United States from Russia. His father's side used construction skills learned in the old world to become successful contractors in the new country, taking advantage of the building boom of the turn of the century. His mother's side was well educated, and Anna Wallenstein Weinstein wanted her son Nathan and her two daughters to have all the perquisites of an upwardly mobile, middle-class life. Soon after settling in New York

City, the Weinsteins learned to enjoy their comforts and to value them highly. They also assumed that their son would receive the finest possible education, pursue a professional career, or at least join the family business. West was an avid reader but a much less ambitious student. He attended a variety of grammer schools before his parents placed him in DeWitt Clinton High School. West, however, preferred exploring Central Park during the day and the theater district in the evenings. He was particularly attracted to the vaudeville shows, his first exposure to techniques such as slapstick and stereotypes which he later used in his fiction.

West was not very disciplined, but his clever and adventurous nature helped to get him into Tufts University without a high school diploma. After one unsuccessful year there, he attended Brown University. West's biographer attributes Brown's acceptance of West to a complicated mismatching of transcripts with another student whose name was also Weinstein, though whether this was planned or accidental is not absolutely certain. Whatever the case, West was graduated from Brown in 1924 with a degree in philosophy, which he earned in only two and a half years.

Neither West nor his parents had much nostalgia for their Jewish Lithuanian roots; instead, they concentrated on rapid assimilation. In 1926, he legally changed his name to Nathanael West. Even so, the subject of roots still appears in most of his work. The degree of corruption in Lemuel Pitkin's hometown in *A Cool Million* is nothing compared to what he finds elsewhere in the country. The protagonist in *Miss Lonelyhearts* suffers from acute isolation despite his efforts to communicate, and this seems to stem from his earliest memories of childhood; he is estranged from his Baptist upbringing and has only a single comforting memory of his youth. Tod Hackett in *The Day of the Locust* leaves the East Coast, where he was an undergraduate at the Yale School of Fine Arts, for Hollywood. He observes other new arrivals and decides that they have come to California to die in one way or another. Although he does not include himself in this category, it is clear that he too succumbs to the superficial glitter and wastefulness.

West's parents encouraged him to pursue a dependable career, but their son was not interested, and he convinced them to send him to Paris in 1926. He enjoyed the artistic and literary circles there, but signs of the coming Depression were being felt in the construction industry and West had to return to New York after three months. Relatives managed to find him a job as a night manager of a midtown hotel, providing West with an income, a place to write, and a steady flow of guests to watch. West found these people fascinating, and so it is not surprising that seedy hotels and their transient occupants find their way into *The Day of the Locust*. Working as a night manager also gave West time to revise *The Dream Life of Balso Snell*, which he had begun while in college. William Carlos Williams liked the manuscript and recommended that Moss and Kamin publish it; five hundred copies were printed in 1931.

S. J. Perelman, also a student at Brown, married West's sister Laura. Through Perelman, who worked at *The New Yorker*, West met other writers and artists. It was also through his brother-in-law that West conceived of the controlling idea for *Miss Lonelyhearts*. Perelman knew a writer named Susan Chester who gave advice to readers of *The Brooklyn Eagle*. The three of them met one evening in 1939, and she read samples of the letters. West was moved by them and eventually used an advice-to-the-lovelorn column and a tormented newspaper columnist for what is probably his most famous novel. *Miss Lonelyhearts* was published by Liveright in 1933.

West soon went to Southern California to work on film scripts. His experience with the less glamorous aspects of Hollywood and the film industry, with the masses of aspiring actors and actresses, with people who had little talent to begin with, but compensated for that with their dreams, helped provide the themes, landscapes, and characters of West's final novel, *The Day of the Locust*. In 1940, West married Eileen McKenney, the sister of Ruth McKenney, who worked with Perelman at *The New Yorker*. West's careless driving was known to all his friends, and a few months after his marriage, he and his wife were killed in an automobile crash.

Analysis

Although all of Nathanael West's fiction is concerned with certain recurring themes, it gradually matures in tone, style, and subject. *The Dream Life of Balso Snell*, his first novel, has a clever but sarcastic and ugly adolescent tone. *The Day of the Locust*, his last novel, is also satirical and sarcastic, but its greater maturity and empathetic tone make it both disturbing and profoundly moving.

West's Miss Lonelyhearts dreams that he is a magician who does tricks with doorknobs: he is able to make them speak, bleed, and flower. In a sense, this conceit explains all of West's work. His protagonists travel across dead landscapes which they try to revivify. In *The Dream Life of Balso Snell*, the landscape is mechanical, wooden, purely farcical; in *A Cool Million*, West shows one American town after another, all equally corrupt. *Miss Lonely-hearts* is set in the dirt and concrete of New York City, and *The Day of the Locust* is set in the sordid but irresistible Southern California landscape. West's typical protagonist is a quester, intent on bringing life wherever he travels; Miss Lonelyhearts especially is obsessed with the challenges of a savior. The task of making a dead world bloom, however, seems hopeless. Life may surface in a moment of communication or lovemaking, but something is likely to go awry, as the moment reverses itself into an unnatural distortion. For example, as Miss Lonelyhearts tries to comfort an old man he meets in Central Park, he suddenly has the urge to crush and destroy him. Shrike, his employer at the newspaper office, compares making love to his wife with sleeping with a knife in his groin. This dichotomy is at the heart of West's vision. Characters driven by benevolent ambitions are thwarted—by themselves, by those in need of their help, by cosmic and divine indifference—until they become grotesque parodies of their original selves. Innocence and success can be recalled only through dreams. At best, the world is passively dead; at worst, it is aggressively violent.

The quester of *The Dream Life of Balso Snell* does not take himself seriously, and the novel itself seems to be an extended literary joke. Balso Snell describes a dream in which he encounters the famous wooden horse of the Greeks in ancient Troy. A brash and distinctly modern tour guide leads him through the interiors of the horse, which quickly become the subject of numerous adolescent witticisms. The inside of the horse expands to a landscape that Balso explores for the rest of his dream. West's purpose is humor and parody, which he accomplishes mercilessly although unpleasantly, beginning even with the the title of this first book. Following his "path," Balso meets a Catholic mystic, and West has the opportunity to mock the literary lives of saints. Then Balso meets a schoolboy who has just hidden his journal in the trunk of a nearby tree. Balso reads its entries, which serve as a parody of the nineteenth century Russian novel. Balso then meets the boy's teacher, Miss McGeeny, who has been busily writing a biography of a biographer's biographer; West parodies another literary genre.

The Dream Life of Balso Snell is not a significant work of fiction, but it is useful for readers to appreciate how quickly West's style and perspective deepened. His later novels have the same piercing quality, and West never lost his tendency to satirize, but the later novels are finely and precisely directed. West's later fiction also has the same motifs—quester, mechanical or obsessive journeys, dreams, and suffering humanity—but West examines them much more seriously in the later novels.

West is in superb control of his material in *Miss Lonelyhearts*, published only two years after *The Dream Life of Balso Snell*. The vituperative tone of the earlier work is balanced by greater development of plot and diversity of character. Following his preference for fast action and exaggeration, West uses comic-strip stereotypes: the meek husband and the bullying wife, Mr. and Mrs. Doyle; the bullish employer, Shrike, and his castrating wife Mary; and Miss Lonelyhearts' innocent but dumb girl friend Betty. Miss Lonelyhearts himself is only somewhat more developed, primarily because he is in almost every episode and because the third-person voice sardonically presents his private thoughts.

As in *The Dream Life of Balso Snell*, a central quester travels a barren landscape. Between the newspaper office and the local speakeasy is Central Park. As Miss Lonelyhearts walks across it, he realizes that there should be signs of spring but, in fact, there are none to be seen. Then he recalls that last year, new life seemed wrenched from the soil only in July. Miss Lonelyhearts' job as a newspaper columnist thrusts him into the position of a quester, and he makes a highly unlikely candidate. Simultaneously attracted to and repelled by his mission to assuage the grief of his readers, he makes attempts to get close to some of them, such as Mr. and Mrs. Doyle, but he then suddenly feels a compulsion to keep separate from them. This dichotomy keeps him in motion, reeling him like a puppet from one person's apartment to another, building a pressure that is released only when Miss Lonelyhearts has a final breakdown.

In each new location, the newspaperman tries to make a meaningful connection with another human being. Strict chronology becomes vague as the protagonist's state of mind becomes increasingly disturbed. He reaches toward Betty when they are sitting on the couch in her apartment but suddenly has no interest in her. He does remain sexually interested in Mary Shrike, but she refuses his advances as long as they stay in her apartment, and in the restaurant she teases him sadistically. He telephones Mrs. Doyle, a letter-writer, saying he will advise her in person. He exploits her unhappiness to satisfy his own need but, not surprisingly, is disappointed in the results. Rather than help others, the quester of this novel uses them as targets for venting his own anger. As he is increasingly frustrated in his task of bringing beauty and gentleness into the world, Miss Lonelyhearts takes to the isolation of his own room.

Another kind of quest occurs here, one that parodies the earlier quest. Rather than embark on further quests from one location to another in New York City, Miss Lonelyhearts hallucinates a journey; his bed serves as his mode of transportation. It appears to him a perfect world and a perfect journey, sanctioned by God, who finally communicates to him that he has chosen the right conclusion to his quest. Miss Lonelyhearts feels that he has become a rock, perfect in its design not because God has helped to create it, but because it is impenetrable to all but its own existence. It is ironic that the driven quester actually drives himself into a blissful delusion of isolation.

Reality intrudes. Mr. Doyle, incensed at being cuckolded, rushes up the stairs to the apartment. Miss Lonelyhearts rushes down the stairs, hoping to meet him and welcome what he assumes is Doyle's conversion. Instead, there is a scuffle and Doyle's gun fires. Only in dreams do doorknobs blossom and human beings turn into gentle and compassionate creatures—at least in West's novels. Miss Lonelyhearts dies, a victim of his own miscalculation.

The protagonist of *A Cool Million: Or, The Dismantling of Lemuel Pitkin*, is another miscalculating quester. Pitkin is an idealistic young man who leaves his hometown to seek his fortune. The fact that the immediate cause of his departure from Ottsville, Vermont, is the dishonest foreclosing of his mother's mortgage does not dampen his enthusiastic belief that his nation is the land of limitless possibilities. He has faith in himself and in those who insist they are using him for his own good.

Mr. Shagpole Whipple, ex-president of the United States and now director of the Rat River National Bank in Ottsville, becomes Lemuel's earliest supporter. He advises his young friend that America "is the land of opportunity," a land that "takes care of the honest and the industrious." Lemuel is inspired and sets out in what becomes a parody of the Horatio Alger myth. On the train to New York City, he enjoys a conversation with a Mr. Mape, who was left "a cool million" by his father. Lemuel is impressed, especially since, he explains, he must make his fortune starting with only the thirty dollars in his pocket. By the end of the trip, he has been divested of that thirty dollars. Lemuel is the fall guy for another scheme, so that he, and not the thief, is apprehended by the police, brought to trial, and declared guilty. Being sent to prison is only the first of a long series of misfortunes. Lemuel is always someone's dupe or prey, but he bounces back to try again, although he repeatedly gets nothing out of his adventures. In fact, the more he travels, the less he has. Lemuel loses his teeth, his scalp, his eye, part of a hand, one leg; each time there is someone close by who can benefit from his new loss. Lemuel is used by entrepreneurs and thieves of all varieties.

A Cool Million is fast-paced and episodic. Its characters are pure stereotypes—the ingenuous dupe, the patriot, the innocent young girl, the deceitful villain. Everyone and everything is satirized: Midwesterners, Jews, Southerners, capitalists, and socialists. *A Cool Million* shows how West was beginning to use his material for clearly defined purposes and to control his sharp-edged humor and black comedy in order to make a point. This novel, however, remains a minor work in comparison to *Miss Lonelyhearts* and *The Day of the Locust*. In these works, pathos emerges from West's stereotypes and seems all the more powerful because of its sources. *A Cool Million* is clever and biting but not poignant or profound.

West is at his best in *The Day of the Locust*. Tod Hackett, the central quester, comes to Hollywood from the East to learn set and costume designing. The people he gets to know are desperately in need of beauty, romance, and renewal, but, as in *Miss Lonelyhearts*, the harder they struggle to achieve these goals, the farther away they are.

The story is about dreamers who have traveled to what they believe is the dream capital of America, which West portrays as the wasteland of America. In addition to Tod, there is Faye Greener, beautiful but exploitative, making up in vanity what she lacks in intelligence. Homer Simpson is a thickheaded but sincere middle-aged bachelor from the Midwest. He has run from his one attempt to break through his dull-witted loneliness because the memory of failure is too painful. Characters such as Faye and Homer are particularly successful; although they are stereotypes, they still have something unpredictable about them. This quality usually manifests itself involuntarily by a spasm or quirk. For example, Faye is obviously a second-rate actress, but Tod sees through her tawdry facade to a deep archetypal beauty. Faye is unaware of any such quality; even if she knew, she would not appreciate it, because it has almost nothing in common with the self she has created. Homer Simpson has difficulty controlling parts of his body. He does not fall asleep easily because waking up is so arduous. His hands seem disassociated from his psyche; he has to put them under cold running water to rouse them, after which his fingers seem to follow their own rhythms. Like Faye, he has a structural purity without means to express it. Like Miss Lonelyhearts, his emotions swell in intensity, causing pressure that eventually must find release.

Faye becomes Tod's obsession. If he is a quester, she is his grail, and a most difficult challenge. Tod can neither support her not further her acting career. Instead, he becomes a voyeur, watching her tease Earle Shoop, the cowboy from Arizona, and Miguel, the Mexican. He settles for simply painting Faye in a mural he calls "The Burning of Los Angeles." Tod observes that people come to California to die, despite their ambitions, and the mural reflects their disappointments. In the mural, a mob chases Faye, who seems oblivious to imminent danger and maintains a calm, detached expression. Those who realize they have failed need to express their anger, and those who think they have succeeded exist in a state of happy but dangerous ignorance. As in all of West's fiction, the challenge is as impossible as turning doorknobs into flowers. As the dreamers recognize the gap between their desires and accomplishments, thwarted ambition leads to frustration, and frustration to violence. The power of *The Day of the Locust* derives from the last few chapters, which describe the mindless and destructive product of such frustrated dreams.

It is the evening of a motion-picture premiere; violet lights run across the sky, and crowds of fans are kept under control by police barricades. The premiere provides the opportunity for fans to see face-to-face the "stars," the ones who have made it. The tension is too great, however, and the control too tenuous. The crowd begins to charge toward the theater, and Tod is caught in the pressure. *The Day of the Locust* is a tight, "pressured" novel, but all gives way at the end. As the crowd surges, it builds up strength from the people whose lives are filled with boredom and mistakes. There is mass pandemonium. Homer, moving like a robot, mechanically and swiftly murders a child who has been teasing him. Tod, submerged in the crowd, is hurt, but steadies himself at the base of a rail. In agony, he begins to think about his mural, "The Burning of Los Angeles," until reality and his thoughts merge. He thinks of the burning city, of mobs of people running into the foreground with baseball bats, and he and his friends fleeing from the mob. He actually believes he is painting the flames when policemen grab him from the rail and lift him into a police car. When the siren begins, Tod is not sure whether he or the siren has been making the noise. In effect, he succumbs to the chaos around him.

The Day of the Locust is a bleak novel, reflecting West's belief that recognizing limitations is difficult for humanity, which prefers to think that all things are possible. West shows limitations to be everywhere: within the masses; within the questers trying to save them; within the arid landscape itself. As the limitations prove insurmountable, natural ambitions and desires for harmony are inverted. Love becomes pantomime and compassion a veil for selfish and sadistic purposes. West's characters and settings desperately need to be renewed, but the job of salvation is difficult, one that West's protagonists fail to achieve.

Bibliography
Comerchero, Victor. *Nathanael West: The Ironic Prophet*, 1964.
Hyman, Stanley Edgar. *Nathanael West*, 1962.
Light, James L. *Nathanael West: An Interpretive Study*, 1961.
Malin, Irving. *Nathanael West's Novels*, 1972.
Martin, Jay, ed. *Nathanael West: The Art of His life*, 1970.
_____ . *Nathanael West: A Collection of Critical Essays*, 1971.
Reid, Randall. *The Fiction of Nathanael West: No Redeemer, No Promised Land*, 1967.

Miriam Fuchs

EDITH WHARTON

Born: New York, New York; January 24, 1862
Died: St. Brice sous Forêt, France; August 11, 1937

Principal long fiction

The Touchstone, 1900; *The Valley of Decision*, 1902; *Sanctuary*, 1903; *The House of Mirth*, 1905; *Madame de Treymes*, 1907; *The Fruit of the Tree*, 1907; *Ethan Frome*, 1911; *The Reef*, 1912; *The Custom of the Country*, 1913; *Summer*, 1917; *The Marne*, 1918; *The Age of Innocence*, 1920; *The Glimpses of the Moon*, 1922; *A Son at the Front*, 1923; *The Mother's Recompense*, 1925; *Twilight Sleep*, 1927; *The Children*, 1928; *Hudson River Bracketed*, 1929; *The Gods Arrive*, 1932; *The Buccaneers*, 1938.

Other literary forms

In addition to her novels, of which several had appeared serially in *Scribners*, *The Delineator*, and *The Pictorial Review*, Edith Wharton published eleven collections of short stories and three volumes of poetry as well as a variety of nonfiction works. She wrote an early and influential book on interior decorating, *The Decoration of Houses* (1897, in collaboration with architect Ogden Codman, Jr.), a short book on the art of narrative, *The Writing of Fiction* (1925) published originally in *Scribner's Magazine*, and a delightful if highly selective autobiography, *A Backward Glance* (1934), which includes among other things an amusing account of Henry James's circumlocutory manner of speech. Wharton, an indefatigable traveler, recorded accounts of her travels in *Italian Villas and Their Gardens* (1904), *Italian Backgrounds* (1905), *A Motor Flight Through France* (1908), and *In Morocco* (1920). During World War I, she wrote numerous pamphlets and letters to inform Americans about French and Belgian suffering and to enlist sympathy and support. Articles she wrote to explain the French people to American soldiers were later collected in the volume *French Ways and Their Meanings* (1919), and accounts of her five tours of the front lines were published under the title *Fighting France from Dunkerque to Belfort* (1915). Wharton also published a great many short stories, articles, and reviews that have never been collected. A number of her stories and novels have been adapted for the stage, motion pictures, and television, and have also been translated into French, Italian, Spanish, German, Danish, Finnish, and Japanese.

Achievements

Unlike Henry James, whose readership was small and intensely discriminating, Wharton managed to attract a large audience of general readers and at the same time command the interest of critics and fellow writers as well. Among her admirers were Sinclair Lewis and F. Scott Fitzgerald; Bernard

Berenson, the art critic; and Percy Lubbock. Wharton's popularity remained high almost to the end of her career in the 1930's, but critical enthusiasm began to diminish after 1920, when the quality of her fiction declined. Even in the early years, 1905 to 1920, when Wharton's best fiction was being published, there were reservations expressed or implied by those who thought her a follower of and to some extent a lesser James, a charge easier to disprove than to eradicate. The truth is, that, though Warton learned from James— and a few of her novels, particularly *Madame de Treymes* reflect Jamesian themes as well as techniques—Wharton had her own manner as well as her own subject, and as she grew older, she continued to discover differences between her fiction and James's. It should also be pointed out (whether in praise or blame will depend on the critic) that James was a more dedicated artist than Wharton; his fiction had a finish and a coherence to be found in only a half-dozen of her novels; moreover, Wharton sometimes skated on the thin ice of superficiality, and in one novel, *The Glimpses of the Moon*, plunged through. Toward the end of her career, she also grew increasingly out of touch with life in the postwar world, much of which offended her. Her long residence in France, moreover, not only cut her off from the life of her fellow countrymen, but also—since she spoke French or Italian almost exclusively— loosened her grasp of English, so much so that a critic such as the young Edmund Wilson could complain that there were awkward phrases even in her masterpiece *The Age of Innocence*.

Wharton's major talent was for social observation. Unlike James, whose interest was ultimately metaphysical and whose novels were often invented from the slightest hints and employed few details, she filled her novels with precise accounts of the decoration of houses, of dress and of dinner parties, describing them often down to the cut of a waistcoat and the contents of the soup tureen. This is not to say that such details were signs of superficiality, but rather that Wharton's fiction depended heavily on the notation of manners and were the result of direct observation. Wharton tended to write—again, unlike James—out of her own direct experience. Even novels such as *Ethan Frome* and *Summer*—both set in provincial New England, and so different from the world she inhabited in New York and Paris—were created with remarkable attention to surface details, of which the famous cut glass, red pickle dish of Zeena's in *Ethan Frome* is a familiar example.

Wharton's fiction, it now appears, was (again, unlike James's) significantly autobiographical. Even the novels of provincial life, so different on the surface, treated issues that came out of the tensions of her own restricted upbringing and her unhappy marriage. Marriage was one of Wharton's principal subjects and provided her with a way of exploring and dramatizing her two main themes: the entrapment of an individual, as R. W. B. Lewis puts it in his *Edith Wharton: A Biography* (1975), and the attempt by an outsider, often a vulgar lower-class individual, to break into an old, aristocratic society. There is a sense in which these two themes are contradictory; the first one implies a point of view that identifies with the individual rather than with society; the second one judges from the point of view of society. The apparent contradiction, however, merely points up the range and boundaries of the author's sensibility. In some novels, *Ethan Frome* and *The House of Mirth*, for example, Wharton writes with sympathy of the trapped individual; in others, *The Custom of the Country*, and *The Children*, she writes from the standpoint of a traditional society. In her best novels, there is both sympathy for the trapped individual and the invocation of an outside claim—marriage vows, moral code, traditional manners—with the balance of sympathy tipped to the individual.

Wharton's major work was written between 1905, the year *The House of Mirth* was published, and 1920, when *The Age of Innocence* appeared. Interesting novels were still to come: *The Mother's Recompense*, *The Children*, and *The Buchaneers*, which has the best qualities of her earlier fiction; but the major works of the 1930's, *Hudson River Bracketed* and *The Gods Arrive*, betray a serious falling off of energy and of talent. In these novels, Wharton was attempting to judge the contemporary world by the values of the past, but was so out of sympathy with the life around her and so out of touch with its manners that her representation of it in these later books can hardly be taken seriously.

Despite this later decline, however, and despite the undeniable influence of James on some of her early work, Wharton produced a considerable body of original fiction, high in quality and superior to most of what was being published at the time. Her fiction also influenced other, younger American writers, notably Sinclair Lewis and F. Scott Fitzgerald. After a long decline in readership and a period of critical indifference, there now appears to be a renewal of interest in her writing, both by critics and scholars of the American novel and by feminist scholars interested in extraliterary issues.

Biography

Edith Wharton was born Edith Newbold Jones on January 24, 1862, in New York City. Her parents, George Frederic and Lucretia Rhinelander Jones, were descendants of early English and Dutch settlers and belonged to the pre-Civil War New York aristocracy, families whose wealth consisted largely of Manhattan real estate and who constituted in their common ancestry, landed wealth, and traditional manners a tightly knit, closed society. With the industrial expansion that occurred during and immediately after the Civil War, the old society was "invaded" by a new class of self-made rich men such as John Jacob Astor and Cornelius Vanderbilt. Whereas the old society had lived unostentatiously, observing, outwardly at least, a strict code of manners—the women presiding over a well-regulated social life and the men making perfunctory gestures at pursuing a profession—the new rich spent lavishly, built expensive, vulgar houses, and behaved in ways the old order found shockingly reprehensible. With its energy, its money, and its easier morality, the new order inevitably triumphed over the old, and this displacement of New York society constituted one of the chief subjects of Wharton's fiction, particularly in *The House of Mirth* and *The Custom of the Country*.

Wharton was educated at home by governesses, and later, tutors, and it was expected that she would assume the role young women of her class were educated to play, that of wife, mother, a gracious hostess. From an early age, however, Wharton showed intellectual and literary talents which, along with an acute shyness, kept her at the edge of conventional social life and later threatened to consign her at the age of twenty-three to a life of spinsterhood—the worst fate, so it was thought, that could befall a young woman of her class. After one engagement had been called off (because the young man's mother opposed it), and a promising relationship with a young lawyer, Walter Berry (who later became a close friend), had failed to develop romantically, Wharton married a man twelve years her senior, Edward ("Teddy") Robbins Wharton, a friend of her favorite brother.

Teddy Wharton was a socially prominent Bostonian without a profession or money of his own; Henry James and other friends in England were later incredulous that Wharton could marry a man so obviously her intellectual inferior and so incompatible in his interests; nevertheless, the marriage in the beginning must have been a liberation, both from the social pressure to marry and from her mother's domination. Wharton was close to her father, but there was a coolness between her and her mother that is frequently reflected in her fiction in the portrayal of mother-daughter relationships. By marrying Teddy, she was at last free to come and go as she pleased, to establish her own residence, which she did on a grand scale at Lenox, Massachusetts, and to travel abroad as often as she liked, In time, however, the marriage to Teddy became irksome, partly from lack of deep affection for him, but also because of his increasing bouts of depression and, later, his financial and sexual irresponsibilities. After revelations of his mismanagement of her estate and his adulterous affairs, she divorced Teddy in 1913. In his research for the biography of Wharton, Lewis uncovered the fact that she herself had had a brief but intense affair in 1908 with an American journalist named Morton Fullerton, and that that relationship had a profound influence on her fiction.

Wharton had lived and traveled in Europe as a child with her parents and after her marriage had visited abroad as often as possible, alternating the seasons between her house at Lenox and an apartment in Paris, with shorter visits to England and rural France. In 1903, when she met James in England, there began an important friendship, with frequent visits and exchanges of letters and motor trips in Wharton's powerful automobile. The Whartons always traveled in luxury, and their style and Edith's energy quite overwhelmed James at the same time he delighted in them. Like James, and for somewhat the same reasons, Wharton became in time an expatriate, giving up the newer, rawer life of America for the rich, deeply rooted culture of Europe. She felt at home in the salons and drawing rooms of Paris and London, where art and literature and ideas were discussed freely, where women were treated by men as equals, and where life itself was more pleasing to the senses and to the contemplative mind. Wharton also felt that in Europe, respect for the family, for manners, for learning, and for culture, even among the poorer classes, was very much alive.

Even before the final break with Teddy, Wharton had lengthened her frequent stays abroad and, finally, in 1911, allowed the house at Lenox to be sold. When World War I broke out, she remained in Paris and devoted her time, energy, and money to the relief of French and Belgian refugees; in 1916, she was officially recognized for her services to her adopted country by being made a Chevalier of the Legion of Honor. After the war, she bought a house just north of Paris and, later, another in the south of France. She made only one more trip home, in 1923, to receive an honorary degree at Yale. The remainder of her life was spent abroad.

According to those who knew her well, Wharton was a highly intelligent, well-read, brilliant conversationalist, somewhat remote at first, though the grand manner that many complained of was apparently a way of covering up her deep shyness. She read and spoke Italian and French fluently, and her salons in both Paris and Saint Claire were gathering places for literary, artistic, and social luminaries of the time, including such well-known figures as F. Scott Fitzgerald, Bernard Berenson, Jean Cocteau, Aldous Huxley, and Kenneth Clark. Despite the hectic pace of her social life and her frequent travels, Wharton continued to write regularly, turning out novels and short stories and articles, most of which sold well and brought her a great deal of money. She suffered a slight stroke in 1935, which for a time curtailed her activities; two years later, she was fatally stricken. After a short illness, she died at her home in St. Brice sous Forêt, August 11, 1937. Her body was buried in a cemetery at Versailles, beside the grave where the ashes of her old friend Walter Berry had been buried earlier.

Analysis

On a surface level, there is a surprising variety in the kinds of characters and the aspects of life with which Edith Wharton was familiar. In *The House of Mirth*, for example, one of her best novels, she was able to create characters such as the Trenors and the Van Osburghs, who belong to opposite ends of the upper level of old New York society, as well as Nettie Struther, the poor working-class girl who befriends Lily Bart when she has sunk from the glittering world of Fifth Avenue social life to a seedy, boardinghouse existence. In *The Fruit of the Tree*, she created not only the world of the fashionable Westmores, but also the factory milieu in which the foreman John Amherst attempts to bring industrial reform. In *The Reef*, she could treat life in a French chateau, as well as in a sordid hotel in Paris, and in her two brilliant short novels, *Ethan Frome* and *Summer*, she managed to depict a life in rural Massachusetts that she could only have known by observation, rather than by direct experience.

It must be admitted, however, that Wharton is at times less than convincing. Some critics consider her attempt to deal with factory life in *The Fruit of the Tree* inept, even ludicrous, though others believe it entirely adequate; and certainly the life of impoverished Nettie Struther is delineated with nothing like the thoroughness of Lily Bart's, whose upper-class milieu Wharton knew at firsthand. Still, the extent of Wharton's social range and her ability to create realistic characters from a background quite different from her own is impressive, unrivaled in American fiction of the time.

As for variety of character types, one might cite in particular those to be found in *The House of Mirth*, in the range of male characters—from the fastidious Selden to the rapacious Gus Trenor and the socially ambiguous and vulgar Simon Rosedale, all of them suitors for Lily's attention. Both *Ethan Frome* and *Summer* present a more limited range, but both contain sharply realized and distinctly differentiated characters, including the powerful Ethan, the pretty young Mattie, and Zeena, the neurasthenic wife of Ethan. In *Summer*, Charity Royall, the mountain girl, is vividly created, as is her feckless young lover and her elderly guardian and attempted seducer, Lawyer Royall.

Despite this surface breadth, this impressive range of social observation, Wharton's novels have a rather narrow thematic focus. It has been said that Edith Wharton's chief theme is entrapment. Blake Nevius, in *Edith Wharton: A Study of Her Fiction* (1953), points out how this theme is implicit in the principal relationships among characters in many of the novels, in which a superior nature is caught in a wasteful and baffling submission to an inferior nature. It was a situation that Wharton herself must have experienced, not only with a mother who was obsessed with fashion and propriety, but also in a society narrowly given up to the pursuit of pleasure. It was a situation in which she later found herself in her marriage to Teddy, who disliked and resented her interest in social and intellectual life. In novel after novel, one sees this same situation treated—superior individuals trapped in relationships with their inferiors and prevented from extricating themselves by a finer sensibility.

In *The House of Mirth*, Lily Bart is impoverished by the bankruptcy and later the death of her father and is obliged to recoup her fortune in the only way open to her, by attempting to marry a rich man. Lily's situation was not Wharton's, but the social pressures on her must have been similar: to make a suitable marriage, with social position certainly, and, if possible, money as well. In the novel, Lily is given a choice that Wharton apparently did not have: an offer of marriage from an emancipated young lawyer of her own class (though Walter Berry, a lawyer, was thought at one time to have been Wharton's suitor). Wharton chose a passionless marriage with Teddy; Lily was not allowed that solution. Selden deserts her at the crucial moment and she dies of an overdose of sleeping medicine.

In her autobiography *A Backward Glance*, Wharton stated that her subject in *The House of Mirth* was to be the tragic power of New York society in "debasing people and ideas," and Lily Bart was created in order to give that power dramatic scope. Lily's entrapment by society and her eventual destruction are not the final story. Lily overcomes the limitations of her upbringing and aspirations and acts on principle. She has in her possession a packet of letters which could be used to regain her social position, but the letters would involve the reputation of Selden. She also has a ten-thousand-dollar inheritance which could be used to establish herself in a profitable business, but she burns the letters and uses the money to repay a debt of honor. Lily dies, but in choosing death rather than dishonor, she has escaped entrapment.

In *The Age of Innocence*, published fifteen years after *The House of Mirth*, the underlying conflict is the same, though the tone of the novel and the nature of the entrapment are somewhat different. Here, the trapped individual is a man, Newland Archer, a young lawyer who is engaged to marry May Welland, a pretty and shallow young woman of respectable old New York society of the 1870's and 1890's. This is the world of Wharton's young womanhood, a society that is narrow and rigid and socially proper. Into this limited and self-contained world, she brings Ellen Olenska, a cousin of May, who belongs to this world by birth but left it years before and has since married a Polish count. Ellen has now separated from her husband, who has been notoriously unfaithful, and has returned to the bosom of her family for support and comfort. Archer is engaged by the family to help her in her quest for a divorce settlement. The inevitable happens. Archer and Ellen fall in love. Archer is attracted by Ellen's European sophistication, her freedom of thought and manners, and her refusal to take seriously the small taboos of New York society. Archer considers breaking with May and marrying Ellen. The family, sensing his defection, contrive with other members of the society to separate the lovers and reunite Archer with May, his conventional fiancée. Social pressure forces Ellen to return to Europe, and Archer is again thinking of pursuing Ellen; then May announces that she is expecting a baby. Archer is finally and permanently trapped.

As though to drive home the extent to which Archer has been defeated, Wharton takes him to Paris years later. His son is grown, his wife dead, and Ellen Olenska is now a widow living alone. Archer makes an appointment to see Ellen but gets only as far as a park bench near her apartment. At the last minute, he decides to send his son to see her, while he remains seated on the bench, telling himself that it would be more real for him to remain there than to go himself to see Ellen. The trap has done its work.

While one can see resemblances between Ellen and Wharton—the expatriation, the charm, the liberated views, perhaps even the slight French accent with which Ellen speaks—Archer is also Wharton, or that side of her that could never entirely escape the past. *The Age of Innocence* was thought by some reviewers to be a glorification of the past, which it clearly is not. Wharton does evoke with some nostalgia the old New York of her youth, but she also sets forth with delicate but cutting irony that society's limitations and its destructive narrowness. Archer has led an exemplary life, one is led to believe, but the happiness he might have had was gently but firmly denied him. Whereas a more popular novelist might have allowed Archer to be reunited with Ellen at the end of the novel, Wharton insists that that would be unreal; for her, personal happiness in the real world is the exception rather than the rule.

Two of Wharton's best novels—also two of her shortest; some critics prefer to call them novellas—both deal with protagonists trapped by passionless marriages. The earliest of these, *Ethan Frome*, is about a Massachusetts farmer married to an older, neurasthenic wife, whose pretty young cousin has come to work for her. The inevitable again happens. Ethan falls in love with Mattie and dreams about running away with her. Ethan's jealous wife, however, arranges for Mattie to be sent away, and Ethan is obliged to escort her to the train station. It is winter, and the lovers stop for a brief time together. They embrace, realize the inevitablity of separation, and decide to kill themselves by coasting down a steep hill into a great elm tree. During the ride down the steep hill, Ethan accidentally swerves the sled; a crash occurs, in which the lovers are seriously injured but survive. Mattie becomes a whining invalid, while Zeena, the neurotic wife, takes over the running of the household, and Ethan, who is severely disfigured, feels himself like a handcuffed convict, a prisoner for life.

As Lewis has pointed out, the situation in *Ethan Frome* is very much like the situation in Wharton's own life at the time. If one shifts the sexes, Frome is Wharton trapped in a loveless marriage with the neurasthenic Teddy and passionately in love with a younger man who shared her interests and feelings, Morton Fullerton. The violent ending, of course, may be seen as Wharton's passionate statement about her own desperate situation. The success of *Ethan Frome*, however, does not depend on making such biographical connections; the book is a brilliantly realized work of realistic fiction that owes its power not to some abstractly conceived pessimistic philosophy of life, but to Wharton's successful transposition of her own emotional life into the language of fiction.

Summer was published six years after *Ethan Frome* and was called by Wharton and her friends the "hot Ethan." As in *Ethan Frome*, there is a triangle: Lawyer Royall, elderly guardian of Charity, a pretty young mountain girl, and a visiting architecture student, Lucius Harney. During the idyllic summer months, an intense and passionate affair takes place between Charity and Harney. Harney returns to Boston, and Charity is left to face her guardian, who is also in love with her, and the prospect of an illegal abortion. The novel concludes with a reconciliation between Charity and her guardian and a secure if passionless marriage with him. While it would be a mistake to overemphasize biographical parallels, they are unmistakable. The affair of Charity and Harney suggests Wharton's earlier affair with Fullerton, while the intrusive presence of the fatherly Lawyer Royall suggests Teddy's irksome claims on Wharton's loyalties. An interesting alteration of chronology is in making the marriage with the older man follow the affair rather than precede it, as it had in Wharton's own life. *Summer* was written four years after the Whartons were divorced, and by then, she may have had time to view her marriage to Teddy more dispassionately, as the practical solution it must originally have been. Like Lily's death, the surrender to marriage is a defeat as well as a moral triumph.

Summer is one of Wharton's finest novels, written according to her own testimony, in a state of "creative joy" and reflecting in its characters, scenes, and symbolic structures, the deep well of the unconscious that seems to nourish the most powerful works of American fiction.

The Reef, published the year before the Whartons' divorce, and commonly acknowledged to be Wharton's most Jamesian novel, again deals with conflicts between the individual and society and the problems of marriage. In this novel, however, the society is remote; the inheritor of the society's standards, Anna Leath, an American widow of a French nobleman, is reunited with an old friend, George Darrow, also an American, a lawyer, living in Europe. Anna and Darrow become engaged and are about to be married when Anna discovers that Darrow has had an affair with Sophy Viner, her daughter's governess, a girl of a lower class, and that Sophy, who is also her stepson's fiancée, is still in love with Darrow. For Darrow, the situation is a matter of diplomatic maneuvering, of steering his way between the two women and the stepson, but for Anna, it presents a moral dilemma involving, on the one hand, an inherited code of conduct, which tells her that Darrow must be abandoned, and a personal one, which tells her not to give him up. The moral complexities of the novel are a good deal more complicated than summary can indicate—indeed, are so ambiguous that one is hard pressed to decide where the author stands. It is possible, however, to see in this novel situations parallel to Wharton's earlier involvement with Fullerton, and a possible moral dilemma over her own infidelity. In a sense, Wharton is Sophy Viner, but Sophy (and Wharton's affair with Fullerton) seen in the light of a later moral judgment; Wharton is also Anna, attempting to accept the break with conventional morality that led to Darrow's affair with Sophy. The trap in which Anna finds herself is doubly baited, and no matter which way she turns, she must fall, either morally or emotionally. The fact that Anna chooses Darrow after all suggests the same kind of compromise other Wharton protagonists have made, Justine of *The Fruit of the Tree* and Charity Royall of *Summer* especially, both of whom were betrayed by the weakness of the men they loved but settled for what was finally available.

The Custom of the Country is a different sort of work, influenced by the French realist Honoré de Balzac rather than by Henry James; it attempts to deal, as did Balzac, with the destruction of an aristocracy by the invasion of uncivilized materialists. The protagonist of the novel, Undine Spragg, is a handsome young woman from Apex, a city in the American Middle West. Undine's father made a great deal of money in Apex and now has come East to try his hand in New York City. The Spraggs move into an expensive, vulgar hotel, and the parents would be content to exist on the fringes of New York society, but Undine, who is as ambitious as she is vulgar, manages to meet and then marry Ralph Marvel, an ineffectual member of old New York society. When life with Marvel grows boring, Undine becomes the mistress of a richer and more aggressive New York aristocrat, Peter Van Degen; when Van Degen drops her, she manages to snare the son of an old aristocratic French family, the Marquis de Chelles. Undine marries de Chelles, but she has learned nothing, being without taste, manners, or ideas; her sole interest is in amusing and gratifying herself. As soon as she gets what she thinks she wants, she becomes dissatisfied with it and wants something she decides is better. She grows tired of having to fit herself into the demands of the feudal aristocracy into which she has married; when she attempts to sell family heirlooms, whose value she does not understand, her husband divorces her. Her third husband is a perfect match, a hard-driving vulgar materialist from Apex, Elmer Moffat, whose chief interest is in buying up European art. Moffat also aspires to an ambassadorial post, but is barred because he is married to Undine, a divorced woman.

The Custom of the Country is regarded by some critics as among Wharton's best fiction, but, as Blake Nevius has observed, during the course of the novel, Undine ceases to be a credible character and becomes an "inhuman abstraction." Clearly, she came to represent everything that Wharton detested in the America of 1912, and, at a deeper and vaguer level, perhaps also expressed Wharton's fear and resentment at the displacement of her own class by more energetic and less cultivated outsiders. The fact that such fears were real enough and the implicit social criticisms valid, does nothing to alter the fact that, measured against books such as *The House of Mirth*, *Ethan Frome*, *Summer*, and *The Reef*, *The Custom of the Country* is crude and unconvincing. James had been right years earlier in advising Wharton to write about that part of the world she knew best, for in attempting to deal with the Middle West in *The Custom of the Country*, and later, in *Hudson River Bracketed* and *The Gods Arrive*, with bohemian circles about which she knew very little, she condemned herself to superficiality and caricature. It is difficult to take seriously Undine Spragg of *The Custom of the Country* or Advance Weston, the protagonist of *Hudson River Bracketed* and *The Gods Arrive*, who is said to be from Pruneville, Nebraska, and later Hallelujah, Missouri, and Euphoria, Illinois. Caricature is an expression of outrage, not understanding.

Fortunately, the last of Wharton's novels, *The Buchaneers*, published the year after her death, was a return to the territory of her earlier fiction, old New York of the 1870's. The novel was unfinished at her death and lacks the coherence of her best early work, but she could still write with the sharpness and scenic fullness that had characterized *The House of Mirth* and *The Age of Innocence.*

Wharton was a novelist of manners, then, not a chronicler of large social movements, and her real subject was the entrapment of superior individuals who keenly feel the pull of moral responsibility. Her talents for social obser- vation, for noting subtleties of dress and decoration, for nuance of voice and phrase, and for language—precise and yet expressive—were essential instru- ments in the creation of her novels. Wharton has been unduly charged with pessimism; her characteristic tone is ironic, the product of a sensibility able to see and feel the claims on both sides of a human dilemma. If her voice faltered in her later years and she conceded too much to the popular taste for which she increasingly wrote, she nevertheless produced some of the finest American fiction published in the first two decades of the century, and her name deserves to stand with those of James and F. Scott Fitzgerald, who outrank her only at their best.

Major publications other than long fiction

SHORT FICTION: *The Greater Inclination*, 1899; *Crucial Instances*, 1901; *The Descent of Man*, 1904; *The Hermit and the Wild Woman*, 1916; *Here and Beyond*, 1926; *Certain People*, 1930; *Human Nature*, 1933; *The World Over*, 1936; *Ghosts*, 1937.

POETRY: *Verses*, 1878; *Artemis to Acteon*, 1909; *Twelve Poems*, 1926.

NONFICTION: *The Decoration of Houses*, 1897 (with Ogden Codman, Jr.); *Italian Villas and Their Gardens*, 1904; *Italian Backgrounds*, 1905; *A Motor Flight Through France*, 1908; *Fighting France from Dunkerque to Belfort*, 1915; *French Ways and Their Meaning*, 1919; *In Morocco*, 1920; *The Writing of Fiction*, 1925; *A Backward Glance*, 1934.

Bibliography

Brenni, Vito J. *Edith Wharton: A Bibliography*, 1966.
Howe, Irving. *Edith Wharton: A Collection of Critical Essays*, 1962.
Lewis, R. W. B. *Edith Wharton: A Biography*, 1975.
Nevius, Blake. *Edith Wharton: A Study of Her Fiction*, 1953.

                                                                            W. J. Stuckey

PATRICK WHITE

Born: London, England; May 28, 1912

Principal long fiction

Happy Valley, 1939; *The Living and the Dead*, 1941; *The Aunt's Story*, 1948; *The Tree of Man*, 1955; *Voss*, 1957; *Riders in the Chariot*, 1961; *The Solid Mandala*, 1966; *The Vivisector*, 1970; *The Eye of the Storm*, 1973; *A Fringe of Leaves*, 1977; *The Twyborn Affair*, 1980.

Other literary forms

Patrick White first attempted to achieve literary success as a playwright in London in the 1930's. His work was largely rejected, partly, he implies in his autobiographical memoir, *Flaws in the Glass: A Self-Portrait* (1982), because of lack of connections in the theatrical world (although he does not deny that his talent was immature at that time). In particular, he notes that an effort to dramatize *The Aspern Papers* (1888), Henry James's famous novella based on an incident in the life of Lord Byron's mistress, might have succeeded had it found a sponsor, thanks to James's dialogue. Later, in his mature Australian years, White published six plays (four of which were published in *Four Plays*, 1965), one play, *The Ham Funeral*, has received much attention. White's short-story collections, *The Burnt Ones* (1964) and *The Cockatoos: Shorter Novels and Stories* (1974), bring together the best of his shorter fiction published originally in Australian literary journals (for the most part); White has also published in *The London Magazine*, where, among others, the fine stories "Clay" and "A Cheery Soul" appeared. White also has experimented with writing film scripts; one has been filmed and received some mildly favorable reviews. White's autobiographical memoir, already mentioned, mixes poetic impressionism with trenchant satire.

Achievements

White's stature as a novelist was already considerable, among discerning critics and discriminating readers in the English-speaking world, before it was confirmed by his reception of the Nobel Prize in 1973. The books which established White's reputation after World War II were *The Aunt's Story*, which has been widely recognized as a masterpiece, *The Tree of Man*, and the virtually unforgettable *Voss*. *Riders in the Chariot*, an impressive but controversial novel, was a harbinger of the ambivalent reaction White has received from critics both in Australia and elsewhere. At the same time, White's fiction, though accessible to the general reader, unlike the work of such modernist masters as James Joyce and William Faulkner (or contemporary "experimental" fiction), has never achieved a wide readership. It is uncompromisingly addressed to the same discerning public which respects Joyce, D. H. Lawrence, Thomas Mann, and Marcel Proust.

If rather philistine criticism from intellectual readers as well as from the general public in Australia and elsewhere began in the 1960's, after *Riders in the Chariot*, such critics were not likely to be molified by White's subsequent books in the decade, which included a volume of short stories, *The Burnt Ones*; *Four Plays*; and *The Solid Mandala*, one of White's most idiosyncratic works, a novel saturated with religious mysticism showing the influence of C. G. Jung and Fyodor Dostoevski. White's social criticism and tragic vision were more pronounced than ever in these books, and his satire on rationalism and sterile intellectualism through the character of the minor critic, Arthur Brown, in *The Solid Mandala* could be read as a calculated affront to his hostile critics. In *Flaws in the Glass*, White contends that his art is imaginative and intuitive, and that the rationalism of some of his academic critics has prevented them from comprehending it fully.

Whatever their faults, the works of the 1960's are impressive and helped to consolidate White's growing reputation as a brilliant, if sometimes eccentric, novelist. White's fame was further enlarged by *The Vivisector*, the first of four massive novels to be published in the 1970's, the first three of them being received very favorably (and regarded by many as near masterpieces). *The Vivisector* provides a powerful portrait of the artist in his travails, a kind of apologia, although White avoids autobiography in the narrow sense of the word, or presents it only through a refracted vision. The second novel of the decade, *The Eye of the Storm*, had the good fortune to appear directly after the Nobel award in 1973, and it received wide acclaim, including praise from reviewers who had until then barely been conscious of White's existence. At the same time, some critics objected that White seemed to write old-fashioned family novels; these readers seemed unaware of White's experiments with form in *The Aunt's Story*, *The Solid Mandala*, and *Riders in the Chariot*, and of his roots in literary modernism. After *The Eye of the Storm*, which combines the novel of manners with an attempt to render a tragic vision of Shakespearean magnitude, White published *A Fringe of Leaves*, a novel of a woman's survival in the Australian wilderness of the early nineteenth century, based on the legend of Eliza Fraser. This work is one of White's most impressive performances, and its stature is likely to increase with time. Finally, *The Twyborn Affair* appeared at the end of the decade; this is White's first novel to make the theme of homosexuality central to its tragic vision, and, like *The Solid Mandala*, it reveals its author at his most eccentric. As though in response to negative or lukewarm reviews, White has pronounced this novel, along with *The Aunt's Story* and *The Solid Mandala*, his most idiosyncratic works, to be his best novels. Whatever final judgments are made about *The Twyborn Affair*, the decade of the 1970's was a highly fertile period for White.

Despite White's faults, there can be little doubt that he has published an impressive body of fiction. *The Aunt's Story* is almost universally admired, and *The Tree of Man*, *Voss*, *Riders in the Chariot*, *The Vivisector*, *The Eye of the Storm*, and *A Fringe of Leaves* all have admirers who regard them as virtual classics. White's transformation of Australian history into epic and tragic vision in *The Tree of Man*, *Voss*, and *A Fringe of Leaves* is brilliant, and his vision of the fragmented world of the twentieth century is equally impressive, especially in *The Vivisector* and *The Eye of the Storm*. White's major successes ultimately assure their author a place beside the masters of prose fiction in English, including James Joyce, D. H. Lawrence, and Graham Greene.

Biography

Patrick Martindale White was born in Wellington Court, London, on May 28, 1912, of parents whose affluence allowed them the opportunity to travel and enjoy the social pretensions available to prosperous Australians able to play the role of landed gentry. White's father, Victor (Dick) White, was one of several brothers who enjoyed prosperity in the family grazier business. Although the Whites could trace their lineage to respectable yeoman stock in Somerset, it was only in Australia that they achieved such success. Ironically, their social aspirations so far as the mother country was concerned were forever tainted by their status as "colonials" and Australians, the former penal colony being one of the least prestigious of the British dominions. White's mother was a Withycomb, and it is to the maternal connection that White attributes most of his imaginative and poetic gifts. At the same time, White disliked and despised his strong-willed and socially ambitious mother, Ruth, the model of self-centered and devouring maternal figure who appears frequently in his fiction. Toward his father, White was more ambivalent: he pitied Victor White for his weakness and found him impossible because he hid his emotions behind his social role as a landed gentleman; White has written that he might have loved his father if the latter had been capable of revealing his feelings or inspiring the affection of his children.

Resenting and distrusting his parents as he did, and contemptuous of their social ambitions and their inclination to conceal their humanity behind public personae, White felt as much an outsider and rebel against the class to which he was born as is his painter hero, Hurtle Duffield, in *The Vivisector*, a working-class child adopted by a prosperous Sydney family.

White tended as a child to identify with his working-class nanny and her husband, a circumstance that helps to account for the persistent scorn and irony in his fiction directed toward the assumptions and manners of the Australian upper class, an attitude that perhaps finds its purest expression in White's treatment of Mrs. Chalmers-Robinson in *Riders in the Chariot*, but which appears in many other novels as well, notably *The Vivisector* and *The Eye of the Storm*. Another important event in White's childhood was his parents' residence at the Gothic home of the poet and dilettante, William Hayley, at Felpham: the place is chiefly noted in literary history as a temporary residence (for three years) of William Blake, whom Hayley tried to assist ineffectually, and with whom he ultimately quarreled, in a classic confrontation of mediocrity and genius. Although White as a child had no awareness of Blake's work, in later life, he tended to reject his parents' identification with Hayley's world and to identify himself with the political sympathies and the urgent religious, visionary spirit of Blake. Indeed, Blake is a major influence on *Riders in the Chariot*.

Not only was White an "outsider" in relationship to Australian affluent class, but also he found that his status in English boarding schools, and later at Cambridge, was that of an "outsider," by virtue of his Australian citizenship and accent. Hence, throughout his career, White as artist has played the role of an outsider in a double sense, a condition intensified by his frequent alternation of residences between Australia and England in childhood and youth. White's major concentration at Cambridge was modern languages, primarily German, an interest augmented by time spent on the Continent, in the Germany of the Weimar Republic in its waning days, and in the early years of Adolf Hitler's rule, during summer vacations from 1932 to 1935. One German city, Hanover, is depicted in White's fiction as the archetypal German cathedral town from which White's characters Voss and Himmelfarb both originate.

After coming down from Cambridge, White spent a bohemian period in London in the middle and late 1930's, lodging mainly in Ebury Street, where he wrote three unsatisfactory novels and attempted without success to begin a career in the theater as a playwright. During this time, White fell under the influence of various intellectual friends and apprentice artists, the most important being the Australian expatriate Roy de Maistre, who was, like White, a homosexual. (White seems to have accepted his homosexuality in his boarding school adolescence, and to have had little difficulty over it at the Cambridge and London of the 1930's.) In 1939, White's unsatisfactory first novel, *Happy Valley*, was published, and soon White voyaged to America to try his hand in New York literary circles and to begin a period of dissipation that lasted for several months. During this New York period, he completed his strong second novel, *The Living and the Dead*, a book that shows him mastering and exorcising some of the literary and cultural influences of his youth. The decision of White's working-class hero, Joe, to go to Spain to fight on the Loyalist side, is a symbol of commitment; it reflects White's own decision, reached after much guilt and self-analysis, to return to England (unlike some other English expatriates, such as W. H. Auden) and to offer himself to the campaign against Hitler.

Receiving a commission in the Royal Air Force's intelligence division, White spent the majority of his war years in North Africa, Alexandria, the

Middle East, and Greece. Although White writes of his military experience with an amused and self-deprecating irony, it is clear that his years in the war were a significant rite of passage for him. He gained decisiveness and self-reliance as well as maturity; equally important, he met Manoly Lascaris, a Greek whose mother had been British; Lascaris was to become White's lover and homosexual spouse from that time until the present. After the war, White considered living in America and Greece, before realizing that an expatriate Englishman might have difficulties finding acceptance in either country, and particularly in Greece. During this time, he also worked on the manuscript of his first mature novel, *The Aunt's Story*, part of which was written in postwar Greece and Alexandria. Eventually, White and Lascaris decided on permanent residence in Australia, and White arrived there in 1947 with the manuscript of *The Aunt's Story* as a kind of "talisman." Hence, White is an Australian by a conscious choice, however reluctant the choice may have been. At the same time, his country has not always been overwhelmed by White's decision, for although White has used the Australian heroic past extensively in his fiction, he has continued to be an outsider whose work does not always display clear relationships with Australian literary traditions.

White's long career in Australia has flourished primarily at two residences: the small "farm" called "Dogwoods," really only a house, some outbuildings, and a few acres at Castle Hill, just outside Sydney and later incorporated into it. In 1963, however, White moved to his present residence at Martin's Road in Sydney. In the Castle Hill period, White and Lascaris kept some cattle and tried to support themselves, at least partially, by some gardening. In later years, White's writing has provided some support.

After five novels and a book of short stories, White was awarded the Nobel Prize for Literature for 1973. He used the money to establish a fund for struggling Australian writers of some talent and literary ambition. His later life has been marked by increasing fame and some travel and by considerable attention from the media and from academic critics and scholars. During his Australian years, White has shown himself to be a man of strong family loyalties. Although his mother chose to leave Australia and spend the rest of her life in London at the time that White had returned to Australia, White attempted to display some filial concern toward her. In fact, an incident involving a nursing home in England to which White and his sister had their mother committed in her last months in the 1960's provided the seminal idea for *The Eye of the Storm*.

Since he has received the Nobel Prize, White's fame has increased, although not necessarily his acceptance with some critics, and he has become something of a celebrity in Australia. Although White has attempted to wear his fame lightly, there is some indication that he finds much of the attention he receives somewhat annoying, and he is as wary and skeptical of it as is the aged painter Duffield at his retrospective exhibition in *The Vivisector*.

Analysis

Patrick White's fiction is concerned with the psychological depth and the emotional density of experience, and with the perceptions of the solitary self. This obsession with the isolated self in its search for fulfillment, its quest for an experience of unity and the divine, and its attempts to resolve the contradictions of its social heritage and its sexual nature, provides the central drama in White's fiction. On the one hand, White's fiction is rich in its command of the nuances of dialogue and social intercourse; it is possible to discuss his work in terms primarily of the novel of manners and social comedy. On the other hand, White's fiction is the work of an author obsessed with tragic vision and a religious quest. After *The Aunt's Story*, White's novels contain characters who struggle and overcome obstacles to understanding and vision, and whose lives culminate in a visionary or mystical affirmation. Stan Parker in *The Tree of Man* testifies to the unity of holiness of being; Elizabeth Hunter finds the eye of God in the center of her storm; Rod Gravenor in his final letter to Eddie Twyborn asserts the reality of love and faith in God. Such affirmations, though they represent White's own beliefs, if his autobiographical statements are to be accepted, are nevertheless to be seen as dramatic statements, paradoxical assertions aimed at overcoming doubts and confusion, and ultimately as aesthetically correct as the statements of faith in the poetry of the seventeenth century metaphysical poets. Despite all the parallels with Victorian novelists who write family novels with complicated plots, White is essentially a religious visionary akin to poets such as T. S. Eliot and W. H. Auden, and one very much at odds with the dominant spirit of his age.

White's first published novel, *Happy Valley*, is regarded by most critics as a failure, and the judgment is accurate. The novel deals with the passions and defeats of a group of characters in an Australian rural setting, but White is not entirely in control of his characters and plot, nor of his own style. The characters are mostly flawed romantics, somewhat obsessed by sex and erotic entanglements, and their emotions are often operatic and even Wagnerian in scope. The novel lacks the saving grace of White's magisterial and sophisticated irony, which tends to control the style in the later books and prevent both author and characters from lapsing into the excesses of emotion. White, however, does use the Australian landscape effectively as a dramatic backdrop for human drama played out under the eye of an inscrutable cosmos—a feature in which the novel anticipates dimly some of the later impressive works, such as *Voss*. Nevertheless, the Australian grazier country is seen primarily as a setting for primitive passions and as a stifling provincial milieu from which the characters long to escape. As some critics have remarked, the influence of D. H. Lawrence, James Joyce, and other modernists has not been assimilated.

The Living and the Dead, the second published novel of White's prewar apprenticeship, shows considerable improvement. The novel, set in England, primarily London, casts a critical and retrospective look at the 1930's, but like many novels of the period by English and American writers, it displays a movement from empty intellectualism and social snobbery to political and ideological commitment on the part of some characters. The central figures in the book are Elyot and Eden Standish and their feckless and snobbish mother. Elyot and Eden provide an ironic contrast: Eloyt is a skeptical rationalist who wants to withdraw from experience, while Eden is a romantic who accepts life with its attendant suffering. Each finds a suitably ironic reward: Eden gains love with a working-class hero, only to lose him when he departs to join the Loyalist cause in the Spanish Civil War. Elyot, fearing involvement with others, is doomed to a life of loneliness until he finds himself exposed to the suffering he has tried to avoid by the death of his mother and the departure of his sister for Spain. Ironically, the experience of tragedy helps to heal Elyot's loneliness and alienation; at the end of the novel, he finds a satisfying release from the prison of himself, although there is no indication that his newfound acceptance of the human community and the human condition will continue or signals a dramatic transformation of his life.

Brian Kiernan in *Patrick White* (1980) has pointed out that there are many influences of T. S. Eliot's early poetry evident in the novel: London is Eliot's "Unreal City" of *The Waste Land* (1922), for example. It might be added that Elyot Standish is White's most Prufrokian character; he represents the same kind of paralyzed and life-evading intellectual that Eliot satirized in his early peotry, and White's portrayal indicates his own aversion to such a figure.

If Elyot is skillfully drawn, his mother, with all her vulgarities and superficialities, is equally effective and her final spasmodic affair with an English jazz musician is poignant, as is the description of her final illness. Less effectively depicted, but still successful, are Eden, Elyot's romantic sister, and Wally Collins, the itinerant jazz musician just back from America, who is presented as representative of the rootless and uncommitted modern urban man. Unfortunately, Eden Standish is portrayed through the eyes of other characters more often than from her own point of view, and hence remains a more remote character than she should have been. (The later White would probably have made her consciousness the central point of view in the novel, or at any rate one equal to Elyot, if such novels as *The Solid Mandala* provide any basis for comparison.) The weakest figure of all is Joe Barnett, the working-class hero, who is too obviously inspired by the abstraction of the virtuous proletarian which afflicted much of the fiction of the 1930's. One of the weaknesses of the conception shows in White's style: whereas White uses a good deal of American slang to characterize Wally, in a kind of tour de force of experiment with the vernacular, he is not able to do anything comparable in his treatment of Joe. Again, the later White would have made Joe's fundamental nobility more credible by making him more human and fallible.

The emphasis on commitment and release from alienation with which the novel concludes is handled with a great deal of aesthetic tact and restraint, particularly when the novel is placed alongside many other works from the period, including some by such distinguished writers as Ernest Hemingway and John Steinbeck. Nevertheless, the adoption of the Loyalist cause in Spain is portrayed as more of a humanist commitment than an acceptance of an ideological or religious imperative, although no doubt White's sympathies were leftist. While White's characters find an exit from the modern wasteland through tragic self-sacrifice, the novel does not provide any assurance that the solution found is an enduring one, either for the characters who accept it or for the author. (Since the novel was finished in America, however, there can be little doubt that the choices made by Joe and Eden in favor of the Loyalist cause embody a fictional parallel to White's own decision to return to England and volunteer for military service against Hitler.)

With his next novel, *The Aunt's Story*, White established himself as a novelist of stature with a mature tragic vision. One of the most difficult things for a novelist to do, White believes, is to make a "virtuous woman" an interesting character. White accomplished this feat with Theodora Goodman, the aunt, who to all outward appearances lives an uneventful life which, save for its tragic denouement, might be considered "without a story." The real "story" of the spinster aunt is rendered through White's depiction of her inner life: despite Theodora's apparently barren existence, her experience is rich indeed. Seldom, in fact, since Joyce and Virginia Woolf, has the ironic contrast between a supposedly sterile existence judged by surfaces and social convention, and a rich and imaginative psychological experience been more impressively presented in fiction.

Theodora's tale is told in three economically narrated sections: an Australian sequence called "Meroe"; a European interlude, "Jardin Exotique"; and a climactic American adventure, "Holstius." In these sections, Theodora's childhood, youth, and maturity are portrayed. She has a strong, rather masculine sensibility, and an imaginative nature with deep psychological insight, in an unprepossessing feminine body. Her fate is to play the role of the understanding observer in the tragedies and romances of others, until she finds her own tragic destiny in Colorado in Part 3.

In Part 1, Theodora's journey from innocence to the experience of young adulthood is chronicled. The contrast between the heroine's strong desire for individuality and the conventional femininity and conformity of her sister is strongly marked. At boarding school in adolescence, Theodora develops one of her strongest relationships, a friendship with the sensitive Violet Adams, who, like Theodora, is fascinated by art and poetry. Theodora here reveals her intense and rather hard inner nature: she would like to be a poet, but her chosen subject would be landscapes and studies of rocks. This ambition is a revelation that Theodora is perhaps more masculine in her psyche than feminine, unlike her friend or her sister, for whom the conventional happiness of marriage, motherhood, and children seems an adequate fulfillment.

In her childhood and youth, too, Theodora shows more love for her father's country estate than for the city: Meroe is the "Abyssinia" or happy valley of innocence which provides a romantic metaphor for her years of growth and maturation. Later, following World War I, when Australia, after a brief emergence from its provincial slumber, relapses into a comfortable vacuous middle-class existence, Theodora lives in Sydney and cares for her mean-spirited and snobbish mother in the latter's failing years. In this period, the mysterious murderer Jack Frost provides some excitement and titillation for a bored middle-class population, and serves as a symbol of the mysterious Jungian shadow she longs to encounter. Her major chance for the conventional felicity of marriage and children occurs when she is courted by the apparently strong and manly Huntly Clarkson. Yet in a role reversal typical of many later White novels, Huntly soon is revealed as weak and somewhat feminine in his relationship with the resolute Theodora. She in turn appears somewhat more masculine than he (if viewed in conventional gender terms), demonstrating a harder will; on one occasion, she humiliates him by proving herself a better shot with a rifle. Her skillfulness and strength strike a deathblow to their courtship.

Released from an unrewarding life by the death of her mother, Theodora finds herself free to seek her destiny abroad, and her journey of initiation to Europe constitutes the central action in Part 2, "Jardin Exotique," where she encounters a group of European eccentrics in a "grand hotel" setting on the French Riviera. Her sojourn with these international exiles evokes obvious parallels with Thomas Mann's *The Magic Mountain* (1924), while Theodora, as a relatively untested seeker, may remind readers of American fiction of similar women in Nathaniel Hawthorne and Henry James.

In the "Jardin Exotique" section, which is notable for its economy of style and incident, Theodora exercises her talent for living, which had been suppressed and frustrated in Australia. She enters imaginatively into the lives of her companions, identifying with them and living their exotic histories vicariously. Her friends, a seedy group of expatriates, all have built up myths of romantic pasts. Theodora is not only a responsive and sympathetic consciousness for them but is also able to enrich their illusions by her own imagination. Ironically, however, each fantasy life proves to have been an artful lie near the end of Part 2, leaving Theodora with the sense of having been cheated when the pathetic reality of a character's past is revealed. The final irony occurs when the Hotel du Midi is destroyed by fire, probably a symbol of the coming war which will end the 1930's.

This section, rich in fine characterizations and virtuoso stylistic divertissements, is White's portrait of the Europe of the 1930's and his moral evaluation of it. Theodora, alternately seduced by Europe and its illusions of a glamorous past and then disillusioned by the emptiness of its reality, emerges from the experience morally tested and unscathed, but still an unfulfilled and psychologically incomplete personality. It is not until Part 3, "Holstius," that Theodora confronts her own tragic destiny.

Part 3 takes place in America, where Theodora is overwhelmed by a sense of the vastness of the American continent and her own sense of isolation (personal solitude is always an important theme in White). A chance encounter with a traveling salesman on a train near Chicago results in a conversation that is symbolic: the salesman boasts of America's size and population in the best Babbitt or booster style, while Theodora is impressed with the abstractness of the individual self in a country where enormous numbers—of square miles, people, and sums of money—seem to dominate.

Leaving the train in the mountains of Colorado, Theodora wanders into a lonely canyon, driven by an urge to confront the unknown side of her inner self at last. Alone, at night, she hallucinates an experience of mythic force: a meeting with a stunted little man, almost like a folklore dwarf, who informs her that his name is "Holstius" (a name that perhaps both combines and caricatures the Jungian "animus" or male self in a woman, and the idea of "wholeness"). In Theodora's encounter with the imaginary Holstius, the masculine side of her nature emerges and speaks to her at last, and her inner conflicts appear to be resolved. The confrontation is traumatic, however, and the cost of it is the loss of Theodora's sanity, for the next day a nearby farmer and his family are forced to take charge of her, regarding her as mad.

The Aunt's Story is an expression of mature tragic vision, a novel which explores the possibilities and anguish of the solitary self in search of wholeness and fulfillment in a more assured manner than White's first two published novels. Unlike *The Living and the Dead*, it envisons self-discovery and self-fulfillment as a private quest, to which the changing political and social winds are incidental, almost irrelevant. In this respect, and in its hints of a symbolism drawn partly from Jungian psychology, as well as in its masterful weaving of a suble texture of imagery, *The Aunt's Story* marks the beginning of White's maturity as an artist.

White's next three novels were much larger in scope and intention, epic in length at least. They also project a vision of the Australian past and of the middle twentieth century present influenced by that past. The first, *The Tree of Man*, has been much praised and admired by many different kinds of readers, probably because its theme and characters are much more unexceptionable to the ordinary reader than those of later White novels. The story told is the saga of Australia's pioneer past, as seen through three generations, but mainly through the experience of Stan and Amy Parker, homesteaders who wrest a farm from the wilderness. Stan and Amy are attractive characters, although rather conventional, and their lives are given a depth not found in most novels of pioneer life. Moreover, White provides splendid comic relief through their foils, the irresponsible O'Dowds, so that despite its length, the novel has considerable popular appeal, unlike much of White's fiction. When examined closely, however, the novel does not make an entirely affirmative statement about the settlement of the Australian continent and the replacing of frontier hardships by twentieth century "progress." On the contrary, while Stan and Amy's life as lonely settlers in the outback often possesses a beauty and quiet dignity, their later lives are frustrating, and their sense of progress and achievement is dissipated in the disappointing lives of their children, and in Amy's later estrangement from her husband.

Like the American writer Wright Morris, and other serious novelists of the American West, White establishes an ironic contrast between the often epic and challenging lives of the frontier past and the stunted and rather empty lives of the pioneers' descendants. This persistent mood of irony dominates the later sections of the novel, until a brilliant reversal of perspective occurs in the closing pages. Here, the aged Stan Parker, apparently a neglected and forgotten failure living in a suburb of Sydney which has replaced the rural world of his heroic labor, rises to heights of tragic dignity. Accosted by an annoying fundamentalist evangelist, Parker rejects the easy formula for salvation the latter offers and asserts his own faith: he identifies God with a gob of spittle. To the evangelist, this is a blasphemous comment, and some have tended to treat it as a defiant and rebellious one, but, as William Walsh and some other critics have claimed, Parker's statement is a confession of faith in the ultimate goodness of life and of the holiness of being. This event marks the beginning of the paradoxical but assured religious affirmation that surfaces at crucial moments in most of White's subsequent novels. It should be noted, however, that whatever one thinks of White's religious beliefs or symbolism, Parker's statement of faith gives his character a tragic stature it has richly earned through *The Tree of Man*.

The sense of an impressive tragic vision is heightened and intensified in White's next novel, *Voss*, which is, like *The Aunt's Story*, one of his better-known works. Like *The Tree of Man*, *Voss* takes its inspiration from the Australian past, and like *The Tree of Man*, it aspires to and attains an epic scope. Whereas, however, *The Tree of Man* is epic in its use of time, drawing on three generations of Australian experience, *Voss* is epic in its treatment of space, for the novel describes its hero's Faustian ambition to be the first to conquer the Australian continent by leading an exploratory expedition across it. Moreover, *Voss* is much more dramatic than *The Tree of Man*, since Voss's noble failure (based on an actual expedition led by the explorer Ludwig Leichardt) is counterbalanced by his mystical love for Laura Trevelyan, which transforms him from an exponent of the heroic and resolute will (like that celebrated by Friedrich Nietzsche in the late nineteenth century) to a more chastened and forgiving spirit. At the end, Voss is ready to accept his failure and death with a sense of Christian (or at any rate, religious) resignation.

Although a humorless and often exasperating character, Voss is a dynamic force who entices stolid Australian businessmen into financing his enterprise. Yet his nature is more complex than most of the unimaginative bourgeois Australians realize; only Laura, a complicated young woman who privately rebels against conventional Christianity and the age's worship of material progress, perceives the hidden sensitivities and beauty of Voss's character.

In the early stages of the novel, Laura and Voss seem to be in conflict, as their opposed but complementary natures seem to strike sparks from each other. Once Voss and his companions embark on their heroic journey in the Australian desert, however, Laura and Voss appear to communicate by a mystical or telepathic bond, and the communication allows each to complete or fulfill his or her nature. Jungian psychology would consider each a person who has partially suppressed his hidden self: Voss has repressed his latent feminine qualities by devotion to the ideals of the masculine will; Laura has suppressed her masculine alter ego in the service of femininity. Their mystic communication enlarges and fulfills both their natures, as Laura serves to an anima to Voss's ego, and Voss becomes an animus for Laura.

The telepathic communication between Voss and Laura is difficult to explain in rationalist terms. Frequently, White departs from the conventions of the traditional realistic novel, but perhaps in no other book does he move so far in the direction of literary fantasy. Since the use of the fantastic event or theme in serious fiction is once again becoming acceptable, and is even being justified by literary theorists such as Eric Rabkin (*The Fantastic in Literature*, 1976), White's daring gamble with telepathy may be defended on purely aesthetic grounds. Indeed, it enriches the drama of *Voss*.

Defeated by the Australian climate and landscape, the treachery of his companions, and his own miscalculations, Voss's expedition culminates in his tragic death. Yet the heroic grandeur of Voss's failure is impressive: White's hero has a strength and ambition beyond that of the protagonists of many modern novels, and in his defeat he gains some of the humanity that he had so obviously lacked. White's achievement in this novel is not unworthy of comparison with the best fiction of William Faulkner or D. H. Lawrence.

Voss's acceptance of the Southern cross as a symbol of his transformation from Nietzschean ideals to a more humane and forgiving outlook prompted some to assume that White himself was espousing doctrinal and institutional Christianity in *Voss*. This is not so, but White does affirm his personal religious vision, a synthesis of Jungian thought, Christian and Jewish mysticism, and poetic vision. His next novel, *Riders in the Chariot*, is perhaps White's most ambitious attempt to present the religious vision that undergirds all the fiction after *The Tree of Man*. *Riders in the Chariot* draws its title from Ezekiel's biblical vision of the chariot, but its prophetic and at times apocalyptic tone comes partially from William Blake, whose visionary conversation with Isaiah and Ezekiel in *The Marriage of Heaven and Hell* (1790) provides an epigraph.

Jungian symbolism conjoins with Jewish and Christian mysticism to provide the synthesis of religious vision White offers in the novel. The four main protagonists, two men and two women (one black or "abo" painter, one Jewish mystic, one evangelical Christian, and one nature mystic) are all outcast visionaries, who combine to make a gigantic and impressive human mandala.

The influence of Jewish mysticism is a major element in the Himmelfarb sections of the narrative, since Himmelfarb is a scholar who turns from enlightened rationalism to the dense but powerful mystical images of the Cabala, including the "blue fire" of some Cabalist treatises. One source for White appears to have been Gerschom Scholem's work on the Cabalists, as Peter Beatson and others have indicated. White's sympathetic treatment of Himmelfarb's religious quest aroused hostile comment from at least one Australian critic, who charged that White had turned to a discredited mystical tradition, although the novel also suggests that Hasidic as well as Cabalistic thought influenced him. This line of criticism is ultimately based on the assumption that all mystical traditions are suspect, and probably on the argument that only modern rationalism provides a sane outlook for an enlightened person. Such a position, whether acknowledged or not, is open to debate.

White's other seekers in the novel are religious questers who follow different and perhaps equally valid paths to their epiphanies and revelations. Miss Hare's nature mysticism is a naïve affirmation of being that resembles the kind of mysticism preached and celebrated by Ralph Waldo Emerson and Walt Whitman in their poetry and essays: the affirmation of the phenomenal world which leads to a perception of the transcendental realm. This mystical acceptance of the world resembles that theorized by Martin Buber in his *I and Thou* (1923) with its emphasis on mystical acceptance of being. By contrast, Mrs. Godbold's way is that of orthodox Christian piety, and Alf Dubbo's path is that of the romantic transcendentalist vision, as proclaimed by Blake and others.

Riders in the Chariot not only asserts the primacy of mystical search over conventional life, but it is also Blakean in its harsh indictment of evil in the modern world and in modern history. Just as Blake in his later years was obsessed with the concept of an apocalyptic work of art separating evil from goodness, the lost from the redeemed, through radical vision, so White attempts to achieve that kind of apocalyptic point of view in *Riders in the Chariot*. Evil is seen in various forms in this novel: it is the anti-Semitism and later the Nazism that Himmelfarb encounters; it is the smug self-righteousness of decaying puritanism in Miss Hare's tormentor, Mrs. Jolley; it is the narcissistic upper-class arrogance and contempt for the less fortunate shown by Mrs. Chalmers-Robinson; it is the feeble and thwarted religiosity of the Reverend Pask and his sister. Above all, it is the working-class bigotry and mule-headed chauvinism with its suspicion of outsiders shown by the Australian workmen, who reenact the crucifixion as a blasphemous joke on Himmelfarb on Good Friday. Primarily, White is inclined in this novel to see evil as a kind of spiritual blindness or lack of vision "of the infinite" as Blake's epigraph says, although the malice demonstrated by Mrs. Jolley and White's laborers is hard to explain in such simple terms. Nevertheless, White's sense of the overwhelming presence of evil in the modern world, especially "moral evil," or evil for which humans are responsible, is one of the most convincing features of the book. Equally strong is the sense of moral goodness or inno-cence in his four central characters, however much they may occasionally surrender to their flaws. Whether one is interested in White's attempt to portray the different paths of mysticism, it is hard to forget the strength of his portraits of four characters who remain admirable while enduring great suffering.

Finally, it should be noted that *Riders in the Chariot*, is structured carefully around dominant metaphors and myths reenacted in a ritualized way. Several critics have noted the use of the crucifixion imagery to describe the passion of Himmelfarb. It is also worth noting that each of the four central characters is associated with certain recurrent motifs; one of the four elements is invoked, for example, in connection with each, Miss Hare being associated with air, Himmelfarb with fire, Mrs. Godbold with earth, and Alf Dubbo with water. This is not the only instance of such patterning, but also it serves to illustrate the care and symbolic weight of the poetic design of this massive and richly textured novel. If *Riders in the Chariot* possesses some minor flaws, such as a certain difficulty in controlling the tone of the description of Himmelfarb's passion, it is nevertheless one of White's most impressive and enduring achievements.

After the three epic novels just discussed, White devoted the early and middle years of the 1960's to works that were smaller in scale and perhaps more appealing to those aesthetic purists who prefer the nearly flawless small masterpiece to a gigantic but more uneven novel of Dickensian vitality. For example, the volume of short stories entitled *The Burnt Ones* describes iron-ically the pathos of victimized innocents much like the four "riders" in the divine chariot of Ezekiel's and Blake's visions depicted in the preceding novel.

In *The Solid Mandala*, which White has considered one of his three best novels, his idiosyncracies emerge more noticeably than in earlier works. This novel affirms White's Jungian religious vision more strongly than ever, and to underscore the theme for the obtuse reader, the noble example of Fyodor Dostoevski is invoked by Arthur Brown, the inarticulate visionary who is in part a spokesman for White. Arthur is set in contrast with his tragic brother, Waldo, a minor fiction-writer and critic hampered by excessive rationalism and rendered creatively impotent by fear of his emotions and imagination. Waldo is White's revenge on unimaginative and spiteful critics who had responded with scorn to his passionate major novels, especially *Riders in the Chariot*. Ironically, after failing as a writer and ruining his own life by aloofness from humanity, Waldo is ambushed by his repressed sexuality near the end: he becomes a pathetic transvestite wearing his late mother's discarded dresses, and thus expressing the thwarted feminine side of his nature.

Although Arthur Brown's life also ends pathetically in a lonely old age, the narrative shows that Arthur, one of White's holy simpletons or divine fools, lives a spiritually fulfilled, if obscure and misunderstood, existence. Arthur has a mystical sympathy with animals and nature and with some of the other less articulate characters, especially Dulcie Feinstein, a rich young woman to whom both brothers are attracted. A close communion also exists between Arthur and Mrs. Poulter, a working-class woman who is a kind of surrogate mother and wife to him. Arthur finds meaning in existence through his apprehension of mandalas, the Jungian symbol for the unity and holiness of all being, and of all innocent and life-enhancing forms of existence. Two major mandala symbols dominate Arthur's experience: a large green marble, or "solid mandala," which appears to him to be symbolic of the holiness toward which humanity should strive; and a mystic dance in the shape of a mandala he performs with Mrs. Poulter.

Arthur and Waldo both lead tragic lives, if judged by conventional human standards, and each is an incomplete person: Arthur, the mystic and visionary, lacks a well-developed rational mind; while Waldo, the rationalist, is dead to all spiritual and transcendental existence. In the story of the unbalanced natures of the two brothers, White has attempted to present a fable about the tragic split in humanity between the rational and the mystical faculties of the mind, between—if some psychologists, like Robert Ornstein, are to be believed—the left and the right sides of the human brain. Yet despite the tragic nature of his novel, White makes Arthur much the more attractive of the two brothers, and reaffirms once more one of the themes of *Riders in the Chariot* and other novels: if a choice must be made between reason and mysticism, the path of the mystic, however despised in a rationalistic and technological age, is nevertheless the more rewarding and redemptive road.

Although beneath the rough and grainy surface of *The Solid Mandala* there are surprising riches and pleasures, its sometimes crabbed and eccentric nature might have suggested to some that White had fallen into a creative decline in the 1960's. The three remarkable novels that followed, however, proved that the converse was true: *The Vivisector*, *The Eye of the Storm*, and *A Fringe of Leaves* testify not only to an impressive sustained surge of creative power, but also show White in more masterful control of his material and of his artistic form than ever before.

The Vivisector describes the life of a rebellious and obsessed painter, Hurtle Duffield, who triumphs over enormous obstacles—an obscure background, a stultifying upper-class education, the cultural sterility of the Australian environment, numerous unhappy love affairs—to achieve triumph as a modern artist, a master of the techniques of impressionism, surrealism, and abstract impressionism, who successfully shapes Australian material into a solid series of enduring works.

The novel is clearly an apologia for White, who brilliantly projects and transforms his experience as an Australian novelist into the struggles of his painter. Indeed, had this novel been by an unknown, rather than by White, it is possible that it would have created much more impact than it did. At any rate, the book deserves a high place in White's canon.

In terms of form, *The Vivisector* is one of White's more daring gambles, for it ostensibly follows the shapeless biographical narrative mode of some of the most primitive works of fiction, tracing Duffield's development from his childhood to his death through a series of selected incidents and periods. Yet the author of *The Aunt's Story* and *Riders in the Chariot* could hardly be considered deficient in the post-Jamesian twentieth century concern for novelistic form, and close inspection of *The Vivisector* shows that White has made a sophisticated use of a naïve narrative form in his treatment of Duffield's struggle. For example, Duffield's experience is rendered in terms of his relationship to a series of Jungian anima figures who serve as lovers, supports, and muses. These range from his crippled foster sister, Rhoda Courtney, a childhood rival but a supporter of his old age, through Ponce Nan, a vital but tragic prostitute, and Hero Pavloussi, the wife of a Greek businessman with whom he enjoys a brief, passionate, but unsatisfying romance.

As a painter, Duffield is a tireless worker and committed visionary whose paintings recapitulate many motifs familiar to White's readers. At one point, Duffield perfects his craft by painting rocks, suggesting Theodora's desire in *The Aunt's Story* to write poetry about rocks: the action suggests the need to come to terms with the intractable and substantial nature of the visible and phenomenal world. In his early stages, Duffield is a rebellious and defiantly blasphemous painter who charges God with being the great "vivisector," an unfeeling and cruel being who experiments with human suffering as a scientist dismembers animals—or, as Duffield and other artists approach human life, seeing it as raw material for art. Guilt over the suicide of Nan, however, for which he feels partially responsible, and compassion for the frustrated homosexual grocer, Cutbush, whom he paints as a surrealist figure machine gunning lovers, changes Duffield to a more tolerant and forgiving nature, and his work at last becomes more a kind of worship than blasphemy. In his last period, weakened by strokes, he becomes obsessed with painting in indigo and is characterized by a wry humility and kindness. Duffield thinks of his final, fatal stroke as a moment when he is "indiggodd," or departing "into God." Once again, as in other novels, White makes a paradoxical affirmation of religious faith through the experience of one of his characters.

If *The Vivisector* is rich in vital characterizations and frequently possesses the exuberance of Duffield's raw energy, *The Eye of the Storm* is a splendidly controlled performance which demonstrates once more that when he chooses,

White can display a sure mastery of the techniques of the English novel of manners as practiced by such writers as E. M. Forster. *The Eye of the Storm* is constructed around the social comedy of the last days of Elizabeth Hunter, a regal but selfish matriarch of Sydney society who at eighty-six is slowly dying in her home on Moreton Drive while her son and daughter scheme to have her removed from the care of her nurses and placed in a nursing home. As is usual with White, however, the social comedy of the novel's surface masks tragedy and religious vision: in this case, the Learesque tragedy of Mrs. Hunter and her two children, and the crisis of faith suffered by her remarkable nurse, Sister Mary de Santis. Although the present time of the novel amounts to only a few days, White's narration re-creates, through the memories of the characters, the spiritual and psychological histories of their entire lives. Elizabeth Hunter, like White himself the talented offspring of a grazier, has during her life grown from a grazier's wife with social aspirations into a lady of poise and charm. At the same time, this majestic woman is portrayed as a dominating and selfish mother whose poise and beauty have given her untalented and unattractive daughter, Dorothy, an inferiority complex and driven her talented but narcissistic son to become both a successful London actor and a pathetic womanizing failure in private life.

Mrs. Hunter in later life, however, has been transformed by her critical experience during the hurricane on Brumby Island, when, abandoned and alone during a hurricane, she had experienced a numinous epiphany in the still of the eye of the storm. As a result, she has become a compassionate, understanding, and deeply religious woman, although her piety is of the unchurched kind. Mrs. Hunter's later life has changed the selfish and devouring existence that her children remember; this transformation lends a Lear-like poignancy to her last days, when the poorly concealed malice of Basil and Dorothy is embodied in their effort to move her to a nursing home. The irony in this situation is heightened by the fact that Basil Hunter longs to play Lear himself, as the capstone of his career, while failing to see that the role is acted in life by his mother. Another tragic irony is Dorothy's idolatry of the Duchess of Sanseverina in Stendhal's *The Charterhouse of Parma* (1839): longing to be a masterful woman like the Sanseverina, Dorothy subconsciously resents her mother, whose social poise and personality recall that Stendhal heroine. The tragic irony in the actions of the children comes to a climax in their sentimental journey to their home ranch, where they finally surrender to their loneliness and huddle together in an act of incest during the night, while staying with the family of the conventional grazier who manages the place.

In contrast to the bleak and loveless lives of Basil and Dorothy, Mrs. Hunter finds solace in the loving care of Mary de Santis, her nurse and a reluctant believer in Greek Orthodox Christianity. Sister de Santis' care aids Mrs. Hunter in her final days, and in turn, Sister de Santis finds her own provisional faith reaffirmed by an epiphany of numinous divine immanence at the end of the novel in a mystic moment of water, birds' wings, and morning light, recalling biblical images of revelation. Both Mrs. Hunter and Sister de Santis are characters whose experience reaffirms White's religious vision, although they are also figures in a tragic drama that White intends to be comparable in magnitude to Shakespearean tragedy.

An interesting and partially comic minor plot in *The Eye of the Storm* involves another of Elizabeth Hunter's nurses, the youthful Flora Manhood, who finds herself caught between resentment of her male lover and a temptation to join her cousin in a Lesbian affair. Yet, despite White's obvious sympathy for Flora and her Lesbian inclinations, the matter is resolved by her decision to remain heterosexual, while lesbianism is treated with a touch of comic irony. It is curious that White, himself a practicing homosexual, is able to treat homosexuality with enormous sympathy, yet finally implies the desirablity of a traditional heterosexual identity.

Without a doubt, *The Eye of the Storm* is one of White's most carefully crafted and formally satisfying novels, and the one that most closely approximates the Jamesian ideal of complete mastery of novelistic form. This novel, which might have been considered the crowning work of a lesser career, was followed by other equally challenging works.

There are many impressive strengths of *A Fringe of Leaves*. Like *Voss*, this epic tale is inspired by the Australian past, specifically the experience of Eliza Fraser, a heroic woman who survived shipwreck, the loss of husband and companions, and captivity by aborigines, to return to civilization and become a legendary heroine. In White's hands, the legend is transformed into a work of psychological fiction which is often harrowing in its depiction of physical ordeals, but finally majestic in its tragic dignity. White's heroine, Ellen Gluyas Roxborough, is a woman of enormous appetite for living, who undergoes numerous metamorphoses on her road to destiny. At first an imaginative Cornish farm girl who longs to journey to some mystical or fabled sacred place such as Tintagel, Ellen marries a dry country squire, Austin Roxborough, and is made over, on the surface at least, into a polished eighteenth century lady and a dutiful adornment to her husband's estate near Winchester. On a sentimental journey to Australia (or "Van Dieman's Land") to visit her husband's rakish brother, Garnet, Ellen's inner self emerges, first in a brief affair with Garnet, then in the ordeal of survival of shipwreck and capture by savages.

The shipwreck and the captivity sections form the heart of the narrative. In the shipwreck, Ellen gradually has her civilized self stripped from her, along with her clothing, which is removed layer by layer. Later, after losing her husband and becoming a captive of the Australian natives, Ellen is obliged to confront her own authentic humanity. Her will to survive is indomitable; to cling to her sense of being human, she weaves a "fringe of leaves" as a kind of primitive clothing and an assertion of her belonging to a human realm above the world of nature. Yet a central question for her is the question of her relationship to her captors. Is she of the same order as the dark-skinned aborigines? The question is answered when she participates in a ritual feast at the center of the novel: it is a rite of cannibalism which not only provides physical nourishment but also, ironically, a sense of religious fulfillment as well. At the center of her "heart of darkness," Ellen finds her essential humanity.

The captivity section—which one critic has compared to the captivity narratives of prisoners of the American Indians—is followed by an idyllic interlude which represents a return to innocence for Ellen. In this episode, Ellen meets an escaped convict, a cockney murderer Jack Chance, who in London had brutally murdered his wife, but atones for that by falling in love with Ellen. With Jack, Ellen enjoys her most satisfying sexual relationship, but this Edenic experience, like all others, must end: the idyll comes to a finish when Ellen crosses the Brisband River (likened to a snake) that separates the Australian wilderness from the settled country.

In the resolution of the novel, Ellen is both a heroine to other pioneers, especially the women, and a penitent. In her own eyes, her guilt over her participation in the cannibal rite and the betrayal of Jack is great, but her will to live triumphs over her sense of unworthiness and self-immmolation. At the close of the novel, it is clear she will return to routine and ordered life by marrying a pleasant, but somewhat inarticulate, Australian settler.

In its depiction of the indestructible will to survive, *A Fringe of Leaves* is a masterpiece, perhaps White's finest novel. Its central character, Ellen Roxborough, may well become one of the unforgettable heroines of literature, and while its affirmation tends to be more humanist than religious, it is nevertheless a testament to White's essential compound of tragic vision with an ultimate affirmation.

Although *A Fringe of Leaves* has received much favorable comment, White's most recent novel, *The Twyborn Affair*, was the object of a different reception, especially in America. This work is likely to be one of White's most controversial, for it attempts to deal with homosexual experience more candidly than ever before in White's fiction. Moreover, the novel is an interesting experiment in technique, because it is constructed of three sections which are essentially self-contained units, yet which also attempt to form a greater unity of a lengthy novel covering several decades. Finally, however successful White may be in achieving his intentions in these respects, the novel also seeks to attain and reaffirm his characteristic tragic vision.

Eddie Twyborn, the hero (and sometimes heroine) of the novel, is presented as a feminine personality in the body of a handsome male: an unusual "prisoner of sex" whose incarceration is indeed tragic. In Part 1, Eddie Twyborn appears as the transvestite lover of a likable older man, a somewhat decadent

Greek living in France in the pre-World War I period. The couple are spied upon by Joanie Golson, a friend of Eddie's upper-class, overbearing Australian mother, and there is a certain amount of rather strained social comedy here until the affair ends with the death of Twyborn's Greek lover. In Part 2, Twyborn returns to Australia after the war as a decorated hero—an idea that White strives to make convincing—and tries living as a working man in the outback on a sheep ranch. There, he becomes emotionally entangled with the brutal foreman, Don Prowse, who finally rapes him, and with the owner's wife, who falls in love with him, misunderstanding his sexual nature while beguiled by his charm and sensitivity. Here, Twyborn appears androgynous, seeming to enjoy both kinds of sexual experience.

The failure to live peacefully as a man in Part 2 is followed by Twyborn's life in London in Part 3, where he surfaces in the late 1930's in female dress. This time, he is the madam of a brothel patronized by the rich and fashionable, and he becomes something of a celebrity. During this period, he suffers from a thwarted love for his patron, Lord Gravenor, who is finally revealed as a homosexual also. A touching reconciliation with his selfish mother, now humbled by age and living in London alone, provides a kind of tragic recognition scene at the novel's end. This is followed by Twyborn's death in the London blitz.

Undoubtedly, Eddie Twyborn—the name is an obvious pun on "twice-born"—is one of the most interesting homosexual heroes in literature, and perhaps White's theme, the irony of a feminine nature in a male body, has never been treated with such insight. The novel's eccentricities, however, are pronounced, and the social comedy in Parts 1 and 3 often becomes tiresome. Like White's other major novels, the work achieves a kind of tragic dignity, despite its flaws, yet it appears vastly inferior to his other novels published in the 1970's. Like White's other major works after *The Aunt's Story*, *The Twyborn Affair* once again affirms, however paradoxically, the power of love and the importance of religious faith, both ideas that are defiant affronts to the intellectual orthodoxies of many of the most vocal of twentieth century intellectuals.

White's strengths as a writer are many. Despite some idiosyncracies, he is a masterful stylist, and his characterizations are psychologically complex and memorable. His skill at depicting social comedy is complemented by his contempt for the arrogance of wealth and power. Beyond these gifts, however, White strives to create tragic fictional works on the Greek or Shakespearean scale in an age of irony and a diminished or disappearing tragic vision. White's fiction also, in the works following *The Aunt's Story*, articulates the author's own prodigious mythology and majestic religious vision. It is a vision drawing on numerous disparate sources—Blake and the Cabala, Carl Jung, Dostoevski, and the Bible—but it forms a synthesis which affirms the importance of a search for transcendence and the significance of mystical experience. White's views are as unfashionable among most modern thinkers as his novels have been in an era of "experimental fiction," but both his vision and his novels are likely to stand the test of time.

Major publications other than long fiction

SHORT FICTION: *The Burnt Ones*, 1964; *The Cockatoos: Shorter Novels and Stories*, 1974.

PLAYS: *Four Plays*, 1965; *Big Toys*, 1978; *The Night the Prowler*, 1978.

POETRY: *The Ploughman and Other Poems*, 1935.

NONFICTION: *Flaws in the Glass: A Self-Portrait*, 1982.

Bibliography

Argyle, Barry. *Patrick White*, 1967.

Beatson, Peter. *The Eye of the Mandala*, 1976.

Blamires, David. "Patrick White: *The Twyborn Affair*," in *Critical Quarterly*. XXII, no. 1 (Spring, 1980), pp. 77-85.

Brissenden, R. F. *Patrick White*, 1966.

Bjorkstén, Ingmar. *Patrick White: A General Introduction*, 1976.

Kiernan, Brian. *Patrick White*, 1980.

Morley, Patricia. *The Mystery of Unity: Theme and Technique in the Novels of Patrick White*, 1972.

Walsh, William. *Patrick White's Fiction*, 1977.

Wilkes, G. A., ed. *Ten Essays on Patrick White: Selected from Southerly, 1964-67*, 1970.

Edgar L. Chapman

THORNTON WILDER

Born: Madison, Wisconsin; April 17, 1897
Died: Hamden, Connecticut; December 7, 1975

Principal long fiction

The Cabala, 1926; *The Bridge of San Luis Rey*, 1927; *The Woman of Andros*, 1930; *Heaven's My Destination*, 1934; *The Ides of March*, 1948; *The Eighth Day*, 1967; *Theophilus North*, 1973.

Other literary forms

Thornton Wilder is as well known for his plays as for his fiction. *Our Town* (1938), *The Merchant of Yonkers* (1939, revised as *The Matchmaker*, 1955), and *The Skin of Our Teeth* (1942) were published with Wilder's own Preface as *Three Plays* (1957). Collections of his short plays were published in *The Angel That Troubled the Waters and Other Plays* (1928) and *The Long Christmas Dinner and Other Plays in One Act* (1931). *The Alcestiad: Or, A Life in the Sun* was published posthumously (1977), as was a collection of his essays, *American Characteristics and Other Essays* (1979).

Achievements

Wilder began his career as a teacher and in a sense never gave up the practice of that profession. He attempted to persuade generations of readers of the power of love, the need for individual integrity, the importance of maintaining faith in man's essential goodness. His clear style and straightforward narrative earned for him a broad readership, transcending categories of age, class, or education. Though detractors have labeled him middle class and middlebrow, he received enthusiastic praise throughout his career from such critics as Edmund Wilson, Malcolm Cowley, Edmund Fuller, Henry Seidel Canby, and John Updike. Wilder has been less a subject of scholarly research than some of his contemporaries—F. Scott Fitzgerald and Ernest Hemingway, for example—yet he has remained widely read since his first novel was published in 1926, and his versatility as a writer—of two Pulitzer-Prize-winning full-length plays and dozens of short plays—has brought him worldwide recognition.

Wilder won a Pulitzer Prize for fiction in 1928, a National Book Award in 1967, and the first National Medal for Literature in 1964, besides being the recipient of several honorary doctorates.

Biography

Thornton Niven Wilder was born in Madison, Wisconsin, on April 17, 1897, the son of Amos Parker Wilder and Isabella Thornton Niven Wilder. His father, a newspaper editor, moved the family to Hong Kong in 1906 when he was assigned a diplomatic post there. The young Wilder attended the Kaiser Wilhelm School, then the China Inland Missionary Boys' School, where he harbored a brief desire to become a missionary himself. When his family returned to the United States, settling in California, he continued his education at the Thacher School in Ojai, then Berkeley High School, where he first began to write plays and act in class productions. In 1915, he entered Oberlin, a school his father chose because it was less socially elite than his own alma mater, Yale. At Oberlin, Wilder continued his involvement in theatrical productions and contributed prolifically to the college's literary magazine. After two years there, Wilder was allowed by his father to enroll at Yale, where, after a period of homesickness for Oberlin, he again proved himself, in the words of professor and literary critic William Lyon Phelps, to be "a star of the first magnitude . . . unusually versatile, original, and clever." Wilder was graduated with no specific career goals in mind. His father, believing a European experience would be broadening, sent him to study at the American Academy in Rome for a summer. Meanwhile, he searched for a suitable job for his son and found one at Lawrenceville, a preparatory school in New Jersey. There, when his French classes were over, Wilder began a novel with the working title *Memoirs of a Roman Student*, to be published as *The Cabala* in 1926. In the same year, Wilder took advantage of Lawrenceville's proximity to Princeton to earn his master of arts degree. He took a year's leave of absence from teaching and began work on a new novel, *The Bridge of San Luis Rey*, published to enormous acclaim in 1927, and earning Wilder his first Pulitzer Prize.

In 1929, Wilder was invited to teach at the University of Chicago by an Oberlin classmate, Robert Hutchins, who had just been named President of the prestigious Illinois university. Wilder was writing intensely: *The Woman of Andros* was published in 1930, a collection of short plays in 1931, and *Heaven's My Destination* in 1934. He remained at the University of Chicago until the mid-1930's, teaching one semester and writing during the next. More and more, he was drawn to the theater. He completed *The Merchant of Yonkers*, later revised as *The Matchmaker* (and still later transformed into the Broadway musical *Hello, Dolly!*) in 1937 and then turned to a more serious play, *Our Village*, soon retitled *Our Town*. This play was met with great enthusiasm when it opened in New York in 1938 and earned Wilder his second Pulitzer Prize.

The political upheaval in Europe, soon to involve America, found its way into Wilder's next play, *The Skin of Our Teeth*, which evoked a deep response in audiences both in the United States and abroad; the play was awarded a Pulitzer Prize in 1942. Wilder served in the army during World War II, and emerged with his optimism intact and his faith in humanity unshaken.

In the late 1940's, Wilder again turned to fiction, dealing with the problem of authority and dictatorship in *The Ides of March*. This novel reflected his talks with Gertrude Stein, whom Wilder had met in 1934 when Stein was lecturing at the University of Chicago. They shared ideas on the problem of identity and the creation of a believable reality for readers. Stein attempted to deal with these problems in her own novel, *Ida* (1941); Wilder took as his subject Julius Caesar.

In 1950, Wilder delivered the Charles Eliot Norton lectures at Harvard, then traveled—always a stimulation and joy for him—and worked on *The Alcestiad*, his retelling of the Greek legend of Alcestis. In the early 1960's, he retreated to Arizona to write *The Eighth Day*. By the end of the decade, his pace had slowed. He worked on short plays and completed his quasi-autobiographical *Theophilus North*. He died in his sleep on December 7, 1975.

Analysis

Thornton Wilder's seven novels, written over nearly fifty years, show a remarkable consistency in theme and tone. His early books, contemporaneous with Theodore Dreiser's *An American Tragedy* (1925) and Sinclair Lewis' *Arrowsmith* (1925), are far from the realism and naturalism which dominated American literature in the 1920's and 1930's. Though he joined groups active in civil rights and social justice, these themes did not find their way into his works in the manner of John Dos Passos or John Steinbeck. His later works, similarly, show none of the interest in psychoanalysis which may be found in the works of Sherwood Anderson, for example, none of the angry intensity of a Norman Mailer.

Wilder chose not to comment on contemporary politics, social problems, psychological *Angst*, or cultural changes, preferring instead to mine those themes he considered of utmost importance: love, brotherhood, tolerance, and faith. His faith was expressed not in strictly Judeo-Christian terms, but in humanistic convictions which incorporated diverse religious beliefs. Without being didactic, Wilder wished to educate, to inspire, to allow his readers to move beyond an obsession with the individual case to a consideration of humankind and its history. His second novel, *The Bridge of San Luis Rey*, is representative of the themes which recur throughout his works, and his final statement in that book well expresses his one abiding conviction: "There is a land of the living and a land of the dead and the bridge is love, the only survival, the only meaning."

Though Wilder drew on his memories of Rome for his first novel, *The Cabala*, the book is a fantasy, only incidentally autobiographical. The "Cabala" is an aristocratic social circle in which two Americans find themselves involved. These two, Samuele and James Blair, represent Wilder's interest in duality of personality which recurs in later works and results in part from his having been born a twin (his sibling was stillborn). Samuele is a typical Wilder character: innocent, sensitive, stable, with a deep strain of common sense. Blair is the dry intellectual so obsessed by books that he fears real life.

Samuele is the vehicle by which a number of episodes are linked, since he is asked by various members of the Cabala to intervene in the lives of others. First, he is called in to restrain the impetuous and licentious Marcantonio, but fails: the young man engages in incest and then kills himself. Then, Samuele must console the lovely young Alix, unfortunate enough to fall in love with James Blair. Finally, he must deal with the royalist Astrée-Luce in her plot to "prop up" and empower cynical Cardinal Vaini. Samuele is baffled by these obsessed and decadent characters, and is hardly satisfied by an explanation offered to him that the group is possessed by ancient gods who have passed on their power to unsuspecting mortals. Finally, on advice from Vergil's ghost, Samuele returns to America. For Wilder, Europe, for all its richness of culture, was too deeply mired in the past to allow the spirit to grow. Samuele could thrive only in America, a country of youth and intellectual freedom.

In his second novel, *The Bridge of San Luis Rey*, Wilder again uses a structure of separate episodes linked by one thread, this time the collapse of an ancient bridge over a chasm in Peru. Again, he offers a religious figure, but instead of the jaded Cardinal, there is the sympathetic brother Juniper, who searches for meaning in the deaths of those who perished: the Marquesa de Montemayor; Pepita, her maid; Esteban, a young Indian; Uncle Pio, an aging actor, and his ward Jaime. Brother Juniper finds that the five were victims of love, and those who survive are forced to a change of consciousness by the deaths of those they spurned or misjudged.

As in *The Cabala*, Wilder explores twinness in the tale of Esteban and his twin brother Manuel. The two are extraordinarily close, and when Manuel falls in love with a woman, Esteban becomes despondent. Yet he nurses his brother faithfully after Manuel is injured, suffering his delirious ravings until Manuel dies. Nearly mad with grief, Esteban first assumes his dead brother's identity, then attempts suicide, only to die when the bridge collapses. A sea captain, Alvarado, had offered to sign him on his crew, and tried to console him by reminding him, "We do what we can. We push on, Esteban, as best we can. It isn't for long, you know. Time keeps going by. You'll be surprised at the way time passes." Wilder was always conscious of the brevity of life and the need, therefore, to cling to love where one finds it. In *The Bridge of San Luis Rey*, he urges the celebration and fulfillment of love as the only meaning in the world.

From eighteenth century Peru, Wilder moved to pre-Christian Greece in his third novel, *The Woman of Andros*, again dealing with love; its theme, as in *The Bridge of San Luis Rey*, is "How does one live? . . . What does one do first?" Society on the island of Brynos was not essentially different, according to Wilder, from that of his own America. When Chrysis, the central character, says "Lift every roof, and you will find seven puzzled hearts," she speaks of man's bewilderment in the face of the unknown, his search for communion, his need for love—basic human struggles which are not rooted in any particular time or place.

In 1930, however, a number of critics were disappointed with this message. In a time of economic and social crisis, Wilder seemed to retreat into yet another esoteric setting, far removed from the urgencies of the day. One critic writing in *The New Republic* dubbed Wilder a "Prophet of the Genteel Christ" who wrote for a wealthy elite not interested in social problems. The article touched off a month of debate, with letters supporting or attacking Wilder appearing in each issue of the journal. At the end of December, Wilder finally received his greatest support when Sinclair Lewis, accepting the Nobel Prize for Literature, praised his fellow writer "who in an age of realism dreams the old and lovely dreams of the eternal romantic."

Throughout the controversy, Wilder remained silent. He was sensitive to the criticism, however, and in his next novel attempted to find a setting and characters which would appear relevant to his own time. *Heaven's My Destination* concerns the misadventures of George Marvin Brush, a salesman of religious textbooks, who travels across Depression-ridden America preaching, moralizing, and interfering in the lives of ordinary citizens. Converted to Bible Belt Christianity by a woman evangelist at Shiloh Baptist College, he has proceeded to spread his own fundamentalist version of the Gospel wherever he goes. Wilder returned to the episodic structure of his first two novels in presenting George's adventures in picaresque form. Unlike Don Quixote, however, with whom George has been compared, Wilder's protagonist is rarely endearing, more often exasperating.

George is different from the "normal" Americans with whom he interacts, yet Wilder is satirizing not only his earnest hero, but also those who spurn him. George, after a while, becomes depressed by his society and exclaims, "It's the world that's crazy. Everybody's crazy except me; that's what's the matter. The whole world's nuts." Why, asks this ardent believer, is God "so slow" in changing things?

For all his misconceptions, George does act upon truly humanistic beliefs. He takes a vow of poverty and occasionally of silence, refuses his interest from the bank and dislikes raises in pay. "I think everybody ought to be hit by the depression equally," he says, as he gives away his money. Like Samuele, George maintains his integrity in an environment which threatens to corrupt him and is selfless in his efforts to aid those who need him—even if they protest against his interference.

George Brush was Wilder's answer to the critics who dismissed his previous works, and in a sense, he gave them what he thought they deserved—a priggish, monomaniacal American overreacting to mundane occurrences. Even with such a cartoon-strip character, however, Wilder could not help but imbue him with gentleness and humility, and for Edmund Wilson, Brush emerged as a "type of saint . . . and therefore a universal character."

In part, it was Brush's earnestness, his reluctance to see evil and his determination to do good, that caused Wilder to exclaim, "I'm George Brush." Certainly, his persistent faith in humanity unites him with his character, but there is further correspondence in Brush's essential isolation, the loneliness which causes him to reach out for companionship. For Wilder, such isolation was characteristically American: solitude was to be treasured, but loneliness was threatening. He once noted an adage which he thought well expressed the American spirit: "If you can see the smoke from your neighbor's chimney, you're too near." In his next novel, thirteen years later, he created yet another lonely, questing character, but this time Wilder eschewed satire and humor to deal seriously with a man powerful before the world, yet powerless before death.

The Ides of March, written just after World War II, deals with an archetypal dictator, Julius Caesar. Here, Wilder aimed to revive the spirit of the man from a palimpsest of historical and fictional treatments. The novel, therefore, becomes a study in identity and a technical challenge in creating for readers a believable reality. In structure, *The Ides of March* differs sharply from Wilder's previous work. He assembles fictionalized letters, diary entries, messages, and documents in an effort to offer a vibrant picture of Roman life. Caesar himself is a man obsessed not only with power but also with death, and he must learn how to celebrate life faced with a dark world and an uncaring universe.

Wilder contrasts Caesar with his friend and counselor Lucius Turrinus, who offers a philosophy which was by then familiar to Wilder's readers: "The universe is not aware that we are here," Lucius tells Caesar. "Hope has never changed tomorrow's weather." Yet love could change the world, and Caesar comes to exclaim, "I wish to cry out to all the living and all the dead that there is not part of the universe that is untouched by bliss."

Caesar's urge to seize life and live it to the fullest causes his companions to label him rash and irreverent; but he feels himself to be above them because he has clearly envisioned his own death, and in so doing believes himself "capable of praising the sunlight." Wilder transfers to the Roman dictator much of the sentiment expressed in his play *Our Town*, where Emily Webb dies and is allowed to return to Earth for one day. Only then does she realize how wonderful life is, how desperately she wants to live, and how foolish most people are in squandering their brief existence. Caesar refuses to be foolish; perhaps he will be ruthless, impetuous, temperamental, passionate— but he will live each moment.

The Ides of March had two major inspirations: the war itself, with its focus on the use and misuse of power, the character of a dictator, and the death of innocents; and a personal confrontation with death—first that of Wilder's friend and mentor Edward Sheldon, a playwright whose character informs

Lucius Turrinus, and upon whose wisdom Wilder often relied; then, and most important, the death of his mother, his most ardent supporter and admirer.

After *The Ides of March* was published, Wilder devoted nearly two decades to his plays; not until 1967 would he write another novel. In *The Eighth Day*, Wilder returned to an American setting, the turn-of-the-century Midwest, and to traditional narrative. He carefully unfolds the tale of John Barrington Ashley, tried for the murder of his neighbor, Breckenridge Lansing, and found guilty. Five days after being sentenced to death, he escapes with the help of an unknown accomplice. Five years later, Ashley is found innocent on the basis of new evidence. Ashley's flight, which takes him to Chile, is contrasted with the life of his wife and children in a small town which barely tolerates the outlaw's family.

Wilder's concern, however, is not with one family's history, but with the archetypal family, and Ashley represents not one wronged citizen, but the man of the Eighth Day, a new man with faith in humanity and a strong commitment to working toward a better future. Wilder tells his readers that faith and action can bring about a better life. Throughout the novel, he assigns several characters to speak for him, most notably Dr. Gillies, a country physician, who observes,

> Nature never sleeps. The process of life never stands still. The creation has not come to an end. The Bible says that God created man on the sixth day and rested, but each of those days was many millions of years long. That day of rest must have been a short one. Man is not an end but a beginning. We are at the beginning of the second week. We are children of the eighth day.

On the eighth day, man must begin to forge his own future, and though Dr. Gillies knows that there will be "no Golden Ages and no Dark Ages," still he believes in the power of each individual to work toward the collective fate of humankind.

Because the novel is concerned essentially with imparting a message, the characters—as in *The Cabala* and *Heaven's My Destination*—are not fully realized individuals, but instead are one-dimensional representations of predictable types. The Ashley family, ignored and rebuffed by their neighbors, never lose their aristocratic elegance. They persist in their nightly reading of William Shakespeare even when economic problems would seem severe enough to lower their morale. Here, Wilder pleads for art as the true salvation of mankind, its highest achievement, "the only satisfactory products of civilization."

Through Dr. Gillies, who echoes the sentiments of Chrysis in *The Woman of Andros* and Lucius in *The Ides of March*, Wilder reminds his readers that they occupy only a brief span of time when contrasted with eternity and so must exhibit proper humility. They are small specks in a vast universe, and their duty is not to enhance their own egos, but to work together toward a higher good. "We keep saying that 'we live our lives,'" Dr. Gillies exclaims. "Shucks! Life lives us." Wilder had sent this message for forty years; he insisted again, in the turbulent, self-conscious, self-indulgent late 1960's, on attempting to awaken his readers to his own values.

Wilder was seventy when *The Eighth Day* was published, the time of a writer's life when he might consider writing his autobiography or memoirs. Wilder, however, chose not to reveal his memories or bare his soul: instead, he wrote a last novel, *Theophilus North*, with a protagonist, he once told an interviewer, who was what his twin brother might have been if he had lived.

Theophilus may be Wilder's imaginary brother, but his life bears striking similarities to that of Wilder himself. He has lived in China, attended Yale, and spent a summer in Rome; after teaching at a boys' preparatory school in New Jersey, he leaves his job to explore life and goes to Newport, Rhode Island—a town where Wilder often vacationed—to set his new course. Like Samuele, Theophilus is gentle, well-mannered, polite, helpful. These traits endear him to the Newport natives, and he is asked to intervene in several lives. The structure here, as in many previous Wilder novels, is one of loosely linked episodes.

Theophilus succeeds in such tasks as separating mismatched lovers, liberating an aging man from the manipulation of his daughter, allowing a shrewish wife to mend her ways, extricating one man from his unwitting involvement with criminals, bringing home a wayward husband, finding a lover for a maimed young man, and impregnating a woman whose husband is sterile. Throughout, Theophilus is a typical Wilder hero—a man of good will, of faith, of sincerity.

Theophilus North is Wilder's only novel in which sexuality is of central importance. The sexual episodes are conducted offstage and seem unbelievable and strained. Theophilus, in his seductions and in his everyday relationships with his neighbors, is curiously unaffected and uninvolved. Though he displays emotion, he seems to lack passion.

Wilder's characters, from Samuele to John Ashley, from the circle of Roman aristocrats to Newport society, remain thin and superficial, emblems rather than specific, rounded human beings. Such characterization was in keeping with Wilder's conviction that each individual was, in the long history of the human race, of but little importance. His trials, anguish, suffering, and joy were not significant when placed in the context of all human suffering and all human joy. Rather than writing about individual human beings, Wilder chose to write about humanity; rather than dealing with the intricacies of individual lives, he chose to compress those lives into brief episodes to demonstrate the multiplicity of life.

Wilder, deeply philosophical and reflective, was always the teacher, the educator, with an abiding concern for the future of humanity. "Hope," he wrote in *Theophilus North*, "is a projection of the imagination; so is despair.

Despair all too readily embraces the ills it forsees; hope is an energy and arouses the mind to explore every possibility to combat them." In all his works, he exuded hope and, even in dark times, urged his readers to work together in faith and in love.

Major publications other than long fiction

PLAYS: *The Angel That Troubled the Waters and Other Plays*, 1928; *The Long Christmas Dinner and Other Plays in One Act*, 1931; *Lucrece*, 1933 (adaptation); *Our Town*, 1938; *The Merchant of Yonkers*, 1939 (revised as *The Matchmaker*, 1955); *The Skin of Our Teeth*, 1942; *Our Century*, 1947; *Three Plays*, 1957; *The Drunken Sisters*, 1957; *Plays for Bleecker Street*, 1960, 1961 (3 volumes); *The Alcestiad: Or, The Life in the Sun*, 1977.

NONFICTION: *The Intent of the Artist*, 1941; *American Characteristics and Other Essays*, 1979.

Bibliography

Burbank, Rex. *Thornton Wilder*, 1961.
Goldstein, Malcolm. *The Art of Thornton Wilder*, 1965.
Goldstone, Richard. *Thornton Wilder*, 1975.
Goldstone, Richard, and Gary Anderson. *A Bibliographical Checklist of Work by and About Thornton Wilder*, 1982.
Grebanier, Bernard. *Thornton Wilder*, 1964.
Simon, Linda. *Thornton Wilder: His World*, 1979.
Stresau, Hermann. *Thornton Wilder*, 1971.
Wilder, Amos. *Thornton Wilder and His Public*, 1980.

Linda Simon

SYLVIA WILKINSON

Born: Durham, North Carolina; April 3, 1940

Principal long fiction
Moss on the North Side, 1966; *A Killing Frost*, 1967; *Cale*, 1970; *Shadow of the Mountain*, 1977; *Bone of My Bones*, 1982.

Other literary forms
In addition to her five novels, Sylvia Wilkinson has written a nonfiction book, *The Stainless Steel Carrot: An Auto Racing Odyssey* (1973), about driver John Morton; an adventure series for young people on auto racing; and has edited a handbook, *Change: The Innovative Teaching of English and Social Studies in Secondary Schools* (1971). She has written articles for numerous periodicals, including *The American Scholar, Sports Illustrated, The Writer, Mademoiselle, True,* and *Ingenue.* She has also worked in Richmond, Virginia, as a consultant to the Henrico County Humanities Center, and has contributed to its publications, *The Turtle and the Teacher, A Borrower Be,* and *Last But Not Least, My Poem.*

Achievements
Often described by critics and reviewers as being in the tradition of Southern women writers such as Flannery O'Connor, Carson McCullers, Katherine Anne Porter, and Eudora Welty, Wilkinson belongs to the generation of novelists which includes Lee Smith, Anne Tyler, Alice Walker, and Gail Godwin. Her first two novels were prominently and favorably reviewed in the popular press as well as in literary quarterlies. Her last three novels, however, have not received the attention they deserve. Though not explicitly feminist, her fiction is alive with dramatized perceptions of what it means to grow up female in the South. Her insights cover the socioeconomic range from wealth to poverty, from the educated to the culturally deprived. She gives voice to the kind of characters not often treated in contemporary fiction by women: poor, rural whites and, to a lesser extent, blacks.

In the inner lives of Wilkinson's people, nature is still a living symbolic force, and her considerable powers of description bring nature alive for the urban reader. She has much to say to and about women that has not been said by other writers. While she explicitly explores the passage of women to adulthood in the South, she also has much to offer all readers, regardless of sex, in her treatment of the human struggle to become creatively, decently adult in spite of cultural constrictions.

Biography
Sylvia Jean Wilkinson was born in Durham, North Carolina, on April 3,

1940, the daughter of Peggy George and Thomas Noel Wilkinson. She received her B.A. in writing and painting in 1961 at the University of North Carolina at Greensboro. At first a painting major, she landed by accident in poet Randall Jarrell's writing workshop when she was supposed to have been placed in a composition course. In 1963, she earned an M.A. in English and writing under Louis Rubin at Hollins College, where she revised her first novel, *Moss on the North Side*, which she had begun in her Blue Horse notebook as a seventh grader. She completed her second novel, *A Killing Frost*, in 1966 while attending Stanford University on a Wallace Stegner Creative Writing Fellowship.

A woman of diverse gifts and interests, Wilkinson, during her high school and college years, played championship tennis, was an avid horseback rider, and became interested in auto racing, now her second profession. She earns a portion of her living as a timer for the formula-car racing team of actor Paul Newman. A talented visual artist, Wilkinson's paintings and other art objects are often modeled on characters and animals in her novels.

In addition to working in writers-in-the-schools programs in Virginia, Kentucky, and North Carolina, Wilkinson has taught or been writer-in-residence at numerous colleges and universities, including the College of William and Mary, Sweet Briar College, and the University of North Carolina at Chapel Hill. Her honors and awards include a Eugene Saxton Memorial Trust Grant (1964), a Mademoiselle Merit Award for Literature (1964), two Sir Walter Raleigh Awards for Fiction (1968 and 1977), a Creative Writing Fellowship from the National Endowment for the Arts (1973-1974), and a Guggenheim Fellowship (1977).

Now living in El Segundo, California, Wilkinson frequently returns to the house she and her sister, the potter Margot Wilkinson, maintain outside Chapel Hill, North Carolina. She divides her time between writing in California and traveling the auto-racing circuit.

Analysis

Each of Sylvia Wilkinson's novels creates a whole world which the reader enters with all five senses attuned. Through a patient accumulation of exact, telling details, she suggests the fabric of actual lives. The real focus of her fiction, much of which is told in the first person, is the psychic life of her characters; vividly drawn nature imagery functions as a metaphor for this inner life.

The development of the female psyche in the modern South is Wilkinson's dominant theme. Her typical protagonist (only one, Cale Jenkins, is a boy) is a Southern girl or young woman, intelligent, sensitive, rebellious, and imaginative. After the asexual freedom of rural girlhood, she struggles to find a way to grow up without losing spontaneity and integrity to the stultifying strictures of Southern femininity. Unable to find among their relatives models for what they might become, Wilkinson's protagonists are forced into lives outside the mainstream of their culture, until in the 1982 novel, *Bone of My Bones*, Ella Ruth Higgins breaks out of the pattern. Against all odds, she finds her vocation as a fiction-writer and manages to realize the possibility of a viable future, a workable womanhood.

In *Moss on the North Side* and *A Killing Frost*, Cary and Ramie respectively emerge from tomboy girlhoods into the forced feminization of adolescence. Both are outsiders, a fact underscored by their illegitimacy and by Cary's half-Indian parentage. In all five novels, girl characters look futilely to their mothers, aunts, and grandmothers for models of how to grow up and be whole; they tend to identify with their fathers as being more at home in the world. Predictably, both Cary and Ramie wish they were boys.

Cary, in *Moss on the North Side*, alienated from the mainstream of life around her by her father's tenant-farmer status and Indian blood, retreats into her own world of vivid perceptions of nature with its constant cyclical impetus toward death. Her father's sudden death from rabbit fever leaves her frighteningly alone, because she totally rejects her mother, a prostitute who never married Cary's father. In several passages of forceful psychological realism, Wilkinson shows how Cary's mother's body denotes to her daughter aspects of physicality and sexuality that she is not able to confront.

After Cary is orphaned, the indulgent widow Strawbright, their landlady, becomes Cary's parent-figure. A fantasy fulfillment, the all-accepting, unconditionally loving mother, she takes Cary into her family on parity with her own two sexually awakening sons. Her boundless nurturing in this situation seems unlikely, and it is difficult to envision how Cary's life will develop from this point. The novel thus loses some psychological momentum at the end.

In *A Killing Frost*, Ramie, like Cary, a girl on the threshold of womanhood, grasps for workable ways of growing up through her relation with Miss Liz, her maternal grandmother. One of the richest of Wilkinson's characters, Miss Liz, a workhorse of a woman, keeps up household and farm by sheer force of will after the death of her less overworked, less overwrought husband, whose intimacy with natural processes shaped Ramie's mind. The dead Maylean, Ramie's retarded mother, totally controlled by her sexuality, is at the opposite extreme from Cecie, Ramie's aunt, who adopts her and does her best to feminize the rebellious child according to accepted standards. Miss Liz alone has sympathy for Ramie's ambivalence about who she is and what she can become; but Miss Liz is dying, hopelessly and somewhat bitterly. Stymied by the inevitability of the physical dissolution of death, Miss Liz is resolutely intolerant of those around her who hold different perspectives from hers: she feuds with her neighbors for taking in Dummy, an aging and severely retarded man who surfaced in the community years before, and she was earlier unable to summon the generosity to allow her husband the joy of his long-anticipated and only trip to the seashore.

Thus, in spite of her nurturing of Ramie's sensibility and her appreciation of her intelligence, Miss Liz is not a workable model either. The farm milieu in which she is wisely competent is giving way to technology; she becomes obsolete as she dies, and Ramie is left alone with these deprivations. Unlike Cary in *Moss on the North Side*, Ramie does not find a model at novel's end, but must squarely face the dilemma of how to grow up with Miss Liz's strengths, but without the constrictions that embittered her. One of the best of Wilkinson's novels, *A Killing Frost* teems with images of realized life, especially the pungently convincing characters of Ramie and Miss Liz.

In *Cale*, Wilkinson probes the possibilities for the future of a boy protagonist who also grows up in cultural and emotional poverty. Cale, however, shares the focus with his mother Falissa, who is something like what Cary and Ramie might grow up to be. The world of *Cale* includes a broader, more various range of characters than the earlier novels, and employs the same imagistically accurate but symbolic use of nature. It also has a stronger ambience of determinism than the others, but the possibility of Cale's breaking out of the dreary repetition of his forbears' miseries mitigates the atmosphere of hopeless enclosure.

In some respects, Falissa is a more interesting character than Cale, who tends toward self-absorption, humorlessness, and lack of imagination, and strikes a macho pose modeled after that of his Uncle Roe, who has escaped the mold that squeezes Cale but in destructive ways that lead to his murder by fellow moonshiners. Falissa, on the other hand, is, at the beginning of the eighteen years the novel covers, vital, sensitive, imaginative; the novel charts the process of the gradual quelling of these qualities.

Falissa's Southern-belle mother, Sarah Ann, shaped her ideas about what it means to be a woman, and her ghost must delight in her daughter's submission to woman's work and in her thorough repression of the healing, unifying influence of her father's gentle, artistic sensibility. Falissa feels that the onset of puberty denied her the only authentic experience she had known, active, direct confrontation with the world outside the confines of the house, permanently alienating her from nature and from straightforward relations with other people. Just as Sarah Ann hid from her daughter the physical facts of her future female life, she, as a married woman herself, dutifully represses her longings for an active state of being and her resentment of her servitude to husband, children, and farm. The novel effectively dramatizes the dwindling away of her spontaneity, and the pathos of the fact that her life reached its peak in the integrity of her childhood experience of the outdoors. By novel's end, when Cale is eighteen, Falissa is scarcely there as a personality; she is esteemed by neither son nor husband, in spite of the fact that she is the source of order in the household and on the farm. To her perception, the only roles possible to her are those of self-denying mother, martyred wife, and slave to the house. She resignedly sees that the hopelessness of her own life will be reenacted in that of her daughter, Pearlie, who at fourteen is already an emotionally repressed religious fundamentalist.

Onto her son Cale, by contrast, Falissa projects all the energy of her own lost potential for joy and life, but vicarious fulfillment through the much-desired boy-child is not possible. Her projections help make him self-centered, surly, and, at last, alienated from her. He despises her submission to the abuse of her husband Jerome, and Roe, Jerome's brother, reappears in their lives just when Cale needs a model for his transition to manhood. Although Cale eventually achieves a balanced perspective on Roe's superficially glamorous outlawry, his unwelcome uncle brings Falissa much grief and further alienates her from Cale. Her powerlessness is almost complete.

Wilkinson, then, projects the boy into his future further than she had yet been able to take her girl characters, because his possibilities are not so thoroughly circumscribed as theirs. Although Cale's upbringing is equally cramped, and though he suffers the same dearth of role-models and carries the additional burden of Falissa's transference to him of her own sense of self and wish to be active in the world, he does, since he is male, retain enough self-esteem to imagine that he wants to be an architect, and to be able to fantasize actual ways of developing into this future. He can conceive of getting out, like Roe, but with creative and constructive, not destructive, results. *Cale*, Wilkinson's most ambitious novel at the time of its publication, is also the most flawed in its near-unrelieved dreariness. Cale's characterization has thin places, too: his intelligence, creativity, and general appeal to others is asserted but never convincingly dramatized. The novel is, nevertheless, vivid and valuable, and contributed significantly to Wilkinson's growing power and widening scope as a novelist.

In *Shadow of the Mountain*, an even more ambitious and also more successful novel, the protagonist for the first time moves outside the tight circle of family to try her identity. Jean Fitzgerald, not poor white, but rather of the Carolina aristocracy, has recently left an expensive Southern women's college. She tours Europe and then settles down as a member of the Appalachian Corps to save the mountain people from poverty. Failing to comprehend the cultural chasm that yawns between her and those she is to help, she is baffled by the suspicion and hostility with which she is confronted.

Slowly, her idealism and optimism give way to cold, stony fear as she is first accused of being a Communist (because Leo Tolstoy and Fyodor Dostoevski are on her bookshelf), and later as she becomes the object of the obscene attentions of Leon, the town drunk. After she locks her door against him, and he dies of exposure in a drunken stupor, her "murder" of him leads to her own violent death.

Written in the form of Jean's journal and letters, with occasional interjection of others' thoughts, the novel charts Jean's struggle to define her womanhood. Just as *Cale* indicates that being male does not guarantee a smooth transition into adulthood, so Jean's character indicates that being rich is likewise not the answer. Her mother, a hysterical society matron with superficial values, offers no model for Jean's urge toward self-expression, or for her conviction that she can and should help others. Her worldly father gives her good advice about her physical safety but has no real sympathy for her values and no idea of the nature of her inner life.

Jean also wrestles with her reactions to Jane Boey, whose body she discovers at a mountain lookout; to her college friend, Christina, who dropped out of school to marry an abusive basketball star; and to Molly, a mountain woman who moved from Kentucky to North Carolina when she was in her seventies, bitterly disappointed with life but still facing it with voracious acceptance. Jean sees their fate reflected in the fact that their own experiences absolutely circumscribe their conceptions of reality.

The startling image at the beginning of the novel of the frozen Jane Boey, sitting as if contemplating the valleys that smothered her existence, typifies all the women in the book. Her figure balances the ultimate position of Jean herself, who escapes many dead ends of traditional femininity but whose compulsions trap her at last, as the less privileged women have been trapped.

A major strength of *Shadow of the Mountain* lies in its metaphorical descriptions, which open into multiple layers of understanding. Wilkinson describes the desolate surf on the Outer Banks as "an ocean that is eating away at [the beach] like a starving dog snapping at a carcass." She makes the landscape, as well as the human scenery, speak its own meanings. Her observations draw into reality a wide range of characters, from snake-handling preachers to a highball-sipping grandfather. She gives voice to the kind of nonintellectual rural people who too seldom are credibly presented in contemporary fiction.

Finally, in *Bone of My Bones*, Wilkinson's most recent novel, Ella Ruth Higgins, born the same year as Cale Jenkins in the same North Carolina town, finds a way to incorporate into herself the images of both her parents and thus is able to conceive for herself a creative adult life. Her intelligence and imagination are more fully realized than those qualities are in Cary, Ramie, Falissa Jenkins, and Jean Fitzgerald. At the beginning of the novel, the ten-year-old Ella Ruth avidly writes stories and stows them in a time capsule, made from kindling and lined with red velvet, that she buries all over her yard. By the time she is eighteen at novel's end, the time capsule has become simply her story box, where she files the fictions she systematically, lovingly constructs. She has partially rejected her "good" mother, an obese and emotionally generous caterer who cannot tolerate change, while she partially embraces her "mean" father, who is constricted and cold but who adapts readily to change. The apprentice novelist, alive and believable, transforms not only her parents but also other people in her experience into complex characters she knows are also partly herself. In Ella Ruth's character and its careful development, Wilkinson believably dramatizes the growth of an artist, a hopeful progress which contrasts markedly with the fate of her earlier protagonists.

The emotional dynamics which focus this novel are brought into symbolic coherence in Ella Ruth's fictional account of the world premiere of the play she has written about the family reunion her mother longed for but which never occurred. The two characters in the play are Elisa Ruth, a young mother who accepts all the conventions of femininity and is a reflection of the side of Ella Ruth which sees this as an alternative, and Katella, an old renegade who rejects the conventions and lives an authentic but painful life of her own. Based partly on two patients Ella Ruth knows in the hospital where she works as an aide, and partly on her own conflicting predilections, Elisa Ruth and Katella dramatize two major possibilities for womanhood. Ella Ruth's affirmation of the values of the old woman, whose real-life counterpart was a barroom crony of her father, signifies her acceptance of her father as part of herself. Her rejection of the values of the young woman, Elisa Ruth, who is totally dependent on her husband and on her primary sexual characteristics for her sense of who she is, signifies Ella Ruth's rejection of the aspects of her mother that have been feminized to the point of psychic paralysis. Other-directed and completely overwhelmed by her husband, her kind mother cannot grasp that Ella Ruth is fundamentally different. She urges her daughter to leave her father, get married as quickly as she can, and have her own babies, not seeing, as Ella Ruth does, that this would simply repeat the pattern of entrapment. Escaping her mother's compulsions, Ella Ruth declines conformity to conventional femininity. Unlike Cary and Ramie, who at the end of earlier novels venture toward sexuality, Ella Ruth foils her would-be boyfriend's attempts to manuever her into mothering him. Instead, she consciously chooses the artist's calling and rejects that of the glands.

With each successive novel, Wilkinson has become more inclusive, creating increasingly real and compelling worlds. The range of her characters and the truth of their voices energize her narratives. *Moss on the North Side* and *A Killing Frost* accomplish more completely their modest aims than *Cale* and *Shadow of the Mountain* do their more ambitious goals, but these later novels, despite their flaws, widen the focus of Wilkinson's fiction. With increased explicitness, she deals with the basic issue of sexual identity and the possibility of a woman becoming a productive, developing person in the difficult milieu of twentieth century Southern society. In *Bone of My Bones*, Wilkinson knits psychological insight, clarity of narration, and complexity and range of character into a living fabric. Her most accomplished novel to date, *Bone of My Bones* confirms Wilkinson's continuing growth as an artist and promises rich works to come.

Major publications other than long fiction
NONFICTION: *Change: The Innovative Teaching of English and Social Studies*

in Secondary Schools, 1971 (edited); *The Stainless Steel Carrot: An Auto Racing Odyssey*, 1973.

CHILDREN'S LITERATURE: *Can-Am*, 1981; *Endurance Racing*, 1981; *Formula Atlantic*, 1981; *Formula One*, 1981; *Stock Cars*, 1981; *Super Vee*, 1981; *Automobiles*, 1982; *Champ Cars*, 1982.

Bibliography

Chappell, Fred. "Unpeaceable Kingdoms: The Novels of Sylvia Wilkinson," in *The Hollins Critic*. VIII, no. 2 (April, 1971), pp. 1-10.

Vance, Jane Gentry. "Fat Like Mama/Mean Like Daddy: The Fiction of Sylvia Wilkinson," in *The Southern Literary Journal*. XV, no. 1 (Fall, 1982), pp. 23-36.

_____ . "An Interview with Sylvia Wilkinson," in *The Kentucky Review*. II, no. 2 (1981), pp. 75-88.

Jane Gentry Vance

ANGUS WILSON

Born: Bexhill, England; August 11, 1913

Principal long fiction

Hemlock and After, 1952; *Anglo-Saxon Attitudes*, 1956; *The Middle Age of Mrs. Eliot*, 1958; *The Old Men at the Zoo*, 1961; *Late Call*, 1964; *No Laughing Matter*, 1967; *As if by Magic*, 1973; *Setting the World on Fire*, 1980.

Other literary forms

Angus Wilson started his literary career in 1946, at the age of thirty-three, by writing short stories. The earliest stories were published in *Horizon*. *The Wrong Set and Other Stories* (1949), *Such Darling Dodos and Other Stories* (1950), *A Bit off the Map and Other Stories* (1957) deal with the same problems and use the same imagery as his novels. Wilson also wrote drama; and in the 1970's, he became a leading reviewer of fiction. His literary journalism and criticism for *The Spectator*, *The Observer*, and *London Magazine* center mainly on the problem of the English novel. The range of writers he has discussed in articles, introductions, or lectures is extremely wide and includes, among others, the Victorians, the Bloomsbury Group, Aldous Huxley, D. H. Lawrence, John Cowper Powys, Leo Tolstoy, Fyodor Dostoevski, Irving Shaw, Robert Penn Warren, and William Golding. He also has published three full-length literary monographs: *Emile Zola: An Introductory Study of His Novels* (1952), *The World of Charles Dickens* (1970), and *The Strange Ride of Rudyard Kipling* (1977). Wilson's many lectures and articles display his concern with a wide range of problems relevant to the second half of the century. Most important for the study and understanding of his art is the volume *The Wild Garden: Or, Speaking of Writing* (1963), which contains his lectures given in California in 1960.

Achievements

Most critics agree that by the 1980's, Wilson has secured a place among the most distinguished contemporary British novelists. He is even recognized outside the English-speaking world, particulary France. In the 1960's and 1970's, the number of interviews with the artist increased, signifying his growing recognition among critics. Whether the critics use Stephen Spender's terminology of "modern" and "contemporary," or speak of experimental, psychological, aesthetic, or modern versus the traditional, sociological English novel, they all try to assess Wilson in relation to these categories. Some contend that Wilson's main concern rests with the sociological aspects of human life, but almost all critics concede that his interest goes beyond social issues. Without abandoning his commitment to depicting reality, Wilson has always been committed to probe deeper into the dark depths of the human self. This concern with the inner self separates him sharply from the "angry" writers who also wrote in the 1950's: Kingsley Amis, John Wain, and Alan Sillitoe. Wilson, however, is dedicated to experimenting both in content and method. In his novels and critical writings, he emerges as a champion for a new type of novel, standing between the traditional and the experimental.

Biography

Angus Wilson was born in Bexhill, Sussex, on August 11, 1913, to a middle-class family as the sixth son. His father was of Scottish extraction; his mother came from South Africa, and he spent some time there as a child. In constant financial troubles, his parents tried to maintain pretense and appearance, which left a deep impression on Wilson: at a very early age, he became aware of the chasm separating the real world and the world of fantasy into which many people escape to avoid the unpleasant facts of their lives. Frequently lonely (he was thirteen years younger than his next older brother), he realized that his clowning ability made him popular with the school children. He attended prep school in Seaford; from there he went to Westminster School and then to Merton College, Oxford. While at Oxford University, his history training was on the Marxist line; that fact, and his left-wing political activities in the 1930's, account for his Labour sympathies.

In 1937, he started work at the British Museum and with a short interruption during World War II, he stayed there until 1955. During the war, he was associated with an interservice organization attached to the Foreign Office, and for a while he lived in the country in a home with a Methodist widow and her daughter. During this time, he had a serious nervous breakdown; his psychotherapist suggested creative writing as therapy. In 1946, Wilson rejoined the staff at the British Museum and, at the same time, started writing seriously. His first published writing, the short story "Raspberry Jam" (1946), reflects his personal crisis and foreshadows the dark atmosphere of most of his work to come. The whole experience at the British Museum, situated in London's sophisticated Bloomsbury district and especially his job as Deputy Superintendent at the Reading Room, provided him with an understanding and knowledge of the cultural establishment and of the management of cultural institutions, which he used later in *The Old Men at the Zoo*. Also, observing scholars, book addicts, and eccentric visitors to the Reading Room gave him material for creating some of his fictional characters, such as Gerald Middleton in *Anglo-Saxon Attitudes*.

In 1952, he published his first novel, *Hemlock and After*, and a critical monograph, *Emile Zola*. He gave talks on the novel for the British Broadcasting Corporation that were later published in *The Listener*. In 1955, a contract with Secker and Warburg as well as his ongoing reviewing activity for *The Spectator* and *Encounter* made it possible for him to resign his post at the British Museum. He then retired to the Sussex countryside, thus reviving his childhood garden-dream. As a result of his freedom from job-related responsibilities, he published four novels in a rapid sequence: *Anglo-Saxon Attitudes*, *The Middle Age of Mrs. Eliot*, *The Old Men at the Zoo*, and *Late Call*. Furthermore, his participation in the cultural and literary life of England as a journalist, critic, and lecturer became more extensive. In 1963, he started his association with the University of East Anglia as a part-time lecturer, becoming Professor in 1966. Also in 1966, he became Chairman of the Literary Panel of the Arts Council of Great Britain. In 1967, he lectured at Berkeley California, as a Beckerman Professor and in the same year *No Laughing Matter* appeared.

In 1968, he was made Commander of the British Empire and Honorary Fellow of Cowell College of the University of California at Santa Cruz. He honored the Dickens Centennial in 1970 with *The World of Charles Dickens*. Between 1971 and 1974, he served as Chairman of the National Book League while receiving two more distinctions in 1972, becoming a Companion of Literature and a Chevalier de l'Ordre des Arts et des Lettres, the latter a sign of his growing reputation in France. A sixth novel, *As if by Magic*, appeared in 1973; in it he made use of his teaching experience and involvement with young intellectuals. He continues to live in the country; his many activities include traveling, and his Asian journey resulted in his book *The Strange Ride of Rudyard Kipling*. In 1974, he was John Hinkley Visiting Professor at The Johns Hopkins University and, in 1977, Distinguished Visiting Professor at the University of Delaware; he has also lectured at many other American universities. In 1980, he published another novel, *Setting the World on Fire*. His manuscripts, deposited at the Library of the University of Iowa, provide ample material for future researchers.

Analysis

"Self-realization was to become the theme of all my novels," declared Angus Wilson in *The Wild Garden*. Self-realization does not take place in a vacuum; the process is closely linked with a person's efforts to face and to cope with the world. His childhood experience, among déclassé middle-class people living in a fantasy world, initiated the novelist's interest in the conflict between two worlds and in the possibility or impossibility of resolving the conflict. The rapidly changing scene in England as the Edwardian Age gave way to the postwar 1920's, with the cultural dominance of Bloomsbury, and then to the radical leftist 1930's, impressed on him the urgency of such a search. His encounter with Marxism at Oxford University intensified Wilson's tendency to see the world as one of opposing forces. The dichotomy of town and country, of the classes, and of old and new form the background of Wilson's fiction as the remnants of Edwardian England disappeared and the dissolution of the British Empire left the island nation searching for its place in the modern world.

In *The Wild Garden*, Wilson describes his creative-writing process in terms of a dialectic; he reveals that he "never felt called upon to declare allegiance to either fantasy or realism," but then he adds that "without their fusion I could not produce a novel." Wilson is desperately looking for syntheses to all kinds of conflicts and insists that self-realization is an absolute necessity to achieve them. His own breakdown as well as Sigmund Freud's impact on his generation pushed Wilson in the direction of psychoanalysis and the search for identity. In an age of tension, violence, and suffering, he insists on the necessity of self-realization in order to overcome despair.

Wilson's heroes all have crippled, wasted lives and broken families, and the novelist explores their "cherished evasions." Bernard Sand in *Hemlock and After* has to be shocked into self-knowledge by facing sadism in his own nature; Gerald Middleton, in *Anglo-Saxon Attitudes*, gets a new chance for a satisfactory, if not happy, life in old age when he is ready to resume responsibility as a scholar and to reveal a shameful hoax. Both of these heroes are presented in their private and public lives because, in Wilson's view, both of these aspects of life are equally important to modern man. This view of human life in the dialectic of the private and the public is even more important for Meg Eliot, the heroine of *The Middle Age of Mrs. Eliot*; after many frustrations she emerges at the end of the novel as a career woman. Similarly, Sylvia Calvert in *Late Call* discovers a meaningful [retirement] life of her own, independent of her family.

Wilson is a very "British" writer with a subtle sense for the typical English understatement, while his Hegelian drive for reconciliation of conflicts agrees with the spirit of the traditional English compromise. He is constantly searching for ways to save the remnants of the liberal, humanistic values that have remained dear to him in a world that does not seem to have any use for them. His heroes and heroines, saved from final disintegration, are restored to some kind of meaningful life through self-knowledge and are brought closer to other people in defiance of loneliness and despair.

In his first novel, *Hemlock and After*, Wilson extends the exploration of the theme of self-knowledge to both the private and public life of his hero. The novel is about Bernard Sand's troubled conscience, a most private matter; but Bernard is an important public figure, described as "the country's own ambassador to the world outside," and a successful, self-confident novelist who organizes a subsidized writers' colony, Valden Hall in order to support young talent. Overtly successful, his family life is in shambles. His wife, Ella, lives in "neurotic misery"; his son is a staunch conservative in strong disagreement with Bernard's liberal views; his unmarried daughter, a journalist, feels lonely and unhappy. As an indication of the overhanging disaster, Bernard's first novel is entitled *Nightmare's Image*.

In the title, "Hemlock" suggests poisonous wrong, evil, and even violence.

Poisoning and violence occur in a "massacre of innocence," as related to Eric, Bernard's young homosexual partner, and to the little girl Elzie, whom the disreputable Mrs. Curry wants to make available to Hugh Rose. Wilson deliberately links the fate of the two young people by calling them both "rabbits." Rose and Mrs. Curry strike their deal at the "Lamb" inn.

The word "After" in the title refers to the aftermath of knowledge: self-knowledge. A crucial scene occurs at the end of Book One when a still complacent and self-confident Bernard watches the arrest of young homosexuals at Leicester Square and is shocked suddenly by the discovery that he experienced sadistic enjoyment in watching the terror in the eyes of those youths. This discovery has a devastating effect on Bernard's life and destroys not only him but also Valden Hall. The long-awaited opening of the young artists' colony becomes a total disaster, as its erupting violence grows into a symbol of the modern predicament. Wilson describes the scene as one of chaos, disorder, disappointment, strain, and hostility.

After this startling event, Bernard's life goes downhill very rapidly; self-knowledge paralyzes his will, and he is entirely unable to act. The discovery of sadistic tendencies makes him suspect of his own motives. He realizes with frightening clarity the abyss of the human soul and is driven to utter despair about the motivation behind any action. He has a horrifying vision of the subtle difference between intention and action, and as a consequence, Bernard loses his determination to deal with Mrs. Curry. At the same time, Ella almost miraculously recovers from her nervous breakdown and, after Bernard dies, acts on his behalf in arranging efficient management at Valden Hall and a prison sentence for Rose and Mrs. Curry. Rose commits suicide in prison, while Mrs. Curry earns an early release with her good behavior. It is briefly indicated that she might continue her former activity; thus the Epilogue ends the novel on an ambiguous note of qualified optimism.

The title *Anglo-Saxon Attitudes*, derived from *Alice's Adventures in Wonderland* (1865), suggests a typically English atmosphere; it is Wilson's most Victorian novel, a broad social comedy. At the same time, it displays experimental technique in the use of the flashback, which provides all the background to Gerald Middleton's crisis in his private and public life. The hero, a sixty-year-old failure, is a historian. In the beginning of the novel, sitting by himself at a Christmas party given by his estranged wife, Inge, Gerald overhears broken sentences of conversation that remind him of the most significant episodes of his life. Wilson makes it very clear that self-knowledge is important for Gerald; it is both a psychological need to him and a matter of "intellectual honesty," a duty to the professional community of historians.

Gerald's crisis of conscience concerns a cruel hoax that occurred back in 1912 when he participated with a team in an excavation. Young Gilbert Stokeway, a disciple of T. H. Hulme and Wyndham Lewis and the son of the leader of the team, put a fake idol in the tomb under research at Melpham.

His hoax was successful, and the fake came to be hailed as a pagan idol. At that time, Gerald was a Prufrock-like antihero: disabled physically by a sprained ankle, and disabled emotionally by his love for Gilbert's wife, Dollie. His affair with her played an important role in his silence about the fake idol. Gerald's feelings of guilt center on "the two forbidden subjects of his thoughts," his marriage and the hoax. His life, "rooted in evasion," appears to him empty, meaningless, and futile. His professional career fell victim to his decision not to reveal the hoax. Because of his affair with Dollie, he evaded dealing with Inge's inefficiencies as a mother.

In fact, none of the minor characters has a happy, self-fulfilling life. While Gerald still believes in the liberal tradition, neither of his sons adheres to his beliefs. His elder son, Robert, a businessman, stands rather to the right and the younger son, John, is a radical; and they have violent clashes whenever they meet. Both sons are unhappy in their personal relationships as well. Robert is married to the conventional Marie-Hélène but loves the more modern Elvira Portway. John has a short-lived homosexual relationship with an unruly young Irishman, Larry, who is killed in a wild drive in which John loses a leg. Gerald's daughter, Kay, has a serious crisis in her marriage to the smart right-wing young sociologist, Donald. Wilson employs specific imagery to drive home to the reader the overwhelming atmosphere of frustration of all these people. Expressions such as "flat and dead" and "deadly heaviness" abound, referring to the behavior of people at parties when communication is impossible. Gerald's house is "noiseless as a tomb," and during the Christmas party at Inge's the "Norse Goddess," all those present "shivered" in spite of the central heating.

Realizing the failure of his family, Gerald has to admit that he is to take the blame; when he selected Inge to be his wife, he decided for second-best. Yet, at the end, Gerald manages to pull himself out of his dead life. By revealing the hoax, he succeeds in restoring his professional status, and after a long silence, he becomes active again in research. The novel, however, like *Hemlock and After*, ends on a note of qualified optimism as Gerald remains estranged from his family. The picture of Gerald's life, combined with the divergent subplots, reveals a world in which relationships do not last, where options are limited.

Critics believe that they can recognize Wilson in most of his central characters; the novelist, however, admits the connection only in the case of Meg Eliot, the heroine of his third novel, *The Middle Age of Mrs. Eliot*. "Meg," he says, "is in large part modelled on myself," while David Parker's nursery recalls to Wilson childhood memories of a garden of a friendly family.

Meg Eliot, a well-to-do barrister's childless, worldly, spoiled wife, experiences sudden tragedy when her husband dies from a gunshot wound as he tries to protect a local minister. The novel depicts Meg's nervous breakdown and painful recovery: her journey to self-knowledge. She is first revealed to be holding desperately to her old friends; yet, their lives are no more secure than hers. Lady Pirie in her "decaying genteel jail" is preoccupied with her son only; Bohemian Polly Robinson lives a kind of "animated death"; and Jill Stokes is obsessed with the memory of her dead husband. These "lame ducks" cannot help Meg nor can drugs. Meg's brother, David Parker, who runs the nursery with his homosexual partner, is sheltered in the pleasant quiet atmosphere which suggests a return to lost innocence. Yet, Wilson is ambiguous about the validity of the garden image since David's nursery is commercial, an irony in itself. Meg cannot share her brother's life-style, his abnegation of action and the human world. Wilson does not censure David for his contemplative life-style, but it is evident that he prefers Meg's choice "to be with people!"

Meg is determined to find meaning in life, in a life with people. Her story is strikingly reminiscent of George Eliot's heroines; similar to them, she used to live in self-delusion and is shocked into consciousness by the "remorse of not having made life count enough" for her husband. Moreover, again like the Victorian woman, she returns to a fuller life. Two factors are important in her recovery. First, she refuses any kind of opium, a George Eliot ideal; second, she is determined to build herself a meaningful, useful life. While she admits that she "used to be Maggie Tulliver," she also resembles Gwendolen Harleth from *Daniel Deronda* (1876). She shares with her an unhappy childhood and the horrors of remorse, but she shares also in Gwendolen's way of redemption. Like the Victorian heroine, Meg too had to learn in a painful way that the outside world could intrude into her life at any time and destroy it if she is taken unaware. As she takes a paying secretarial job, Meg is full of confidence in her farewell letter to David: "At any rate in a few years at least, the modern world won't be able to take me by surprise so easily again."

From the omniscient narrator of his early works, Wilson shifts to a more modern device in *The Old Men at the Zoo* by creating a first-person narrator in Simon Carter. In the beginning of the novel, Simon is a gifted, dedicated yet disabled naturalist, very much like Gerald Middleton at the time of the excavation. He is prevented from continuing research in Africa because of amoebal dysenteria. He joins the London Zoo as an administrator at a crucial time when the zoo itself becomes a battleground of conflicting ideas, reflecting a conflict of values in British politics. Wilson creates an armed conflict between England and Allied Europe, followed by a Fascist invasion of England when all standards of civilized behavior collapse and give way to brutality. When the war breaks out, the Fascists want to put on a spectable with prisoners of war fighting the zoo animals. Simon is horrified, but as he later tries to drive the animals to safety, he finds himself killing his favorite badgers to feed a boy and his mother.

Almost an antihero, trying to avoid any kind of involvement with people, an administrator following orders, Simon emerges at the end of the novel ready to face the world, to be involved with people, even running for director. Because of his loyalty to the zoo under three different administrations, representing three different political ideologies, some are inclined to view him as a Vicar of Bray. In the twentieth century, however, many people had to face Simon's fundamental dilemma: whether to follow orders or to take up independent responsibility. Simon's American-born wife, Martha, disapproves of his behavior; she would like him to give up his job. Simon refuses, saying, "What do you think I am, a weathercock?" There is cruel irony in this remark; however, Wilson's irony is not pointed at Simon but rather at the general human predicament of a rapidly changing world in which choices are limited and people are continuously bombarded with dilemmas.

Simon's only independent action is his attempt to save the animals, which ends in disaster. In him, Wilson presents modern man struggling with despair in a desperate race to catch up with challenges. Simon's painful adjustment commands respect; he almost achieves heroic status when, after all the horrors and violence, he describes this modern world as "a demie-paradise." In this sense, *The Old Men at the Zoo* is Wilson's least pessimistic novel.

No Laughing Matter is one of Wilson's most complex novels and requires close reading. The narrative is interwoven with dramas, enacted by the characters and reflecting various dramatic styles, including the absurd. Pastiches and parody of writers are important features of the novel, and literary references abound. A *Forsyte Saga*-like family chronicle of the Matthews family, the novel is also a historical document covering the twentieth century to 1967. The father, Billy Pop, a Micawber of the twentieth century, is a failure in his writing profession and ineffectual in his family life, letting his selfish wife dominate the children. All six of them have a crippled childhood and are deprived of privacy. By the end of the novel, they all achieve some kind of success in their professional lives; some even attain fame, such as Rupert, the actor, and Quentin, the political journalist, later a celebrated television commentator. Success does not make him lovable and his cynicism enjoyed by a million common viewers questions the role of the media.

The final scene, in 1967, brings the whole clan together. While Margaret and her brother Marcus, a homosexual art dealer, are discussing and quarreling about Margaret's art, and Hassan, who will inherit Marcus's cooperatively run scent factory, makes a final statement; the last words of the novel. He considers Marcus's ideas of a cooperative absurd. Hassan admires "ambition, high profit and determined management." His coldly calculating, ruthless thoughts cast a dark shadow on the future; they underline once again Wilson's skepticism about the survival of liberal humanistic ideals in the modern world.

A strong moral sense links Wilson to George Eliot, and his sense of the caricature and the grotesque shows affinities with his favorite author, Charles Dickens. At the same time, his fiction is full of experiments into new literary methods. With almost each novel, Wilson made an important step forward in his search for new techniques. Tragedy and laughter coexist in his novels; there is tragedy in the private lives of the characters, but Wilson has a grotesque view of man's behavior, and his ability to create atmosphere through concentrating on speech habits promotes laughter.

In his commitment to duty, in his moral seriousness, Wilson is definitely akin to George Eliot, but he differs from the Victorian in that he cannot believe in "meliorism." George Eliot firmly maintained that self-awareness would lead to self-improvement and in consequence, to the individual's improved performance in the human community. Wilson is much more skeptical. Like E. M. Forster, he, too, is painfully aware of the decline of liberal hopes. In *The Middle Age of Mrs. Eliot*, he came to the sad conclusion that "self-knowledge had no magic power to alter," and in his sixth novel, he killed magic with finality.

In *As if by Magic*, magic, the ultimate evasion, is destroyed forever for the two central characters. Moreover, this time they are not middle-aged or elderly intellectuals paralyzed by frustration; they are young people. Wilson's teaching experience in Britain and America caused him to concentrate on the young, the future generation. Hamo Langmuir is a dedicated young scientist on a worldwide fact-finding tour to study the benevolent affects of his "magic" rice, destined to solve the problem of starvation in underdeveloped countries. His goddaughter, Alexandra Grant, in the company of her fellow hippies, is also on a world tour in search of an occult answer to all human problems. A bewildered Hamo must find out that his magic rice solution has introduced a farming method for which natives are not yet prepared and, consequently, it is causing more damage than good. Hamo falls victim to the anger of a crowd at a moment when he is ready to get involved in the human aspects of research. He, like Alexandra, who gets to Goa at the same time, had to learn through experience that the intrusion of Western ways into radically different cultures can cause disruption and many unnecessary tragedies. At the end of the novel, a sober Alexandra, cured of her hippie ways, resumes the responsibility of building a normal life for her son, a legacy of the hippie venture. A millionaire through an inheritance, she is ready to support and subsidize food research, but she knows by now that the possibilities are limited and that no easy answers are available; magic of any kind is only for the neurotics who are unable to face reality or for the power-hungry who use it to dominate others.

Wilson's concern with human nature and with what it means for the future of the world dominates *Setting the World on Fire*. This novel is a family chronicle like *No Laughing Matter* but more condensed, more limited in time (1948-1969) and in the number of characters. Indeed, the writer concentrates on two brothers, Piers and Tom, the last generation of an old aristocratic family. Literary references are replaced by other arts: theater, music, architecture, and painting. Piers hopes to dedicate his life to the theater, and as a promising student, he earns the admiration of family, friends, and teachers with his stage-managing and directing abilities. The final part of the novel is about the preparations for the first performance of a new play, with the younger brother Tom supporting Piers as best he can in the hectic work. Everything is set for success when, unexpectedly, Scotland Yard intervenes and orders the premises emptied because of a bomb threat. The author of the play, an old employee of the family, masterminded the plot, simultaneously aimed at the family and at the government.

Tom saves Piers's life by knocking him down, but he himself gets killed. On his way home from the hospital where Tom died, Piers is on the verge of a breakdown and about to give up hope as well as artistic ambitions, because what good are the wonders of art in "a chaotic universe"? He calms down, however, and decides to stage the play anyway; he must not "lose the power to ascend the towers of imagination," he says. The tragedy brought Piers to a fuller realization of his duty as an artist, which means doing the only thing left to him: to create in, and for, a world threatened by chaos, violence, and destruction.

Wilson, a mixture of a twentieth century Charles Dickens, George Eliot, and E. M. Forster, and with his increasingly dark vision of the modern predicament, rededicates himself, the artist, to his moral obligation. He continues writing in a desperate attempt to impose some kind of order on chaos and, by making men aware, to try to save mankind from itself.

Major publications other than long fiction

SHORT FICTION: *The Wrong Set and Other Stories*, 1949; *Such Darling Dodos and Other Stories*, 1950; *A Bit off the Map and Other Stories*, 1957; *Death Dance: 25 Stories*, 1969.

PLAY: *The Mulberry Bush*, 1956.

NONFICTION: *Emile Zola: An Introductory Study of His Novels*, 1952; *For Whom the Cloche Tolls: A Scrapbook of the Twenties*, 1953 (with Philippe Jullian); *The Wild Garden: Or, Speaking of Writing*, 1963; *Tempo: The Impact of Television on the Arts*, 1964; *The World of Charles Dickens*, 1970; *The Strange Ride of Rudyard Kipling*, 1977.

Bibliography

Faulkner, Peter. *Angus Wilson: Mimic and Moralist*, 1980.
Grandsden, K. W. *Angus Wilson*, 1969.
Halio, Jay. *Angus Wilson*, 1964.
Wogatzky, Karin. *Angus Wilson: "Hemlock and After," A Study in Ambiguity*, 1971.

Anna B. Katona

ETHEL WILSON

Born: Port Elizabeth, South Africa; January 20, 1888
Died: Vancouver, Canada; December 22, 1980

Principal long fiction
Hetty Dorval, 1947; *The Innocent Traveller*, 1949; *The Equations of Love*, 1952; *Lilly's Story*, 1953; *Swamp Angel*, 1954; *Love and Salt Water*, 1956.

Other literary forms
Eleven short stories and eight essays by Ethel Wilson were published in magazines between 1937 and 1964. Two of the stories, "Hurry, Hurry!" and "Mrs. Golightly and the First Convention," were later anthologized, and two others, "I Just Love Dogs" and "The Window," were selected for *Best British Short Stories of 1938* and *Best American Short Stories: 1959*, respectively. These four stories, three of the others, and one of the essays, along with nine stories and an essay not previously published, were collected in *Mrs. Golightly and Other Stories* (1961). Besides the stories and essays, seven excerpts from novels also appeared separately as short stories in magazines. One of these, "Miss Tritt," from *The Equations of Love*, was anthologized as a short story.

Achievements
Wilson was among the Canadian authors of the 1930's who broke away from the frontier tradition of provincial and didactic romances. She adapted to Canadian backgrounds the universal themes and methods of the realistic and psychological novel. She was one of the first Canadians to achieve a critical reputation abroad, not indeed as a major novelist, but certainly as an important minor one. Her novels are in the main current of the British and French realistic tradition, especially that of the early twentieth century, showing affinities with the works of E. M. Forster, Virginia Woolf, Arnold Bennett, Ivy Compton-Burnett, and Marcel Proust. Nevertheless, she maintained strong individuality in both theme and form. She wrote that authors can be "endangered by the mould or formula becoming apparent, and then the story has no life." Without being innovative, therefore, her novels have a great deal of variety of theme and approach, so that they are difficult to classify.

Perhaps because Wilson did not attempt to follow literary trends, and perhaps also because she began publishing relatively late in her life, when she was nearly fifty, her works did not have a dramatic impact on Canadian letters. She was publishing out of her generation, and her realism and understatement seemed somewhat old-fashioned to those authors of the 1930's who were following naturalistic trends. Still, she was influential in raising the quality of the art in Canada and in quietly introducing the theme of women "finding themselves" in some sense, well before the theme became popular among feminists. Her heroines are not necessarily strong or aggressive but they mature, meet the vicissitudes of their lives with determination and ingenuity, and for the most part succeed in small but important ways. Wilson's treatment of this theme and her impeccable craftsmanship contributed significantly to the maturing of the novel in Canada.

Biography

Ethel Davis Wilson was born in Port Elizabeth, South Africa, on January 20, 1888, to Robert William Bryant and Lila (Malkin) Bryant. Her mother died when she was only two, and her father took her to Staffordshire, England, to be reared by her maternal grandmother and successive aunts and uncles. Her family members were involved in a number of literary activities, including reading, journalism, and translation, and were acquainted with Matthew Arnold and Arnold Bennett. This literary atmosphere no doubt stimulated her interest in letters, and the literary allusions and quotations in her works demonstrate a comprehensive familiarity with the English tradition. Her father died when she was ten, and she went to Vancouver, British Columbia, to join her grandmother, who had moved there. Many of these family and early personal experiences are recounted in *The Innocent Traveller*, the semibiographical novel based on the life of her aunt.

In Vancouver, Wilson attended Miss Gordon's School, but she was sent to Trinity Hall School in Southport, England, for her secondary education. In 1907, she was graduated from Vancouver Normal School with a Second Class Teacher's Certificate. Between 1907 and 1920, she taught in Vancouver elementary schools.

On January 4, 1921, Wilson married Dr. Wallace Wilson. Their marriage was a happy one, marked by a good deal of traveling in Canada, Europe, and around the Mediterranean, and the successful development of both their careers. Dr. Wilson became a respected physician; he studied internal medicine in Vienna in 1930, represented Canada at the British Medical Association's convention in 1938 and at the World Health Organization in Paris in 1947, and was president of the Canadian Medical Association in 1946 and 1947. The relationship between the Wilsons may have provided details for the happy marriages and the deepening love relationships in *Hetty Dorval*, *Lilly's Story*, and *Love and Salt Water*. The love of travel is also obvious in her work; travel is healing, broadening, and sensitizing to her characters, and Wilson's ability to describe the essential atmosphere of various locales is one of her strongest attributes.

Wilson published her first short story in 1937, and another in 1939 before her career was interrupted by World War II. Although Dr. Wilson was in the Canadian Army and Wilson herself served by editing a Red Cross magazine between 1940 and 1945, she made little use of wartime experiences in her novels, except tangentially in *The Innocent Traveller* and *Love and Salt Water*.

Only the short story "We Have to Sit Opposite" deals specifically with wartime problems.

It is likely that Wilson's career in writing was encouraged by ill-health. She was a victim of arthritis, which by 1956 had become so severe that she could not walk around in London, as she described in her essay "To Keep the Memory of So Worthy a Friend." She wrote, "One of the advantages of being lame is that one can sit and think. . . . And so I often think and think." In her last three novels, several major characters suffer handicaps, either physical or psychological, which affect their relationships with others in various ways and which must be transcended. No doubt her own disability enabled her to interpret this theme sympathetically.

The late 1940's and the 1950's were Wilson's most productive years, all of her novels and most of her short stories and essays being written or published during that period. At the peak of her success, after the publication of *Swamp Angel*, she received three awards: an honorary doctorate from the University of British Columbia in 1955, a special medal from the Canada Council in 1961 for contributions to Canadian Literature, and the Lorne Pierce Gold Medal from the Royal Society of Canada in 1964.

Dr. Wilson died in 1966, and Ethel Wilson lived in retirement in Vancouver until her death in 1980.

Analysis

Although Ethel Wilson's canon is small, it is of high quality. The writing style is direct, simple, and expressive. Only occasionally, in the early books, does the diction or syntax call attention to itself as excellent. In general, only if one should try to paraphrase a passage or change a word would he become aware of that rightness of style that is typical of an artist. Passages describing the beauty of nature are most immediately impressive. Wilson's account of the train journey of the Edgeworths across Canada to Vancouver, in *The Innocent Traveller*, offers a vivid impression of the countryside and evokes the haunting vastness of the plains and forests stretching northward from the train track to the arctic circle. Magnificent descriptions of the Northern Lights occur in more than one book, and the mist-shrouded or sun-brightened mountains of the Vancouver area are sketched with a sensitive pen. Less frequent but equally impressive are descriptions of unsightly scenes, such as the interior of the slovenly Johnson apartment in *Tuesday and Wednesday* (published in *The Equations of Love*). It is not only in description, however, that Wilson excels; her humor is deft, ironic, and humane in passages such as the chapter "Nuts and Figs," from *The Innocent Traveller*, in which Great-Grandfather Edgeworth, in his declining days, proposes to two worthy lady friends in one afternoon and is refused, to the gratification of all three. Thoughtful and philosophical passages are also subtly presented, so that except for a few intrusive statements in the early, less integrated books, the concepts are suggested through economical language and apt symbols.

For Wilson, nature is not only a major inspiration for description, but also a method of characterization. Most of her protagonists are close to nature. Their ability to love and the essential civilization of their emotions are measured by their appreciation of the beauties and dangers of the Canadian mountains, forests, and waters. One notable exception is the garrulous Topaz Edgeworth, who exists in her human relationships rather than in nature, and the other is Hetty Dorval, an antagonist, whose appreciation of nature is one of the deceptive charms of her evil. Wilson's characters are firmly rooted in their environments and grow out of them. Her attitude toward them is dispassionately empathetic; they are clearly and humorously drawn, with subtle complexities. All are believable, and the best of them are memorable. She develops understanding of even her most unsympathetic characters, to the extent that plot is often weakened because she is drawn into digressions about the characters, about whom she cares more than she cares about careful plot structure. Topaz Edgeworth, Nell Severance, Lilly Hughes, and Maggie Lloyd are her most convincing creations, and it is the success of their characterization which causes *The Innocent Traveller*, Lilly's Story, and *Swamp Angel* to be her best novels.

If style and characterization are what make Wilson's novels outstanding, the plots are what keep them from being great. Plotting appears always to have been difficult for Wilson. Her admirers defend the inconsequentiality of her plots as true to life, expressing a philosophy about the fortuitous connections, or lack of connections, between the events in a person's history. Wilson minimizes suspense as a plot device; in fact, she often uses a technique of revealing future events, since causality interests her more than suspense. Still, the novels that are most effectively plotted, *Lilly's Story* and *Swamp Angel*, are recognized to be her best.

The title of Wilson's third book, *The Equations of Love*, suggests her recurring themes as a novelist. The typical protagonist of a Wilson novel is orphaned or otherwise separated from her family, as Wilson herself was as a child. Deprived of parental love, she becomes independent but lonely. This typical protagonist usually takes a journey, which is both a literal "trip"— aboard ship or into the Canadian wilderness—and an interior voyage of self-discovery. She is both soothed and awed by her insignificance in the natural world, which is beautiful but indifferent. Out of her new self-awareness, she learns to give of herself and to build a relationship, usually but not necessarily marriage, that brings new meaning to her life, either happiness or philosophical maturity. Love is the solution to this symbolic orphanhood, yet love, too, is imperfect. Orphanhood leaves its mark, and people make do with various "equations of love." This sense of irrevocable loss, of necessary compromise, saves Wilson's love-stories from sentimentality without veering toward cynicism. There is nobility in the aspiration toward love and self-subordination, triumph in even the flawed achievement of those graces. Wilson is impressed by the human ability to transcend egotism through whatever equation of love is possible to each individual.

For a first novel, *Hetty Dorval* is exceptionally good, although a melodramatic climax undercuts the subtleties of its characterization. It introduces Wilson's recurring themes: orphanhood, egotism, and love; the tempering of the ego by nature or travel; the lasting impact of momentary impressions or casual coincidences; the emotional maturation of a young woman. It is the story of Frances Burnaby, and the influence of Hetty Dorval on her maturation. Hetty crosses Frankie's path only a half-dozen times, but the temptation that she represents is very strong. The two are parallel in certain important respects: both are only children, and both are reared with considerable protection and privilege. Both are attracted by elements of wildness, such as the turbulent Thompson River and the flight of wild geese. Frankie, however, has been reared by her parents with friends and loving discipline. By contrast, Hetty's illegitimate mother, Mrs. Broom, has hidden her maternal role, and with it her model of a loving relationship, to give Hetty a superior social standing: she has pretended to be Hetty's nurse and later her lady's maid, so that Hetty has learned tyranny and self-indulgence. Hetty is seraphically beautiful, with selfish charm, concerned only with her own pleasures. Frankie's mother calls her "The Menace" even before she knows Hetty's full story. Hetty's beauty and charm and her elemental wildness attract Frankie as a child. Even though the younger girl gives up the older woman's friendship, in obedience to her parents' orders, she does not understand the evil in Hetty's character. As she grows up and gains experience, however, in each subsequent contact with Hetty she learns more and comprehends more fully the destructiveness of Hetty's egotism. Frankie's full comprehension of what is morally wrong with Hetty's way of life comes when Richard Tretheway, the man she loves, falls in love with Hetty, and she has to decide what action she should take.

Three of the major characters in the story are orphaned: Frankie loses her father during the course of the story; Richard has lost his mother before Frankie meets him; and Hetty is a psychological orphan, having no publicly acknowledged father or mother. Each has dealt with the problems of isolation in a different way. Frankie grows to love the Tretheway family and builds new familial relationships with them; Richard has tried to substitute as a mother to his younger sister Molly; and Hetty has turned to self-indulgence and the collection and abandonment of men. Each of these compensatory behaviors is one possible equation of love, but Hetty's is not honest or giving. The traits in Frankie's character that are similar to Hetty's are finally subordinated in Frankie as she learns to love. Although Hetty comments near the end of the book about their kinship, Frankie has moved beyond Hetty in self-control and compassion, and has thus ended her egocentric solitude.

Wilson's second novel, *The Innocent Traveller*, is a radical departure from her archetypal plot line. Topaz Edgeworth is not a solitary orphan, but a beloved child in a large and close family. Family is an all-pervasive concept throughout the book; characters are designated according to their role in the family, which changes as they age. Father becomes Grandfather and finally Great-Grandfather Edgeworth. Topaz herself is defined successively in terms of child, daughter, sister, aunt, and great-aunt. Topaz does lose her mother when she is young, but Father marries Mother's sister, and the family continues with virtually imperceptible interruption. Topaz continues to live with her father until she is middle-aged, and after his death, she lives with her older sister in much the same role of dependent daughter. Even with the death of the sister, she lives with her niece in virtually the same role, as if she were daughter to her niece. Although she moves to Canada, the wilderness does not impress her, nor does the new environment broaden her sympathies. *The Innocent Traveller* is a happy book, Topaz a happy woman, with a sense of warmth and security very different from the solitary mood of the other novels. Complementing this happy mood are glowing descriptions of the English and Canadian landscapes and sensitive expressions of a generous, witty, and perceptive philosophy.

What this book contributes to analysis of Wilson's thematic development is the contrast it provides with her recurring story of orphanhood and reconciliation. Topaz is never orphaned; she also never matures. Topaz is characterized as a delightfully irrepressible child, a lovable nonconformist, but gradually (and only between the lines), an irresponsible eccentric, and finally an irritating, futile burden on her family. She is loved, but she does not love deeply in return; she is an affectionate family member, but she does not feel the needs and tragedies of others. She remains childishly egocentric to the last of her life. After her death, "there is no mark of her that I know, no more than the dimpling of the water caused by the wind . . . and when we met together . . . perhaps no one remembers, until afterwards, to mention her name." The contrast between Topaz and Wilson's typical orphaned protagonists is striking. Topaz is never independent and never feels solitary; therefore, she never comes to value loving relationships. She never goes off alone to come to terms with herself and her universe; therefore, she never comes to terms with society. She never feels insignificant in nature; therefore, she never feels the need to establish significance through commitment and love. Having realized these themes from the converse and happy side, Wilson was prepared to use them more powerfully in *The Equations of Love* and *Swamp Angel*.

Tuesday and Wednesday, a novella, the first part of *The Equations of Love*, deals with grotesque and pitiable "equations" in a mood of dark humor or satire. It is the story of the marital reelationship of Myrt and Mort Johnson, no longer a marriage of love, but an equation of shared resentment and frustration, lightened by moments of sensuality and a habitual tender impulse. Mort is shiftless, envious, self-deceived, but good-natured and capable of friendship. Myrt is self-pitying, domineering, lazy, sporadically sensual, often spiteful, but kind when it is no trouble to be kind. They live apart from most human contacts; Mort is too feckless and Myrt too lazy to entertain. They have no family except one aunt and one orphaned cousin, Victoria May Tritt, to whom they are indifferently kind because she is even more lonely and repressed than they are. This kindness passes in her mind as beneficence, and her gratitude constitutes a kind of love for them. Mort has a friend, Eddie, whom Myrt dislikes because of his drinking and brawling, but the two men share a bond of camaraderie and wishful thinking. These are the relationships which pass for love in the seedy near-slums of the city.

One evening, Mort meets Eddie, drunk; during a search in the dark for Eddie's lost suitcase, the inebriated Eddie falls off a pier and drowns. Mort, in his efforts to save his friend, falls into the water and is dragged under by Eddie to his death. Witnesses testify to Eddie's drunkenness, and the police conclude that both men were drunk, reporting the accident to Myrt in those terms. In her typical spite and self-pity, Myrt is not grieved, but affronted by Mort's drinking, abandoning her, and damaging her reputation by his association with the brawling Eddie. To salvage her self-esteem, she bitterly adopts the role of martyr. Victoria May has seen the meeting of Eddie and Mort, however, and knows that Mort was not drunk. In her love for both Myrt and Mort, she tells not only that part of the story but also the fiction that Mort dived after Eddie in a heroic attempt to save his friend. Thus, in her love for this unlikely pair, she both redeems Mort and comforts his wife by recalling Myrt's love for Mort, restoring her self-esteem, and establishing her right to grieve.

Even though *Tuesday and Wednesday* is darkly satirical, the story is in some ways the clearest of Wilson's statements about the success, however flawed, of the human drive for love as a solution to loneliness. Antagonistic though they may be, Myrt and Mort nevertheless love each other in their own way and cling together against their isolation. Mort's love for Myrt, with so little to thrive on, is sad and admirable. Myrt's need for Mort to pierce the shell of her egotism is believable and moving. Victoria May is almost heroic in her lie for Mort. Such unsatisfactory substitutes for love are pitiable, but they transcend the dingy and uninspiring atmosphere in which these characters live.

Lilly's Story, the second half of *The Equations of Love*, approaches the equations in a more positive way, although the heroine begins even more unpromisingly than Myrt and Mort. Lilly is an abandoned child, growing up like an alley cat. Never having experienced love, she expects none, and her first equation of love is the lust she excites to acquire food and stockings from men. Running away from the police, she gets a job as a waitress in a small town some distance from Vancouver and finds another equation of love, a man who provides her some temporary security, like "a kennel into which a bitch crawls." When this man leaves, and she finds she is pregnant, she goes to another small town farther into the wilderness and gets a job as a maid.

In this new environment, Lilly knows love for the first time, her love for her baby; and for her baby's sake, she invents a dead husband and behaves with such circumspection that she earns the respect of the couple whom she serves. Respect is a new equation of love. In this wilderness location, she also learns a new identification with nature which she could not have known in the slums of Vancouver. She lets Eleanor grow up in touch with this natural environment. Lilly also admires the pretty home and gentle manners of her employers, and she allows Eleanor, her child, to receive training from Mrs. Butler, determined that Eleanor will have a better life than her own. Eventually, Lilly leaves the Butlers and finds employment as housekeeper in a hospital. She and the Matron become close friends, and Lilly begins to build relationships that are overcoming her circle of self-protection. Eleanor grows into a lady and goes to nursing school, where she meets and marries a young lawyer. It is from this marriage that Lilly learns what love can be and what she has missed, when she sees Eleanor "come up to her husband with her face raised, and on her face a revealed look that Lilly had never seen on Eleanor's face nor on any face. . . . She had lived for nearly fifty years, and she had never seen this thing before. So this was love, each for each, and she had never known it." Soon after this, a threat from Lilly's past drives her to Toronto, where she meets a widower and marries him, not with the passion that she has observed in Eleanor, but at least with "the perfect satisfaction which is one equation of love."

Lilly could be another Mrs. Broom (*Hetty Dorval*), but instead of hiding her motherhood and spoiling her child, Lilly drags herself out of that egocentric circle in order to prevent egocentrism in Eleanor, and in so doing, she finds loving relationships which almost transform her. Lilly starts off too badly and is too warped by her orphanhood ever to be totally transformed by love, but at least her story is a triumph of the power of love over egocentrism.

Maggie Lloyd, is triply solitary: the protagonist of *Swamp Angel*, her mother died when she was a baby, her young husband in the war, and her baby and her father shortly thereafter. Maggie, unlike Wilson's other orphaned heroines, is never trapped in egocentrism by her loneliness. She has too much giving in her nature, and makes a second marriage out of compassion. Her story opens when she leaves that mistaken equation of marriage and goes into the wilderness, not to find but to reestablish herself. She finds a job as cook and assistant manager to a fishing lodge owner who has been lamed and can no longer manage alone. His wife, Vera, is the orphan in this story who has been warped and damaged by her loneliness.

Vera finds no comfort in the beauty of the wilderness that restores Maggie after her separation. Vera, to the contrary, longs to return to the city from which she came, and instead of building new relationships that might redeem her, she nags at her husband and grows jealous of his admiration for Maggie. She eventually tries to commit suicide but cannot, and the story ends with Maggie trying to think how to break through Vera's egocentrism to help her. Another pair of "orphans" in this story are Maggie's friends Nell Severance and her daughter Hilda. Although their story constitutes a subplot, in some ways they are more important to the theme than is Vera. Nell is a widow who has had more than her share of excitement and romance. She used to be a juggler on the stage, and she met and married a man she loved deeply. Because of her career and eventful marriage, however, she neglected Hilda to the extent that Hilda has always felt a degree of isolation and alienation from her mother. Nell's loved memento from her past life is a small revolver, the Swamp Angel, which was part of her juggling act. Hilda has always resented the revolver, as it reminds her of her neglect as a child, but she has never told her mother of her feelings: this is her gift of love to her mother. Nell is aware of Hilda's aversion to the gun, although she does not know the reason; one day she boxes it and sends it to Maggie: this is her gift of love to her daughter. Hilda goes away on a vacation, and comes back with new self-knowledge and recognition of her love for Albert Cousins, whom she marries not long before Nell dies. Thus, she builds new relationships to end her sense of solitude. These are very loving relationships, successful resolutions to the problems of isolation.

Swamp Angel makes use of two important symbols which specify more clearly than any of Wilson's earlier books the meanings of wilderness/egotism and orphanhood/love. While in the wilderness, Maggie goes swimming. She feels happy, strong, elemental, and in control of her movements. She can swim wherever she wishes; she is alone and completely independent. She also realizes, however, that this feeling is an illusion: she is not a god. The water is sensual and comforting, but it could drown her as impartially as it now buoys her. She swims back to her boat and returns to the lodge, to the things of civilization and the friends she serves in her job. The other key symbol is the Swamp Angel itself. It is a symbol of Nell's past, and she clings to it until she realizes that it makes Hilda uncomfortable. She gives it to Maggie to discard, reflecting that the symbol is less important than the reality, which cannot be taken away, but which grows less important as she grows nearer to death. Like the water in which Maggie swims, the gun symbolizes independence and control, but it also symbolizes egotism. In giving it away, Nell severs herself from the past in order to build a better relationship with her daughter. Unlike Maggie and Nell, Vera clings to her past, cannot find herself in nature, and so cannot build loving relationships with her husband and son. She tries to drown herself in the same lake where Maggie swims and where she throws Nell's gun.

Ethel Wilson's books can be summed up as minor masterpieces of style, insightful, witty, believable, and intelligent. They are prevented from being major works by faults in plotting, and they have not had a great influence upon literary trends. Nevertheless, they are all readable and entertaining, and the best are compelling. They deserve renewed attention in this age of increased receptivity to literature by and about women.

Major publications other than long fiction
SHORT FICTION: *Mrs. Golightly and Other Stories*, 1961.

Bibliography
Clarke, Rita. "Appearance and Reality in the Fiction of Ethel Wilson," 1964 (dissertation).
Livesay, Dorothy. "Ethel Wilson: West Coast Novelist," in *Saturday Night*. LXVII (July 26, 1952), pp. 20, 36.
Pacey, Desmond. *Ethel Wilson*, 1967.
_____ . "The Innocent Eye: The Art of Ethel Wilson," in *Queen's Quarterly*. LXI (Spring, 1954), pp. 45-52.
Sonthoff, H. W. "The Novels of Ethel Wilson," in *Canadian Literature*. XXVI (Autumn, 1965), pp. 33-42

Carol I. Croxton

P. G. WODEHOUSE

Born: Guildford, England; October 15, 1881
Died: Long Island, New York; February 15, 1975

Principal long fiction

The Pothunters, 1902; *A Prefect's Uncle*, 1903; *The Gold Bat*, 1904; *The Head of Kay's*, 1905; *Love Among the Chickens*, 1906; *The White Feather*, 1907; *Not George Washington*, 1907 (with Herbert Westbrook); *The Swoop: How Clarence Saved England*, 1909; *Mike: A Public School Story*, 1909; *The Intrusion of Jimmy*, 1910; *Psmith in the City: A Sequel to "Mike,"* 1910; *The Prince and Betty*, 1912; *The Prince and Betty*, 1912 (different book from previous title); *The Little Nugget*, 1913; *The Man Upstairs*, 1914; *Something New*, 1915; *Uneasy Money*, 1916; *Piccadilly Jim*, 1917; *The Man with Two Left Feet*, 1917; *My Man Jeeves*, 1919; *Their Mutual Child*, 1919; *A Damsel in Distress*, 1919; *The Little Warrior*, 1920; *Indiscretions of Archie*, 1921; *The Clicking of Cuthbert*, 1922 (published in the United States as *Golf Without Tears*, 1924); *Three Men and a Maid*, 1922; *The Adventures of Sally*, 1922 (published in the United States as *Mostly Sally*, 1923); *The Inimitable Jeeves*, 1923 (published in the United States as *Jeeves*); *Leave It to Psmith*, 1923; *Ukridge*, 1924 (published in the United States as *He Rather Enjoyed It*, 1926); *Bill the Conqueror: His Invasion of England in the Springtime*, 1924; *Carry On, Jeeves*, 1925; *Sam the Sudden*, 1925 (published in the United States as *Sam in the Suburbs*); *The Heart of a Goof*, 1926 (published in the United States as *Divots*, 1927); *The Small Bachelor*, 1927; *Meet Mr. Mulliner*, 1927; *Money for Nothing*, 1928; *Mr. Mulliner Speaking*, 1929; *Fish Preferred*, 1929; *Very Good, Jeeves*, 1930; *Big Money*, 1931; *If I Were You*, 1931; *Doctor Sally*, 1932; *Hot Water*, 1932; *Mulliner Nights*, 1933; *Heavy Weather*, 1933; *Thank You, Jeeves*, 1934; *Right Ho, Jeeves*, 1934 (published in the United States as *Brinkly Manor*); *Blandings Castle: And Elsewhere*, 1935; *The Luck of the Bodkins*, 1935; *Young Men in Spats*, 1936; *Laughing Gas*, 1936; *Lord Emsworth and Others*, 1937 (published in the United States as *Crime Wave at Blandings and Other Stories*); *Summer Moonshine*, 1937; *The Code of the Woosters*, 1938; *Uncle Fred in the Springtime*, 1939; *Eggs, Beans and Crumpets*, 1940; *Quick Service*, 1940; *Money in the Bank*, 1942; *Joy in the Morning*, 1946; *Full Moon*, 1947; *Spring Fever*, 1948; *Uncle Dynamite*, 1948; *The Mating Season*, 1949; *Nothing Serious*, 1950; *The Old Reliable*, 1951; *Barmy in Wonderland*, 1952 (published in the United States as *Angle Cake*); *Pigs Have Wings*, 1952; *Ring for Jeeves*, 1953 (published in the United States as *The Return of Jeeves*, 1954); *Jeeves and the Feudal Spirit*, 1954 (published in the United States as *Bertie Wooster Sees It Through*, 1955); *French Leave*, 1956; *Something Fishy*, 1957 (published in the United States as *The Butler Did It*); *Cocktail Time*, 1958; *A Few Quick Ones*, 1959; *How Right You Are, Jeeves*,

1960; *The Ice in the Bedroom*, 1961; *Service with a Smile*, 1961; *Stiff Upper Lip, Jeeves*, 1963; *Biffen's Millions*, 1964; *The Brinkmanship of Galahad Threepwood*, 1965; *Plum Pie*, 1966; *The Purloined Paperweight*, 1967; *Do Butlers Burgle Banks?*, 1968; *A Pelican at Blandings*, 1969 (published in the United States as *No Nudes Is Good Nudes*, 1970); *The Girl in Blue*, 1970; *Much Obliged, Jeeves*, 1971 (published in the United States as *Jeeves and the Tie That Binds*); *Pearls, Girls and Monty Bodkin*, 1972 (published in the United States as *The Plot That Thickened*, 1973); *Bachelors Anonymous*, 1973; *Aunts Aren't Gentlemen*, 1974 (published in the United States as *The Cat-Nappers: A Jeeves and Bertie Story*); *Sunset at Blandings*, 1977.

Other literary forms

In addition to writing more than ninety novels, P. G. Wodehouse wrote hundreds of short stories, some eighteen plays (of which ten were published), the lyrics for thirty-three musicals, and a vast, uncollected body of essays, reviews, poems, and sketches. So much of Wodehouse's early work has been lost that it is impossible to measure his total literary output, and collections of his stories published under the title "Uncollected Wodehouse" are likely to appear with some frequency for the next twenty years. He also wrote two comic autobiographies, *Performing Flea: A Self Portrait in Letters* (1953) and *America, I Like You* (1956).

Achievements

Wodehouse has always been regarded as a "popular" writer. The designation is just. "Every schoolboy," wrote Ogden Nash, "knows that no one can hold a candle to P. G. Wodehouse." His novels and short stories were among the best-selling works of their generation, but it should be remembered that Wodehouse's appeal transcended his popular audience. Many of the major writers of the twentieth century have professed a deep admiration for the art of "Plum," as Wodehouse was known to his friends and family. T. S. Eliot, W. H. Auden, Bertrand Russell—all were fanatic enthusiasts of Wodehouse. Hilaire Belloc said that he was the greatest writer of the twentieth century, and Evelyn Waugh offered the following tribute to his genius: "Mr. Wodehouse's idyllic world can never stale. He will continue to release future generations from captivity that may be more irksome than our own." It is unfortunately true that critics and readers who expect high seriousness from their literary pleasures will never quite approve of one who makes a light-hearted mockery of most of England's and America's most sacred cows. F. R. Leavis, the celebrated English scholar, pointed to the awarding of an honorary doctorate to Wodehouse as proof of declining literary standards. Other critics have been even more emphatic in their deprecation of Wodehouse's lack of seriousness. For sheer enjoyment, however, or what Dr. Johnson called "innocent recreation," no one can touch P. G. Wodehouse.

Biography

Pelham Grenville Wodehouse was born in Guildford, Surrey, on October 15, 1881, the third of four sons born to Henry Ernest and Eleanor Deane Wodehouse. Wodehouse's father was a member of the English Civil Service and spent most of his working years in Hong Kong; indeed, it was a mere chance that Wodehouse was not born in Hong Kong. Whether it was miscalculation or the event was premature, his birth occurred during one of his mother's rare and rather brief visits to England.

Wodehouse was reared away from his parents; they were, he often remarked, like distant aunts and uncles rather than parents. Wodehouse entered Dulwich College at the age of twelve and remained there for the next six years. The school was not prominent in the sense that Harrow and Eton were prominent; it was simply a good middle-class school. The headmaster was the most impressive figure, and may have served as the model for Wooster's nemesis, the Reverend Aubrey Upjohn; the headmaster was not impressed with his student. He once wrote to Wodehouse's parents: "He has the most distorted ideas about wit and humour. . . . One is obliged to like him in spite of his vagaries." The vagaries, apart from the student's drawing match figures in his classical texts, are unrecorded. In those final years at Dulwich, Wodehouse had found his vocation. He was appointed editor of the school paper and sold his first story to a boy's weekly, *The Public School Magazine*. The story won first prize for fiction in that year.

Following graduation in 1900, Wodehouse went to work for the London branch of the Hong Kong and Shanghai Bank. His work there was not a complete disaster for the banking industry, but very nearly so. Wodehouse was no good at checks and balances and served only as an unpleasant distraction for those who were. At night, he continued to write fiction and reviews or plays and was given a position on the *Globe* in 1902, the year the first of his many novels was published. *Punch* accepted an article from him the next year, and a second novel was also published in 1903. From that time, Wodehouse averaged more than a novel, several short stories, and either a play or musical a year. In 1914, Wodehouse married Ethel Rowley, a widow with one child. The marriage was a happy one, and the author frequently expressed his gratitude to his wife for the support she had given to his work. For the Wodehouse reader, however, the following year had a much greater significance: *Something New*, the first of the Blandings novels, was published. A few years later, *My Man Jeeves* (1919) appeared, the first of the Jeeves and Wooster saga.

Novels and stories appeared with an unfailing regularity, and in the next two decades, Wodehouse became an acknowledged master. In 1939, Oxford paid tribute to his greatness by conferring on him the honorary Doctorate of Letters (D.Litt.). The doctorate meant that Jeeves, Wooster, Emsworth, and the rest were accepted as part of the heritage of English literature. The London

Times supported the Oxford gesture, noting that the praise given to Wodehouse the stylist was especially apt: "Style goes a long way in Oxford; indeed the purity of Mr. Wodehouse's style was singled out for particular praise in the Public Orator's happy Horatian summing up of Mr. Wodehouse's qualities and achievements."

Wodehouse and his wife had lived in France throughout much of the 1930's, and though war with Germany was believed imminent, he returned to France after he received the doctorate at Oxford. In 1940, he was taken prisoner by the Germans. In various prison camps, he made a series of broadcasts over German radio which were interpreted as a form of collaboration with the enemy. Wodehouse was innocent of all the charges, but it was perhaps his innocence, the vital ingredient in most of his heroes, that almost undid him. The closest Wodehouse came to collaboration was his remark to the effect that he was not unhappy in prison, for he was able to continue his work. One scholar has called that broadcast "clearly indiscreet," but those who have read the Wodehouse letters know that he scarcely thought about anything else beside his work.

After his release, Wodehouse eventually returned to America, where he took permanent residence; he was naturalized in 1955. In 1973 he was knighted, and he died in 1975 at the age of ninety-four.

Analysis

Few of P. G. Wodehouse's novels are ever far from the school environment, for the plots of the later Jeeves and Blandings series of novels frequently derive from the desire of one schoolmate, usually Bertie Wooster, to help another. Yet the early school novels represent a distinct type within the body of Wodehouse's fiction. Perhaps, as one scholar has observed, these eight school novels are no more than "bibliographical curiosities," in that only the most ardent fan of Wodehouse would be led to read them after the later work had been written. Still, the works are different in tone and theme. The novels are set at Wrykyn College, which seems to closely resemble Dulwich, the author's alma mater. The emphasis is on sports, and this emphasis gives a serious tone to the work. Boys are measured largely by their athletic skills. One might suggest that the ever-present sports motif was a symbol of the particular virtues of youth: comaradeship, loyalty, and perseverance. Enlarging upon these virtues, Wodehouse was following what was almost a cliché in the boy's fiction of the time. The cliché, however, was one particularly congenial to the author, who once noted that he would never be able to write his autobiography, for he had not had one of the essentials in the background of an autobiographer—"a hell of a time at his public school."

Wodehouse loved Dulwich College, and the eight school novels are a record of his affection. The schoolmasters are a decent group, the boys with few exceptions are generous and loyal, and the setting of the college is one of great beauty. The distinctive element in the novels is the happiness which pervades them, and the reader need only remember George Orwell's, Graham Greene's, and Evelyn Waugh's accounts of their own school days to notice the sharp difference between Wodehouse and many of his contemporaries. The only curiosity about the novels is not the absence of horror and malice, but that no one in the school novels seems to have learned anything at Wrykyn. It should also be remembered that many of Wodehouse's most celebrated idiots are graduates of Oxford and Cambridge.

Wodehouse once said of his work: "I believe there are two ways of writing novels. One is mine, making a sort of musical comedy without music and ignoring life altogether." The Blandings series of novels is perhaps the best example of the author's determined resistance to "real life." These twenty-odd novels are centered on the beautiful estate of Lord Emsworth, who serves as unwilling host to almost everyone who goes in and out of his ancestral home. Lord Emsworth is old and absentminded, and his affections are limited to his younger brother Galahad, his roses, and his pig, the Empress of Blandings. This pig, as Emsworth remarks several times in each of the novels, has won the silver prize for being the fattest in Shropshire County. Only Galahad can really appreciate the high distinction that has been conferred on the Empress, and one feels that even he is not very serious about the pig. Yet the Empress is very nearly the catalyst for all of the actions that take place in the novels. She is stolen, which makes it imperative to effect a rescue; she is painted an outrageous color and introduced into strange bedrooms to make the recipients of such favors "more spiritual" in their outlook; and on one occasion, her portrait is done at the behest of Lord Emsworth.

This last episode in the life of the Empress occurs in one of the best of the Blandings novels, and is a fair measure of the formula used by Wodehouse in the series. *Full Moon*, in which the portrait is commissioned, has all of the characteristics of the Blandings novels. Emsworth has the insane idea that the pig's portrait should be done by an eminent painter, but they have all turned down his request. While this action is debated, Lady Constance, Emsworth's sister, has come to the castle with a young lady in tow. Her intent is to keep the young woman away from the man to whom she has become foolishly engaged, foolishly because the fellow does not have any money, which is the essential requisite for a good marriage in the mind of Lady Constance. Galahad arranges to have the young man invited to the castle on the pretext that he is Edwin Landseer, celebrated painter of animal pictures, including "Pig at Bey." Galahad's ruse works for a while, but the young man's painting is rejected by Emsworth, who complains that the painting makes the Empress look as if she had a hangover. The young man is ejected from Blandings but soon returns, wearing a beard resembling an Assyrian monarch. He makes a tragic mistake when he gives a love note to one of Emsworth's other sisters, thinking that she is a cook. He is again thrown out. By the novel's end, however, he has successfully won the hand of his beloved, and the sisters are all leaving the estate. Galahad has once more succeeded in spreading "sweetness and light" in all directions, except that of his usually irate sisters.

There are few variations in the Blandings series. At least one and sometimes as many as three courtships are repaired; the pig is safe from whatever threatens it; the sisters have been thwarted in usually about five ways by Galahad; and Lord Emsworth has the prospect of peace and quiet in front of him at the novel's end. Yet Emsworth, Galahad, the sisters, and a host of only slightly less important or interesting characters are among the most brilliant comic figures in the whole of English literature. In writing the Blandings novels, Wodehouse followed his own precept: "The absolute cast-iron rule, I'm sure, in writing a story is to introduce *all* your characters as early as possible—especially if they are going to play important parts later." Yet his other favorite maxim that a novel should contain no more than one "big" character—is seldom observed in the Blanding's series. Each of the characters has his own element of fascination, and each is slightly crazy in one way or another. As absurd and funny as is Lord Emsworth's vanity about his pig, it is only a little more so than his sisters' vanity about their social position and wealth. If the formula for this series does not vary, neither does the uniform excellence of each novel in the series.

There are more than a dozen novels which use Jeeves and Bertie Wooster as the main characters. These novels have commonly been regarded as Wodehouse's "crowning achievement," but the author once noted that the idea of the latent greatness of Jeeves came to him very slowly. In his first appearance in a short story, he barely says more than "Very good, Sir." Jeeves is the manservant to Bertie Wooster, who is preyed upon by aunts, friends, and women who wish to help him improve his mind as a prerequisite to marriage with him. Wooster has been dismissed as silly and very stupid. Compared to Jeeves, perhaps he is both, but he is also extremely generous with both his money and time, and it is his unfailing willingness to help others which invariably places him in the precarious situation which is the main plot. Wooster is an Oxford graduate, but detective novels are most demanding reading. He never uses a word of more than two syllables without wondering whether he is using the word properly. Wooster is the "big" character in the Jeeves series, and such a character, according to Wodehouse, is worth "two of any other kind."

The marriage motif is very much a part of the Wooster and Jeeves saga, but frequently the central issue of this series is helping Bertie keep away from the wrong woman. It is not quite accurate to describe him as one of "nature's bachelors," for he has been engaged to nearly a score of females and is threatened with marriage in nearly every one of the novels in the series. Some of these women are insipid and poetic, others are coarse and athletic; the worst are intellectual women who want to improve his mind. He is assigned books to read which he finds boring and incomprehensible, told never to laugh aloud, and threatened, after marriage, to have his membership in the Drones Club revoked. Bertie is quite content with the state of his mind and soul. At the threat of marriage and all the other threats that the novels present, Jeeves comes to the rescue. In spite of Bertie's chronic need of Jeeves' aid, he is ostensibly the main character in the novels and one of Wodehouse's most brilliant creations. It is through the eyes of Bertie that the reader observes and passes judgment on what is taking place in the novel. Such a process was an enormous technical difficulty for his creator: Wooster must be stupid and generous in order for the plot to develop, but not so stupid that the reader casts him off.

The character of Jeeves, perfect as it is, is one of the most traditional aspects of Wodehouse's craft, for the wise servant of a stupid master is a hoary cliché. Jeeves has never been to Oxford, and he has no aristocratic blood flowing in his veins to spur him into action. His central motive for rescuing Bertie and the legions of others who come to him for counsel is a manifestation of what is called in this series of novels "the feudal spirit." Though not a university man, Jeeves knows French, Latin, and the whole of English literature. He quotes freely from the Shakespearean tragedies, and even has at his disposal a host of obscure lines from obscure poets in Latin and English. He is not a gloomy person, but Benedictus de Spinoza is his favorite author. He is well acquainted with psychology, and his rescue of Bertie or others in trouble frequently derives from his knowledge of the "psychology" of the individuals in question. He is moved by the feudal spirit, but he is tipped in a handsome way by his employer for services rendered, and he accepts the just praises of all whom he serves.

The series is also distinguished by a host of lesser figures who threaten to jostle Bertie out of his role as the main character. Gussie Fink-Nottle is an old schoolmate of Bertie, and he is engaged to a particularly insipid woman, Madelaine Basset, a romantic intellectual. She has a poetic phrase for every-thing, and drives Bertie and all who know her crazy merely by opening her mouth. Madelaine is one of Bertie's ex-girl friends, and she imagines that Bertie is still in love with her. The hero's duty is to see that the pending nuptials between Gussie and Madelaine take place, but Gussie, who is even less intelligent than Bertie, keeps fouling things up. Bertie goes at once to his aid, but nothing works until Jeeves puts his brain to the trial.

Jeeves never fails in his destined role as guardian angel to Wooster, but the plots frequently have an additional twist. Jeeves, though not omniscient as a character, has recourse to a body of information that none of the others shares. As a butler and member of a London club for butlers, he has access to a private collection of anecdotes supplied by other butlers about their masters. It is a point of honor for a manservant to supply all vital information

about his employer—tastes, eccentricities, and even weaknesses—so that others will be well advised before taking employment with the same person. The ·
collection has something about almost every rich male in England, and when affairs take on a desperate note, Jeeves is dispatched to London to find out something about the adversary that might serve as blackmail. Thus, one of the silliest of Wodehouse's creations, a proto-Fascist named Spode who is inclined to bully everyone and especially Wooster, is disarmed when it is discovered that he designs ladies' underwear. As Wooster is being threatened with decapitation by Spode, he mentions the name of Spode's company, *Eulalie Soeurs*, and the man is silent and servile, though it is only at the very end and with the bribe of a trip around the world that Jeeves tells Wooster the meaning of that magic phrase.

The Jeeves novels, then, have at least three plots running through them, and it is in his scrupulous concern for the development of the plot that the author exhibits one of his greatest talents. The key to Wodehouse's concerns for the logic and probability of his plots derives, perhaps, from his lifelong interest in detective novels; Wodehouse frequently avowed that they were his favorite kind of reading. The plots of the great Wodehouse comedies develop like that of a superb mystery: there is not an extraneous word or action in them.

For most Wodehouse readers, the Blandings and Jeeves series of novels represent the highest level of Wodehouse's art, but there are many other novels that do not fit into either category. In 1906, Wodehouse published *Love Among the Chickens*, which has in it the first of Wodehouse's several "nonheroes," Ukridge. Ukridge has almost no attractive qualities. He does not work; rather, he lives by his wits and is able to sponge off his friends and from many who scarcely know him. Another character who figures prominently in several novels is Psmith. The name is pronounced "Smith," and its owner freely admits that he added the *P* to distinguish himself from the vast number of Smiths. The name is one mark of the young man's condescending arrogance, but he is helpful toward all who seek his assistance. A Psmith novel usually ends with the marriage of a friend or simply a bit of adventure for the central figure. Psmith does not hold a regular job, and like many of the other young male protagonists in a Wodehouse novel, he seems to be a textbook study in the antiwork ethic. The heroes in the Psmith series, like the central figure himself, are not ignorant or stupid men, but the novelist's emphasis is on their old school ties and on physical excellence. They are, as one critic noted, "strong, healthy animals." They are good at sports and they triumph over poets and other intellectual types. On occasion, they may drink heavily, but they make up for an infrequent binge by an excess of exercise.

Evelyn Waugh once suggested that the clue to Wodehouse's great success was the fact that he was unaware of the doctrine of original sin. In the Wodehouse novel, virtue is inevitably triumphant, and even vice is seldom punished with anything that might be called severity. In Wodehouse's catalog of bad sorts, one group alone stands out: intellectual snobs. In his frequent descriptions of such types, Wodehouse may have consciously been responding to the disdain with which intellectuals have usually treated his work; in turn, the author had almost no sympathy for the group that he often described as "eggheads." Whatever may have been his motivation, the athletes and the innocents invariably triumph over those who carry on about their own minds or some esoteric art form. It is therefore hard to agree with critics such as George Orwell who find elements of snobbery in the Wodehouse novels. It is true that the creator of Blandings Castle loved big houses and grand vistas, but the aristocrats are too obviously flawed in intellect or temper for any to assume Wodehouse was on their side. It may be, however, that Wodehouse was an inverse snob in his treatment of intellectuals, both male and female. None of them succeeds in his fiction.

There is nothing like a consensus over the source or qualities of Wodehouse's greatness as a writer. Scholars have traced Wooster and Jeeves back through English literature to authors such as Ben Jonson, but source studies do not account for Wodehouse's genius. He has been called the laureate of the Edwardian age, but there is little resemblance between the Edwardian world and that of P. G. Wodehouse. For most readers, the triumph of a Wodehouse novel is in its artistry of presentation. All the aspects of fiction— good story, effective characters, and dialogue which is often brilliant—are present. Wodehouse once summed up his career as well as anyone ever has: "When in due course Charon ferries me across the Styx and everyone is telling everyone else what a rotten writer I was, I hope at least one voice will be heard piping up: 'But he did take trouble.'" Wodehouse did indeed take trouble with his work, but given the rich abundance of that work and the incredible smoothness of each volume, the reader would never know.

Major publications other than long fiction

SHORT FICTION: *Tales of St. Austin's*, 1903; *Mulliner Omnibus*, 1935 (revised as *The World of Mr. Mulliner*, 1972); *Dudley Is Back to Normal*, 1940; *Selected Stories*, 1958; *The Golf Omnibus: Thirty-One Golfing Short Stories*, 1973; *The World of Psmith*, 1974.

PLAYS: *Hearts and Diamonds*, 1926 (adaptation with Laurie Wylie); *The Play's the Thing*, 1927 (adaptation); *Good Morning, Bill*, 1928 (adaptation); *A Damsel in Distress*, 1930 (adaptation with Ian Hay); *Baa, Baa, Black Sheep*, 1930 (with Ian Hay); *Leave It to Psmith*, 1932 (adaptation with Ian Hay); *Candlelight*, 1934 (adaptation); *Anything Goes*, 1936 (with others); *The Three Musketeers*, 1937 (with Clifford Grey and George Grossmith); *Carry On, Jeeves*, 1956 (adaptation).

NONFICTION: *William Tell Told Again*, 1904 (with additional fictional material); *The Globe "By the Way" Book: A Literary Quick Lunch for People*

Who Have Got Five Minutes to Spare, 1908 (with Herbert Westbrook); *Louder and Funnier*, 1932; *Performing Flea: A Self-Portrait in Letters*, 1953 (revised as *Author! Author!*, 1962, W. Townend, editor); *America, I Like You*, 1956 (revised as *Over Seventy: An Autobiography with Digressions*, 1957).

MISCELLANEOUS: *Hethuen's Library of Humour: P. G. Wodehouse*, 1934; *A Century of Humour*, 1934 (edited); *The Best of Modern Humor*, 1952 (edited with Scott Meredith); *The Week-End Book of Humor*, 1952 (edited with Scott Meredith); *Bring on the Girls: The Improbable Story of Our Life in Musical Comedy, with Pictures to Prove It*, 1953 (with Guy Bolton); *The World of Jeeves*, 1967; *A Carnival of Modern Humor*, 1967 (edited wtih Scott Meredith).

Bibliography

Hall, Robert. *The Comic Style of P. G. Wodehouse*, 1974.

Jason, David. *P. G. Wodehouse: Portrait of a Master*, 1974.

Usborne, Richard. *Wodehouse at Work*, 1963.

Vaugh, E. "An Act of Homage and Reparation of P. J. Wodehouse," in London *Sunday Times*. July 19, 1916, pp. 21-23.

Voorhees, Richard. *P. G. Wodehouse*, 1966.

John R. Griffin

THOMAS WOLFE

Born: Asheville, North Carolina; October 3, 1900
Died: Baltimore, Maryland; September 15, 1938

Principal long fiction

Look Homeward, Angel, 1929; *Of Time and the River*, 1935; *The Web and the Rock*, 1939; *You Can't Go Home Again*, 1940; *The Short Novels of Thomas Wolfe*, 1961.

Other literary forms

During his lifetime Thomas Wolfe published four major works: two novels, *Look Homeward, Angel* and *Of Time and the River*; a collection of short stories, *From Death to Morning* (1935); and his description of his life as a creative artist, *The Story of a Novel* (1936). In addition to his major works, he also sold a few lengthy stories to magazines; *Scribner's Magazine* published "A Portrait of Bascom Hawke" (April, 1932) and "The Web of Earth" (July, 1939). Both of these have since been republished as short novels in *The Short Novels of Thomas Wolfe* (1961), a collection edited by C. Hugh Holman. Because Wolfe viewed each piece of his writing as only a part of some larger design, he frequently adapted past material to meet a present need. For example, he modified "A Portrait of Bascom Hawke" for later inclusion in *Of Time and the River*, and "The Child by Tiger" (1937), a short story he published in the *Saturday Evening Post*, appeared two years later with changes in point of view in *The Web and the Rock*. After his death, Wolfe's editor at Harper's, Edward Aswell, put together three posthumous books from two large packing cases of unfinished manuscript that Wolfe left behind. Two of these books—*The Web and the Rock* and *You Can't Go Home Again*—are novels; the third is a volume of stories, entitled *The Hills Beyond* (1941). Wolfe began his career (unsuccessfully) as a playwright with *The Mountains*, which he wrote in 1920 but which was not published until 1940 by the University of North Carolina at Chapel Hill, Wolfe's alma mater. *Thomas Wolfe's Purdue Speech* (1964), delivered by Wolfe in 1938, is a statement of his development as an artist. Wolfe's letters and notebooks have also been published, allowing for first-hand insight into his personal and creative life.

Achievements

Wolfe captured the essence of what it meant to be young in his time with the publication of *Look Homeward, Angel*. He further influenced readers of the Depression-plagued 1930's with stories he published in magazines such as *The New Yorker*, *Harper's Bazaar*, *Redbook*, *Scribner's Magazine*, and the *Saturday Evening Post*. Widely read in America and abroad, Wolfe was a well-respected author during his lifetime, a man who in a very real sense lived the part of the driven artist. Wolfe is still read, even if not to the extent of his more significant contemporaries, Ernest Hemingway, William Faulkner, and F. Scott Fitzgerald. In retrospect, Wolfe's achievement is especially remarkable when one considers that his literary life spanned little more than a decade. In 1957, Faulkner ranked Wolfe above all of his contemporaries: "My admiration for Wolfe is that he tried the best to get it all said; he was willing to throw away style, coherence, all the rules of preciseness to try to put all the experience of the human heart on the head of a pin." Wolfe's weaknesses are now recognized, but he is still praised for his strengths. A balanced view of his work has emerged, and his reputation as an important figure in twentieth century American literature is secure.

Biography

Born on October 3, 1900, in Asheville, North Carolina, Thomas Wolfe was the youngest of the seven surviving children of Julia Elizabeth Westall and William Oliver Wolfe. Of Pennsylvania Dutch-German stock, Wolfe's father was a man of intense vitality, a stonecutter who instilled in Wolfe a love of language, whether it be the high rhetoric of Elizabethan poetry or the low vernacular of the mountain people surrounding Asheville. Wolfe's mother was more attuned to the values of commerce than her husband (she was forever speculating in real estate). In fact, one biographer has termed the match an "epic misalliance." Domestic relations in the Wolfe household were often strained; young Wolfe grew up a witness to his father's drunken rampages and his mother's ensuing resentment. From this family cauldron came much of the autobiographical material Wolfe poured forth in *Look Homeward, Angel*.

In September of 1912, Wolfe entered the North State Fitting School, where he came under the influence of his teacher, Margaret Roberts (Margaret Leonard in *Look Homeward, Angel*). Roberts encouranged Wolfe's voracious appetite for reading by introducing him to the best of English literature. In 1916, at the precocious age of fifteen, Wolfe entered the University of North Carolina at Chapel Hill. Six feet tall and still growing (he would eventually reach six feet six inches), Wolfe was a skinny, long-legged youth, sensitive to the criticism of his older classmates. Wolfe's first year at Chapel Hill was unremarkable, but he eventually made a name for himself as an excellent student and a campus literary figure. In March of 1919, *The Return of Buck Garvin*, a play Wolfe had written in a dramatic writing course, was performed by the Carolina Playmakers, with Wolfe performing in the title role.

After graduating in 1920, Wolfe entered Harvard University to pursue his interests as a playwright. He was especially attracted by the famous workshop given by playwright George Pierce Baker (whom he would later depict as Professor Hatcher in *Of Time and the River*). Wolfe hoped to make a literary name for himself, but after a series of setbacks, he accepted an appointment as an Instructor in English at the Washington Square College of New York University and began teaching in February of 1924, continuing to do so intermittently until 1930.

In October of 1924, Wolfe made his first trip to Europe. Many of his experiences there he later incorporated into *Of Time and the River*. Returning to New York in August of 1925, Wolfe met Aline Bernstein, a wealthy married woman who was involved in the theater world of New York. For the next seven years, Wolfe participated in a stormy on-and-off again affair with Bernstein, who was seventeen years his elder. She was the mother-mistress Wolfe seemed to need; certainly, she inspired *Look Homeward, Angel*, which he commenced while abroad with Bernstein in July of 1926.

The popular image of Wolfe as a literary lion is in part caused by the critical success he achieved with *Look Homeward, Angel*, but mostly owing to his personal appearance and habits. Often dressed in shabby clothes, he was known to prowl the streets of Brooklyn, where he had settled after another trip abroad in 1931. One night while wandering the streets he was overheard to say, "I wrote ten thousand words today! I wrote ten thousand words today!" Although Wolfe resented efforts to publicize his eccentricities, it was inevitable that his behavior and fame would make him a legendary figure.

In December of 1933, Wolfe began work on what was to become *Of Time and the River*. It was also during this period that Maxwell Perkins, Wolfe's editor at Scribner's, worked closely with the author on the formation of the novel. Wolfe incorporated his experiences at Harvard, in Europe, and with Bernstein into *Of Time and the River*, which picks up the Eugene Gant story where *Look Homeward, Angel* concludes. In 1937, after critics had raised questions concerning Perkins' influence on his work, Wolfe left Scribner's for Harper and Brothers. His editor at Harper's was Edward C. Aswell, and Wolfe left two large crates containing nearly a million words of manuscript with him before leaving on a tour of the West in May of 1938. In July, Wolfe fell ill with pneumonia and was hospitalized near Seattle. In September, having been transferred to The Johns Hopkins Hospital in Baltimore, he underwent brain surgery for complications he suffered from tuberculosis. He died on September 15, 1938.

Analysis

Throughout Thomas Wolfe's fiction there is evidence of a powerful but sometimes uncontrolled mind at work. Few would argue Wolfe's genius, but many have questioned how well he directed it. Part of the difficulty may have come from his self-professed intention to create an American mythology. The result would be the record of an individual, lonely and lost in the flux of time, forever exploring the diversity of American life. Partly because of his early death and partly because of his own difficulties in giving form to ideas, Wolfe never managed to unify the vast body of his work. Add to this the considerable amount of influence his editors exerted upon his manuscripts, and there still remain some intriguing questions about the interrelationship of segments in the writings and the final form of his novels.

Wolfe wrote with passionate intensity, producing vast quantities of manuscript. His central themes focus on a lonely individual, the isolated artist, in search of self-discovery and the true meaning of the American experience. In *Look Homeward, Angel*, the first of these themes is most pronounced, for this is autobiography very thinly veiled. The story of Eugene Gant is in many ways the story of Thomas Wolfe. After the publication of *Look Homeward, Angel*, which was generally well-received, some critics began to raise questions concerning the novel's weaknesses, especially the obvious attempt by Wolfe to capture experience at the expense of artistic control. It was not until 1936, however, that the landmark case against Wolfe would be launched with the publication in the *Saturday Review* of "Genius Is Not Enough," Bernard DeVoto's indictment of Wolfe and his fiction.

DeVoto was responding to *The Story of a Novel*, Wolfe's extremely frank account of his own life as a writer and the work that went into *Of Time and the River*. For Wolfe, writing was a chaotic experience, something done with great pain and toil. DeVoto acknowledged that Wolfe was a genius "of the good old-fashioned, romantic kind, possessed by a demon, driven by the gales of his own fury, helpless before the lava-flood of his own passion"; he further argued, however, that such genius was in and of itself not enough. Today the legacy of DeVoto's remarks remains manifest in a series of stereotypes: by some readers (especially academics), Wolfe is still thought of as one who never controlled his rhetoric, as one who was unable to organize his work, and as one who sometimes pushed autobiography to the limits of reporting.

To illustrate Wolfe's lack of rhetorical restraint, DeVoto pointed to *Of Time and the River*, commenting that Wolfe invested each experience he described with so much raw emotion that a midnight snack took on the same importance as the death of Oliver Gant. As DeVoto stated, "If the death of one's father comes out emotionally even with ham-on-rye, then the art of fiction is cockeyed." As for the charge that Wolfe was a writer who never exerted sufficient control over his material, DeVoto and others have cited the sprawling sections of his mammoth novels where there is supportive evidence that episodes stand by themselves rather than in relation to others. The extent of Wolfe's involvement with his editors (Maxwell Perkins at Scribners from 1928 to 1937; Edward Aswell at Harper's from 1937 to 1938) also raises questions about his own ability to revise and organize his novels.

Perhaps the most revealing example of editorial influence on Wolfe's fiction concerns *Of Time and the River*. While Wolfe was working on the novel, Perkins met with him day and night for more than a year in an attempt to help him gain control over the voluminous amount of material he had written. Often Perkins would ask Wolfe to go home and cut a section, only to find that he would return with an episode thousands of words longer. In one of the most dramatic decisions any editor has made with a figure as significant as Wolfe, Perkins, without Wolfe's final approval, sent the manuscript of *Of Time and the River* to the printer in September of 1934. Perkins made the decision because he felt the novel was as complete as Wolfe could make it and that Wolfe needed to get on with other work. Whatever the reasons, the ultimate responsibility for the publication of any book rests squarely upon the writer. Because Wolfe was so deferential to his editor and because he was unable or unwilling to see his novel through to the end, he opened himself to questions concerning his craftsmanship, questions which are still being asked today.

Finally, there remains the issue of autobiography in Wolfe's novels. Wolfe himself claimed that autobiography was a part of any serious creative work, but there are in his novels, especially *Look Homeward, Angel*, sections that read like a mere diary. There is also a great deal of artistic invention in his novels, and certainly almost all writers use material based on their own experiences; nevertheless, many of Wolfe's depictions were so thinly fictionalized that individuals were easily recognized, and many were hurt and embarrassed by what they thought were the unflattering portraits Wolfe rendered of them. Wolfe's use of autobiography pushed to journalistic limits raises more questions about his fictional method.

Although Wolfe's rhetoric, his conception of structure, and the autobiographical element within his work have been discussed as weaknesses, these three elements can also be cited as the strengths of his writing. For example, it is true there is ample evidence to support DeVoto's claim that Wolfe's rhetoric is often artificially heightened, but at the same time, one of his most compelling attributes is his ability to depict something as insignificant as a "ham-on-rye" so clearly that readers may suddenly find themselves hungry. More to the point, however, are passages such as the Laura James sections of *Look Homeward, Angel*, where Wolfe manages to capture as well as any writer what it means to be young and in love. There are also numerous passages within his other novels that stand as some of the most poetic set pieces to be found in prose. In large measure, Wolfe is still read today because of the magnificence of his style, however extravagant it may be at times.

Wolfe held to an organic theory of art, one in which content dictates form. He was constantly searching for new ways to communicate experience; in this sense, the criticism directed at him for being a "formless" writer may in some ways be unfair. Certainly there is no doubt that in his attempts to depart from traditional formats he sometimes lost control of his material—*Of Time and the River*, for example, is marred by this flaw. On the other hand, he did manage to find an effective structure in "The Web of Earth," his lengthy story written under the influence of James Joyce. The entire work is filtered through the consciousness of an old woman engaged in reminiscence, and it is the finest example of artistic unity in Wolfe's work. In *Look Homeward, Angel*, Wolfe modified a traditional novelistic form, the *Bildungsroman* (the story of a youth initiated by experience into maturity), organizing the novel not around a unified sequence of events but instead around a series of sense impressions. In this way, the loose structure serves to complement the rhapsodic style. The result is a powerful rendering of the book's central theme—that of an artistic youth lost and in search of self-knowledge and self-definition.

As for the contention that Wolfe is too highly autobiographical, that his writing too often approaches mere reportage, there can be no denying that on occasion, he is guilty as charged. In most instances, however, he was by no means a mere reporter of events. His fiction is memorable because he was such an apt interpreter of human beings and everyday experiences. He was able to synthesize experience into art; he himself claimed that everything in a work of art is changed, that nothing is a literal representation of actual experience. Whether he always achieved this transmutation, it can safely be said that Wolfe is still read today because his novels stand as a testimony to human experience artistically rendered from a unique and personal vision.

Look Homeward, Angel, Wolfe's first and most significant novel, made use of extensive autobiographical material. In many ways, it is the story of his own life, the life of his family, his neighbors, and the region in which he lived. For those who know something of Wolfe's background, there are unmistakable connections between the fictional characters in *Look Homeward, Angel* and the real people among whom Wolfe grew up in Asheville, North Carolina. After the novel's publication, many from his hometown—and indeed many in his own family—were angered by what they took to be unflattering depictions of themselves in the novel. Wolfe's own account of the reaction to his novel can be found in *The Story of a Novel*, wherein he describes the uproar in Asheville and provides his own defense of his fictional method. Essentially, Wolfe believed that the people he described, whatever their faults, were magnificent. As magnificent as he thought his characters were, however, he often described them (no doubt truthfully) with all their faults made highly visible.

The ethics of his method can be questioned when one considers how it must have been to have lived in Asheville at the time the novel was published, to have opened its pages and to have found the characters so thinly fictionalized that their real counterparts could be easily identified. The ethical issue is not so much whether Wolfe was accurate in his depictions of the whole range of humanity he described, but rather how one would feel if he were identified as the model for the town drunk or as the counterpart of the unscrupulous businessman. It did not take long for the people of Asheville to start pointing fingers at one another after figuring out who was who in the novel. Perhaps with some justification, all fingers eventually pointed toward Wolfe himself; the controversy over what he had done to his town and the people in it was so pronounced that he was unable to return to Asheville until seven years after the publication of *Look Homeward, Angel.*

Wolfe departed from the development of a traditional plot in *Look Homeward, Angel* and instead made use of impressionistic realism to tie events and characters together. The narrator moves in and out of the consciousness of the principal characters, giving readers impressions of their inner feelings and motivations. As much as anything else, *Look Homeward, Angel* is the story of a quest, a search for self-knowledge and for lasting human interaction. The subtitle of the novel is *A Story of the Buried Life*, and much of what Wolfe depicts concerns itself with the inner lives of the characters in the novel—what they really think and feel as well as how isolated and alienated they are from one another. In this sense, the novel explores the relationship of time, change, and death as elements which will always frustrate man's desire for happiness and fulfillment.

Look Homeward, Angel was initially entitled *O Lost* and then *Alone, Alone.* The title on which Wolfe finally settled comes from "Lycidas," John Milton's poem in which the archangel Michael is asked to look back toward England to mourn a young man's death and all the unfulfilled potential it signifies. Eugene Gant, is, like most of Wolfe's protagonists, the isolated and sensitive artist in search of meaning and companionship in a hostile world. Given this theme, it is ironic that some of Wolfe's least effective passages are the results of his attempts to describe Eugene's feelings of loneliness and despair. In such segments (which recur in almost all of Wolfe's works), he often lapses into contrived language; rather than arising from natural consequences or from the interplay between one character and another, feelings seem forced by authorial intervention. On the other hand, the novel does contain some of his finest writing, especially when he describes people, places, and things with visionary intensity.

Look Homeward, Angel covers the first twenty years of Eugene Gant's life—his adolescence, his four years at the private school of Margaret Leonard, and his four years at the university. A pattern of potential fulfillment destroyed by frustration is personified in Eugene's parents, Eliza and Oliver, who are modeled after Wolfe's own mother and father. Oliver Gant is a stonecutter who passionately desires to create something beautiful, to carve an angel's head. He is an unfulfilled artist, a man of intense vitality who desires a full and sensuous life. His intensity, his capacity for life, is checked by his wife, Eliza, who is his antithesis; parsimonious, cold, and materialistic. This pattern of frustrated potential recurs throughout the novel. In one example, after spending his first year at the university and losing his innocence in a brothel, Eugene returns home to spend the summer at Dixieland, his mother's boardinghouse. There he meets and falls in love with Laura James (based on his own first love, Clara Paul). In his descriptions of the young, passionate love that develops between them, Wolfe's prose becomes a lyrical celebration that turns to tragic frustration as Eugene learns that Laura is engaged to marry another young man back home, that she will never be a part of his life again. Thus, potential (in this example, physical and spiritual union between Eugene and Laura) is checked by reality (separation and isolation). This pattern manifests itself in varying ways throughout the novel. The story of a youth coming of age by initiation into experience, *Look Homeward, Angel* is a comprehensive account of the inner life of a sensitive and artistic youth.

With the publication of *Look Homeward, Angel*, Wolfe was thrust (not unwillingly) into the limelight as a legend, a novelist who demonstrated enormous potential. His success was spectacular, but because he was a driven artist (much like his fictional counterpart, Eugene Gant), his initial success created a good many subsequent problems. He immediately felt the burden to surpass his first effort with an even better second novel. At the same time, he ran into difficulty giving form to his expansive ideas (a problem with which he would grapple for the remainder of his life). During this same period, he also began leading a turbulent private life. He was involved with Aline Bernstein (the "A. B." to whom *Look Homeward, Angel* is dedicated), and their relationship—as tempestuous as any could conceivably be—would figure heavily in the remainder of his life and work.

Composed of eight sections, each of which is named after some epic or mythic figure, *Of Time and the River* exceeds nine hundred pages in length and spans two continents, continuing the story of Thomas Wolfe as personified in the character of Eugene Gant. Wolfe continues the story with Eugene's departure from Altamont for study at Harvard. He stated his ambitious theme for *Of Time and the River* in *The Story of a Novel*; his central idea was to depict the search for a father, not only in a literal but also in a figurative sense. While trying to exemplify his theme, Wolfe also struggled to form *Of Time and the River* out of the vast amount of manuscript he had written (a detailed discussion of that struggle is related in *The Story of a Novel*). The struggle reached its peak when his editor, Maxwell Perkins, sent the novel to press without Wolfe's knowledge. In one of his letters to Perkins, Wolfe claimed that another six months' work would have allowed him to complete the necessary revisions that would have made the book less episodic. There can be no doubt that had Wolfe written *Of Time and the River* without Perkins' influence, it would have been a very different novel—perhaps a better one than it is. As it stands, it is, as Wolfe himself noted, episodic; its parts are not always aligned to form a unified plot. Even so, there are fine passages throughout that more than compensate for its ponderous pace and meandering plot. In *The Story of a Novel*, Wolfe describes how he wrote one scene that ran to eighty thousand words (about two hundred pages). He was attempting to capture "the full flood and fabric" of four people simply talking to one another for four continuous hours. This scene, as good as he thought it was, eventually was cut, but it illustrates the massive amount of writing he did for the novel as well as the extensive amount of cutting he did to get it into publishable form.

Perhaps the novel's most magnificent scene is that which describes the death of Eugene's father, who has been slowly dying of cancer. Gant, the paternal figure whose presence was so unforgettable in *Look Homeward, Angel*, is now old and enfeebled. His death, which comes in a final moment of traquility, stands in stark contrast to his life, which was lived with violent gestures and howling protests. Often drunk, sometimes violent, he was a hard man to live with, but his death comes as a reminder that life lived intensely—however excessively—is life worth living. The death of his wife, Eliza, would not begin to elicit the intensity of emotion aroused by his final moments, for she stands as a testimony to all that opposes the force and fury of his life.

Other memorable scenes in the novel include those that take place in Boston with Eugene's uncle, Bascom Pentland. Uncle Bascom and his demented wife are two of the more finely drawn eccentrics in the novel. These segments as well as others involving Eugene's dreams to become a playwright, his time spent as an English instructor at a city university in New York, and his eventual travel to Europe, all contribute to Wolfe's attempt to describe the vast array of people, places, and things unique to the American experience.

While working out his central theme of a search for a father, Wolfe developed a three-part vision of time: time present, time past, and time eternal. The first, time present, is the time in which the actual events in the novel take place, the time of reality. The second, time past, represents all of the accumulated experience that affects time present. The third, time eternal, stands for the lasting time of oceans, forests, and rivers, of things that form the permanent backdrop for man's experiences. These three levels of time allow Wolfe to contrast, in a vast and symbolic scale, the relationship of past, present, and eternal experience with the experience of Eugene Gant. The result is an intensely personal search for meaning, an attempt to reconcile opposites, to find something lasting and meaningful.

Throughout the novel, a scene that takes place in the present may be linked with past scenes and eternal scenes. In this way, all three levels of time are united. For example, a train ride taking place in present time provides Eugene with the opportunity to recall the travelers of earlier days, their epic searching, their longing for discovery, for movement. During the same segment, Eugene speculates that other men in the future (eternal time) will also travel the earth in search of one another. The novel frequently develops itself in this way, and it is these segments which give the novel its mysterious, almost haunting, quality. At the same time, however, these same passages become repetitious (if not tedious), and illustrate once again the lack of restraint so evident throughout Wolfe's work. In contrast to these overwritten segments are a good many specific characterizations as well as a variety of satiric passages aimed at mediocre people, middle-class values, and intellectual pretenders.

This is a vast and comprehensive book that ends when Eugene sets sail back to America. Aboard ship he meets Esther Jack (Aline Bernstein), who, although certainly not the father for whom he is searching, is nevertheless someone who can help him transcend the tormented youth he has endured to this point in his life.

Both *The Web and the Rock* and *You Can't Go Home Again* were put together by Edward Aswell, Wolfe's editor at Harper's, and published posthumously as novels. It was not until 1962, when Richard S. Kennedy published *The Window of Memory: The Literary Career of Thomas Wolfe*, that the extent of Aswell's influence on the two novels became fully known. Just before his death, Wolfe left a large packing crate of manuscript with Aswell. From that collection of manuscript, it was generally assumed that Aswell found two separate narratives, which he then published as the two posthumous novels. Surprisingly, however, Professor Kennedy discovered, after an extensive study of Wolfe's papers and manuscripts at Harvard University, that Aswell constructed *The Web and the Rock* and *You Can't Go Home Again* from what was a massive—but fragmentary—amount of manuscript that Wolfe apparently intended to condense into a single narrative. Had Wolfe lived, he most certainly would not have published the two novels as Aswell published them. In a very real way, they are as much the product of Aswell's editorializing as they are a product of Wolfe's imagination. Even so, the two novels represent a significant part of Wolfe's creative output, and analysis of them can help put his entire achievement into a clearer perspective.

Wolfe claimed that he was turning away from the books he had previously written, that *The Web and the Rock* would be his most "objective" work to date. It should be noted that at that time, Wolfe had become particularly sensitive about the criticism he had received from DeVoto and others concerning his alleged inability to exert artistic control over his material. As a result, not only did he claim his new novel to be objective, but also he abandoned his previous protagonist, Eugene Gant, in favor of a new one, George "Monk" Webber. The change was more in name than in substance, however, for Webber, like Eugene Gant, bears a close resemblance to Wolfe himself. Indeed, *The Web and the Rock* is quite similar to Wolfe's earlier works: its first half parallels *Look Homeward, Angel*, while its second half stands as a sequel to *Of Time and the River*.

One of the strongest chapters in the novel is enlightening insofar as it illustrates how Wolfe continually reshaped past material. "The Child by Tiger" was first published in 1937 as a short story, but in the eighth chapter of *The Web and the Rock*, Wolfe reworks the story with changes in character and point of view. It is a moving story about the nature of good and evil, innocence and experience. Dick Prosser, a black man of ability and potential, is the object of the racial prejudice that was so pronounced in the South during the early part of the twentieth century. He is a man who befriends several young white boys; he teaches them how to throw a football, how to box, and how to make a fire. In short, he becomes a kindly father-figure who initiates them into experience. There is, however, another side to Prosser. Driven to the point of madness by prejudicial treatment, by his own apocalyptic brand of religion, and by his involvement with a woman, he goes on a shooting spree one night, killing blacks and whites alike. Eventually shot by the mob formed to hunt him down, his bullet-riddled body is hung up for display in the window of the undertaker's parlor. In the course of these events, the young men who were Prosser's friends are initiated into a world full of violence and death. For the first time in their lives, they experience profound loss, and they witness evil as it is personified in the bloodthirsty mob. Woven within the story are stanzas from William Blake's poem, "The Tiger," from which the chapter title is derived.

In what comprises the second half of the novel, Wolfe deals with his own experiences in New York City. He explores his relationship with Bernstein, depicting her as a sophisticated mistress and himself as a brilliant but egocentric genius. Their relationship is described in detail—from their lovemaking and eating to their quarrels and reconciliations. These segments are remarkable for their candor and intriguing because of the insight they provide into the tempestuous relationship between the two. Webber's past experiences, the environment in which he was reared, and his ancestry symbolically form the web in which he is snared, and, as Esther Jack becomes a part of that web, he escapes to Germany. His search for the rock, the strength and beauty of vision that is represented by the father figure for whom he longs, is interrupted by his realization at the end of the novel that "you can't go home again." In short, he knows that he must look to the future to escape the past.

Continuing the chronicle of George Webber's life and artistic development, *You Can't Go Home Again* metaphorically develops the theme that Webber cannot go "home," cannot return to past places, old ideas, and former experiences because time and change have corrupted them. In this sense, "home" is an idealized vision of America as it appeared to George in his youth. These youthful visions come into abrupt contact with reality, and the resulting clash allows Wolfe to explore the very fabric of American society.

The novel begins approximately six months after *The Web and the Rock* ends. Webber has returned home to America and, against his better judgment, he decides to resume his relationship with Esther Jack. He also resumes work on his novel *Home to Our Mountains* (*Look Homeward, Angel*) and finds a publisher, James Rodney & Co. (Scribner's) as well as a sympathetic editor and father-figure, Foxhall Edwards (Maxwell Perkins). Before his book is published, however, he returns home for the first time in years to attend the funeral of his Aunt Maw. Home in this novel is Libya Hill (like the Altamont of *Look Homeward, Angel*, the locale still represents Asheville (North Carolina). On the train trip home, he meets his childhood friend Nebraska Crane, a one-time big-league baseball star. Crane, a Cherokee Indian, is now satisfied to lead the simple life of a family man and part-time tobacco farmer, standing in contrast to Webber, whose intellectual drive and literary ambition make him a driven "city" man.

Also on the train is Judge Rumford Bland, a blind syphilitic whose corruption serves to symbolize the corruption in Libya Hill toward which Webber is traveling. Upon his arrival, Webber finds that his quiet boyhood town has become crazed from a land-boom mentality that has everyone making huge paper fortunes in real estate (these events parallel those immediately preceding the Depression). Thus, his idealized expectations of home are shattered by the reality of corruption and madness running rampant throughout Libya Hill.

After the publication of his novel, Webber receives abusive letters from the residents of Libya Hill. Typically, Wolfe incorporated his own experiences into his fiction. In this instance, he drew upon his unpleasant memories of what happened after he published *Look Homeward, Angel*. An entire book in the novel ("The World That Jack Built") is devoted to the wealthy lives of Esther and Frederick Jack (the Bernsteins). Writing about his own breakup with Aline Bernstein, Wolfe describes Webber's move to Brooklyn and the end of his relationship with Esther Jack. In Brooklyn, Webber learns to love the low-life characters who inhabit the streets—the prostitutes, the derelicts, and the petty criminals—for they are very much a part of the American experience. To ignore them—or worse yet, to explain them away somehow—would be to deny the underbelly of America that Webber (and Wolfe) found so compelling.

After his years in Brooklyn (with scenes devoted to his relationship with Foxhall Edwards, his editor), Webber tires of New York and sails for Europe. In Germany, he is welcomed with the fame and notoriety he has sought for so long, but he also witnesses the darker side of Nazi Germany. The novel is the story of one man's pilgrimage, a search for a faith that will endure within a society so corrupt that each individual is destroyed by it. *You Can't Go Home Again* is not an entirely cynical book, however, for it concludes with a sense of hope and faith in the future.

Throughout his novels, Wolfe explored isolation, death, and the changes wrought by time—themes that exemplify his interest in the darker elements of life. In his attempts to capture the essence of a moment, he often overlooked the artistic demands that the novel imposes upon any writer. He was not a craftsman of the novel because he often sacrificed form, unity, and coherence to capture experience. His reputation is linked directly to his ambitious attempts to say it all, and *Look Homeward, Angel*, although only the beginning of the story Wolfe desired to tell, stands as his most satisfying and fully realized work.

Major publications other than long fiction

SHORT FICTION: *From Death to Morning*, 1935; *The Hills Beyond*, 1941.

PLAYS: *Mannerhouse*, 1948; *Welcome to Our City*, 1962 (published only in Germany as *Willkommen in Altamont*); *The Mountains*, 1970.

POETRY: *The Face of a Nation: Poetical Passages from the Writings of Thomas Wolfe*, 1939; *A Stone, a Leaf, a Door: Poems by Thomas Wolfe*, 1945.

NONFICTION: *The Story of a Novel*, 1936; *Thomas Wolfe's Letters to His Mother*, 1943; *The Portable Thomas Wolfe*, 1946; *The Letters of Thomas Wolfe*, 1956; *The Notebooks of Thomas Wolfe*, 1970; *The Thomas Wolfe Reader*, 1982.

Bibliography

Field, Leslie A., ed. *Thomas Wolfe: Three Decades of Criticism*, 1968.
Holman, C. Hugh, ed. *The World of Thomas Wolfe*, 1960.
Payne, Ladell. *Thomas Wolfe*, 1969.
Rubin, Luis D., Jr. ed. *Thomas Wolfe: A Collection of Critical Essays*, 1973.
Turnbull, Andrew. *Thomas Wolfe*, 1967.

Philip A. Luther

VIRGINIA WOOLF

Born: London, England; January 25, 1882
Died: Lewes, Sussex, England; March 28, 1941

Principal long fiction
The Voyage Out, 1915; *Night and Day*, 1919; *Jacob's Room*, 1922; *Mrs. Dalloway*, 1925; *To the Lighthouse*, 1927; *Orlando: A Biography*, 1928; *The Waves*, 1931; *Flush: A Biography*, 1933; *The Years*, 1937; *Between the Acts*, 1941.

Other literary forms
To say that Virginia Woolf lived to write is no exaggeration. Her output was both prodigious and varied; counting her posthumously published works, it fills more than forty volumes. Beyond her novels her fiction encompasses several short-story collections. As a writer of nonfiction, Woolf was similarly prolific, her book-length works including *Roger Fry: A Biography* (1940) and two influential feminist statements, *A Room of One's Own* (1929) and *Three Guineas* (1938). Throughout her life, Woolf also produced criticism and reviews; the best-known collections are *The Common Reader: First Series* (1925) and *The Common Reader: Second Series* (1932). In 1967, the four-volume *Collected Essays* was published. Additional books of essays, reviews, and sketches continue to appear, most notably the illuminating selection of autobiographical materials, *Moments of Being* (1976). Her letters—3,800 of them survive—are now available in six volumes; when publication is completed, her diaries will run to five.

Achievements
From the appearance of her first novel in 1915, Virginia Woolf's work was received with respect—an important point, since she was extremely sensitive to criticism. Descendant of a distinguished literary family, member of the avant-garde Bloomsbury Group, herself an experienced critic and reviewer, she was taken seriously as an artist. Nevertheless, her early works were not financially successful; she was forty before she earned a living from her writing. From the start, the rather narrow territory of her novels precluded broad popularity, peopled as they were with sophisticated, sexually reserved, upper-middle-class characters, finely attuned to their sensibilities and relatively insulated from the demands of mundane existence. When in *Jacob's Room* she first abandoned the conventional novel to experiment with the interior monologues and lyrical poetic devices which characterize her mature method, she also began to develop a reputation as a "difficult" or "high-brow" writer, though undeniably an important one. Not until the brilliant fantasy *Orlando* was published did she enjoy a definite commercial success. Thereafter, she

received both critical and popular acclaim; *The Years* was even a bona fide best-seller.

During the 1930's, Woolf became the subject of critical essays and two book-length studies; some of her works were translated into French. At the same time, however, her novels began to be judged as irrelevant to a world beset by growing economic and political chaos. At her death in 1941, she was widely regarded as a pioneer of modernism but also reviewed by many as the effete, melancholic "invalid priestess of Bloomsbury," a stereotype her friend and fellow novelist E. M. Forster dismissed at the time as wholly inaccurate; she was, he insisted, "tough, sensitive but tough."

Over the next twenty-five years, respectful attention to Woolf's work continued, but in the late 1960's, critical interest accelerated dramatically and has remained strong. Two reasons for this renewed notice seem particularly apparent. First, Woolf's feminist essays *A Room of One's Own* and *Three Guineas* became rallying documents in the growing women's movement; readers who might not otherwise have discovered her novels were drawn to them via her nonfiction and tended to read them primarily as validations of her feminist thinking. Second, with the appearance of her husband Leonard Woolf's five-volume autobiography from 1965-1969, her nephew Quentin Bell's definitive two-volume biography of her in 1972, and the full-scale editions of her own diaries and letters commencing in the mid-1970's, Woolf's life has become one of the most thoroughly documented of any modern author. Marked by intellectual and sexual unconventionality, madness, and suicide, it is for today's readers also one of the most fascinating; the steady demand for memoirs, reminiscences, and photograph collections relating to her has generated what is sometimes disparagingly labeled "the Virginia Woolf industry." At its worst, such insatiable curiosity is morbidly voyeuristic, distracting from and trivializing Woolf's achievement; on a more responsible level, it has led to serious, provocative revaluations of the political and especially the feminist elements in her work, as well as to redefinitions of her role as an artist.

Biography

Daughter of the eminent editor and critic Sir Leslie Stephen and Julia Jackson Duckworth, both of whom had been previously widowed, Virginia Woolf was born in 1882 into a solidly late Victorian intellectual and social milieu. Her father's first wife had been W. M. Thackeray's daughter; James Russell Lowell was her godfather; visitors to the Stephens' London household included Henry James, George Meredith, and Thomas Hardy. From childhood on, she had access to her father's superb library, benefitting from his guidance and commentary on her rigorous, precocious reading. Nevertheless, unlike her brothers, she did not receive a formal university education, a lack she always regretted and that partly explains the anger in *Three Guineas*, where she proposes a "university of outsiders." (Throughout her life she declined all academic honors.)

In 1895, when Woolf was thirteen, her mother, just past fifty, suddenly died. Altruistic, self-sacrificing, totally devoted to her demanding husband and large family, the beautiful Julia Stephen fulfilled the Victorian ideal of womanhood and exhausted herself doing so; her daughter would movingly eulogize her as Mrs. Ramsay in *To the Lighthouse*. The loss devastated Woolf, who experienced at that time the first of four major mental breakdowns in her life, the last of which would end in death.

Leslie Stephen, twenty years his wife's senior and thus sanguinely expecting her to pilot him comfortably through old age, was devastated in another way. Retreating histrionically into self-pitying but deeply felt grief, like that of his fictional counterpart, Mr. Ramsay, he transferred his intense demands for sympathetic attention to a succession of what could only seem to him achingly inadequate substitutes for his dead wife: first, his stepdaughter Stella Duckworth, who herself died suddenly in 1897, then, Virginia's older sister Vanessa. The traditional feminine role would eventually have befallen Virginia had Leslie Stephen not died in 1904. Writing in her 1928 diary on what would have been her father's ninety-sixth birthday, Woolf reflects that, had he lived, "His life would have entirely ended mine. . . . No writing, no books;— inconceivable."

On her father's death, Woolf sustained her second incapacitating breakdown. Yet she also gained, as her diary suggests, something crucial: freedom, which took an immediate and, to her parents' staid friends and relatives, shocking form. Virginia, Vanessa, and their brothers Thoby and Adrian abandoned the Stephen house in respectable Kensington to set up a home in the seedy bohemian district of London known as Bloomsbury. There, on Thursday evenings, a coterie of Thoby Stephen's Cambridge University friends regularly gathered to talk in an atmosphere of free thought, avant-garde art, and sexual tolerance, forming the nucleus of what came to be called the Bloomsbury Group. At various stages in its evolution over the next decade, the group included such luminaries as biographer Lytton Strachey, novelist E. M. Forster, art critic Roger Fry, and economist John Maynard Keynes. In 1911, they were joined by another of Thoby's Cambridge friends, a colonial official just returned from seven years in Ceylon, Leonard Woolf; Virginia Stephen married him the following year. Scarcely twelve months after the wedding, Virginia Woolf's third severe breakdown began, marked by a suicide attempt; her recovery took almost two years.

The causes of Woolf's madness have been much debated and the treatment she was prescribed—bed rest, milk, withdrawal of intellectual stimulation— much disputed, especially since she apparently never received psychoanalytic help, even though the Hogarth Press, founded by the Woolfs in 1917, was one of Sigmund Freud's earliest English publishers. A history of insanity ran in the Stephen family; if Virginia were afflicted with a hereditary nervous condition, it was thought, then that must be accepted as unalterable. On the other hand, the timing of these three breakdowns prompts speculation about more subtle causes. About her parents' deaths she evidently felt strong guilt; of *To the Lighthouse*, the fictionalized account of her parents' relationship, she would later say, "I was obsessed by them both, unhealthily; and writing of them was a necessary act." Marriage was for her a deliberately sought yet disturbing commitment, representing a potential loss of autonomy and a retreat into what her would-be novelist Terence Hewet envisions in *The Voyage Out* as a walled-up, firelit room. She found her own marriage sexually disappointing, perhaps in part because she had been molested both as a child and a young woman by her two Duckworth stepbrothers.

More recently, feminist scholars especially have argued as a cause of Woolf's madness the burden of being a greatly talented woman in a world hostile to feminine achievement, a situation Woolf strikingly depicts in *A Room of One's Own* as the plight of William Shakespeare's hypothetical sister. Indeed, the young Virginia Stephen might plunder her father's library all day, but by teatime she was expected to don the role of deferential Victorian female in a rigidly patriarchal household. Yet once she settled in Bloomsbury, she enjoyed unconventional independence and received much sympathetic encouragement of her gifts, most of all from her husband.

Leonard Woolf, himself a professional writer and literary editor, connected her madness directly with her genius, saying that she concentrated more intensely on her work than any writer he had ever known. Her books passed through long, difficult gestations; her sanity was always most vulnerable immediately after a novel was finished. Expanding on his belief that the imagination in his wife's books and the delusions of her breakdowns "all came from the same place in her mind," some critics go so far as to claim her madness as the very source of her art, permitting her to make mystical descents into inner space from which she returned with sharpened perception.

It is significant, certainly, that although Woolf's first publication, an unsigned article for *The Guardian*, appeared just two months after her 1904 move to Bloomsbury, her first novel, over which she labored for seven years, was only completed shortly after her marriage; her breakdown occurred three months after its acceptance for publication. Very early, therefore, Leonard Woolf learned to keep a daily record of his wife's health; throughout their life together, he would be alert for those signs of fatigue or erratic behavior that signaled approaching danger and the need for her customary rest cure. Rational, efficient, uncomplaining, Leonard Woolf has been condemned by some disaffected scholars as a pseudosaintly nurse who benignly badgered his patient into crippling dependency. The compelling argument against this extreme interpretation is Virginia Woolf's astonishing productivity after she recovered from her third illness. Although there were certainly periods of instability and near disaster, the following twenty-five years were immensely fruitful as she discarded traditional fiction to move toward realizing her unique vision, all the while functioning actively and diversely as a fine critic, too.

After Woolf's seventh novel, *The Years*, was finished in 1936, however, she came closer to mental collapse than she had been at any time since 1913. Meanwhile, a larger pattern of breakdown was developing in the world around her as World War II became inevitable. Working at her Sussex home on her last book, *Between the Acts*, she could hear the Battle of Britain being fought over her head; her London house was severely damaged in the Blitz. Yet strangely, that novel was her easiest to write; Leonard Woolf, ever watchful, was struck by her tranquility during this period. The gradual symptoms of warning were absent this time; when her depression began, he would recall, it struck her "like a sudden blow." She began to hear voices and knew what was coming. On February 26, 1941, she finished *Between the Acts*. Four weeks later, she went out for one of her usual walks across the Sussex downs, placed a heavy stone in her pocket, and stepped into the River Ouse. Within minutes Leonard Woolf arrived at its banks to find her walking stick and hat lying there. Her body was recovered three weeks later.

Analysis

In one of her most famous pronouncements on the nature of fiction—as a practicing critic, she had much to say on the subject—Virginia Woolf insists that "life is not a series of gig lamps symmetrically arranged; but a luminous halo, a semi-transparent envelope surrounding us from the beginning of consciousness to the end." In an ordinary day, she argues, "thousands of ideas" course through the human brain; "thousands of emotions" meet, collide, and disappear "in astonishing disorder." Amid this hectic interior flux, the trivial and the vital, the past and the present, are constantly interacting; there is endless tension between the multitude of ideas and emotions rushing through one's consciousness and the numerous impressions scoring on it from the external world. Thus, even personal identity becomes evanescent, continually reordering itself as "the atoms of experience . . . fall upon the mind." It follows, then, that human beings must have great difficulty communicating with one another, for of this welter of perceptions that define individual personality, only a tiny fraction can ever be externalized in word or gesture. Yet, despite—in fact, because of—their frightening isolation as unknowable entities, people yearn to unite both with one another and with some larger pattern of order hidden behind the flux, to experience time standing still momentarily, to see matches struck that briefly illuminate the darkness.

Given the complex phenomenon of human subjectivity, Woolf asks, "Is it not the task of the novelist to convey this varying, this unknown and uncircumscribed spirit . . . with as little mixture of the alien and external as possible?" The conventional novel form is plainly inadequate for such a purpose, she maintains. Dealing sequentially with a logical set of completed past actions that occur in a coherent, densely detailed physical and social environment, presided over by an omniscient narrator interpreting the significance of it all, the traditional novel trims and shapes experience into a rational but falsified pattern. "Is life like this?" Woolf demands rhetorically. "Must novels be like this?"

In Woolf's first two books, nevertheless, she attempted to work within conventional modes, discovering empirically that they could not convey her vision. Although in recent years some critics have defended *The Voyage Out* and *Night and Day* as artistically satisfying in their own right, both novels have generally been considered interesting mainly for what they foreshadow of Woolf's later preoccupations and techniques.

The Voyage Out is the story of twenty-four-year-old Rachel Vinrace, a naïve and talented amateur pianist who sails from England to a small resort on the South American coast, where she vacations with relatives. There, she meets a fledgling novelist, Terence Hewet; on a pleasure expedition up a jungle river, they declare their love. Shortly thereafter, Rachel falls ill with a fever and dies. The novel's exotic local, large cast of minor characters, elaborate scenes of social comedy, and excessive length are all atypical of Woolf's mature work. Already, however, many of her later concerns are largely emerging. The resonance of the title itself anticipates Woolf's poetic symbolism; the "voyage out" can be the literal trip across the Atlantic or up the South American river, but it also suggests the progression from innocence to experience, from life to death, which she later depicts using similar water imagery. Her concern with premature death and how survivors come to terms with it prefigures *Jacob's Room*, *Mrs. Dalloway*, *To the Lighthouse*, and *The Waves*. Most significant is her portrayal of a world in which characters are forever striving to overcome their isolation from one another. The ship on which Rachel "voyages out" is labeled by Woolf an "emblem of the loneliness of human life." Terence, Rachel's lover, might be describing his creator's own frustration when he says he is trying "to write a novel about Silence, the things people don't say. But the difficulty is immense."

Yet moments of unity amid seemingly unconquerable disorder do occur. On a communal level, one such transformation happens at a ball being held to celebrate the engagement of two English guests at the resort's small hotel. When the musicians go home, Rachel appropriates the piano and plays Mozart, hunting songs, and hymn tunes as the guests gradually resume dancing, each in a newly expressive, uninhibited way, eventually to join hands in a gigantic round dance. When the circle breaks and each member spins away to become individual once more, Rachel modulates to Bach; her weary yet exhilarated listeners sit quietly and allow themselves to be soothed by the serene complexity of the music. As dawn breaks outside and Rachel plays on, they envision "themselves and their lives, and the whole of human life advancing nobly under the direction of the music." They have transcended their single identities temporarily to gain a privileged glimpse of some larger pattern beyond themselves.

If Rachel transforms briefly through her art the lives of a small community, she herself privately discerns fleeting stability through her growing love for Terence. Yet even love is insufficient; although in the couple's newfound sense of union "divisions disappeared," Terence feels that Rachel seems able "to pass away to unknown places where she had no need of him." In the elegiac closing scenes of illness (which Woolf reworked many times and which are the most original as well as moving part of the novel), Rachel "descends into another world"; she is "curled up at the bottom of the sea." Terence, sitting by her bedside, senses that "they seemed to be thinking together; he seemed to be Rachel as well as himself." When she ceases breathing, he experiences "an immense feeling of peace," a "complete union" with her that shatters when he notices an ordinary table covered with crockery and realizes in horror that in this world he will never see Rachel again. For her, stability has been achieved; for him, the isolating flux has resumed.

Looking back on *The Voyage Out*, Woolf could see, she said, why readers found it "a more gallant and inspiring spectacle" than her next and least-known book *Night and Day*. This second novel is usually regarded as her most traditional in form and subject—in its social satire, her obeisance to Jane Austen. Its dancelike plot, however, in which mismatched young couples eventually find their true loves, suggests the magical atmosphere of William Shakespeare's romantic comedies as well. References to Shakespeare abound in the book; for example, the delightfully eccentric Mrs. Hilbery characterizes herself as one of his wise fools, and when at the end she presides over the repatterning of the couples in London, she has just arrived from a pilgrimage to Stratford-upon-Avon. Coincidentally, *Night and Day* is the most conventionally dramatic of Woolf's novels, full of dialogue, exits and entrances; characters are constantly taking omnibuses and taxis across London from one contrived scene to the next.

Like *The Voyage Out*, *Night and Day* does point to Woolf's enduring preoccupations. It is too a novel depicting movement from innocence to maturity and escape from the conventional world through the liberating influence of love. Ralph Denham, a London solicitor from a large, vulgar, middle-class family living in suburban Highgate, would prefer to move to a Norfolk cottage and write. Katharine Hilbery measures out her days serving tea in her wealthy family's beautiful Chelsea home and helping her disorganized mother produce a biography of their forebear, a great nineteenth century poet. Her secret passions, however, are mathematics and astronomy. These seeming opposites, Ralph and Katharine, are alike in that both retreat at night to their rooms to pursue their private visions. The entire novel is concerned with such dualities—public selves and private selves, activity and contemplation, fact and imagination; but Woolf also depicts the unity that Ralph and Katharine can achieve, notwithstanding the social and intellectual barriers separating them. At the end, as the couple leaves Katharine's elegant but constraining home to walk in the open night air, "They lapsed gently into silence, travelling the dark paths side by side towards something discerned in the distance which gradually possessed them both."

The sustained passages of subtle interior analysis by which Woolf charts the couple's growing realization of their need for each other define her real area of fictional interest, but they are hemmed in by a tediously constrictive traditional structure. Except for her late novel, *The Years*, also comparatively orthodox in form, her first two books took the longest to finish and underwent the most extensive revisions, undoubtedly because she was writing against her grain. Nevertheless, they represented a necessary apprenticeship; as she would later remark of *Night and Day*, "You must put it all in before you can leave out."

Woolf dared to leave out a great deal in the short experimental novel she wrote next. Described in conventional terms, *Jacob's Room* is a *Bildungsroman* or "novel of formation" tracing its hero's development from childhood to maturity: Jacob Flanders is first portrayed as a small boy studying a tide pool on a Cornish beach; at twenty-six, he dies fighting in World War I. In structure, style, and tone, however, *Jacob's Room* defies such labeling. It does not move in steady chronological fashion but in irregular leaps. Of the fourteen chapters, two cover Jacob's childhood; two, his college years at Cambridge; the remainder, his life as a young adult working in London and traveling abroad. In length, and hence in the complexity with which various periods of Jacob's existence are treated, the chapters range from one to twenty-eight pages. They vary, that is, as the process of growth itself does.

Individual chapters are likewise discontinous in structure, broken into irregular segments that convey multiple, often simultaneous perspectives. The ten-page Chapter 8 for example, opens with Jacob's slamming the door of his London room as he starts for work in the morning; he is then glimpsed at his office desk. Meanwhile, on a table back in his room lies his mother's unopened letter to him, placed there the previous night by his lover, Florinda; its contents and Mrs. Flanders herself are evoked. The narrator then discourses on the significance of letter-writing. Jacob is next seen leaving work for the day; in Greek Street, he spies Florinda on another man's arm. At eight o'clock, Rose Shaw, a guest at a party Jacob attended several nights earlier, walks through Holburn, meditating bitterly on the ironies of love and death. The narrator sketches London by lamplight. Then, Jacob is back in his room reading by the fire a newspaper account of the Prime Minister's speech on Home Rule; the night is very cold. The narrator abruptly shifts perspective from congested London to the open countryside, describing the snow that has been accumulating since mid-afternoon; an old shepherd crossing a field hears a distant clock strike. Back in London, Jacob also hears the hour chiming, rakes out his fire, and goes to bed. There is no story here in any conventional sense, no action being furthered; in the entire ten pages, only one sentence is direct dialogue. What Woolf delineates is the *texture* of an ordinary day in the life of Jacob and the world in which he exists. Clock time moves the chapter forward, while spatially the chapter radiates outward from the small area Jacob occupies. Simultaneously, in the brief reference to the Prime Minister, Woolf suggests the larger procession of modern history that will inexorably sweep Jacob to premature death.

Such indirection and understatement characterize the whole novel: "It is no use trying to sum people up," the narrator laments. "One must follow hints." Thus, Jacob is described mainly from the outside, defined through the impressions he makes on others, from a hotel chambermaid to a Cambridge don, and by his surroundings and possessions. Even his death is conveyed obliquely: Mrs. Flanders, half asleep in her Yorkshire house, hears "dull sounds"; it cannot be guns, she thinks, it must be the sea. On the next page, she stands in her dead son's London room, holding a pair of Jacob's old shoes and asking his friend pathetically, "What am I to do with these, Mr. Bonamy?" The novel ends.

To construct Jacob's ultimately unknowable biography out of such fragments, Woolf evolves not only a new structure but a new style. Long, fluid sentences contain precise physical details juxtaposed with metaphysical speculations on the evanescence of life and the impossibility of understanding another person. Lyrical descriptions of nature—waves, moths, falling snow, birds rising and settling—are interspersed to suggest life's beauty and fragility. Images and phrases recur as unifying motifs: Jacob is repeatedly associated with Greek literature and myth and spends his last fulfilling days visiting the Parthenon. Most important, Woolf begins to move freely in and out of her characters' minds to capture the flow of sense impressions mingling with memory, emotion, and random association, experimenting with that narrative method conveniently if imprecisely labeled "stream of consciousness."

Jacob's Room is not a mature work, especially with its intrusive narrator, who can be excessively chatty, archly pedantic, and sententious. Woolf protests the difficulties of her task ("In short, the observer is choked with observations") and cannot quite follow the logic of her new method; after an essay-like passage on the necessity of illusion, for example, she awkwardly concludes, "Jacob, no doubt, thought something in this fashion. . . ." Even the lovely passages of poetic description at times seem self-indulgent. The book definitely shows its seams. Woolf's rejection of traditional novel structure, however, and her efforts to eliminate "the alien and the external" make *Jacob's Room* a dazzling advance in her ability to embody her philosophic vision: "Life is but a procession of shadows, and God knows why it is that we embrace them so eagerly, and see them depart with such anguish, being shadows."

Within three years, Woolf had resolved her technical problems superbly in *Mrs. Dalloway*. The intruding narrator vanishes; though the freedom with which point of view shifts among characters and settings clearly posits an omniscient intelligence, the narrator's observations are now subtly integrated with the thoughts of her characters, and the transitions between scenes flow organically. Woolf's subject is also better suited to her method: whereas *Jacob's Room* is a story of youthful potential tragically cut off, *Mrs. Dalloway* is a novel of middle age, about what people have become as the result of choices made, opportunities seized or refused. Jacob Flanders had but a brief past; the characters in *Mrs. Dalloway* must come to terms with theirs, sifting and valuing the memories that course through their minds.

The book covers one June day in the life of Clarissa Dalloway, fifty-two years old, an accomplished London political hostess and wife of a Member of Parliament. A recent serious illness from which she is still recovering has made her freshly appreciate the wonder of life as she prepares for the party she will give that evening. Peter Walsh, once desperately in love with her, arrives from India, where he has had an undistinguished career; he calls on her and is invited to the party, at which another friend from the past, Sally Seton, formerly a romantic and now the conventional wife of a Manchester industrialist, will also unexpectedly appear. Running parallel with Clarissa's day is that of the mad Septimus Warren Smith, a surviving Jacob Flanders, shell-shocked in the war; his suicide in the late afternoon delays the arrival of another of Clarissa's guests, the eminent nerve specialist Sir William Bradshaw. Learning of this stranger's death, Clarissa must confront the inevitability of her own.

Mrs. Dalloway is also, then, a novel about time itself (its working title at one point was *The Hours*). Instead of using chapters or other formal sectioning, Woolf structures the book by counterpointing clock time, signaled by the obtrusive hourly tolling of Big Ben, against the subjective flow of time in her characters' minds as they recover the past and envision the future. Not only does she move backward and forward in time, however; she also creates an effect of simultaneity that is especially crucial in linking Septimus' story with Clarissa's. Thus, when Mrs. Dalloway, buying flowers that morning in a Bond Street shop, hears "a pistol shot" outside and emerges to see a large, official automobile that has backfired, Septimus is standing in the crowd blocked by the car and likewise reacting to this "violent explosion" ("The world has raised its whip; where will it descend?"). Later, when Septimus' frightened young Italian wife Rezia guides him to Regents Park to calm him before their appointment with Bradshaw, he has a terrifying hallucination of his dead friend Evans, killed just before the Armistice; Peter Walsh, passing their bench, wonders, "What awful fix had they got themselves in to look so desperate as that on a fine summer morning?" This atmosphere of intensely populated time and space, of many anonymous lives intersecting briefly, of the world resonating with unwritten novels, comic and tragic, accounts in part for the richly poignant texture of nearly all Woolf's mature work.

In her early thinking about *Mrs. Dalloway*, Virginia Woolf wanted to show a "world seen by the sane and the insane, side by side." Although the novel definitely focuses on Clarissa, Septimus functions as a kind of double, representing her own responses to life carried to an untenable extreme. Both find great terror in life and also great joy; both want to withdraw from life into blissful isolation, yet both want to reach out to merge with others. Clarissa's friends, and indeed she herself, sense a "coldness" about her, "an impenetrability"; both Peter and Sally believe she chose safety rather than adventure by marrying the unimaginative, responsible Richard Dalloway. The quiet attic room where she now convalesces is described as a tower into which she retreats nunlike to a virginal narrow bed. Yet Clarissa also loves "life; London; this moment of June"—and her parties. Though some critics condemn her party-giving as shallow, trivial, even corrupt (Peter Walsh could make her wince as a girl by predicting that she would become "the perfect hostess"), Clarissa considers her parties a form of creativity, "an offering," "her gift" of bringing people together. For Septimus, the war has destroyed his capacity to feel; in his aloneness and withdrawal, he finds "an isolation full of sublimity; a freedom which the attached can never know"—he can elude "human nature," "the repulsive brute, with the blood-red nostrils." Yet just watching leaves quivering is for him "an exquisite joy"; he feels them "connected by millions of fibres with his own body" and wants to reveal this unity to the world because "communication is health; communication is happiness."

Desperate because of his suicide threats, Septimus' wife takes him to see Sir William Bradshaw. At the center of the novel, in one of the most bitter scenes in all of Woolf's writing (certainly one with strong autobiographical overtones), is Septimus' confrontation with this "priest of science," this man of "lightning skill" and "almost infallible accuracy" who "never spoke of 'madness'; he called it not having a sense of proportion." Within three minutes, he has discreetly recorded his diagnosis on a pink card ("a case of complete breakdown . . . with every symptom in an advanced stage"); Septimus will be sent to a beautiful house in the country where he will be taught to rest, to regain proportion. Rezia, agonized, understands that she has been failed by this obtuse, complacently cruel man whom Woolf symbolically connects with a larger system that prospers on intolerance and sends its best young men to fight futile wars. Septimus' suicide at this point becomes inevitable.

The two stories fuse when Bradshaw appears at the party. Learning of the reason for his lateness, Clarissa, deeply shaken, withdraws to a small side room, not unlike her attic tower, where she accurately imagines Septimus' suicide: "He had thrown himself from a window. Up had flashed the ground;

through him, blundering, bruising, went the rusty spikes. . . . So she saw it." She also intuits the immediate cause: Bradshaw is "capable of some indiscriminate outrage—forcing your soul, that was it"; seeing him, this young man must have said to himself, "they make life intolerable, men like that." Thus, she sees, "death was defiance," a means to preserve one's center from being violated, but "death was also an attempt to comunicate," and in death, Septimus' message that all life is connected is heard by one unlikely person, Clarissa Dalloway. Reviewing her own past as she has reconstructed it this day, and forced anew to acknowledge her own mortality, she realizes that "He had made her feel the beauty." Spiritually regenerated, she returns to her party "to kindle and illuminate" life.

In her most moving, complexly affirmative novel, *To the Lighthouse*, Woolf portrays another woman whose creativity lies in uniting people, Mrs. Ramsay. For this luminous evocation of her own parents' marriage, Woolf drew on memories of her girlhood summers at St. Ives, Cornwall (here transposed to an island in the Hebrides) to focus on her perennial themes, the difficulties and joys of human communication, especially as frustrated by time and death.

The plot is absurdly simple: an expedition to a lighthouse is postponed, then completed a decade later. Woolf's mastery, however, of the interior monologue in this novel makes such a fragile plot line quite sufficient; the real "story" of *To the Lighthouse* is the reader's gradually increasing intimacy with its characters' richly depicted inner lives; the reader's understanding expands in concert with the characters' own growing insights.

Woolf again devises an experimental structure for her work, this time of three unequal parts. Approximately the first half of the novel entitled "The Window," occurs during a single day at the seaside home occupied by an eminent philosopher, Mr. Ramsay, his wife, and a melange of children, guests, and servants, including Lily Briscoe, an amateur painter in her thirties, unmarried. Mrs. Ramsay is the dominant consciousness in this section. A short, exquisitely beautiful center section, "Time Passes," pictures the house succumbing to time during the family's ten-year absence and then being rescued from decay by two old women for the Ramsays' repossession. Periodically interrupting this natural flow of time are terse, bracketed, clock-time announcements like news bulletins, telling of the deaths of Mrs. Ramsay, the eldest son Andrew (in World War I), and the eldest daughter Prue (of childbirth complications). The final third, "The Lighthouse," also covers one day; the diminished family and several former guests having returned; the lighthouse expedition can now be completed. This section is centered almost entirely in Lily Briscoe's consciousness.

Because Mr. and Mrs. Ramsay are both strong personalities, they are sometimes interpreted too simply. Particularly in some recent readings by feminist critics, Mr. Ramsay is seen as an insufferable patriarch, arrogantly rational in his work but almost infantile emotionally, while Mrs. Ramsay is a Victorian Earth Mother, not only submitting unquestioningly to her husband's and children's excessive demands but actively trying to impose on all the other female characters her unliberated way of life. Such readings are sound to some extent, but they undervalue the vivid way that Woolf captures in the couple's monologues the conflicting mixture of motives and needs that characterize human beings of either sex. For example, Mrs. Ramsay is infuriated that her husband blights their youngest son James's anticipation of the lighthouse visit by announcing that it will storm tomorrow, yet his unflinching pursuit of truth is also something she most admires in him. Mr. Ramsay finds his wife's irrational habit of exaggeration maddening, but as she sits alone in a reverie, he respects her integrity and will not interrupt, "though it hurt him that she should look so distant, and he could not reach her, he could do nothing to help her." Lily, a shrewd observer who simultaneously adores and resists Mrs. Ramsay, perceives that "it would be a mistake . . . to simplify their relationship."

Amid these typical contradictions and mundane demands, however, "little daily miracles" may be achieved. One of Woolf's finest scenes, Mrs. Ramsay's dinner, provides a paradigm (though a summary can scarcely convey the richness of these forty pages). As she mechanically seats her guests at the huge table, Mrs. Ramsay glimpses her husband at the other end, "all in a heap, frowning": "She could not understand how she had ever felt any emotion of affection for him." Gloomily, she perceives that not just the two of them but everyone is separate and out of sorts. For example, Charles Tansley, Mr. Ramsay's disciple, who feels the whole family despises him, fidgets angrily; Lily, annoyed that Tansley is always telling her "women can't paint," purposely tries to irritate him; William Bankes would rather be home dining alone and fears that Mrs. Ramsay will read his mind. They all sense that "something [is] lacking"—they are divided from one another, sunk in their "treacherous" thoughts. Mrs. Ramsay wearily recognizes that "the whole of the effort of merging and flowing and creating rested on her."

She instructs two of her children to light the candles and set them around a beautiful fruit centerpiece that her daughter Rose has arranged for the table. This is Mrs. Ramsay's first stroke of artistry; the candles and fruit compose the table and the faces around it into an island, a sheltering haven: "Here, inside the room, seemed to be order and dry land; there, outside, a reflection in which things wavered and vanished, waterily." All the guests feel this change and have a sudden sense of making "common cause against that fluidity out there." Then the maid brings in a great steaming dish of *boeuf en daube* that even the finicky widower Bankes considers "a triumph." As the guests relish the succulent food and their camaraderie grows, Mrs. Ramsay, serving the last helpings from the depths of the pot, experiences a moment of perfect insight: "There it was, all around them. It partook . . . of eternity." She affirms to herself that "there is a coherence in things, a stability; something, she meant, that is immune from change, and shines out . . . in the face of the flowing, the fleeting." As is true of so much of Woolf's sparse dialogue, the ordinary words Mrs. Ramsay then speaks aloud can be read both literally and symbolically: "Yes, there is plenty for everybody." As the dinner ends and she passes out of the room triumphantly—the inscrutable poet Augustus Carmichael, who usually resists her magic, actually bows in homage—she looks back on the scene and sees that "it had become, she knew . . . already the past."

The burden of the past and the coming to terms with it are the focus of Part III. Just as "a sort of disintegration" sets in as soon as Mrs. Ramsay sweeps out of the dining room, so her death has left a larger kind of wreckage. Without her unifying artistry, all is disorder, as it was at the beginning of the dinner. In a gesture of belated atonement for quarreling with his wife over the original lighthouse trip, the melodramatically despairing Mr. Ramsay insists on making the expedition now with his children James and Cam, although both hate his tyranny and neither wants to go. As they set out, Lily remains behind to paint. Surely mirroring the creative anxiety of Woolf herself, she feels "a painful but exciting ecstasy" before her blank canvas, knowing how ideas that seem simple become "in practice immediately complex." As she starts making rhythmic strokes across the canvas, she loses "consciousness of outer things" and begins to meditate on the past, from which she gradually retrieves a vision of Mrs. Ramsay that will permit her to reconstruct and complete the painting she left unfinished a decade ago, one in which Mrs. Ramsay would have been, and will become again, a triangular shadow on a step (symbolically echoing the invisible "wedge-shaped core of darkness" to which Mrs. Ramsay feels herself shrinking during her moments of reverie). Through the unexpectedly intense pain of recalling her, Lily also comprehends Mrs. Ramsay's significance, her ability "to make the moment something permanent," as art does, to strike "this eternal passing and flowing . . . into stability." Mrs. Ramsay is able to make "life stand still here."

Meanwhile, Mr. Ramsay and his children are also voyaging into the past; Cam, dreamily drifting her hand in the water, begins, as her mother did, to see her father as bravely pursuing truth like a tragic hero. James bitterly relives the childhood scene when his father thoughtlessly dashed his hopes for the lighthouse visit, but as they near the lighthouse in the present and Mr. Ramsay offers his son rare praise, James too is reconciled. When they land, Mr. Ramsay himself, standing in the bow "very straight and tall," springs "lightly like a young man . . . on to the rock," renewed. Simultaneously, though the boat has long since disappeared from her sight and even the lighthouse itself seems blurred, Lily intuits that they have reached their goal and she completes her painting. All of them have reclaimed Mrs. Ramsay from death, and she has unified them; memory can defeat time. "Yes," Lily thinks, "I have had my vision." Clearly, Woolf had achieved hers too and transmuted the materials of a painful past into this radiant novel.

Although Woolf denied intending any specific symbolism for the lighthouse, it resonates with almost infinite possibilities, both within the book and in a larger way as an emblem of her work. Like the candles at the dinner party, it can be a symbol of safety and stability amid darkness and watery flux, its beams those rhythmically occurring moments of illumination that sustain Mrs. Ramsay and by extension everyone. Perhaps, however, it can also serve as a metaphor for human beings themselves as Woolf portrays them. The lighthouse signifies what can be objectively perceived of an individual—in Mrs. Ramsay's words, "our apparitions, the things you know us by"; but it also signals invisible, possibly tragic depths, for, as Mrs. Ramsay knew, "beneath it is all dark, it is all spreading, it is unfathomably deep."

In *The Waves*, widely considered her masterpiece, Woolf most resolutely overcomes the limits of the traditional novel. Entirely unique in form, *The Waves* cannot perhaps be called a novel at all; Woolf herself first projected a work of "prose yet poetry; a novel and a play." The book is a series of grouped soliloquies in varying combinations spoken by six friends, three men and three women, at successive stages in their lives from childhood to late middle age. Each grouping is preceded by a brief, lyrical "interlude" (Woolf's own term), set off in italic type, that describes an empty house by the sea as the sun moves across the sky in a single day.

The texture of these soliloquies is extremely difficult to convey; the term "soliloquy," in fact, is merely a critical convenience. Although each is introduced in the same straightforward way ("Neville said," "Jinny said"), they obviously are unspoken, representing each character's private vision. Their style is also unvarying—solemn, formal, almost stilted, like that of choral figures. The author has deliberately translated into a rigorously neutral, dignified idiom the conscious and subconscious reality her characters perceive but cannot articulate on their own. This method represents Woolf's most ambitious attempt to capture the unfathomable depths of separate human personalities which defy communication in ordinary life—and in ordinary novels. The abstraction of the device, however, especially in combination with the flow of cosmic time in the interludes, shows that she is also concerned with depicting a universal pattern which transcends mere individuals. Thus, once more Woolf treats her theme of human beings' attempts to overcome their isolation and to become part of a larger stabilizing pattern; this time, however, the theme is embodied in the very form of her work.

It would be inaccurate, though, to say that the characters exist only as symbols. Each has definable qualities and unique imagery; Susan, as an example, farm-bred and almost belligerently maternal, speaks in elemental images of wood smoke, grassy paths, flowers thick with pollen. Further, the characters often evoke one another's imagery; the other figures, for example, even in maturity picture the fearful, solitary Rhoda as a child rocking white petals in a brown basin of water. They are linked by intricately woven threads of common experience, above all by their shared admiration for a shadowy seventh character, Percival. Their gathering with him at a farewell dinner before he embarks on a career in India is one of the few actual events recorded in the soliloquies and also becomes one of those miraculous moments of unity comparable to that achieved by Mrs. Ramsay for her dinner guests; as they rise to leave the restaurant, all the characters are thinking as Louis does: "We pray, holding in our hands this common feeling, 'Do not move, do not let the swing-door cut to pieces this thing that we have made, that globes itself here. . . .'" Such union, however, is cruelly impermanent; two pages later, a telegram announces Percival's death in a riding accident. Bernard, trying to make sense of this absurdity, echoes the imagery of encircling unity that characterized their thoughts at the dinner: "Ideas break a thousand times for once that they globe themselves entire."

It is Bernard—identified, significantly, throughout the book as a story-teller—who is given the long final section of *The Waves* in which "to sum up," becoming perhaps a surrogate for the author herself. (As a young man at school, worrying out "my novel," he discovers how "stories that follow people into their private rooms are difficult.") It is he who recognizes that "I am not one person; I am many people," part of his friends as they are part of him, all of them incomplete in themselves; he is "a man without a self." Yet it is also he who on the novel's final page, using the wave imagery of the universalizing interludes, passionately asserts his individuality: "Against you I will fling myself, unvanquished and unyielding, O Death!" Life, however obdurate and fragmented, must be affirmed.

The Waves is without doubt Woolf's most demanding and original novel, her most daring experiment in eliminating the alien and the external. When she vowed to cast out "all waste, deadness, and superfluity," however, she also ascetically renounced some of her greatest strengths as a novelist: her wit and humor, her delight in the daily beauty, variety, and muddle of material existence. This "abstract mystical eyeless book," as she at one point envisioned it, is a work to admire greatly, but not to love.

The six years following *The Waves* were a difficult period for Woolf both personally and artistically. Deeply depressed by the deaths of Lytton Strachey and Roger Fry, two of her oldest, most respected friends, she was at work on an "essay-novel," as she first conceived of it, which despite her initial enthusiasm became her most painfully frustrating effort—even though it proved, ironically, to be her greatest commercial success.

In *The Years*, Woolf returned to the conventional novel that she had rejected after *Night and Day*; she planned "to take in everything" and found herself "infinitely delighting in facts for a change." Whereas *The Waves* had represented the extreme of leaving out, *The Years* suggests the opposite one of almost indiscriminate putting in. Its very subject, a history of the Pargiter clan spanning fifty years and three generations, links it with the diffuse family sagas of John Galsworthy and Arnold Bennett, whose books Woolf was expressly deriding when she demanded, "Must novels be like this?"

Nevertheless, *The Years* is more original than it may appear; Woolf made fresh use of her experimental methods in her effort to reanimate traditional form. The novel contains eleven unequal segments, each standing for a year; the longest ones, the opening "1880" section and the closing "Present Day" (the 1930's), anchor the book; the nine intermediate sections cover the years between 1891 and 1918. Echoing *The Waves*, Woolf begins each chapter with a short panoramic passage describing both London and the countryside. Within the chapters, instead of continuous narrative, there are collections of vignettes, somewhat reminiscent of *Jacob's Room*, depicting various Pargiters going about their daily lives. Running parallel with the family's history are larger historical events, including Edward VII's death, the suffrage movement, the Irish troubles, and especially World War I. These events are usually treated indirectly, however; for example, the "1917" section takes place mainly in a cellar to which the characters have retreated, dinner plates in hand, during an air raid. It is here that Eleanor Pargiter asks, setting a theme that suffuses the rest of the novel, "When shall we live adventurously, wholly, not like cripples in a cave?"

The most pervasive effect of the war is felt in the lengthy "Present Day" segment, which culminates in a family reunion, where the youngest generation of Pargiters, Peggy and North, are lonely, cynical, and misanthropic, and their faltering elders are compromised either by complacency or failed hopes. Symbolically, Delia Pargiter gives the party in a rented office, not a home, underscoring the uprooting caused by the war. Yet the balancing "1880" section is almost equally dreary: the Pargiters' solid Victorian house shelters a chronically ailing mother whose children wish she would die, a father whose vulgar mistress greets him in hair curlers and frets over her dog's eczema, and a young daughter traumatized by an exhibitionist in the street outside. One oppressive way of life seems only to have been superseded by another, albeit a more universally menacing one.

The overall imagery of the novel is likewise unlovely: children recall being scrubbed with slimy washcloths; a revolting dinner of underdone mutton served by Sara Pargiter includes a bowl of rotting, flyblown fruit, grotesquely parodying Mrs. Ramsay's *boeuf en daube* and Rose's centerpiece; London is populated with deformed violet-sellers and old men eating cold sausages on buses. Communication in such a world is even more difficult than in Woolf's earlier books; the dialogue throughout is full of incomplete sentences, and a central vignette in the "Present Day" section turns on one guest's abortive efforts to deliver a speech toasting the human race.

Despite these circumstances, the characters still grope toward some kind of transforming unity; Eleanor, the eldest surviving Pargiter and the most sympathetic character in the novel, comes closest to achieving such vision on the scale that Lily Briscoe and Clarissa Dalloway do. At the reunion, looking back over her life, she wonders if there is "a pattern; a theme recurring like music . . . momentarily perceptible?" Casting about her, trying to connect with her relatives and friends but dozing in the process, she suddenly wakes, proclaiming that "it's been a perpetual discovery, my life. A miracle." Answering by implication her question posed fifteen years earlier during the air raid, she perceives that "we're only just beginning . . . to understand, here and there." That prospect is enough, however; she wants "to enclose the present moment . . . to fill it fuller and fuller, with the past, the present and the future, until it shone, whole, bright, deep with understanding."

Even this glowing dream of eventual unity is muted, though, when one recalls how Eleanor's embittered niece Peggy half pities, half admires her as a person who "still believed with passion . . . in the things man had destroyed," and how her nephew North, a captain in the trenches of World War I, thinks, "We cannot help each other, we are all deformed." It is difficult not to read the final lines of this profoundly somber novel ironically: "The sun had risen, and the sky above the houses wore an air of extraordinary beauty, simplicity and peace."

Woolf's final work, *Between the Acts*, also deals with individual lives unfolding against the screen of history, but her vision and the methods by which she conveys it are more inventive, complex, and successful than in *The Years*. Covering the space of a single day in June, 1939, as world war threatens on the Continent, *Between the Acts* depicts the events surrounding a village pageant about the history of England, performed on the grounds of Pointz Hall, a country house occupied by the unhappily married Giles and Isa Oliver. The Olivers' story frames the presentation of the pageant, scenes of which are directly reproduced in the novel and alternate with glimpses of the audience's lives during the intervals between the acts. The novel's title is hence richly metaphorical: the acts of the drama itself are bracketed by the scenes of real life, which in turn can be viewed as brief episodes in the long pageant of human history. Equally ambiguous, then, is the meaning of "parts," connoting clearly defined roles within a drama but also the fragmentation and incompleteness of the individuals who play them, that pervasive theme in Woolf's work.

In *The Years*, Woolf had focused on the personal histories of her characters; history in the larger sense made itself felt as it impinged on private lives. This emphasis is reversed in *Between the Acts*. Though the novel has interesting characters, Woolf provides scant information about their backgrounds, nor does she plumb individual memory in her usual manner. Instead, the characters possess a national, cultural, *communal* past—finally that of the whole human race from the Stone Age to the present. That Woolf intends her characters to be seen as part of this universal progression is clear from myriad references in the early pages to historical time. For example, from the air, the "scars" made by the Britons and the Romans can be seen around the village as can the Elizabethan manor house; graves in the churchyard attest that Mrs. Haines' family has lived in the area "for many centuries," whereas the Oliver family has inhabited Pointz Hall for "only something over a hundred and twenty years"; Lucy Swithin, Giles's endearing aunt, enjoys reading about history and imagining Piccadilly when it was a rhododendron forest populated by mastodons, "from whom, presumably, she thought . . . we descend."

The pageant itself, therefore, functions in the novel as more than simply a church fund-raising ritual, the product of well-meaning but hapless amateurs (though it exists amusingly on that level too). It is a heroic attempt by its author-director, the formidable Miss La Trobe, to make people see themselves playing parts in the continuum of British history. Thus, the audience has an integral role that blurs the lines "between the acts"; "Our part," says Giles's father, Bartholomew, "is to be the audience. And a very important part too." Their increasing interest in the pageant as they return from the successive intermissions signals their growing sense of a shared past and hence of an identity that both binds and transcends them as individuals.

The scenes of the pageant proceed from bathos to unnerving profundity. The first player, a small girl in pink, announces, "England am I," then promptly forgets her lines, while the wind blows away half the words of the singers behind her. Queen Elizabeth, splendidly decorated with six-penny brooches and a cape made of silvery scouring pads, turns out to be Mrs. Clark, the village tobacconist; the combined applause and laughter of delighted recognition muffle her opening speech. As the pageant progresses from a wicked though overlong parody of Restoration comedy to a satiric scene at a Victorian picnic, however, the audience becomes more reflective; the past is now close enough to be familiar, triggering their own memories and priming them for the last scene, Miss La Trobe's inspired experiment in expressionism, "The Present Time. Ourselves." The uncomprehending audience fidgets as the stage remains empty, refusing to understand that they are supposed to contemplate their own significance. "Reality too strong," Miss La Trobe mutters angrily from behind the bushes, "Curse 'em!" Then, "sudden and universal," a summer shower fortuitously begins. "Down it rained like all the people in the world weeping." Nature has provided the bridge of meaning Miss La Trobe required. As the rain ends, all the players from all the periods reappear, still in costume and declaiming fragments of their parts while flashing mirrors in the faces of the discomfited audience. An offstage voice asks how civilization is "to be built by orts, scraps and fragments like ourselves," then dies away.

The Reverend Streatfield, disconcerted like the rest of the audience, is assigned the embarrassing role of summing up the play's meaning. Tentatively, self-consciously, he ventures, "To me at least it was indicated that we are members of one another. . . . We act different parts; but are the same. . . . Surely, we should unite?" Then he abruptly shifts into a fund-raising appeal that is drowned out by a formation of war planes passing overhead. As the audience departs, a gramophone plays a valedictory: "Dispersed are we; we who have come together. But let us retain whatever made that harmony." The audience responds, thinking "There is joy, sweet joy, in company."

The qualified optimism of the pageant's close, however, is darkened by the bleak, perhaps apocalyptic postscript of the framing story. After the group disperses, the characters resume their usual roles. Lucy Swithin, identified earlier as a "unifier," experiences a typically Woolfian epiphany as she gazes on a fishpond, glimpsing the silver of the great carp below the surface and "seeing in that vision beauty, power and glory in ourselves." Her staunchly rational brother Bartholomew, a "separatist," goes into the house. Miss La Trobe, convinced that she has failed again, heads for the local pub to drink alone and plan her next play; it will be set at midnight with two figures half hidden by a rock as the curtain rises. "What would the first words be?"

It is the disaffected Giles and Isa, loving and hating each other, who begin the new play. In a remarkable ending, Woolf portrays the couple sitting silently in the dark before going to bed: "Before they slept, they must fight; after they had fought they would embrace." From that embrace, they may create another life, but "first they must fight, as the dog fox fights the vixen, in the heart of darkness, in the fields of night." The "great hooded chairs" in which they sit grow enormous, like Miss La Trobe's rock. The house fades, no longer sheltering them; they are like "dwellers in caves," watching "from some high place." The last lines of the novel are, "Then the curtain rose. They spoke."

This indeterminate conclusion implies that love and hate are elemental and reciprocal, and that such oppositions on a personal level are also the polarities that drive human history. Does Woolf read, then, in the gathering European storm, a cataclysm that will bring the pageant of history full circle, back to the primitive stage of prehistory? Or, like W. B. Yeats in "The Second Coming," does she envision a new cycle even more terrifying than the old? Or, as the faithful Lucy Swithin does, perhaps she hopes that "*all* is harmony could we hear it. And we shall."

Eight years earlier, Virginia Woolf wrote in her diary, "I think the effort to live in two spheres: the novel; and life; is a strain." Miss La Trobe, a crude alter ego for the author, is obsessed by failure but always driven to create anew because "a vision imparted was relief from agony . . . for one moment." In her brilliant experimental attempts to impart her own view of fragmented human beings achieving momentary harmony, discovering unity and stability behind the flux of daily life, Woolf repeatedly endured such anguish, but after *Between the Acts* was done, the strain of beginning again was too great. Perhaps the questions Virginia Woolf posed in this final haunting novel, published posthumously and unrevised, were answered for her in death.

Major publications other than long fiction

SHORT FICTION: *Monday or Tuesday*, 1921; *A Haunted House and Other Short Stories*, 1943; *Mrs. Dalloway's Party*, 1973 (Stella McNichol, editor).

NONFICTION: *The Common Reader: First Series*, 1925; *A Room of One's Own*, 1929; *The Common Reader: Second Series*, 1932; *Three Guineas*, 1938; *Roger Fry: A Biography*, 1940; *The Death of the Moth and Other Essays*, 1942; *The Moment and Other Essays*, 1947; *The Captain's Death Bed and Other Essays*, 1950; *A Writer's Diary*, 1953; *Granite and Rainbow*, 1958; *Collected Essays, Volumes 1-2*, 1966; *Collected Essays, Volumes 3-4*, 1967; *The Flight of the Mind: The Letters of Virginia Woolf, Vol. I, 1888-1912*, 1975 (published in the United States as *The Letters of Virginia Woolf, Vol. I: 1888-1912*, 1975; Nigel Nicholson, editor); *The Question of Things Happening: The Letters of Virginia Woolf, Vol. II, 1912-1922*, 1976 (published in the United States as *The Letters of Virginia Woolf, Vol. II: 1912-1922*, 1976; Nigel Nicolson, editor); *Moments of Being*, 1976 (Jeanne Schulkind, editor); *The Diary of Virginia Woolf*, 1977, 1978, 1980 (Anne Olivier Bell, editor, 3 volumes); *A Change of Perspective: The Letters of Virginia Woolf, Vol. III, 1923-1928*, 1977 (published in the United States as *The Letters of Virginia Woolf, Vol. III: 1923-1928*, 1978; Nigel Nicolson, editor); *A Reflection of the Other Person: The Letters of Virginia Woolf, Vol. IV, 1929-1931*, 1978 (published in the United States as *The Letters of Virginia Woolf, Vol. IV: 1929-1931*, 1979; Nigel Nicolson, editor); *The Sickle Side of the Moon: The Letters of Virginia Woolf, Vol. V, 1932-1935*, 1979 (published in the United States as *The Letters of Virginia Woolf, Vol. V: 1932-1935*, 1979; Nigel Nicolson, editor); *Leave the Letters Till We're Dead: The Letters of Virginia Woolf, Vol. VI, 1936-1941*, 1980 (Nigel Nicolson, editor).

Bibliography

Bell, Quentin. *Virginia Woolf: A Biography*, 1972.
Bennet, Joan. *Virginia Woolf: Her Art as a Novelist*, 1964.
Fleishman, Avrom. *Virginia Woolf: A Critical Reading*, 1975.
Forster, E. M. *Virginia Woolf*, 1942.
Guiguet, Jean. *Virginia Woolf and Her Works*, 1965. Translated by Jean Stewart.
Lee, Hermione. *The Novels of Virginia Woolf*, 1977.
Marder, Herbert. *Feminism and Art: A Study of Virginia Woolf*, 1968.
Naremore, James. *The World Without a Self*, 1973.
Rose, Phyllis. *Woman of Letters: A Life of Virginia Woolf*, 1978.
Woolf, Leonard. *The Autobiography of Leonard Woolf*, 1960-1969.

Kristine Ottesen Garrigan

HERMAN WOUK

Born: New York, New York; May 27, 1915

Principal long fiction
Aurora Dawn, 1947; *City Boy*, 1948; *The Caine Mutiny*, 1951; *Marjorie Morningstar*, 1955; *Slattery's Hurricane*, 1956; *Youngblood Hawke*, 1962; *Don't Stop the Carnival*, 1965; *The Winds of War*, 1971; *War and Remembrance*, 1978.

Other literary forms
Herman Wouk has written three plays; the first, *The Traitor*, was produced on Broadway in 1949 and was published by Samuel French the same year. His most successful theatrical work, *The Caine Mutiny Court-Martial* (based upon the novel published in 1951), appeared on Broadway in 1954 and was published by Doubleday the same year. *Nature's Way* was produced on Broadway in 1957, and was published by Doubleday the following year. Eric Bentley, speaking of *The Caine Mutiny Court-Martial*, said that Wouk showed a gift for crisp dialogue that no other regular writer for the American theater could rival. Wouk collaborated with Richard Murphy Slattery in writing the screenplay for *Slattery's Hurricane* (1949). *This Is My God*, which Wouk first published in 1959 and followed with a revised edition in 1973, is a description and explanation of the Jewish way of life. The volume was a Reader's Digest Condensed Book Club selection, and an alternate selection for the Book-of-the-Month Club in 1959.

Achievements
It is a peculiarity of American criticism to denigrate popular success in literature. Almost from the outset of his career, Wouk has been a very popular writer; putting aside prejudicial presuppositions, this can be acknowledged as a genuine achievement, for Wouk has not attained his popular status by catering to the baser tastes of his readers. Beginning with *The Caine Mutiny* (1951), his books have appeared regularly on the best-seller list. Several of his titles have been selections of the country's major book clubs. Wouk was awarded the Pulitzer Prize for Fiction in 1952 for *The Caine Mutiny*. That same year, Columbia University presented him the Medal of Excellence, an honor extended to distinguished alumni. Three universities have awarded him honorary doctoral degrees.

Wouk might be described as a traditional novelist, in that his writing does not reflect the experimental qualities that are to be found in so much twentieth century American fiction. Like John Updike, he has chosen to give primacy of place to the narrative element in fiction; he has brought to the novel his own peculiar brand of rough-hewn vigor. At a time when the conventional wisdom judges it bad form for a novelist to take a clear stand on moral issues—as if ambiguity itself were a virtue—Wouk has consistently declared his moral position in his writings. This has not always been to the benefit of his fiction, but by and large, his novels are stronger for his conviction that literary art does not subsist in a vacuum but is part of a larger moral universe.

Biography

Herman Wouk was born in New York City on May 27, 1915. He is the son of Abraham Isaac and Esther (Levine) Wouk. Wouk's father, an industrialist in the power laundry field, started out as an immigrant laundry worker earning three dollars a week. Wouk was educated at Townsend Harris Hall and at Columbia University, where he was graduated with honors in 1934. While at Columbia, he studied philosophy and was editor of the *Columbia Jester*. From 1934 to 1935 he worked as a gag writer for radio comedians, and from 1936 to 1941, he was a scriptwriter for Fred Allen. In 1941, Wouk moved to Washington, D.C. following his appointment to the United States Treasury Department as a dollar-a-year man; his job was to write and produce radio shows to sell war bonds. He left this work to join the navy. After completing Officer Candidate School, he was commissioned an ensign and assigned to mine sweeper duty in the Pacific fleet. He served in the navy from 1942 to 1946. Three of those years were spent aboard the destroyer-minesweeper *U.S.S. Southard*, and eventually he was to be promoted to the position of Executive Officer of that ship. He was decorated with four campaign stars during the war, and received a Unit Citation as well. When Wouk was processed out of the navy in 1946, he held the rank of lieutenant.

Wouk married Betty Sarah Brown in December, 1945. They have had three sons, Abraham Isaac (who died before reaching his fifth birthday), Nathaniel, and Joseph.

Wouk began his career as a serious writer while he was in the navy; before his release from the service, he had completed a good portion of his first novel. That novel, *Aurora Dawn*, was published by Simon and Schuster in 1946. Two years later, his second novel, *City Boy*, was published. Neither of these works gained a great deal of attention for Wouk, but with the publication of *The Caine Mutiny* in 1951 (awarded the Pulitzer Prize the following year), he was quickly established as a writer of consequence. His play, *The Caine Mutiny Court-Martial*, began its successful run on Broadway in 1954. *Marjorie Morningstar* appeared in 1955, and his nonfiction work on Jewish culture and religion, *This Is My God*, in 1959. The 1960's saw the publication of *Youngblood Hawke* (1962) and *Don't Stop the Carnival* (1965). His sprawling two-volume fictional account of World War II, which he began writing in 1962, was published in the 1970's; the first volume, *The Winds of War*, appeared in 1971, and the second, *War and Remembrance*, in 1978.

Wouk's great popular success has enabled him to devote his full time to his craft, but he has on occasion taken academic or semiacademic positions. From 1953 to 1957, he was a visiting professor of English at Yeshiva University, and during 1973-1974, he was scholar-in-residence at the Aspen Institute for Humanistic Studies. He has served on the board of directors for institutions and organizations such as the College of the Virgin Islands, the Washington National Symphony, and Kennedy Center Productions. He is a member of the Authors Guild and the Dramatists Guild.

Analysis

Herman Wouk is a novelist in the tradition of the great English novelists of the nineteenth century; he is also a spiritual descendent of such American writers as James Fenimore Cooper, William Dean Howells, Theodore Dreiser, and James T. Farrell. What he has in common with these writers is narrative prowess, a commitment to realism, and a lively moral consciousness. Furthermore, like these writers, Wouk addresses himself to the population at large. Since World War II, there has been detectable in American fiction a distinction between writers who seem to be inclined to write primarily for other writers or for academic critics, and those inclined to write for a general audience. That Wouk is numbered among the latter would appear to be traceable to a definite decision on his part. His first novel, *Aurora Dawn*, has the flavor of the experimental fiction that began to proliferate in the postwar period. If one were to have speculated in 1946 upon the course that Wouk's literary career was going to take, it would have been a safe guess to say that he would probably continue down the road of experimentation, that he would become more and more concerned with language as an end in itself, and that eventually, he would be writing books destined to be read only in upper-division English courses in universities. This was not what happened, however; in his second novel, *City Boy*, Wouk followed a conventional narrative pattern and told his story in language which was not constantly calling attention to itself.

In *Aurora Dawn* and *City Boy*, Wouk was still stretching his muscles and attempting to find his proper level as a writer. He came into his own with *The Caine Mutiny*. In that novel, and in every novel that has followed it, there can be recognized the presence of a central theme, treated in various ways and from varying perspectives. The theme is the conflict between traditional values and a modern consciousness which is either indifferent to those values or flatly antipathetic toward them. The conflict is not treated in abstract terms, but in terms of individuals who are caught up in it, and how the individual fares is in great part determined by the side with which he chooses to ally himself.

Wouk's first novel, *Aurora Dawn*, which he began while serving as an officer in the navy, is an effort at satire. The butt of the satire is the advertising industry and, more generally, the foolishness of anyone in business whose ethical consciousness is dimmed by avarice. The moral of the story is explicit: greed is the root of all evil. Andrew Reale, the novel's young protagonist, is bright, energetic, and imaginative, but until he undergoes a conversion at novel's end, his primary concern is getting ahead. He wants to be successful above all else, and to him, success means money. In his scramble to get to the top as quickly as possible, his myopia becomes acute and his values are severely twisted. He is willing to make compromises where compromises should not be made. A connection is intimated between Reale's moral weakness and his failure to continue to adhere to the religious principles according to which he was reared, a recurring theme in Wouk's fiction.

Reale's obsessive pursuit of success leads him to jilt his fiancé, the beautiful and innocent Laura Beaton, so that he can take up with the beautiful but frivolous Carol Marquis, daughter of the despicable but very rich Talmadge Marquis. It leads him to be crassly manipulative in his dealings with the Reverend Calvin Stanfield, who is simple, straightforward, and a good man. Finally, it leads him, in a move of pure expediency, to quit an employer who has been generous with him so that he can join forces with Talmadge Marquis. All Reale's machinations, however, are to no avail. The hastily courted Carol Marquis runs off with an eccentric painter, and Laura Beaton, brokenhearted at Reale's rejection of her, marries an older man. In the end, Reale gets better than he deserves. His thwarted attempt to blackmail Father Stanfield proves to be the occasion of a conversion experience for him. He suddenly sees the wickedness of his ways and decides to alter his course. Laura Beaton is miraculously released from her unconsummated marriage, so that Reale is able to get the woman of his dreams after all. Fleeing the wicked city, the bride and groom go off to live together in New Mexico.

The novel is not realistic and cannot be judged according to the criterion of verisimilitude. It is a light, playful work in which humor plays an important part. Despite several brilliant passages, however, the novel does not come across as successful satire, and that would seem to be attributable to the fact that Wouk is vacillating and hesitant in what he wants to say. What he takes with one hand, he gives back with the other. The novel is clever, in both good and bad senses. While its language is often lively, it can as well be pretentious and self-conscious at times. The anachronistic devices of addressing the reader directly, inserting explicit authorial commentary on the action, and interspersing the narrative with short philosophical asides do not always work to maximize the effect. The humor of the novel is capable of being right on the mark, but for the most part it is a bit forced; Wouk, the radio gagman, is too much in evidence. The flaws to be found in *Aurora Dawn* are flaws which are not uncommon in a first novel. Despite its weaknesses, however, already in evidence in this work are the two traits that have subsequently become the chief strengths of Wouk's fiction: a vigorous talent for narrative and a lively sensitivity to moral issues.

Perhaps the most striking thing about Wouk's second novel, *City Boy*, is that, stylistically, it represents a marked departure from the standards he had established in his first novel. The language of the work does not call attention to itself; it is clear, straightforward, and unpretentious. The novel is humorous in tone, and its plot structure is loose. It revolves around the adventures— most of which take place in an upstate summer camp—of a New York City boy, Herbie Bookbinder. John P. Marquand's comparison of this novel with Mark Twain's *The Adventures of Tom Sawyer* (1876) is well-founded. In many respects, Herbie is an urban version of the scamp from the Midwestern frontier. He is a bright and enterprising lad, and if he is mischievous at times, it is seldom with malice of forethought. Much of what he does is calculated to impress Lucille Glass, the object of his single-minded puppy love. Herbie is unlike Tom Sawyer in that he is an outsider as far as other boys are concerned, this because of his poor athletic skills and his penchant for things intellectual. A goodly amount of Herbie's efforts in the novel are given over to his attempts to gain the status of a regular guy. He succeeds, finally, and as a result is welcomed into the full fellowship of his peers. *City Boy* is a light novel—in some respects a boy's book—but in it, Wouk's moral consciousness is manifested by his underscoring the difference between good and evil in the actions of the characters.

The Caine Mutiny is Wouk's best novel, the work on which his reputation rests. The novel takes place against the backdrop of war, but it cannot be regarded as a "war story" in any simplistic sense. It is a story about the subtle and complicated relationships that exist among men who are part of the enclosed world that constitutes the military establishment. One of its central themes concerns the matter of authority—how it is exercised within a military context, and how it is abused. The novel explores the manner in which various personality types act and react within a hierarchical, authoritarian structure. In addition, it examines the ways in which the lives of those caught up in the trauma of war are altered, sometimes profoundly. Other themes which the novel treats are loyalty and disloyalty, patriotism, doers versus sayers, personal integrity, and the process by which young men are tested in stressful situations.

The Caine Mutiny can easily be misread. One might conclude that its chief concern is the everlasting battle between despotism and democracy, that Captain Queeg therefore is clearly the villain of the piece, and that its heroes are Lieutenant Maryk, Willie Keith, Tom Keefer, and the others who were involved in the mutiny. It is not that simple. If it were, *The Caine Mutiny* would be little more than a melodrama. Captain Queeg is not a hero, but neither is he a diabolical type. He is a sorry human being; he has serious personal problems (his eccentricity is not amusing—he is, in fact, a sick man); and, perhaps most serious, given his status as a commanding officer, he is incompetent professionally. For all that, he is consistent in trying to do his job to the best of his ability. Queeg's problem is that he is a man who is in over his head; he can at times scarcely cope with situations which are his duty to control. The circumstances surrounding the event which led to the mutiny are sufficiently ambiguous as to render doubtful the claim of the mutineers that, had they not relieved Queeg of command when they did, the ship would have been lost.

Wouk's assessment of the situation seems to be communicated most directly through the character of Lieutenant Greenwald, the young aviator-lawyer who defends Maryk at the court-martial. Greenwald is a dedicated navy man, and he is not sympathetic with the mutineers, but he decides to defend Maryk because he respects the Executive Officer's personal integrity and because he is convinced that Maryk, in assuming command of the *Caine* during the typhoon, was acting in good faith. Greenwald succeeds in having Maryk acquitted of the charge of mutiny, mainly by drawing out of Queeg in the courtroom telltale signs of his emotional instability, but he takes no joy in his victory. After the trial, he puts the damper on the victory celebration being staged by the *Caine*'s officers when he gives them a stinging tongue-lashing. His ire is directed particularly at Tom Keefer, whom he perceives correctly as being the chief instigator of the mutiny, but one who refused, when the matter came to a head, to put himself on the line. Greenwald's position seems to be that, while the *Caine*'s officers are legally innocent, they are morally guilty. However sophisticated a rationale they might provide for their actions, what was at the bottom of those actions, in his view, was disloyalty, and disloyalty, for a military officer, is an unforgivable sin. One might say that the trial does not prove either clear-cut guilt or innocence. If anything, it demonstrates the complexity and ambiguity of all human situations. Greenwald's position is that, given the ambiguity, it is always better not to second-guess legitimately constituted authority. It is the chief responsibility of the naval officer to do his duty through thick and thin.

If there is a clear villain in *The Caine Mutiny*, Tom Keefer would appear to be the most likely candidate for the role. Keefer is, in many respects, the preeminently modern man. He is committed to what he presumably regards as the absolute truths of Freudian psychology, which he employs in a reductionist way, as weapons against those who do not share his world view. He is in the navy, but not of it, and, in fact, he rather enjoys and exploits his position as an iconoclastic outsider. He maintains an attitude of supercilious superiority toward people such as Queeg, and toward everything that the navy represents. His view is narrow, restricted by the dictates of his overriding egotism. Keefer is a carping critic of the navy, but he does not hesitate to take selfish advantage of what the navy can offer him at every turn. His hypocrisy allows him to talk a big game, but when the pressure is on and when circumstances call for words to be translated into action, he invariably backs off. Perhaps the most damning thing that could be said of Keefer is that he is a coward, as he demonstrates when he is captain of the *Caine* and precipitously abandons ship. By the novel's end, however, Keefer seem to have arrived at a degree of self-awareness which hitherto had eluded him; he confesses to Willie Keith, succeeding him as commanding officer, that Keith is a better man than he. He is right.

Willie Keith is the central character of the novel; his moral education is the real subject of *The Caine Mutiny*. Willie is an aristocratic rich kid from New York who comes to learn, among other things, the value of democracy. His relationship with Maria Minotti, alias May Wynn, can be interpreted in this way. The bulk of Keith's education, however, takes place in the navy. When he first comes aboard the *Caine*, he is very much under the influence of Tom Keefer, and he accepts Keefer's cynical interpretation of things as the correct one. Eventually, Keith realizes that the navy, though imperfect, is not a bad organization. What is more, given the realities of the modern world, it is a necessary organization. Unlike Keefer, Keith is prepared to acknowledge that the navy in World War II is contributing toward the preservation of the way of life into which both men have been born and to which they are devoted, and that, excepting a total transformation of human nature, navies will probably always be needed to insure the protection of men's freedom. Keith is not changed into a mindless patriot and militarist, but his criticism of the navy and its personnel becomes more discriminate, more intelligent, more responsible. He learns to judge matters according to criteria which are not self-centered, and develops an appreciation for the larger scheme of things. He takes pride in his work, and as he rises in rank, his conscientiousness increases; he tries to be the best officer he can.

The world of the navy, in *The Caine Mutiny*, is in certain respects a microcosm of the world at large. It is beset by all sorts of problems, but there is no perfect alternative somewhere to which one might flee. A man's maturity is measured by his ability to establish standards of excellence and to work assiduously to achieve them in spite of various limitations, sometimes severe— limitations in himself, in others, and in the situation.

On the surface, Wouk's fourth novel, *Marjorie Morningstar*, would seem to lead nowhere. It is the story of a young Jewish woman, the daughter of immigrants established comfortably in the middle class of New York, who has been sufficiently Americanized as to have for her chief ambition the desire to become a famous actress, a star. Marjorie Morningstar (née Morgenstern) is a beautiful woman whose theatrical talent, while not scintillating, is probably sufficient to underwrite the realization of her dream, given a lucky break here and there. She is willing to make the sacrifices, within certain bounds, and to invest the hard work which the ascent to stardom inevitably entails. If Marjorie is determined about anything, it is that she is not going to allow herself to lapse into the staid, conventional life that is the destiny of the vast majority of nice, middle-class Jewish girls. She is going to be different; she is going to break out of the mold. After several fruitless efforts to break into the theater and to make it big, after a sequence of adventures with an assortment of men, chiefly with Noel Airman, she ends up doing what she vowed she would never do. She marries a Jew, a successful lawyer by the name of Milton Schwartz, and she retires to a plush suburb to live the most conventional of conventional lives. The novel, then, would seem to end on an almost laughably anticlimactic note, but only if one fails to perceive the kind of statement that it is attempting to make.

If *The Caine Mutiny* delineates the education of Willie Keith, the education of Marjorie Morningstar is the primary concern of the novel that bears her name. If Marjorie comes full circle, as it were, and ends by embracing the conventional, it is because she discovers that the conventional is worthy of being embraced, the conventional not only as representing middle-class morality, but also, and much more important, as embodying traditional cultural and religious values. The glamorous life to which Marjorie aspired, whether or not she was always fully conscious of the fact, was a life that repudiated traditional values. As a teenager and young woman, she fought her own tradition, particularly as manifested in the Jewish religion; she looked upon it as crude and superstitious, a carry-over from humankind's primitive past. This tradition, however, was more deeply embedded in her, was more integral a part of her identity than she was willing to admit, and throughout her various experiences it guided her actions more than she knew.

Marjorie's failure to realize her dream of becoming a star actually represents the triumph of her better, truer self. Her concern shifts from thin, superficial values to those with substance and depth. The drama of her quest for self-realization is played out principally around her long and erratic affair with Noel Airman. When she first meets Airman, who is some ten years her senior, she is scarcely more than a girl, and she is completely enamored of him. He is handsome, intelligent, urbane, and witty, a talented composer of popular songs who shows promise of becoming a success in the theater. Noel represents much of what she wants to become, and all of what she has decided is most valuable in life, which is emphasized by the fact that she throws decorum to the winds and pursues him actively. When she finally catches him, however, she realizes that she does not really want him. The man who was once her ideal, her hero, the man whom she wanted to marry more than anyone else, is at last perceived, albeit faintly, as a god with clay feet.

Who is this Noel Airman? He is Saul Ehrmann, a man who has actively repudiated his Jewish identity and its associated traditions, but who has failed to come up with a viable substitute for either. He is a rootless vagabond, a shameless Casanova, a man who eschews commitment as a matter of principle, and who tries hard to make a profession of cynicism. It would be wrong, however, to think of him entirely in negative terms. He is not a character lacking in complexity, and he is not devoid of critical self-knowledge, which at times can be acute and penetrating. Still, this self-awareness serves only to accentuate the pathetic quality of the man, for in the final analysis, he is impotent to act upon his better impulses. He does not have the moral stamina to follow through, and this is so, Wouk implies, precisely because he has cut himself off from his tradition.

The fact that Marjorie arrives at a new state of consciousness which allows her to see Airman for what he is, and accordingly to reject him, is attributable in part to her brief but fateful acquaintance with Michael Eden. Eden, like Airman, is a Jew, but, unlike Airman, he is not in flight from the fact. He is a strong, taciturn man whose personal sufferings have led him to dedicate himself to a melancholy but determined altruism. He is involved in the very risky business of rescuing Jews from Nazi Germany. Here is a man who is every bit as bright and talented as Airman but who has what Airman lacks—integrity and a sense of purpose in life. Although it is not Marjorie's destiny to marry Eden, meeting him has the effect of altering her perception of Airman. Milton Schwartz, the man she marries, has in common with Eden a fundamental decency.

Wouk's sixth novel, *Youngblood Hawke*, based to some extent on the life of Thomas Wolfe, could be the story of many a young American writer of this century, and for that reason, the novel, besides its intrinsic worth as a work of fiction, has considerable value as a historical document. The story of Arthur Youngblood Hawke is a success story, but it is a story of failure as well. Indeed, Hawke's case is in many respects a tragic one. Hawke is a lanky, down-home Kentuckian who, after being released from the navy at the end of World War II, moves to New York to conquer the city and the country, by his pen. He comes to his task with a spotty education, with an explosive imagination, and with a seemingly boundless store of energy. Writing is his life, and his engagement in it is passionate. There is much about Hawke which smacks of the all-American boy. He is crude and unpolished, but straightforward and gentle in his dealings with people—except with those who deserve otherwise. He is an honest man, in his way, and an assiduous worker. He wants to be a success as a writer. He wants to become a millionaire, not so that he can give up writing but so that, freed from financial worries, he can devote himself to it without distractions. Hawke is in the mold of the rustic innocent who has long played a part in American literature.

His early success works against him in the long run. His first novel, though receiving rough treatment at the hands of the critics, gains a large popular audience; his second novel wins the Pulitzer Prize and increasing respect from the critics. He is associated with a solid, respectable publishing house whose head values his work, has faith in his future, and is willing to be very generous in making contractual arrangements with him. Hawke's obsessional longing for financial independence, however, prompts him to break ties with his publisher and begin publishing his own books; he also makes some risky investments. His luck turns, and in a matter of months he finds himself on the threshold of bankruptcy. He determines that he is going to write his way out of his debts; leaving behind the plush life that he enjoyed only too briefly in New York, he returns to Kentucky, and there, living in a cabin in the woods, he works furiously to complete what proves to be his final novel. In fact, he overworks, devoting himself not only to the novel but also, earlier, to a theatrical production which he hopes will strike it rich. The strain brought about by his frenetic activities exacerbates an old head injury, and, after a wild chase to South America made in a state of delirium, he ends up back in New York. He is hospitalized there and dies at the age of thirty-three.

As Youngblood Hawke lies dying, his vaguely addressed prayer is that he might be given more time so that he can work. Everything that he has done he considers as only preparatory exercises to his great multivolume *Comedy*. That the *Comedy* was never written is not simply attributable to the fact that Hawke showed poor business sense or that he was careless of his health. There is evidence in the novel to warrant the conclusion that Hawke's failure to fulfill his chief artistic ambition amounts to an exacting payment he has had to make for his sins. There have been two principal women in his life, but, by his own admission, there should have been only one. In the beginning of the novel, before he bursts upon the American literary scene, he meets a young editor, Jeanne Green, who subsequently becomes for him what Maxwell Perkins was for Thomas Wolfe. Jeanne, besides being a very talented editor, is, like Hawke, essentially a small-town person. She is simple, unpretentious, genuine. Hawke falls in love with Jeanne almost immediately—his better self tells him that this is the woman in his life, the woman he should marry—but he becomes involved in a torrid affair with a wealthy, sophisticated, fundamentally selfish New Yorker, Frieda Winters. Frieda is older than he; she is married, has three children, and is no stranger to adulterous affairs. Hawke is honest enough with himself to admit that he is involved in adultery; the reader is told that he hates both the word and the fact. He does not have the moral courage, however, to extricate himself from the affair—not until, as it turns out, it is too late. His relationship with Frieda proves to be an enervating experience; if it does not exactly destroy him, it contributes substantially toward his destruction.

What allowed Hawke to become involved in an affair which he knew to be wrong? One explanation is that he failed to be true to the basic religious principles which he had been taught as a boy but which in his impetuous youth he attempted to reject. Unlike Marjorie Morningstar, whose roots in a religious tradition were sufficiently deep and tenacious to carry her through the hard times, Hawke succumbs to the facile moral standards of a secularized society.

Wouk's next novel, *Don't Stop the Carnival*, is the weakest of his entire corpus. It is a comic novel and it would seem to have some kind of satiric intent, but the humor, instead of carrying the moral import of the tale, more often than not obstructs it. The work's humor is hampered by obtrusive, heavy-handed moralizing, and its seriousness is trivialized by a humor which too often degenerates into tedious slapstick. Most damaging for the novel is the fact that Wouk's narrative talent, which is his forte, serves him poorly here. The plot is too often based upon contrivance, and in some instances blatant authorial manipulation is very much in evidence. Add to this fact that characterization is unconvincing, and the sum total is a generally undistinguished piece of fiction that holds the reader's attention only by an adamant act of will. It is not that the novel is completely lacking in substance, but the detectably substantive elements are not allowed to emerge fully. There is, for example, a statement being made about the haplessness of "liberal" types who are awash in a world that in many respects is the result of their own brand of thinking, but the message is befuddled by static of various kinds and one must strain to detect it.

Wouk's two most recent novels, *The Winds of War* and *War and Remembrance* published in 1971 and 1978, respectively, are in effect a single, sustained work of fiction, and therefore can be discussed together. Wouk spent sixteen years in completing the work, and it seems likely that he regards it as his *magnum opus*. *The Winds of War* is focused primarily on the European theater, beginning with the German invasion of Czechoslovakia and Poland, putting special emphasis upon the latter. The Battle of Britain is also treated at close range. The book ends with the bombing of Pearl Harbor, the point at which *War and Remembrance* takes up the story. This book, while continuing to trace the course of events in Europe, especially those events having to do with the systematic extermination of the Jews by the Nazis, shifts attention to the Pacific theater and provides poignant descriptions of the major naval battles fought there. The book ends with the dropping of the atomic bombs and the Japanese acceptance of unconditional surrender. In these two massive volumes which constitute a single work, an ambitious fictional history of World War II, Wouk once again shows himself to be a master of narrative. This is not a mere chronicle of events; rather, major events of the war are given dramatic immediacy by the tactic of having one of the many key characters in the narrative involved in those events. One is even provided access to the Axis point of view through excerpts from the analytic histories of the German General Armin von Roon, interspersed throughout the work.

The key character in the work is Victor Henry, a naval officer who has given thirty years of his life to military service. He is a staid, conservative man, a patriot but not a jingoist, dedicated to professional excellence and quietly guided by deeply embedded religious principles. Following his various adventures in Europe and in the Pacific, one is not only brought into direct contact with important historical personages but treated to his thoughtful reactions to them as well. Wouk is the type of artist who likes to paint on a large canvas, but the canvas he is covering in this work is of mammoth proportions. All the more remarkable, then, is the control he exercises here; nothing gets away from him. There is about this wide-ranging tour de force a satisfying unity and completeness. It is thickly peopled with a vast array of characters, and their attitudes toward the war run the full gamut from self-sacrificing heroism to cold-blooded murderousness.

One of the most interesting characters in the work is Aaron Jastrow, a Jewish-American, world-renowned scholar and former Yale professor who at the outbreak of the war is living in active retirement in Italy. In tracing the story of Aaron Jastrow, and that of his Polish cousin Berel, Wouk recounts in moving fashion the sickening circumstances of the infamous "final solution." Aaron himself was born in Poland and reared in a strict Orthodox tradition. As he reached young manhood, he put aside his religion and settled into a benevolent agnosticism. Accompanied by his niece Natalie, he is hounded by the Nazis throughout Europe for years, until he finally ends up in the land of his birth, in a death camp. His life is choked out in the gas chambers. He speaks to the reader directly through *A Jew's Journey*. What one learns from this document is that the most significant journey in the waning months of Jastrow's life is a spiritual one. His personal confrontation with the horrors of Nazism has the effect of returning him to the religion of his birth. When he comes to die, he is possessed of an inner peace his murderers could never know, and he represents a basic human dignity which they have chosen to abandon for themselves and to attempt to destroy in others.

The Winds of War and *War and Remembrance* are about a specific war, but they are about war in general as well. Wouk does not romanticize World War II, but he suggests that it was absolutely essential that the Allied forces emerged as victorious. It was an unspeakably grim yet nevertheless necessary struggle. The bombs that ended the war, however, changed the nature of war forever. If mankind were capable before Hiroshima and Nagasaki of arguing that all-out war, however cruel and crude, was a workable solution to human problems, that argument proved no longer tenable. World War II was perhaps the most gruesome war that human beings have ever inflicted upon themselves. Wouk's thesis is that wars in the future will not be avoided simply by proclaiming them to be unthinkable. One must think about them; one must think especially about the most gruesome of wars. Through memory, perhaps a pathway to peace can be found.

Despite his broad popular appeal, Wouk has generally not found favor with the critics, especially academic critics. The common response of the latter has been simply to ignore him. It is difficult to explain precisely why this is so. Perhaps Wouk's very popularity militates against him, as if there existed a necessary relationship between popularity and artistic worth: the more popular a writer, the poorer the quality of what he writes. Perhaps Wouk's traditionalist world view and forthright advocacy of Judeo-Christian moral principles, to which many critics today are hostile, account in part for the critical neglect of his work. In any case, Wouk deserves more critical attention than he has received. He is not the greatest among the many fine novelists to appear in the United States since World War II, but neither is he an inconsequential figure. His prose is solid and vigorous, eschewing precosity and self-indulgence. Writing with intelligence and sensitivity, he appeals neither to a small clique of literary aesthetes nor to the lowest common denominator of a general audience. His attitude toward fiction is that shared by all the major novelists of literary history; his fiction is not concerned with itself but with the world at large. His fiction does not attempt the irrelevant task of creating a moral universe from scratch, but accepts and responds to the moral universe which is already in place.

Major publications other than long fiction
PLAYS: *The Traitor*, 1949; *The Caine Mutiny Court-Martial*, 1954, *Nature's Way*, 1958.
NONFICTION: *This Is My God*, 1959, 1973.

Bibliography
Carpenter, Frederic I. "Herman Wouk," in *College English*. XVII (January, 1956), pp. 211-215.
_____ . "Herman Wouk and the Wisdom of Disillusion," in *English Journal*. XLV (January, 1956), pp. 1-6, 32.
McElderry, B. R., Jr. "The Conservative as Novelist: Herman Wouk," in *Arizona Quarterly*. XV (Summer, 1959), pp. 128-136.

Dennis Q. McInerny

RICHARD WRIGHT

Born: Natchez, Mississippi; September 4, 1908
Died: Paris, France; November 28, 1960

Principal long fiction

Native Son, 1940; *The Outsider*, 1953; *Savage Holiday*, 1954; *The Long Dream*, 1958; *Lawd Today*, 1963.

Other literary forms

In addition to his five novels, Richard Wright published collections of essays and short stories and two autobiographical volumes. Two collections of short stories, the early *Uncle Tom's Children* (1938) and the posthumously collected *Eight Men* (1961), represent some of Wright's finest fiction. Wright himself felt that the characters in *Uncle Tom's Children* were too easily pitied and that they elicited from readers a sympathy that was unlike the tough intellectual judgment he desired. Wright later wrote that his creation of Bigger Thomas in *Native Son* was an attempt to stiffen that portrayal so that readers could not leniently dismiss his characters with simple compassion, but would have to accept them as free, fully human adults, whose actions required assessment. Nevertheless, the stories of *Uncle Tom's Children* are carefully written, and the characters, though sometimes defeated, embody the kind of independence and intractability that Wright valued in his fiction.

Two stories from *Eight Men* reveal the themes to which Wright gave sustained development in his novels. In "The Man Who Was Almos' a Man," the main character learns that power means freedom, and although he first bungles his attempt to shoot a gun, his symbol of power, he lies to his family, keeps the gun, and at the conclusion of the story leaves home to grow into manhood elsewhere. In "The Man Who Lived Underground," the main character, nameless at first, is accused of a crime he did not commit. Fleeing underground to the sewers of the city, he becomes a voyeur of life, seen now from a new perspective. The values that served him badly above ground do not serve him at all below. By the end of the story, he has come to understand that all men are guilty; his name is revealed, and with his new values, he ascends once more to accept responsibility for the crime. Since all men are guilty, it is less important to him that the crime is not his own than that he acknowledges freely that he shares in human guilt.

Even more important than these two collections is the first volume of Wright's autobiography, *Black Boy* (1945), which opens up a world of experience to the reader. It traces the first seventeen years of Wright's life—from his birth in Mississippi and the desertion of the family by his father, through years of displacement as he travels from one relative to another with his ill mother·and religious grandmother. The early years find Wright, like his later protagonists, an outsider, cut off from family, from friends, from culture. He is as out of place among blacks as among whites, baffled by those blacks who play the roles whites expect of them, himself unable to dissimulate his feelings and thoughts.

Although the work is nonfiction, it is united by powerful metaphors: fire, hunger, and blindness. Wright's inner fire is mirrored throughout the work by actual fires; indeed, his first act is to set afire the curtains in his home. His physical hunger, a constant companion, is an image of his hunger for knowledge and connection, and his two jobs in optical factories suggest the blindness of society, a blindness given further representation in *Native Son*.

What Wright learns in *Black Boy* is the power of words. His early life is marked by physical violence: he witnesses murders and beatings, but it is the violence of words which offers liberation from his suffocating environment. Whether it is the profanity with which he shocks his grandmother, the literalness with which he takes his father's words, or the crude expressions with which he taunts Jewish shopkeepers, he discovers that words have a power which make him an equal to those around him. When he feels unequal, as in his early school experiences, he is speechless. The culmination of this theme occurs when Wright acquires a library card and discovers through his readings in the American social critics of the early part of this century, men such as H. L. Mencken and Sinclair Lewis, that he is not alone in his feelings and that there are others who share his alienation and discontent.

When Wright finally sees his father many years after his desertion, his hatred dissolves: he realizes that his father, trapped by his surroundings, with neither a cultural past nor an individual future, speaks a different language from his own, holds different thoughts, and is truly a victim and therefore not worthy even of his hatred. Wright's characters must never be victims, for as such they hold no interest. At the end of the book, he goes north, first to Memphis and, when that fails, north again to Chicago, pursuing the dream, having now the power of words to articulate it and to define himself.

The record of his years in Chicago is found in the posthumously published second autobiographical volume, *American Hunger* (written in 1944, published in 1977). Largely a record of his involvement and later disillusionment with the Communist party, this book is interesting for its view of a later, mature Wright who is still struggling with institutions which would limit his freedom.

Achievements

In his best work, Wright gives American literature its strongest statement of the existential theme of alienated man defining himself. Wright's use of the black American as archetypal outsider gives his work a double edge. On the one hand, no American writer so carefully illuminates the black experience in America: the ambivalence of black feeling, the hypocrisies of the dominant culture, and the tension between them find concrete and original manifestation in Wright's work, a manifestation at once revealing and terrifying.

It is not only in his revelation of black life, however, that Wright's power lies, for as much as his writing is social and political, it is also personal and philosophical. The story of alienated man is a universal one; because the concrete experiences of the outsider are so vividly rendered in Wright's fiction, his books have an immediate accessibility. Because they also reveal deeper patterns, they have further claims to attention. Much of Wright's later fiction seems self-conscious and studied, but it cannot diminish the greatness of his finest work.

Biography

Born in Mississippi of sharecropper parents, Richard Wright had a lonely and troubled childhood. His father deserted the family early, and after his mother suffered a stroke, Wright was forced at a young age to work to help support the family, which moved frequently from one relative to another. His portrayal of his mother is of a stern but loving parent, unable to contend with the stronger personality of his extremely religious grandmother. Wright's grandmother believed that all fiction was "the devil's lies"; her chief goal was to force Wright into a religious conversion, a goal in which she was singularly unsuccessful.

Wright moved from school to school, attempting to make friends and make his talents known. Though both tasks were difficult, he became valedictorian of his class. Even this accomplishment was spoiled when the principal insisted that Wright read a speech which the principal himself had written, and Wright refused. An uncle told Richard, "They're going to break you," and society, both black and white, seemed intent on doing so. Wright was determined to resist, not to be claimed by his environment as he felt so many blacks around him were.

Wright left Mississippi for Memphis, Tennessee, had little luck there, and—with money stolen from the movie theater where he worked—moved to Chicago. When others stole, Wright disapproved—not for moral reasons, but because he felt stealing did not change the fundamental relationship of a person to his environment. When it offered a chance to change that environment, Wright accepted it.

In Chicago, Wright became involved with others who viewed the country as he did, first in a federal theater project and then with the Communist John Reed Club, which supported his writing until Wright's goals differed from their own. In 1937, he moved to New York City to become the editor of the *Daily Worker*. A year later, he published his first important work, *Uncle Tom's Children*, after which he won a Guggenheim Fellowship, which provided him with the time and funds to write *Native Son*. The novel was published to great acclaim and was followed by a second major work, *Black Boy*.

Although his writing career was a success, Wright was arguing more frequently with the Communist party, with which he finally broke in 1944, and was becoming less optimistic about the hope of racial progress in America.

In 1946, Wright moved to France, where he spent the rest of his life. Although he wrote a great deal there, nothing in his later work, with the possible exception of *The Outsider*, approaches the strength of *Native Son* and *Black Boy*. The existentialism which was always implicit in his work became the dominant theme, but—displaced from his native environment—Wright never again found a convincing dramatic situation in which to work out his preoccupations.

Wright died in France of a heart attack on November 28, 1960. Since his death, three of his works, *Eight Men*, *Lawd Today*, and *American Hunger*, have been published.

Analysis

Richard Wright's best work is always the story of one man's struggle to define himself and by so doing make himself free and responsible, fully human, a character worthy not of pity but of admiration and horror simultaneously. Typically, the character is an outsider, and Wright uses blackness as a representation of that alienation, though his characters are never as interested in defining their blackness as in defining their humanity. Although many characters in Wright's works are outsiders without being aware of their condition, Wright is never interested in them except as foils. Many of them avoid confronting themselves by fleeing to dreams; religion and liquor are two avoidance-mechanisms for Wright's characters, narcotics that blind them to their surrounding world, to what they are and what they might be.

Even Wright's main characters must not think about that world too often: to let it touch them is to risk insanity or violence, and so his characters strive to keep the fire within in check, to keep the physical hunger satisfied. Thus, all of Wright's protagonists are initially trapped by desire and by fear—fear of what might happen to them, what they may do, if they risk venturing outside the confines of black life in America, and the desire to do so. The life outside may be glimpsed in movies; Bigger Thomas, for example, goes to a film and watches contrasting and artificial views of black and white society. Yet as untruthful as both views are, they remind Bigger of a reality beyond his present situation. Desire is often symbolized by flight; Bigger, like other Wright characters, dreams of flying above the world, unchained from its limitations.

Most of Wright's stories and novels examine what happens when the protagonist's fear is mastered for a moment when desires are met. The manifestation of desire in Wright is almost always through violence (and it is here, perhaps, that he is most pessimistic, for other, more positive manifestations of desire, such as love, can come only later, after the protagonists have violently acted out their longings). Violence is central to Wright's fiction, for as important as sex may be to his characters, power is much more so, and power is often achieved through violence; in Wright's world, beatings and murders are frequent acts—central and occasionally creative.

Once the character has acted, he finds himself trapped again in a new set of oppositions, for in acting, he has left the old sureties behind, has made himself free, and has begun to define and create himself. With that new freedom comes a new awareness of responsibility. He is without excuses, and that awareness is as terrifying as—though more liberating than—the fears he has previously known. Although Wright does not always elaborate on what may follow, the characters open up new possibilities for themselves. If one may create one's self by violence, perhaps, Wright sometimes suggests, there are other, less destructive ways as well.

Some of Wright's novels end on this note of optimism, the characters tragically happy: tragic because they have committed violent and repulsive acts, but happy because for the first time they have *chosen* to commit them; they have freed themselves from their constraints, and the future, however short it may be, lies open. Others end simply with tragedy, the destruction achieving no purpose, the characters attaining no illumination.

Lawd Today, written before *Native Son*, but not published until after Wright's death, tells the story of Jake Jackson from his awakening on the morning of February 12, 1936, to that day's violent conclusion. Jackson is Wright's most inarticulate protagonist: he has a banal life, undefined dreams, and a vague sense of discontent which he is unable to explain. Violent and prejudiced, he speaks in clichés, a language as meaningless as his life.

Technically, the book incorporates a montage of radio broadcasts, newspaper articles, and religious and political pamphlets into the narration of Jake's day. Divided into three sections, *Lawd Today* opens with Jake's dream of running up an endless staircase after a disappearing voice. That dream gives way to the reality of his life: hunger, anger, and recrimination. Tricked by Jake into an abortion for which Jake still owes five hundred dollars and now claiming to have a tumor which will cost another five hundred dollars to remove, Jake's wife represents his entrapment. In the first section, "Commonplace," Jake reveals his brutish and trivial character: his anger at his wife, a jealousy and resentment that lead him to bait her so he can hit her, a mock-battle straightening his hair, and a meeting with friends who work with him at the post office. As they play bridge to pass the time until work, Wright presents without comment their stupid, cliché-ridden conversation.

Section two, "Squirrel Cage," shows the men at work. They are all alienated in meaningless, routine jobs, but Jake's position is the most desperate, for his wife has been to see his boss, and he is now threatened with the loss of his job. Falling deeper into debt by borrowing more money and making mistakes on the job, Jake is trapped by his work—despite his own protestations, as a self-proclaimed Republican and capitalist, that work is liberating. This section, too, ends with a long, rambling, and banal conversation among the men at work.

In the concluding section, "Rat's Alley," the men go to a brothel for a good time on some of Jake's borrowed money. There, Jake is robbed and then beaten for his threats of revenge. Finally, Jake stumbles homeward, his day nearing an end. The February weather, pleasant when the book began, has turned bad. All of Jake's frustration and anger finally erupt; he beats his wife, whom he finds kneeling asleep by the bed in an attitude of prayer. As they struggle, he throws objects through the window. She grabs a shard of broken glass and slashes him three times. The book ends with Jake lying in a drunken stupor, bleeding, while his wife is on her knees, also bleeding, praying for death. Outside, the wind blows mercilessly.

Although some of the experimentalism of *Lawd Today* seems artificial, and although the protagonist is too limited to sustain the reader's interest, this early work is powerful and economical. The situation, if not the character, is typical of Wright's work, and the reader understands Jake's violent frustration. *Lawd Today* has its flaws, but it foreshadows the strengths of Wright's best work and in its own right is a daring and fascinating novel.

Along with *Black Boy*, *Native Son* is one of Wright's finest achievements: a brilliant portrayal of, as Wright put it, the way the environment provides the instrumentalities through which one expresses himself and the way that self becomes whole despite the environment's conspiring to keep it divided.

The book parallels Theordore Dreiser's *An American Tragedy* (1925): both are three-part novels in which there is a murder, in part accidental, in part willed; an attempted flight; and a long concluding trial, in both cases somewhat anticlimactic. Both novels are concerned with the interplay of environment and heredity, of fate and accident, and both have protagonists who rebel against the world which would hold them back.

In the first part of *Native Son*, Bigger Thomas is a black man cut off from family and peers. Superficially like his friends, he is in fact possessed of a different consciousness. To think about that consciousness is for him to risk insanity or violence, so Bigger endeavors to keep his fears and uncertainty at a preconscious level. On the day of the first section, however, he is required by welfare to apply for a job as a menial at the home of the rich Dalton family. Mr. Dalton is a ghetto landlord who soothes his conscience by donating sums of money for recreational purposes. That it is a miniscule part of the money he is deriving from blacks is an irony he overlooks. Mrs. Dalton is blind, a fact that is necessary to the plot as well as being symbolic. Their daughter, Mary, is a member of the Communist party, and from the moment she sees Bigger, who wants nothing more than to be left alone, she begins to enlist his support.

The first evening, Bigger is to drive Mary to a university class. In reality, she is going with Jan Erlone, her Communist boyfriend, to a party meeting. Afterward, they insist that Bigger take them to a bar in the black part of town. Jan and Mary are at this point satirized, for their attitudes toward blacks are as limited and stereotyped as any in the novel. Bigger does not want to be seen by his friends with whites, but that fact does not occur to Mary. After much drinking, Bigger must carry the drunken Mary to her bedroom. He puts her to bed, stands over her, attracted to the woman he sees. The door opens and Mrs. Dalton enters. When Mary makes drunken noises, Bigger becomes frightened that Mrs. Dalton will come close enough to discover him, so he puts a pillow over Mary's face to quiet her. By the time Mrs. Dalton leaves, Mary is dead.

Wright wanted to make Bigger a character it would be impossible to pity, and what follows is extremely grisly. Bigger tries to put Mary's body in the furnace and saws off her head to make her fit. However accidental Mary's death may appear to the reader, Bigger himself does not regard it as such. He has, he thinks, many times wanted to kill whites without ever having the opportunity to do so. This time there was the act without the desire, but rather than seeing himself as the victim of a chance occurrence, Bigger prefers to unite the earlier desire with the present act, to make himself whole by accepting responsibility for the killing. Indeed, not only will he accept the act, but also Bigger determines to capitalize on it by sending a ransom note. Later, accused of raping Mary as well, an act he considered but did not commit, he reverses the process, accepting responsibility for this, too, even though here there was desire but no act. His only sign of conscience is that he cannot bring himself to shake the ashes in the furnace; this guilt is not redemptive, but his undoing, for, in an implausible scene in the Dalton basement, the room fills with smoke, the murder is revealed to newspaper reporters gathered there, and Bigger is forced to flee.

He runs with his girl friend, Bessie Mears. She, like Bigger, has a hunger for sensation, which has initially attracted him to her. Now, however, as they flee together, she becomes a threat and a burden; huddled with her in an abandoned tenement, Bigger wants only to be rid of her. He picks up a brick and smashes her face, dumping her body down an airshaft. His only regret is not that he has killed her, but that he has forgotten to remove their money from her body.

The rest of the plot moves quickly: Bigger is soon arrested, the trial is turned into a political farce, and Bigger is convicted and sentenced to death. In the last part of the novel, after Bigger's arrest, the implications of the action are developed, largely through Bigger's relations to other characters. Some of the characters are worthy only of contempt, particularly the district attorney, who, in an attempt at reelection, is turning the trial into political capital. Bigger's mother relies on religion. In a scene in the jail cell, she falls on her knees in apology before Mrs. Dalton and urges Bigger to pray, but toughness is Bigger's code. He is embarrassed by his mother's self-abasement, and although he agrees to pray simply to end his discomfort, his attitude toward religion is shown when he throws away a cross a minister has given him and throws a cup of coffee in a priest's face. In his view, they want only to avoid the world and to force him to accept guilt without responsibility.

Bigger learns from two characters. The first is Boris Max, the lawyer the Communist party provides. Max listens to Bigger, and for the first time in his life, Bigger exposes his ideas and feelings to another human. Max's plea to the court is that, just as Bigger must accept responsibility for what he has done, so must the society around him understand its responsibility for what Bigger has become and, if the court chooses to execute Bigger, understand the consequences that must flow from that action. He does not argue—nor does Wright believe—that Bigger is a victim of injustice. There is no injustice, because that would presume a world in which Bigger could hope for justice, and such a world does not exist; more important, Bigger is not a victim, for he has chosen his own fate. Max argues rather that all men are entitled to happiness. Like all of Wright's protagonists, Bigger has earlier been torn between the poles of dread and ecstasy. His ecstasy, his happiness comes from the meaningfulness he creates in his existence, a product of self-realization. Unhappily for Bigger, he realizes himself through murder: it was, he feels, his highest creative act.

If Max articulates the intellectual presentation of Wright's beliefs about Bigger, it is Jan, Mary's lover, who is its dramatic representation. He visits Bigger in his cell and, having at last understood the futility and paucity of his own stereotypes, admits to Bigger that he too shares in the responsibility for what has happend. He, too, addresses Bigger as a human being, but from the unique position of being the one who is alive to remind Bigger of the consequences of his actions, for Bigger learns that Jan has suffered loss through what he has done and that, while Bigger has created himself, he has also destroyed another.

Native Son ends with the failure of Max's appeals on Bigger's behalf. He comes to the cell to confront Bigger before his execution, and the novel closes with Bigger Thomas smiling at Max as the prison door clangs shut. He will die happy because he will die fulfilled, having, however terribly, created a self. *Native Son* is Wright's most powerful work, because his theme, universal in nature, is given its fullest and most evocative embodiment. In the characterization of Bigger, alienated man at his least abstract and most genuine, of Bigger's exactly rendered mind and milieu, and of Bigger's working out of his destiny, *Native Son* is Wright's masterpiece.

Wright's next novel, *The Outsider*, written in France and published thirteen years after *Native Son*, suffers from a surplus of internal explanation and a failure to provide a setting as rich as that of *Native Son*. Still, its portrayal of Cross Damon and his struggle to define himself, while too self-conscious, adds new dimensions to Wright's myth.

As the novel opens, Damon is trapped by his life. His post-office job is unfulfilling, his wife is threatening, and his underage mistress is pregnant. He "desires desire," but there is no way for that desire to be completed. "A man creates himself," he has told his wife, but the self Damon has created is a nightmare. He broods, his brooding as close as he comes to religion. Another underground man, Damon gets his chance for new life on the subway. Thought dead after his identification papers are found near the mangled body of another, Damon gets a chance to create himself anew. He must invent, he thinks, not only his future, but also a past to fit with his present; this new opportunity brings with it a different and more potent sense of dread.

From the beginning of this new life, Damon is remarkably successful at the mechanics of creating a past. He easily obtains a birth certificate and a draft card. At a deeper level, however, he traps himself as surely as he has been trapped in his old life, so that his new one becomes a continuous act of bad faith. Even before he leaves Chicago, he hides in a brothel where he encounters a co-worker who recognizes him. Damon murders the man and throws his body out a window. The pattern of violence, so typical of Wright's characters, begins in earnest for Damon

Taking a train to New York, Cross meets two people who will influence his new life, a black waiter who introduces him to the world of Communist politics in New York City, and Ely Houston, the district attorney, who is the most articulate person in the novel and the only one fully to understand Damon. Houston asks Damon why, when all blacks are outsiders, so few seem conscious of this fact. Wright suggests that being man is too much to be borne by man, that the struggle to define oneself is too difficult; the novel is a testament to that suggestion.

The Communist party members, too, are outsiders, and there is nothing unified about their company. Each one that Damon meets is playing god, hoping to protect and extend his personal power. Their awareness of their motives varies, but they are a threat to Damon, and the action of the book is propelled by a series of murders: Damon himself wants to act like a god. Near the end of the book, Houston comes to understand that Damon is the killer, but—rather than indicting and punishing him legally—Houston allows him to go free, alone with his knowledge of what he is. Damon is horrified by his fate, but he is robbed of even that when he is killed by two Communist party members who fear him.

The Outsider is both an extension and a modification of Wright's earlier views; it is far more pessimistic than *Native Son*, and the influence of the French existentialists is more pervasive. Like earlier Wright heroes, Damon is engaged in defining the world and himself. "The moment we act 'as if' it's true, then it's true," he thinks, because each man, in the absence of a god, it able to create the world and its truth. From Fyodor Dostoevski, Wright again borrows the notion of underground man and the idea that without a god, all is permitted. Yet as each man plays god, as each becomes criminal, policemen, judge, and executioner, there are no longer limits. Man desires everything, and desire is described as a floating demon. Men are jealous gods here—the worlds they create are petty, their jealousy destructive. Cross Damon is loved in the novel, but that love, unlike the love in *Native Son* which is held up as potentially meaningful, is here without promise. Although he creates himself and his world in *The Outsider*, all that is made is violent and brutal, a world without redemption even in the act of self-realization.

At the end of the novel, Cross Damon dies, not with Bigger Thomas' smile, but with the knowledge that alone, man is nothing. Searching in his last moments of freedom for a clean, well-lighted place in which to rest before he confronts the world again, Cross finds only death. Before he dies, he admits his final act of bad faith: he has thought that he could create a world and be different from other men, that he could remain innocent. Like Joseph Conrad's Kurtz in *Heart of Darkness* (1902), Damon dies realizing the futility of that hope; having looked into his own heart of darkness, he dies with the word *horror* on his lips.

It is Wright's bleakest conclusion, the book his most relentless examination of the consequences of his own philosophy. If *The Outsider* lacks the narrative drive of *Native Son*, it remains a strongly conceived and troubling piece of fiction.

Wright's last novel, *The Long Dream*, despite some effective scenes, is one of his weakest. The story of Rex "Fishbelly" Tucker's growing up and coming to terms with his environment is a pale repetition of earlier themes. The first section describes Tucker's youth. His father, an undertaker, is the richest black man in town, but his money comes also from a brothel he runs on the side. Tucker admires his father's success while detesting his obsequiousness with whites. When, however, Fishbelly is arrested, he twice faints at the white world's threats. Having presented himself as a victim, he becomes one. Walking home after his father has arranged his freedom, Fishbelly sees an injured dog, which he puts out of its misery. Fishbelly then comes upon a white man, pinned to the ground with a car door in his body. When the white man calls out to Fishbelly, using the term "nigger," Fishbelly walks on, leaving the man to die.

In the second section, Fishbelly finds a woman, but she and forty-one others are burned to death in a fire at the bar. The rest of the novel is an unconvincing story of the police who want the return of the cancelled checks that Fishbelly's father has used to pay them off, the police's arranged murder of the father, the subsequent framing and imprisoning of Fishbelly for rape, and Fishbelly's keeping the checks for his future use. All of this is badly contrived. At the end, Fishbelly is on a plane leaving for France, where his childhood friends are stationed in the army which they describe as exciting. He is talking to an

Italian whose father has come to America and found a dream, where Fishbelly himself has known only a nightmare. France, he dreams, will offer him what America has not.

In Fishbelly's attempt to understand himself and his environment, he is a typical Wright protagonist. He is weaker than Wright's usual characters, however, and that shallowness, coupled with an implausible plot, prevents Wright's last work of long fiction from succeeding.

Unlike many highly acclaimed books of the 1940's, *Native Son* and *Black Boy* have not dated. They are a lacerating challenge to contemporary readers and writers—a challenge to share the relentless integrity of Richard Wright's vision.

Major publications other than long fiction

SHORT FICTION: *Uncle Tom's Children*, 1938, 1940; *Eight Men*, 1961.

NONFICTION: *Twelve Million Black Voices*, 1941; *Black Boy*, 1945; *Black Power*, 1954; *The Color Curtain*, 1956; *Pagan Spain*, 1957; *White Man, Listen!*, 1957; *American Hunger*, 1977.

Bibliography

Bone, Robert. *Richard Wright*, 1969.

Brignano, Russell. *Richard Wright: An Introduction to the Man and His Works*, 1970.

Fabre, Michel. *The Unfinished Quest of Richard Wright*, 1973.

Kinnamon, Keneth. *The Emergence of Richard Wright*, 1972.

Margolies, Edward L. *The Art of Richard Wright*, 1969.

McCall, Daniel. *The Example of Richard Wright*, 1969.

Walker, Margaret. *The Demonic Genius of Richard Wright*, 1982.

Webb, Constance. *Richard Wright: A Biography*, 1968.

Howard Faulkner

FRANK YERBY

Born: Augusta, Georgia; September 5, 1916

Principal long fiction

The Foxes of Harrow, 1946; *The Vixens*, 1947; *The Golden Hawk*, 1948; *Pride's Castle*, 1949; *Floodtide*, 1950; *A Woman Called Fancy*, 1951; *The Saracen Blade*, 1952; *The Devil's Laughter*, 1953; *Bride of Liberty*, 1954; *Benton's Row*, 1954; *The Treasure of Pleasant Valley*; 1955; *Captain Rebel*, 1956; *Fairoaks*, 1957; *The Serpent and the Staff*, 1958; *Jarrett's Jade*, 1959; *Gillian*, 1960; *The Garfield Honor*, 1961; *Griffin's Way*, 1962; *The Old Gods Laugh: A Modern Romance*, 1964; *An Odor of Sanctity*, 1965; *Goat Song*, 1968; *Judas, My Brother*, 1968; *Speak Now: A Modern Novel*, 1969; *The Dahomean*, 1971; *The Girl from Storyville*, 1972; *The Voyage Unplanned*, 1974; *Tobias and the Angel*, 1975; *A Rose for Ana Maria*, 1976; *Hail the Conquering Hero*, 1977; *A Darkness at Ingraham's Crest*, 1979; *Western*, 1982.

Other literary forms

In addition to his novels, Frank Yerby has written poetry and short stories that are often found in anthologies of black literature. One story, "Health Card," first published in *Harper's Magazine*, won a special O. Henry Memorial Award in 1944.

Achievements

Yerby has written many best-selling historical novels over a long career beginning in the 1940's. Most of his best work, however, dates from the 1960's, after he had established himself as a prolific popular novelist. Yerby excels at creating complicated, fast-moving plots that give vivid impressions of historical eras and periods. Often the novels contradict myths and stereotypes of the periods in question. Almost every novel, too, suggests the futility of finding real truth in the universal confusion of the human condition. While Yerby's protagonists are flawed, often by ruthlessness and infidelity, they are also characterized by a fierce sense of dignity of the worth of a human life.

Biography

Frank Garvin Yerby, a black American novelist, was born in Augusta, Georgia, on September 5, 1916. He received an A.B. at Paine College in 1937 and an M.A. at Fisk College in 1938. Subsequently, he did graduate work in education at the University of Chicago.

From 1939 to 1941, Yerby taught English, first at Florida A. & M. and then at Southern University and Agricultural and Mechanical College. Married in 1941, he worked from 1941 to 1944 at the Ford Motor Company at

Dearborn, Michigan, as a technician and then as an inspector at Fairchild Aircraft from 1944 to 1945. In 1944, he won an O. Henry Memorial Award for the short story, "Health Card," a story that dealt sensitively with black issues. In 1945, he started work on a novel, *The Foxes of Harrow*, which he aimed to make a commercial success. Thereafter, Yerby wrote many similar melodramatic best-sellers. His books have sold millions of copies and have been translated into at least fourteen languages.

Divorced in the 1950's, Yerby moved to France and then to Spain, where he still resides. He has four children from his first marriage. His second wife is his researcher and general manager; some of his later novels give evidence of considerable research. He is widely traveled, and sometimes his travels have involved investigating locales of works in progress.

Analysis

Frank Yerby is a best-selling author, and much of what he has done has clear commercial appeal, a point on which Yerby has made inconsistent remarks. His plots are intricate and involved, but in many of his novels, the characterizations are basically flat. His most-used era is that of the nineteenth century South, yet he has written about many other places and times in his more than thirty novels. Occasionally, he has set a novel in modern times. The superficial reader of best-sellers will find in Yerby's novels fast-paced narrative with appropriate amounts of violence and sex.

Yerby is more, however, than a mere best-selling writer. His short stories written early in his career show promise and develop radically different themes from those of his costume novels. In the 1960's, secure after many commercial successes, Yerby began to do his best work, dealing with larger issues of race and religion which figure less prominently in his earlier novels. The characters in these later novels are no longer cardboard figures, while the backgrounds are as richly detailed and vividly re-created as ever. Yerby's historical novels must be evaluated within the context of that often unappreciated genre. His novels almost always show the conflict between two worlds or orders, as great historical novels do. Yerby rarely deals with actual historical figures but rather creates characters who have to deal with the essential conflicts of their eras. Often his novels, even the early ones, destroy widely held myths and stereotypes; Darwin Turner suggests that this revisionism might be Yerby's most significant contribution as a novelist. While extensive research is not evident in his early work, many of Yerby's later novels have been thoroughly researched. Yerby is at his best in creating the color and movement of a particular era.

Yerby's typical protagonist is, in the words of his main character in *The Serpent and the Staff*, an *auslander* or outsider, excluded from the ruling social order. The protagonist experientially develops a philosophy that often approaches modern existentialism, an attitude that life has no answer but that man still must cope with the bleakness of human existence with both dignity and humanity. This pattern emerges in Yerby's first novel, *The Foxes of Harrow*, and is developed in three of his best novels: *Griffin's Way*, *An Odor of Sanctity*, and *The Dahomean.*

The Foxes of Harrow, Yerby's first novel, is set in the South and covers the years from 1825 to just after the end of the Civil War. Superficially, it is a novel about a clever schemer who rises to own a plantation with a neo-classical mansion, Harrow, and who has marriages to beautiful white women and a liaison with a stunning mulatto. Much of the novel is composed of stock devices of pulp fiction, and Yerby himself recently said of *The Foxes of Harrow* that he set out to write a popular novel that would make him a lot of money, regardless of literary merit. Yerby added, however, that he became strangely involved with the writing of the novel and, despite himself, exceeded the ambitions of the pulp genre. Stephen Fox, the protagonist, is an outsider, originally shanty Irish. He is not merely the rogue that early reviewers took him for, whose success and eventual fall conform to a predictable pulp outline. Fox sees all values and ideals slip from him, so that at the end, he is a failure despite his humanity and perception. He is superior to the Southerners with whom he sympathetically deals. More than merely a novel of stock devices, *The Foxes of Harrow* is a story about the failure of a culture.

In the opening of the novel, Yerby's authorial voice establishes a pensive tone as he describes a visit to Harrow, now in ruins, in the twentieth century. Harrow is the symbol of a lost cause. Thus, for symbolic purposes, Harrow is cut off from the modern world. Bathed in moonlight, the ruins of Harrow have a decadent grandeur. The visitor feels driven from room to room and finally away from the house, never wanting to look back. The shortness of the opening, six brief paragraphs, makes the tone all the more striking, and the mood shifts quickly into the dialogue and description of the arrival of Stephen Fox in New Orleans in 1825.

Yerby is at his best in the novel in creating vivid images and scenes of the region during the forty or so years the novel spans. New Orleans appears as a lush feudalistic world where color is measured by degrees, given the novel's constant references to mulattos, quadroons, and octaroons, references which are historically true to the setting. New Orleans emerges as a backward society that refuses to drain the marshes where the mosquitoes carrying yellow fever breed and instead fires cannon to disperse the plague. The society also destroys the creativity of freed blacks. In one case, a thoroughly educated black returns from France and is killed for acting as if he were equal to whites. The most poignant scene occurs at the end of the novel, when the young heir to Harrow returns after the war to New Orleans to be confronted by a former slave of Harrow now in control. This former slave presents the heir's unknown half brother (by a beautiful mulatto) to his former master, who sees the image of his father as a young man—but the half brother is mentally retarded. As the scene concludes, Yerby deftly shows the social history of the next one hundred years of the South. The former slave, now the ruler, knows that power will again return to the whites but suggests that blacks and whites can live together and respect one another. The heir, a combination of the worst of his father's roguish tendencies and the excesses of New Orleans, emphatically denies that such equality and reconciliation between the races is possible.

Yerby is weakest in his creation of character in *The Foxes of Harrow*, for the characters are one-dimensional and move woodenly through a convoluted, overheated plot. Stephen Fox is the fox, the rogue set off from Southern society by his birth, whose goals are riches and the most beautiful woman in New Orleans, Odalie Arceneaux, a cold, haughty belle. Her sister Aurore is a foil to her, for she is warm and beautiful and in love with Stephen, who is too blind at first to see her love. As pulps have it, Odalie dies in childbirth, and Stephen then marries gentle Aurore, but only after having fathered a child by a beautiful mulatto when Odalie had spurned his strong sexual drives.

Underneath this claptrap, though, is an author working with social issues not to be found in the typical 1946 pulp novel. In one scene, a black woman recently inducted into slavery throws herself into the Mississippi rather than live in bondage. Old Calleen, a trusted slave at Harrow, later tells her grandson Inch (the son of the drowned slave) that someday, the rightness of their freedom will be made apparent. More significantly, in understated dialogue Stephen talks to his son Etienne about freeing slaves and says that the country must treat all people equally, including the blacks and the poorest whites. When his son dismisses the poor, white or black, Stephen uses history as a defense, mentioning the French Revolution, Haiti, and Nat Turner. It is in his sympathy and balance in treating social matters that Yerby's "moral mobility" appears, a phrase that a London *Times* writer used in reviewing a later Yerby novel.

Griffin's Way was published in 1962, sixteen years after *The Foxes of Harrow*, and is a departure in some respects from Yerby's work up to that time. It treats the Mississippi of the 1870's unglamorously, highlighting squalor, inbreeding among whites, and the violence of the Klan in a manner more characteristic of William Faulkner than of the standard best-selling author. The novel shows the paralysis of humane white society after the war, a paralysis symbolized by the central hero's amnesia and invalid status.

Much of the novel debunks the grandeur and opulence of the old South which Yerby himself had occasionally exploited in earlier novels. The ruined South appears first through the eyes of a Northerner, Candace Trevor, a New England minister's daughter married to a paralyzed Southerner and hired as a nurse for Paris Griffin as the novel opens. She despises the Southern "courtesy" to which women are subjected, dismisses the neoclassical architecture in the poorly constructed homes, and comments on how most planters lived in squalor even before the war. Unlike her father, she believes in a Darwinian theory of evolution and sees the darker forces in herself as part of the ape still remaining in man. Candace knows that to cure Paris of his amnesia she must find the key to it from Paris' oversexed wife Laurel. Ferreting out answers with the right leading questions, she discovers the tawdry, twisted story that led to Paris' amnesia and emotional paralysis. It is only her austere moral upbringing that allows her to control her love for Paris to use her knowledge to help him.

When Candace does cure him, Paris tries to return to his home, Griffin's Way, and to his wife Laurel, but while his cure is a rebirth, it does not allow a return. To begin with, he has returned to a world changed by the war, a world of political corruption and violence, a world that has regressed, so that even a sixty-mile trip, once possible in three hours, now involves an arduous three-day journey because the railroads remain unrepaired even five years after the war. Three years later, with the railroad rebuilt, Paris and Laurel visit Vicksburg, where Paris, despite his humanity, appears troubled by the apparent ascendancy of blacks. Yerby balances the situation by having Paris also see the obvious corruption of the black superintendent of schools, who lives in the grand style of the old South on money intended for the schools. Paris is thus caught between two worlds: he rejects the Klan as apes but resents a black man wearing a suit as if he is accustomed to it. Even renewed, Paris still represents the paralysis of the humane white during the Reconstruction.

Yerby entitled the last third of the novel "Apocalypse," and this part has unresolved elements, unresolved on account of Yerby's honesty in dealing with his material. Paris watches the new world tumble around him, powerless to do anything. Black militants and white Klansmen fight all over the South, but Paris can only catalog the battles; he cannot change events. His moment of action does allow him to rescue Samson, a former slave, and Samson's wife by helping them escape to the North. He can do nothing to help his brother, his mulatto wife, and their children, who are burned in their house except for one daughter, who dies after being repeatedly raped, all of them victims of the Klan. He also helps a black minister escape, but only after the dynamiting of the minister's house, which killed a daughter. At his daughter's funeral, the minister delivers a stern sermon to the Klan members, who then threaten his life so that Paris must again help him. The Klan members finally back off from Paris' house when one accidentally shoots Laurel, still very much a symbol of Southern womanhood. The novel ends with dawn imagery, the night having been endured and the humane whites now waiting for the light of morning. Whether the whites threatened by the Klan can start anew is unclear. Given the implied parallel to modern events, Yerby seems to be saying that it is too soon to tell if the twentieth century can rise above racial violence; nevertheless, the concluding imagery does suggest hope.

In *An Odor of Sanctity*, Yerby is at his best as a historical novelist. It is a long, deftly paced novel which, while using many of the stock elements of Yerby's novels of the 1940's and 1950's, also deals intelligently with a religious theme. Once again, Yerby creates an outsider, Alaric Teudisson, as hero; he is set off by his odor of sanctity, a saintly force in him of which he is not fully aware for most of his life. Teudisson must deal with the complex culture of medieval Spain, a battleground for Christians, Moors, and numerous bands of marauding barbarians.

Like earlier Yerby protagonists, Teudisson is involved in many liaisons and several marriages. Teudisson is a striking blond of Visigoth extraction who, before the male hormones take effect, is so "beautiful" that at one point he is almost made a catamite. Thereafter, Teudisson has numerous sexual encounters, one unconsummated marriage, and finally a marriage to a woman who has been repeatedly raped by bandits, a marriage which shows Teudisson's magnanimity and one which also brings Teudisson genuine happiness and a family.

The religious motif of *An Odor of Sanctity* adds depth to what would otherwise be an entertaining but rather shallow melodrama. Despite himself, Alaric Teudisson becomes a saint by the end of the novel. As a man, Teudisson is handsome but scarred by battle, but as a boy, his beauty, so unlike the usual rough Goth face, led his mother and others to think he was marked for the priesthood. He turns from his religious impulses to lead a secular life, however, and while doing so, he finds his saintliness. In dealing with women, he shows a compassion and love that is the basis of his profound sexual appeal; at one point of seeming dissolution, he has numerous prostitutes loving him because he has talked to them and treated them as human beings and not merely as sex objects. Misused by a woman, he always responds with kindness. By the end of the novel, Teudisson becomes the arbiter between Moor and Christian factions when a certain group of fanatic Christians want to destroy all tolerance for the predominant Moors. Throughout the novel, Teudisson has been a genuine ecumenist. At the end, Teudisson, doubting his saintly powers because he is unable to save his wife, willingly seeks crucifixion and thus enters sainthood and legend. In losing himself, he gains sainthood.

As in most of his novels, Yerby's greatest strength in *An Odor of Sanctity* is his re-creation of a time, a re-creation imbued with color and action. Again, a humane authorial voice speaks throughout the novel. The book shows that the diversity of medieval Spain is indeed its glory. While the Moorish culture encourages learning and recognizes Christ as a prophet, the contrasting Christian culture (except for Teudisson and a few Church fathers) is dark and intolerant. In showing the clash between these cultures, *An Odor of Sanctity* is first-rate historical fiction.

If one of Yerby's novels is destined to last, it is *The Dahomean*, a novel unlike any of his others. It is a simple, moving tale of the life of a black man in his African culture before he was sold into slavery. Yerby neither idealizes nor sensationalizes his material but presents a story composed of love, envy, and hatred that reads as a legend, a story of characters and events drawn larger than life. The protagonist, Nyasanu, is like other Yerby protagonists because he is an alien or outsider: he is far less violent and far more handsome than most men of his society. Caught in the ugliness of the American slave-system, he has the tragic quality of some of the great existentialist heroes.

Yerby begins the chronological narrative of Nyasanu as he is about to enter manhood, a passage marked by the painful ritual of circumcision. The early parts of the novel present such rituals in convincing detail. Yerby moves the reader from Nyasanu's initiation to an enemy's attempt to destroy his guardian tree to his wedding and the deflowering of his bride. In "A Note to the Reader," Yerby explains that the novel is based on research into the customs of the Dahomeans of the nineteenth century, but Yerby adds to his research his own respect of this African culture.

As Nyasanu moves through his period of manhood, Yerby depicts the society of the Dahomeans as a stage for the great primal emotions and forces of life. Nyasanu has encounters with numerous women, but his sexual experiences are never merely sensational, the stuff of popular fiction: Nyasanu has a reality which sets him apart from Yerby's typical protagonists. In addition to his sexual encounters, Nyasanu also has the experience of real brotherhood, for his society expects each male to have his three closest friends identified in order. Battles with warring tribes give Nyasanu the chance to show bravery and also to distinguish himself as more sensitive to violence than the average Dahomean. In addition, Yerby shows the diversity of Dahomean society, which includes both male homosexuals and Amazonian warriors.

In a moving discussion with his number one friend, Kpadunu, Nyasanu learns that the generations are all of one fabric. Each generation faces the same problems of love, the family, and death. The old priests, therefore, give answers based on the past to the young and the unsure, and—given the coherence of their society—the answers generally hold. Facing the problem of belief in the gods which these old priests try to inculcate in the young, Nyasanu realizes that their wisdom is not divine but experiential, that the past of his society answers the present needs. Ironically, his friend Kpadunu is trying to help Nyasanu rise above the control of priests by showing where their wisdom resides, yet he actually makes the skeptical Nyasanu believe more than he did, so that he must face the priestly prediction that his life will end in Dahomey but will begin again in another place.

Nyasanu does learn that he can count on the inexorability of fate and not the protection of the gods. In quick succession, he loses his friend Kpadunu, his wife in childbirth, and his father. He comes to see his heroism as mere foolishness in taking risks. Rather than listening to the gods, he simply faces life as chieftain and husband of Kpadunu's widow. Far more than the ritual of circumcision, his acceptance of life and his rejection of the illusion of divine protection marks Nyasanu's adulthood. When Nyasanu next appears in the novel, he is chieftain and has four wives. His life is successful until he is sold into slavery with the aid of his homosexual brother and rival.

The betrayal of Nyasanu has the archetypal pattern of tragedy, the hero fallen from great heights, undone by his own blindness in not facing the evil of his brother and his incestuous brother-in-law and by his pride in not following the past and living with his extended family in the same compound. He faces the guns of his attackers with his sword, only to be told to put his sword down, for in the modern era, swords are powerless against guns. First, he must watch the murder of his mother (the slavers see that she is too old to have children), the subsequent murder of all his children (the slavers know that they would die on the voyage across the Atlantic), and the subjugation of his wives, the rape of some and the suicide of one. His response is disassociation, a silence which lasts the rest of his life.

Like a classical tragedy, *The Dahomean* treats terrible despair in its conclusion but leads to an illumination, Nyasanu's enlightenment. He recognizes the evil of blacks selling blacks into American slavery, although they have no conception of the degradation of this foreign slavery, their domestic slavery being gentle and indulgent. Philosophically, Nyasanu faces the bleakness of life with the realization that there are no answers. Truth is only that there is no truth. Nyasanu acquits himself with honor; like a great tragic hero, he has his dignity, the dignity of silence in the face of the emptiness of the human condition.

Bibliography

Hemenway, Robert, ed. *The Black Novelist*, 1970.

Kinsman, Clare D., and Mary Ann Tennenhouse, eds. *Contemporary Authors*, 1974.

Mendelson, Phyllis Carmen, and Dedria Bryfonski, eds. *Contemporary Literary Criticism*, 1977.

Dennis Goldsberry

JOSÉ YGLESIAS

Born: Tampa, Florida; November 29, 1919

Principal long fiction

Island of Women, 1962 (translation, published in England as *Sands of Torremolinos*); *Villa Milo*, 1962 (translation); *A Wake in Ybor City*, 1963; *The Party's Over*, 1966 (translation); *An Orderly Life*, 1967; *The Truth About Them*, 1971; *Double Double*, 1974; *The Kill Price*, 1976.

Other literary forms

In addition to his five novels, José Yglesias has contributed many articles and short stories to such respected journals as *The New Yorker*, *The Nation*, *Esquire*, *The Atlantic*, and *The Sunday Times Magazine*. He has also translated novels by Juan Goytisolo and Xavier Domingo from Spanish into English. His four major nonfictional works have been praised for their clear narrative prose. Focusing on Spain and Latin America, these works provide the American reader with the all too rare opportunity to meet individual Spaniards and Latin Americans, to see their socioeconomic and political situation from their own perspective. In *The Goodbye Land* (1967), which first appeared in serial form in *The New Yorker* in the spring of 1967, Yglesias recounts his 1965 trip to Galicia, Spain, where his father, a native Galician, returned home to die. Some forty years after his father's death, Yglesias visits his father's birthplace in search of the many unanswered questions concerning his last years. In uncovering the truth about his father, Yglesias also discovers the captivating beauty of the Galician people. His second book of nonfiction, *In the Fist of the Revolution* (1968), describes the everyday life of a small town, Mayarí, in post revolutionary Cuba, while *Down There* (1970) is a broader analysis of Latin-American reality. Based on interviews he conducted in 1969 with various groups of politically involved Latin Americans (in Cuba, Brazil, Chile, and Peru), the book captures many of the hopes and frustrations experienced by Latin America's militantly anti-American youth. In *The Franco Years* (1977), Yglesias presents a candid analysis of the controversial Spanish dictator, Generalísimo Francisco Franco, and the alternatives facing post-Franco Spain.

Achievements

José Yglesias' many contributions to magazines such as *The New Yorker* have made his name both known and respected throughout the American literary establishment. Several of his stories have appeared in *Best American Stories* (1972 and 1975). His books on Spain and Latin America have been recognized not only for their documentary value but also for their literary merit. Yglesias' fluid narrative style and seemingly effortless ability to describe the complex and diverse realities of the Spanish-speaking world, have brought him several prestigious academic awards. He was the recipient of a John Simon Guggenheim Memorial Foundation Fellowship both in 1970 and 1976. As a result of these grants, he produced a penetrating analysis of Francisco Franco's waning influence in contemporary Spain, *The Franco Years*. In 1974, he was awarded a grant from the National Endowment for the Arts. Because of his bilingual upbringing (his father was Spanish and his mother Cuban), he was the ideal writer to visit postrevolutionary Cuba. He spent three months there in the spring of 1967 with the people of Mayarí. On the basis of this unique experience, he wrote *In the Fist of the Revolution*, a rare glimpse of the Cuban people as they truly are, and not as Americans prefer to imagine them. Curiously, it is Yglesias' nonfiction that has received the greatest praise from reviewers and critics. His novels, for the most part, have not enjoyed such acclaim. Possibly, since each novel deals with a Cuban-American or Mexican-American protagonist, a better understanding and appreciation of Hispanic-American reality would allow the American critic to view these works with a broader perspective, opening areas of literary investigation.

Biography

José Yglesias was born in Tampa, Florida, on November 29, 1919. Reared in a Spanish-speaking home in the Cuban sector of Tampa known as Ybor City, his mixed Hispanic heritage was to play a major role in his development as a writer. Perhaps it was the fact that his father left home to return to his beloved Galicia when Yglesias was only a child, or perhaps it was the schizophrenic experience of growing up in America as a Cuban-American that planted the first seeds of interest in his Hispanic-American heritage. Whatever the cause, Yglesias' enthusiastic quest to learn all he could about his background is evident throughout his fiction. His novels generally center around the fragmented psyche of a Hispanic-American protagonist who is searching for his spiritual center. Two days after he was graduated from high school in Tampa, Yglesias left for New York City, where he experienced the freedom that always accompanies the abandonment of one's hometown environment; on the other hand, mistaken frequently for a Puerto Rican, he became even more conscious of his identity as a Hispanic American. During World War II, he served in the United States Naval Reserve for three years, where he received the Naval Merit Citation. After the war, he decided to go back to school. He attended Black Mountain College for one year (1946-1947) before returning to New York City, where he met his wife-to-be, Helen Bassine. They were married on August 19, 1950. Before devoting himself full-time to writing, he worked in New York City for a pharmaceutical company, rising from an entry-level job to an executive position. His initial attempts at writing consisted almost entirely of reviews or articles for literary magazines; he also translated several books from Spanish into English. It was not until 1963, with the publication of his first novel, *A Wake in Ybor City*, that he began to utilize fully the rich material that his Tampa/Manhattan connection provided him. Presently living in North Brooklin, Maine, he continues to be active both in the world of fiction and nonfiction. His wife, Helen, and his son, Rafael, are both accomplished novelists.

Analysis

There is a special quality to each of José Yglesias' novels, a kind of aura that seems to tell the reader that he or she is entering a fictional world radically different from the Anglo-American tradition. Although each novel is unique unto itself, there is in all of his novels a definite tension underlying the seemingly natural flow of events, a kind of double vision that stems from Yglesias' diverse and at times conflicting heritage. Brought up in a Cuban-American environment that was more Latin than American, he moved to New York City while still young. There, he encountered head-on the rather old and impersonal but nonetheless captivating charm of mainstream America. Having experienced the tenuous acceptance that is given to all those who succeed in Anglo-America's melting pot, Yglesias has never rejected his Latin roots. The result is a unique mestizo portrayal of American reality. The vision presented in *A Wake in Ybor City*, *An Orderly Life*, *The Truth About Them*, *Double Double*, and *The Kill Price* is at once reminiscent of the seventeenth century Spanish *picaro* and the twentieth century New York intellectual. Like the Peruvian novelist Jose Maria Arguedas, who committed suicide in 1969, Yglesias presents the world through the eyes of one who belongs simultaneously to two distinct realities. Thus, the reader is treated to a rare opportunity: an inside view of the world as seen from the perspective of a semi-outsider.

Yglesias returns to the place of his youth, Ybor City, for the setting of his first novel, *A Wake in Ybor City*. An omniscient third-person narrator recounts three days in the life of a Cuban-American family in 1958. The novel's simple structure and fluid style pose no problem to the reader, who quickly finds himself more and more involved in a moving depiction of a family's struggle to face several crises that threaten to destroy their uncommonly close ties with one another.

The story is simple. An aging widow, Dolores, anxiously awaits the arrival of her children, who will be visiting her from Havana, Cuba. Elena, the eldest daughter, is married to a wealthy and influential Cuban aristocrat, Jaime. They are scheduled to arrive the next day with Dolores' other daughter, Clara, and her son, Jimmy. During the two days following their arrival, several unforeseen events occur that rock the very foundation of Dolores' family, perhaps foreshadowing the political upheaval that was to undo Batista's Cuba the following year.

Almost immediately, the reader is introduced to Dolores' extended family. First, there are her two widowed sisters, Mina and Clemencia. Then come the children and their families. Mina's son Feliz is a weak man, totally dominated by his mother and equally unsuccessful with other women. He has been married four times. Clemencia's son Roberto is visiting for the summer from New York City with his Jewish-American (non-Cuban) wife, Shirley, and their two children. Roberto is a struggling artist who, in his idealistic youth (he is now thirty-seven) was involved with the political left. Of all the characters, Roberto comes closest to being Yglesias' alter ego. Dolores, besides her two daughters who are visiting from Cuba, has two sons, one in Miami (Mario) and another one, her youngest, Armando. Although Armando is living at home, he previously had served in the Army, during which time he was married to and later divorced from an American (non-Cuban) girl named Katie. Of all the children, Armando seems the most lost. His association with a local gangster, Wally Chase, distresses his mother. One of the two reasons for Elena's visit to Ybor City is to offer Armando a lucrative position in Cuba. Armando initially refuses this offer but later is forced to accept it when his boss is mysteriously killed. Armando is suspected of involvement in the slaying and flees, with the help of his family, to Cuba. The other reason for Elena's return is to obtain permission from her sister's ex-husband, Esteban, to adopt Jimmy. Jimmy's sudden and unexpected death, a result of complications that arise after an emergency appendectomy, shocks the reader as well as Dolores' entire family.

What might, at first reading, appear to be a typically melodramatic story, whose unexpected and tragic ending leaves the reader stunned and therefore properly entertained, takes on a somewhat deeper significance upon further reflection. What Yglesias has done in fabricating his tale about a wake in Ybor City is to introduce the Anglo-American reader to some of the characteristic elements of Cuban-American life that ordinarily are not accessible to mainstream Americans. In particular, *A Wake in Ybor City* focuses on two important aspects of Cuban-American life: the family, and the male's ambivalent role in the family structure.

From the outset, it is clear that Dolores, Mina, and Clemencia are the spiritual as well as the political authorities of this Cuban-American family. The fact that the reader never learns their surnames suggests that the matriarchal structure portrayed here is representative of the Cuban-American family in general. Moreover, their given names reveal some of the qualities of the typical matriarch. Of the three, Mina (a mine of hidden wealth) is the realist. She is a practical woman whose earthy wisdom constantly returns the family to everyday reality where difficult decisions must be made and their consequences accepted. Clemencia ("Mercy") is a compassionate and understanding woman. Dolores ("Sorrows") is the dominant one among the three and embodies the role of the suffering mother. She is a romantic, a writer of heroic dramas and pastoral poems that reflect her subjective and distorted vision of her family. Together, these three women are the heart, head, and loving arms that control and sustain the life of this Cuban-American family. Living as an isolated island within the American mainstream, their primary mission is to protect the family at all costs. As the novel progresses, it becomes clear that the new matriarch who is to succeed the three aging women is Elena. It is her responsibility to take the reins of authority so that the family structure can continue to exist in relative peace and security. Elena has already helped set up her brother Mario in Miami. It is she who arranges Armando's escape to Cuba, and it is she who is organizing the legal adoption of her nephew Jimmy before his untimely death. Perhaps Elena's failure to save Jimmy, the family's youngest, from death is a foreshadowing of the eventual breakdown of the matriarchal family structure. To the extent that the younger members, such as Roberto, decide to leave the security of Ybor City and enter into the mainstream of American (non-Cuban) society, the inhibiting influence of the dominant mother figure will diminish.

The undisputed primacy of women in the Cuban-American family gives rise to a particular problem concerning the men, commonly referred to as machismo. Since the male's role in the family is ambivalent at best, he feels pressured to prove his manhood outside the family structure. This machismo is expressed by extramarital sexual conquests or by even more violent manifestations of strength and superiority. Except for Roberto, who has abandoned the matriarchal environment of Ybor City, the other male characters fail miserably in their quest for manliness within the family structure. Feliz, who has been married four times, is still an adolescent psychologically. For him, it is baseball which allows a man to prove his worth. Esteban, although a highly committed revolutionary, can only relate to women as sex-objects. Armando, whose marriage to Katie failed shortly after he brought her back home to live with his mother, fears any form of adult responsibility. Even Roberto, who is the strongest of the male characters, has difficulty looking directly at women. Jimmy, the youngest grandson, is virtually smothered by the attention given to him by all the women of the family. Perhaps the best indication of female superiority is Dolores' criticism of God for having allowed her grandson to die. According to Dolores, her status as one of the family's matriarchs has given her the right to scold God. In such a female-dominated environment, there is little place for the man to feel useful, let alone important. With these insightful vignettes of Cuban-American life, *A Wake in Ybor City* introduces the American (non-Cuban) reader to a part of America normally outside his experience.

Unlike Yglesias' first novel, which described an entire family's struggle to maintain its Cuban-American identity in the threatening ambience of a changing Tampa, Florida, *An Orderly Life* focuses on one individual. His name is Rafael Sabas. In many ways, Rafe resembles Roberto of *A Wake in*

Ybor City. If Jimmy's death prefigured the family's eventual loss of Latin-American identity by allowing itself to be absorbed into America's amorphous mass of humanity, Rafe represents the extreme to which one may fall prey to the great American dream while still carrying within him the seeds of his Latin heritage. Narrated in the first person, *An Orderly Life* allows the reader an intimacy with its protagonist that is absent in Yglesias' first novel. The year is 1963, and Rafe has just been offered the vice-presidency of a prestigious New York pharmaceutical house; Yglesias employs repeated flashbacks so that the reader can come to know Rafe as he climbs the social ladder of success.

In a sense, the novel presents Rafael Sabas' definition of a happy man. In the final sentence of the book, Rafe defines himself in just those terms. When the reader considers that this "happy man" has spent the last twenty years of his life using and abusing friends and business partners alike so that he might continue to climb the corporate ladder, it is clear that *An Orderly Life* is meant to be a stinging indictment of the American way of life.

Rafe is the epitome of the cold and calculating executive who will not rest until he has made it to the top. There was a time, however, when his zeal to get ahead in life was relatively uncontaminated by the lust for wealth and power. In the 1930's, while attending City College in New York he joined the Young Communist League, where he came to know and later to develop a deep friendship with two politically active students, Jerry and Gloria. During World War II, he served in the Navy, where he spent much of his free time trying to improve himself by reading grammar books and college composition texts. While still in the service, he married a lovely young woman named Betty Evans, whom he first met while at City college. After leaving the service, he joined his father-in-law's pharmaceutical firm, Smith-Jonas, where he gradually worked his way to the vice-presidency. Blessed with two children, a loving wife, and a beautiful home in Scotch Plains, Rafe at age forty-two seems to be what he claims—a happy man. The reader, however, is aware of the numerous betrayals, compromises, and lies that Rafe was pressured into making in order to protect his professional career. At one point, the reader hears him say that he would never let sex or friendship get in the way of his professional advancement. When given the opportunity to help his poverty-stricken cousin Abel in Cuba, he calmly rationalizes that his cousin was anti-Castro, and therefore deserving of his plight. The list of betrayals is long, to the point of seeming contrived. What would be merely another saga concerning a ruthless executive's struggle in the corporate jungle of New York City takes on a deeper significance, however, when one remembers that Rafael Sabas comes out of the Cuban-American community of Tampa, Florida. As such, *An Orderly Life* is not only a powerful statement against the inherent evils of the corporate milieu, but also a sensitive portrayal of a Cuban-American male's struggle for manhood (machismo).

Rafe's inordinate need to "win," be it in friendship, love, or business, is less difficult to understand if the reader looks upon these affairs and betrayals as the adventures of one who is struggling to prove his worth as a man. Yglesias provides many subtle reminders that Rafe is basically an insecure man whose search for self-affirmation is hidden by his many seemingly "manly" acts of conquest. For example, Rafe's constant need to demonstrate his sexual prowess outside marriage is but a mask concealing his true feelings of inferiority in his relationship with women. Although quick to "enjoy" a woman, any woman, he is unable to look directly into her eyes. Moreover, in choosing the woman he wants as his wife, he selects a virgin whose purity and innocence inhibits him when expressing his love sexually. From the traditional Latin male's perspective, Rafael Sabas is truly a happy man, for he has proven himself to be *macho*—on the one hand, a loving father who provides his family with a comfortable and secure environment, on the other hand, a successful business executive who has managed to play at the game of life and win.

Yglesias' third novel, *The Truth About Them* focuses once again on the family history of a Cuban-American clan, whose American experience dates from 1890, when the narrator's aristocratic grandmother first arrived in Tampa, Florida. Although much of their life in America is associated with the up-and-down fortunes of Florida's cigar industry, this working-class family displays a pride and cohesiveness that defies all obstacles. During the lean years of the 1930's, some members of the clan are forced to go north to New York City in search of jobs. Before long, however, they find themselves drifting back to Ybor City, owned and controlled by the cigar company. The narrator, much like Roberto of *A Wake in Ybor City*, is truly a Cuban-American. Brought up in the very Latin atmosphere of Ybor City, he eventually becomes a left-wing journalist and learns to swim freely in America's traditionless mainstream. Eager to learn more about his Latin roots, however, he visits postrevolutionary Cuba, an experience that engenders a newfound pride in his Cuban background.

In a sense, *The Truth About Them* is a very straightforward reconstruction of a family's history. It is neither more nor less than what is proclaims itself to be—an attempt at uncovering and relating the truth about one's heritage. Since this novel covers a greater time-span than that of *A Wake in Ybor City*, it serves to fill in the historical background lacking in Yglesias' first novel. Written in an episodic style (several adventures were first published separately in *The New Yorker*), this fictionalized family portrait with its rich and varied characters, its fast-moving plot, and its free-flowing style, offers a panoramic vision of a part of America generally unknown to non-Cuban Americans. Its detailed and loving depiction of a specific ethnic group seems to say that America is that much greater for having accepted as its own such resolute and distinctive communities.

As the years separate the 1960's from the present, the value of *Double Double*, Yglesias' tongue-in-cheek depiction of this turbulent decade, continues to increase. The focus, once again, is on one main character, Seth Evergood. Through Yglesias' skillful use of interior monologues, the reader comes to know Seth very well and, more important, comes to experience the excitement, the energy, the confusion, the hypocrisy, and above all, the naïve innocence that characterized the 1960's.

The reader follows Seth Evergood, a politically avant-garde author-lecturer, through a series of adventures that recall many of the so-called movements of the 1960's: student rights, draft resistance, the Black Panthers, Third World involvement, the Puerto Rican Liberation movement, Flower Power, and so on. What makes *Double Double* a truly valuable re-creation of the 1960's, however, is not merely its many references to specific historial events or people, but rather its double perspective on an age that has come to be looked upon both as the best of times and the worst of times.

The reader first encounters Seth as he is completing a lecture at a small Pennsylvania college to a group of intensely idealistic young students. They respond to his call for more student involvement and possible draft resistance by enthusiastically accompanying him to the town bus depot, where he supposedly must catch the next bus to New York City in order to arrive on time for an important meeting concerning the political upheaval in Bolivia.

On the surface, Seth Evergood seems to be what his name indicates—a man standing for all that is good and wholesome in life. Once the reader is permitted to enter into Seth's heart and head, however, it becomes obvious that he is an extremely insecure man. Although attracted by the chaotic social ferment of the 1960's and capable at times of believing his own revolutionary rhetoric, Seth is fundamentally a confused and disillusioned individual. Wanting desperately to stand above his fellow men and to lead them in their quest for freedom, Seth has difficulty accepting his own reality. Dependent on amphetamines and aspirin to help him through each day, undergoing psychoanalysis regarding his marriage, he nevertheless allows himself to become involved in a dangerous adventure. His friend Gary asks Seth to accompany him on a trip to Vermont to pick up contraband for the Black Panther organization. In the meantime, Seth is offered a contract to write a book about his father, James Evergood, who led the International Brigade in the Spanish Civil War. The trip to Vermont brings Seth and Gary to a commune, where they spend an unforgettable night replete with drugs, sex, and heavy "existential rapping." On the following day, when Seth turns the ignition of his car to begin their trip back to New York, there is an explosion, and *Double Double* comes to a sudden end, much like the era of the 1960's—with a roar, but with little evidence that such a reality or unreality ever existed.

For the most part, reviewers have failed to see Yglesias' deliberate attempt to capture the Camelot atmosphere that pervaded this decade. Resembling a bubble that floats effortlessly through the air enchanting all who see its delicate, transparent beauty, the 1960's captured the imagination and aspirations of many people. Like all bubbles, however, this euphoric time in American history was destined to come to an abrupt and violent end. *Double Double* has been criticized as a "cliché-ridden" depiction of the 1960's. If one focuses, however, on the schizophrenic world of the protagonist, Seth Evergood, it becomes clear that what appears to be a superficial portrayal of the 1960's is actually a highly original re-creation of an era that was both defined and destroyed by the unbalanced interplay between idealism and realism—with Seth Evergood as the embodiment of this conflict.

In his fifth novel, *The Kill Price*, which focuses on a theme that is too frequently avoided—death and dying—Yglesias displays a growing mastery over the narrative form. The few but well developed characters (a dying man named Wolf, his wife, and three friends) and the concentration of place and time (Wolf's apartment on the night of his death) permit the reader to share in the fear, the frustration, and ultimately the personal revelation that one inevitably experiences on witnessing the death of a loved one. The feeling of immediacy that is created by such an intense convergence of time and place is counterbalanced by Yglesias' timely retreats into the thoughts and feelings of the protagonist, Jack Moreno, Wolf's closest friend. Besides the intimacy that Jack's interior monologues allow the reader, the necessary distance for reflection is also established. It is Yglesias' skillful juxtaposition of cinematiclike close-ups and fade-outs that make *The Kill Price* a superbly written novel. Whereas the close-ups capture the magnitude of the moment, subsequent fade-outs transport the reader away from the immediate situation and allow for internalization of events.

The first third of the novel recounts Jack's memories as he walks over to Wolf's West Side apartment. Jack is a successful New York journalist whose cosmopolitan, jet set life-style is in conflict with the values of his Chicano upbringing in El Paso, Texas. He reflects about his past, how he abandoned his story on César Chávez and the Farm Worker's movement in Los Angeles to be with T. D., Wolf's wife, when Wolf was forced to return a second time to the hospital, and how his efforts to comfort T. D. eventually led to their having an affair. Further reflections inform the reader about Wolf's past, how he was previously married to Mary Anne, had a son by her, and eventually went through a painful divorce which he later used as material for his novel, *Breaking Away*.

When Jack arrives at Wolf's apartment, he is greeted by Carol, a New York actress who was Wolf's girl friend before he and T. D. were married. Although Wolf is suffering from an advanced case of lung cancer and is near death, the three closest people in his life (Jack, T. D., and Carol) act as if there is nothing terribly wrong, for Wolf has been told that he is recuperating from an attack of pleurisy. Although it is obvious that Wolf is aware of the seriousness of his condition, he, too, plays along in the charade. Wolf's former brother-in-law, Perry, arrives shortly after Jack. A long-time acquaintance of both Wolf and Jack, Perry has never managed to penetrate into their inner circle of friendship. He joins in the tacit deception concerning Wolf's illness, directing Wolf's attention from his present condition by requesting the film rights to his novel. He further distracts Wolf by offering to arrange to have his son, whom Wolf has not seen in more than a decade, come and stay with him and T. D. The charade comes to a sudden end, however, when Wolf dies, leaving his friends behind to deal with death's seemingly unchallenged dominion over life.

Although the actions seems to center around Wolf's untimely death, the novel's true focus is on Jack. His friend's death is but the catalyst that awakens him to his own inner emptiness. Wolf's terminal illness is the most dramatic reminder of death to appear in the novel. There is the death of a neighborhood, depicted by the West Side's deterioration; there is the death by drugs of the black celebrity Tiny Dick, whom Jack had once encountered while flying back to New York; there is the death of a lost love, as experienced by Wolf in his painful divorce from Mary Anne; moreover, the nation itself, presently embroiled in the Watergate fiasco, is in a state of moral decay.

Of all the forms of death present in *The Kill Price*, none is more devastating than the death one experiences on rejecting the truth about oneself. In leaving El Paso, first to go to Iowa for his college education and then on to New York for his career as a journalist, Jack was not going *to* some place as much as he was fleeing *from* some reality—his Chicano heritage. It takes the harrowing experience of seeing his best friend unable to express openly the truth of his imminent death, to force Jack to acknowledge that the life he has been living in New York is no life at all, but a lie. As his surname indicates (*Moreno* means "dark"), he is Chicano, and it is by embracing his Mexican-American heritage that he will truly begin to live, and therefore know how to die—in dignity and peace.

The vision presented in *A Wake in Ybor City*, *An Orderly Life*, *The Truth About Them*, *Double Double*, and *The Kill Price* allows the reader a rare glimpse into the schizophrenic existence of the Cuban-American as he attempts to enter the mainstream of American society. Yglesias draws deeply from the well of his dual heritage and shares a refreshingly different perspective on American reality. American society may be likened to a finely woven tapestry whose cultural threads weave in and out, creating an endless array of patterns. Yglesias' novels, by focusing on one particular thread, the Cuban-American reality, help the reader to appreciate the unfathomable richness of America's multicultural heritage.

Major publications other than long fiction
NONFICTION: *The Goodbye Land*, 1967; *In the Fist of the Revolution*, 1968;

Down There, 1970; *The Franco Years*, 1977.

Bibliography
"José Yglesias," in *Contemporary Authors*, 1974.
Nelson, Milo G. "Review of *Double Double*," in *Library Journal*. XCIX, no. 10 (May 15, 1974), p. 1410.
"Review of *Double Double*," in *Kirkus Reviews*. XLII (February 15, 1974), p. 211.
"Review of *The Kill Price*," in *Booklist*. LXXII, no. 17 (May 1, 1976), p. 1244.
"Review of *The Kill Price*," in *Kirkus Reviews*. XLIV (March 15, 1976), p. 349.
"Review of *An Orderly Life*," in *Kirkus Reviews*. XXXVI (July 1, 1968), p. 720.

Richard Keenan

AL YOUNG

Born: Ocean Springs, Mississippi: May 31, 1939

Principal long fiction

Snakes, 1970; *Who Is Angelina?*, 1974; *Sitting Pretty*, 1976; *Ask Me Now*, 1980.

Other literary forms

In addition to his fiction, Al Young has produced several volumes of poetry, the first being *Dancing: Poems* in 1969. His twin themes are the American family and individual maturation. Early in this century, Ezra Pound warned modern poets that music separated from dance will atrophy, as will poetry separated from music; accordingly, Al Young's love of the rhythms of life places music between poetry and dance. His second volume of poems is entitled *The Song Turning Back into Itself* (1971). Here, the singer of life confronts images of a Whitmanesque America less musical, choral perhaps, certainly panoramic: the singer's song becomes the poet's vision. In *Geography of the Near Past* (1976) and *The Blues Don't Change: New and Selected Poems* (1982), the music and the dancing continue along Young's thematic lines of loving and growing.

In 1981, Young published his autobiographical *Bodies and Soul: Musical Memoirs*, which makes use of specific pieces of music to provide continuity and to set the tone for related essays, each based on personal recollection. *The Blues Don't Change* incorporates musical rhythms and quotations of Chinese poets into a collection of poems designed to dance with "laughter in the blood."

Besides work represented in major anthologies such as the *Heath Introduction to Poetry* (1975) and *How Does a Poem Mean?* (1976), edited by John Ciardi and Miller Williams, Young has written articles and stories for *New Times*, *Rolling Stone*, *Evergreen Review*, *Journal of Black Poetry*, *Essence*, *Massachusetts Review*, and other national publications. He has also written screenplays and scenarios for Laser Film Corporation and Stigwood Corporation in New York and Verdon Productions, First Artists Ltd., and Universal Pictures in California.

Achievements

During the mid-1960's, Young founded and edited *Loveletter*, an avant-garde review which has received awards from the National Arts Council. He is the West Coast editor of *Changes*, and in 1975 was guest fiction editor of the *Iowa Review*. With Ishmael Reed, he edits the biennial anthology *Yardbird Reader*, and was coeditor of *Yardbird Lives*, published in 1979.

A selection of Young's poems and an introductory essay are included in the 1979 anthology *Calafía: The California Poetry*. *Calafía* is a widely recognized project that examines the poetry of the West Coast, with recognition of a regional tradition extending back through the nineteenth century.

Young was a Wallace E. Stegner fellow in 1966, and in 1969, he was the recipient of the Joseph Henry Jackson Award for his first collection of poetry, *Dancing*. The California Association of Teachers of English selected Young to receive a special award in 1973. He was a Guggenheim fellow in 1974, received a National Endowment for the Arts fellowship in 1975, and the Pushcart Prize for poetry in 1980.

Biography

Albert James Young, the son of Mary (Campbell) and Albert James Young, attended the University of Michigan from 1957 to 1961 and received his A.B. in Spanish from the University of California at Berkeley in 1969. He and his wife Arline June (Belch) were married in 1963 and have a son, Michael James.

Young taught writing at the San Francisco Museum of Art during the late 1960's and was linguistic consultant for the Berkeley Neighborhood Youth Corps. From 1969 to 1973, he held the Stanford University Edward H. Jones lectureship in creative writing. He was the 1979 director of Associated Writing Programs, an organization of graduate university administrators, teachers, and students of creative writing, was writer-in-residence at the University of Washington in Seattle from 1981 to 1982, and served as consultant to the New York writer's organization *Poets & Writers* from 1974 to 1975. He has read his work at the Cooper Union Forum for the Academy of American Poets in Manhattan and the Young Men's and Women's Hebrew Association Poetry Series.

Having lectured at numerous universities in the United States, and having traveled extensively in Canada, Mexico, Portugal, Spain, and France, Young has also had presentations of his work produced and broadcast by KQED-TV, San Francisco, and the Pacifica Radio Network—appropriately, since, among various other jobs, his early career included an acting role in a television documentary about Archie Moore, a year as a disc jockey, and, prior to that, eight years as a professional jazz musician.

Analysis

Al Young's concern for language, a concern that embraces mistrust and love, is clearly evinced in his prose. Unfortunately, his second novel *Who Is Angelina?*, and his fourth, *Ask Me Now*, have third-person narrative personae who stand distractingly close to their author; they appear hesitant to act freely for want of purpose. Readers of the first and third novels, however, will quickly recognize Young's ability to render in his first-person narrative personae a vibrant male voice of new adulthood (*Snakes*), or sagacious middle-age (*Sitting Pretty*).

The author's background as a professional musician enables him to use music descriptively as well as metaphorically; the reader shares the experience of making music and feeling music make life known. The music of language also affects Young's style. Sparingly, he alters standard syntax and diction, sometimes punctuation, in order to set the speech closer to its natural human tone. His objective is not merely to create contemporary dialect, but also to create an enduring contemporaneity, to offer rhythmically, as the poet-musician should, the nonverbal meanings that language can carry in its sounds. Young accomplishes this quality of speech through narrative personae who speak softly or stridently, sometimes too literally, yet with voices constant and sincere.

Love, like a curse or a whimper, extends most intensely from the individual to those nearby. The contemporary American social dilemma is thereby represented in Young's prose just as it appears in his poetry: each person must somehow maintain the unity, fidelity, and consistency love requires while grappling for the freedom and oneness that American mythology promises. Although *Snakes* and *Sitting Pretty* are more successful, all of Young's novels contain graphic portrayals of mainstream urban America—middle-class people who try to be good at being themselves. They emote, they dream, and they reason. At worst, they stand too large on the page; at best, they find purpose to complement the dignity they feel. Whether he narrates with commentary from a third-person point of view, or with the immediacy of first-person sensory experience, Young confronts the problems of individuals growing into their individuality, and the qualities of life central to the congregate American family.

The narrative persona of Young's first novel, *Snakes*, is M. C. Moore, who recollects his youth and adolescence in the mature, seasoned voice of the novel's master-of-ceremonies. A novel of formation, *Snakes* is in the *Bildungsroman* tradition and is rendered in a tone of voice at once nostalgic and fatherly. Although he has only snapshots of his true parents by which to remember them, M. C. gradually finds their love implanted in his own initialed name, "so it sound[s] like you had some status, his first lover explains, "whether you did or not." For M. C., the process of learning who he is becomes the composition of his own music.

M. C. discovers music in his soul and he makes music the core of his world. He finds music everywhere, "in the streets, in the country, in people's voices" . . . and "in the way they lead their lives." Providing counterpoint, M. C.'s grandmother Claude offers guidance and family history, and M. C. is her captive audience: "I could listen to Claude talk all day long, and did, many a time. Her voice was like music." The association expands as his views of love and music merge, and women ultimately become "lovable fields of musical energy."

While living with relatives in the South, M. C. learns at the age of ten that music will be his life. His Uncle Donald, a "night rambler" with a "talent for getting hold of a dollar," turns their impoverished household into a "blind pig," or a Meridian, Mississippi, version of a speakeasy. During his first exposure to the amoral world of adults, M. C. meets Tull, an itinerant jazz pianist who in effect provides the novel's premise: "You'll get it if you keep at it. Listen, just take your time, one note a time over here with your right hand. Just take your time, that's all it is to playin' the piano or anything else. Take your time and work it on out." The impression lasts; M. C. goes on to structure his life around his love of music and his faith that music will help him grow.

Literature also has a formative effect on him. It is not literature as found in the classroom or in books—M. C. attends high school in body only, and barely earns his diploma—rather, literature personified in Shakes, his closest friend, whose name is short for Shakespeare. Shakes has a "greedy memory and a razor tongue." He is bright, musical, and funny: "You hip to Cyrano de Bergerac? Talk about a joker could talk some trash! Cyrano got everybody told! Didn't nobody be messin with Cyrano, ugly as he was."

Yet there is more to know about life than its music and its literature; such knowledge appears in the person of Champ, who exposes M. C. to contemporary jazz and the business hemisphere of that musical world. In his bemusing, self-sacrificial way, Champ also demonstrates his worsening drug addiction and the consequential brutalization of his sensibilities. "Poor Champ," M. C. soon observes while he learns to jam, to feel his music come alive inside himself and issue forth, "who wanted to play an instrument so badly, would stand around working his arms and fingers for hours sometimes, shaping the smoky air in the room into some imaginary saxophone. . . . We all wanted to get good."

The evil to which Champ submits himself opposes the good that he gives M. C.—music as growth and expression. "Up until Champ, I was pretty lame. . . ." M. C.'s band, "The Masters of Ceremony," discovers in their art a meaning that transcends the music they produce, and although the group separates after one demo and some local gigs, M. C.'s early success provides him with a clearer view of the possibilities of his life and a deep sense of wonder. He emerges from his plain, ordinary background complete, communicative, and capable of more, having also achieved his own narrative voice, that husky, now masculine voice the reader has heard maturing since the story's outset. He boards the New York bus a musician, grown: "I don't feel free . . . but I don't feel trapped." Awkwardly, painfully, naturally, M. C. has learned to look for the subtle ironies that enrich both life and art. Ready at last for the rest of what he will be, the young adult takes with him his guitar, his music, and precious recordings of his song "Snakes," which throughout the novel parallels his experience of youth: "The tune sounded simple the first time you heard it, but it wasn't all that simple to play."

While the narrative voice of *Snakes* provides contrast and consistency—a gradual merging of the maturing young man with his adult consciousness—the narrative voice of *Who Is Angelina?* accomplishes neither. Angelina is already grown, but her adult life has entered a phase of meaningless triviality. This she blames on the shifting cultural milieu of Berkeley, California. Life in Berkeley seem different now—dangerous—and the people's sense of freedom and fun, that community spirit of festivity, is gone. She uses the burglary of her apartment as the justification, and a friend's convenient cash as the means, to skip town—an act she considers the prerequisite for introspection. She flees not only her fictional problems but also her reader as well; a character with both brains and beauty who struggles with mere communal ennui is less than sympathetic. Moreover, even the reader who can overlook her escapist behavior needs to know more about her, and most of her background is provided through recollection and reminiscence. The novel's principal events—travel in Mexico, some romantic sex, an emergency trip home to Detroit, an encounter with a street thief—facilitate reflection by the viewpoint character, and the reader must simply accept her gradual appraisals. Dramatically, little takes place. Most of this novel is exposition; what little action there is consists of Angelina's consideration of an adaptation to what goes on around her.

The unifying thematic metaphor of *Who Is Angelina?* is the act of taking away: Angelina is robbed (her reaction is passive); her lover's mysterious occupation suggests more of the same; her father is robbed and nearly killed; a friend's purse is stolen (her reaction this time is spontaneous and violent). Eventually, Angelina's searching appears to reach some sort of resolution that makes her worthy of new self-esteem. Yet the reader can only observe, not participate in this search, because—unlike *Snakes*'s composer-narrator—Angelina does not experience within the narrative a process of growth.

Plainly, Angelina is a woman experiencing a crisis of self-identity during a series of events that propel her toward introspection. What she ultimately discovers within herself is a typical American complex of contradictions, such as the one she describes to a fellow traveler early in her journey, the contradiction Americans create by equating individuality with isolation: "Angelina explained that in America it's the individual who matters most and that she and her family, such as it was, lived at separate ends of what's called reality. She too was lonely and fed up with a kind of life she'd been leading."

Whether the narrator addresses the reader directly or through the medium of a letter to a former lover, the exposition continues: "Everyone nowadays is busy digging for roots. Well, I know them well and it doesn't make a damn bit of difference when it comes to making sense of who I am and why I make the kinds of mistakes I do. In the end, I've discovered, it all comes down to being in competition with yourself." At moments, Angelina's concern waxes angry and the culturally contemplative author intrudes: "I'm not so sure that all those chitlins, hamhocks, hog maws, pigsfeet, spareribs and cooking with lard—soulfood so-called—isn't contributing more toward bringing about black genocide, as the phrasemongers would have it, than Sickle Cell Anemia." An important discovery about herself does take place, however, and this is what her wandering is all about. The exploration has been a contemporary one that many young, single Americans never complete: "The truth was that, most of all, she loved open-hearted vulnerable strangers for whom she wasn't strictly obliged to feel anything."

In the end, Angelina also learns that she has been changing at the same time that her surroundings have been changing. Because she has confused one process with another, separation followed by a reassertion of self followed by a return to her point of departure appear to be cathartic. If so, the reader hopes that she also learns that life is and continues to be a process of change, some small part of which is subject to each individual's conscious control. Angelina's recognition of this consciousness is both the special story and the ordinariness of Young's second novel.

Sidney J. Prettymon, the narrative persona of *Sitting Pretty*, is streetwise, sardonic, and ironically self-conscious. He establishes early a mock superstitious mentality—astronauts may mess up the moon so that it can no longer be full—and verbalizes "the integral aspects of [his] personal philosophy to be cool." Prettymon is dangerously learned: "I cut this article out of the National Inquirer that maintain how you can succeed and develop yourself and transformate your whole personality by the buildin' up your vocabulary." His inborn sense of linguistic sound combines comically with his interest in discovering associative meanings (*radical chic* connotes to him the concubine of a politically motivated Arab husband of many wives), but the best humor to be found in *Sitting Pretty* is derived from Prettymon's command of the text. The reader is at all times close to Prettymon, and he exploits the closeness. Having pondered his plot-situation at the story's outset, he describes himself to himself as being "on the threshold of destiny, temptation, and fate." Turning aside, he speaks directly to the reader: "Now, that's bad! [good] Let me run through that one again so yall can savor it. . . ."

The narrative opens below the closing sentence of Mark Twain's *The Adventures of Huckleberry Finn* (1884); in many ways, Sidney J. Prettymon is a contemporary, self-possessed Jim. As Twain's narrative control allowed him to elevate linguistic puns through burlesque to high satirical levels, Young's narrative is successful here by virtue of its consistently controlled authorial distance: "All I mean by imagination," Prettymon says, "is the way stuff look when you pull back from it and give it some reflection room." Prettymon as first-person narrative persona allows the author to work most effectively; because his imagination provides Prettymon with overview, it allows him to construct connotative ironies.

The incongruous coexistence of common insight and aesthetic misinterpretation (Huck does not misinterpret aesthetic qualities; he misses them entirely) works through sarcastic understatement: "Carpe Diem, like they say in Latin. Save the day." The author's hand moves subtly, characterizing by misquotation.

Like M. C.'s unknown parents, Prettymon has given his son an inspirational name with which to command respect—Aristotle: "He is a lawyer." Professionally successful, Aristotle is a son ungrateful for his name, and working-class Prettymon must struggle to disguise his pride as resentment: "He go around callin hisself A. Winfred Prettymon. I'm the one give him his first name and that's his way of gettin back at me. I wanted him to stand out and be distinguished and be the bearer of a name that smack of dignity." Telephoning his daughter, Prettymon again creates linguistic pandemonium, quoting Ralph Waldo Emerson in order to reinforce some fatherly advice, then addressing the reader as the individualistic, pro-consumer Henry David Thoreau: "I hung up fast, then taken the receiver back off the hook again so the operator couldn't ring me back for that extra ten cent. I ain't go nothing but the vastest contempt for the Phone Company. Leeches and rascals! Need to be investigated."

Sitting Pretty is Young's best novel in three ways: consistency of viewpoint, ingenuity of the narrative-persona, and control of the language. The last must be perfect for an author to choose suggestive, convincing variations consistent with popular speech. Young's rendering of black dialect for artistic purpose is found throughout his fiction, and it works effectively here. The novel's language is an unconcealed treasure:

> What with all that racket and commotion and the drink I'd just taken, I was startin to feel randy—a term the Professor use, British word for horney—randy for my own private bottle of sweet wine. Got a job lines up and just *know* Aristotle gon spring my Plymouth loose. Clebratin time! Time to do that quiet furlough down to Adamo's again.

Surprised, uniquely joyful, Sidney J. Prettymon rediscovers his treasure again and again.

Whereas Young's first and third novels may be paired according to their points of view and the consistency of their narrative voices, *Ask Me Now*, Young's fourth novel, contains narrative weaknesses similar to those found in *Who Is Angelina?* Like Angelina, Woody Knight also finds himself in a world changing at a pace inconsistent with his own ability to change, a major source of frustration for this retired pro-basketball player who has always depended upon the musical, built-in rhythms of his game. In life on the outside, it seems to Woody, the court lines keep shifting.

The sequence of events that brings crisis and reunion to Woody's middle-class family is, like the catalytic changes Angelina experiences, rather improbable. As the narrative opens, Woody is not trying to control the ball and the players in motion, but a double arm-load of groceries, rain, a raucous crowd in a shopping mall, the theft of his car. and his wife's winning of a sweepstakes raffle, all in the time it takes to report his loss to a security man who mistakes him for someone he is not. This complexity of absurd events may be American, middle-class normality, but the mid-life, change-related distance Woody discovers growing between himself and his wife (the prize she wins is a trip to Reno, America's emblematic city of the free and the damned), his children, and society becomes less believable as the plot progresses.

The kidnaping of his daughter by the street gang who stole his car and hid cocaine in one of its tires provides crisis and denouement, but at the cost of increasing the distance between Woody and the reader. Secondary characters quickly become contemporary types that provide color, not credibility, and a final chase scene produces climactic anger, not release. On Woody's mind as the final seconds tick away—the police and the mobsters in the mysterious limousine move aside—is the "elbow room" he valued so highly on the court, the kind of elbow room Angelina sought in her flight to Mexico City. Although this moment contains a great burst of energy—Woody charging in to rescue his daughter, his family, and himself—the climax rings false: he finds and then abandons his daughter in order to pursue the criminal, whom the police ultimately must rescue from a murderous Woody. Despite rather than because of his heroics, all ends well. New insights are gained by all, including that minority of readers for whom the fiction maintains its illusion of reality.

The unbelievable crime and the stock family crisis notwithstanding, Young's control of language is complemented by the twin metaphors of basketball as dance and music as movement. Woody works the ball along the novel's narrative line with eloquence and style. If what he does and what others do to him is too pat, too contrived, his responses are genuine. Woody is a man both worthy of respect and capable of love. He proves himself. The crisis past, he finds himself renewed, as did Angelina, yet, for the reader, there remains at best an evanescent certainty that Woody's reaction to events, not himself, and his reaction to selected alternatives, not decisions, have brought resolution. Unlike the courageous M. C. and the umbrageous Prettymon, Woody is yet incompletely his own. His story ends, but his score remains tied with time remaining on the clock.

Al Young's main characters experience their passages with a fortitude that becomes their personal style. As M. C. copes with adolescence and Angelina seeks alternatives, while Prettymon nurtures his middle-age pride and Woody deals clumsily with midlife crisis, their stories are less important than their thoughts and expression. The music and love in their living is heard and felt; the reader wants to dance with them, to celebrate. "Celebratory" is a good word to describe Al Young's style. His major characters are able to seek and find better versions of themselves when they become able and willing to celebrate what they already are.

Major publications other than long fiction
POETRY: *Dancing: Poems*, 1969; *The Song Turning Back into Itself*, 1971; *Geography of the Near Past*, 1976; *The Blues Don't Change: New and Selected Poems*, 1982.
NONFICTION: *Bodies and Soul: Musical Memoirs*, 1981.

Bibliography
Page, James A., ed. *Selected Black American Authors*, 1977.
Reed, Ishmael, ed. *Calafía: The California Poetry*, 1979.
Rush, Theressa G., et al. *Black American Writers Past and Present: A Bio-graphical and Bibliographical Dictionary*, 1975.

Joseph F. Battaglia